ENCYCLOPEDIA
OF
AMERICAN
SOCIAL
MOVEMENTS

VOLUME THREE

EDITED BY
IMMANUEL NESS

SHARPE REFERENCE
an imprint of M.E.Sharpe, Inc.

SHARPE REFERENCE

Sharpe Reference is an imprint of M.E. Sharpe INC.

M.E. Sharpe INC.
80 Business Park Drive
Armonk, NY 10504

© 2004 by M.E. Sharpe INC.

Library of Congress Cataloging-in-Publication Data

Encyclopedia of American social movements / Immanuel Ness, editor.
  p. cm.
  Includes bibliographical references and indexes.
  ISBN 0-7656-8045-9 (set: alk. paper)
  1. Social movements—United States—History—Encyclopedias. 2. Social change—United States—History—Encyclopedias. 3. Social justice—United States—History—encyclopedias. I. Ness, Immanuel.
HN57 .E594 2004
303.48'4'097303—dc21

2002042613

Printed and bound in the United States of America

The paper used in this publication meets the minimum requirements of American National Standard for Information Sciences—Permanence of Paper for Printed Library Materials,
ANSI Z 39.48.1984.

BM (c) 10 9 8 7 6 5 4 3 2 1

Publisher: Myron E. Sharpe
Vice President and Editorial Director: Patricia Kolb
Vice President and Production Director: Carmen Chetti
Executive Editor and Manager of Reference: Todd Hallman
Project Manager: Wendy E. Muto
Editorial Assistant: Cathleen Prisco
Cover and Text Design: Jesse Sanchez

Contents

6

RURAL, SOCIAL, AND POLITICAL MOVEMENTS

INTRODUCTION

For most of its history, America has been mostly a rural society. Indeed, from the early seventeenth century to the early twentieth century, the majority of Americans lived and worked in the countryside. Many of the nation's most significant rural social movements developed in these years. The essays in this section tell the stories of fifteen such social movements from the late colonial era to the late twentieth century and from the completely local to those nationwide in scope. The following writings, though not a definitive accounting of America's rural social movements, include the most important ones. All bear on fundamental themes of political and economic power, class and race, and, at least in one case, gender roles in the countryside.

Readers may note a common thread in the essays explaining rural political and economic protest movements. With only a handful of notable exceptions, America's rural common people usually lost their battles. Their experience, then, is at odds with the dominant American national myth of triumph through virtue. Their setbacks made them in a sense—as historian C. Vann Woodward observed of Southerners in particular—"un-American." Rural Americans shared something important in common with the rest of the world: firsthand knowledge of defeat. Yet, these movements are not essentially about defeat but about struggle. Rural people, like others elsewhere, struggled throughout their history for the sometimes contradictory goals of autonomy, security, and comfort.

These struggles began early in the American experience. In the late colonial era, a series of rural protests in western Massachusetts and in the Appalachian and Southern backcountry united country people in "Regulator" uprisings, Shays' Rebellion, and the Whiskey Rebellion. In each case, these social movements resorted to violence to achieve their goals in much the same manner as those in the East which had just resulted in the winning of independence from the British Empire. Yet, contesting elites defeated these resistance movements in part because of their reliance on violence. Violence as well as other forms of political struggle accompanied the New York State Anti-Rent movement of the 1820s and 1830s, which fought the hereditary land barons of the Hudson River Valley whose claims to tenant farmers' land dated from the seventeenth century. From the same era, various antebellum American communities explored perfectionist social models from the 1820s through the 1850s. Far from using violence, most of these utopian movements sought ordered perfectionism through experimental cooperative social structures.

The decades following the Civil War saw a dramatic increase in rural social movements. Freedmen from the South fled from oppression to opportunity in the 1870s, and a host of protest movements flowered among disgruntled small farmers in the Midwest, South, and Great Plains. In the 1860s, a century of cooperation, protest, and education began with the formation of the Patrons of Husbandry, known as the Grange. While the cataclysm of Civil War permanently dampened utopian dreams, its outcome created some uncertain opportunities for formerly enslaved African Americans. Hopeful "Exodusters" fled white supremacy in the South to Great Plains settlements during the 1870s and 1880s with varying outcomes. Another social movement took political form in the 1870s and 1880s with the Greenbacker Party seeking to forge links between rural and urban labor militancy. In the 1870s, rural Texans founded an organization that became the Farmers' Alliance whose branches would reach throughout the South, the West, and Midwest during the 1880s. On its deathbed, the Farmers' Alliance combined with the Knights of Labor to create the most significant rural protest movement in American history with the formation of the People's Party (Populists). The Populists of the 1890s represent the highwater mark of rural social movements in the United States in total numbers for good reason. The conditions against which they protested would inexorably empty out the people of the countryside into the working class of the great twentieth-century American cities. Yet, in spite of diminishing numbers, the most discontented of those remaining on the land would seek to voice their point of view in a number of militant twentieth-century rural social movements.

The twentieth century saw the virtual elimination of the rural "plain folk" as an economic class, with the most painful adjustments occurring in the first forty years of the century. These economic changes provoked a variety of responses among rural people, but most endured the transformation in social silence. Some, perhaps, even rejoiced at its demise. A vocal minority, however, expressed disagreement with the trends of the nationwide marketplace. Discontented farmers produced a brief, but radical, critique of the new economic order in the agrarian Socialist movement of the Southwest. While World War I-era repression killed off the Socialist movement, remnants survived and briefly flourished on the northern plains and upper Midwest in the rural Nonpartisan League of the Dakotas and Minnesota. The coming of the Great Depression created misery in the American South, where profoundly impoverished black and white sharecroppers fought their landlords, the Depression, and unintended consequences of the New Deal through the Southern Tenant Farmers' Union. And in the midst of such generally hard times for rural people, American farmwomen struggled to provide for their families with the aid of the U.S. Department of Agriculture's Home Demonstration movement.

World War II diverted even more rural people into the new jobs of the cities, especially in the South, but rural social movements continued among the remaining rural population. In some cases, such movements grew from early twentieth-century roots but persisted into the late twentieth and early twenty-first centuries. A uniquely Minnesotan rural social movement arose in the Farmer-Labor Party. Unlike many other rural movements, this expression of rural-urban working-class solidarity experienced significant long-term success, eventually becoming the majority political party throughout much of the twentieth century. Perhaps the longest-lived rural social movement in U.S. history is that of West Coast farm workers whose movement stretches from the late nineteenth century into the twenty-first century, from the first struggles for improved treatment to the gains and losses of the United Farm Workers. By the late twentieth century, rural Americans were few in number. Yet, enough remained—and remained discontented—to produce the late-twentieth-century phenomenon of rural protest by otherwise conservative farm owners known as the American Agricultural Movement from 1979 to the present.

The essays in this section suggest the complexity and richness of America's rural past—where disparate movements have struggled to define, control, reshape, or maintain various groups' places in that countryside since the late colonial era.

Kyle Wilkison

REGULATOR MOVEMENTS AND OTHER REBELLIONS   1760s–1790s

Agrarian protest movements were a regular feature of late colonial and early republican politics, taking place in every colony or state during the last half of the eighteenth century. These protests were driven by complex and sometimes overlapping issues, such as disputed land titles, burdensome debt and taxation, and ineffective or corrupt government. They had a class dimension, often pitting poor and middling family farmers against wealthy merchants and land speculators. They also had a sectional or geographic element, with residents of the backcountry (the rural, developing, recently settled region in the western parts of the colonies/states) challenging a coastal establishment that monopolized political and economic power. Although protesters typically used legal channels to state their grievances, they did not hesitate to resort to violence, including broadly organized armed insurrection, to achieve their ends. Yet the "radicalism" of these agrarian movements is ambiguous. In one sense they were cut from the same fabric as the American Revolution, appropriating its language and seeking to extend its benefits more broadly. In another sense, they hearken back to the traditional crowd rituals of early modern Europe, seeking to change local conditions but not challenging the social and political system more broadly.

North Carolina Regulators

Among the earliest agrarian protest movements was the North Carolina Regulation, which had its origins in part in the land wars of the mid-1760s. During the preceding decades, Henry McCulloh, an English merchant and Crown favorite, had amassed some 1.2 million acres of land in North Carolina, much of it in the piedmont or backcountry. By the time McCulloh sorted out his surveys after the Seven Years' War, hundreds of small farmers had migrated into the piedmont and established themselves on his claims, some with legal title, others with surveys only, and still others claiming squatters' rights. McCulloh pressed his claims all the same, sparking violent opposition from farmers who resented the efforts of an absentee speculator to control land they had improved. Angry farmers in Anson County seized and beat McCulloh's agents, but in the end his claims prevailed, forcing farmers to purchase lands they still believed they owned. Resentment from these land wars would fuel the much broader and more explosive Regulator movement later in the decade.

This second phase of the movement was driven by class antagonism, ineffective government, and political corruption. By the late 1760s, backcountry farmers were complaining to Governor William Tryon about a whole host of abuses: local officials were corrupt, they claimed, charging extortionate fees for services, seizing farms and jailing farmers for delinquent taxes and debt, and monopolizing local political control through multiple officeholding. Taxation was also an issue: provincial taxes were especially burdensome for people who lived in a cash-poor region, whose economy was based primarily on barter, who saw little in the way of government services, and who were underrepresented in the colonial assembly. Led primarily by Herman Husband, a prosperous yeoman farmer and passionate evangelical who fused country politics with millennarian thinking, backcountry farmers organized as the Regulators. At its height, the Regulation numbered around 6,000 members, approximately three-fourths of the backcountry's adult white male population. Between 1766 and 1771, Regulators repeatedly petitioned provincial leaders, openly refused to pay taxes, destroyed property, disrupted government, and even took up arms against the colonial militia. In September 1770, an angry mob assaulted local officials and judges at the Orange County courthouse in Hillsborough, destroyed the home of one particularly detested official, and staged a mock court. In the wake of the Hillsborough riot, Husband was arrested, acquitted, and released, but Tryon, determined to put an end to the insurgency, marched into the backcountry with 1,200 provincial militia and arrest warrants for key Regulation leaders. On May 16, 1771, Tryon's forces engaged a poorly armed and undisciplined Regulator army at Alamance Creek. Within three hours his forces had routed the Regulators; thirty were killed, 200 wounded, twelve were tried, and seven were later executed. The remaining Regulators were pardoned. Herman Husband escaped to Pennsylvania, where he would later play a minor role in the Whiskey Rebellion. Tryon's heavy-handed approach ended the insurgency but did not address its causes; unresolved Regulator grievances would surface again in the coming years, fueling Revolutionary sentiment in the North Carolina backcountry.

SOUTH CAROLINA REGULATORS

Whereas local political corruption drove agrarian protest in North Carolina, the absence of local political control fueled conflict in the South Carolina backcountry. This conflict had its origins in South Carolina's unique demographic makeup. After 1710, coastal rice planters comprised a shrinking white minority surrounded by hostile slaves at home and potentially hostile Indians in the interior. Seeking to create a human buffer zone on the frontier and increase the colony's white population, after 1730 provincial authorities in Charleston sponsored a settlement scheme that brought thousands of white farmers into central and upper South Carolina. By the mid-1760s, the majority of South Carolina's white population was concentrated in the interior, but both political power and the center of provincial government remained in Charleston, some 200 miles from some of the most densely populated backcountry communities. In the absence of local courts, upcountry settlers could not convey property, prosecute debts, or resolve boundary disputes without traveling to Charleston. Law enforcement was weak; warrants were issued from Charleston, and suspected criminals were transferred to lowcountry precincts to await trial.

This institutional vacuum became acute in the wake of the Seven Years' War, when a crisis of law and order erupted in the upcountry. Settlers reported that gangs of bandits were roaming the countryside, stealing livestock, kidnapping women, harboring slaves, and beating, torturing, and robbing settlers. Among these outlaws were veterans of the recent Cherokee War, farmers who had been bankrupted by drought and crop failure, and career criminals capitalizing on the region's weak law enforcement. In addition to these outlaws, backcountry settlers complained of hunters who subsisted through foraging and killing game and whose way of life went against the emerging social order centered on family farms; the settlers demanded vagrancy laws to control the hunting population. When the General Assembly was slow to act on these grievances, upcountry farmers took matters into their own hands. In 1767, they organized as the Regulators. Led by storekeepers, militia captains, and prosperous planters like Moses Kirkland and Patrick Calhoun, the Regulators whipped, banished, and arrested suspected bandits and forced hunters to work on farms. For the most part, provincial authorities in the lowcountry were sympathetic with Regulator goals and methods. However, in July 1768, a lowcountry militia unit clashed with Regulators at Marrs Bluff when a constable tried to arrest Regulator leader Gideon Gibson. In the pitched battle that ensued, Regulators wounded a number of lowcountry militiamen and whipped several others. Although such conflict raised tensions between coastal and upcountry authorities, it also prodded the General Assembly to move swiftly. That year the Assembly extended political representation into the upcountry, and in 1769 it passed the Circuit Court Act, which established district courts and sheriffs in the interior. Thus, whereas the North Carolina Regulator affair only deepened sectional tensions, in South Carolina the grievances of backcountry settlers were amicably resolved and served to build solidarity between the regions.

SHAYS' REBELLION—MASSACHUSETTS REGULATORS

A different kind of agrarian uprising took place in Massachusetts in the wake of the Revolutionary War. As in the Carolinas, rural Massachusetts was populated by independent family farmers. These yeomen relied largely on family labor to work their small freehold farms, exchanged their meager surpluses with neighbors and storekeepers for goods and services, and participated in a rich communal life based on interdependency and neighborliness. By contrast, in the urban trading centers along the coast, wealthy merchants dominated a commercial money economy centered on profits and long-distance trade. An elaborate credit network extended from these coastal merchants to inland storekeepers and increasingly to small farmers.

Two developments occurred after the war to produce an economic crisis and fuel sectional conflict in Massachusetts. First, American merchants reestablished trade with the British. Encumbered with massive inventories, British merchants were only too willing to accommodate American demands for English goods, offering easy credit and reasonable prices. At the same time, however, the British shut American merchants out of the West Indian trade, leaving them with few markets for their exports and little cash to pay for British goods. The resulting trade deficit siphoned off the supply of hard money in the United States, creating an economic depression. When British merchants called in their loans, a debt crisis ensued. Coastal merchants sued country storekeepers, who in turn sued and jailed farmers for debts. (The idea was to force friends and family to pay these debts in order to free the head of household from jail.) Second, the state's need to retire the huge war debt led to increased property taxes. These taxes were especially burdensome to inland farmers, who were accustomed to paying in goods and services and had little hard money, especially as the postwar depression deepened. Thus, while creditors were jailing farmers for unpaid debts, state officials were seizing and selling their farms to recover delinquent taxes.

Inland farmers initially responded to this crisis by organizing county conventions and petitioning for relief and reform through legal channels. Between 1784 and 1787, they pleaded with the state to print paper currency, enact tender laws that permitted in-kind payment of debts, and replace the Court of Common Pleas with elected committees of arbitration to mediate tax and debt delinquency suits. They also called for more equitable taxation through reductions in property taxes and increases in poll taxes. However, the state sided with the mercantile interests and rejected these petitions. Wild rumors circulated about the insurgent farmers—that they were backed by the British, that they were levelers seeking to engender equality, that they were bent on destroying commerce—leaving little room for conciliation between the two parties. In late 1786, farmers organized as the Regulators, forcefully closing several inland courts and freeing jailed debtors. In January 1787, the movement turned more violent when some 1,200 men, led by Daniel Shays, a captain in the Revolution, advanced on the federal arsenal at Springfield. The governor mustered a force of 4,400 coastal militia to meet the "Shaysites" and routed them with little difficulty. Thereafter, the Shays' rebels resorted to guerrilla tactics, leading raids on merchants, lawyers, and storekeepers through the summer of 1787. Violence ceased soon thereafter, when an economic upswing put an end to the depression and brought peace to the countryside. Moreover, the new state legislature proved more sympathetic to Regulator demands, lowering government fees, passing tender laws, and providing tax relief. Similar debt insurgencies took place throughout New England as well as in Maryland, Virginia, South Carolina, and Pennsylvania. This agrarian unrest fueled support for the new federal constitution, with its powerful chief executive and its standing federal army.

THE WHISKEY REBELLION

The new federal government would soon get its first opportunity to test its strength against agrarian protesters in western Pennsylvania. This movement, too, was rooted in the postwar economic crisis. As part of his vision for a strong national economy, Alexander Hamilton, secretary of the Treasury under George Washington, proposed to secure the nation's credit by retiring the national debt and assuming the remaining war debts of the states. Hamilton's plan had several controversial elements. First, it benefited New England states disproportionately because, unlike most Southern and Mid-Atlantic states, they were still mired in debt. (Hamilton won Southern support for his plan by agreeing to relocate the national capital to Virginia.) Second, it benefited wealthy speculators who had purchased bonds from poor, cash-starved veterans at a fraction of their value but who now stood to receive the full face value of these bonds from the federal government. (Hamilton made no apologies for seeking to win the support and trust of the wealthy.) Third, Hamilton proposed to raise the revenue for retiring the debt from a new excise tax on distilled spirits. This whiskey tax gave a break to large producers—the more they produced, the lower the tax per gallon—and hurt small, home-based distillers the most. Despite these controversial measures, Congress enacted Hamilton's credit program in 1791.

The whiskey tax was especially hard on small backcountry farmers who depended on whiskey sales for their livelihood. Corn was too bulky and cheap to ship profitably to coastal markets, but corn liquor could be traded to distant markets for profits or among neighbors as a key commodity in the local barter economy. In the eyes of poor Western distillers and farmers, the excise tax took a big bite out of their already meager incomes; it was imposed by a federal government that did not represent the interests of common people and from which much of the Western

The Massachusetts militia rebuffs an attack by Daniel Shays and his agrarian rebels at the federal arsenal in Springfield in January 1787. Although Shays' Rebellion failed militarily, it induced the state legislature to enact laws providing relief to farmers and galvanized support for a new federal constitution. *(Brown Brothers)*

region was already alienated; and the revenues it produced went to service the debts of other states or line the pockets of rich bond speculators. To further fuel class tensions, large landowners and absentee land speculators frequently served as excise tax collectors. From Georgia to Pennsylvania, agrarian protesters resisted the excise tax through petitions, nonpayment, and violence. Resistance culminated in western Pennsylvania in 1794, when protesters tarred and feathered tax collectors, closed county courts, burned the home of one exciseman, and marched on Pittsburgh, vowing to destroy the town and kill its leading citizens. In September, President George Washington declared western Pennsylvania in rebellion and ordered 12,950 militiamen—a larger force than he had commanded during the Revolution—to occupy the region, put down the rebellion, and arrest the leading insurgents. Although clearly an exaggerated response to an ex-

aggerated problem, Washington's show of force was effective: the protesters dispersed, twenty were arrested, and two were convicted of treason and later pardoned by the president. For the agrarian rebels, the lesson of the Whiskey Rebellion was all too clear: the federal government had proved itself fully capable of dealing with local resistance. On the other hand, Hamilton's whiskey tax was never adequately enforced, even after the rebellion was put down, and the insurgents had shown that the tradition of agrarian protest and the Revolution's spirit of political dissent was still alive and well.

LIBERTY MEN

Many agrarian protest movements turned on issues of land ownership that pitted small freeholders against wealthy, often-absentee speculators or proprietors. Such was the case in post-Revolutionary Maine,

Pennsylvania farmers opposed to the whiskey tax carry a tax collector they have tarred and feathered. Although Americans had long protested higher taxes and economic injustices, the Whiskey Rebellion of 1794 proved the first major insurrection under the new U.S. government. President George Washington sent nearly 13,000 troops to suppress the uprising. *(Brown Brothers)*

where thousands of poor farmers clashed with distant but powerful proprietors (landlords) in the 1790s and early 1800s. A series of proprietary grants for large tracts in Maine had been issued under Charles I in 1632, and they were extremely problematic: there were no precise surveys, claims overlapped, and the proprietors' tendency to contest titles deterred potential buyers and settlers. This changed during the Revolutionary War. Under the assumption that Massachusetts would confiscate the proprietary lands (most proprietors were also Loyalists) and redistribute them to common people, tens of thousands of settlers poured into Maine from southern New England and established themselves on the proprietors' claims. These immigrants were among the poorest of New England's poor; their lives turned upside down by the war, they were desperate for land. Massachusetts did not confiscate these lands, however, and after the war the proprietors regrouped. Recruiting powerful allies like Henry Knox and Josiah Little, both of whom were American military leaders with extensive political connections, the proprietors redrew their boundaries precisely and reasserted their claims to the Maine lands, aiming to lease, sell, or eject the "squatters" from their lands. The region's growing population and its improved farmsteads now promised lucrative returns for the absentee proprietors, who wielded nearly absolute political power in the assembly as well as in the courts.

Much of the subsequent contest between proprietors and farmers turned on the meaning of land ownership. The proprietors' claims rested on legal title that was conferred by a sovereign, regardless of actual physical possession. For their part, farmers argued that legitimate ownership was conferred through their use of the land: it was rightfully theirs because they took only what they needed to support their households and more importantly because they possessed and improved it with their labor. Moreover, they viewed land ownership as essential to a democratic society; only as freeholders could they maintain their autonomy and avoid the slavish dependency of tenancy. Speculators and absentee landlords were in their view parasites profiting from the labor of the common people. Settlers petitioned the state, but they could not match the costly, high-pressure legal tactics used by the proprietors. Instead, they quickly turned to extralegal solutions aimed at intimidating local supporters of the proprietors and terrorizing the proprietors' agents. Disguised as Indians, agrarian insurgents beat and mutilated surveyors, destroyed property of the proprietors' local allies, and vowed to kill anyone who tried to evict farmers or who harbored proprietary agents. Dubbed White Indians by their enemies, agrarian protesters were seen as half-savage, the enemies of civilization and social order. Deeming themselves Liberty Men, militant farmers claimed the heritage of the Revolution and its promise of liberty and local autonomy. The ongoing struggle between proprietors and Liberty Men was not resolved until the Jeffersonian Republicans defeated the Federalists in 1800–1801 and achieved a compromise on the question of land ownership: labor would not confer title, but neither could landlords extort the improvements of settlers. The proprietors were forced to offer a just price. Nonetheless, agrarian conflict would continue in parts of Maine for more than a decade after the Jeffersonian revolution.

THE CONTEXT OF AGRARIAN CONFLICT

Geography interwove with class and cultural differences to create a complex context for agrarian conflict in the late colonial and early national periods. The backcountry was by definition a developing region. Western communities often lacked access to navigable rivers and were forced to ship their goods over poor roads, limiting their access to commercial markets. Farmers were preoccupied with clearing land and providing for the basic survival needs of their families; they exchanged their surpluses locally, but commercial markets took time to develop. Most immigrants were poor, many were desperate, and nearly all were poorly educated. Few owned slaves or servants, depending on family labor and, during peak periods, on the shared labor of neighbors. Not until the second or third generations would these backcountry households achieve a comfortable subsistence or "competence." Even the wealthiest and most ambitious planters and merchants were modest by Eastern standards. Socially and economically, Westerners stood in stark contrast to the established communities to the East, with their rich commercial markets and extremes of wealth and poverty. Furthermore, backcountry communities were far from the centers of power; they were politically alienated, with little or no voice in the decisions that affected their lives. The peculiar economic, social, and political geography of eighteenth-century America provides the context through which agrarian conflict must be understood.

But there was also an important cultural gap between East and West. Religious differences played a role in agrarian conflict. Most North Carolina Regulators belonged to dissenting churches and resented paying taxes to support a distant and, to them, anti-Christian Anglican establishment. In Maine, the insurgent evangelicalism of the Liberty Men glorified the poor and produced charismatic leaders who fused religion and politics, making the land war into a holy war. Cultural differences also surfaced around economic issues. Backcountry communities used a borrowing system based on personal, face-to-face exchanges of goods and labor, not the impersonal money economy based on cash transactions that prevailed along the seaboard. Although grounded in strong notions of private property and economic autonomy, these communities survived because of neighborliness and interdependence. In South Carolina, the absence of local courts made for a low level of litigiousness in the upcountry and forced residents to turn to informal ways of resolving disputes, through their churches or among neighbors. In fact, agrarian protesters frequently targeted the courts, viewing them as the tools of wealthy creditors, distant speculators, and powerful taxmen, not as dispensers of justice. In Maine, Liberty Men fashioned a theory of use-value to justify their property claims, while the proprietors relied on notions of legal right and saw land purely as a commodity or source of profit, not as the source of livelihood and autonomy. These cultural differences deepened the conflict between East and West by making it about basic values, assumptions, and social relationships, not simply about resources.

HOW RADICAL WERE AGRARIAN PROTESTERS?

Eighteenth-century agrarian protest movements were not radical in the sense that insurgents hoped to overturn or transform an unjust system. Instead, agrarian rebels typically sought to redress specific local grievances. They regarded the political and social system itself to be sound, but believed it had been betrayed by specific monied interests intent on enriching themselves at the expense of the common good. This was as true under the colonial "patronage" system, where the ruling class was expected to serve the interests of the whole and protect the common people from abuse, as it was under the new "republican" system, where virtuous and enlightened citizen-leaders protected democracy from any who sought to exploit or betray it. When such men failed to protect the interests of the whole, it fell to the people (the "mob," as they were known to the elite) to set things aright. In the absence of interest group or party politics—political parties were viewed as a threat to national unity before 1800—the only workable alternative for oppressed farmers was violence. They thus stood within a long tradition that regarded violence as a necessary and legitimate part of the political process (a sentiment echoed by Jefferson himself). After the Jeffersonian triumph of 1800–1801, it became increasingly clear that partisanship and interest-group politics would not destroy the republic. As agrarian protesters were absorbed into the Jeffersonian Republican fold, they abandoned violence as a political weapon. Consequently, agrarian protest movements declined with the emergence of party politics.

Peter N. Moore

BIBLIOGRAPHY

Brown, Richard Maxwell. *The South Carolina Regulators*. Cambridge, MA: Belknap Press of Harvard University Press, 1963.

Ekirch, A. Roger. *"Poor Carolina": Politics and Society in Colonial North Carolina, 1729–1766*. Chapel Hill: University of North Carolina Press, 1981.

Kars, Marjoleine. *"Breaking Loose Together": The Regulator Rebellion in Pre-Revolutionary North Carolina*. Chapel Hill: University of North Carolina Press, 2002.

Klein, Rachel. *Unification of a Slave State: The Rise of the Planter Class in the South Carolina Backcountry, 1760–1808*. Williamsburg, VA: Institute of Early American History and Culture, 1990.

Slaughter, Thomas P. *The Whiskey Rebellion: Frontier Epilogue to the American Revolution*. New York: Oxford University Press, 1986.

Szatmary, David P. *Shays' Rebellion: The Making of an Agrarian Insurrection*. Amherst: University of Massachusetts Press, 1980.

Taylor, Alan. *Liberty Men and Great Proprietors: The Revolutionary Settlement on the Maine Frontier, 1760–1820*. Williamsburg, VA: Institute of Early American History and Culture, 1990.

The Anti-Rent movement convulsed several counties in upstate New York in the period between 1839 and 1865, as tenants living on the estates of wealthy landlords, called "patroons," revolted against leases that were essentially feudal tenures. Through a combination of political activity, rent strikes, and violent action, the Anti-Renters built a movement that at its height threatened not only public order but also the status of land as a commodity to be traded in freely. Divisions in the Anti-Rent movement between those who thought of land as a natural right and those who simply sought to question particular land titles condemned the movement to instability, however, and this, combined with government opposition, led to the decline of the movement in the early 1850s.

Like the populist movement of the late nineteenth century, the Anti-Rent movement was primarily one of small farmers facing untenable economic change. The hill-country tenant farmers of Albany, Delaware, Rensselaer, and surrounding New York counties were united by a common ideology and experience. The tenant farmers were linked to the wealthy families whose manor houses dotted the valleys of upstate New York through a peculiar device called the "lease-in-fee." Through these contracts, most of which had been signed before the Revolutionary War, the land of the farms was conveyed as if outright, but the tenants were contractually obligated to pay a perpetual rent in the form of crops to the landlords. They also owed something approaching feudal service, in the form of an agreement to provide "four fat fowls" per year, along with one day's horse-and-cart hire and personal work for the patroon. Nor were they allowed to sell the farms they occupied, unless they remitted to the patroon families one-quarter of the purchase price. If the occupier of the land violated any of these stipulations, the patroon had the right to reoccupy the land.

The "lease-in-fee" was a legal structure that ex-

isted nowhere else in America, and did not even exist in monarchical Britain, where such feudal services had been abolished in the 1200s. Nonetheless, because ancestors of tenants or occupiers of the land had once freely contracted with the patroons, there seemed to be no legal way for the tenants to free themselves from the disagreeable and undemocratic elements of their contracts. The United States Constitution specifically prohibited even legislatures from interfering with the freedom of free individuals to create contracts.

Despite the disagreeable nature of the leasehold system, the tenants had created what historian Reeve Huston has called "independent, productive, patriarchal households ... marked by rough economic equality, household autonomy, and widespread access to natural resources." They insisted on their version of property rights, having rebelled in the 1750s in support of the Lockean idea that he who actually lived on and cultivated the land should own it. They cooperated with their neighbors through exchanges of labor and produced much of what they needed through the labor of the female members of their families. Like English peasants, they exploited the local woods for fuel and building materials, and allowed their livestock to graze on the common lands of the patroon's estate. Access to the commons meant that poverty was either a life stage or perhaps due to bad luck, but it was not endemic. The rough equality of the hill-country households cohered well with Americans' ideas about economically independent citizens.

PRECIPITATING FACTORS IN ANTI-RENTISM

The relative contentment of the hill farmers changed with the death of Stephen Van Rensselaer III, one of the area's largest landlords. For several generations, the Van Rensselaer family, recognizing that during

THE ANTI-RENT MOVEMENT

Anti-Rent activism in upstate New York lasted from 1839 to 1865. Tenants living on the estates of landlords were granted property rights analogous to feudal estates. Tenants living on the land revolted, organizing rent strikes and mass action against their landlords, even calling for the end of land as a commodity to be traded freely. The following is an excerpt from "The 'Anti-Rent' Movement and Outbreak in New York," chronicling resistance by tenants against landlords.

Last winter the sheriff was resisted in Cattaraugus by an armed force, when attempting to execute a writ of possession. The writ was against a man who had taken a contract for his farm of 150 acres in 1821, nearly a quarter of a century before, when he had paid one dollar. He paid neither interest nor principal till 1837, when he was induced to take a new contract, and pay *fifty dollars*; and after that he utterly refused to pay any more. He had a most valuable farm, for which he was required to pay, principal and interest, at a rate rather below than above the value of new land. And this was

regarded in that quarter, quite extensively, as a case calling for sympathy, if not for violence. The truth is, not that particular form of indebtedness for land which is called rent—it is indebtedness *for land* in any and every form—which makes the trouble. The agrarian spirit of the times is alive with a special hostility to this indebtedness. The claim is for land to every man without paying for it. Property in land, beyond what a man can personally occupy and cultivate, is especially denounced; and so is property, or debts, due for land. It is denounced as monopoly, it is branded as "feudal," and inconsistent, therefore with "the spirit of our institutions!"

We think it not unimportant to put to silence so far as truth can do it, the customary clamor in which many persons indulge about feudal tenures in the "Manor" of Rensselearwyck. Many, we doubt not, are deceived; but some, who use this "argument" most freely, must know better, or they ought to know better.

Source: "The 'Anti-Rent' Movement and Outbreak in New York." *The American Whig Review* 2:6 (December 1845): 587–598.

hard times it was impossible for tenant farmers to pay high rents, had been accepting whatever the tenants could pay and carrying the rest as arrears. This strategy could no longer be followed by the next generation, since Stephen Van Rensselaer IV also had creditors eager to collect mortgage payments. Social and economic changes taking place in the hill towns accelerated the accumulation of rent arrears. The transportation revolution that opened up canals and roads in the 1820s and 1830s enabled the easy transportation of grain from far Western lands to Eastern markets, putting New York tenant farmers with their exhausted soils at a competitive disadvantage. Tenants who did own land were passing regulations that barred the landless from access to the commons. This also made it difficult for marginal farmers to supplement their home production with products gleaned from nature.

In 1839 the tenant farmers appointed a committee to represent them to Stephen Van Rensselaer IV. These were no landless proletarians; the men who were chosen to speak were largely good burghers, 65 percent of whom were forty years of age or older. They were almost all farmers of some wealth, chosen to represent the area's ethnic diversity (English, Dutch, and German immigrants). They had political experience, through leadership positions in their churches, in

town offices, or in county-level political parties. They called for their rent arrears to be forgiven, and they also hoped that they would be able to convert their rental contracts to mortgages. They were unwilling to grant the patroon families any compensation for the feudal services they would lose, although they did agree to mortgage values that represented the loss of the perpetual rents. Stephen Van Rensselaer refused their request, adding insult to injury by accusing them of attempting to renege on legal contracts.

On July 4, 1839, the aggrieved tenants crafted their reply—a manifesto in the form of the Declaration of Independence, which set forth their grievances and promised that the rent would not be paid. It was the first, rhetorical, shot fired in what came to be called the Helderberg War, after the Helderberg Mountains of the region. Men who had been deputized to serve warrants on behalf of the landlords were threatened with tar and feathers. Others had to perambulate from one tavern to another, buying drinks for the angry mob. On other occasions, people with sympathy for the landlords were held captive until they agreed to shout the motto of the Anti-Renters: "Down with the Rent!" The war finally abated when Governor William H. Seward threatened the rebels with violence and promised legislative action to consider their concerns.

ANTI-RENT AND POLITICS

When Governor Seward appointed the Manor Commission to consider the question of the leases-in-fee, the concerns of the Anti-Renters began to intersect with larger political changes taking place in the nation. The 1840s were a key moment for reformers; white men of little property now had the vote, and the political parties were in flux, so that reform groups could court either party, or both. Ideologically speaking, rank-and-file Anti-Renters had most in common with the Democrats, who argued against monopolies of all kinds. The Bank War of the mid-1830s had been predicated on just this type of opposition. But the tenants were not completely given over to the Democrats. Many of the landlords were Democrats. The landlords insisted on strict construction in interpreting the Constitution because the Contracts Clause prevented any legislative meddling with the power of free individuals freely to contract.

Furthermore, many Anti-Renters believed, along with the Whig party, that government intervention in the economy was necessary to promote social happiness. As the Anti-Rent war developed, the Whigs set forth a potent justification for opposing the feudal titles: that they interfered with a free market in land, the only thing that would ensure the proper economic development of upstate New York. The Manor Commission, populated largely by Whigs, endorsed the Anti-Renters' view of the contracts as oppressive and suggested that the government's power of eminent domain might be used in order to assume stewardship of the land. Unfortunately for the Anti-Renters, these ideas were not successfully translated into action.

ANTI-RENT AS A POPULAR MOVEMENT

In 1843, William Van Rensselaer, one of Stephen Van Rensselaer's heirs, began to sue his tenants for back rents. The tenants fought the lawsuits with lawsuits of their own. They investigated the patroons' titles and found many areas of weakness in them, including the absence of certain boundaries and the failure of the grantors to fulfill all of their responsibilities. But they were unable to use these weaknesses against the patroons because nothing could excuse the tenants from their obligation to pay rent. Legislative attempts to abrogate the contracts failed when, in 1843, the Supreme Court found unconstitutional any legislation that tended to hinder the enforcement of contracts.

The inability of the Anti-Renters to gain redress through the legislature or the courts caused them to switch tactics again in 1844. Charismatic speakers like Smith Boughton, a doctor with previous radical experience fighting to free Quebec, circulated through the mountain towns, encouraging the tenants to withhold their rent and to form organizations for the promotion of the cause. They also promoted Anti-Rent candidates for the New York State Assembly. By 1845, there were between 25,000 and 60,000 Anti-Rent supporters in eleven counties.

The Anti-Renters also began to model their movement after highly successful evangelical reform movements such as temperance and abolition. They had their own newspaper, the *Albany Freeholder*, which reported on the movement's doings and encouraged Anti-Renters through its documentation of their united strength. Balladeers wrote songs and poems that celebrated Anti-Rent ideas and commemorated the Helderberg War. People who identified with the Anti-Rent cause could express this element of their identities by joining the legally focused Anti-Rent associations, supporting the nexus between Anti-Rent and party politics, or even joining the enforcement arm of the movement—the "Indians."

The Indian bands were coordinated groups of neighbors, presided over by "chiefs" at the neighborhood and town level. Unlike members of the Anti-Rent associations, who were older and more respectable, more than half of the "Indians" were under thirty and owned little property. Their relative poverty was only partly a function of life stage, since the Indians were coming of age at a time when earning a competency from the land was becoming more and more difficult. Since their function was to intimidate and act in raucous ways, the Indians had a lot in common with the early modern ritual of the charivari, a ceremonial harassment of newlyweds or similar notables by local men and boys. The ritual was a holdover from premodern Europe that persisted in rural America. The rite was designed to accommodate change in a community and used as an ad hoc form of social control with a complex ritual world. The Indians concocted their own language. They created their own costumes, which were more than just feathered headdresses; they wore full masks with ears that resembled animals or devils, and long, nightgown-like outfits of multicolored calico decorated with furs and beads. Indian identity provided a focus for young men in the mountain towns to celebrate their masculinity and, since Indians were thought of as "pre-political," to hark back to a time before the patroon land grants.

The Indians were not benign and quaint relics of

early modern Europe; contemporaries both within and outside the movement saw them as a threat to the public order. In December 1844, two men were killed in separate incidents by Indians firing guns at Anti-Rent rallies. Then, on August 7, 1845, Indians interrupted a distress sale of farm equipment intended to satisfy creditors, and killed Sheriff's Deputy Osman Steele. In the wake of this homicide, Governor Silas Wright declared three New York counties to be in rebellion. Posses circulated through the towns of Delaware County, arresting suspected Indians and forcing others to flee. Two of the eighty-four Indians convicted were sentenced to hang for the murder of the deputy, and the Indian violence, which had been a highly effective deterrent to distress sales, stopped.

THE ANTI-RENT IDEOLOGY

In 1844 and 1845, at the same time that the Indians were being stamped out, the Anti-Renters began in earnest to express an ideology as well as a grievance. They developed their ideology in tandem with the National Reform Movement to gain homesteads for workers—a movement founded in New York in 1844. The National Reformers numbered among their ranks gifted writers and working-class theorists like George Henry Evans, trade unionists like John Commerford, and even the former Newcastle Chartist Thomas Devyr, whose close connection with Anti-Rent would bring to the movement a world of British radical experience. The National Reformers, through their newspaper, the *Working Man's Advocate*, later *Young America!*, drew from a whole genealogy of theorists who propounded people's natural right to the soil. The fact that a person was alive, they claimed, meant that one had a right to the wherewithal needed to live—and this included the soil.

The National Reformers recognized the opportunity to expand their constituency, and sent their own lecturers to upstate New York, where they promoted Anti-Rent as a natural part of a larger movement against land monopoly. Thus, the Anti-Renters not only were able to develop their ideology in more detail, but also signed their names to petitions calling for free homesteads, exemption of the homestead from distraint for debt, and limitation on the amount of land that any one man could own. What had started as a provincial movement in response to some discrete conditions in upstate New York was becoming a national—and with the Chartist connection, an international—land reform movement.

By spring 1845, the Anti-Renters had decided that their only entry into politics would be by running in-

dependent Anti-Rent candidates; Whigs or Democrats were simply not amenable to the discipline that was necessary to get Anti-Rent goals accomplished. In the autumn of 1845, Anti-Rent candidates won control of the governments of three counties and seven seats in the New York State legislature. The Anti-Rent movement was able to achieve the passage of two laws in 1846 that limited landlords' right to oppress distressed tenants and also taxed landlords' rental income. Even more was accomplished at the 1846 New York Constitutional Convention, which promoted short leases and free trade in land. Unfortunately for the leaders of the Anti-Rent movement, however, many constituents had moved on to consider the essential injustice of land monopoly and feared that these changes would do little to address underlying inequalities.

Throughout 1846, there were attempts—successful in some counties—to fuse Anti-Rent with the more thoroughgoing critique of private land ownership put forth by the National Reformers. Some of the most prominent Anti-Renters, including Smith Boughton and Thomas Devyr, led this shift. But it would be wrong to accuse these men of "agrarianism" or lack of respect for private property, or to see them as backward looking. They were strong believers in economic development, yet they knew that a free market in land would prevent the widespread independent proprietorship that could create a level playing field in America. The year saw a second electoral victory for the Anti-Renters, with eleven seats captured in the assembly, but the split between radicals and more moderate reformers remained.

DECLINE OF THE ANTI-RENT MOVEMENT

During the 1847 legislative session, Anti-Renters saw a New York Assembly Select Committee on leasehold estates endorse not only specific anti-leasehold legislation, but also the general natural-rights argument that the National Reformers propounded. Despite this support, Anti-Rent bills repeatedly failed in the legislature. The energy of the movement began to dissipate in various directions. Some Anti-Renters began to renew their support of the National Reform movement, and some combined land reform with abolition to endorse the new Free Soil Party. At the same time, landlords continued to be effective at fighting off any challenges to the legitimacy of their titles.

Having met permanent obstacles in the legislature and been transformed on its radical wing into the quest for free homesteads, the Anti-Rent movement took a long time to die out. The radical wing of the

Anti-Rent movement went further than denouncing rents and called for free homesteads for every farm family. In 1851, the Supreme Court of New York dismissed lawsuits against the patroons' titles, acknowledging that, although old frauds were bad, allowing the state to tinker with contracts was worse. Some challenges to the rent system persisted into the 1880s, but for the most part the 1851 decision deflated the movement. Its remaining newspaper, the *Anti-Renter*, which had been ably led by Thomas Devyr, folded, leaving the movement without feedback or direction.

In the end, the social revolution promised by Anti-Rent was incomplete. The landholding patterns of the manor towns did change, but the value of independent proprietorship and the importance of contracts did not. Once the depression of 1837–1842 had abated, some of the more prosperous farmers bought their lands outright from the landlords. Other, more marginal farmers had been forced off their lands after the Indians were no longer around to protect them. Landholding in upstate New York was substantially more democratic and fitting of a republic than it had been, but change was achieved through continued recognition of the hated contracts. Even so, the more idealistic land-reforming ideas of the Anti-Renters and the National Reformers did not die. One of the most radical ideas in the movement, that every free white American had a natural right to the soil, persisted into the 1850s. By the middle of that decade, "land for the landless" and "homes for the homeless" had become part of the platform of the new Republican Party. The old New Yorkers who had railed against land monopoly lived to see their ideology encapsulated in the Homestead Act of 1862.

Jamie L. Bronstein

BIBLIOGRAPHY

Bronstein, Jamie L. *Land Reform and Working-Class Experience in Britain and the United States*. Stanford, CA: Stanford University Press, 1999.

Christman, Henry. *Tin Horns and Calico: A Decisive Episode in the Emergence of Democracy*. New York: Henry Holt, 1945.

Huston, Reeve. *Land and Freedom: Rural Society, Popular Protest, and Party Politics in Antebellum New York*. New York: Oxford University Press, 2000.

Kubik, Dorothy. *A Free Soil—A Free People: The Anti-Rent War in Delaware County, New York*. Fleischmanns, NY: Purple Mountain, 1997.

McCurdy, Charles. *The Anti-Rent Era in New York Law and Politics, 1839–1865*. Chapel Hill: University of North Carolina Press, 2001.

SOUTHERN EXODUSTERS MOVEMENT

1860s–1870s

In 1879, an African-American man from Louisiana wrote a letter to the governor of Kansas that read in part: "I am very anxious to reach your state, not just because of the great race now made for it but because of the sacredness of her soil washed by the blood of humanitarians for the cause of black freedom."

This man was not alone. Thousands of African Americans made their way to Kansas and other Western states after Reconstruction. The Homestead Act and other liberal land laws offered blacks (in theory) the opportunity to escape the racism and oppression of the postwar South and become owners of their own tracts of private farmland. For people who had spent their lives working the lands of white masters with no freedom or pay, the opportunities offered by these land laws must have seemed the answer to prayer. Many individuals and families were indeed willing to leave the only place they had known to move to a place few of them had ever seen. The large-scale black migration from the South to Kansas came to be known as the "Great Exodus," and those participating in it were called "exodusters."

CONDITIONS IN THE POSTWAR SOUTH

The post-Civil War era should have been a time of jubilation and progress for the African Americans of the South. Slavery, officially abolished in 1865, was nothing more than a bad memory; the Fourteenth Amendment to the Constitution had granted them citizenship; and the Fifteenth Amendment outlawed suffrage discrimination based on race, color, or previous slave status. However, many Southern whites sought to keep blacks effectively disenfranchised and socially and economically inferior.

One way whites in power attempted to prevent black equality was through denial of African-American participation in the political process. Freed blacks were great supporters of the Republican Party, which was the party of Abraham Lincoln and eman-

cipation. Much of the white South, however, remained loyal to the Democratic Party and professed hatred for all Republicans, black or white. When blacks turned out in droves to cast their ballots for Republican candidates, they were often met at the polls by whites employing creative means to keep the African Americans from ever seeing the inside of the voting booth. Many African Americans were prevented from cast-

Ho for Kansas! is a representation of African-American farmers migrating from the South to Kansas and other Western states to stake out land for their own farms. *(Library of Congress)*

ing their ballots and assuming their places as full members of the society. In addition to maintaining some semblance of the postwar balance of power, these methods also helped elect white Democrats.

Economic obstacles unique to their condition also prevented many freed blacks from moving ahead. After having been slaves for most of their lives, they knew only how to be farmers. Even for those who did possess or acquire alternative skills, the region's lack of alternatives to farming as well as determined white supremacy blocked the freedmen's advance. As farmers, they had no money to purchase land of their own, and many were actually forced to go back to work for the very same whites who had held them in bondage for so many years. The only difference was that the white landowners now paid them with a share of the crop which, after deductions for food and other necessities, amounted to a ridiculously low wage for their work. Although this did not technically constitute a master-slave relationship, it likely seemed hardly better than one to the African Americans who had to endure such humiliation and frustration. Many of the freed blacks had few other skills, however, and often had families of their own to support. It must have seemed a no-win situation.

The era of Reconstruction in the South lasted from 1865 to 1877. During these years, federal troops occupied the states of the former Confederacy to ensure compliance with the laws and regulations governing the Southern states' reentry into the Union. Although the protection these troops provided to African Americans was often minimal, it had been better than nothing. When President Rutherford B. Hayes ended Reconstruction in 1877 and pulled the U.S. troops out of the South, the white ruling class of the South had free reign to terrorize and oppress freed blacks without interference from the U.S. Army or anyone else. Murders, lynchings, and other violent crimes against blacks increased dramatically. It was likely at this point that many African Americans began to feel that leaving the South forever was their only real chance to begin new lives. Movement to parts further west, such as Kansas, began almost immediately after the end of Reconstruction.

BLACK MIGRATION TO KANSAS PRIOR TO THE GREAT EXODUS

What was it about Kansas that particularly attracted African Americans to that state? At the time many blacks began to consider abandoning the South, there was certainly a good deal of frontier land available elsewhere. Besides slick (and often misleading) promotion of town sites, what drew freedmen and -women to Kansas?

First, purely logistical and geographic factors must be considered. Kansas, though certainly never considered a part of the South (except by pro-slavery Missourians prior to the Civil War), is much closer to the South than far-off spots like California and Oregon. Getting to Kansas was a much simpler and less expensive task than getting to such faraway places. For those coming from many parts of the South, a boat or train ride to St. Louis was the real beginning of their journey to Kansas. Although conditions on these boats and trains were never ideal, riding in any form was certainly preferable to walking. Many arrived in St. Louis with little idea about how they would get across Missouri and into Kansas. They must have felt, however, that whatever hardships they faced on that leg of the journey would be less onerous than those left behind in the South.

Another factor—a human one—also played a role in the selection of Kansas as the new Promised Land. The exploits of antislavery activists like John Brown gave Kansas an almost holy sacredness to many African Americans. In Kansas, blood had been spilled to keep slavery out. The memories of John Brown and other abolitionist warriors lived on in the hearts and minds of freedmen and -women and made Kansas seem the ideal place to begin anew.

Many of the African Americans who migrated to Kansas prior to the 1879 exodus came from Tennessee. There a popular movement had sprung seemingly from nowhere in 1874, leading to a "colored people's convention" in Nashville in May 1875. Many town promoters, including the notable Benjamin "Pap" Singleton, saw this convention as a way to convince people to migrate to Kansas. The convention resulted in the designation of a board of commissioners to officially promote migration to Kansas. This board would later stipulate that would-be migrants needed at least $1,000 per family to relocate to Kansas; very few interested in doing so had such funds. Nevertheless, many freed blacks determined to leave Tennessee anyway. Promoters like Singleton became known as "conductors" and began leading African American families to Kansas.

Obviously, black migration to Kansas did not begin (or end) with the exodus of 1879. Thousands of freed blacks made their way to Kansas throughout the 1870s. Since their migration was more gradual, however, few whites took notice. This was certainly not the case when the well-publicized exodus took place in 1879.

THE EXODUS OF 1879

The great exodus of African Americans in 1879 was largely influenced by the outcome of the elections of 1878 in the state of Louisiana, in which the Democratic Party made major gains by winning several congressional seats and the governorship. Freed blacks, largely Republican supporters, were coerced, threatened, assaulted, and even murdered to keep them away from the ballot box. When the final tallies were in and the Democrats claimed almost total victory, many black Louisianans knew that the time had come for them to abandon their state and join those already in Kansas. Senator William Windom, a white Republican from Minnesota, introduced a resolution on January 16, 1879, which actually encouraged black migration out of the South. The Windom Resolution, together with Southern white bigotry and the letters and newspaper articles of those blacks already in Kansas, led many Southern freedmen and -women to finally decide to make their way to Kansas. By early 1879, the "Kansas Fever Exodus" was taking place.

The 1879 exodus removed approximately 6,000 African Americans primarily from Louisiana, Mississippi, and Texas. Many had heard rumors of free transportation all the way to Kansas, but they were sorely disappointed when they discovered that such a luxury did not exist. Very few, however, were dissuaded by this inconvenience.

Many Southern whites had a racist and patronizing attitude about blacks in general and the exodus in particular. As much as whites hated dealing with freed blacks, they still wanted the former slaves there as a cheap labor force. Many Southern whites became so alarmed by the exodus that they began to pressure their elected officials to put a stop to it. They eventually succeeded, and a U.S. Senate committee met for three months in 1880 to investigate the cause of the exodus. The committee disintegrated into partisan bickering and accomplished little.

Nonetheless, blacks continued to leave for Kansas. By early March, about 1,500 had already passed through St. Louis en route to Kansas. Back in Mississippi and Louisiana, thousands more crowded onto riverbanks to wait for passing steamers to give them passage to St. Louis. One white man stated that the banks of the Mississippi River were "literally covered with colored people and their little store of worldly goods [sic] every road leading to the river is filled with wagons loaded with plunder and families who seem to think that anywhere is better than here."

Once in St. Louis, many of the exodusters had little idea how to continue their flight with no resources. Some were so destitute that they could not feed themselves or their families. In response, St. Louis clergy and business leaders formed committees to assist the freed blacks so that they could survive and get to Kansas. Food and funds were collected from the local community as well as from sympathizers from Iowa to Ohio. Lack of shelter, however, became the most serious problem, and many blacks were forced to sleep outside near the waterfronts to which the steamships had delivered them. Care of the exodusters in St. Louis became a political issue, especially after the Democratic-leaning *Missouri Republican* began running antiblack stories and tales of mishandling of donated funds. By the time the last of the exodusters departed St. Louis by rail, wagon, boat, or on foot, even the most sympathetic citizens were likely happy to see them go.

Back in the South, more African Americans continued to plan to depart for Kansas. Black social leaders and ministers often sang the praises of the exodus, comparing it to Moses and the Israelites' escape from Egypt. Of course, some black leaders spoke out against the exodus as well, stating that those leaving for Kansas were jeopardizing the future of those who chose to stay behind and that democracy should be given more time to work. Among the most notable of those who tried to dissuade blacks from fleeing the South was Frederick Douglass.

Southern whites continued to oppose the exodus as well. Many went to extreme measures to try to keep blacks from emigrating, including arrest and imprisonment on false charges and the old standby of raw, brute force. African Americans suffered beatings and other forms of violence at the hands of whites desperate to keep them in the South. Although these typical forms of intimidation did not deter many freed blacks from leaving, the eventual refusal of steamship captains to pick them up did. One can only guess that at least some of these sailors had been threatened or paid not to offer blacks passage to St. Louis.

END OF THE EXODUS

The exodus began to subside by the early summer of 1879. Although some African Americans did continue to head for Kansas, the massive movement known as the exodus basically ended with the decade of the 1870s. That ten-year period had witnessed great changes for blacks both in the South and in Kansas. In 1870, Kansas had hosted a black population of approximately 16,250. Ten years later, in 1880, some 43,110 African Americans called Kansas home. Between the earlier gradual migrations and the 1879 exodus, Kansas had gained nearly 27,000 black residents in ten years. Though a far greater number of blacks remained in the South, this number still represents 27,000 individual dreams of a better life and 27,000 people who acted on their desires and their rights to enjoy the freedoms to which they supposedly had been entitled since the Emancipation Proclamation. Few found Kansas to be the Promised Land for which they hoped; yet it was a place that enabled them to live freely and with much less racial interference than in the South.

B.T. Arrington

BIBLIOGRAPHY

Athearn, Robert G. *In Search of Canaan: Black Migration to Kansas, 1879–80.* Lawrence: Regents Press of Kansas, 1978.

Crockett, Norman L. *The Black Towns.* Lawrence: Regents Press of Kansas, 1979.

Hamilton, Kenneth Marvin. *Black Towns and Profit: Promotion and Development in the Trans-Appalachian West, 1877–1915.* Urbana: University of Illinois Press, 1991.

Katz, William Loren. *The Black West: A Documentary and Pictorial History of the African-American Role in the Westward Expansion of the United States.* New York: Touchstone, 1996.

Painter, Nell Irvin. *Exodusters: Black Migration to Kansas after Reconstruction.* New York: W.W. Norton, 1976.

Taylor, Quintard. *In Search of the Racial Frontier: African-Americans in the American West, 1528–1990.* New York: W.W. Norton, 1998.

Grange Movement

The Order of Patrons of Husbandry, as its founders named it in 1867, is generally called the Grange, which is officially the term for its local, county, state, and national units. Members, both men and women, have always been farmers and a variety of other, mostly rural, people. Its purposes, also diverse, have been social, educational, broadly reformist, and briefly, in some of its early years, economically radical. Its size has varied enormously. In 1875, it claimed to have 858,050 members, which was close to its all-time peak. Late in that year the National Grange *Proceedings* reported 761,263 members spread over thirty-six states, several western territories, the District of Columbia, and Canada. Numbers had begun to move downward then, but they were still big, especially in the Ohio River Valley. The allure of its cooperatives and the discounts members received from Montgomery Ward and other vendors had made the Order popular. Then, as the longest depression that the United States had yet experienced dragged on, the Order's economic attractions weakened. Membership dropped precipitously, but the Order did not die. It recovered, becoming what historians have called the Second Granger Movement. Although it inspired enthusiasm among a wide range of reformers, including women who wanted suffrage for themselves and moral betterment for their communities, its growth was slow through the 1890s, perhaps because many rural people who wanted economic reforms were then drawn to the Farmers' Alliances and the People's Party. The Order grew more rapidly in the twentieth century. In 1952, according to Grange leader and historian David H. Howard, membership reached a new high: 858,105. Then it fell. Now, according to the Order's website, membership is about 300,000. It remains, as the Second Granger Movement has consistently been, a social organization with a wide range of reform interests that are connected mostly with rural life.

The First Grange Movement

Oliver Hudson Kelley, a restless Bostonian who became a Minnesota farmer in 1849, was the Order's principal founder. Kelley had claimed Minnesota land near Itasca, which he hoped would become the territory's capital, but Minnesota's legislature decided to let St. Paul keep that honor. Defeated as real estate speculators, Oliver and Lucy Kelley made a difficult start as farmers; she died while delivering their first child early in 1851. But Oliver stayed on the land and soon married Temperance Lane, a fellow Massachusetts migrant who had been teaching in Anoka, Minnesota. Though a novice farmer, Oliver tried to be progressive. He studied agricultural literature, which was burgeoning then, and helped to found Minnesota's first agricultural organization, the Benton County Agricultural Society, in 1852. He hoped, as did organizers of a great many other agricultural societies in his time, that it would help to educate farmers.

In 1864, Senator Alexander Ramsey got Kelley appointed a clerk in the U.S. Department of Agriculture. Trying to farm in Minnesota and work in Washington, with a great deal of help from Temperance who stayed on the land, Kelley wrote articles for the Department of Agriculture and several newspapers. Then, in 1866, he was called upon to survey the condition of Southern agriculture. Kelly, a Democrat sympathetic to the defeated South, spoke with Andrew Johnson before the president's Southern tour. Johnson wanted Kelley, whose writings urged migration to Minnesota, to similarly promote the South and so contribute to its recovery. Kelley tried to do that. Moreover, historians have often taught, his Southern tour inspired him to found the Grange.

Inspiration is said to have begun with the cordiality that fellow Masons in the South showed to Kelley as a fraternal brother, Yankee though he was. Freemasonry, brought to Britain's American colonies from Europe, had about 446,000 American members in 1870, which was more than twice the number in 1860. The great fraternity, with its rituals and secrets, was enjoying an enormous boom. Kelley recalled in his book, *Origin and Progress of the Order of the Patrons of Husbandry in the United States* (1875), that something like it could be a healing bond between Southern and Northern Americans and, like the existing agricultural societies, an instrument of agricultural education and progress. Those ideas, as historians have repeatedly reported, following Kelley's book, inspired him to found the Grange.

Other historians, informed by Kelley's journal as well as his book, have suggested that he envisioned an agricultural fraternity before visiting the South. His purposes, in their view, were not only social and educational. Historian Thomas A. Woods argued in 1991 "that the Grange originated as a radical organization," which sought "legislative controls on monopoly capitalism."

Kelley did not shape the organization alone. His friends in Washington, D.C., where he worked for the Post Office Department in 1867, also played important founding roles. William Saunders, chief horticulturist for the U.S. Department of Agriculture, wrote the Order's national constitution, including its eloquent preamble, which lauded agriculture and knowledge in the style of contemporary agricultural societies. John R. Thompson, a high-ranking Mason, helped to shape Grange ritual. The Rev. Aaron B. Grosh, a Universalist minister, wrote prayers and collected songs for use in Grange meetings. Francis M. McDowell was the Order's financial planner.

Caroline Hall, Kelley's niece, was not among the founders in Washington, but in 1892 the National Grange honored her as "equal to a founder." In his own history, Kelley recalled that full membership for women "ORIGINATED WITH HER." All of those founders and the near founder gave the Order a moral tone and a focus on social, cultural, and educational objectives. From late 1867 through January 1868, that tone and focus prevailed when the organization was being shaped in Washington. There the Potomac Grange became its first local unit, and its members began the National Grange.

Then, in April 1868, Oliver Kelley left Washington. He founded only one durable local grange, in Fredonia, Chautauqua County, New York, on his way home to Minnesota. Other attempts to start granges on that trip failed, so Fredonia's grange has sometimes been honored as the "First Farmers' Grange in the World." Few of its members, however, were farmers. The organization's first Lecturer, responsible for

educational programs, later recalled that he took his office because the other members were also "village people, who cared no more about farming than I did." Woods believes that "Only when Oliver Kelley reached Minnesota" did the Order's "lasting work among the farmers themselves" finally begin. Then, too, Charles M. Gardner, Grange leader and inside historian of the mid-twentieth century tells us, Temperance Kelley "probably saved the Grange" by giving her husband a $500 legacy which she had received during his long absence and which might have been enormously helpful to her and the farm for which she had taken day-to-day responsibility.

Soon Kelley organized two granges near that farm: Granite and Cascade Grange. Neither lasted through 1868, and neither demonstrated that Kelley's movement was exciting widespread or grassroots interest. Most of the Granite Grange members—thirteen men and an unstated number of women—were personal friends of Kelley's. Apart from J.S. Pillsbury, a miller who had already achieved business importance and would later be Minnesota's governor, everyone in the Cascade Grange had become acquainted with Kelley in 1866, when he and they started the Minnesota Fruit Growers' Association. Despite the cooperation that Kelley got from newspapers, notably the *St. Paul Pioneer*, and from agricultural journals, and despite Kelley's passionate class appeals to farmers, his movement had no durable results through the summer of 1868. Then, in September, he started North Star Grange in St. Paul, with fifteen male members.

North Star Grange was important not only because it lasted, soon becoming the state's Grange No. 1 when the first two granges collapsed, but because Daniel A. Robertson, one of its leaders, joined Kelley in rewriting the Order's circular to farmers, promising to build a "co-operative association for individual improvement and common benefit." Then the Order began to grow. It had thirty-six local granges in Minnesota, where it had also formed a state organization, by the end of 1869. By that time, too, it had five local units in other parts of the Midwest: two in Illinois, two in Indiana, and one in Iowa.

The Order began to boom in the 1870s. Daniel A. Robertson volunteered to serve as a deputy and a traveling recruiter; many more deputies, all over the United States and moving into Canada, then enlisted. In 1873, the most spectacular year of growth, 8,667 granges were founded.

At the end of 1873, the Order had more than 10,000 granges in thirty-one states, Quebec, and On-

Grangers assemble at a meeting in Ohio in 1873 to air their grievances and increase their influence. Founded in 1867, the Order of Patrons of Husbandry, as the group was formally known, consisted largely of farmers and rural residents. *(Brown Brothers)*

tario. Growth continued, at a slower pace, into 1875 when the National Grange nearly reached the all-time peak of its membership. Growth owed much to enthusiasm for a wide range of cooperative enterprises that began in 1869 when some leaders of the Minnesota State Grange created a business agency. Hoping to create an assortment of cooperatives, the agency got its first practical results by approaching businesses that dealt with farmers and, in exchange for discounts, helping them to reach grange members. Montgomery Ward, which called itself the "Original Grange Supply House," was not alone in seizing that opportunity. In 1875, Indiana's State Grange agent claimed to have participated in distributing more than $300,000 worth of farm implements, sewing machines, footwear, groceries, and other goods. A year later, his counterpart in the Ohio State Grange claimed that the people he served were getting discounts of 50 percent on sewing machines, 45 percent on garden seeds, 25

percent on footwear and fruit trees, and abundant savings on lots of other goods. However much grangers really saved, such claims surely helped to sell membership in the Order.

Rising membership also inspired entrepreneurial and political interest. In 1874, Master of the National Grange Dudley W. Adams, an Iowa farmer, protested that the Order was infested with "speculators, demagogues, small politicians, grain-buyers, cotton-factors, and lawyers." He wanted to purify the Order, making it an organization of farmers exclusively.

Perhaps that goal was consistent with what William Saunders, author of the Order's constitution, had in mind when he wrote that membership was for people "engaged in Agricultural pursuits." But when the St. Paul, Minnesota, North Star Grange asked whether city folks could join, Kelley welcomed them warmly. Urban ladies who "love flowers and summer visits to their rural friends" were, Kelley thought, particularly valuable to the Order. Then the constitution was amended to state that members had to be "interested in agricultural pursuits." Of course, flower-loving ladies and the sorts of members who irked Dudley W. Adams had many ways of being interested in agriculture.

The Order was a diverse collection of people, both in its early days and when membership boomed. It only lacked recent immigrants, Catholics, members of the Protestant denominations that distrusted fraternal societies, and black people. Some Southern grangers created a parallel black organization, the Council of Laborers; D. Sven Nordin, an important historian of the Grange who studied in Mississippi, tells us that the Grange there "was often a front for the Ku Klux Klan." Then in the mid-1870s, the Order tried to limit its diversity much further. In 1875, its constitution's original phrase, "engaged in Agricultural pursuits," reappeared. Then the executive committee of the Wisconsin State Grange told a local grange master that he should not admit a rural minister. Grangers had to be farmers.

That lasted very briefly. The Order recruited people who were "interested" in agriculture again after membership took a dramatic drop beginning in 1875. It was down to 124,420 in 1880. People left for several reasons, some of which were surely related to the big depression that started late in 1873 and continued for sixty-five months, longer than any previous American economic downturn. Hard-hit farmers became reluctant to pay dues, which some felt state and national Grange leaders to be wasting, and they turned away from Grange cooperatives, which suffered because of both the depression and falling Grange membership. Some members left the Grange, D. Sven Nordin suggests, because they thought that it had achieved all that it could. A few state and federal laws, notably railroad regulations, satisfied some members. Other people, including Grange founders, left for simply personal reasons. William Saunders, author of the Grange constitution, left in 1875 when the Order moved its headquarters from Washington to Kentucky; Oliver Kelley stopped being secretary of the National Grange in 1878 because, he explained, he wanted to devote his time to Florida real estate speculation. He had been losing influence and interest in the Grange for several years by then. Members and some leaders wandered away, but the Order did not die.

THE SECOND GRANGE MOVEMENT

D. Sven Nordin persuasively suggests that the "second Granger Movement" was "in the long run quite probably more significant than the first one." Its significance came in the "long run" because it did not grow rapidly in the late nineteenth century. According to the figures collected by Charles M. Gardner, who was High Priest Emeritus of the National Grange when the Order published his *The Grange-Friend of the Farmer, 1867–1947* (1949), membership was just above 200,000 in 1893 but did not stay above that level for successive years until 1902. Then it moved rather steadily upward. Soon after World War II, the Second Movement became approximately as big as the first had been at its height in 1875. Before that happened, while its numbers were still down in the nineteenth century, it experienced important changes in its regional distribution.

D. Sven Nordin tells us that the first movement at its height had only 13 percent of its members in Ohio, Pennsylvania, New York, and New England. That region had 41 percent of the members in 1880 and 83 percent when the twentieth century began. Oregon Grange leader David H. Howard reports, in his 1992 history of the Order, that membership at the end of the 1960s was greatest in the Northeast, the Northwest, Kansas, and Ohio. Long an important Grange state, Ohio had the largest membership then, but not in the 1970s, when leadership passed to Washington. As membership began what has since been a rather steady decline, a problem shared with many voluntary organizations, most of the states with increasing membership were in the Northwest. The other states where the Order mattered were mostly in the Northeast.

The second movement also differed from the first in terms of women's importance. When the Order began, women held few offices. Their only important activities, other than food preparation, were recitations as the Roman graces Ceres, Pomona, and Flora, on the blessings of grain, fruit, and flowers. The 1869 handbook for local granges called the "graces" officers, which they do not seem to have been at the outset, but gave them no functions other than speaking a few prescribed words about the glories of flowers, fruit, and grain at local meetings. Women had nothing to do or say in state and national granges until 1873 when "four ladies honored" the National Grange by attending its meeting in Oliver Kelley's home, which was then in Georgetown, D.C. The Order's constitution, revised at that meeting, said that women who had "taken the degree of Pomona," the most advanced then available to them, and were married to state grange masters, were welcome at future National Grange meetings.

Clearly, women's participation in early Grange meetings was purely ceremonial and essentially unimportant. That was illustrated in 1875 when participants in the Wisconsin State Grange meeting cast 253 votes for their master and 35 for Pomona. Scant votes for women officers meant that men, the big majority of participants in early meetings, let women choose their own officers. Perhaps men considered women's roles practically unimportant, but they did not act upon the suggestion that the Order should eliminate women from membership. Women stayed in the Order and soon, in a few places, carved out important roles.

That was notably true in Michigan where Mary Mayo played just such a role. Mayo started her Grange career in Pomona's ceremonial role but began lecturing on the Chautauqua Literary and Scientific Circle in 1877. She later addressed granges all over Michigan and often wrote for the *Grange Visitor*, the monthly Michigan State Grange journal. Founder and long chair of the Michigan State Grange Committee on Woman's Work, and deputy lecturer and chaplain of the State Grange, she was active in the Order almost until she died in 1903. She spoke and wrote mostly about morality, education, food, and housekeeping. Politics and suffrage for women little interested her. Mayo's successor, on the other hand, boldly embraced such causes.

Mayo's successor as chaplain of the Michigan State Grange, Olivia Woodman, was a Universalist minister and a vigorous Progressive. Woodman advocated women's suffrage, prohibition, conservation of nature, laws to protect children from dangerous exploitation as workers, and other Progressive causes. Another contemporary, Jennie Buell, brought her literary energy to all of the reforms that interested both Mayo and Woodman and to Swedenborgian philosophy as well. Her books, including a reverent little biography of Mary Mayo, and her articles in Michigan's *Grange Visitor*, *National Grange Monthly*, *Good Housekeeping*, *American Agriculturist*, and other magazines reached a widespread audience. Other women who were important to the Order became masters of local granges, starting in Howard County, Indiana, in 1877. More big steps came in 1895, when Sarah G. Baird began her seventeen years as master of the Minnesota State Grange, and 1986, when Jeanne Davies, master of the Colorado State Grange, became the first woman member of the National Grange executive committee.

Although regional distribution and gender roles changed, the Order stuck to its broad range of traditional concerns. They included and still include what Master of the National Grange Robert Barrow called in 1987 the "increasing concentration" of American agriculture which "poses a threat to the continued viability of the small- and medium-size family farmers and the rural communities they support." A banker and professional singer, not a farmer, Master Barrow resembled many other grangers, who were and continue to be "interested" rather than "engaged" in agriculture. Such nonfarmer Grange members have demonstrated a desire to help farmers economically and to meet their needs for education, healthcare and insurance, and roads. Moreover, grangers have been and remain conservationists of nature's beauty and resources; Gifford Pinchot, President Theodore Roosevelt's chief forester, was a granger. His tradition continues. Finally, as the resolutions passed at the 135th Annual Convention in 2001 demonstrated, grangers have broad public policy concerns that reach beyond farming. They called for "more prominent alcohol warning labels" and endorsed "stem cell research that involves naturally aborted fetuses and unused harvested embryos."

CONCLUSION

The Order of Patrons of Husbandry has now existed for well over a century. Membership, regional distribution, women's roles, and the particular issues that engage its attention have varied over time, but some traditions have continued with fair consistency. Predominantly rural but not exclusively for farmers, despite the purist hope of some early leaders, the Order has always wanted to serve farmers' economic interests. That goal meant a kind of radicalism in its early days; today it means lobbying Congress for policies that may help to block the concentration of agricultural wealth in fewer and fewer hands. Moreover, the Order has always interested itself in a wide range of issues, not all directly connected with farming, and has offered its members a diverse assortment of services. Now Montgomery Ward is gone, but other merchants give grangers discounts on computers, pharmaceutical products, hearing aids, and a good many other products and services. The Order itself offers credit cards, insurance, and, of course, a cookbook. Abundant information about current ideas and services is available to prospective members and the inquisitive public at http://www.nationalgrange.org.

The Order has made available a great deal of information about Grange history, and has published several historical studies. In 1961, it donated Oliver, Lucy, and Temperance Kelley's farm to the Minnesota Historical Society to serve as a museum. Despite the Order's many efforts to explain its organization and objectives and win adherents, membership is not presently at one of its peaks. But grangers, knowing their history, are aware that they have faced that problem before.

Donald B. Marti

BIBLIOGRAPHY

Ander, Fritiof. "The Immigrant Church and the Patrons of Husbandry." *Agricultural History* 8:4 (October 1934): 155–168.

Atkeson, Thomas Clark. *Semi-Centennial History of the Patrons of Husbandry.* New York: Orange Judd, 1916.

Barns, William D. "Oliver Hudson Kelley and the Genesis of the Grange: A Reappraisal." *Agricultural History* 41 (July 1967): 229–242.

Buck, Solon Justus. *The Granger Movement.* Cambridge, MA: Harvard University Press, 1933.

Buell, Jennie. *One Woman's Work for Farm Women, The Story of Mary A. Mayo's Part in Rural Social Movements.* Boston: Whitcomb and Barrows, 1908.

Gardner, Charles M. *The Grange, Friend of the Farmer, 1867–1947.* Washington, DC: National Grange, 1949.

Howard, David H. *People, Pride and Progress: 125 Years of the Grange in America.* Washington, DC: National Grange, 1992.

Kelley, Oliver Hudson. *Origin and Progress of the Order of the Patrons of Husbandry in the United States: A History from 1866 to 1873.* Philadelphia: J.A. Wagenseller, 1875.

Marti, Donald. *Women of the Grange: Mutuality and Sisterhood in Rural America, 1866–1920.* Westport, CT: Greenwood Press, 1991.

Nordin, D. Sven. *Rich Harvest: A History of the Grange, 1867–1900.* Jackson: University Press of Mississippi, 1974.

Robinson, W.L. *The Grange: First Century of Service and Evolution.* Washington, DC: National Grange, 1966.

Woods, Thomas A. *Knights of the Plow: Oliver H. Kelley and the Origins of the Grange in Republican Ideology.* Ames: Iowa State University Press, 1991.

FARMERS' ALLIANCE MOVEMENT

The Farmers' Alliance was the first mass agrarian protest movement in the history of the United States and one of the largest mass movements in American history. The brief life of the Alliance left an enduring legacy of economic self-help, political activism, and moral reform, and led directly to the rise of the Populist Party.

The Farmers' Alliance had its beginnings in Lampasas County, Texas, in 1874–1875 as a way to address essentially Western issues such as government land policy, land fraud, restriction on fencing, and the control of cattle thieves. A dispute over the issue of political involvement in the Greenback Party resulted in its demise, but the idea had spread to other areas, including Parker County where farmers reorganized the Alliance in 1879 to promote self-help strategies such as cooperatives, boycotts, land reform, and other locally based mass action. The growth of the Alliance was painfully slow in the early years. In 1880, the Alliance had twelve local organizations (later called suballiances) in three contiguous counties in North Central, Texas. By 1882, there were only 120 suballiances in twelve Texas counties. By 1886, however, the state meeting of the Texas Alliance reported 104 Texas counties organized. Eventually, in the late 1880s, after it spread throughout the Southwest, Great Plains, and Midwest, the organization would claim a membership of over one million members.

THE CROP LIEN SYSTEM AND RURAL POVERTY

Most historians have attributed the popularity of the Alliance to a rational Southern response to adverse economic conditions among cotton and tobacco farmers. These adverse conditions included a chronic lack of capital and credit in the postbellum South, the emergence of the crop lien system, and the dependence on cotton production in defiance of dropping prices. The crop lien system, which affected both ten-

ants and some landowners, pushed Southern farmers deeper into debt. Local merchants and plantation owners furnished farmers with the necessary supplies for the year for making a crop, taking collateral in the form of a lien on the future crop. Seldom, however, did the sale of the crop pay off the debt incurred to the local merchants or landowners. Because of the crop lien system and low prices, farmers sank deeper and deeper into indebtedness. A report in 1889 showed that 75 percent of the farms in Arkansas were on the verge of insolvency, and another report revealed 70 percent of farmers in the hill counties of Louisiana faced insolvency.

A dissenting voice to the economic cause theory of the rise of the Farmers' Alliance comes from Richard Hofstadter in his influential book *The Age of Reform: From Bryan to FDR* (1976). Hofstadter attributes the farmers' protest movement to status anxiety with the rise of powerful, wealthy, and intellectually sophisticated urban elites and the modernization of industry and commerce with the declining importance of the farm population.

RURAL REBELLION

Whatever the exact motivation for farmers to join in protest, the Alliance took a rather circuitous route to national prominence. In the early 1880s, these local county groups combined in Texas to form a statewide organization that enabled the movement to enter new areas of economic cooperation beyond the local level, to mobilize a larger number of members, and to prepare for further expansion. In 1884 at the state convention, W.L. Garvin, president of the Alliance, appointed S.O. Daws to full-time salaried "Alliance Lecturer" to tour Texas to increase membership, a decision that paid rich returns in the next couple of years. His speeches on the need for cooperative efforts to overcome the effects of monopoly struck a responsive chord among many farmers in Texas. At the same time, the state leadership promoted cooperative economic strategies such as joint stock cooperative stores, cottonseed oil mills, and corn mills, as well as cooperative cotton gins. Suballiances set up trade agreements with local merchants to provide the lowest possible prices in return for the guarantee of Alliance members' trade on a cash basis. These efforts to establish financial independence meant vigorous opposition from local merchants, retailers, and manufacturers. Furthermore, the poorest farmers, enmeshed in the crop lien system, were unable to take advantage of the cash-only trade agreements.

The state convention of 1886 in Cleburne marked yet another key turning point in the history of the Texas Alliance. With the local-based activities of co-ops and trade agreements having reached a point of diminishing returns, the stage was set for a new approach to solving the plight of farmers through new cooperative efforts and political activism. The delegates approved a list of political demands of which the most radical were an overhaul of the monetary system to increase the amount of money in circulation and a demand for government regulation of the railroads. However, a group of economic self-help advocates that included the president, treasurer, and others bolted and called a rival convention to denounce what they thought was too partisan a political approach of the Cleburne meeting.

Those who insisted on avoiding partisan politics feared that this might result in the organization of a third party that would ultimately destroy the one-party system in the South. Rather quickly, Charles William Macune, who took over leadership of the Alliance when the economic self-help group left, worked out a compromise based on three proposals: unification of the local cooperatives into a state exchange, spread of the Alliance to the surrounding states, and the development of a national organization. Macune's "State Exchange" idea appeased those who wished to stay with economic strategies and yet caught the attention of farmers trapped in the crop lien system and those suffering from the low prices of cotton. The Exchange (funded by two assessments on each member) was to act as the agent for supplying the farmers with necessities and to function as a marketing agent for the sale of the farmer's cotton after it had been harvested.

This exchange would reduce the cost of supplies by negotiating directly with manufacturers, thus eliminating the local merchants and the middleman; on the other end of the farmer's economy, bulk marketing of crops would increase the prices farmers got for their crops. The idea spread to other Southern states, with exchanges organized in Georgia and Florida. After a year, the Texas Exchange went bankrupt, in part, for the lack of capital, while the other exchanges, after some initial successes, also failed because of a starvation of money and inexperienced management. The second initiative of the 1886 convention was to take the organization to a new regional level. A plan to send some 350 lecturers throughout the South to organize new local suballiance chapters and state organization became the ultimate logical step to increase the size of the alliance. Implicit in this move to transform the group from a state or regional institution to a national movement was that the problems of the farmer could be addressed at the national level more effectively than at local or state levels.

At the same time as the Alliance experienced a phenomenal increase, Macune recognized the value of consolidating with like-minded groups throughout the South and Great Plains and with labor unions, including the Knights of Labor. In 1887, the Texas Farmers' Alliance merged with a similar group in Louisiana; in 1888, the National Farmers' Alliance merged with the Agricultural Wheel. By 1890, the Alliance, with its name changed to the National Farmers' Alliance and Industrial Union, claimed membership and suballiances in thirty-three states.

THE ALLIANCE EXPANDS

During the period of rapid expansion of membership, the Alliance recruited diverse and, often, conflicting classes of farmers: tenants, yeoman farmers, and large plantation owners. The interests of the large landowners often worked against those of the poorer farmers, an inherent conflict that weakened the overall efforts to institute meaningful change. The Alliance also took hesitant steps to join forces with African Americans in the South by supporting the creation of the Colored Farmers' National Alliance. The Colored Farmers' Alliance was organized in Houston County, Texas, in late 1886. By 1891, the black organizers had chartered groups in every Southern state except Arkansas and had organizations outside the South. Farmers, both black and white, realized that they too shared common economic interests and goals, and tentative cooperative strategies were worked out at the national meetings in Ocala, Florida, in 1889. However the two alliances remained separate. Although historians praise the efforts, they conclude that the white Alliance's overall attitude represented paternalism rather than a sincere attempt toward racial equality.

A similar source of ambiguity arose with the inclusion of women in the movement. Unlike the Grange, which insisted that women participate in membership and provided a separate and complementary organization, the Alliance encouraged female membership without clearly defining their role and extent of involvement in activities. In many local chapters and state alliance organizations, women faced no obstacles to joining, but a few local suballiances showed less willingness to accept female members;, some even prohibited them from joining. Those women who belonged to the Alliance joined because they believed in the goals and objectives of the group, not to create changes for the role of women in society. By 1890, women constituted 11 percent of the total membership of the Alliance.

SOCIAL MOVEMENT AND THIRD-PARTY POLITICS

Responding to pressure from below, the Alliance inevitably moved closer to political activism, first at the state level by putting pressure on the Democratic Party and then in states where a two-party system existed, on the Republican Party to incorporate their reforms. On the state level, they experienced some success and then turned to the national level with new schemes to relieve the economic difficulties of farmers. These proposals took the form of monetary reform to bolster the amount of money in circulation to relieve debt and push up the price of agricultural commodities. The subtreasury idea, hailed by some historians as a noble approach, called for the abolition of the national bank system for the deposit of federal money and the establishment of government warehouses by the U.S. Treasury Department to store the crops. The treasury would loan farmers 80 percent of the market value at the local prices of the stored crops at a very low interest rate. This solved the problem of cash-strapped farmers being forced by debt to sell crops immediately after harvesting when prices tended to be traditionally low, and at the same time increased the amount of money in circulation. The Alliance also demanded increases in the coining of silver, which was another way of putting more money into circulation. Like the Exchange, the subtreasury offered farmers a way to end their dependence on the crop lien as a source of credit and held out the promise of control of their commodity market.

In 1890, after failing to induce the Democratic Party to support their subtreasury idea, after being unable to generate cooperative support from the Democrats for Alliance demands, and after initial suc-

cess in endorsing candidates for state office, the Alliance leaders decided the time was auspicious for the third-party movement. The members and leadership went en masse to the new political party, along with the political platform and ideology of the Alliance. With the creation of the Populist Party, the demise of the Alliance came quickly. The Alliance did not hold national conventions after 1890, and the suballiances and state organizations soon followed in closing out their activities. The death of the Populist Party at the national level came as a result of their 1896 endorsement of the Democratic presidential candidate William Jennings Bryan.

Historians of the movement have debated the extent to which the farmers' movement challenged the existing status quo. Some hold that the movement had a backward looking approach to reform by emphasizing the Jeffersonian myth of the small, independent, landowning farmer. Nevertheless, the demands for government regulation of railroads, monopolies, and the subtreasury plan represented a radical alternative to the capitalist industrial economy. At least several historians argue that moral reforms were equally important as the economic and political objectives of the farmers. Among those concerns expressed in the Alliance newspapers and demands issued at state and national meetings were the regulation of the sale of alcohol, the need for renewal of piety, prohibition of Sunday labor, and control of pornographic material.

ECONOMIC DEPRESSION AND RURAL CRISIS

Whether radical or conservative, in the final analysis, the self-help economics programs failed to improve the permanent condition of farmers, even though Alliance efforts were more sweeping than those of the Grange. The rate of tenancy, indebtedness, and insolvency jumped in the late 1880s and early 1890s, in part as a result of the economic depression that swept the country in the early 1890s. On the other hand, benefits from the political reforms called for by the Alliance resulted in more far-reaching changes for farmers and American citizens. Alliance and Populist political demands included the regulation of railroads, the regulation or destruction of monopolies and trusts, the institution of more democratic election laws, and various social reforms, most of which were implemented under the Progressives.

CONCLUSION

Perhaps the enduring lesson that farmers learned from the Alliance was that a mix of self-help, lobbying, and political pressure on the two major parties worked best in the long run. The third-party venture that killed both the Farmers' Alliance and Populist Party proved a dead end.

The later successes of the National Farmers Union (formally called the Farmers Educational and Cooperative Union of America) best illustrate this point. This third mass-farmers' organization in American history was established near Point, Texas, in 1902. The movement initially experienced phenomenal growth with a membership of 120,000 in 1910 and over 140,000 in 1919, mostly in the Gulf States but eventually spreading to the Midwest and Far West. Following in the footsteps of the Grange and the Alliance, the union promotes cooperative warehouses, grain elevators, stores, and grain and corn mills, establishes plants for manufacture of farm products, and advocates diversification in the production of agricultural commodities, good farm-to-market roads, and improved farm management techniques. These essentially economic and social reforms have been balanced with effective lobbying of the two po-litical parties for programs and public policies to benefit farmers.

James H. Conrad

BIBLIOGRAPHY

Barnes, Donna A. *Farmers in Rebellion: The Rise and Fall of the Southern Farmers Alliance and People's Party in Texas.* Austin: University of Texas Press, 1984.

Goodwyn, Lawrence. *Democratic Promise: The Populist Movement in America.* New York: Oxford University Press, 1976.

Hicks. John D. *The Populist Revolt: A History of the Farmers' Alliance and the Populist Party.* Minneapolis: University of Minnesota Press, 1931.

Hofstadter, Richard. *The Age of Reform: From Bryan to FDR.* New York: Knopf Publishing Group, 1976.

McMath, Robert C., Jr. *Populist Vanguard: A History of the Southern Alliance.* Chapel Hill: University of North Carolina, 1975.

Schwartz, Michael. *Radical Protest and Social Structure: The Southern Farmers' Alliance and Cotton Tenancy, 1880–1890.* New York: Academic, 1976.

GREENBACKER MOVEMENT

1870s–1880s

Greenbackers proposed the government issuance of paper money in order to break the private banks' monopoly over the money supply. This approach was the broadest and most popular manifestation of antimonopolist sentiment, which was central to the politics of the post–Civil War period. Greenbackers built the largest unsuccessful third-party movement in American history, representing a complex movement in terms of its origins, scale, and legacy.

ROOTS OF GREENBACKISM

Greenbackism originated in three currents. First, only a generation before, discontented voters had built the most successful third-party movement in the American experience, bringing the Republicans to power. Older policy had created a tight money supply largely controlled by banks, but the Lincoln administration met its unprecedented expenses by having the government print "greenbacks." This move created an inflation that fueled wartime prosperity and minimized the seasonal indebtedness of farmers and rural people. Some Civil War Republicans had also advocated black civil rights, a shorter working day, and woman suffrage. Such topics faded, however, with the presidency of Ulysses S. Grant, notable for its corruption and its plans to restore the gold standard. Midwestern farmers, as well as many abolitionists, saw their party as having sold itself to business interests and contemplated a repeat of their earlier third-party movement.

The second current important to originating the Greenbacker Movement flowed from the Democrats. "New Departure" Democrats understood that dwelling on their constitutional hostility to the excesses of wartime and Reconstruction Unionism would gain them nothing against Republican efforts to depict Democrats as disloyal. Their approach was new in that they favored reforms like the Granger laws, but most importantly because they avoided "dwelling on their constitutional hostility to the excesses of wartime and Reconstruction Unionism."

Thus far, the Democrats had established a "Solid South" at the price of holding a permanent minority status elsewhere in the country. Those urging a "New Departure" tapped the older antimonopolist rhetoric of Andrew Jackson to criticize the Republican fostering of industrial and commercial privileges.

Third, Greenbackism had clearly radical origins. Before the Civil War, Cincinnati stovemaker Josiah Warren had formulated his version of anticapitalist communitarianism by establishing cooperative stores based upon "Labor Notes" that offered to exchange labor on an equitable basis. He also founded the community of "Modern Times," where he worked with Edward Kellogg who urged adopting paper money as a means to blunt the excesses of antebellum capitalism. Another antebellum writer, William B. Greene, urged cooperative banking as an alternative. For such thinkers, money had ceased to represent wealth and had now become a means of controlling economic life, as well as something of an allegory for representative politics.

THE 1872 ELECTIONS

Such ideas captured the growing movement of trade unionists and labor reformers who began pressing on the legislative agenda such matters as industrial working conditions and a shorter workday. By 1868, adherents of the postwar National Labor Union formed state Labor Reform parties in Massachusetts and New Hampshire and, in 1871, launched a National Labor Reform Party (NLRP). It faced a presidential election in 1872, even as the Republican Party split between the "Liberal" critics of Grant and the regulars, largely leaving Democrats to bloc with the Liberals.

In this context, the prospect of power politics seduced the NLRP convention at Columbus on February 21–22, 1872. It adopted a lackluster platform that embraced "the Ohio idea" of limited paper money advocated by that state's Democrats, and it nominated an Illinois Democrat, David Davis, who after the convention predictably declined the nomination in order to avoid losing his strength with his Democratic Party comrades. The Democrats nominated the Liberal Republican, Horace Greeley. Those that did not want to support Greeley held their own convention and nominated Charles O'Conner on what they called a "Straight-Out Democratic" ticket, which the NLRP leaders endorsed.

The more radical insurgents subsequently convened on May 9–11, in New York's Apollo Hall where they launched the Equal Rights Party. It nominated "the Women's, Negroes, and Workingmen's ticket," Victoria Woodhull and Frederick Douglass. A flattered but loyally Republican Douglass declined, while Woodhull faced arrest over alleged libels in her paper. Woodhull was always facing arrest over libels in her newspaper, *Woodhull and Clafflin's Weekly,* most famously in the Beecher-Tilton scandal.

MIDWESTERN THIRD-PARTY MOVEMENTS

The "hard times" that swept the Midwest with the Panic of 1873 politicized mass organizations like the Patrons of Husbandry, "the Grange." When the elected Supreme Court of Illinois declared unconstitutional the state's efforts to regulate its railroads, angry farmers built a Peoples' Antimonopolist Party that defeated the combined efforts of the more well-heeled parties to reelect the justices. So, too, a similar Independent Party emerged in Indiana. By 1874, there appeared Missouri's Peoples' Party, Michigan's National Reformers, Nebraska's Independents, and the Antimonopolists of Iowa and Minnesota, in addition to the Independent Reformers of Kansas and Wisconsin.

With the exception of Missouri, these parties emerged in states with Republican majorities. Since they posed the clearest possibilities for Democratic victories in these states, adherents of that party, along with "fusionists" within the third party eager to broker power, pressed continually for a shared agenda. For genuine insurgents, a stable third party required a national movement, which seemed to require a unifying issue like the Kansas-Nebraska Act of twenty years before. The government's decision to replace wartime "Greenbacks" with a "resumption" of metal specie and "the gold standard" supplied the unifying issue.

CURRENCY AND THE NATIONAL THIRD PARTY

On June 10, 1874, coordinated state conventions in Illinois and Indiana adopted the call to save paper money. When the Democratic conventions did not address the issue, a small but important conference met on November 25 at Indianapolis. It united the new rural insurgents with former NLRP groups from Illinois, New York, Ohio, Connecticut, Pennsylvania, and West Virginia. Some NLRP leaders favorable to a broader platform met at Harrisburg on March 3, 1875, but failed to win much support.

The new party called itself the "Independent Party" or the "National Party" to distinguish itself from the state parties in Illinois and Indiana and the sectionalized Republican and Democratic parties. Nevertheless, the press called their creation the "Greenback Party," and most insurgents readily accepted the name.

THE 1876 COOPER-CARY CAMPAIGN

A presidential nominating convention gathered on May 17–18, 1876, at the Academy of Music in Indianapolis. As with the earlier NLRP, larger delegations nominated "favorite sons," mostly prominent "New Departure" Democrats, Ohioans pressing for former Ohio governor William Allen and many Illinoisans still wanting to name David Davis, who had beached the NLRP four years before. Eager to get beyond the impasse and to reach potential voters in the Eastern cities, the convention turned to the "Greenback Democrats" of New York City, who had briefly stopped at the convention while seeking allies for the upcoming Democratic National Convention.

Oddly, a party of mostly rural Midwesterners predisposed to vote Republican nominated an octogenarian urban Jacksonian, Peter Cooper, and Democratic Senator Newton Booth of California. When Booth declined, he was replaced with Samuel F. Cary, the popular Cincinnati Democrat. The Greenback Party ultimately won nearly 82,000 votes in the presidential election of 1876, about 1 percent of the turnout. In the end, the Greenback ticket represented little more of a serious third-party effort than had the earlier NLRP slate.

More generally, American politics faced a crisis in the "Stolen Election" of 1876. Several Southern states filed conflicting returns. The Democrats and Republicans each turned in different vote counts in three states, on which the election would turn. Setting aside the question of which returns were valid, the Federal authorities established a national Electoral Commission to decide who would be the president. Ultimately, this solution allowed Republican Rutherford B. Hayes to become president if he abandoned any further federal Reconstruction of the South.

LABOR POLITICS

In the wake of the NLRP, advocates of a more independent and radical strategy had continued on to socialism. The ethnic self-fragmentation of the International Workingmen's Association had continued into 1874 when various suspended sections combined with a Newark labor party to launch the Social Democratic Workingmen's Party of North America, which in 1876 led to the Workingmen's Party of the United States.

By then, broader numbers of workers had turned to political action. In 1877, after several years of worsening economic conditions, the railroads announced yet another round of pay cuts in July. Driven to desperation, railroad workers walked off the job, detonating a national "general strike" that led to the seizure of cities by strike committees at Toledo and St. Louis. Often over the objection of local officials, the national authorities sent troops against the strikers; this was in sharp contrast to their unwillingness to protect the rights of the Southern freedmen. The national authorities used U.S. troops against striking workers, even as they withdrew the last of those troops in the South to sustain the Reconstruction project.

In the wake of the strikes, working-class organizations proliferated. The Knights of Labor began growing rapidly, subsuming preexisting unions and organizations. At the polls, they began electing Socialist and labor candidates in numerous communities. In places, they became Greenbackers or formed a natural alliance with the earlier insurgents.

THE GREENBACK-LABOR PARTY

Insurgents met again in a drafty schoolhouse on Washington's birthday during the bitterly cold winter of 1878. Embracing their new composition, strategy, and orientation, the rebuilt coalition called itself the Greenback-Labor Party (GLP). A coalition of "Greenback" and "Labor" organizations, this represented a rebuilding of the groups that had attempted the National Labor Reform Party in 1872, but on a vastly greater scale. Notably, an important coalition of clubs chose to keep their Union Greenback organization independent of the GLP. So did the Socialists who reorganized as the Socialistic Labor Party (SLP) that winter. One faction of the Workingmen's Party of California, which blamed the oppression of labor on the presence of the Chinese, was interested in the national movement, but much of its leadership was drawn inexorably toward the Democratic Party. So, too, the triumph and hegemony of the white "Redeemer" Democratic governments in the South inspired a series of independent splits from the Democrats, including such statewide formations as the Readjusters' Party, which sought to renegotiate the payment of Virginia's indebtedness. Freethinkers, hostile to a rising tide of militant Protestantism, had also launched a National Liberal Party.

Nevertheless, in places the GLP subsumed the social and community functions of groups like the Grange. It also gained some localized strength beyond the Midwest, winning elections in places as diverse as northern Alabama or the more isolated parts of northern New England. If a successful national movement required such successes, the strategy of fusion seemed to offer a shortcut. Fusion involved making joint nominations with the weaker of the two major parties, a process that generally allied Southern Greenbackers with Republicans and Northern Greenbackers with Democrats.

THE 1878 PEAK

The off-year national elections saw the largest third-party movement in twenty years and proportionately the largest in U.S. history. Although the insurgents claimed 1 million votes for their congressional candidates that year, accurate numbers reveal a more complex reality. Between 802,000 and 852,000, ballots went to the exclusively Independent, National, Greenback, or Independent Greenback tickets, with another 25,000 divided roughly equally between Prohibitionists and Socialists. In addition, third-party candidates running either with Democratic endorsements or, at least, no Democratic opposition, added another 303,400, while another 217,000 went to insurgents with apparent Republican support. Independent Democrats running against Democratic candidates won another 150,000, and Independent Republicans, by the same criteria, gained over 18,000. Such additions nearly doubled the purely insurgent vote to a total of about 1,600,000.

This deluge of independent ballots elected twenty-two independent congressmen, most of whom had some ties to the third party. The Midwestern heartland of the movement elected several new representatives, including: Adlai E. Stevenson and Albert Palaska Forsythe of Illinois; Rev. Gilbert De La Matyr of Indiana; and James B. Weaver and Edward Hooker Gillette of Iowa. In addition, voters in the Northeast elected the following to Congress: Hendrick B. Wright, William D. Kelley, and Seth H. Yocum of Pennsylvania; Hezekiah B. Smith of New Jersey; Daniel O'Reilly of New York; Bradley Barlow of Vermont; and George W. Ladd and Thompson Murch of Maine. More surprisingly, the GLP also cracked the solid Democratic South before it had even hardened: Nicholas Ford of Missouri; Daniel L. Russell of North Carolina; William M. Lowe of Alabama; and George W. Jones of Texas. (Other victorious independents included Henry Persons, William H. Felton, and former Confederate Vice President Alexander Hamilton Stephens in Georgia, and Noble A. Hull, who won a Florida district with no party affiliation.)

THE 1880 ELECTION

On January 8, 1880, sixteen of these independently elected congressmen invited "all classes of people, of men and of women, too, who . . . are willing to act with us" to join in planning united action in the upcoming presidential election. The June national convention at Chicago's Exposition Hall moderately expanded the GLP platform and adopted the SLP's plank: "We declare that land, air, and water are the grand gifts of nature to all mankind, and the law or custom of society that allows any person to monopolize more of these gifts of nature than he has a right to, we earnestly condemn and demand shall be abolished."

The GLP nominated for president Representative Weaver, who shared the ticket with the elderly Texan Barzillai J. Chambers. Weaver spoke of Greenbackism as opposition to the idea not only of a monopoly over the money supply, but of land and the means of transportation as well. Weaver also stumped the country and directly confronted the nationally untenable nature of fusion. State parties like that in Maine hoped to continue winning victories through an alliance with the Democrats, which would doom the party in Alabama. Making a direct issue of genuine independence

(and the Democratic denial of black civil rights in the South), Weaver found himself marginalized, then misreported, and finally rendered invisible in the national press, even as many state leaders tore the national party to pieces. In the end, fusion in Maine, for example, reclassified the 65,310 ballots cast for mostly GLP electors into officially Democratic votes, and reporting of the official insurgent totals as merely 306,867, a considerable decline from the total of two years before.

LEGACY

The GLP survived, particularly at the edges of the large insurgency, in places like Kansas. However, in the wake of the election, the National Antimonopoly League declared itself a National Antimonopoly Party, which stole a march on the remnants of the Greenbackers in 1883 and 1884. This left the GLP simply to endorse Benjamin F. Butler, the Antimonopolist candidate, who openly did the inverse of Weaver by actively courting funding from factions of both major political parties. Again in 1887 and 1888, a nominally insurgent Union Labor Party acted before the Greenbackers and got their endorsement.

Perhaps the real legacy of the Greenbackers was their role in becoming the proponents of a People's Party (the Populists) after 1890. The Populists ran an older but energetic Weaver for president in 1892, and found itself succumbing to the same problems with regard to fusion.

Mark Lause

BIBLIOGRAPHY

Buck, Solon J. *The Granger Movement: A Study of Agricultural Organization and Its Political, Economic, and Social Manifestations, 1870–1880.* Cambridge, MA: Harvard University Press, 1913.

Destler, Chester M. *American Radicalism, 1865–1901.* New London: Connecticut College, 1946.

Fine, Nathan. *Labor and Farmer Parties in the United States, 1828–1928.* New York: Rand School of Social Science, 1928.

Haynes, Fred E. *Social Politics in the United States.* Boston and New York: Houghton Mifflin, 1924.

Lause, Mark A. *The Civil War's Last Campaign: James B. Weaver, the Greenback-Labor Party & the Politics of Race & Section.* Landham, MD: University Press of America, 2001.

Montgomery, David. *Beyond Equality.* New York: Knopf, 1967.

Ritter, Gretchen. *Goldbugs and Greenbacks: The Antimonopoly Tradition and the Politics of Finance in America, 1865–1900.* Cambridge and New York: Cambridge University Press, 1997.

Populist Movement

Populism is the common name for an agrarian democratic political movement of the 1890s, formally identified with the People's Party of America. The Populist movement attracted veterans of earlier reform movements, including Greenbackers, Prohibitionists, union organizers, and dissident Republicans and Democrats. But the party's most significant forerunner was the Farmers' Alliance, which initiated an agrarian revolt in the 1880s. The Alliance attempted to influence the two major political parties, but by 1891, when the national parties had failed to champion the reforms advocated by the Alliance, many within the movement argued for the creation of a party that reflected their interests.

ORGANIZATION

From 1889 to 1891, efforts were made to unite farmer and labor organizations into a single political lobby. In December 1889, sectional Alliance organizations met in St. Louis to discuss the development of a national political strategy to resolve the struggle between organized capital, corporations, and organized labor, unions, and farmer alliances. In June 1890, Alliance members in Kansas formed the statewide People's Party and challenged the dominance of the Republican Party in that state. Six months later, representatives of the Southern Farmers' Alliance, the Farmers' Mutual Benefit Association, and the Colored Farmers' Alliance met in Ocala, Florida, where they compiled a list of demands that resembled the interests debated in St. Louis. These interests included cheap currency, the abolition of national banks, and the adoption of a subtreasury plan. The subtreasury plan held the most interest for farmers.

Developed by Texan Charles Macune, the subtreasury plan called for the federal government to build and operate warehouses, which could hold non-perishable crops that enabled farmers to obtain government loans of up to 80 percent of their crop values at 1 percent interest. Leaders at the meeting advised their members to support candidates of either major party who would pledge themselves to the list of demands drawn up in Ocala.

The failure of the two major political parties to enact the demands of the Alliance organizations led to the call for a national meeting by Leonidas Lafayette Polk of North Carolina. President of the Southern Farmers' Alliance since 1889, Polk argued that the only viable alternative for his members was the formation of a third political party. In May 1891, more than 1,400 delegates from thirty-two states met at Cincinnati. Resolutions to create a new political party to represent farmers' interests passed easily. Formally organized in February 1892 at St. Louis, the People's Party of the United States of America held its first national convention at Omaha in July 1892. Many of the most ardent advocates for labor and farmer rights attended the meeting, including Tom Watson of Georgia, who argued that "you must organize, agitate and educate." The new party attempted to educate the public through the publication of 150 newspapers and by using experienced lecturers from the Alliance movement who traveled to forty-three states reaching over 2 million farmers. Members expected Polk to be the party's nominee for the presidency, but he became ill following his return from St. Louis and died in North Carolina in June, one month before the party selected its standard-bearer.

THE PARTY

The Populists, as the new party quickly became nicknamed, nominated James B. Weaver of Iowa, a former Union general and Greenback presidential candidate, as president. Joining him on the ticket for vice president was James G. Field of Virginia, who had served the Confederacy during the Civil War. The sectional flavor of the ticket was a deliberate attempt to overcome the animosity that lingered from the war and to undercut the Republican political strategy of "waving the bloody shirt," calling attention to the sacrifices of the Civil War to promote their political agenda. The new party wanted to focus voter attention on contemporary economic and political issues and not relive the Civil War.

The new party's platform made this position very clear. Written by Ignatius Donnelly of Minnesota, the platform consisted of twelve short paragraphs that included quotations from the U.S. Constitution and a call for immediate action to save the nation from a "vast conspiracy against mankind." He reminded the delegates that "we meet in the midst of a nation brought to the verge of moral, political and material ruin." Since the two political parties no longer represented the interests of the people but the interests of profit, Donnelly called upon the new party to restore democracy to the nation.

Following Donnelly's preamble, the party's platform listed the specific measures to be taken in order to achieve the restoration of democracy by focusing upon finance, transportation, and political reform. Among the list of demands was a national currency, to be issued by the federal government without the use of banking corporations, government ownership of all transportation and communication lines, a graduated income tax, the establishment of a postal savings system, direct election of U.S. senators, the adoption of the secret ballot, the initiative and referendum, restrictions on immigration and immigrant ownership of land, and an eight-hour working day for industrial labor.

POLITICAL DEVELOPMENT AND REACTION

Although Weaver was defeated in the 1892 presidential election, the new party received over a million votes (8.2 percent of the popular vote) and demonstrated considerable strength in Texas, Georgia, North Carolina, Nebraska, and the Dakotas. The party won the governors' races in Kansas and Colorado. Most affected by Populist support were Southern Democrats who became alarmed by the People's Party's attempt to recruit black farmers to their cause. Democratic leaders in the one-party region could not afford a division of the Southern white vote between Democrats and Populists, for that would allow the black vote to determine the balance of power in the old Confederacy. By the mid-1890s, Southern Democrats took action to disenfranchise the black community. The use of such measures as the "Grandfather clause" (if your grandfather could not vote neither could you, thereby disenfranchising descendants of

slaves), literacy tests, and the poll tax resulted in dramatically decreased black participation in the electoral process in the South. In Louisiana, for example, the number of black voters decreased from a historic high of 130,000 in 1896 to just over 5,000 four years later. Alabama saw its black participation drop from 121,159 to 3,742 during that same four-year period.

Southern Democrats had reason to be alarmed. Shortly after the 1892 election, the Philadelphia and Reading Railroad collapsed, initiating a Wall Street panic and resulting in the worst depression the nation had suffered since the end of the Civil War. By 1894, millions were out of work, 500 banks closed their doors, 16,000 business firms collapsed, 750,000 workers went out on strike, and demands that the federal government take action climaxed with a march on Washington. The Army of the Commonwealth of Christ, led by Jacob Coxey, a former wealthy businessman turned Populist who organized Coxey's Army of the unemployed and poor, arrived in the nation's capital to demand that the government respond to the needs of the people. Although Coxey and some of his followers were arrested shortly after they arrived, the march suggested the level of frustration that citizens felt and the desperate measures they were willing to take. Both major political parties realized that the upcoming mid-term elections could not be reduced to re-fighting the Civil War.

In 1894, the People's Party received 1.5 million votes in the congressional elections, sending to Washington six Populist senators and seven Populist representatives. But party leaders had hoped for better results and were disappointed by the strength of the Republicans. Democrats, however, saw more defections from their party and felt pressured to respond to the demands of the Populists, especially those in Southern states. As a result, many Democrats began to publicly endorse much of the platform of the People's Party. Their actions initiated a national debate over silver.

As a result of a drain on the gold reserve of the country, President Grover Cleveland asked for and received from Congress the repeal of the Sherman Silver Purchasing Act. The gold reserve of the country continued to decline, however, and the president negotiated with private corporate leaders, most notably J.P. Morgan, to purchase gold in exchange for federal bonds. Many in the country saw the deal as evidence of the predominance of private business interests over the interests of the people. As the depression worsened, silver advocates argued for a return to a bimetallic currency. Publications such as William H.

Harvey's *Coin's Financial School* (1894) and Ignatius Donnelly's *The American People's Money* (1895) became required reading for Populists and Democrats. The Republican Party remained loyal to the gold standard.

THE ELECTION OF 1896

As the election of 1896 approached, the Populists debated whether to concentrate on the silver issue at the expense of their other interests. Pro-silver Populists argued that the People's Party should hold their nominating convention after the two major parties met in order to attract "silverites" who might abandon their parties following their own conventions. But pro-silver Democrats captured their convention and nominated William Jennings Bryan. The young former congressman from Nebraska galvanized the convention with his "Cross of Gold" speech. Bryan's speech, which endorsed silver and much of the People's Party platform of 1892, presented a problem for silver Populists who held their convention two weeks later in St. Louis. Suddenly, the Democrats provided an opportunity to secure the goals of those who favored a return to silver. Led by the national chair of the party, Herman E. Taubeneck, pro-silver Populists advocated dropping the Omaha platform and building a coalition with the Democratic Party on the issue of free coinage of silver. Ignoring a minority in the party who argued that fusion with the Democrats would result in the death of the Populists, the new party endorsed Bryan as their presidential candidate. To soothe those who feared that the party might lose their identity, the People's Party nominated one of their own, Tom Watson, as Bryan's running mate.

Silver, however, was not the sole issue in the election of 1896. As in 1860, the differences between the two candidates were sectional and economic, but they were also social and cultural. Bryan cast himself as a crusading prophet who would reform not only his party but the country as well. The Republican candidate, William McKinley of Ohio, followed the direction of his party boss, Mark Hanna, who recognized the need to create a coalition of business and labor in the urban Northeast, thus presenting a campaign that would not offend the rising Protestant middle class, Catholic immigrants, or the economic elite of Wall Street. Thus, the campaign conducted by Bryan and McKinley pitted the promise of moral reform against the promise of the melting pot. The Republicans assured those who had aspirations of economic and social mobility that their platform offered more opportunity. This strategy and changing demographics resulted in a Republican victory. McKinley carried the industrial Northeast, which had increased its population over the previous twenty years, thus increasing its electoral count. Bryan won in the South and the West, but the population of those regions produced fewer electoral votes. Just over 7 million people chose McKinley, resulting in 271 electoral votes, while 6.5 million people cast their ballots for Bryan, producing 176 electoral votes.

DECLINE AND LEGACY

Those who feared that fusion with the Democratic Party would destroy the People's Party proved correct. By the end of the campaign, many state Populists had lost control of their organizations to Democrats, especially in the South. The economy recovered in 1897, as discoveries of gold in South Africa and Alaska inflated the currency. The following year, the country went to war against Spain. A wave of patriotism swept the country, and Americans showed little patience with critics of the nation. As Tom Watson put it, "the blare of the bugle drowned the voice of the reformer." Economic prosperity, patriotism, and political fusion explain the rapid decline of the Populist movement. The party would remain an organized entity for three more elections. In 1900, the fusion Populists once again endorsed Bryan, with the results the same as four years earlier. In 1904 and 1908, the party turned to Tom Watson.

Watson's political career suggested an inherent problem faced by Southern Populists. Western Populists risked little more than political failure in challenging those who held political power. Southern Populists, on the other hand, not only challenged the economic and political relationships of their region but the racial relationship as well. As a result of their attack on the political establishment of the old Confederacy, Southern reformers risked not just their political security but also their personal security. By the early 1900s, the race-baiting tactics of New South politicians created an atmosphere that resulted in the monthly lynching of black citizens and segregation as a way of life, convincing many reformers, including Watson, that making overtures to the black community would be a political liability. As a result, Watson and others convinced themselves that a biracial political partnership was the source of the failure of the People's Party. Watson ended his political career by using the same race-baiting techniques as the New South leaders that he opposed in the previous decade.

The Populist movement proved to be successful in the long run, however. The party's critique of the modern corporate industrial state created the political

Following his "Cross of Gold" speech at the 1896 Democratic National Convention, presidential candidate William Jennings Bryan tries to ride three parties to victory. His loss to Republican William McKinley spelled the doom of the Populist Party. *(Brown Brothers)*

agenda for the country for the next thirty years and proved to be the forerunner of the reform movements of the twentieth century—Progressivism, the New Deal, and the Great Society. Much of the Omaha platform of 1892 became a reality, including the direct election of senators, the initiative and recall measures, a personal income tax, a Warehouse Act that allowed farmers to store produce as collateral for short-term loans, and a Federal Farm Loan Board.

The words "populism" and "populist" took on new meanings in the last four decades of the twentieth century. After World War II, populism migrated from the political left to the political right as public figures began to refer to themselves as populist to distance themselves from those entrenched in Washington, D.C. Individuals such as Senator Joe McCarthy (R-WI) in the 1950s, Governor George Wallace in the 1960s, and Reform Party candidate Ross Perot in 1992 presented themselves not as advocates for economic and social change, but as defenders of the status quo. In reality, figures like McCarthy, Wallace, and Perot had little in common with the Populists of the 1890s and were, instead, self-proclaimed crusaders who thrust themselves into the role of savior. In contrast, Populist leaders of the 1890s were members of the class they sought to represent, and they challenged the economic and political assumptions of those in power.

David O'Donald Cullen

BIBLIOGRAPHY

Clanton, Gene. *Populism: The Humane Preference in America*. Boston: Twayne, 1991.

Goodwyn, Lawrence. *Democratic Promise: The Populist Moment in America*. New York: Oxford University Press, 1976.

Hicks, John D. *The Populist Revolt: A History of the Farmers' Alliance and the People's Party*. Minneapolis: University of Minnesota Press, 1931.

Kazin, Michael. *The Populist Persuasion: An American History*. New York: Basic Books, 1995.

McMath, Robert. *American Populism: A Social History, 1877–1898*. New York: Hill and Wang, 1992.

Sanders, Elizabeth. *Roots of Reform: Farmers, Workers and the American State, 1877–1917*. Chicago: University of Chicago Press, 1999.

AGRARIAN SOCIALIST MOVEMENT
1890s–1920

THE BIRTH OF SOUTHWESTERN SOCIALISM

Early twentieth-century agrarian socialism was an extension of and yet fundamentally different from the Populist movement. Agrarian socialism would be centered in the Great Plains and Southwest, with its most active leaders and voters in Oklahoma and Texas. The first voices to call for dissident Populists to make the break to socialism, indeed, came from Oklahoma and Texas. Radicals in northern Oklahoma formed a local Socialist Party in 1895 and briefly flirted with the Socialist Labor Party (SLP). They soon discovered, however, that the SLP had no interest in farmers. Dominated by its founder, the orthodox Marxist Daniel De Leon, this group made little effort at electoral politics and concentrated instead on enforcing doctrinal purity within a rank-and-file of mostly Northeastern, immigrant industrial workers. Socialist thought and organization also flickered to life here and there among laborites and intellectuals, either in Marxian ideology or in uniquely American hybrids such as the Knights of Labor.

Most of the early Socialist impetus among agrarians came during and after their failed struggle against fusion with the Democratic Party in 1896. Their disagreement with conservative, pro-Bryan elements of the party forced the dissidents to consider their alternatives. Disgusted with fusion, ex-Populist William Farmer of rural north Texas soon founded the first Texas Socialist Party. Of even greater import to the Great Plains and Southwest, in 1895 ex-Populist editor Julius A. Wayland moved *The Appeal to Reason* to Girard, Kansas, specifically to preach socialism to farmers. Wayland's *Appeal to Reason* and its message of socialism would reach tens of thousands of rural readers every week well into the second decade of the twentieth century.

Near the same time that Farmer was announcing his party in rural Texas, former American Railway Union (ARU) president Eugene V. Debs announced the formation of a similar loosely knit group in the Midwest. Debs's railroad union had been crushed by its defeat in the Pullman strike of 1894, but in 1898 Debs began to reassemble the fragments of the ARU as the Social Democracy of America. Debs toured the country organizing party locals and found a number of ex-ARU members now homesteading in Oklahoma. Together with Farmer's Texans, Debs gathered them into the somewhat utopian Social Democracy.

In 1901, however, Debs's Social Democracy joined New York dissidents bolting the SLP in a coalition with Midwestern Socialists led by Victor Berger to form the Socialist Party of America (SPA). Meeting in 1902, Farmer and other Texas Socialists formally joined their state party with the new Socialist Party of America. Thus, from the most radical Populists and through Debs's Social Democracy, the new Socialist Party of America gained a coterie of militant Southwestern agrarians. Consequently, this new coalition became the vehicle of protest in the last widespread agrarian political revolt in United States history. It would be nearly a decade, however, before it became a significant rural movement.

SLOW GROWTH IN THE COUNTRYSIDE

The Socialist Party of America would grow slowly during its first decade of existence among rural Americans. It grew slowly because of contradictions between rural values and the SPA's central message of collectivization. That it grew at all among rural people testified to increasing levels of dismay among farmers. The rapid triumph of turn-of-the-century nationwide capitalism displaced culturally entrenched structures. Although country people's values and expectations regarding economic behavior sprang from their old culture, their new societal reality was a nationwide marketplace impervious to face-to-face relationships or moral codes.

In the Southwest, angry middle-aged farmers found it increasingly difficult to acquire ownership of land. Considered a normal but temporary step up the "agricultural ladder," sharecropping and tenancy had become the permanent occupation for the majority of southwestern farmers by 1910. Most tenants and sharecroppers continued to hope that they would someday work themselves into ownership of their own land. Others, more embittered, began to consider alternatives.

The Socialists' critique of the new marketplace—if not necessarily their proposed solutions—resonated with the rural poor majority's belief that all behaviors, including economic behavior, should conform to locally defined moral standards. At the same time, belief in the individual ownership of land remained a nonnegotiable cornerstone within their culture. Furthermore, the values within rural culture that found the most resonance in the Socialists' message of radical economic equality tended to grow from the plain folk's religious beliefs. Yet, one of the most oft-repeated and effective criticisms of socialism was that it emanated from an atheistic scientific materialism. In the Southwest, at least, by 1910, local Socialists had taken action to minimize the aspects of socialism that were most objectionable to rural people, while emphasizing those aspects with which they would most agree. Culturally, this meant an energetic emphasis on "Bible socialism" through a heavy reliance on rural preachers as lecturers, organizers, and candidates. In the case of land ownership, this meant changing the party's platform to protect the property rights of family farmers.

Eugene Debs carried the Socialist banner in five of the first six presidential elections of the twentieth century. At the Socialists' highwater mark in 1912, Debs's best state percentages came from the West where sparse urban middle-class populations gave the militant unionized workers' votes relative clout. Historians ascribe Debs's 1912 double-digit percentages in the Mountain and Pacific states to the militant Western Federation of Miners and other radical industrial workers in the six-year-old Industrial Workers of the World (IWW). Debs also scored tens of thousands of votes in the industrialized Midwestern and Northeastern states among organized workers, especially old railroaders. Historians also have been fascinated with the Socialists' short-lived burst of support among rural voters in Oklahoma, Arkansas, Louisiana and Texas. Yet, until Oklahoma and Texas Socialists changed their party's land policy in 1910–

1912, the SPA made few gains among these former radical Populists. Only Texas and Oklahoma have had precinct-level analysis of SPA support in the early 1900s, and most of the scholarly exploration has focused on Oklahoma where Debs won 16.4 percent of the vote in the presidential election of 1912. The most comprehensive of these studies, historian James R. Green's *Grass-Roots Socialism: Radical Movements in the Southwest, 1895–1943* (1978), includes Arkansas, Louisiana, Oklahoma, and Texas.

At the 1908 SPA national convention, agrarians and pragmatists tried to soften the party's stance on land collectivization. Agrarians at the convention sought to reassure farmers that socialism did not require the seizure of land from the farmer "which he himself occupies and tills." These moderates argued that small landowning farmers were indeed not members of the capitalist class, as doctrinaire Marxists insisted, but were fellow workers. Ironically, Southwestern delegates led the fight against a land compromise and made some of the most rigidly collectivist speeches offered at the convention. Texan Jake Rhodes cast the land question as a contest between landlords and tenants. As a former organizer for the Farmers' Union—a movement taken over by landlords in Oklahoma, Texas, and elsewhere—he warned of the dire consequences of landlord influence. Those who bemoaned calls for land collectivization did not really farm, Rhodes claimed, but, instead, were those "who farms the farmer." Rhodes argued that if railroads should not be exempted from public ownership in order to woo the votes of railroad stockholders, then land should not be treated any differently. Texan Laura B. Payne and Oklahoman Stanley Clark took similar vocal stands at the 1908 SPA convention and helped to persuade the delegates to reject the agrarians' land compromise.

ZENITH OF THE AGRARIAN PERIOD: OKLAHOMA LEADS THE WAY

Before it could prosper in Oklahoma, the Socialist Party had to "get right" with "Jefferson and Jesus." In *Agrarian Socialism in America: Marx, Jefferson and Jesus in the Oklahoma Countryside, 1904–1920* (1999), historian Jim Bissett shows that the party had to democratize and embrace the property rights of small farmers (Jefferson) and adopt the morality of the rural, Protestant, evangelical church (Jesus) before it could effectively appeal to rural people. The orthodox Marxists who had founded the party in Oklahoma proved unequal to this task and gave way to an indigenous radicalism led by ex-Farmers' Union veterans. First, these local agrarians successfully fought to democratize and decentralize their party. Having accomplished that by 1910, they sought their next goal—winning over the rural poor majority—with a two-pronged strategy. On the one hand, Oklahoma Socialists attacked the excesses of monopolistic early twentieth-century American capitalism in a Bible-based critique, while, on the other they revised their Socialist creed to protect the property rights of small farmers who worked their own land.

The Rev. J.T. Cumbie, a small farmer and ordained Baptist minister, typified this effort with nominations for governor and for congressman. Furthermore, in a critical move to expand their appeal, Oklahoma Socialists promised the redistribution of government-controlled land to the growing class of sharecroppers and tenant farmers. Inspired in part by the Homestead Act, the Oklahomans promised future government renters the right of permanent occupancy—if not ownership—of the land that they worked. The Oklahoma Socialist rank-and-file had taught their state leadership a crucial lesson that migrated to other state platforms, most notably Texas.

THE AGRARIAN PLANK IN TEXAS

Texans showed little interest in rural radicalism—SPA style, at least—before adjustments similar to Oklahoma's were introduced. Battles between the orthodox Marxists and the democratic agrarians colored Texas' early Socialist experience. While party zealots sorted out their differences, rural Texans stayed away from the party on Election Day. In 1908, Jake Rhodes received only 1.6 percent of the total vote for governor. By 1910, however, the agrarians were in the ascendancy and had adopted a compromise land plank in the platform assuring farmers that Socialists did not seek total collectivization of land. In a move very similar to Oklahoma's, the Texas party promised to respect the property rights of farmers who themselves had "use and occupancy" of their land and who did not exploit another's labor.

The 1910 Texas platform contained eighteen separate provisions. The first of these called for increased democracy through the initiative, referendum, recall, female suffrage, abolition of the poll tax, and "the unrestricted right of peaceable assembly, free speech, and free press." The platform also promised relief to industrial labor through the adoption of labor's traditional wages, hours, child labor, workplace safety, and insurance demands. The Socialists promised "humane and scientific" treatment of prisoners and the insane, a system of socialized healthcare, free public school textbooks, maintenance of "destitute children," and the extension of political asylum to oppressed peoples.

The platform also prominently featured the new land policy. The Socialists called for an end to sales of public lands and the reclamation of all leased land after the current leases expired. The platform demanded that all lands sold for taxes should be bought by the state and added to the public domain, and that foreign landowners should appraise their own holdings for taxation purposes, with the state having the right to purchase such holdings at the appraised value plus 10 percent. Any land held for "exploitation and speculation" (i.e., land farmed by tenants or hired labor or unoccupied land owned by individual speculators or corporations) would be subject to an annual "graduated" land tax roughly equal to a year's rental income, thus forcing the landlord to sell on reasonable terms to tenants or forfeit ownership to the government. Tenants could apply for ownership of farms and pay a normal rent-share to the state until one-half the land's market value had been met. At that time, the tenants would stop making payments and would be issued "a permanent right of occupancy." Furthermore, the Socialists promised that their election would mean tax exemption for the "tools, teams, and implements of landless farmers" up to $800. The platform also called for public ownership of gins and other agricultural processing facilities that were "in their nature public."

THE PARADOX OF AGRARIAN SOCIALISM

Of course, herein lay the paradox of agrarian socialism. Of all those who have written on the subject, historian Jim Bissett most closely captures the internal tension of the movement. Bissett finds that agrarian Socialists sought a "marriage of Jefferson and Marx." Steeped in Southern yeoman culture, Oklahoma agrarian Socialists' first choice would have been widespread ownership of the land among working farmers. As changing societal and economic structures impinged upon their ability to achieve their first goal, a significant minority proved willing to use Marxian analysis and ideology to achieve widespread "use and occupancy" of the land for the benefit of the rural majority. But this substitute for outright ownership proved too bitter a pill for most of Oklahoma's rural voters to swallow.

THE AGRARIAN SOCIALIST PRESS AND CAMP MEETINGS

More than through any other medium, agrarian socialism spread throughout Texas and Oklahoma through Socialist "camp meetings" and through the writings of radical newspaper publishers. The Socialist camp meetings were drawn directly from the Populists before them who got the idea from rural outdoor religious revivals. Sometime in the summer, usually in July after the crops had been "laid by," the plain folk would often gather to sing, preach, and pray together in great "protracted meetings" with the worshippers, of necessity, camping on the meeting grounds. The Populists had recruited preachers from plain folk religious traditions—Baptist, Methodist, and various Holiness sects—who first politicized the rural camp meeting in the 1890s. By the 1910s, Southwestern Socialists had perfected such gatherings throughout Oklahoma and Texas. The largest such gathering in East Texas boasted an attendance of 50,000 during a week's worth of preaching, singing, and propagandizing. For those not religiously or politically inclined, the East Texas Socialists promised a hamburger stand, a Socialist rodeo, and a Ferris wheel.

Perhaps of even greater importance in spreading the message were rural Socialist newspapers. It would be difficult to exaggerate their number, which must have been over three dozen in the Southwest; only a few, however, had significant readership and influence. Kansan Julius Wayland's *Appeal to Reason* claimed a circulation greater than the *Saturday Evening Post* nationwide with over 70,000 subscribers in Oklahoma and Texas alone. Oklahoma also produced more than its share of influential Socialist newspapers, including Oscar Ameringer's *Oklahoma Pioneer* and Pat Nagle's *Tenant Farmer*. The Socialist press in Texas likewise thrived for about a decade. Former East Texas farmer Joshua Hicks published the *Farmer's Journal*. A primitive Christian, Socialist, and pacifist, Hicks also argued that believers should take a stand against racism and poverty. The successor publication to the *Farmer's Journal* was publisher E.O. Meitzen's and editor Thomas A. Hickey's *The Rebel*. Begun in 1911, *The Rebel* would eventually claim a circulation of over 30,000 before wartime repression shut it down in 1917. From its inception, *The Rebel* concentrated almost exclusively on the task of appealing to rural readers, especially tenant farmers and small farm owners.

THE RENTERS' UNIONS

Socialists in the Southwest attempted to organize the rural working class. As rates of tenancy shot upward, Socialists reached out to landless farmers who now made up the majority of all farmers. Oklahoma Socialists organized a Renters' Union in 1909; that group called for militant, class-conscious cooperation among sharecroppers and tenant farmers. *The Rebel*'s Tom Hickey organized a Texas Renters' Union in 1911 with calls for a "confiscatory tax" on absentee landlords. The Texas union at first excluded blacks, but, according to James Green, union organizer Hickey saw the error of his ways after witnessing black-white solidarity among East Texas IWW timber workers in 1912. Whatever real chances such organizations had were weakened by relatively low membership totals and the inexorable rise of land ownership concentrations among the most highly capitalized farmers and landlords. These organizations either died out completely during World War I (1914–1918) or existed in name only and in the imaginations of the remaining faithful. Yet, such memorable embers died hard; some would be fanned back into ignition in the form of the Southern Tenant Farmers Union during the Great Depression of the 1930s.

SUPPORT IN ARKANSAS, LOUISIANA, OKLAHOMA, AND TEXAS

Socialist voting in the Southwest peaked in 1912–1914. The largest rates of SPA voting occurred in the poorest agricultural counties in Arkansas, Louisiana, Oklahoma, and Texas. In Texas, Socialist votes also tended to come from former Populist and agrarian protest strongholds. Lavaca County Judge E.O. Meitzen exemplified this tendency with his sojourn from Greenbacker, Allianceman, and Populist to, finally, Socialist. Socialists did not manage to win any statewide elections anywhere in the country in 1912. One congressman, Victor Berger, was elected from Wisconsin. And in 1912 and 1914, voters across the Southwest elected a number of Socialist local officials such as a justice of the peace, a constable, and a county judge in Texas to a mayor in Arkansas. In 1914, Oklahoma elected six state legislators, five representatives, and a state senator.

The 1912 presidential vote gives some idea of the effect of the agrarian compromise within the Southwestern SPA, at least on the state level. Arkansas gave 6.5 percent of its presidential vote to Debs, up from 3.8 percent in 1908. Louisiana reported a 6.6-percent Socialist vote, exactly double the 1908 showing. Oklahomans voted for Debs at the rate of 16.4 percent, over 40,000 votes. This almost doubled the Socialists' 1908 finish in Oklahoma. In Texas, Debs received 8.3

percent statewide, a 207-percent increase over 1908. Analysis of rural versus town precincts shows that in one typical county where the Socialist vote mirrored the statewide SPA share of 8 percent, rural dwellers voting Socialist at almost the same rate as Oklahomans at 15.7 percent.

Reddin Andrews, Texas' SPA gubernatorial candidate in 1912, finished with slightly more votes than Debs with a little over 25,000. Andrews exemplified all of the elements the Socialists sought to bring together in the Southwest. Backed by a suitably agrarian platform, Andrews also packed plenty of appeal for rural Texans. A Baptist minister, the candidate had pastored country churches throughout central and East Texas and had served briefly as president of the state's largest Baptist college, Baylor University. His status as a Confederate veteran, his gray beard and Stetson hat, only served to further strengthen his cultural credentials with rural voters. Andrews did almost as well in 1914; thereafter, the Texas Socialist vote declined precipitously as it did in Oklahoma, Arkansas, and Louisiana.

Why did few Southwestern rural voters support J.T. Cumbie and Reddin Andrews at the height of the movement? First, the Socialist Party stood against absolute property rights and for a fundamental restructuring of the economy. No amount of maneuvering could obscure that issue or change the fact that belief in property rights lay at the heart of rural culture. Second, tradition favored the Southern Democrats who represented themselves as the party of the Lost Cause, the Confederacy. The Civil War still defined partisan loyalty for many voters, North and South. And, finally, the Socialists were not to be trusted with protecting white supremacy.

RACE AND SOUTHERN SOCIALISM

Of all the charges their critics might level, for Socialists in the South the most devastating was the charge of sympathy to the cause of African-American equality. Because of the region's recently passed disenfranchisement laws (poll taxes, etc.), Socialists were facing a seriously truncated electorate. For example, Texas' 1902 poll tax eliminated much more than the 12 percent of Texans who were black; it effectively cut the Texas voting lists in half. Consequently, those among the rural poor majority most likely to be attracted to the SPA were no longer members of the polity. As a result, agrarian Socialists in Texas faced an electorate of only the economic top half of the population and one that was virtually all white as well. Furthermore, many agrarian Socialists came from a staunchly

white-supremacist culture and adhered to such views themselves. Herein lay another killing contradiction for agrarian Socialists. The clearly elucidated antiracist ideals of international socialism—and the declarations against racism by such SPA leaders as Debs—were about to run afoul of the intractability of culture. This hurt the Socialists' chances of winning elections in two ways. Obviously, lukewarm stands for racial equality would win few of the remaining handful of black votes. Even more critical, the suspicion of even scant sympathy for racial equality guaranteed the loss of many, perhaps most, of the Socialists' potential white support in the countryside.

The Oklahoma Socialist Party came closest to upholding Socialist ideals concerning race. In his excellent study of southwestern radicals, Green shows that the Oklahoma SPA wholeheartedly defended voting rights for African Americans. Others in the region tended to avoid the topic when they could and finesse their party's position when they could not.

PATRIOTISM, REPRESSION, AND DECLINE

The outbreak of World War I (1914–1918) forced a momentous crisis within the ranks of international socialism. Purists urged the national parties to reject their countries' war efforts. They argued that the working class had no vested interest in the outcome of a battle between imperialist, capitalist regimes. Yet, in most cases, European Socialists compromised their ideals in the name of pragmatism or patriotism and more or less heartily supported their individual nations. Only the SPA stuck to its ideals and remained staunchly antiwar throughout, thereby committing political suicide. The SPA's symbolic spokesman, Debs, eventually would be convicted under the wartime Sedition Act and sent to federal prison for speaking against the war. Opening themselves and the party to charges of cowardice, disloyalty, and even treason, Socialists never recovered from their failure to support the American war effort. U.S. Postmaster General Albert S. Burleson, a Texas cotton landlord, energetically used his special wartime mandate to shut down the Socialist press. Arrested and questioned in connection to a crackdown on draft resistance in the Southwest, Tom Hickey was soon released but saw his newspaper effectively repressed by Burleson's denial of the use of the mails. The last issue of *The Rebel* came out in June 1917.

The death of the Socialist Party of America in the Southwest did not mean the end of agrarian discontent. It did, however, mean the end of the last significant agrarian electoral protest in that region. A few rural protesters elsewhere carried on through the Nonpartisan League of the Dakotas in the 1920s and in the Farmer-Labor Party in 1930s–1940s Minnesota. Perhaps the closest successor to Southwestern socialism came with the 1930s-era Southern Tenant Farmers Union, founded in Arkansas by agrarian veterans of the Socialist Party of America.

Kyle Wilkison

BIBLIOGRAPHY

Adams, Graham. "Agrarian Discontent in Progressive Texas." *East Texas Historical Journal* 8 (March 1970): 24–28.

Bissett, James. *Agrarian Socialism in America: Marx, Jefferson, and Jesus in the Oklahoma Countryside, 1904–1920*. Norman: University of Oklahoma Press, 1999.

Burbank, Garin. "Agrarian Radicals and Their Opponents." *Journal of American History* 58 (June 1971): 5–30.

————. *When Farmers Voted Red: The Gospel of Socialism in the Oklahoma Countryside, 1910–1924*. Westport, CT: Greenwood Press, 1976.

Dyson, Lowell K. *Red Harvest: The Communist Party and American Farmers*. Lincoln: University of Nebraska Press, 1982.

Green, James R. *Grass-Roots Socialism: Radical Movements in the Southwest, 1895–1943*. Baton Rouge: Louisiana State University Press, 1978.

Kipnis, Ira. *The American Socialist Movement, 1897–1912*. New York: Columbia University Press, 1952.

Lipset, Seymour M. *Agrarian Socialism: The Cooperative Commonwealth Federation in Saskatchewan*. Berkeley: University of California Press, 1950.

Lipset, Seymour M., and Gary Marks. *It Didn't Happen Here: Why Socialism Failed in the United States*. New York: W.W. Norton, 2001.

Quint, Howard H. *The Forging of American Socialism: Origins of the Marxist Movement*. New York: Bobbs-Merrill, 1953.

Weinstein, James. *The Decline of Socialism in America*. New York: Monthly Review, 1969.

NONPARTISAN LEAGUE 1915–1920s

The Nonpartisan League (NPL) was a rural political organization active in thirteen states between 1915 and the 1920s. Feeding on the discontent of exploited farmers, the League operated through the political primaries of the old parties in a nonpartisan spirit. It enjoyed great success for a time, especially in North Dakota, where sweeping reforms ameliorated conditions for small producers. Founded and initially run by Socialists, the Nonpartisan League made state intervention in the market economy widely acceptable and thus laid the foundation for modern Midwest liberalism.

RURAL POVERTY

Ever since the late 1800s, North Dakota farmers should have been making good money growing wheat. While their product was high quality, many did not own their own land and nearly all of them had high debts—and conditions only grew worse with time. Grain brokers and railroads headquartered in Minnesota controlled the market (and North Dakota's political elite), leaving the state weak economically. Without terminal markets in their home state, farmers had no choice but to sell their grain through the Minneapolis Chamber of Commerce (a grain exchange) and the Duluth Board of Trade.

Once their grain went to market, farmers lost all control over the product; middle men and processors docked them at every turn. Wheat was not weighed fairly. Brokers often sold it to each other several times, taking a commission every time. They graded the wheat low and then regraded it upward once sold, thus taking a little more out of farmers' pockets. Railroads charged exorbitant fees, as did local banks in North Dakota, two thirds of which charged usurious (more than 10 percent) rates. The Granger movement of the 1880s and the Populist uprising of the 1890s had little impact on late-developing North Dakota, al-though some historians have argued that Populism was a vital social precursor of the NPL.

FARMER ACTIVISM

By 1915, North Dakota stood ready for change. Arthur C. Townley wanted farmers to form a nonpartisan organization to bring about reform. A former school teacher, plasterer, and small farmer, Townley and his brother started growing flax in 1907 and expanded to 8,000 acres before losing everything when frost destroyed most of their crop and speculators caused prices for the rest to plummet. Farmers like Townley became attracted to the Socialist Party (SP) and a platform that included immediate demands for rural credit, state-owned mills and grain elevators, state insurance on crops, and help to the unemployed. Several Socialists had been elected to local offices, but the program became more popular than the party. So the SP tried an experiment designed to reach out to non-Socialists drawn to the immediate demands. Townley and others toured the state with party-owned Ford automobiles filled with literature and talked farmers into voting for Socialist candidates who supported the platform without pushing party membership on them. The drive was a success but was stopped by the North Dakota SP in early 1915, much to Townley's disgust.

NONPARTISAN FARMERS LEAGUE

Historians disagree about what happened next. In his seminal work on the League, *Political Prairie Fire: The Nonpartisan League, 1915–1922* (1985), Robert Morlan asserts that Townley came up with the idea of creating a nonpartisan league for farmers after a conference with Socialist leader Albert E. Bowen. More recent scholarship asserts that Bowen himself should be given credit for the League scheme. In any event, Townley and Fred B. Wood of the American Society of Equity went on to found the Nonpartisan League, with the ambitious goal of capturing all three branches of state government by putting up League candidates in both Republican and Democrat primary elections, a recent Progressive reform designed to make the old parties more democratic. The League platform said that the state should own the elevators, mills, and storage facilities, inspect the grain and how it was moved, provide tax breaks for farm improvements, insurance against hail damage, and nonprofit rural credit banks.

Townley recruited organizers, training them in what he understood to be proper psychology. Recruiters bought Fords on installment from the League and followed systematic routes throughout the state. Farmers paid dues in the form of checks postdated to October, after their harvests. At first, most all of the League organizers and leaders were men who had been Socialists, but unlike the SP, which tended to view farmers as small-time capitalists, the NPL blamed all the farmers' problems on big business. Townley understood that the League needed its own press to keep the movement together, so by September 1915 the *Nonpartisan Leader* was up and running, with leading Socialist journalist Charles Edward Russell recruited to write. The paper provided news directly to members, offered guidance, and countered anti-League propaganda. Most all North Dakota newspapers denounced the NPL, which made little difference to members forearmed with the *Leader*'s version of the truth. League opponents refused to recognize farmers' problems and thus had no solutions of their own. Farmers felt a burning sense of loyalty to a cause reinforced by literature, songs, and art that set down roots in their culture.

Electoral Politics

The NPL prepared to take over the state government in 1916 by holding a series of election rallies. Lynn Frazier, university graduate, small farmer, and rock-ribbed Republican, emerged as the League's candidate for governor. Most NPL candidates ran in the Republican primary, although some stood for nomination in the Democrat contests. Frazier overwhelmed all opponents in the spring primary and kept his momentum up through the summer at a series of all-day picnics for farmers. In September, the NPL took control of the Republican State Central Committee, writing a platform that reflected the League agenda. The Democratic State Central Committee's platform proved to be remarkably similar.

Faced with a political juggernaut, conservative opponents of the League focused on keeping the NPL

out of the state Supreme Court, but League men prevailed anyway. Frazier won the fall race in a landslide, while NPL candidates won 62 percent of the seats in the state House. However, the League failed to capture the state Senate.

Wasting little time, Governor Frazier asked the new legislature to pass the entire NPL agenda, as well as reduce the legal limit on interest rates, set a minimum wage for women and children, create a labor bureau and a system of nonpartisan primaries and elections, start civil service reform, and come up with a lot more money for rural education. The NPL schooled new legislators in public speaking and parliamentary procedures. Members lived together in the same hotel, with their leaders controlling political caucuses from the top down. The League agenda was rolled up into House Bill 44, a new state constitution; it passed the lower house easily but failed in the Senate. In the end, the legislature passed many laws, including state grain grading, farm tax breaks, state woman suffrage, a nine-hour day for women, banking reform, regulation of railroads, and better financing for rural schools. The Senate refused to pass a nonpartisan election scheme, workers' compensation, a slashing of railroad freight rates, and a minimum wage for women.

World War I

In the spring of 1917, a hysterical patriotism spawned by American entry into World War I derided everything German. Still, millions of people were unsure about the great departure from traditional American isolationism, especially in the rural Midwest. Many NPL members opposed the war as did most Socialists. In the end, the League generally supported the war but wanted to pay for it by taxing the rich. Like the Progressives, the League favored expanded government control over food, prices, railroads, utilities, and energy. Superpatriotism proved to be a rallying point for conservatives who hated the NPL.

North Dakota attracted attention from all over the country from conservatives, Socialists, and Progressive reformers alike. Responding to inquiries, NPL organizers went to Montana, Washington, Kansas, and Wisconsin. The Land League of Texas dispatched Ernest R. Meitzen to North Dakota in the spring of 1917, and he became a convert to the NPL. Meitzen's partner in the popular Socialist weekly, *The Rebel*, Thomas A. Hickey, worked for the League too, but in the end, Southwestern tenant farmers and sharecroppers were too poor and had little in common with grain farmers far to the North. The NPL leadership thought all

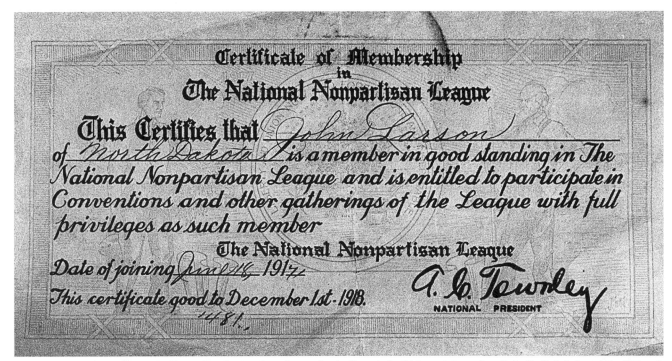

Certificate of Membership in The National Nonpartisan League

This Certifies that *John Larson* of *North Dakota* is a member in good standing in The National Nonpartisan League and is entitled to participate in Conventions and other gatherings of the League with full privileges as such member

The National Nonpartisan League

Date of joining *June 16, 1917*

This certificate good to December 1st-1918.

1481

A. C. Townley
NATIONAL PRESIDENT

Founded by Socialists in 1915, the Nonpartisan League drew thousands of adherents in thirteen states, primarily in North Dakota and the Midwest. The group favored many Populist and Progressive reforms, including increased government aid and protection for farmers, state regulation of railroads, a minimum wage, and workers' compensation. *(State Historical Society of North Dakota A5623)*

along that it would be easy to capture South Dakota, although farmers there did not share the same sense of political urgency. Self-styled "Theodore Roosevelt Republican" South Dakota governor Peter Norbeck proved to be a formidable opponent, co-opting the League with Progressive-style reforms, including rural credits, workers' compensation, and state marketing.

The League also targeted Minnesota where farmers faced problems similar to those in North Dakota. Beginning in the fall of 1916, a small army of Fords (the only car at the time) and recruiters began crisscrossing the Gopher State. A rival group of reactionaries formed the Minnesota Nonpartisan League to sow confusion among farmers, but the effort flopped. A more dangerous adversary arose in the Minnesota Public Safety Commission, a committee consisting of the governor Joseph A. Burnquist, the attorney general, and five cronies given unlimited power to persecute those perceived as disloyal to the war. The commission branched out county by county and created its own Bureau of Intelligence, modeled after the new federal agency headed by young J. Edgar Hoover. Needless to say, the conservative commission, fi-

nanced in part by the Minneapolis Chamber of Commerce, saw the NPL as disloyal.

OPPOSITION TO NONPARTISAN LEAGUE

Violent attacks on the NPL led to a series of resolutions to clarify the League's position. It supported American intervention and free speech, but opposed war for the purpose of annexation of territory and denounced indemnities and secret diplomacy. NPL speakers invoked the name of President Woodrow Wilson whenever possible to further blunt charges of disloyalty. Townley was attacked verbally because he denounced war profiteers in angry terms. The NPL accepted the Food Administration's setting low prices for wheat out of patriotism. Still, the League faced criticism even in North Dakota, where newspapers accused it of being behind the appearance of Kate Richards O'Hare, an outspoken antiwar Socialist sentenced to five years in prison for making a speech in Bowman.

Townley toured in the East to educate Americans about his organization. He and President Wilson both spoke to an American Federation of Labor Convention in Buffalo. Townley also lectured at Cooper Union in New York City and received good press notices. He stopped in Washington, D.C., for private meetings with Wilson, George Creel of the Committee on Public Information, and Food Administration czar Herbert Hoover.

In Minnesota, opposition to the NPL organized swiftly, with the loyalty issue proving to be a handy club. The governor gave sheriffs a blank check to break up meetings so that they could not become riots. In a subsequent reign of terror, organizers and speakers received severe beatings followed by tar and feathers. Farmers who dared to attend NPL meetings were pelted with eggs, stones, and yellow paint. By the spring of 1918, the Minnesota Public Safety Commission had shut the League out of many counties. Townley appealed to George Creel, who regarded the League as a significant voice of farmers, and so supplied loyalty speakers under NPL auspices. League spokesmen attacked the commission for supporting war for democracy while denying free speech to its own citizens. Eventually, Townley and Joe Gilbert, League organization manager, were indicted in Minnesota for sedition. After the war, the U.S. Supreme Court upheld Minnesota's sedition law with an eloquent dissent from Justice Louis Brandeis that would serve as a basis for an eventual reversal.

NONPARTISAN LEAGUE IN NORTH DAKOTA

It was a different story in North Dakota, where little blood was shed because the NPL controlled the government. The League remained active in Montana during the war with only a few incidents of violence. In South Dakota, Governor Norbeck ordered no interference with League activities, but he looked the other way when local vigilantes broke up meetings. Self-appointed secret police hassled NPL organizers in Iowa, while Washington and Texas saw much violence. In April 1918, east Texas vigilantes whipped three organizers, doused them with salt water, and shot at them as they fled for their lives. The terror subsided after the spring primary election season in most states. The Nonpartisan League did not use violence against its enemies, and members were not actively disloyal. On the contrary, they bought liberty bonds and grew lots of grain for the war effort.

Undaunted, the North Dakota NPL drew up new plans to achieve what had been proposed the year before in House Bill 44. Again, the spring election campaign revolved around the Republican primary, where loyalty did not prove to be an issue. With Townley at the height of his popularity, the League enjoyed a great victory, emerging in control of all three branches. Few realized it at the time, but in los-

ing, conservative Stephen Joseph Doyle had put together a coalition that would eventually put an end to League dominance.

In Minnesota, the League backed popular Congressman Charles A. Lindbergh, Sr. for governor. (Lindbergh's son, Charles A. Lindbergh, Jr., would later become famous as the first aviator to fly from New York to Paris.) The ambitious platform resembled North Dakota's with its plan for state-run enterprises in meatpacking, dairy, and wood products. Lindbergh supported the war once the United States took the plunge, but he had been vehemently opposed to entry. Conservatives amassed a huge war chest (paid for by Public Safety Commission) to beat the man who was a hero in some areas of the state and a villain in others. At several stops, vigilantes bombarded Lindbergh with garbage and even shot at him. The incumbent defeated Lindbergh by 50,000 votes. Elsewhere the League made little headway, owing to the strategy of concentrating on North Dakota and Minnesota because most of the other eleven states had some Progressive laws on the books already and farmers needed more education on what needed to be done next.

The fall elections brought few surprises, with the NPL triumphing in North Dakota and losing in Minnesota and South Dakota. In Idaho, the League elected several members as state legislators, while Colorado, Nebraska, and Montana also sent some members to their state houses. The new national NPL was held together at the center by the National Executive Committee, with Townley having the deciding say. All dues (minus commissions to organizers) went directly to the committee, which passed funds out to the states.

At last, in early 1919, the North Dakota League could implement its full economic agenda: a comprehensive nonprofit state-ownership system for farmers, paid for by state credit, and authority to run the system through a powerful new board. The caucus still made decisions behind closed doors, with Townley's opinions carefully considered. Even at the height of the postwar Red Scare, the NPL legislators refused to consider passing laws criminalizing syndicalism (aimed at the Industrial Workers of the World) or making it a crime to fly a red flag.

Opponents tried to smear the League with accusations of sexual immorality because women were encouraged to play an active role outside of their homes. In 1919, the NPL created a Women's Auxiliary that gave an opportunity for improved networking among rural women. The League supported full suffrage and, once in power, ratified the Nineteenth Amendment to the Constitution, which granted women the right to vote nationally. The NPL devoted significant space to women's issues in its publications as well. In 1922, Minnie D. Craig became one of two women elected to the North Dakota state legislature, where she worked on banking reform. She would eventually rise to a position of leadership as speaker of the state house.

The most important law under consideration would create an Industrial Commission to oversee co-operative state organizations. As proposed, the commission would be made up of the governor, the attorney general, and the secretary of agriculture and labor, responsible for every state agency except schools, prisons, and charitable organizations. A new Bank of North Dakota, keystone to the entire scheme, would loan money to farmers, regulate other banks, and finance state agencies. Virtually every bill passed by more than two-thirds in both houses, which meant that they would come into effect immediately after the adjournment of the legislature. The NPL legislative agenda was complete, with every platform plank having been turned into law. Yet in several of the other twelve states where the NPL operated, conservative forces successfully countered the League by banning direct primaries.

Shortly after its legislative triumph, schisms developed in the North Dakota NPL. Three leaders, Attorney General William Langer, Secretary of State Tom Hall, and State Auditor Carl Kosizky, began to attack the League in bitter terms to prepare the ground for a takeover. Conservative opposition coalesced around the Independent Voters Association (IVA), which attacked the NPL as Socialist. The League proved to be vulnerable after all. While the Bank of North Dakota began its business quickly, other parts of the scheme would take some time to construct. During the Red Scare, many violent acts were perpetrated against the NPL. Ensconced in power, League leaders sometimes overreacted to criticism, as when they created an investigating committee with broad powers to acquire information on any person or group attempting to bring about harm to others, especially the NPL.

In 1920, the NPL renominated Frazier to run in the primary. Opponent William Langer was tough because as a former insider he could claim the League had lost its way due to corruption. Frazier won easily, but voters also passed an anti-Red flag law, an ominous sign that the tide was turning against the League. In the nationwide Republican landslide that fall, the North Dakota NPL won again but took a beat-ing in all other states. Governor Frazier saw no need for new reforms as some existing programs, especially the Bank of North Dakota, came in for criticism. Several investigations in the state legislature proved critical of the administration. The next year, the IVA led a drive to recall NPL-elected officials even as a full-fledged fight for control of the organization in North Dakota weakened the insurgency further. Townley stayed on the sidelines, as did many members preoccupied with a farm recession. The voters recalled Frazier and two other high officials.

With the IVA in charge of the government, conservatives discovered that the Bank of North Dakota had some virtues after all. The NPL decentralized, shifting more of the dues and real power to state organizations in 1921. Townley finally served his ninety days in jail for his wartime conviction and then resigned as president. In 1922, Lynn Frazier was elected to the U.S. Senate, while the NPL lost control over both Houses in North Dakota. Conservatives lost a U.S. Senate race in Minnesota, not to the NPL but the Farmer-Labor Party. Clearly, the League was on its way out, folding the *Leader* in the summer of 1923. The national office closed its doors two years later. The League lived on as a major force in the North Dakota GOP for a few more years. William Langer bought his way back into the NPL and made it his personal power base for twenty years. He served two scandal-ridden terms as governor before moving on to the U.S. Senate. In the 1950s, the NPL merged with the Democratic Party in North Dakota, where it has continued to work on behalf of farm interests.

CONCLUSION

The NPL was never as radical as its conservative opponents wished to believe. If anything, it provided a more moderate alternative to the Socialist Party and the Industrial Workers of the World. Farmers and former Socialists created the League as part of a struggle between small capitalists and bigger ones—in other words, people who farmed for profit and the capitalist bankers, railroads, and grain brokers who made money off of the land indirectly. Using modern sales techniques and making effective use of print media, the League entered state government through the old political parties in primary elections. In North Dakota, where the NPL takeover of government was complete for a short time, the League expanded state government to reform the system of marketing so that farmers could make higher profits and live more stable lives. The League is perhaps best seen as a rural variation of Progressivism, which was also nonpartisan, reformist, and effective in alleviating some of the grosser abuses of the capitalist system.

Peter Buckingham

BIBLIOGRAPHY

Claus, Maren K. "Minnie D. Craig: Gender and Politics in North Dakota." *North Dakota History* 63:2–3 (1996): 28–41.

Coleman, Patrick K., and Charles R. Lamb, eds. *The Nonpartisan League, 1915–22: An Annotated Bibliography*. St. Paul: Minnesota Historical Society, 1985.

Fite, Gilbert C. "Peter Norbeck and the Defeat of the Nonpartisan League in South Dakota." *Mississippi Valley Historical Review* 33:2 (1946): 217–236.

Junker, Rozanne Emerson. *The Bank of North Dakota: An Experiment in State Ownership*. Santa Barbara, CA: Fithian, 1989.

Morlan, Robert L. *Political Prairie Fire: The Nonpartisan League, 1915–1922*. St. Paul: Minnesota Historical Society, 1985.

Moum, Kathleen. "The Social Origins of the Nonpartisan League." *North Dakota History* 53:2 (1986): 18–22.

Nielsen, Kim E. " 'We All Leaguers by Our House': Women, Suffrage, and Red-Baiting in the National Nonpartisan League." *Journal of Women's History* 6:1 (1994): 31–50.

North Dakota Democratic-NPL Party. http://www.demnpl.com.

Remele, Larry. " 'Things as They Should Be': Jeffersonian Idealism and Rural Rebellion in Minnesota and North Dakota, 1910–1920." *Minnesota History* 51:1 (1988): 15–22.

Starr, Karen. "Fighting for a Future: Farm Women of the Nonpartisan League." *Minnesota History* 48:6 (1983): 255–262.

Whaley, Richard. "The Other Side of the Mountain: Stephen Joseph Doyle and Opposition to the NPL in 1918." *North Dakota Quarterly* 56:4 (1988): 192–210.

WOMEN'S HOME DEMONSTRATION MOVEMENT

1920s–1930

The Home Demonstration movement was a confluence of the domestic economy movement and the scientific farming movement in the early Progressive Era (1890–1910). Reformers became alarmed by the attrition rate of American farmers, whom they saw as the Jeffersonian core of U.S. society. They believed that by improving rural living conditions, they could turn back the growing tide of urbanization. Agricultural extension education was a means of showing rural Americans better ways to farm and to live, with an eye toward middle-class values. Spurred by the boll weevil invasion throughout the South—an infestation that destroyed cotton crops—individual states began sponsoring agricultural extension agents to work with male farmers. Some states recognized the significant impact that food, shelter, and clothing had on the lives of rural people, and they engaged home demonstrators to improve women's homemaking skills. Schools of agriculture, established under the Morrill Act (1862 in the North; extended to the South in 1890), embraced extension work as one of their primary functions.

At farmers' institutes across the nation, expert agronomists showed farmers how to create larger yields, and domestic science professionals began lecturing to farm women. The U.S. Department of Agriculture established a national extension service in 1907. The Smith-Lever Act of 1914 further institutionalized the extension service, appropriating $10,000 annually to each school of agriculture and stipulating that a portion of the money go for home demonstration. Local counties supplemented federal and state payments for salaries and supplies. Recognizing the value of home demonstration work, organizations such as urban women's clubs lobbied vigorously for adequate funding for women's work.

WOMEN'S CRUCIAL WORK

Although agricultural reformers acknowledged the importance of farm women's work, they strongly believed in the separation of men's and women's work.

In the reformers' conception of farm life, men raised the crops while women took care of all domestic duties. Accordingly, the Smith-Lever Act divided men's and women's programs with little recognition of the symbiotic nature of the farm family. Extension work was also completely segregated by race, with separate programs for whites and blacks. In some Southern states, African-American programs began shortly after white ones. But in other areas, such as Durham County, North Carolina, work by and with African Americans did not begin until the 1930s. African-American programs were uniformly underfunded and, consequently, understaffed.

WOMEN'S PROGRAMS

Reflecting the pressing need in the rural South where most extension work began, women's programs at first emphasized the most basic aspects of life: food, shelter, and clothing. With increasing knowledge about nutrition, home demonstration agents sought to improve farm families' diets. They often began by working with girls, encouraging them to plant small garden plots of tomatoes and to can the results for home consumption. The young charges, sometimes organized into "corn clubs" and "canning clubs," competed on the size and quality of their yields. For farm women, activities such as planting year-round vegetable gardens, canning vegetables and meats, and drying fruits extended the time when home-grown food would be available.

Canning was particularly important, and women enthusiastically embraced the hot work of preserving produce over wood stoves. In many communities, the home demonstration agents sponsored community canning centers, with up-to-date equipment, receiving a portion of the canned goods as payment for the use of the equipment. In 1924, for example, black Texas women canned more than 224,000 quarts of fruit and vegetables and more than 46,000 quarts of meat and fish. Aspiring cooks also learned improved techniques for such difficult procedures as bread making. Agents

Members of the Housewives' League gather at Washington Market in New York City. Women played the central role in the Home Demonstration movement in the early 1900s. *(Library of Congress)*

introduced an array of goods to make cooking more convenient. One homemade appliance was an early-day slow cooker, known as a fireless cooker. Often, agents stressed the purchase of goods, bringing farm women into the world of consumption. National emergencies, such as World War I, also provided fodder for agents, as they taught about the use of wheat, sugar, and meat substitutes.

SUPPLEMENTING INCOME

In the South and Southwest, where lack of income was particularly acute, farm women learned to develop home industries, manufacturing goods that could be produced and sold to bring cash into the family economy. They sought to improve chickens,

eggs, and butter, the petty commodities most typically sold by farm women. Farm women also learned to make crafts such as baskets and rugs. The home demonstration agents sought to improve marketing for all of these products.

Home improvements were also a significant part of home demonstration work. Some of the issues were basic matters of public health, such as installing window screens, building sanitary privies, and constructing home water systems. Needs for food and shelter united in an emphasis on more efficient kitchens. Clubs sponsored competitions such as "better kitchen contests" for women who made improvements on limited budgets. Farm women learned to make mattresses for their families. For more prosperous clients whose basic needs had been met, home demonstration agents stressed aesthetic and decorative elements such as making curtains and rugs and reupholstering furniture. Others emphasized yard beautification with transplanted plants.

Farm women also received instructions on clothing. Agents believed that the farm women would fare better socially and economically in dealing with city-dwellers if they looked less "country." Thus, agents taught sewing techniques, including ways to make over old garments, which often emphasized style and appearance.

DEMONSTRATION CLUBS

For some farm women, home demonstration clubs had profound impacts on their lives. In some areas, however, home demonstration clubs had limited effectiveness. In the South, clubs were strictly separated by race, and significantly fewer services were offered to African Americans than to white women. Locations with concentrations of recent European immigrants sometimes rejected the efforts of the government workers, preferring to keep their knowledge within the circle of their kin. And class often divided farm women. Poorer women lacked the cooking utensils, stoves, sewing necessities, and garden implements needed to carry out the programs of work, and they lacked the time to attend meetings. In many instances, the work failed to reach the people who could have benefited from it most.

With the coming of the New Deal and World War II, rural areas of the nation lost population, and membership in home demonstration clubs peaked. No more than a quarter of farm women belonged to home demonstration clubs, but for their members, their impact could be profound. The women whose husbands owned land and adapted to business-oriented agriculture after World War II continued to enjoy sessions on canning, cooking, and sewing throughout the 1950s. Like many agricultural reforms, however, home demonstration's goal of a decent farm home for all farm families was accomplished not by the agency itself but by the departure from farming of those people who had most needed the assistance.

Rebecca Sharpless

BIBLIOGRAPHY

Hilton, Kathleen C. " 'Both in the Field, Each with a Plow': Race and Gender in USDA Policy, 1907–1929." In *Hidden Histories of Women in the New South*, ed. Virginia Bernhard et al., pp. 114–133. Columbia: University of Missouri Press, 1994.

Holt, Marilyn Irvin. *Linoleum, Better Babies, & the Modern Farm Woman, 1890–1930.* Albuquerque: University of New Mexico Press, 1995.

Jones, Lu Ann. *Mama Learned Us to Work: Farm Women in the New South.* Chapel Hill: University of North Carolina Press, 2002.

———. " 'The Task That Is Ours': White North Carolina Farm Women and Agrarian Reform, 1886–1914." Master's thesis, University of North Carolina at Chapel Hill, 1983.

McCleary, Ann Elizabeth. "Shaping a New Role for the Rural Woman: Home Demonstration Work in Augusta County, Virginia, 1917–1940." Ph.D. diss., Brown University, 1996.

Reid, Debra Ann. "Reaping a Greater Harvest: African Americans, Agrarian Reform, and the Texas Agricultural Extension Service." Ph.D. diss., Texas A&M University, 2000.

Rieff, Lynn A. " 'Go Ahead and Do All You Can': Southern Progressives and Alabama Home Demonstration Clubs, 1914–1940." In *Hidden Histories of Women in the New South*, ed. Virginia Bernhard et al., pp. 134–149. Columbia: University of Missouri Press, 1994.

———. " 'Rousing the People of the Land': Home Demonstration Work in the Deep South, 1914–1950." Ph.D. diss., Auburn University, 1995.

Waalkes, Mary Amanda. "Working in the Shadow of Racism and Poverty: Alabama's Black Home Demonstration Agents, 1915–1939." Ph.D. diss., University of Colorado, 1998.

Walker, Melissa. *All We Knew Was to Farm: Rural Women in the Upcountry South, 1919–1941.* Baltimore, MD: Johns Hopkins University Press, 2000.

SOUTHERN TENANT FARMERS' UNION

For a few years during the Great Depression, African-American and white tenant farmers in the Arkansas Delta's cotton country fought for relief from their economic misery through the vehicle of a potentially radical biracial organization called the Southern Tenant Farmers' Union. Tenants were galvanized into action after the federal government's New Deal Agricultural Adjustment Act provided for paying cotton planters to reduce crop production and the planters (the landlords) systematically denied tenants their share of the payments. Historians agree that the Southern Tenant Farmers' Union (STFU) was a reaction to the operation of the Agricultural Adjustment Act (AAA), but they differ about the meaning of and ideological commitment of the movement the STFU tried to become. Almost all agree that the basic goal of the STFU was to secure tenants' portions of AAA benefits paid to planters as part of the Act's crop-reduction program. Other analysts see the STFU as going further and attempting to lead agricultural laborers in the economic and political overthrow of the planter class. For their part, Delta cotton planters chose—through mass tenant evictions—to sever the relationships through which they had traditionally maintained their social and economic power. When they evicted tenants to reap the benefits of the AAA, they sacrificed the economic leverage so critical to their control. Thus, when former tenants began to join the STFU, planters could not rely on traditional modes of economic coercion to defeat the organization. Instead, they relied solely on methods that brought national attention to the plight of the union's membership and tenants throughout the South.

Union leaders H.L. Mitchell, Clay East, and others hoped to build a more democratic society in the Arkansas cotton-growing country, but the membership, for the most part, had more limited goals. Rank-and-file members wanted a division of AAA benefits consistent with the division of profits from crops under the tenancy system. If the union could win more for them, tenants would take it, especially if they secured their own land. But the story of the STFU is one of a desperate struggle by men and women to stop the unraveling of tenant farming inadvertently triggered by a government aid program.

UNINTENDED CONSEQUENCES: THE AGRICULTURAL ADJUSTMENT ACT

The AAA's designers hoped to aid agriculture through a program of crop restriction. Government officials told producers how much acreage to take out of production and paid them for each restricted acre. Theoretically, crop restriction would aid both landlords and tenants by forcing price increases while sustaining all producers until such price increases occurred. But, through various methods, the planters managed to keep the tenants' share of government payments. Planters often persuaded tenants to sign agreements waiving their rights to benefit payments. More often, planters simply renamed their tenants as laborers, who were not entitled to benefits. Furthermore, restriction of the number of acres in production reduced the planters' need for tenants, thereby encouraging widespread evictions of tenants.

Planters in the Arkansas Delta counties joined this trend away from tenancy. From 1930 to 1940, the number of tenants in Cross, Crittenden, Lincoln, and St. Francis counties fell 20 percent. Indicative of the relationship between the AAA crop-restriction program and this decline in tenant population is the fact that most of the decrease occurred between 1936 and 1940. Those ex-tenants who were retained as wage laborers were, to be sure, more fortunate than those who were evicted and could find no work in the crowded labor market. In a letter to the New Deal's chief relief administrator Harry Hopkins, one of these unemployed former tenants described his plight: "I have Bin farming all my life But the man I live with Has Turned me loose taking my mule all my feed. . . . I have 7 in family. I ploud up cotton last yeare I can rent 9 acres and plant 14 in cotton But I haven't got a mule no feed. . . . I want to farm I have Bin on this farm 5 years. I can't get a job So Some one said Rite you." Tenants and ex-tenants in many parts of the South apparently accepted their losses with little protest. In northeastern Arkansas, however, they joined the STFU in an effort to preserve the social relationships that held the Southern plantation system together. They did not enter the union because tenancy assured them of comfortable lives; they did so because the alternatives were so much worse.

ARKANSAS SOCIALISTS AND A BIRACIAL UNION

Arkansas Socialists organized African-American and white tenants into the union beginning in 1933. That year, a group of displaced tenants and unemployed workers complained to H.L. Mitchell, the operator of a dry cleaners in Tyronza, Arkansas, about plantation owners' practice of placing their favorite tenants in Civil Works Administration projects during the winter to reduce the planters' costs, thereby keeping the genuinely unemployed from getting the jobs. Mitchell, his friend Clay East, and the Tyronza Socialist Party led in the formation of an Unemployed League to protest this practice. When the League held a meeting to present its grievances to the state relief director, over 600 people attended, many of whom were former tenants. At the meeting, the relief director promised to take care of the people's complaints. Mitchell then disbanded the organization.

As a result of its leadership in the formation of the Unemployed League, the Tyronza Socialist Party gained a few more members. The protest of the League is more important, however, as an early expression of the growing discontent in northeastern Arkansas as plantation owners began to trim their workforce in response to the Depression. With the passage of the AAA and mandatory crop restrictions, planters evicted and/or reduced to day labor more of their tenants. Discontent grew with the number evicted. Mitchell and East met with representatives of the families at Sunnyside School on Fairview plantation and suggested that they organize a union. The men representing the Fairview families agreed with Mitchell and East that through a union they might be able to force an end to displacement.

From the beginning, the STFU included African-American members. Fairview's owner evicted black families and white families from his lands, as did other landowners in northeastern Arkansas. If the union could not win the support of both races, planters would use one against the other to undermine union activities. In the past, Southern labor organizations had tried to bridge the racial divide by organizing blacks and whites into separate organizations. Rarely had this approach proved successful in the long term. Isaac Shaw, one of the African Americans at the Sunnyside schoolhouse meeting, warned Mitchell and East against such a policy. He stated that blacks feared that if they joined an organization that did not include whites, they would become the targets of planter retribution. Shaw's argument convinced the founders of the STFU that African Americans and whites would have to be organized within the same organization.

Although the STFU did not adopt separate black and white organizations, most locals were still not integrated. The racial makeup of a local depended upon the racial makeup of the plantation from which members came. Because most plantations were either all white or all black, STFU locals were either all white or all black. If the union had pursued a more aggressive policy of integration, it would have had much more difficulty securing the white support that was a prerequisite for African-American participation. As it was, the two races joined together for major union functions, such as large protest meetings. This level of racial cooperation distinguished the STFU in the South.

RELIGION AND THE STFU

Having decided upon a racial policy, the founders turned to the task of recruiting members. From the beginning, the STFU used the evangelical Protestant religious idiom and traditions of most tenants to spread its message. Meetings resembled camp-meeting revivals as preacher-organizers such as Ward Rodgers, Claude Williams, and E.B. McKinney spoke about the sins of the planters and the righteousness of the tenants' cause. Claude Williams, stressing the importance of such appeals, observed that "religion speaks a language that southern people understand. Southern people know more about Moses and the children of Israel in bondage than about Jefferson and Washington." African-American preachers were especially important in the STFU's recruitment of members. Mitchell urged organizers to include ministers, such as A.B. Brookins, in their appeals to blacks as well as whites. White tenants and laborers felt that African-American preachers understood the conditions in which they lived better than did most white ministers.

The STFU's use of religion and its racial policy reflected the leadership's understanding of the South in general, Arkansas in particular. All of the leaders were natives of the area or had lived there for extended periods of time before organizing the union. Mitchell, a native Southerner, had been in Tyronza for seven years. East had lived in the Delta all his life. E.B. McKinney had been a tenant and a long-time circuit-riding preacher in Arkansas as was Ward Rodgers. J.R. Butler, another Socialist who joined the union shortly after its formation, was from Pangburn, Arkansas, and had been active in labor organizing in Arkansas for years. Only Howard Kester, a West Virginian and Vanderbilt graduate who began working for the union in 1935, could be considered an outsider.

HOPES FOR INTERVENTION—FEARS OF PLANTER REPRESSION

Union leaders did not initially embrace direct action in their efforts to roll back evictions. Instead, they appealed for government intervention on behalf of evicted tenants and sought relief in the courts. Throughout the South, people believed that President Franklin D. Roosevelt's administration would take the side of those who suffered from the effects of the Depression. Government officials were concerned about the unintended consequences of the AAA, but for political reasons would not challenge local control of New Deal programs. Mitchell and the union's Executive Council then filed a lawsuit on behalf of the tenants evicted from the Norcross plantation based on Section 7 of the cotton acreage reduction contract, which, in theory, protected tenants both from being dismissed or displaced from their homes except for bad conduct. Both provisions protecting tenants were weak. As planters pointed out, Section 7 did not, in fact, compel them to do anything; they only had to "endeavor in good faith" to prevent displacement. Who could prove they had not been at least trying to retain the same number of tenants they had before the AAA? In addition, some would later argue that membership in or sympathy with the STFU constituted bad conduct. Therefore, those who were guilty of union activity could legally be put off the plantation. C.T. Carpenter, the union's attorney, argued that Section 7 provided legal protection against eviction for tenants, not just an expression of the government's hope that planters would provide that protection. He also contended that union activity alone did not constitute

bad conduct and that tenants who joined could not, under the law, be evicted.

In the meantime, Ward Rodgers conducted public gatherings at which he denounced the actions of planters. These meetings triggered a campaign to destroy the union. The deputy prosecuting attorney for Marked Tree, Arkansas, had Rodgers arrested and jailed in Jonesboro, Arkansas. He charged Rodgers with conspiracy to overthrow the government, anarchy, and intimidation of landowners. Because Sheriff J.D. Dubard empaneled a jury of planters, Carpenter, who defended Rodgers, realized that a vigorous defense would be an exercise in futility. For this reason, he brought forth no evidence or witnesses. The prosecutor, on the other hand, introduced witnesses who testified that Rodgers threatened to lynch planters and to lead in the overthrow of the plantation system. The prosecutor also noted, for good measure, that Rodgers addressed a "nigger" as "mister" at a union meeting. As was expected, the jury found Rodgers guilty. The publicity the Rodgers case brought to the union proved to be vital to its continued existence. Socialist Party and liberal groups such as the American Civil Liberties Union (ACLU) and the Southern Organizing Committee (SOC) for Economic and Social Justice began protesting against the Rodgers verdict and the conditions of which the STFU complained. These groups, as well as the Strikers' Emergency Relief Committee, the Church Emergency Relief Fund, and others provided the union direct financial help.

Recognizing the problem the STFU posed, planters stepped up their campaign against the organization. Having failed to intimidate members and prospective members through disruption of meetings, illegal arrests, and other forms of harassment and now lacking the economic sanctions that had been fundamental to their control of the rural South, planters resorted to more brutal methods. This new phase of the planters' anti-union campaign began in a town named Birdsong. On March 16, a crowd of tenants gathered to hear the most prominent supporter of the STFU, Norman Thomas, speak. When Thomas began his speech, a group of planters and riding bosses, reportedly drunk, pulled Thomas from the platform and said "that they would take care of their labor, and weren't gonna have no outside interference from any white haired Yankee son-of-a-bitch." The mob then escorted Thomas and his entourage to the Tennessee line. After the attack on Thomas at Birdsong, attacks on prominent union members were numerous. Gangs fired into the homes of A.B. Brookins and C.T. Carpenter shortly after the Birdsong incident. On March

30, a mob fired on an African-American church near Lepanto and attacked a group of church members.

Planters also employed more subtle tactics in their war against the union. They encouraged Abner Sage, the minister of the Marked Tree Methodist Church, to set up an alternative organization called the Marked Tree Cooperative Association (MTCA). Although Sage denied that he was a puppet of the planters, a *New York Times* reporter noted that Sage consistently spoke for the planters through his letters to newspapers and to Senator Joe Robinson (D-AR). But the support for Sage's organization revealed more than the reporter understood. In his remarks, Sage expressed alarm at the STFU's racial policy that many white tenant farmers in the area shared. Although the MCTA attracted few followers in the beginning, it reminded Mitchell and other union leaders of the tenuous nature of the racial accord they had negotiated. Without progress in their struggle to redress their members' grievances, appeals such as Sage's might gain more widespread support from white members.

THE STRIKE OF 1935

Such concerns moved Mitchell to propose a strike in April 1935. As Mitchell wrote in July, the membership wanted "action and has for some time," and a strike would give them what they wanted. He proposed that cotton pickers demand $1.00 per hundred pounds of cotton picked, a 40- to 50-cent increase in the rate. If planters refused, pickers would go on strike. By the time Mitchell submitted the proposal to the membership, planters had announced their intention of reducing the picking rate. Not surprisingly, union members supported the strike plan. The action would begin at the end of September 1935 when the cotton had to be picked or it would die in the fields.

On the night of September 22, representatives from locals began spreading handbills throughout Crittenden, Cross, and Poinsett counties announcing the beginning of the strike. The next day, 4,000 to 5,000 pickers failed to report to work. H.C. Malcolm, Arkansas deputy labor commissioner, reported that he could only find five pickers working. Planters quickly began to grant wage increases to strikers rather than watch their crops rot in the fields. By October 4, when leaders called the strike off, most locals had won at least $0.75 per hundred pounds and many had won the full $1.00. Because the walkout surprised planters and strikers never directly confronted their employers, little violence occurred during the strike.

The ease with which the STFU won the 1935 strike fostered confidence in the union among eastern Ar-

kansas tenants. Mitchell received more requests for organization of new locals than he and other organizers could handle. Those clamoring for organization knew they faced more evictions in the coming year and looked to the union to assist them.

EVICTIONS

In early January, the expected new wave of evictions began. Letters to union leaders from displaced tenants pleading for help indicate the misery they suffered. J.J. Lynn, for example, wrote that since his eviction, he had no food, no money, and only a self-built shack with a dirt floor in which to live. He stated in a letter to Mitchell that he was "in the worst shape I ever were in in my life." As planters reduced the number of tenants on their lands before the 1936 planting season began, the number of people in similar circumstances would increase. Indeed, a plantation owner named C.H. Dibble intended to evict all the tenants from his place on January 16. In the first two weeks of January, STFU leaders concentrated on stopping the evictions of these families but failed. Dibble forced tenants out of their homes, onto roadsides in freezing weather, with no shelter or food. Other plantation owners offered them places if they would sever their ties to the STFU, but they refused to accept.

After Dibble evicted his tenants, union leaders appealed for donations to be used to provide the families with shelter and food. Kester wrote James Myers of the Church Emergency Relief Committee, Charles Garland of the Garland Fund, and Mary Fox of the League for Industrial Democracy to request relief funds from these organizations. Myers, who had already sent money for use in the union's relief effort, sent food and some tents and assured Kester of continued support as needed; the others soon sent money to assist the union. A few of the Dibble families were fortunate enough to be allowed to live in the Mount Zion church near Parkin, Arkansas; those for whom there was not enough room in the church lived in the churchyard in the tents Myers sent. For the next two months, the church and the tents would be home for the Dibble group as well as other displaced tenants. In addition, the Parkin church colony provided the union with dramatic evidence of planter tyranny with which to mobilize tenants and laborers. For some, such symbols were unnecessary. On the day Dibble ejected the tenants from his plantation, the St. Peters local of the STFU met to protest the planter's action and to demonstrate their determination to fight evictions. Unfortunately, plantation owners and local law enforcement agencies were just as determined to fight

A former Arkansas sharecropper builds a new house in Mississippi after being evicted from his land for joining the Southern Tenant Farmers' Union. The interracial union of poor farmers and laborers fought for higher wages and better working conditions and attracted thousands of members in the 1930s. Their actions were often met with violent resistance from planters. *(Library of Congress)*

the STFU. Shortly after the meeting began, a deputy sheriff arrived, disarmed those guarding the proceedings, entered the church, and ordered everyone to leave.

Union officials continued to appeal for assistance from the federal government, doubting the prospects of assistance from state and local authorities. Mitchell and the others thought they had convinced government officials to assist evicted tenants and to do more to prevent further such actions by planters. But when some in Cross and Wynn counties applied for government relief, they were rejected unless they were widows, orphans, or elderly. Local officials controlled relief programs and generally were reluctant to follow direction from Washington. STFU officials demanded

more direct intervention from Washington but elicited little more than promises to investigate violations of the civil liberties of union members.

Such promises won for the union some national media coverage but offered little of substance to tenants facing eviction. Henry Craft, Jr. of Proctor, Arkansas, evicted twenty-four families from his plantation in early February. When planter George Berry ordered several families off his place, twenty-nine men, women, and children were left without food or shelter. On February 21, the STFU reported that hundreds had lost their places on plantations since the beginning of the month. Landlords told many of their former tenants that they could return in March if they wanted to work as day laborers. In the meantime, they relied on more fortunate neighbors, and the STFU provided food, shelter, and clothes to displaced families; by the end of February, however, its resources were almost exhausted. Now the euphoria of the months following the successful 1935 strike gave way to doubts about the viability of the union. Tenants fearing eviction did not want to antagonize their landlords when the STFU proved helpless to do anything for them. A union official near Trumann informed Mitchell in early February that people there would not join the union. At least one union local folded during this period because its tenants lost interest in the activities of the STFU. Union leaders, understanding the need to act, in early March decided that the union would have to fight "with its only weapon," a general strike of all tenants and laborers in northeastern Arkansas.

THE STRIKE OF 1936

Mitchell distributed a strike proposal to locals that met with a tepid response. The unfavorable reaction of tenants to the strike proposal exposed a more deeply felt skepticism concerning union activities than union leaders thought. For example, J.J. Lynn, a union official in Poinsett county, the only county in union territory in which tenancy did not decline between 1935 and 1940, stated that tenants there did not consider a strike to be in their interest. Tenants on the Golightly plantation, in another county, would not even meet to vote on the strike proposal because they feared the owner would evict them. In mid-March, a local union official reported that two-thirds of his tenant members quit the union completely because they feared they would lose their places on the plantations if caught openly participating in union activities of any kind.

Predictably, evicted tenants were much more supportive of the strike proposal. After eviction they had no place to live and often had no food, shelter, or clothes. Even if a displaced tenant could find work as a day laborer, he usually could not earn enough to pay rent on a house, or to purchase food and clothing sufficient to his needs. People in this condition were quick to take the opportunity to strike back at those responsible for their misery. Although union records do not indicate what percentage of the over-6,000 votes for the strike came from evicted tenants, certain evidence suggests a relationship between loss of tenant status and support for direct action tactics. A local secretary, for instance, reported to union offices that four families did not decide to support the strike until a planter kicked them off of his plantation. More re-

vealing of the connection between eviction and support for the strike was union leaders' decision to hold the strike only in St. Francis, Crittenden, and Cross counties, where displacement was the greatest in northeastern Arkansas, and to limit the action to day laborers. If the laborers could win a victory, the STFU leadership hoped, tenants might renew their commitment to the union.

During March and April, support for the proposed strike grew as the number of homeless people in northeastern Arkansas increased. On March 9, Henry Peters wrote Mitchell to report the eviction of four families from the H.J. Johnson, a plantation near Parkin. M.E. Holland reduced the number of tenant families on his land by four several days later. These and thirty to forty other families set up another tent colony on Highway 64 near Wynne, Arkansas. Lula Parchman, secretary of the STFU local at St. John, Arkansas, was among those who lost their places on plantations during April. She had been on the J.H. Blunt place since 1933, she wrote Mitchell, and did not want to start working as a day laborer. Parchman, like hundreds of other tenants, who suffered the same fate, believed that she could only gain from a strike against those responsible for her misery.

STFU leaders planned to hold the strike in May when cotton had to be "chopped" to keep grass from taking it. Day laborers would demand $1.00 per day for a ten-hour day and 15 cents for overtime. Usually, planters paid day laborers 75 cents to $1.00 for a day that began at sunrise and lasted until the sun went down. If planters entered into negotiations with the union before the May deadline, the strike would be canceled. Union leaders also would cancel the walkout if, as Jackson stated in a memorandum to President Franklin D. Roosevelt, the federal government took action on their complaints against planters. As expected, plantation owners refused to negotiate with the STFU. For a short while, however, it appeared that the federal government would act. Since becoming the STFU's representative in Washington, Jackson had lobbied for a presidential inquiry into conditions in northeastern Arkansas. He and Norman Thomas persuaded Rexford Tugwell to discuss the matter with President Roosevelt. In early March, the president brought up the Arkansas tenant problem at a cabinet meeting. Frances Perkins, the secretary of labor, urged the president to dispatch a government mediator to Arkansas to settle disputes between landlords and tenants. Because Vice President John Nance Garner feared such an investigation would embarrass Senator Joseph Robinson in an election year, little came of Perkins's suggestion or Mitchell's proposal for a government commission to investigate conditions in Arkansas. Officials at the Agriculture Department informed Mitchell that complaints had been investigated and found to be exaggerated; nothing more would be done.

Because further efforts to find solutions failed, the STFU leaders and rank-and-file were committed more than ever to a strike at the end of April. As in 1935, Mitchell had union officials in the three strike counties set up strike committees. Each committee consisted of a representative from every organized plantation in a local's territory. The committees were responsible for explaining the union's demands to members and for informing them of the time and date of the walkout. In addition, the local strike committee would negotiate with planters if they decided to negotiate with the STFU.

On May 18, 1936, strike committees began spreading leaflets announcing the start of the strike. Although the union claimed 4,000 to 5,000 strikers, reports from members, organizers, and others revealed limited participation. The events of the early part of the year, division within the union, and planters' preparation for the strike all contributed to its failure. Those who remained on the land or even had work as day laborers understood the risk they took if they joined the union. Clearly, planters were willing and able to simply dismiss strikers, thereby depriving them of a means to survive. Internecine bickering also undermined the union's credibility among many.

Under the circumstances, planters' well-planned response had maximum effect on those who did strike. Unlike 1935, planters made arrangements to import unemployed workers from Memphis to replace strikers. Mitchell, anticipating this strategy, enlisted the assistance of the Memphis Workers' Alliance in trying to discourage those who would go into the Arkansas cotton fields, but he failed to stop the replacement of strikers. Local law enforcement officers assisted the planters by arresting anyone who interfered with "strikebreakers." Deputy Sheriff Paul Peacher arrested thirty-five strikers for vagrancy and put them to work on a "county farm." By the end of May, the strike was hardly noticeable. Mitchell and union officials decided to call it off.

CONCLUSION

The Southern Tenant Farmers' Union would continue to exist in various forms through the remainder of the 1930s. But the failure of the 1936 strike marked the end of its effectiveness in fighting the effects of agricultural change in the South. Even if they had temporarily succeeded in rolling back evictions and other immediate effects of New Deal farm policy, they could not preserve the farms of rural Arkansas, or their ability to subsist in rural areas. The AAA began a long-term process in the South that encompassed mechanization of the cotton harvest, production of less labor-intensive crops, and the end of tenancy. Tenants and rural laborers rendered superfluous by such fundamental changes found their ways to the factories of the South's expanding the urban-industrial economy, if they were fortunate. Others joined the ranks of the chronically underemployed in the countryside and in the city. With its struggle to control this revolution in Southern agriculture for the people who worked the land, the STFU joined a lengthy list of similar failed movements.

Henry M. McKiven, Jr.

BIBLIOGRAPHY

Conrad, David Eugene. *The Forgotten Farmers: The Story of Sharecroppers in the New Deal.* Westport, CT: Greenwood Press, 1982.

Fannin, Mark. *Labor's Promised Land: Radical Visions of Gender, Race, and Religion in the South.* Knoxville: University of Tennessee Press, 2003.

Grubbs, Donald H. *Cry from the Cotton: The Southern Tenant Farmers' Union and the New Deal.* Chapel Hill: University of North Carolina Press, 1971.

Kester, Howard. Introduction by Alex Lichtenstein. *Revolt Among the Sharecroppers.* Knoxville: University of Tennessee Press, 1997.

Korstad, Robert, and Nelson Lichtenstein. "Opportunities Found and Lost: Labor, Radicals, and the Early Civil Rights Movement." *The Journal of American History* 75 (December 1988): 786–811.

Martin, Robert F. "A Prophet's Pilgrimage: The Religious Radicalism of Howard Anderson Kester, 1921–1941." *The Journal of Southern History* 48 (November 1982): 511–530.

Mitchell, H.L. Foreword by Michael Harrington. *Mean Things Happening in This Land: The Life and Times of H.L. Mitchell, Co-Founder of the Southern Tenant Farmers Union.* Montclair, NJ: Allanheld, Osmun, 1979.

Saloutos, Theodore. "New Deal Agricultural Policy: An Evaluation." *The Journal of American History* 61 (September 1974): 394–416.

Venkataramani, M.S. "Norman Thomas, Arkansas Sharecroppers, and the Roosevelt Agricultural Policies, 1933–1937." *The Mississippi Valley Historical Review* 47 (September 1960): 225–246.

FARMER-LABOR PARTY

Minnesota's Farmer-Labor Party, and the larger movement of which it was a part, represents one of the most successful progressive third-party movements in American history. For about a twenty-year period, in the 1920s and 1930s, workers and farmers combined to elect hundreds of candidates to public office and promote an agenda that included fair prices for farmers and fair treatment of workers.

Although the seeds of third-party activism existed in many states, few movements flowered as the Farmer-Labor Party did in Minnesota. Situated at the boundaries of the industrial East and the agricultural West, Minnesota had both well-developed farmer organizations and strong labor unions. Leaders from both groups came forward at critical times to promote the formation of the party. The Minnesota movement, therefore, was in a position to take advantage of circumstances favorable to third-party formation—namely, an unpopular war and economic depression.

The history of the Farmer-Labor Party can best be understood in four stages: emergence (1917–1924), consolidation (1924–1930), high tide (1930–1938), and decline (1938–1948).

EMERGENCE
In the first stage, emergence (1917–1924), two broad-based organizations, the Farmer's Nonpartisan League and the Working People's Nonpartisan League, joined forces to challenge Minnesota's ruling Republicans by running opposition candidates in the primaries. Although their immediate aims were different, the two movements found little trouble agreeing on a political program. Both opposed the state's business and political elites who controlled the agricultural markets and viciously fought workers' attempts to organize unions. Both favored programs to curb corporate powers through state regulations and public ownership.

In autumn 1917, organizers from the Farmer's Nonpartisan League crisscrossed the state, signing up 50,000 farmers on an antimonopoly program patterned after the successful effort of North Dakota farmers the year before. From the beginning, opposition was intense. League organizing took place during the heat of U.S. involvement in World War I. Main Street "patriots" broke up meetings and ran organizers out of town. The Republican administration carried on a campaign of harassment, branding both farm and labor militants as disloyal and jailing leaders for sedition.

Still, the organizing continued. In 1918, Congressman Charles Lindbergh Sr., father of the famous aviator, came within 50,000 votes of defeating Governor Joseph A. Burnquist in the primary. The Farmer-Labor coalition elected a respectable number of state legislators and firmly established itself as the second-most powerful political force in the state—well ahead of the hapless Democrats.

Key players in the formation of the Farmer-Labor movement were farmer Henry Teigan and labor leader William Mahoney. United by their Socialist political views, they saw the coalition as a natural step toward achieving real political power. In 1918, Mahoney convinced leaders of the Minnesota Federation of Labor to abandon the electoral philosophy of American Federation of Labor President Samuel Gompers and pursue an independent political course. Teigan wrote frequently for both farm and labor publications on the need for unity. Both men ultimately became elected officials—Teigan as a member of the U.S. House of Representatives in 1936 and Mahoney as mayor of St. Paul in 1932.

Other Farmer-Labor advocates came to Farmer-Laborism through religion, particularly the Social Gospel, and the Prohibition movement. The Rev. Howard Y. Williams, a Congregational minister from St. Paul, and Susie W. Stageberg, an evangelical Lutheran crusader from Red Wing, were attracted to Farmer-Laborism's high purpose and moral activism. Stageberg would be remembered, Millard Gieske wrote in *Minnesota Farmer-Laborism: The Third-Party Alternative* (1979), as "the very personification of the religious disciple in politics."

CONSOLIDATION

The position of these activists and others who favored the creation of a genuine third party was strengthened by success in the 1920 and 1922 elections. In 1924, the two organizations founded the Farmer-Labor Federation—renamed the Farmer-Labor Association the following year. This event marked the beginning of the second stage of the movement's history, consolidation, (1924–1930).

The Farmer-Labor Association was the year-round, participatory body of the movement; the Farmer-Labor Party was its electoral arm. The development of a Farmer-Labor Party did not at first result in any dramatic improvement in Farmer-Labor fortunes. In 1924, the charismatic Hennepin County attorney, Floyd B. Olson, fell short in his bid to win the governorship. Throughout the rest of the decade, the association found itself swimming upstream, keeping its "loyal opposition" status in the legislature but unable to catch up with the Republicans.

Unlike many third-party efforts, however, the Farmer-Labor Party held together, less as a "movement" now with all the unfettered energy and participation the term implies, but as a viable organization. The continued support of the labor unions and the widespread network of ideologically committed Farmer-Laborites from both city and country kept the program and spirit alive.

HIGH TIDE

In 1930, the steady work paid off. Olson was elected governor, beginning the third and most successful period of Farmer-Labor history, the high tide (1930–1938). A gifted orator, Olson articulated the feelings of the one in five Minnesotans in search of work during the Great Depression and the many more who experienced both insecurity about their own situations and outrage about poverty and social injustice. The immensely popular Olson was elected governor three times and was a shoo-in for U.S. Senate before he died of a stomach tumor in 1936.

Olson's success was paralleled throughout the organization. Dues-paying membership in the association rose to almost 40,000 as organizers set up clubs across the state. Hundreds of Farmer-Laborites held elected offices at all levels of government—from city council to U.S. Senate. In 1936, Farmer-Laborites captured five of eight congressional seats, the governor-

A former dockworker and member of the Industrial Workers of the World, Floyd B. Olson served as governor of Minnesota from 1930 to 1936. Under his leadership, the state legislature passed many laws favored by the Farmer-Labor Party, including securities regulation, expansion of public works, conservation of natural resources, and aid to farmer and worker cooperatives. *(Minnesota Historical Society/St. Paul Daily News)*

ship, and a solid majority in the Minnesota House of Representatives.

Political success was buoyed by the spectacular reemergence of mass movements. The Farm Holiday movement revived the dormant populist spirit of Minnesota farmers as thousands participated in strikes and direct action tactics to resist foreclosures. In Minneapolis, the Teamsters Union faced down the Citizens Alliance, the country's most notorious anti-labor organization, and won an epic battle that opened up the state's largest city to the labor movement. In 1936–1938, the newly organized Congress of Industrial Organizations (CIO) set northern Minnesota's Iron Range on fire with militant campaigns among timber workers and iron ore miners.

Labor and farm organizing was complemented by other efforts as well. The Workers Alliance set up councils of the unemployed across the state, leading the fight for adequate relief and modern social security programs. Cooperatives of all kinds sprung up in town and country alike: electric power cooperatives, food cooperatives, marketing cooperatives, hardware stores, gas stations, and grain elevators. All of these movements allied themselves with the Farmer-Labor Association, oftentimes formally, as affiliated organizations. The association became the political extension of the great social movements of the 1930s.

Although the Farmer-Labor Party controlled the governorship for eight years, it was never able to control the state senate and was thus stymied in its efforts to enact its agenda. Pieces of the platform did become law, however, putting Minnesota in the forefront of New Deal–era reform. Successful Farmer-Labor legislation included a moratorium on farm foreclosures, ratification of the national child labor amendment, passage of the state income tax, and creation of thirteen new state forests.

DECLINE

The late 1930s signaled the end of the glory days of the Farmer-Labor movement. In 1938, Olson's successor, Elmer Benson, was overwhelmingly defeated by a reform Republican named Harold Stassen. The inability of successive Farmer-Labor administrations to solve the economic problems of the Great Depression; the people's weariness of class confrontation politics; a systematic anti-Semitic and anti-Communist campaign from both within and outside the association; and serious divisions within the association itself were all factors in the overwhelming Farmer-Labor defeat. The period of decline (1938–1948) set in.

With the United States' entry into World War II, the economy improved, and most Farmer-Laborites joined enthusiastically in support of the war effort. There was little inclination—and less of a constituency—for vintage Farmer-Labor antimonopoly politics while the war continued. In 1944, the association merged with the Democrats to become the Democratic-Farmer-Labor Party (DFL). Unity prevailed until the war's end.

In 1946, the struggle for the political direction of the new party began. Farmer-Labor opposition to the consolidation of corporate power and the Cold War politics of President Harry Truman's administration met head on with the corporate liberalism of the Democrats. When Farmer-Laborites moved to endorse the independent presidential candidacy of Henry Wallace in 1948, the Democrats, led by young Hubert Humphrey, united behind Truman. In a brutal six-month battle fought in precinct and district caucuses across the state, the Democrats soundly defeated their opposition. The Farmer-Labor wing never recovered its influence and was soon subsumed by the Democratic forces within the party.

But the Farmer-Labor movement was far more than an electoral party. It was a genuine social movement with its own educational and cultural components. It was *participatory*, the collective expression of thousands: farmers, workers, professionals, and small businesspeople. Many had inherited their outlook from parents, participants in earlier populist movements and labor struggles. Thousands more came to the association through their own experiences.

CONCLUSION

The Farmer-Labor movement encompassed but extended beyond the association itself. The movement included the Farm Holiday, the CIO, and the cooperatives. In an organizational sense, these movements often connected directly to the association as affiliates. But even when they did not, the collective energy of popular protest in Minnesota formed the social soil in which the Farmer-Labor Association could take root and grow.

As participants in progressive social movements, Farmer-Laborites developed a political viewpoint and program that were far to the left of both the New Deal of the 1930s and the Democratic Party today. The Farmer-Labor program contained "socialistic" proposals (public ownership of utilities, banks, packing houses, railroads) without advocating socialism as a total system. Farmer-Laborites believed that economic democracy was a necessary component of political democracy, that the unchecked power of monopolies was the greatest threat to both economic security *and* individual freedom, and that workers and farmers had the courage and intelligence to reshape society.

To be sure, some Farmer-Laborites were indeed Socialists. Veterans of the Socialist Party formed the nucleus of the Nonpartisan League, organizing efforts among farmers in both North Dakota and Minnesota. Socialists were prominent in the Twin Cities labor movement as well. They provided much of the ideological leaven for the foundation of the Farmer-Labor Federation in 1924.

The fullest expression of the Farmer-Labor Socialist current was the famous "Cooperative Commonwealth" platform of 1934. The term itself, "Cooperative Commonwealth," was vintage American socialism. It symbolized an economic-political system based on individual freedom and the common good. It countered the dominant cultural image of a free individual in a free market with a vision of a free *people* controlling both their political and economic institutions. The program itself, with its emphasis on grassroots economic organization through producer and consumer cooperatives, as well as state ownership, further reinforced this image.

But the imagery and poetry of the 1934 platform, while reflecting a continuous current within Farmer-Labor thought, was the exception. More typical was the platform of the Working People's Nonpartisan League in 1919. It would serve as a prototype for Farmer-Labor platforms throughout the 1920s and 1930s. It called for the eight-hour day and forty-four-hour week; the establishment of cooperatives; state compensation for injured workers; equality of men and women and equal pay; abolition of unemployment; and public ownership of railroads, banks, terminal grain elevators, and public utilities. The Farmer-Labor movement was nourished by diverse social traditions: the radicalism of the Finns on the Iron Range; the reform tradition of the Norwegians; the moral fervor of the Social Gospel; the crusading spirit of the temperance and suffrage movements; the populism of the Red River Valley wheat farmers; and the democratic dream of the Jeffersonian tradition itself.

The relationship between Communism and Farmer-Laborism was a matter of controversy throughout Farmer-Labor history. The American Communist Party supported the formation of the movement in the early 1920s, only to move to active opposition by 1924. Beginning with the United Front period in the latter half of the 1930s, the party once again actively supported the Farmer-Labor Association, adding strong organizing energy to the movement, but also creating conflict within movement ranks. Given the strength of anti-Communism in Minnesota and elsewhere, participation by party members provided the Republican opposition with a powerful political issue against Farmer-Laborites.

The Farmer-Labor movement had a lasting effect on Minnesota politics, not only in conventional political terms and in ideology, but also on the culture of civic participation itself. Not only did it elect hundreds to public office, keeping Minnesota's Democrats in their place, and challenging the dominant Republican Party for the top rung, but it produced in Floyd

Olson a political leader of national stature—"presidential timber" according to the era's pundits. Even after the merger creating the DFL Party, the progressive populism that was at the heart of the Farmer-Labor movement influenced the careers of such exemplars of postwar liberalism as Hubert Humphrey, Eugene McCarthy, Walter Mondale, and, more recently, Paul Wellstone. Minnesota's Republican Party changed fundamentally as it coped with the Farmer-Labor challenge. From the election of Harold Stassen in 1936 until the emergence of President Ronald Reagan's conservatism in 1980, Minnesota Republicans accepted a positive role for state government—a core value of Farmer-Laborism. The success of the Farmer-Labor Party established a tradition of third-party efforts in Minnesota, the political space for electoral success by Green Party candidates at the local level and Reform Party (later Independence Party) governor Jesse Ventura in the early twenty-first century.

Students of American political culture credit Minnesota with a high level of civic participation and an underlying commitment to public action for the public good. This "moralistic" approach to politics and public life has multiple roots. Chief among them is the progressive legacy of Minnesota's Farmer-Labor tradition.

Tom O'Connell and Barbara Kucera

BIBLIOGRAPHY

"Farmer-Labor Movement Owes Much to Mahoney." *The Union Advocate*, May 19, 1997. http://www.workdayminnesota.org.

Faue, Elizabeth. *Community of Suffering & Struggle: Women, Men, and the Labor Movement in Minneapolis, 1915–1945.* Chapel Hill: University of North Carolina Press, 1991.

Gieske, Millard L. *Minnesota Farmer-Laborism: The Third-Party Alternative.* Minneapolis: University of Minnesota Press, 1979.

Keillor, Steven J. *Cooperative Commonwealth: Coops in Rural Minnesota, 1859–1939.* St. Paul: Minnesota Historical Society Press, 2000.

Mayer, George H. *The Political Career of Floyd B. Olson.* Minneapolis: University of Minnesota Press, 1951.

O'Connell, Thomas G. "Toward the Cooperative Commonwealth: An Introductory History of the Farmer-Labor Movement in Minnesota (1917–1948)." Ph.D. diss., The Union Graduate School, 1979. http://www.freenet.msp.mn.us/people/fholson/fla-hist.html.

FARM WORKERS LABOR MOVEMENT

One of the poorest occupations in the United States is that of the landless, migrant farm worker. During the twentieth century, most seasonal workers labored on the enormous farms and ranches in California. Historically, how have members of America's rural proletariat responded to their lack of steady work and income? By what collective actions have they sought to change the conditions that they face? Have their efforts been, on the whole, successful or not?

THE ECONOMIC CONTEXT

Prior to World War I, agriculture in the United States was by and large family based and small scale. Independent family farmers, tenant farmers, and sharecropping families lived on the land that they cultivated. They directly consumed a goodly portion of what they raised. Production was fairly diversified, with a few specialized products, such as wheat and cotton, raised for domestic and international markets.

For historical reasons, California was an exception. After winning the Mexican-American War, the United States signed a treaty that promised to respect Mexican deeds for haciendas and ranchos, where large herds of cattle grazed on thousands of acres. Shortly after statehood was achieved in 1850, the California government, in hopes of encouraging economic development, sold much of the territory's unclaimed public lands. The government also sold a fair amount of land previously owned by Mexican citizens (partly because of real and alleged confusions over the content and location of deeds).

During the massive transfer of property, former Mexican estates were only partially broken up. Wealthy private investors, such as the Southern Pacific Railroad, shrewdly amassed prime farming property from the government, often through graft and corruption. A few thousand of California's wealthiest private proprietors soon owned most of the state's 128 million acres of arable land. Sometimes a company's real estate exceeded 100,000 acres, and single "plots" could take a day or more to walk across. As political historian and activist Carey McWilliams has noted, Henry George wrote in 1871: "California is not a country of farms but a country of plantations and estates."

By the time the government had completed its decisions about whether and how to transfer former Mexican landholdings, America's second industrial revolution had begun in earnest. After the Civil War, electrically powered machines were being invented and rapidly refined; and the transcontinental railroad was almost complete. Intrigued by the sales potential of America's enormous market, owners of California's gigantic farms soon invested in electrical-powered irrigation and underground pumps, harvesting machinery, storage facilities, and fertilizers, pesticides, and other chemicals. Modern railway technology (including refrigerated cars) enabled large landlords to focus on perishable fruits and vegetables that were in great demand and to ship them quickly to urban consumers in the Midwest and along the Eastern seaboard. Some ambitious growers branched out into ancillary businesses, such as food processing and preparation. (In the upper Midwestern states, in contrast, a clear division of labor developed between private farmers and large private processing companies, such as Campbell, Heinz, and Vlasic.)

The new machinery and facilities required lots of capital, which few of California's largest growers could amass by themselves. The state's financial institutions soon developed close ties with major growers. Complementary economic interests also led to friendships between leaders in California's booming agricultural sector and leaders of its transportation and utility sectors, creating a network of interlocking directorates among the state's wealthiest companies.

The titular owners of California's gigantic agribusinesses seldom resided on their lands or directly worked the ground. Large growers, visiting their holdings from time to time, usually lived and worked in cities, where they helped set production goals and planned market strategies, and dickered with banks, railroad companies, and retailers on prices and rates. To run the farms, owners hired supervisors and small year-round crews that maintained machines and watched the crops. In addition, growers authorized the hiring of large temporary workforces to harvest crops for a few weeks each year.

Except for grains, which could be harvested by machines, many commercial crops needed to be harvested within days by hand (and in the cases of some fruits, within hours). Otherwise, the crop would spoil. An inadequate number of workers thus could create an immediate financial crisis for a large farmer—a crisis whose dimensions few private industrialists could appreciate.

The transient laborers were paid piecemeal for the number of pounds they harvested each day. Workers either rented housing from the growers (which sometimes might be merely a tattered tent) or huddled at night in makeshift camps along public roads. Often pickers were not allowed to leave the ranches in the evening and were forced to buy groceries, toiletries, and other daily goods at exorbitant prices in company stores. Temporary workers sometimes were paid in scrip. This was done partly to encourage purchases on the ranch, partly to deter workers from leaving early for better paying jobs, and partly to cover damage to property, which was deducted from the field hand's pay when the scrip was exchanged for cash at the conclusion of the harvest.

As soon as a harvest was completed, a large grower usually had no further need for the hundreds (and sometimes more than a thousand) field hands. They were quickly pushed and pulled to new ranches. Vagrancy laws punished stragglers, but the need for food and wages usually provided enough incentive to prompt workers to move constantly up and down the state, according to the harvest schedules of different crops.

TRAITS OF FARM WORKERS

California's system of agriculture, featuring both large land holdings and a huge migrating workforce, has persisted for almost a century and a half. During that time, the ethnic and racial composition of the rural proletariat has changed dramatically.

At first, California's large agribusinesses recruited down-on-their-luck miners, Native Americans, bank-

rupt former farmers, and newly arrived Europeans. Toward the turn of the century, growers began to import laborers from China, Japan, Mexico, and Hawaii. By the 1880s, Chinese field hands made up more than half of the state's rural workforce. Later, waves of Japanese, Filipino, Mexican, and Middle Eastern immigrants provided most of the transient workforces that California's agribusinesses required. In the middle of the twentieth century, approximately two-thirds of the workforce was Spanish speakers from Mexico and the Philippines. In the late 1980s, growers began to rely on large numbers of non-Spanish speaking Native Americans from southern Mexico. Only for a few years in the late 1930s were a majority of the rural proletariat U.S citizens of northern European descent.

The ethnic diversity of the migrant workers has in some ways compounded their economic troubles. Not only are most of California's field hands very poorly paid and without secure jobs. They are shunned by most of white California, denied equal treatment when looking for housing and loans, and compelled to send their children to inferior schools and medical centers.

Throughout the twentieth century, members of the rural proletariat—regardless of national origins—tried to improve their material circumstances through individual and group actions. During boom years, many field hands migrated to cities in hopes of securing better paying jobs and, in the long run, of purchasing small amounts of property and joining the middle class. (Conversely, during early twentieth-century depressions, desperate urban workers in California sometimes would migrate to the countryside and seek work as pickers.) Of those who remained in the countryside, a large minority participated in local and spontaneous strikes and slowdowns in hopes of securing better pay and working conditions. A few farm workers attempted to create permanent labor organizations.

Partly because of the constant turnover among field hands (inasmuch as most workers leave sooner or later for the cities), the history of rural labor movements has been episodic. Different ethnic groups have become active at different times and have pursued different strategies and goals. There has been little organizational, ideological, or tactical continuity.

One can demarcate three periods in the history of California's farm workers' collective efforts to change working conditions. The first predated the New Deal and arguably was the most radical in terms of activists' aspirations. Chinese, Japanese, and Mexican immigrants, without outside support, launched strikes and walkouts; and members of the Industrial Workers of the World (IWW) tried to organize a grand anti-capitalist, quasi-Anarchist labor movement across skill levels.

The second period coincided roughly with the New Deal. Once again, Mexican workers initially spearheaded local acts of resistance; but the social and political landscape had changed, partly because of the newly arrived field hands who formerly were small farmers in southwestern states, such as Oklahoma and Arkansas. The widely publicized sufferings of these workers prompted the federal and state governments to intervene in California agriculture and to provide services, such as resident camps, that would make the lives of citizens more bearable. Government interest in the plight of farm workers waned, however, once the United States entered World War II and white laborers found better paying jobs in military-related industries.

The final period of farm-worker resistance began in the 1960s and flourished in the early 1970s, when Cesar Chavez used boycotts to defeat growers and temporarily broke through big business's grip on California's government. The final period of activism ended in the mid-1980s, after George Deukmejian, a conservative Republican, became governor of California and rolled back many of the political rights secured by Chavez's movement organization, the United Farm Workers (UFW).

WALKOUTS AND WOBBLIES

Many California growers in the nineteenth and early twentieth centuries believed that rural workers from Asia and Latin America were culturally passive and therefore more controllable than white-skinned laborers. Growers therefore repeatedly lobbied the federal government for the right to import field hands from abroad. Once on U.S. soil, non-European workers faced multiple forms of discrimination, ranging from daily exclusion from movie theaters and restaurants to the denial of opportunities to purchase stores and rent homes. Many white-skinned workers, competing with Chinese and Japanese immigrants for low-paying jobs, and many owners of smaller businesses, competing with larger companies that relied heavily on inexpensive Asian labor, formed the California's Workingmen's Party in the late 1870s and 1880s. The party called for an end to immigration from Asia, the deportation of Asians and the seizure of their property, and the strict restrictions on foreigners' rights to own businesses. As early as the depression of 1894, bands of unemployed white rural workers, partly out

of resentment and partly in hopes of generating jobs, attacked the homes of Chinese and Japanese workers, forcing them to flee to cities, where they were attacked by urban white workers and small shopkeepers.

Despite their vulnerability, immigrant field hands organized local strikes and attempted to establish unions. In the 1880s, disgruntled Chinese workers staged brief walkouts to protest landowners' policies. Some labor leaders asked for recognition and support from the American Federation of Labor (AFL). The AFL refused to help, partly to protect its meager financial resources for winnable strikes and partly because AFL members held anti-Chinese prejudices and wished to protect jobs for "white" Americans.

In 1902 and 1903, Japanese and Mexican sugar beet harvesters joined forces and formed a union, despite growers' efforts to promote ethnic rivalries. The AFL once again refused the workers' requests for help, partly because it viewed workers from non-European descent as unfair competitors, who undermined the wages and employment opportunities of U.S. citizens. Meanwhile, the large landowners increasingly used the threat of deportation to reinforce the purportedly "naturally" passive propensity of nonwhite workers.

In 1905, a group of Socialist-leaning labor activists met in Chicago to form the Industrial Workers of the World (IWW). The so-called Wobblies advocated the creation of one large union that would unite workers across craft and skill levels, races, and ethnic heritage. According to the union's theoreticians, workers should secure new rights through general strikes, in which workers across all crafts and skills, in a spirit of solidarity, would stop working at once. The Wobblies were not of one mind about violence, despite their critics' frequent accusations to the contrary. Some Wobblies considered violence counterproductive and therefore advocated nonviolent actions. Some believed that violence could on occasion be productive but was usually unnecessary. A vocal minority of Wobblies believed that violence, when applied wisely by workers, could be productive and in America probably was necessary.

Most Wobblies, regardless of their outlook on violence, considered themselves bitter rivals of the AFL. According to IWW spokespersons, the American Federation of Labor pursued only winnable strikes and was inspired by a narrow dream: the improvement of wages for skilled workers. The AFL (the Wobblies said) simply wanted to reinforce the economic status quo, to nurture quiescence among well-paid skilled workers, and to ignore the plight of the most vulnerable workers in the land, who were overwhelmingly either low-skilled or unskilled.

The AFL's behavior partly accorded with the Wobblies' analysis. Seeing farm workers in California as too indigent, transient, and legally vulnerable (because of their immigrant status) to organize, the AFL's leadership decided early in the twentieth century to abandon the countryside and to focus on organizing artisans and skilled factory workers in the cities. Seeing a political opportunity, the Wobblies soon began to communicate with and organize farm workers in California, especially those of Asian and Mexican descent.

In 1913, approximately 100 Wobblies joined a spontaneous strike at a ranch outside Wheatland, a small agricultural town in northern California. The Durst brothers, the state's largest single employer of agricultural labor, owned the ranch and, to secure a large enough workforce for the one-month hops harvest, advertised widely for workers. More than 2,800 workers arrived, but only half that number was in fact needed. This situation contributed to depressed wages and left hundreds of hungry and desperate families stranded in Wheatland without employment. The field workers who were hired were angered by the absence of toilets and drinking water in the fields (where temperatures exceeded 100 degrees by noon). At night, no shelter was provided, save dirty straw and ragged tents that the ranch rented to workers at exorbitant rates. Last but not least, the wages for harvesting at the Dursts' ranch were far less than the newspaper ads had promised and were appalling even by the standards of California agriculture. Facing unusually demeaning working conditions, many pickers in Wheatland planned to protest even before the IWW activists arrived.

The Wobblies quickly organized a general strike in the roughly dozen rural communities surrounding the Dursts' ranch. The Wobblies also held public meetings, circulated radical literature, and aided the workers in drafting a list of demands. At one rally, a sheriff's posse arrived and tried to disperse the crowd. In the heat of the moment, some members of the posse accidentally fired their guns, prompting a melee, in which four people (including a deputy sheriff and a district attorney) died.

California's political elite was stunned by the turn of events. Large growers were outraged and declared that a revolution was taking place, not because of deplorable wages and working conditions, but because of outside agitators spreading anti-American beliefs. Growers quickly hired a private detective agency to search for Wobblies throughout the state. Meanwhile, to restore order to Wheatland, the governor dispatched four companies of the National Guard. Over the following months, more than 100 Wobbly organizers were arrested, beaten, and held in prisons on grounds of fomenting violence for the purpose of undermining established patterns of property (even though many had in fact counseled nonviolence). State judges sentenced two of the Wobbly activists who had been present at Wheatland to life imprisonment.

The so-called Wheatland riot was in many ways a turning point in the history of farm workers' movements. In the course of covering the events, the popular press began to investigate the plight of field hands. This, in turn, led to growing popular outrage toward big growers. According to journalist Dick Meister and labor historian Anne Loftis, an editorial in the *Sacramento Bee* denounced the growers' "absolute disregard of the rights of others." Even the relatively conservative AFL openly denounced the condition of farm workers as well as the governments' and growers' undue repression of the Wobblies.

The public outcry prompted action by Governor Hiram Johnson and his fellow Progressive Party members in the state legislature. They created a Commission on Immigration Housing that investigated the events at Wheatland. The Commission's report denounced the growers' treatment of harvest workers. The government also began to enforce labor statutes more rigorously. Backpedaling, large growers began to improve work conditions—for example, installing bathhouses, water hydrants, and enclosed toilets—in hopes of obviating further legislative action.

Meanwhile, IWW activists, afraid that the owners' actions would placate farm workers, criticized the government's investigations and businesses' actions as illusory and minimal. Allegedly, such reforms might distract workers and prevent them from understanding the need to form independent unions and sooner or later to seize property from private growers through general strikes. Workers should be able, according to Wobbly literature, to tell a boss where, when, and for what compensation they would work. This would require, sooner or later, a complete transfer of property from absentee landlords to those who directly tilled the land. To recruit and motivate members, IWW writers and speakers employed incendiary language that exaggerated the purposes and consequences of local acts of everyday resistance. For example, they talked about workplace "sabotage" when referring to a simple slowdown to pressure owners to raise wages.

In 1915, a group of Wobblies formed the Agricultural Workers Organization (AWO), the first broadly based farm workers' union in U.S. history. Unlike earlier IWW organizations, the AWO played down radical rhetoric and concentrated on winning short-term benefits for workers. For a few years the union succeeded in organizing strikes leading to basic pay raises, overtime pay, and better housing. At one point, more than forty IWW and AWO locals were functioning in California.

In some ways, 1915 was the zenith of California farm-workers' resistance. The actions of California's Progressive politicians and the successful strikes organized (but seldom initiated) by the Wobblies had led to a significant improvement in the material standards of living of California's farm workers. The formation of the AWO seemed to foreshadow the creation of a permanent workers' organization with political clout. But the workers' victories proved to be short-lived.

The California government, which temporarily had sided with workers and had challenged the prerogatives of growers, returned to its old ways. By 1915, the Progressive movement had begun to disintegrate, partly because of members' disagreements over economic policy and over the wisdom of the United States' plans to enter World War I. In 1919, California governor William Stephens, a politician with socially conservative views, helped the state legislature pass the so-called Criminal Syndicalism Law. This piece of legislation prohibited not only acts of violence, but also the teaching of doctrines that encouraged changes in industrial ownership through the use of force. With this law in hand, state and local government officials began to arrest, try, and convict labor organizers who were planning violent attacks on growers and illegal seizures of property.

Meanwhile, California's growers, in the wake of the Wheatland debacle, formed several political organizations, perhaps the most famous of which was the Farmers' Protective League. The League hired private guards and detectives to spy on and harass union activists, lobbied the state legislature to pass laws against the IWW, and pressured newspapers to publish stories favorable to the growers' particular view of agricultural conditions and unions.

Last but not least, the United States' decision in 1917 to enter World War I effectively ended the Wobblies. Since 1915, the IWW had vigorously opposed U.S. entry into the war and had called it "a business-

man's war" motivated by profits and indifferent to the working-class lives that would be lost. After 1917, the Wobblies carefully avoided openly opposing U.S. participation; but their ongoing support of strikes was viewed as unpatriotic and detrimental to the war effort. In the popular press and on the floors of the state and national legislatures, Wobblies were denounced as traitors and, at worst, German spies and, at best, spineless draft evaders. Police and other security agencies invaded the Wobblies' offices and seized union funds.

After the war ended in 1918, opponents took advantage of the Wobblies' open support for the Bolshevik revolutionaries in Russia to brand them, once again, as disloyal and anti-American. William Stephens received a bomb in the mail, which he attributed to the work of IWW assassins (an accusation that was never proven valid). According to Meister and Loftis, Stephens and his aides characterized the Wobblies as "huns of industry" and "the bitter enemy of all honest workers." Federal and state prosecutors, meanwhile, charged the Wobblies with engaging in "Bolshevik conspiracies." The Wobblies' legal rights to mail union and party literature were suspended, and their opportunities to raise funds for legal defense were severely reduced. By 1926, both the IWW and AWO were bankrupt and were rapidly losing members, partly because many key leaders had been deported. Most key theoreticians and tacticians who had neither died nor been imprisoned left the movement and joined either the more conservative AFL or the more explicitly pro-Russian Communist Party.

Shortly after 1920, real wages for farm workers plummeted, and living conditions once again worsened. The new laws that set higher standards for housing for transient workers no longer were enforced. Growers no longer feared strikes, for radical activists were deterred by fears of arrest; and the increasing use of vigilantes had intimidated most field hands.

Nonetheless, the first wave of farm-worker activism had not totally failed; for the Wobblies and the Asian-Mexican alliances had clearly demonstrated that farm workers in California could be organized despite their poverty and economic vulnerability. The Wobbly activists left behind a large body of songs, stories, speeches, and experiments in grassroots organizing from which later farm-worker activists would creatively borrow. Finally, the dramatic collapse of the Wobbly movement taught some farm workers that only with the support of government could the growers be defeated. Without support from government, any concession from growers was likely to be short-lived.

NEW DEALS

During the early 1920s, California's farm workers were largely passive, even though their standards of living dropped steadily. Real wages, for example, declined 50 percent between the beginning and end of the decade. But proletarian quiescence was short-lived. Farm-worker activism became more common and frequent during the 1930s. More than 140 strikes, involving more than 125,000 field workers, took place in that decade.

Economic disaster partly explains the abrupt revival of protests. With the advent of the Great Depression, starvation became an immediate problem; and cities no longer offered a viable alternative for the rural poor. The countryside was filled not only with traditional field hands, but also with hungry former city dwellers in need of work, and with former small farmers from the Midwest and Southwest who had been evicted from their lands. Basic biological need fueled workers' demands for better wages, decent housing, and reasonable prices in company stores.

In addition, approximately half of California's farm workers between 1935 and 1940 were white-skinned, and many came from the American heartland and carried with them the expectations and pride of small farmers. These poor field hands were not social radicals, for they remembered independently managing their own property and retained hopes of one day earning enough to purchase a small farm or urban business. But they were hostile to big businesses (including banks), and believed that land should belong to those who labored on it.

Although reputed to be passive, Mexican field hands were the first to protest against the steady deterioration of wages. Because of new legal restrictions on the immigration of Asian workers, by the mid-1920s Mexicans had become the largest nonwhite contingent of field workers in California. Excluded from Anglo schools and barred from restaurants and movie theaters, Mexican laborers and their families established their own *barrio* settlements, in which Spanish-speaking mutual-aid societies, defense lawyers, and local unions thrived. Beneficiaries of organizing spaces and ties of loyalty, Mexican field hands began to stop working if they felt that wages were too low or that working conditions were too brutal. By 1928, the numerous strikes by immigrants from Mexico had prompted growers to call in government officials to arrest and deport strike leaders.

The actions attracted the attention of a new radical labor organization, the Trade Union Unity League (TUUL), which the Communist Party had established in 1929. The League's long-term goals resembled those of the IWW, as both organizations were devoted to the creation of a single, large union that crossed ethnic, racial, and craft lines. In 1930, TUUL members began working with Mexican strikers, led a few strikes, and tried to hold a conference with representatives for field hands and packing-shed workers. These actions troubled growers and government officials. California's Criminal Syndicalism Law gave the authorities the legal instrument that they needed. More than 100 TUUL activists were arrested and convicted of fomenting the violent overthrow of established property relations.

Shortly afterward, the Communist Party established a new political action group, called the Cannery and Agricultural Workers' Industrial Union (CAWIU), which attempted to assume the leadership of wildcat strikes, usually at the request of strikers. Typically, CAWIU activists would hear of an upcoming labor action, travel to the site, and set up so-called tent cities with armed guards to keep nonworkers away. Within these proletarian settlements, workers elected racially mixed strike committees, which drew up demands and planned collective actions, such as caravans of trucks with huge strike signs that would drive along the borders of farms and ranches.

The CAWIU and Mexican activists jointly launched several major strikes during the early 1930s. At first, the strikes typically failed. Growers brought in hungry strikebreakers from Mexico, and organized vigilantes who, with the tacit support of local police, attacked picketers with lead pipes, chains, and guns.

As time passed, the CAWIU learned how to mobilize a more effective antigrower coalition by appealing to and drawing resources from small growers and urban sympathizers. As a result, most local crop-wide strikes were successful by 1933.

Growers were not easily defeated, however. The Great Depression had severely reduced sales and profits, and many growers found themselves deeply in debt. Higher wages were not a luxury that the growers could easily afford. In 1934, a group of major rural and urban business groups in California—including Pacific Gas and Electric, the Southern Pacific Railroad, and the Bank of America—funded a new business association, called the Associated Farmers. Members of the Associated Farmers insisted that unions were "un-American" and represented the first step in the overthrow of the U.S. system of government and society. The organization kept files on union activists, refused to hire known labor activists, and regularly turned over lists of names to the federal government and to local law enforcement agencies. The organization also financed local paramilitary units, such as the California Cavaliers, whose job was to stamp out un-American activity by force.

On the whole, local governments supported the Associated Farmers and banned workers' meetings and car caravans. Local police also openly aided and abetted the vigilantes, who used tear gas bombs and guns to break up peaceful gatherings of workers.

Suffering increasing violence and widespread arrests, farm workers began to doubt the wisdom of resistance; and strikes began to collapse by the late 1930s. It momentarily seemed that the growers would win the day and that workers would once again glumly but quietly accept their circumstances. In fact, the Communist Party, wishing to avoid an unpatriotic appearance during World War II, adopted a moderate Popular Front strategy and dissolved the CAWIU.

During this discouraging period, the hundreds of thousands of white field workers who recently had lost their farmland in Southwestern states suddenly became visible. Attracted to California because of handbills that described plentiful job opportunities, the so-called Okies (the name came from Oklahoma, though the migrants came from many different states) discovered both that the number of field hands in California vastly exceeded the number growers needed and that wages often dropped below subsistence level.

Literally starving, Okies on occasion launched spontaneous strikes. But more often the Okies, being former small farmers, scrupulously respected property rights.

The suffering of the Okies drew attention from an unexpected source: the New Deal reformers in Washington and in Sacramento. In 1938, Culbert Olson became the first Democrat in the twentieth century to be elected governor of California. Once in office, Olson revived the Commission on Immigration and Housing that had originally been created in the aftermath of the Wheatland riot. Olson appointed Carey McWilliams, a lawyer with strong sympathy for field workers and strong antipathy toward big business, to be the executive secretary of the Commission. McWilliams toured the countryside to publicize the plight of field hands, used radio announcements to encourage citizens to report on the growers' failure to meet housing standards, and supported numerous

bills to improve working conditions for field hands. Most of the legislative initiatives, however, were blocked by California's Republican-dominated legislature and by the lobbying efforts of the Associated Farmers. Through indefatigable efforts to publicize conditions in the countryside, McWilliams succeeded in influencing how many Californians viewed the behavior of growers and the suffering of field hands. Temporarily, public opinion shifted against those who owned factories in the fields.

The popular uproar generated by John Steinbeck's immensely popular novel, *The Grapes of Wrath* (1939), drew the attention of citizens outside California to the economic plight of the state's migrant workers. New Dealers in the nation's capital were shocked to read about the sufferings of white-skinned Okies. First Lady Eleanor Roosevelt traveled to California to see for herself if the conditions described by Steinbeck were true. She returned saying that, if anything, conditions were far worse than Steinbeck had reported.

Prompted by pro-union staffers, U.S. Senator Robert La Follette, Jr. (R-WI) reluctantly announced in the late 1930s that his Senate Committee on Education and Labor would travel to California and hold investigations into possible violations of workers' civil rights. After several weeks of public hearings, the La Follette commission concluded that California's local governments and growers had indeed flagrantly violated the rights of workers through blacklisting, strikebreaking, and vigilantism. Like President Franklin D. Roosevelt, La Follette recommended that the New Deal's National Labor Relations Act, which guaranteed industrial workers the right to assemble, form unions, and negotiate contracts, be extended to farm workers.

By the end of the 1930s, the nation's middle-class conscience had been pricked. The federal government, working with the California state government, created approximately forty camps where workers could live while searching for jobs. Within these camps, union organizers could speak with workers and plan collective actions, while the paramilitary groups funded by growers were banned.

Growers viewed these government centers as places where "Reds" could plan the overthrow of America's economy. Growers therefore used their political clout to limit the further development of migrant workers' camps, as well as to prevent passage of a broader national labor relations act that would give farm workers the rights to form unions, engage in collective bargaining, and participate in binding arbitration. In addition, rural communities and local

After spraying tear gas to break up a crowd of striking lettuce workers in Salinas, California, on September 16, 1936, authorities patrol the streets. Workers were attempting to block trucks carrying lettuce from the fields to the packing sheds. *(© Underwood Photo Archives, Inc.)*

associations that were supported by the Associated Farmers held outdoor book burnings, in which copies of *The Grapes of Wrath* were destroyed.

For a brief period toward the close of the 1930s, it looked once again as if California's field hands finally would secure permanent improvements in their living conditions and significant increases in their legal rights to challenge growers' policies. However, the government's concern about farm workers was soon overshadowed by the United States' entrance into World War II. Many California farm workers who were U.S. citizens either were drafted into the armed forces or left the fields for better paying jobs in the war industries. The federal government, meanwhile,

was loath to discourage agricultural productivity or to promote economic conflict, and therefore backed away from forcing agribusinesses to allow unions.

The war, however, created an unexpected labor shortage in the countryside. California's growers argued that if they were to feed a nation at war, they would need a new batch of inexpensive harvesters. The U.S. government tried to alleviate the shortage by approving in 1942 the so-called Bracero program, which allowed Mexican nationals to work temporarily on U.S. farms but with the understanding that after the harvest season, the immigrants would return to their homeland. Once implemented, the Bracero program proved highly controversial. Its defenders ar-

Seeking to register and find work, Mexican farm laborers line up outside a Migratory Processing Office. The Bracero program permitted Mexican citizens to find temporary agricultural employment in the United States during the mid-twentieth century. *(Brown Brothers)*

gued that it sensibly gave growers the sizable labor force that was needed if Americans were to eat at affordable prices. Without the braceros (which loosely translated means "those who work with their arms"), growers allegedly would not find enough U.S. citizens willing to engage in stoop labor. Critics of the Bracero program argued that it kept wages artificially low by recruiting desperate workers who were too terrified and legally vulnerable to protest mistreatment by growers. In effect, a pliable workforce had been recruited.

In 1964, the Bracero program officially ended. By this time, the farm workers in California were overwhelmingly either Mexican Americans or Mexican citizens. The following year, the United Farm Workers, the largest and most successful farm workers' movement in California history, was officially established.

CHAVEZ: SUCCESSES AND FAILURES

In 1962, a middle-aged community activist named Cesar Chavez founded a labor organization, the Farm Workers Association (FWA), which a few years later would be rechristened the United Farm Workers.

As a child, Chavez lived on a small farm, which his father lost in 1937 when he was unable to pay taxes and irrigation bills. The dispossessed family eked out an existence as migrant laborers, and young Chavez, after spending year after frustrating year in more than fifty segregated schools, dropped out of formal education and through books taught himself about the Mexican Revolution and the ethical reasoning of Mohandas Gandhi, Henry David Thoreau, and various Christian saints.

Returning from military service during World War II, Chavez joined philanthropic organizations that worked for the betterment of poorer Americans.

CESAR ESTRADA CHAVEZ (1927–1993)

Chavez was born on March 31, 1927, near Yuma, Arizona, the son of a migrant worker. His childhood was spent moving about in Arizona and California, and he had an inconsistent education that ended after eighth grade. He became a migrant worker to help his family.

After two years in the Navy (1945–1946), Chavez returned to farm work, married, and settled in Delano, California. After moving to San Jose, he began reading about the use of nonviolence for social change. In 1952, Chavez met Fred Ross and became involved in the self-help Community Service Organization (CSO) in California, working among Mexicans and Mexican Americans. From 1958 to 1962, he served as its general director. During his service he also met Dolores Huerta.

In 1962, he and Huerta left the CSO to organize wine grape pickers in California and formed the National Farm Workers Association. Using strikes, fasts, picketing, and marches, Chavez was able to obtain contracts from a number of major growers. During a strike by the Agricultural Workers Organizing Committee of the American Federation of Labor-Congress of Industrial Organizations (AFL-CIO) in 1966, his organization merged with it to form the United Farm Workers Organizing Committee, which later became United Farm Workers of America (UFW). Chavez served as president of the UFW for the remainder of his life. Embracing nonviolent tactics, he conducted fasts that focused national attention on the farm workers' problems, as did the 340-mile march from Delano to Sacramento in 1966.

Chavez also launched a 1968 boycott against the table grape growers, mobilizing consumer support throughout the United States. By 1970, the UFW got grape growers to accept union contracts and effectively organized most of that industry. By then, the UFW claimed 50,000 dues-paying members, the most ever represented by a union in California agriculture. The UFW boasted a union-run hiring hall, a health clinic and health plan, a credit union, a community center and cooperative gas station, as well as higher wages. The hiring hall meant an end to discrimination and favoritism by labor contractors.

In 1972, the United Farm Workers, with Chavez as president, became a member union of the AFL-CIO. Chavez expanded its efforts to include all California vegetable pickers and launched a lettuce boycott, as well as extending his organizational efforts to Florida citrus workers. His successes in California were sharply diminished, however, as the result of a jurisdictional dispute with the International Brotherhood of Teamsters over the organization of field workers that began in 1970. In 1973, the Teamsters cut heavily into UFW membership by signing contracts with former UFW grape growers, but Chavez renewed the grape workers' strike. In 1977, the two unions signed a pact defining the types of workers each could organize.

In 1976, Chavez reorganized the union to improve efficiency and outreach to the public. He led another boycott in 1984 over the grape industry's refusal to control the use of pesticides. Membership in the UFW later declined, in part due to disputes between Chavez and his followers, some of whom accused him of nepotism. But the accusations did not harm his work or his legacy as a leading figure in the American labor movement. He died on April 23, 1993, while working to defend the union from a lawsuit filed by a major grower.

James G. Lewis

One group was the Community Service Organization (CSO), a Saul Alinsky-inspired assemblage that believed in organizing the poor into self-governing political blocks that then could make demands on local governments for improvements in public services. The key, according to this strategy, was to have members of an impoverished community discuss common problems and debate possible political solutions. Once they discovered how to formulate their own demands, members of a self-governing committee would develop confidence, which would lead to further demands and ultimately to greater political clout (or so the theory went). As long as they had outsiders speak for them, the poor would remain passive supplicants, abjectly dependent on the kindness of strangers.

After working on primarily urban projects, such as registering low-income voters and investigating discrimination in rental housing, Chavez decided to leave the CSO. He wanted to return to the fields and organize desperately poor migrant workers.

With family members and friends, Chavez established the Farm Workers Association. Chavez decided to avoid the term *union* because of the suspicions it might generate among growers and workers alike. At first, the FWA promoted self-help institutions within Mexican-American communities, such as credit unions and consumers' cooperatives. Needing financial

Cesar Chavez, speaking into a microphone, urges consumers not to purchase lettuce and grapes picked by nonunion labor. Chavez and Dolores Huerta, founders and leaders of the United Farm Workers, organized boycotts, strikes, marches, and other nonviolent actions to gain higher pay and better working conditions for agricultural laborers. *(Karen Eberhardt/Walter P. Reuther Library, Wayne State University)*

resources, meeting places, and legal contacts, FWA began to work closely with the Migrant Ministry, an arm of the National Council of Churches dedicated to helping the rural poor.

In 1965, Mexican-American field hands spontaneously struck for better wages against a group of powerful vineyards. The strikers asked the FWA to support the strike, and Chavez agreed to help, despite his reservations about possibly squandering his organization's limited finances. The Migrant Ministry, the leadership of the United Automobile Workers, and other labor organizations soon swung their support behind the strikers.

The strike against grape growers unexpectedly lasted more than five years, as growers once again engaged in armed intimidation. In the face of likely defeat, Chavez coined a novel strategy: the promotion of consumer boycotts of the growers' products. Chavez, a master motivator, also changed his orga-

nization's name to the United Farm Workers and proposed that a black eagle against a red and white background become the union's daring emblem. UFW activists traveled throughout the United States and spoke to students and parishioners about the need to boycott grapes and wines. Supermarkets that stocked the growers' products were boycotted until they stopped.

Because of past experiences and personal convictions, Chavez distrusted armed action and preferred moral suasion, electoral politicking, and legal action. To dissuade workers from engaging in violence and to draw outsiders' attention to the strikers' cause, Chavez led dramatic marches, featuring popular religious symbols, through the blistering heat of central California and undertook public fasts, some of which lasted more than three weeks. The UFW began to lobby legislators and endorse political candidates. By the end of the decade, Chavez had become arguably the most famous Mexican American of his time. *Time* magazine selected him as the magazine's "Man of the Year." Martin Luther King, Jr. and presidential candidate Robert Kennedy not only praised Chavez's commitment to nonviolence but also pledged to support the farm workers.

In the mid-1970s, Jerry Brown, the liberal governor of California, publicly endorsed Chavez's aim of unionizing all farm workers and helped pass California's Agricultural Labor Relations Act (ALRA), which granted farm workers the legal right to unionize and to elect their own spokespersons. The Act, among other things, created the Agricultural Labor Relations Board (ALRB) with powers to investigate the fairness of union elections, to judge possible contract violations, and to identify and resolve the sources of stalemate during contract negotiations.

For approximately five years California's farm workers used ALRA provisions to secure concessions from growers. Growers were required by law to allow union activists to enter fields at specified times and to inform laborers about their rights and legal options. Frustrated by Chavez's success in attracting outside supporters, some growers tried to avoid negotiating with the UFW by quietly signing contracts with the Teamsters. But the ALRB declared the Teamster contracts illegal and insisted that workers should vote on who would represent them, the UFW or the Teamsters. The UFW usually won these elections, allowing it by 1982 to negotiate 162 contracts that affected 75,000 farm workers.

In 1983, political conditions in California once again changed drastically. The newly elected governor

DOLORES HUERTA (1930–)

Born on April 10, 1930, in Dawson, New Mexico, Dolores Fernández moved as a child to Stockton, California, with her mother and siblings after her parents' divorce. After graduating from Stockton High School, she married, had a family, and divorced but eventually received an A.A. degree and a teaching certificate from the University of Pacific's Delta Community College. After teaching only a few months, she decided that she could do more for the impoverished farm workers' children in her class by helping their parents win more equitable working conditions.

Huerta cofounded the Stockton branch of a Mexican-American self-help association called the Community Service Organization (CSO) and began lobbying California state legislators to enact such progressive legislation as old-age pensions for noncitizens. While working for the CSO, she met and married another community activist, Ventura Huerta, but this marriage also ended in divorce.

In the late 1950s, Huerta met Cesar Chavez, a CSO official. Both eventually left that organization because the CSO refused to organize farm labor. In 1962, they cofounded the National Farm Workers Association (NFWA), forerunner of the United Farm Workers (UFW). In 1963, she was instrumental in securing Aid for Dependent Families (AFDC), for the unemployed and underemployed, and disability insurance for farm workers in California. By 1965, Huerta and Chavez had recruited farm workers, and their families, throughout the San Joaquin Valley. On September 16, 1965, the NFWA voted to join in the strike by the Agricultural

Workers Organizing Committee for higher wages. The two organizations merged in 1966 to form the United Farm Workers Organizing Committee, which later became the United Farm Workers of America (UFW). The strike lasted five years. In 1966, Huerta negotiated the first UFW contract with the Schenley Wine Company. The grape strike continued, and Huerta, as the main UFW negotiator, successfully negotiated contracts that established the first health and benefit plans for farm workers.

In 1973, when the grape contracts expired, Huerta organized picket lines and continued to lobby. She was instrumental in securing unemployment benefits for farm workers the following year. The UFW organized the workers in the vegetable industry as well. When anti-union violence erupted, the UFW called for another consumer boycott. Huerta directed the East Coast boycott of grapes, lettuce, and Gallo wines, which led to the passage in 1975 of the Agricultural Labor Relations Act, the first law recognizing the rights of California farm workers to bargain collectively. In 1975, Huerta lobbied against federal guest worker programs and spearheaded legislation granting amnesty for farm workers who had lived, worked, and paid taxes in the United States for many years but were unable to enjoy the privileges of citizenship. This resulted in the Immigration Act of 1985. In the 1980s, Huerta cofounded the UFW's radio station and continued to speak and raise funds on behalf of a variety of causes, including immigration policy and farm laborers' health.

James G. Lewis

of California, a conservative Republican named George Deukmejian, denounced the ALRA, the UFW, and Chavez. According to Deukmejian, Chavez was a demagogue, unwilling to compromise and unable to speak truthfully about workers' conditions. Once in office, Deukmejian drastically cut the budget of the ALRB, appointed a pro-business politician to head it, and named judges to the California Supreme Court who lacked backgrounds in labor law. The cumulative impact of these actions was that the ALRB investigated fewer complaints by workers, and the Supreme Court frequently favored growers whenever the growers appealed decisions made by the earlier ALRB.

Cut from the political loop, the UFW began to splinter. Some rank-and-file members were discouraged by the failure of the highly legalistic ALRA strat-

egy and lost faith in collective bargaining. By 1987, the UFW still held only thirty-one contracts. Other activists, such as Meta Mendel-Reyes, were frustrated by Chavez's refusal to delegate responsibility to mid-level union officials. Chavez insisted on personally overseeing almost all facets of his organization, which made it difficult for other UFW officials to make policy decisions in a timely manner. This ultimately contributed to the union's failure to complete many of its tasks, such as maintaining its medical clinics, certifying union elections, and administering retirement plans. Finally, more than a few leaders were troubled by Chavez's religiosity and his close ties to church groups. Some wanted him to be more of a secular trade-unionist. Others who held Chicano political beliefs wanted Chavez to make the union first and foremost an organization to help and protect Mexican

Americans and Mexican immigrants. The Chicanos were particularly troubled by Chavez's hostility to illegal immigrants from Mexico who, in Chavez's opinion, were too easily used as strikebreakers and who threatened the job security and opportunities of U.S. workers.

When Chavez died in 1993, many former farmworker activists, despite their admiration for his courage and spirit, expressed reservations about his authoritarian leadership, his non-Chicano and highly religious beliefs, and his legalistic style. Activists were not of one mind about why their movement had shrunk from 60,000 members in 1982 to less than 20,000 members in 1993, or about why the UFW had not sponsored a wildcat strike, major grassroots protest in over a decade. Few disagreed, however, that in the 1990s field hands were once again among the poorest paid of U.S. workers and that rural workers had yet to discover effective ways with which to advance their interests.

CONCLUSION

The history of farm-worker protests and movements in California highlights both the ongoing powerlessness of the state's rural workers and the economic and political power of California's agribusinesses. After a century of struggles, California farm hands remain among the poorest paid workers in America and still lack effective labor-law protection.

Political-process theorizing and resource-mobilization theorizing—two standard approaches to the study of social-movement development—illuminate important aspects of the history of California's farmworker movements. Workers, when striking, were often aided by outside organizers, such as the Wobblies in the 1910s, the Communists in the 1930s, and Chavez and his followers in the 1960s and 1970s. These groups helped local acts of spontaneous resistance become more large-scale and more successful. Moreover, as political-process writers would predict, changes in the political climate—especially shifts in California's party politics—help explain the surges and ebbing of slowdowns, strikes, and union activity.

Nonetheless, the resource-mobilization and political-process models of social-movement politics fail to highlight the impact of racism and foreign policy on the evolution of farm workers' movements, and fail to recognize the remarkable political resources of California's agribusinesses. Accusations of treason during World War I and World War II had a chilling effect on the development of farm workers' movements. Anglo-Americans' distrust of nonwhites hindered the development of coalitions between farm workers and other sectors of American labor. Meanwhile, growers' ability to promote paramilitary units, to shape media coverage of events, and to finance and lobby party politicians repeatedly offset farm workers' initial political and economic victories.

Such factors, not yet central themes in social-movement theorizing, must be kept in mind if we are to explain why farm workers' victories were so few and so brief. Although the movements enjoyed short-term successes, in the long run the power of California's growers (vis-à-vis farm workers) was never significantly diluted. The story of farm workers' movements thus cannot be separated from other "American" stories of racism, Cold War ideologies, and countermobilizations by agribusinesses.

Cyrus Ernesto Zirakzadeh

BIBLIOGRAPHY

Bardacke, Frank. "Cesar's Ghost: Decline and Fall of the UFW." In *Cesar Chavez: A Brief Biography with Documents*, ed. Richard W. Etulain, 106–116. Boston: Bedford/St. Martin's, 2002.

Etulain, Richard W. *Cesar Chavez: A Brief Biography with Documents*. Boston: Bedford/St. Martin's, 2002.

Jenkins, J. Craig. "The Transformation of a Constituency into a Social Movement Revisited: Farmworker Organizing in California." In *Waves of Protest: Social Movements Since the Sixties*, ed. Jo Freeman and Victoria Johnson, 277–299. Lanham, MD: Rowman and Littlefield, 1999.

Loftis, Anne. *Witnesses to the Struggle: Imaging the 1930s California Labor Movement*. Reno: University of Nevada Press, 1998.

McWilliams, Carey. *California: The Great Exception*. Berkeley: University of California Press, 1999.

———. *Factories in the Field: The Story of Migratory Farm Labor in California*. Boston: Little, Brown, 1939.

Meister, Dick, and Anne Loftis. *A Long Time Coming: The Struggle to Unionize America's Farm Workers*. New York: Macmillan, 1977.

Mendel-Reyes, Meta. *Reclaiming Democracy: The Sixties in Politics and Memory*. New York: Routledge, 1995.

Mooney, Patrick H., and Theo J. Majka. *Farmers' and Farm Workers' Movements: Social Protest in American Agriculture*. New York: Twayne, 1995.

Starr, Kevin. *Endangered Dreams: The Great Depression in California*. New York: Oxford University Press, 1996.

AMERICAN AGRICULTURE MOVEMENT

The American Agriculture Movement (AAM) was a dramatic, short-lived farmers' protest movement that has, in recent decades, transformed itself into a more subtle, long-term farm and rural life issues organization. The movement sprang to life first among Colorado grain growers in the fall of 1977 and spread across the nation's farm belt on the wings of a call for an agricultural strike. The movement dramatized in stark relief the grievances of family farmers: a depressed farm economy, low prices, high operating costs, an unrealistic government policy, and weak farm advocacy groups. Organizers and supporters were reacting to the recent passage of President Jimmy Carter's Food and Agriculture Act of 1977, but they were also decrying historically ineffectual government farm policies that had ruinously promoted fencerow-to-fencerow production. The short-term solution was to strike and not plant in 1978 so as to bring about higher commodity prices. At the core of AAM's objectives, then and now, was the demand for 100 percent parity prices for all domestic and foreign consumer agricultural products. Neither the strike nor higher commodity prices materialized, however, and momentum and cohesiveness faded with failed legislative actions and the loss of media coverage in the early 1980s. AAM's political activism developed from early shortsighted demonstrations into more results-oriented political lobbying; because of this shift in strategy, AAM remains a voice in agricultural policymaking today.

CRISIS IN AGRICULTURE

What compelled farm people of the late 1970s and early 1980s to politicize their situation was the disastrous economic state of agriculture following decades of major changes and shifts. AAM represented as much a protest against where farming stood and where it was likely to go, as it did a protest against how it had deteriorated to this level. By the 1970s, for example, farm families were laboring under staggeringly high—and relentlessly increasing—fixed costs (surging up nearly 200 percent) and interest rates (as high as 18 percent annually), while commodity prices had fallen by 50 percent.

During the course of the twentieth century, farming had become increasingly complex, industrialized, efficiency-oriented, mechanized, capitalized, international, and productive. These changes strained the structure of agriculture, subjecting it to chronic overproduction, low prices, and a greater need for capital, all of which worked to undermine farm economics and, ultimately, the prospects of affordable, let alone profitable, family farming. In its demands for price parity, AAM was reaching for a federal policy tradition that dated back to the 1920s when policymakers began measuring agricultural prosperity against the prosperous years of 1909 to 1914, also known as the "golden age of agriculture." Parity is an economic relationship characterized by strong agricultural prices that boost farmers' purchasing power to at least equal (on a *par*) with that of other laborers in the economy. AAM sought a remediation of the farm crisis through a federal policy commitment to 100 percent parity.

Despite the structural changes, the farm economy was relatively stable during most of the two decades following the 1950s; interest rates held at 5 or 6 percent, and farmers were able to meet their operating needs through low interest loans. Commodity prices had dipped after 1951, but parity was largely maintained with the assistance of government program price supports and production controls. These were also designed to reduce the number of smaller producers in the economy and thus sparked a significant rural outmigration that was still apparent into the 1970s. Unfavorable domestic and international changes beginning with the Food and Agriculture Act of 1965 soon created the context for protest throughout the Great Plains, Midwest, and other regions.

The Food and Agriculture Act of 1965 sought to bring American commodity prices in line with those on the world markets. As such, the Act lowered the price supports farmers had been receiving, and the strength of American commodity prices subsequently declined. American grain exports more than doubled, however, and prices jumped between 1968 and 1973 when the international market experienced crop failures, particularly in the Soviet Union. To fill this vacuum, the U.S. government urged farmers to increase fertilizing and planting. Unfortunately, petroleum prices, gasoline, farm machinery, and petroleum-based fertilizers were all on the rise as a result of escalating conflicts in the Middle East. Although the U.S. economy had begun displaying encouraging signs by 1976, the restoration of international grain production levels caused American farm prices to drop precipitously.

FARM CRISIS GROWS

That was also the year that presidential candidate Jimmy Carter promised farmers a program that would assure them cost of production prices. Yet when Carter became president and his Food and Agriculture Act of 1977 clearly only amended the Food and Agriculture Act of 1965, farmers realized that they were locked into another four-year term of unresponsive farm policy. The Act established a price floor much lower than the 1973–1975 average. Moreover, the contracts that the government proposed entailed that farmers would receive a combination of loans and direct payments toward a government-determined "target price" that was considerably lower than U.S. Department of Agriculture cost of production figures. It was this political and economic reality that dominated the conversations of Western grain growers Gene and Derrel Schroder, Jerry Wright, Lynn Bitner, and Alvin Jenkins who came together in September 1977, in Campo, Colorado, to discuss the possibility of an agricultural strike.

AGRICULTURAL ACTIVISM

Under these conditions, strike talk took root in fertile ground. Originally calling their group the American Agricultural Strike, the movement founders quickly organized a public meeting in Springfield, Colorado. They generated interest and support through extensive use of flyers and the media such that 700 farm men and women, coming from as far away as Texas, came together and agreed to set December 14 as the strike date and to establish Springfield as the national farm strike headquarters. On September 22, 1977,

2,000 movement supporters participated in a nationally televised rally in Pueblo, Colorado. U.S. Secretary of Agriculture Bob Bergland was in attendance and heard not only the concerns of the farm people but also their demand for 100 percent parity on all domestic and foreign agricultural products, as well as their threats to strike, to halt agricultural production and distribution, and to stop purchasing farm equipment on or after the strike date. Besides 100 percent parity, AAM's subsequent five-point demands included the halting of all imports of agricultural products that were domestically produced until 100 percent parity was achieved, and the creation of an entity that involved agricultural producers in policy formation.

EMERGENCE OF A MOVEMENT

AAM launched a movement strategy that made excellent use of demonstrations, rallies, tractor parades ("tractorcades"), a variety of publicity, and local activism to advance its cause. A rally held in Amarillo, Texas, on October 14, 1977, drew 5,000 supporters, while a smaller, though obviously symbolic, protest in President Carter's rural hometown of Plains, Georgia, brought in hundreds of farmers and tractors. Meetings and rallies were staged through the coordinated efforts of state and local organizers as well as traveling speakers. Together, according to AAM, they succeeded in establishing 1,100 local offices nationwide by January 1978. Cofounder Alvin Jenkins was also one of the movement's most effective speakers, reportedly pointing out to the farmers that without a change in farm policy and without their activism, "You're going to look awful silly five years from now, trying to chase down 3 dollars a bushel wheat in your $100,000 combine!" AAM's activities gained the support of the National Farmers Union and the National Farmers Organization, but not that of the American Farm Bureau, which prompted much bitterness among farmers and considerable confusion on the part of legislators.

From the outset, AAM strove to maintain a movement that was at once centralized and decentralized. The Springfield national headquarters planned for the impending nationwide strike and the upcoming January protest in Washington, D.C., while the state and local offices oversaw the local activism aimed at recruitment. Although the movement's founders and leaders managed the business side of AAM with the assistance of volunteers, any sort of formal structuring ended there. AAM avoided membership dues and lists, appointing officials, and devising regulations, and anyone could speak on the group's behalf.

AAM successfully mobilized participants and was able to cultivate an initial commitment to the cause through a number of ways, especially by linking participation to the winning of political concessions. Public policy educator William P. Browne found that AAM's impressive organizing and recruitment owed much to the "social incentives" that AAM held out to farm men and women in terms of camaraderie and common interests at the meetings. Conversely, the incurring of negative social benefits, such as criticism or even intimidation by AAM, proved to be motivating factors toward participation as well. According to Browne, farm people also joined because of the tremendous early successes in gaining publicity and large audiences that seemed to suggest that the winning of political rewards was quite possible. Finally, many supporters believed it was necessary to confront and protest a political system that they held responsible for devising ineffectual agricultural policies that had financially abused them. The strength of these convictions explains why so many farm people would take part in the January 1978 Washington, D.C., protest, although the severity of their financial situation would ultimately weaken their commitment to the strike.

Farm Strikes

Despite nearly three months of media hype, mushrooming member participation, effective demonstrations, and tractorcades held throughout the country, in state capitals and Washington, D.C., the December 14 strike date passed by as a whisper, with Congress taking little notice. Farmer activism increased in response. To many farmers winter meant no planting, and the unresolved question of the strike and spring planting was as yet a ways off. AAM now began a series of tractor picketing at packinghouses and food distribution warehouses, wholesalers, and some railroads. Farm implement dealers and fertilizer companies supported AAM's goals but were concerned about the consequences to them of the threats to stop buying machines and supplies. Most importantly, AAM leaders were determined to quickly force some kind of congressional action by a show of solidarity and strength if necessary. From various points across the country in early January 1978, farm people and tractorcades converged upon Washington. The Texas tractorcade alone contained thousands of tractors and campers. When Congress convened on January 18, an estimated gathering of 50,000 farm men and women were on hand to greet them.

Lobbying Government Officials

Over the next four months, AAM state delegates and supporters aggressively lobbied for favorable legislation and appeared to have gained Congress's ear. They met with Senate and House Agriculture Committees, the U.S. Department of Agriculture (USDA), and President Carter, making officials personally acquainted with the problems of the farm economy. Subsequently, Congress approved a new farm loan program and a moratorium on Farmers Home Administration foreclosures. It could not, however, create long-term legislation for a new farm program in time for the 1978 growing season; instead it worked with AAM delegates in their call for short-term legislation to amend the 1977 Farm Act. In mid-March, Kansas Senator Robert Dole offered an encouraging compromise proposal for a flexible parity plan that was passed by the Senate (H.R. 6782). The act stipulated that wheat growers who set aside a percentage of their land would receive a target price of three dollars a bushel through so-called deficiency payments, with 5 percent price increases until the acreage set aside equaled 50 percent. Corn, cotton, and soybean growers were offered similar terms. Unfortunately for AAM, the Carter administration ably worked to defeat the bill in the House, pointing toward the USDA's March 3 report which depicted AAM's parity objectives as particularly threatening to retail food prices. When the bill reappeared as the Emergency Agriculture Act of 1978, it merely offered an upward adjustment in price supports of 11 percent. AAM saw the Act's passage as nothing short of a political sellout.

By spring, many AAM supporters had filtered back to their agricultural enterprises. The movement showed signs of suffering from both external and internal defeat. In reality, total adherence to the strike against planting would have imposed financial consequences that few farm families could have tolerated. When forty-nine prominent AAM participants were later asked if they themselves had reduced production in support of the strike, only 20 percent responded in the affirmative. Disillusionment began depleting the movement of its members even as it emboldened some of the remaining activists. The latter maintained AAM's public visibility through various means, including the publishing of a sharply critical newsletter, *American Agriculture News*, which was sent to several thousand subscribers. AAM's second major protest in the nation's capitol in January 1979, with its traffic-

To protest low milk prices, dairy farmers dump 80,000 pounds of milk on a Wisconsin farm on July 4, 2000. While the American Agriculture Movement has declined since its peak years in the late 1970s and early 1980s, it remains active in support of farmers' economic interests. *(AP Wide World Photos)*

snarling tractorcades and destructive behavior, put off supporters, officials, and the general public alike. At AAM's June 1979 convention, delegates reported that between 60 and 90 percent of their state locals were now in fact inactive.

THE FARM ECONOMY WORSENS

As long as the farm economy remained in crisis as it did, even worsening in the 1980s, AAM had a rallying cause and a constituency. At the August 1979 convention, AAM restructured as AAM, Inc., firmed up its organization and strategies, and designated Texas cotton farmer Marvin Meek as chair. Meek made little inroads with the Carter administration, and even less with the Reagan administration under whose leadership farmers watched helplessly as parity fell to a meager 61 percent. In the early 1980s, AAM turned its energies to pressuring state governments and

sought mortgage moratorium laws as well as commodity blockade laws designed to bolster commodity prices. AAM activists formed the American Agriculture Movement Political Action Committee in Washington, and they also began running for office. The October 4, 1986, *Economist* reported that at least five AAM farmer-activists were campaigning for House seats that year.

Although AAM continues to lobby for agriculture today, it has not survived intact. During the 1980s, several factions left AAM, Inc., to form Grassroots AAM, with original AAM founder Alvin Jenkins as chair. Little is known about this smaller group except that some members appeared to espouse more disruptive action, and that its strength emanated from eastern Colorado, western Kansas, and parts of Texas. AAM, Inc., developed a three point program to preserve independent farming based on minimum commodity prices, inventory control, and supply management, as well as a plan involving production quotas resembling one proposed in the 1930s by Milo Reno of the Farm Holiday Association. Currently, AAM, Inc., also lobbies for rural issues and is part of the National Family Farm Coalition, an organization committed to promoting a unified farm program.

Ginette Aley

BIBLIOGRAPHY

Browne, William P. "Mobilizing and Activating Group Demands: The American Agriculture Movement." *Social Science Quarterly* 64:1 (March 1983): 19–34.

Browne, William P., and John Dinse. "The Emergence of the American Agriculture Movement, 1977–1979." *Great Plains Quarterly* 5 (Fall 1985): 221–235.

Dyson, Lowell K. *Farmers' Organizations.* Westport, CT: Greenwood Press, 1986.

Greene, Donald Miller. "The American Agriculture Movement: Its Cause, Spread, and Impact." Ph.D. diss., University of Oklahoma, 1979.

Hurt, R. Douglas. *American Agriculture: A Brief History.* Ames: Iowa State University Press, 1994.

McCathern, Gerald. *Gentle Rebels: The Story of the Farm Protest of 1977 thru 1982 by Members of the American Agriculture Movement.* Hereford, TX: Food for Thought Publications, 1982.

"Ploughing a Furrow to Washington." *The Economist*, October 4, 1986.

7

MORAL REFORM MOVEMENTS

INTRODUCTION

Temperance, anti-vice, and social purity campaigns are an integral element of the history of American social movements. As the essays in this section explore, campaigns against alcohol, drugs, prostitution, homosexuality, sexually explicit materials, contraception, and abortion reflect deep-seated concerns about changing family structures, the role of women, the economic climate, industrialization, urbanization, and immigration. For two centuries, moral panics around these shifting dynamics have played a significant role in the formation of American social and governmental policy.

This section addresses the significant influence of a gathering social force from the late 1800s to 1920, comprised of a majority of middle- and upper-class Americans interested in social "progress" and "reform" known as the "Progressives." The movement was instrumental in changing the political, social, and economic landscape of the United States by injecting their form of moral superiority on working-class and poor Americans.

Common Prohibitionist Themes

In *Themes in Chemical Prohibition* (1979), drug addiction expert William L. White identified eight themes that pervade prohibitionist campaigns: association of the target substance (or activity) with a hated subgroup of society or a foreign enemy; identification of the substance (or activity) as being responsible for unrelated social problems such as crime, violence, and insanity; the idea that cultural survival depends on prohibition; a "domino theory" whereby the targeted substance (or activity) is said to lead to worse vices, addiction, or ruined health; an association between the substance (or activity) and the corruption—especially the sexual corruption—of children; the idea that the substance (or activity) is "contagious" and that users are recruiters; the idea that the substance (or activity) must be totally banned—rather than intelligently regulated—lest it overwhelm society; and attacks on those who question prohibition as themselves part of the problem. Although White focused on crusades against illicit substances, the same themes can be seen in campaigns to control stigmatized behavior, "deviant" sexual activity, sexually explicit materials, and politically unpopular speech.

Two Centuries of Anti-Vice Activism

In the 1800s, campaigns against prostitution, sexually explicit literature, and alcohol took place against the backdrop of industrialization and changing family roles as women entered the public sphere—both as workers and reformers—in increasing numbers. Early efforts against prostitution, alcohol, and drugs had a public health focus, but later took on an abolitionist tone.

The Comstock Law of 1873 set the stage for a century of battles against sexually explicit representation. Although the original Comstock laws were overturned by the mid-1960s, later laws against pornography and explicit music and art were often based on similar themes of social purity.

In the late 1800s and early 1900s, the Prohibition movement associated alcohol with crime, insanity, irresponsibility, and the corruption of youth. Similar themes carried over to the War on Drugs that entered the public consciousness in the 1980s—as did many of the unintended adverse effects of Prohibition, such as the development of underground markets and widespread lawbreaking. Alcohol and drugs were linked to immigrants and racial and ethnic minorities, from German brewers to Chinese opium addicts to Mexican marijuana users to black cocaine fiends. Alcohol and drug use were also linked to youth subcultures that challenged authority and prevailing social mores. The repeal of Prohibition in 1933 illustrated the shallow sentiment underlying the ban on alcohol, demonstrating that the mainstream was concerned with curbing excess, not eliminating all use.

World War I, the Great Depression, and World War II ushered in major social changes and greatly influenced moral purity campaigns. Both war periods brought changes in the roles of women and intensified anti-foreigner sentiment. During the McCarthy era of the 1950s, middle-class women were driven back into the home and crusades raged against communism and sexual depravity, especially homosexuality.

The 1960s and 1970s saw a major period of liberalization, with the flowering of the civil rights movement, the women's movement, youth empowerment, and gay liberation. During these years, the Comstock Law banning contraception was overturned, the *Roe v. Wade* decision legalizing abortion was handed down, and several court cases narrowed prohibitions against sexually explicit materials. But as drug use became widespread and several types of crime increased, the stage was set for President Richard Nixon's "tough on crime" campaign and the intensification of the War on Drugs.

The election of President Ronald Reagan in 1980 signaled a new culture war, with renewed campaigns against abortion, pornography, and homosexuality. The Religious Right, with their traditional values agenda, became a major player on the national political stage. Multiple state and federal laws whittled away the right to abortion. Despite lack of evidence that pornography caused societal harm, religious conservatives and some feminists joined forces to promote increasingly restrictive anti-pornography legislation. Under the leadership of Senator Jesse Helms (R-NC), Congress stepped up efforts to deny federal funding for sexually explicit art and to ban AIDS education efforts that were seen as promoting homosexuality and drug use. The War on Drugs continued apace, with the public panic against drugs and drug users reaching a crescendo in the mid-1980s. As a consequence, the prison population exploded and the anti-drug crusade increasingly became a factor in U.S. foreign policy.

By the turn of the twenty-first century, the tide appeared to be turning once again. As happened during Prohibition, an increasing number of people began to decry the excesses of the War on Drugs and its unintended consequences. Harm-reduction policies, which attempt to minimize drug-related problems without insisting on abstinence, were increasingly ac-

cepted by the public health establishment. The Religious Right lost much of its political clout, and the Catholic Church became mired in a scandal over sexual abuse by priests. Nevertheless, conservatives were still able to employ fears about the corruption of children to push through abstinence-only sex education. The effects of the September 11, 2001 terrorist attacks remain to be seen, although the target of public panic and government control appears to have shifted away from sex and drugs to focus on foreigners, immigrants, and political dissidents.

THE MAKING OF MORAL PANICS

The nineteenth- and twentieth-century campaigns against alcohol, drugs, prostitution, pornography, explicit popular entertainment and art, homosexuality, pedophilia, and public sex have elements of classic moral panics. In his book *Sexuality and Its Discontents* (1985) sociologist Jeffrey Weeks defined moral panics as political moments in which diffuse social fears are channeled into agitation against an unpopular minority. "Sex panics, witch-hunts, and red scares are staples of American history," wrote historian Lisa Duggan in *Sex Panics* (1989). "While often promoted by powerless but vocal minorities hostile to cultural difference, they have been enthusiastically taken up by powerful groups in an effort to impose a rigid orthodoxy on the majority."

In *Thinking Sex* (1984), Anthropologist Gayle Rubin stated, "The criminalization of innocuous behaviors such as homosexuality, prostitution, obscenity, or recreational drug use is rationalized by portraying them as menaces to health and safety, to women and children, to national security, to the family, or to civilization itself." Judith Levine noted in *Harmful to Minors* (2002) that such panics tend to arise in times of transformation when people are anxious about social changes, traditional institutions are unstable, and authorities feel they are losing control. According to Rubin, "During a moral panic, such fears attach to some unfortunate activity or population. The media become ablaze with indignation, the public behaves like a rabid mob, the police are activated, and the state enacts new laws and regulations. When the furor has passed, some innocent erotic group has been decimated, and the state has extended its power into new areas of behavior."

Liz Highleyman and Benjamin Shepard

MORAL REFORM MOVEMENTS IN POSTWAR AMERICA

World War II brought a new round of social changes to the United States. In the prewar years, isolationist sentiment was prominent, but after the bombing of Pearl Harbor on December 7, 1941, mainstream America was ready for war. The rampant xenophobia of the day was most clearly exemplified by the forced relocation of people of Japanese descent—primarily from California—and their internment in concentration camps. Women entered the labor force in large numbers to replace men who had gone to war. For many women, this allowed an unprecedented degree of freedom and economic participation. Military leaders, well aware that soldiers would frequent prostitutes, promoted the use of condoms so that the men would not contract syphilis and pass it on to their wives and girlfriends back home. In the grip of patriotic fever and economic hardship, the country took a break from moral crusades; while vice was still unquestionably condemned, a more practical approach prevailed.

The end of the war sparked the beginning of a new backlash, ushering in what is widely regarded as the most conservative period in contemporary U.S. history. Middle-class women were forced out of the workplace and back into the domestic sphere. Aided by the GI Bill, many who could afford to do so left the cities for the suburbs. The idealized American nuclear family arose, and any diversion from this image was condemned. In the 1940s and 1950s, xenophobia, fear of left-wing radicals—in particular, "godless" Communists—anxieties about nuclear war, and renewed concerns about sexual immorality intersected in countless ways.

THE RISE OF MCCARTHYISM

The first major American "red scare" began in 1919 in the wake of the Russian Revolution; before it ended, thousands suspected of holding dangerous radical sentiments were arrested, held without trial, and in some cases deported. But McCarthyism—a period of anti-Communist hysteria—was more far-reaching, extending into all areas of American life and ensnaring many who had no connection with political dissent. In 1952, deepening xenophobia led to the passage of the McCarran-Walter Act, which imposed more rigid entry restrictions for immigrants. In 1947, the House Un-American Activities Committee (HUAC) began to target Hollywood, attempting to root out any suggestion of anti-American sentiment. Academia was another favorite realm of anti-Communist crusaders. Before it was over, McCarthyism had ruined countless careers and lives.

Under the leadership of Senator Joseph McCarthy (R-WI) and Federal Bureau of Investigation (FBI) director J. Edgar Hoover, the dragnet rapidly expanded to focus on all forms of "sexual depravity," especially homosexuality. In 1948, Alfred Kinsey and co-authors published *Sexual Behavior in the Human Male,* followed in 1953 by *Sexual Behavior in the Human Female;* the books altered social discourse about homosexuality and other sexual variations. Kinsey and his Institute for Sex Research were accused of weakening the moral fiber of the country and rendering Americans more vulnerable to Communist influence. Homosexuality—which had only come to be seen as a distinct sexual identity around the turn of the century and was rarely mentioned in the social purity movements of the late 1800s—became a key target of moral crusaders. During this era, the government restricted employment of known or suspected homosexuals in federal jobs. Police raids of gay and transgender bars and surveillance and sweeps of cruising and commercial sex areas continued through the 1960s. In many cases, those netted in such operations were publicly exposed in the media.

Yet the increased repression galvanized homosexuals to fight for their rights. In 1951, at the height of the McCarthy era, Harry Hay—a Communist and la-

On October 23, 1947, a youthful Ronald Reagan, president of the Screen Actors Guild, attends a hearing of the House Un-American Activities Committee prior to testifying. A fervent anti-Communist, Reagan was elected president of the United States in 1980. *(AP Wide World Photos)*

bor activist—and others formed the Mattachine Society in Los Angeles. In 1954, the postal service banned the shipment of the group's *ONE* magazine under the still intact Comstock Law, the 1873 federal anti-obscenity law that prohibited the passage through the mail of "obscene, lewd, or lascivious" material. The 1958 *ONE Inc. v. Olesen* Supreme Court decision declaring that homophile literature could not be banned as obscene was the first ever high court ruling favoring homosexuals. The Daughters of Bilitis, a group for lesbians, formed in San Francisco in 1955. The San Francisco–based Council on Religion and the Homosexual, a civil rights organization comprised of early gay activists and progressive Protestant ministers, formed in 1964.

THE 1960S: BIRTH OF AN ERA

Although the countercultural Beatnik movement began in the late 1940s, it was not until the 1960s that a confluence of sweeping social changes ushered in a new era of liberalization in most aspects of American life. The civil rights movement for racial equality grew during this period. Major riots broke out in several U.S. cities. Rejecting the mandatory nuclear family of the 1950s, women increasingly entered the workforce and demanded social equality. The National Organization for Women formed in 1966. Middle-class youth on campuses became increasingly radicalized, and massive protests against the war in Vietnam—and against the ruling establishment in general—exploded across the country. The new "unisex" fashion in clothing and hairstyles set off anxieties about gender-role nonconformity. Hippie youth flocked *en masse* to San Francisco's Haight-Ashbury district during the 1967 "Summer of Love," where they experimented with drugs, communal living, and new types of sexual relationships. After police raided the Council on Religion and the Homosexual's 1965 New Year's Eve costume ball, the American Civil Liberties Union (ACLU) sued and all charges were dropped, ushering in a new era of gay political power in San Francisco. The gay liberation movement burst into public consciousness nationwide with the Stonewall Riots in New York City in June 1969, when gay, lesbian, bisexual, and transgender bar patrons and bystanders fought back against police who raided the Stonewall Inn in Greenwich Village.

By the time Richard Nixon resigned in disgrace in 1974 following the Watergate scandal, respect for authority and traditional social mores was perhaps at its lowest ever ebb.

CONTRACEPTION AND ABORTION

The U.S. Food and Drug Administration's approval of the first birth control pill in 1960 is widely credited with sparking the sexual revolution. But battles over contraception and abortion continued apace. Moral crusaders not only played on fears about the changes in middle-class women's traditional roles that would be brought about by the ability to control fertility, but also exploited anxieties about rapidly reproducing immigrants and blacks overwhelming Anglo-Saxon whites.

In the 1936 case *U.S. v. One Package of Japanese Pessaries* (a device similar to a diaphragm), federal judge Augustus Hand ruled that birth control could not be classified as obscene and loosened laws forbidding the importation of contraceptive devices. But it was not until the 1965 *Griswold v. Connecticut* decision that the U.S. Supreme Court, citing marital privacy, ruled that married couples had the right to use contraceptives. The 1972 *Eisenstadt v. Baird* decision extended this right to unmarried people. In the late 1960s, Pope Paul VI issued an encyclical condemning abortion and all forms of artificial birth control. Seen as a representative of foreign interests, the Catholic Church had not been instrumental in the social purity campaigns of the nineteenth century, but gained increasing influence—especially in cities such as New York and Boston—with the influx of Catholic immigrants. In the latter half of the twentieth century, the

Catholic Church played a major role in the anti-abortion movement.

Roe v. Wade

The most celebrated victory in the fight for reproductive rights was the landmark 1973 *Roe v. Wade* decision, in which the U.S. Supreme Court ruled that abortion was legal during the first three months of pregnancy. As with the *Griswold vs. Connecticut* decision, the court based its ruling on the right to privacy. The first state laws against abortion had been passed in the mid- to late 1800s, and by 1910 most states had laws criminalizing abortion unless necessary to save the mother's life. Before the 1973 court decision, many women availed themselves of illegal abortions; while wealthy women sometimes could obtain legal abortions in other countries, women with fewer resources were consigned to "backroom" or self-administered procedures that led to many deaths.

Anti-abortion Movement

In the final decades of the twentieth century, religious and political conservatives stepped up their campaign against abortion. The National Right to Life Committee, spearheaded by the Catholic Church, was organized in 1973 to overturn *Roe v. Wade*. Both presidents Ronald Reagan and George H.W. Bush were sympathetic and politically indebted to the anti-abortion movement. Groups such as Operation Rescue targeted abortion providers, utilizing tactics such as blockades, which had been pioneered by progressive activists. In response, pro-choice activists—a coalition of women's rights advocates—responded by organizing "clinic defense" efforts. In the 1990s, there were numerous incidents of anti-abortion extremists bombing family-planning clinics and several shootings of abortion providers.

Anti-abortion activists succeeded in whittling down the scope of *Roe v. Wade* even while they failed to outlaw abortion entirely. Public funding of abortions for poor women in the United States was removed by the 1976 Hyde Amendment. Reagan's 1984 Mexico City Policy—better known as the "gag rule"—banned U.S. aid to international organizations that provide or discuss abortion. Most states enacted laws requiring women under age eighteen to obtain parental or judicial consent for an abortion. In the 1989 *Webster v. Reproductive Health Services* decision, the U.S. Supreme Court ruled that states could bar the use of public facilities for abortion. In the late 1990s, anti-abortion advocates began lobbying for laws banning late-term, so-called partial birth abortions. Fewer medical schools provided training in abortion procedures; by the end of the decade, an estimated 85 percent of U.S. counties had no abortion providers. Concern about the appointment of conservative Supreme Court justices who could potentially shift the balance against *Roe v. Wade* was a major issue in the 2000 presidential campaign. The two major successes for pro-choice advocates in these years were the increased availability of emergency contraception (the "morning-after pill") in the late 1990s and the approval of RU-486 (the "abortion pill") in 2000, both of which had the effect of privatizing decisions about abortion.

In the latter decades of the twentieth century, moral crusaders were more successful in campaigns to restrict abortion than in efforts against sexual "deviance." This comparative success can perhaps be attributed to the fact that on the abortion issue, the value mainstream Americans place on privacy and individual liberty clashes with the emphasis they place on protecting children. Nevertheless, today many U.S. women use contraception, and polls show that—although support for choice has declined—a majority of Americans do not favor banning abortion.

DEFINING AND CONTROLLING OBSCENITY

Since the enactment of the 1873 Comstock Law, moral crusades related to sex have continued to play an important role in the history of U.S. social policy. Through the first half of the twentieth century, obscenity restrictions were leveled against many written works, including literary classics such as Geoffrey Chaucer's *Canterbury Tales,* James Joyce's *Ulysses* (1922), D.H. Lawrence's *Lady Chatterley's Lover* (1928), Henry Miller's *Tropic of Cancer* (1934), Allen Ginsberg's *Howl* (1956), and William Burroughs's *Naked Lunch* (1959). Explicit literature was associated with all manner of social ills ranging from obsessive lust to disregard for family responsibilities to the promotion of homosexuality and various forms of depravity. Following the familiar pattern, moral panics about sexual material were often linked to immigrants and racial and ethnic minorities—particularly Jews—who operated venues such as dance halls, produced objectionable films, and published erotic books.

One of the most infamous targets was Samuel Roth, a Jewish immigrant from Austria who produced and distributed by mail both sexually explicit and mainstream publications. In the mid-1950s, Roth was subpoenaed to appear before moral crusader Estes Kefauver's Senate committee to answer charges that his "lewd and lascivious" materials contributed to ju-

venile delinquency. Roth was arrested and prosecuted on several occasions for obscenity law violations. In the key 1957 *Roth v. United States* case, the U.S. Supreme Court struck a blow against the Hicklin test (the outcome of a British case from the 1800s), which held that a work was obscene if it was likely to corrupt children. Another strike against the Hicklin test was delivered earlier that year when the Supreme Court ruled in *Butler v. State of Michigan* that the adult population could not be limited to materials that are fit for children.

The 1973 *Miller v. California* case established the well-known three-prong test for determining whether material is obscene and thus not constitutionally protected: the average person, applying contemporary community standards, would find that the work, taken as a whole, appeals to the prurient interest; the work depicts or describes, in a patently offensive way, sexual conduct; and the work, taken as a whole, lacks serious literary, artistic, political, or scientific value. Under this decision—which remains the basis for today's obscenity laws—the most prudish standards of a minority cannot be used to determine what materials are suitable for an entire community.

With the *Roth* and *Miller* decisions, the Supreme Court affirmed that obscenity—that which appeals to "prurient interest" and is without "redeeming social importance"—is not protected by the First Amendment. However, it left obscenity rather ill-defined, as reflected in Justice Potter Stewart's famous remark that while he could not define smut, he knew it when he saw it. In the years that followed, the Supreme Court refined the three-prong test, defining "prurient interest" as a "shameful or morbid interest in sex"—not "normal lust"—and specifying that the "average person" does not include children. The Court also affirmed that indecent materials—defined as those in "nonconformance with accepted standards of morality"—are protected as long as they meet the conditions set forth in the *Miller* decision.

The Meese Commission

Much of the debate surrounding sexually explicit materials concerned the purported negative societal effects of pornography such as crime, the oppression of women, and harm to children. During the Kefauver Commission hearings, psychiatrist Dr. Benjamin Karpman testified that pornography leads boys into gangs and juvenile delinquency. According to the FBI's Hoover, "The increasing number of sex crimes is due precisely to sex literature madly presented in certain magazines. . . . It is creating criminals faster than jails can be built." But by 1970, the President's Commission on Obscenity and Pornography (the Lockhart Commission) had found "no reliable evidence to date that exposure to explicit sexual materials plays a significant role in the causation of delinquent or criminal sexual behavior among youth or adults."

Sixteen years later, the Attorney General's Commission on Pornography—better known as the Meese Commission—revisited the issue. The Meese Commission amassed a collection of materials found in several adult bookstores—including hundreds of books and thousands of magazines and films. In fact, the Meese Commission's 1,960-page report may be the most extensive pornography database ever compiled.

The Meese Commission hoped to find scientific evidence to refute the conclusion of the 1970 commission that pornography does not lead to negative social consequences, but it had little success. Researchers such as Edward Donnerstein of the University of Wisconsin had found a connection between certain types of violent pornography and aggressive behavior, but did not find similar effects for sexually explicit but nonviolent material. Sociologist Edna Einsiedel, who was hired by the commission, concluded that "no evidence currently exists that actually links fantasies with specific sexual offenses." Some of the most negative testimony came from moral crusader Judith Reisman, who despite questionable methodology in her studies of sexually explicit cartoons in men's magazines still was unable to find much damning evidence.

Released after a year of hearings, the 1986 Meese Commission report contained several recommendations for restricting obscenity and pornography, including stepped-up enforcement, forfeiture provisions similar to those of anti-drug laws, definition of the hiring of porn actors as an unfair labor practice, use of pandering laws against pornography producers, and requirements against doors on peep show booths—which also became an issue in struggles over gay male sex establishments. In 1987, the federal government established the Obscenity Enforcement Unit, later renamed the Child Exploitation and Obscenity Section.

The Feminist Sex Wars

The Meese Commission hearings took place against the backdrop of a battle within the feminist movement that has come to be known as the sex wars. After the birth of feminism, tensions arose between moral reformers, who prioritized protection of women, and others, who emphasized women's right to self-determination. These tensions intensified in the late 1970s and early 1980s and led to bitter battles within academic and activist feminist circles. Groups such as San Francisco's Women Against Violence in Pornography and Media and New York City's Women Against Pornography promoted the anti-pornography view, while the Feminist Anticensorship Task Force, Feminists for Free Expression, and others—a tendency that came to be known as "pro-sex" feminism—argued against censorship. Anti-pornography feminists defined opposition to pornography as an essential tenet of feminism and in some cases acrimoniously attacked feminists who disagreed. Before they were over, the "sex wars" also came to encompass other areas of controversial sexual expression including sadomasochism, public sex, lesbian butch/femme roles, and sex work.

The crux of the feminist anti-pornography argument was that pornography objectified and degraded women, negatively influenced how women were viewed and treated by men, and ultimately led to violence against women. Perhaps the best known and most extensively developed anti-pornography position is that of author Andrea Dworkin and legal scholar Catharine MacKinnon. Dworkin and Mac-Kinnon developed a so-called civil rights legal strategy that defined pornography as discrimination against women. Laws based on this theory would ban material that is "degrading" to women and allow women who felt they had been harmed by pornography to sue the producers and purveyors of such material. An ordinance along these lines was passed in Indianapolis, Indiana, but was invalidated as unconstitutional by the U.S. Supreme Court. In 1992, the Senate considered, but failed to pass, the Pornography Victims Compensation Act (nicknamed the "Bundy Act" after serial killer Ted Bundy, who blamed his crimes on exposure to pornography). A civil rights interpretation of anti-pornography law was established by Canada's 1992 *Regina v. Butler* high court decision; ironically—but not surprisingly—the first materials to be targeted were lesbian and gay erotica.

Anti-pornography feminists made sexually explicit material a scapegoat for the unequal position of women in society, seemingly ignoring the evidence that rape, violence, oppression, and exploitation of women long predated commercial erotica. Although they attacked nonviolent sexually explicit material, they rarely focused on the much more ubiquitous violent material that was not sexually explicit. Anti-pornography feminists did not call for less sexist pornography made by well-compensated and well-treated talent, but rather demanded its total elimination. As had occurred in earlier decades, some moral reform feminists joined forces with religious and political conservatives. By the turn of the twenty-first century, the pro-sex faction appeared to have gained the upper hand within the feminist movement—pro-sex feminism is now well represented within academia and among younger activists—but the antipornography feminists' views have had considerable influence on mainstream thought and government policy, especially in the areas of prostitution and international sex trafficking.

Social Conservatives and Popular Entertainment and Art

Moral purity proponents have been particularly critical of the corrupting influence of popular entertainment and art. In the nineteenth and early twentieth centuries, most of the furor about sexually explicit and other objectionable expression revolved around printed materials and live performances. But with the development of new technologies, recorded music, radio, film, television, and the Internet also became targets.

In 1930, the Hays Production Code governing the content of studio movies was introduced; it was replaced with the current Motion Picture Association of America movie rating system in 1968. As was the case during World War I, materials considered politically subversive, as well as those considered obscene, drew major repression in the 1940s and 1950s. In the 1960s, comedian Lenny Bruce, known for his social satire on topics such as race, homosexuality, drugs, and the criminal justice system, was arrested and tried repeatedly for obscenity law violations. In 1978, the U.S. Supreme Court, in *FCC v. Pacifica Foundation*, ruled against the broadcast of comedian George Carlin's monologue featuring "seven dirty words" that could not be aired on radio or television.

Music, too, was not safe from moral crusaders. In the Roaring Twenties, social purity advocates targeted jazz, which was seen as emblematic of an out-of-control black, urban, and youth subculture. In the 1950s, fears about rock-and-roll music defiling the innocence of youth were rife, as exemplified by complaints about Elvis "the Pelvis" Presley and his sexually suggestive dance moves. In the 1960s and 1970s, concerns revolved around allegations that songs such as "Puff the Magic Dragon" and "Yellow Submarine" promoted drug use. In the 1980s and

1990s, attention turned to punk, heavy metal, "gangster" rap, and hip-hop. In 1985, vice-presidential wife Tipper Gore and other wives of politicians and business leaders founded the Parents' Music Resource Center, which pressured record companies to put ratings or warning stickers on albums with violent or sexual content. In 1985, Jello Biafra of the controversial punk band the Dead Kennedys—known for songs critical of religion, politicians, and U.S. policy—was brought up on charges of distributing material harmful to minors: the band's "Frankenchrist" album which featured explicit art by H.R. Giger. In 1991, the rap group Two Live Crew (with their hit single "Me So Horny") were prosecuted for obscenity violations in Broward County, Florida, and later in several other states; both Biafra and Two Live Crew were eventually acquitted. With the campaigns against offensive music, creative expression became a focal point for concerns about political radicalism, anxieties about youth sexuality and drug use, and fears about black men.

This theme carried over to visual and performance art, but here religion, feminism, and homosexuality were the key areas of concern. In 1989, Dr. James Dobson of Focus on the Family held a press conference to denounce Andres Serrano's representation of a crucifix in a jar of urine, claiming it was anti-Christian. In June 1989, the Corcoran Gallery in Washington, D.C., canceled an exhibit by photographer Robert Mapplethorpe, a gay artist who died of AIDS in March 1989. Both artists had received funding through the National Endowment for the Arts (NEA). In 1990, obscenity charges were brought against the Cincinnati Contemporary Arts Center and its director for displaying the Mapplethorpe exhibit; a jury later voted for acquittal. Civil libertarians, artists, and other activists protested the attempts at censorship; numerous demonstrations took place, and in Washington, D.C., activists projected slides of Mapplethorpe's most controversial works on the side of the Corcoran building. Such work included sadomasochistic images, nude black men, religious imagery, a candid shot of a young girl with her genitals visible, and images that showed his physical deterioration as his illness progressed. Mapplethorpe's work played on the combined anxieties surrounding children and homosexuality, and his images of black men seemed tailor-made to bring out the racial insecurities of white men. Yet despite the objections of a vocal minority, Mapplethorpe was quite popular, and coffee-table books featuring his sexually explicit imagery became a staple of many middle-class living rooms.

In a crackdown on Internet-based child pornography, the FBI arrests former New York City police officer Brian Matthews on March 21, 2002. *(AP Wide World Photos)*

When a small Washington, D.C., gallery picked up the exhibition rejected by the Corcoran, some 4,000 viewers turned out the first weekend.

Conservative legislators, under pressure from the Religious Right, took up the crusade against indecent art and demanded investigation into NEA funding. The NEA, founded in 1965 to provide financial support for the arts, was mandated to consider cultural diversity in its funding decisions. In the summer of 1989, Senator Jesse Helms (R-NC) proposed a bill requiring the NEA to award funding not just on the basis of artistic merit, but also taking into account "general standards of decency and respect for the diverse beliefs and values of the American public." Later that year Congress passed legislation that barred the agency from supporting work that "may be considered obscene, including, but not limited to, depictions of sadomasochism, homoeroticism, the sexual exploitation of children, or individuals engaged in sex acts and which, taken as a whole, do not have serious literary, artistic, political, or scientific value." In 1990, NEA director John Frohnmeyer withdrew grants from four performance artists: Karen Finley,

John Fleck, Holly Hughes, and Tim Miller—respectively, a feminist, a gay man, a lesbian, and a bisexual. A Los Angeles federal judge struck down the congressional decency provision as unconstitutional, but in its 1998 *NEA v. Finley* decision the U.S. Supreme Court reversed the lower court and allowed the decency provision to stand.

New Technologies, New Battles

Perhaps the most notable feature of the censorship debate at the turn of the twenty-first century was the new possibilities for sexual expression opened up by the Internet. Although the Internet was officially born in 1969, it was not until two and a half decades later that the widespread availability of electronic mail and the World Wide Web extended cyberspace beyond university laboratories and into millions of homes. Internet pornography became an issue in the mid-1990s in part as a result of a sensationalistic 1995 *Time* magazine cover article based on a later largely discredited study by Marty Rimm about the extent of sexually explicit material available online. The first attempt to censor the Internet was the 1996 Communications Decency Act (CDA), which made it illegal to transmit indecent or patently offensive material. Challenged by the ACLU and a coalition of plaintiffs in *Reno v. ACLU,* the CDA was struck down by the U.S. Supreme Court in June 1997. The plaintiffs—including several LGBT, AIDS, and sex education organizations as well as civil libertarian groups such as the Electronic Frontier Foundation—successfully argued that "indecency" and "offensiveness" were too vague, that valuable sexually explicit but nonobscene material would be restricted, and that adults would be limited to materials suitable for children. In the years to follow, Congress passed more narrowly tailored laws, hoping to find one that would pass constitutional muster. The 1998 Child Online Protection Act (COPA), which requires age verification measures to prevent the transmission of sexually explicit material to minors, was halted by the Supreme Court in May 2002. The similarly named Children's Internet Protection Act of 2000, which requires that public libraries and schools install filters on computers to prevent access to sexually explicit content or face the loss of federal funding, was ruled unconstitutional by a district court in 2002, but was upheld by the Supreme Court in June 2003. As use of the Internet continues to grow, online pornography remains a contentious issue.

The New Culture War: The Rise of the Religious Right

The Meese Commission hearings and the NEA furor were a microcosm of what conservative candidate Patrick J. Buchanan, speaking at the 1992 Republican National Convention, dubbed the "culture war." The culture war was a backlash against the increasing social liberalization and gains made by feminists, gay people, and ethnic and racial minorities in the 1960s and 1970s. Proponents of this agenda came to be called the New Right or the Religious Right. The beginning of the war can perhaps be dated to Anita Bryant's 1977 Save Our Children campaign, which resulted in Dade County, Florida, voters repealing a gay antidiscrimination ordinance. The Dade campaign was soon followed by California's 1978 Briggs Initiative, which sought to prohibit gay men and lesbians from teaching in public schools. Moral concerns moved from the fringes to the center of public debate, and with the election of Reagan in 1980 the Religious Right became a major force in American politics. Key New Right leaders included Donald Wildmon's American Family Association, Pat Robertson's Christian Coalition, Beverly and Tim LaHaye's Concerned Women for America, Dobson's Family Research Council and Focus on the Family, Jerry Falwell's Moral Majority, and Louis Sheldon's Traditional Values Coalition. The membership of these groups was largely made up of fundamentalist or "born-again" Protestants, and their support was particularly strong in the southern Bible Belt.

The primary targets of the Religious Right included feminism, homosexuality, abortion, sexually explicit popular entertainment and art, sex education, and school prayer. Cultural changes associated with immigrants and racial and ethnic minorities were also a concern, but some conservative African-American and Latino religious and political leaders were drawn into the movement. The central message was the need to restore "traditional family values"—that is, to reverse recent changes in family structure, conventional gender roles, and sex hierarchies. An underlying message of the New Right was that the culture wars were largely responsible for many of the problems of American society. Some of the new wave of moral reformers began their careers in the successful campaign to prevent the passage of the Equal Rights Amendment. The movement placed much importance on "traditional" marriage and the nuclear family—arguing that premarital sex, nonmarital partnerships, and same-sex marriages would undermine these institutions. Under pressure from the Religious Right, in 1996 Congress

passed the Defense of Marriage Act (DOMA), which for the first time instituted a federal definition of a marriage as a "legal union between one man and one woman as husband and wife." Homosexuality—seen by social conservatives as an assault on religion, the family, and traditional gender roles—increasingly became a target of moral crusaders as the LGBT movement grew in numbers and political influence.

PROTECTING CHILDREN

By the 1980s and 1990s, the political climate had shifted appreciably to the right. Social conservatives demanded an end to sex education that actually educated about sex, and pushed for laws giving parents greater control over their children. Abstinence-only sex education in schools became a primary focus. The 1981 Adolescent Family Life Program was a federal effort to promote teen chastity. In 1994, the Religious Right prompted then-president Bill Clinton to dismiss Surgeon General Joycelyn Elders for suggesting that information about masturbation should be included as part of sex education. In 1996, as part of a major welfare reform law, Congress authorized funding for programs that exclusively teach the "social, psychological, and health gains" of abstinence. In 2002, the United States—in alliance with the Vatican and several Islamic countries—was instrumental in modifying United Nations treaties concerning the rights of women and children to remove provisions related to abortion, contraception, and sex education.

Yet even as social conservatives spoke of the importance of families and children, political conservatives opposed public funding for education, child care, and healthcare. Federal welfare funding was dramatically cut, and efforts were made to tie benefits to marriage; several states proposed measures to reduce benefits to women who had additional children while receiving welfare. Notably, laws increasingly required poor women to work full-time jobs; it was middle-class, white women who were being pushed back into the home.

Child Sexual Abuse Panics

The 1980s and 1990s were characterized by fears about pedophilia, sexual abuse by strangers and homosexuals, and child pornography. Sexual abuse of children is widespread, but it is most often committed by family members or acquaintances of the children, and the majority is by men against girls. Yet while intrafamily abuse remains largely unspoken, fears about the "other" and the "outsider" are loud and clear. Pedophiles became the most demonized target in late-twentieth-century America. They remain the one group that even the most ardent proponents of civil and sexual liberties are loath to defend. Penalties for child sexual abuse or statutory rape were increased dramatically during this period, including "Megan's laws" (named after murder victim Megan Kanka), sex offender registries, and proposals for indefinite confinement in mental institutions after the completion of prison sentences. The furor over pedophilia came to a head in 2002 when a large number of Catholic priests were accused and convicted of sexual abuse and their superiors were charged with a cover-up; in response, some Church leaders blamed the scandal on homosexuals within their ranks. Unlike the case in many previous child panics in which rumor swirled without foundation, there was real evidence that inappropriate sexual conduct by priests was a widespread problem.

One of most extreme manifestations of the child sex panic concerned the McMartin preschool in Manhattan Beach, California, near Los Angeles. In 1983, a parent complained to police that her son had been molested at the school, which was run by Peggy Buckey and Virginia McMartin and employed Raymond Buckey as an aide. After the local police chief sent letters to parents warning that their children may have been abused, a media frenzy ensued. Hundreds of children were interviewed by the Children's Institute International, and by 1984 over 300 had been identified as victims and some 100 staff had been accused. The investigation was marked by interview techniques that allegedly coached children about what to say and rewarded them for desired responses. Upon investigation, minimal physical evidence for these charges was found. Although the case was one of the longest and most expensive criminal trials in U.S. history, most charges were dropped. In 1990, Peggy Buckey was cleared by a jury, and two juries deadlocked on charges against Raymond Buckey.

An important feature of the McMartin case—and one that marks it as a classic panic—is how many people believed the allegations and joined in the calls for vengeance, no matter how bizarre the accusations or how little evidence there was to support them. A 1994 U.S. government report analyzing over 12,000 accusations of Satanic ritual abuse in this and other cases found "not a single case where there was clear corroborating evidence." The McMartin case joins the Salem witch trials and the McCarthy-era red scare as a major example of mass hysteria. One outcome of this panic was a generalized suspicion concerning adult men and children.

Child Pornography

Child pornography has never been as prevalent as opponents have claimed, and much of what has been available was provided through the government as part of various entrapment operations such as the FBI's "Innocent Images." Still, with increased access to pornography through the Internet, the opposition to child pornography escalated to such an extent that images not intended as pornography were sometimes targeted. Laws and corporate policies were put into place requiring commercial photo developers to report suspect material. In 1990, police and the FBI raided the San Francisco home of Jock Sturges, a fine art photographer whose work includes nude images of minors; although Sturges was never indicted, he was accused in the media of being a child pornographer. Throughout the decade, reports periodically surfaced of parents being reported to authorities for developing nonsexual nude photos of their own babies and young children.

In 1977, Congress passed the Sexual Exploitation of Children Act, which prohibits the use of minors in the making of pornography, taking pornographic pictures of minors, and interstate transactions involving child pornography. The 1982 *New York v. Ferber* U.S. Supreme Court decision set a new standard for child pornography, permitting greater restrictions of sexual material involving children and essentially waiving the three-prong *Miller* test for child pornography. The Child Sexual Abuse and Pornography Act of 1986 banned advertisements for child pornography and raised minimum sentences for repeat offenders. With the explosion of the Internet, child pornography—much of it produced and distributed from outside the United States—became more widely available, including unsolicited "spam" mailings to unsuspecting recipients. The 1988 Child Protection and Obscenity Enforcement Act prohibited transmission of child pornography using a computer. In 1990, Congress made it illegal to possess three or more pieces of child pornography obtained through interstate or foreign commerce or via computer. And in 1996, Congress passed the Child Pornography Prevention Act (CPPA), which prohibited "virtual" child pornography—computer-generated images of children or images in which adults are made to look like children. In April 2002, the U.S. Supreme Court ruled in *Ashcroft v. Free Speech Coalition* that the CPPA was overbroad and unconstitutional, but legislators soon introduced a new law, the Child Obscenity and Pornography Prevention Act (COPPA), in an attempt to circumvent the ruling. In

On April 19, 1999, picketers in East Amherst, New York, demonstrate at a Barnes & Noble bookstore that sold books depicting nude children by photographers Jock Sturges and David Hamilton. Picketers were divided fairly evenly between supporters and opponents. *(AP Wide World Photos)*

April 2003, Congress passed the PROTECT Act, which included the proposed COPPA provision banning digitally morphed sexual images of children, as well as a prohibition against misleading Internet domain names that could direct children to pornographic Web sites.

AIDS AND ITS IMPACT

The late 1980s and 1990s were a time of increasing visibility for gay men and lesbians, and later for bisexual and transgender people. Several gay rights and antidiscrimination laws had been passed, the federal government began to pay attention to AIDS after nearly a decade of neglect, and the 1987 March on Washington demonstrated the burgeoning movement's growing political strength. One outcome of the march was the birth of the AIDS Coalition to Unleash Power (ACT UP), followed in 1990 by Queer Nation. The upsurge in LGBT activism was spurred in part by outrage over the U.S. Supreme Court's 1986 *Bowers v.*

Hardwick ruling, which upheld a conviction under Georgia's sodomy law of two gay men for having sex in their home. Although many states had abolished their sodomy laws in the sexually liberal 1960s and 1970s, at the turn of the century a dozen states still retained laws prohibiting oral and anal sex—some targeting same-sex activity only and others encompassing everyone, including married heterosexual couples. Although sodomy laws are not often enforced, they sometimes come into play in child custody, statutory rape, and prostitution cases. Arguing that they are discriminatory, gay rights advocates have had some success in overturning sodomy laws that ban sexual activity between same-sex but not opposite-sex partners. The LGBT rights movement also achieved a major victory with the U.S. Supreme Court's 1996 *Romer v. Evans* decision, which declared that a state could not prohibit local sexual orientation antidiscrimination laws.

The moral crusade of the 1980s and 1990s cannot

be understood without taking into account the impact of AIDS, which first came to public attention in 1981. Jerry Falwell and other leaders of the Religious Right began to equate AIDS with homosexuality, prostitution, and drug use in the mid-1980s, contending that AIDS was a punishment for immoral behavior. The New Right associated it with crime, diseases, and mental illness. In 1987, Helms proposed an amendment—which came to be known as "no promo homo"—that prohibited the use of federal funds for HIV/AIDS education or prevention materials and activities that "promote, encourage, or condone, directly or indirectly, homosexual activities or intravenous use of illegal drugs." "No promo homo" rested on the idea that promotion of immorality was more dangerous to society than the transmission of a deadly disease.

AIDS has had a profound effect on gay identity and sexual practices. The language of AIDS would serve as a battleground for a decade of culture wars surrounding sex. ACT UP's slogan was "Silence Equals Death." One of the lessons of the AIDS crisis was that speech and identity are intimately entwined. AIDS has been used to reinforce the old idea—prominent in the crusade against prostitution in the mid- and late 1880s—that sexual deviation leads to disease and death. In the words of Gayle Rubin in her essay "Thinking Sex" (1984), "The history of panic that has accompanied new epidemics, and of the casualties incurred by their scapegoating, should make everyone pause and consider with extreme skepticism any attempts to justify antigay policy initiatives on the basis of AIDS."

Gay Sex Panics

Although the increased visibility and political clout of the LGBT community curtailed police raids on gay bars and cruising spaces relative to their levels in the 1940s through the 1960s, increased uncertainty about gender roles, anxieties about unrestrained sexual expression, and fear of AIDS ushered in new gay sex panics in the 1980s and 1990s. But unlike panics of the past, this round often pitted members of the LGBT community against one another.

San Francisco faced a major battle over gay bathhouses in the early 1980s. Although many such establishments had gone out of business as a result of a decline in clientele as the AIDS epidemic spread, Mayor Dianne Feinstein was determined to close those that remained. The attempt brought about an intracommunity struggle that resembled the "sex wars" taking place at the same time. Some gay men saw bathhouses as a symbol of newly won gay liberation and vociferously opposed their closure. Other, more "respectable," gay men were quick to dissociate themselves from those who were more promiscuous and overtly sexual. LGBT leaders and public health officials were genuinely concerned about the massive illness and death affecting their community and were willing to sacrifice some sexual liberties to stop it. In October 1984, health department director Dr. Mervyn Silverman issued an emergency order closing the baths.

A similar struggle once again came to the fore in the mid-1990s. In a quirk of regulatory bureaucracy, San Francisco had banned bathhouses with private rooms while allowing sex clubs where men could engage in sexual activity in public common spaces. In the fall of 1996, the Coalition for Healthy Sex—a group of local sex club proprietors, sex educators, AIDS activists, and public health workers—proposed a set of standards they hoped would make for a safer sex club experience; these included mandating condoms and HIV education materials and restricting locked private spaces that could not be monitored. Despite opposition, the Department of Public Health implemented the regulations in early 1997. Opponents of the standards—who also included sex club proprietors and AIDS activists—formed a group called Community United for Sexual Privacy to attempt to have the guidelines thrown out. They argued that gay men have a right to privacy in commercial sex venues and that such spaces are ideal locations for AIDS prevention efforts. By 1999, a local gay Democratic club, the city's Human Rights Commission, and the city's HIV Prevention Planning Council voted to withdraw the guidelines; these votes were not binding, however, and the city's health department declined to rescind the regulations. The furor then died down as quickly as it had started.

New York City had a different experience. In that city, bathhouses with private spaces were not banned, but city health regulations prohibited sex—with or without condoms—in public establishments. Here again, debate about public sex spaces divided the LGBT community. A group called Gay and Lesbian HIV Prevention Activists pressed the city to more strongly enforce its ban on sex in commercial venues. Well-known gay authors such as Michelangelo Signorile and Gabriel Rotello called for gay men to be less promiscuous, suggesting that monogamous long-term relationships were key to preventing HIV transmission.

The Battle for Public Space

The debate over gay sex venues in New York City took place against the backdrop of a more general battle over public space. In the mid-1990s, the city undertook an effort to "clean up" Times Square, the blocks surrounding Manhattan's theater district and the Port Authority bus terminal, which had become an infamous center of low-budget sexual entertainment. The city hoped to bring money into its coffers by making the district more attractive to corporations, wealthy residents, and middle-class family-oriented tourists—as exemplified by Disney chairman Michael Eisner's renovation of the New Amsterdam Theater as a venue for Broadway versions of Disney children's movies. In exchange for his investment, Eisner called on the city to get rid of the surrounding X-rated theaters, strip clubs, and adult stores. Although begun under Democratic mayor David Dinkins, the Times Square cleanup became the cornerstone of Republican mayor Rudolph Giuliani's citywide "quality of life" campaign, which targeted the homeless, panhandlers, honking drivers, protesters without permits, unauthorized gatherings, and the punk, transgender, LGBT, and racial and ethnic minority youth who populated the city's public spaces.

In 1995, the New York City Council passed amendments to the city's existing zoning law intended to eliminate commercial sex establishments. The new law targeted businesses that had a "substantial portion" of their stock devoted to sexual merchandise. Although most of the targeted venues catered to heterosexual men, the law was so vague that opponents feared gay-oriented book and novelty stores could fall within its purview. In addition, no adult businesses could be located within 500 feet of a church, a school, a residential district, or another such business. (Similar laws are in place throughout the United States to restrict adult business, but in Manhattan nearly everything is within 500 feet of a school, a church, or a residence.) In order to pass constitutional muster, the city would have to prove that adult businesses could relocate to other areas, and also that they were clearly linked to negative "secondary effects" such as crime—a link the Meese Commission was never able to establish.

New York City mayor Giuliani argued that commercial sex establishments hurt other business and eroded public morality in the city. Some opponents accused the mayor of generating a sex panic, claiming the plan was a real estate land grab cloaked in the guise of a moral campaign. The zoning law engendered debate about cultural diversity and the nature of the public sphere. While some activists were more concerned about what was being lost, others were more angry about what would take its place. Immediately after the zoning law passed, Harold Price Ferringer, former attorney for Larry Flynt, the self-styled smut peddler, challenged its constitutionality. In 1999, the U.S. Supreme Court rejected Ferringer's final appeal, but by then the law had already been implemented. Even in the aftermath of September 11, 2001, the New York City Council took time to pass additional amendments to the zoning code aimed at further restricting public spaces for erotic performance and merchandise (which were ruled unconstitutional in September 2003).

INTO THE TWENTY-FIRST CENTURY

At the turn of the twenty-first century, social conservatives appeared to have lost much of its previous influence. Falwell was ridiculed in 1999 when he complained that Tinky Winky, a children's television character, was gay. Ridicule turned to outrage when he suggested—and Pat Robertson agreed—that pagans, abortionists, feminists, gays and lesbians, and civil liberties activists were to blame for the September 11 terrorist attacks.

The attempted impeachment of Bill Clinton following revelations of his extramarital affair with a White House intern was perhaps one of the last major shows of strength by the Religious Right. Clinton's "permissive" attitudes and unseemly behavior came to symbolize everything wrong with liberal America. Republican leaders, Religious Right spokespersons, and the media spent months dwelling on every detail of "Monicagate," but the public seemed to soon tire of the issue. Unlike preceding Republican administrations, the Religious Right did not play a major role in the election of George W. Bush, who was more closely aligned with business interests (although Ashcroft's ascendance as attorney general exemplified the Religious Right's continuing influence).

Just as the moral crusade of the 1980s and 1990s reflected a backlash against the liberalization of the 1960s and 1970s—which was itself a reaction to the conservativism of the 1950s—by the end of the century the tide again appeared to be turning. Increasing numbers of lesbian, gay, bisexual, and transgender people "came out of the closet," and demonization does not work as well when an enemy is known and stereotypes are shown to be wrong. The adoption of domestic partner legislation or policies by many local and state governments and corporations, and the introduction of civil unions that closely approximate marriage, have led some to predict that same-sex marriage may be a reality by the end of the decade (despite stepped-up efforts to amend the Constitution to define marriage as including only one man and one woman).

Still, throughout the past decade, state sodomy laws were steadily overturned. Most notably, in June 2003 the U.S. Supreme Court ruled against a Texas sodomy law that banned oral and anal sex between same-sex but not opposite-sex partners, overturning its 1986 *Bowers v. Hardwick* decision. In the majority opinion in *Lawrence and Garner v. Texas,* Justice Anthony Kennedy wrote that it is unconstitutional to single out homosexuals for moral disapproval, and that "[t]he state cannot demean their existence or control their destiny by making their private sexual conduct a crime." Recognizing the broad implications of the ruling, which invalidates the thirteen remaining state sodomy laws against both same-sex and opposite-sex sexual conduct, dissenting justice Antonin Scalia asserted that the court had "taken sides in the culture war" and "largely signed on to the so-called homosexual agenda."

On the whole, compared to the War on Drugs, recent moral crusades against stigmatized sexual behavior and expression have generated more sound than fury. Crackdowns against prostitution and gay male cruising still happen with some regularity, but sentences do not approach those for drug infractions.

But this was before September 11, 2001, and subsequent wars in Afghanistan and Iraq. Social panics have always been used to erode opposition to hitherto unacceptable impositions on civil liberties. Following the terrorist attacks, this tendency was exemplified by the efforts of the Bush administration, led by Attorney General John Ashcroft, to institute control of immigrants (especially Arabs and Muslims) and surveillance of citizens that previously would have been untenable. However, the laws put into place since 2001 have for the most part focused on security rather than smut. In the months after September 11, images of an epic battle between good and evil once again were called forth, but this time—as happened during previous times of war—the focus was on foreigners, immigrants, and political dissidents rather than on sex, drugs, and rock-and-roll.

Conclusion

Social purity movements in the United States reflect a paradox inherent to American society: the country was born with a strong Puritan streak, but also has traditionally espoused the values of liberty and privacy. It is therefore not surprising that social movements reflect these conflicting elements. The anti-vice activism of the late nineteenth century combined the progressive drive for social reform with the evangelical hope of making America a religious country. Despite their often-coercive methods, many early efforts to eliminate vice anticipated Progressive Era reforms in the areas of labor law, food and drug regulation, hygiene improvements, and better healthcare for immigrants. In both the social reform movements of the nineteenth century and the anti-pornography activism of the 1980s, some feminists made alliances with religious leaders and other conservative forces. Concerning women's rights, sexual equality, and the structure of the family. Feminists have repeatedly found themselves split between those promoting greater protection for women and social control of men, and those seeking greater autonomy and self-determination for women. Similar tensions have also been evident in movements for the rights of children, people of color, immigrants, and the poor.

Anti-vice movements and intervening periods of liberalization reflect the ongoing battle between the values of Puritanism and liberty. On the whole, mainstream America is a society of moderates, favoring a "live and let live" attitude. Yet periodically—especially during periods of social upheaval—a minority of "true believers" (religious crusaders, hard-core drug warriors, and the like) is able to sway a majority of fed-up moderates and the opportunistic politicians that surround them. During the late 1800s and early 1900s, moderates were mobilized against the excesses of saloon culture, aided by the increased xenophobia of World War I, leading to Prohibition. The social changes brought about by World War II spurred the political and moral panics that set the stage for the McCarthy witch hunts. And fears about societal breakdown in the wake of the cultural liberalization of the 1960s and 1970s ushered in the social conservative "traditional values" campaigns. Moral panics have been most successful in areas in which the mainstream perceives concrete societal harm, especially harm to children.

Loud moral crusades often give the appearance of deeper sentiment than actually exists. Despite their best efforts, social purity proponents have never been able to do away with the demand for alcohol, drugs, prostitution, sexually explicit materials, or contraception—which the market has always found a way to supply. When the pendulum swings too far in the direction of moral purity, mainstream sentiment again pushes toward moderation. As demonstrated with

Prohibition, the typical American has an interest in curbing excess, but not in allowing the state or the church to police his or her own behavior.

Liz Highleyman and Benjamin Shepard

BIBLIOGRAPHY

Associated Press. "Supreme Court Strikes Down Texas Law Banning Sodomy." *New York Times*, June 26, 2003.

Attorney General's Commission on Pornography. *Final Report.* Washington, DC: U.S. Department of Justice, 1986.

Califia, Pat. *Public Sex: The Culture of Radical Sex.* San Francisco: Cleis, 1994.

Crimp, Douglas, Ann Pelligrini, Eva Pendleton, and Michael Warner, eds. *This Is a Sex Panic!* New York: Sheep Meets Sheep Collective, 1997.

Dangerous Bedfellows, eds. *Policing Public Sex: Queer Politics and the Future of AIDS Activism.* Boston: South End, 1996.

Delany, Samuel R. *Times Square Red, Times Square Blue.* New York: New York University Press, 1999.

Dewit, Clyde. "A History Lesson: How the Adult Industry Has Fared in the United States Supreme Court—Part I." *Adult Video News* (June 2001). http://www.adultvideonews.com/legal/leg0601.html.

Duggan, Lisa, and Nan Hunter. *Sex Wars: Sexual Dissent and Political Culture.* New York: Routledge, 1995.

Dworkin, Andrea. *Pornography: Men Possessing Women.* New York: Perigree, 1981.

Eigo, Jim. "The City as Body Politic/The Body as City unto Itself." In *From ACT UP to the WTO: Urban Protest and Community Building in the Era of Globalization*, ed. Benjamin Shepard and Ron Hayduk. New York: Verso, 2002.

Gertzman, Jay A. *Bookleggers and Smuthounds: The Trade in Erotica, 1920–1940.* Philadelphia: University of Pennsylvania Press, 1999.

Gilfoyle, Timothy J. *City of Eros: New York City, Prostitution, and the Commercialization of Sex, 1790–1920.* New York: W.W. Norton. 1992.

Goldstein, Richard. "Porn Free: The City's War on Sex Shops Isn't about Morality. It's about Developers' Dollars." *The Village Voice*, September 1, 1997.

Goode, Erich, and Ben-Yehuda, Nachman. *Moral Panics: The Social Construction of Deviance.* Cambridge, MA: Blackwell, 1994.

Hamlin, Leo. *Secret Careers of Samuel Roth.* Saratoga Springs, NY: Harian, 1969.

Highleyman, Liz. "New Sex Club Legislation Proposed." *Bay Area Reporter*, October 17, 1996.

———. "Supremes Reject 'Decency' on Internet." *Bay Area Reporter*, July 3, 1997.

———. "Courts Render CIPA, COPA Verdicts." *Bay Area Reporter*, June 6, 2002.

———. "Supreme Court Upholds Internet Filters." *Bay Area Reporter*, June 26, 2003.

Kinsey, Alfred, Wardell Pomeroy, and Clyde Martin. *Sexual Behavior in the Human Male.* Philadelphia: W.B. Saunders, 1948.

Kinsey, Alfred, Wardell Pomeroy, Clyde Martin, and Paul Gebhard. *Sexual Behavior in the Human Female.* Philadelphia: W.B. Saunders, 1953.

Kipness, Laura. "(Male) Desire and (Female) Disgust: Reading Hustler." In *Cultural Studies*, ed. Lawrence Grossberg, Cary Nelson, and Paul Treichler. New York: Routledge, 1992.

Koch, Cynthia. "The Contest for American Culture: A Leadership Case Study on the NEA and NEH Funding Crisis." *Public Talk: Online Journal of Discourse Leadership*, 1998. http://www.upenn.edu/pnc/ptkoch.html.

Lederer, Laura, ed. *Take Back the Night: Women on Pornography.* New York: William Morrow, 1980.

MacKinnon, Catharine A., and Andrea Dworkin. *Pornography and Civil Rights: A New Day for Women's Equality.* Minneapolis: Organizing Against Pornography, 1988.

Nathan, Debbie, and Michael Snendeker. *Satan's Silence: Ritual Abuse and the Making of a Modern American Witch Hunt.* New York: Basic Books, 1995.

Nobile, Philip, and Eric Nadler. *United States vs. Sex: How the Meese Commission Lied about Pornography.* New York: Minotaur, 1986.

Nuzum, Eric. *Parental Advisory: Music Censorship in America.* New York: HarperCollins, 2001.

Ockerbloom, John Mark. Banned Books Online, 1993–2002. http://onlinebooks.library.upenn.edu/banned-books.html.

Planned Parenthood Federation of America. *Family Planning in America: Narrative History*, 1998–2003. http://www.plannedparenthood.org/about/narrhistory/fpamnar.html.

Planned Parenthood Federation of America. *A History of Contraceptive Methods*, 1998–2003. http://www.plannedparenthood.org/library/birthcontrol/020709_bchistory.html.

Price, Deb, and Joyce Murdoch. *Courting Justice: Gay Men and Lesbians v. the Supreme Court.* New York: Basic Books, 2001.

Rofes, Eric. *Dry Bones Breathe: Gay Men Creating Post-AIDS Identities and Subcultures.* Binghamton, NY: Harrington Park, 1998.

Rubin, Gayle. "Thinking Sex: Notes for a Radical Theory of the Politics of Sexuality." In *Pleasure and Danger: Exploring Female Sexuality*, ed. Carol S. Vance. New York: Routledge, 1984.

———. "Misguided, Dangerous and Wrong: An Analysis of Anti-Pornography Politics." In *Bad Girls and Dirty Pictures: The Challenge to Reclaim Feminism*, ed. Alison Assiter and Carol Avedon. London: Pluto, 1993.

Shepard, Benjamin. "Culture Jamming a Sex Panic!" In *From ACT UP to the WTO: Urban Protest and Community-Building in the Era of Globalization*, ed. Benjamin Shepard and Ron Hayduk. New York: Verso, 2002.

Shilts, Randy. *And the Band Played On: Politics, People, and the AIDS Epidemic.* New York: St. Martin's, 1987.

Strossen, Nadine. *Defending Pornography.* New York: Scribner, 1995.

Toy, Vivian S. "Panel Votes Zoning Rule on Sex Shops." *New York Times*, October 24, 1995.

Vance, Carol S., ed. *Pleasure and Danger: Exploring Female Sexuality.* New York: Routledge, 1984.

Victor, Jeffrey S. "Moral Panics and the Social Construction of Deviant Behavior: A Theory and Application to the Case of Ritual Child Abuse." *Sociological-Perspective* 41:3 (Fall 1998).

Watney, Simon. *Policing Desire: Pornography, AIDS and the Media.* Minneapolis: University of Minnesota Press, 1996.

PROSTITUTION REFORM

Vice and prostitution were considered a permanent feature of American life for much of the eighteenth and early nineteenth centuries. In some parts of the West during the frontier and Gold Rush days, prostitution was widely accepted, and prominent madams played an active role in many a town's social scene. But changes in the structure of the American family and society during the mid-nineteenth century created a shift in social understandings. As early industrialization drove women's work outside the home, women's roles in traditional domestic economies began to change. Commercialization altered both families and social networks. Some women became wage earners, while others became social reformers. Outside of domestic private spaces, discrimination and exploitation marked women's work experiences. Far from family and community, there was no redress for labor-management problems. Pregnancy outside of marriage was condemned, and many women turned to prostitution as a means of survival. Industrialization intensified the shifts in family life, contributing to the rise in prostitution and calls for social reform. Concurrently, some of the same societal changes that drove working-class women into the labor force provided upper- and middle-class women the leisure time to focus their attention beyond the domestic sphere; these women came to play a major role in the century's social reform movements.

THE ANTI-PROSTITUTION MOVEMENT

The first wave of anti-prostitution reform in the United States, as in Britain, conceived of prostitution as a social problem of public health and morality, with female polluters and male victims. The year 1864 saw the passage of the British Contagious Diseases Act, a law aimed at controlling venereal disease. Paradoxically, the same social purists who saw women as the victims of male lust offered a solution that punished women by sanctioning the state to examine and in-spect those accused of prostitution. Opponents of the new laws—a coalition of feminists, radical working-class men, and evangelists—fought the legislation on the grounds that it sacrificed female liberties while supporting state-sanctioned rape. Reflecting social fears about immigration and racial diversity, the first anti-prostitution laws in San Francisco in the mid-nineteenth century were aimed at controlling Chinese prostitutes.

Not all reform efforts were aimed at punishing "fallen" women. In the mid-1800s, groups such as the Providence Association for Employment of Women, the New York Moral Reform Society, and the Boston Society for Employing the Poor worked to raise women's wages so that they would not be forced to turn to prostitution. So-called Magdalene Societies sought to rehabilitate prostitutes and discourage male lust; some favored "anti-seduction" laws to prevent men's exploitation of vulnerable women. But many U.S. prostitution abolitionists followed the British model, describing prostitutes as "malevolent, cruel, and vengeful women" who were thought to corrupt their male victims. Men rarely were arrested or incarcerated for their involvement with prostitutes. The double standard of punishing women for providing a service that men sought and paid for thus became an issue with which feminists would grapple well into the next century. Women's rights were rarely the driving force behind anti-vice campaigns.

EARLY 1900S REFORM

"Ladies . . . Dante is dead . . . and I think it's time we dropped the study of his inferno and turned our attention to our own," Sara Decker, the president of the General Federation of Women's Clubs, urged members in 1904. The General Federation of Women's Clubs won a federal charter in 1901, thus sparking an exodus of middle-class women from the private domestic sphere of the home into the public sphere of the broader world with its various "social evils."

The second wave of prostitution reform in the United States was set between a coalition of abolitionists and social purity advocates who defined prostitution in moral terms, and reformers who defined prostitution in functional terms as a social necessity (or inevitability) that should be regulated to prevent disease and the exploitation of women. While conservative social purity advocates opposed women's suffrage, employment, and education—instead focusing on male depravity—more socially progressive feminists argued that such an agenda had little to do with feminism. As the social purity movement and Victorian mores intersected, reformers called for a change not of men's hearts, but of the nation's laws. Although it was appealing to call for reform of male sexual urges—which some conservatives and radicals alike suggested turned women into "prostitutes" at home—others felt that legal remedies were the best solution.

PROSTITUTION AND PUBLIC SPACE

To the extent that prostitution was defined in terms of public health, morality, and public space, the voices of those who argued for its abolition persisted. In 1911, in Hartford, Connecticut, for example, a group of suffragists attacked the "social necessity" argument for prostitution, challenging a core ideology of public space that allowed prostitution to thrive in cities across the country. They understood that vice districts existed within the contradictions of the nineteenth-century ideology of separate spheres for middle-class women and men, under which virtuous women were thought to belong within the private domestic sphere of the home while men belonged in the more dangerous terrain of public spaces. The public arena was thought to be an immoral space equated with evil and sin, while the private sphere was equated with goodness, chastity, and safety. Feminists challenged this ideology. In doing so, they called for closing brothels and fighting prostitution within the city's public spaces as part of their struggle for women's access to and safety within these spaces. Many states passed laws against vagrancy and bawdy houses in the early 1900s, and in the World War I era, a majority of the country's brothels were shut down. Yet as reformers succeeded in shutting down vice districts and houses of ill repute, prostitution instead dispersed throughout cities, producing new institutions within the commercial sex economy. In the end, the public sphere was no more purified. It is notable that the very neighborhood street prostitution that spurs the most

complaints today is a result of closing brothels and launching crackdowns on red-light districts.

Other social reformers focused on so-called white slavery—the capturing or selling of "innocent" white women into prostitution or sexual slavery—which was the subject of considerable moral panic but never proven to exist on a wide scale. Again, concerns about prostitution reflected fears about immigration, racial and ethnic differences, urbanization, industrialization, and the entry of women into the workforce, often under deplorable conditions. Just as the temperance movement was able to propel the eventual passage of national alcohol prohibition, women's agitation around prostitution created momentum toward the passage of the 1910 Mann Act, better known as the White Slave Traffic Act. Debate about prostitution led to a massing of information on the subject, which helped propel trade and wage reforms. In many respects, the temperance movement laid the groundwork for reforms witnessed during the Progressive Era.

As Emma Goldman outlined in her essay, "The Traffic in Women" (1917), the link between sweatshop conditions and easy recruitment into the black market economy became a visceral reality that few could deny. Goldman's was a critique of marriage and patriarchy within the capitalist social framework. Goldman saw marriage as no less a form of prostitution than street solicitation for women who had no other options for work. Given the lack of vocational opportunities for women, Goldman said, it is:

> inevitable that she would pay for her right to exist, to keep a position in whatever line, with sex favors. Thus it is merely a degree whether she sells herself to one man, in or out of marriage, or to many men. Whether our reformers admit it or not, the economic and social inferiority of women is responsible for prostitution.

Goldman noted that sweatshop workers received $6 per week, or an average wage of $280 per year. Under such conditions, Goldman asked, why would anyone be surprised at the rise of prostitution? Thus, prostitution could be viewed as "the direct result, in many cases, of insufficient compensation of honest labor" and functioned as the only way out of a second-class life as a sweatshop worker, a mistress, or a servant. As such, Goldman called for workers' solidarity with prostitutes.

THE SEX WORKER MOVEMENT

Although prostitutes' spaces could be shut down, the practice (and the market demand for it) rarely disappeared. Attacks on prostitutes as threats to public space, morality, and health would remain a long-term fixture of discourses on prostitution. Today, Nevada is the only state that permits legal prostitution in certain counties. In the latter years of the twentieth century, the right of women in the sex industry to earn their living as they saw fit was a major area of contention. Sex worker activists and groups such as Call Off Your Old Tired Ethics (COYOTE) and Prostitutes of New York (PONY)—run by sex workers themselves rather than by outside reformers—demanded self-determination for women and men in the sex industry and spoke out against laws that penalize sex workers. The issue of sex work became one of the arenas of the feminist "sex wars" of the late 1970s and early 1980s. The spread of AIDS in the 1980s and 1990s led to many laws restricting prostitution and punishing HIV-positive prostitutes, but at the same time had the effect of galvanizing prostitutes' rights activism and led to the development of many harm reduction and safer sex education programs for sex workers.

Recalling the anti-prostitution crusade of the early 1900s, by the turn of the twentieth century trafficking in women and children had again become a major focus of the campaign against the sex industry. Increased globalization allowed people to move more freely across international borders, but the attendant economic dislocation made it more likely that women and children would enter prostitution for lack of other options. Some feminists and social reformers defined prostitution as inherently exploitative and called for the abolition of the sex industry rather than improving its conditions. Like the Magdalene Societies, abolitionists dedicated themselves to rescuing women from the sex industry and helping them to find other employment—rarely acknowledging that the garment industry, domestic labor, and other available alternatives could be equally problematic. Whereas organizations such as Women Hurt in Systems of Prostitution Engaged in Revolt (WHISPER) oppose the legitimization of prostitution, liberationist sex worker activists focus on improving working conditions, reducing legal persecution, and instituting harm reduction measures. An important victory for the sex worker rights movement was the establishment in 1996 of the first closed-shop sex worker union, the Exotic Dancer's Union, at San Francisco's Lusty Lady peepshow.

Today the issue of prostitution—especially on a global scale—remains contentious. Reformers who wish to abolish prostitution and those who seek to improve working conditions and eliminate social stigma against sex workers remain at odds. But having evolved past the stage of seemingly glorified sex work as an expression of women's sexual autonomy, prostitutes' rights activists increasingly acknowledge the negative effects of sex work in certain social contexts and focus on the distinction between those who choose a career in sex work and those who are forced into prostitution, whether by threats and violence or due to the lack of viable economic alternatives.

Benjamin Shephard and Liz Highleyman

BIBLIOGRAPHY

Baldwin, Peter. "Antiprostitution Reform and the Use of Public Space in Hartford, Connecticut, 1878–1914." *Journal of Urban History* 23:6 (September 1997): 709–738.

Bernstein, Elizabeth. "What's Wrong with Prostitution? What's Right with Sex Work? Comparing Markets in Female Sexual Labor." *Hastings Women's Law Journal* 10:1 (Winter 1999). Symposium Issue: Economic Justice for Sex Workers.

Degler, Carl N. *Out of the Past: The Forces That Shaped Modern America*. New York: Harper & Row, 1984.

Gilfoyle, Timothy J. *City of Eros: New York City, Prostitution, and the Commercialization of Sex, 1790–1920*. New York: W.W. Norton, 1992.

Goldman, Emma. "The Traffic in Women." In *Anarchism and Other Essays*. New York: Dover, 1917.

Hobson, Barbara. *Uneasy Virtue: The Politics of Prostitution and the American Reform Tradition*. Chicago: University of Chicago Press, 1990.

Rosen, Ruth. *The Lost Sisterhood: Prostitution in America, 1900–1918*. Baltimore, MD: Johns Hopkins University Press, 1982.

Rubin, Gayle. "Thinking Sex: Notes for a Radical Theory of the Politics of Sexuality." In *Pleasure and Danger: Exploring Female Sexuality*, ed. Carol S. Vance. New York: Routledge, 1984.

Walkowitz, Judith. "Male Vice and Female Virtue: Feminism and the Politics of Prostitution in 19th Century Britain." In *Powers and Desire: The Politics of Sexuality*, ed. Ann Snitow et al. New York: Monthly Review, 1983.

EARLY ANTI-VICE CAMPAIGNS

After the Civil War, as young men arrived in cities away from family influences, reformers feared they would fall prey to urban vices. Pervasive municipal corruption and the persistent presence of increasingly popular gambling dens, brothels, and saloons left many New Yorkers convinced that the time had come to contend with the social evil of sexual commerce.

One of the most well-known opponents of prostitution and obscenity was Anthony Comstock. Working with a group of reformers including Charles Parkhurst, Comstock organized a group of preventive societies, the most famous of which was the Society for the Suppression of Vice. Comstock and fellow anti-vice crusaders saw connections between various vices such as alcohol, prostitution, and sexually explicit materials. In Comstock's major treatise *Traps for the Young* (1883), he described lust as:

> the boon companion of all other crimes. There is no evil so extensive, none doing more to destroy the institutions of free America. It sets aside the laws of God and morality; marriage bonds are broken, most sacred ties severed, State laws ignored, and dens of infamy plant themselves in almost every community and then, reaching out like immense cuttlefish, draw in, from all sides, our youth to destruction.

Comstock successfully lobbied for the passage in 1873 of federal anti-obscenity legislation dubbed the "Comstock Law." The law prohibited the passage through the mail of "obscene, lewd, or lascivious" matter, including educational materials about venereal disease and literature or devices related to contraception or abortion. The law did not specify what was to be considered obscene; as a result, certain scientific and medical works were censored, and sex education was excluded from schools. In the years that followed, half the states in the Union passed similar laws.

COMSTOCK'S TARGETS

Appointed by the federal postmaster as a special agent in charge of enforcement of the 1873 law, Comstock dedicated himself to the task of investigating, researching, and prohibiting obscene materials. Although he focused on printed matter, Comstock also railed against live sexual performances, venturing into the "dens of iniquity" where live sex acts were performed for an audience. On one typical occasion, he spent some four hours witnessing, taking notes on, and describing every detail of the evening's "Busy Flea" performance in New York City. His notes described three women stripping, exposing themselves to patrons, and engaging in and mimicking various sex acts. After sitting through the entire show, Comstock announced that everyone in the house was under arrest. Comstock did not limit himself to sexually explicit performances. One of his most famous targets was Chicago belly dancer Farida Mahzar, better known as Little Egypt.

On some evenings Comstock's appearance at a brothel was greeted by the fist of an owner. One such reception sent him reeling down a flight of stairs. Yet none of this deterred the crusader.

Another victim of Comstockery was Ida Craddock, a counselor who wrote several marriage manuals with titles such as *Right Marital Living*. She argued for sexual self-control and urged men not to force sexual intercourse upon their wives. Ironically, Craddock herself was somewhat of a moral purist, opposing prostitution, masturbation, and contraception. Craddock was imprisoned in 1902 under New York City's anti-obscenity law. Arrested again under the federal Comstock Law soon after her release, she committed suicide rather than face another prison term.

But perhaps the best-known target of Comstock's efforts was birth control advocate Margaret Sanger. Sanger, a nurse, wrote a birth control pamphlet titled *What Every Girl Should Know* in 1916 and opened the first family planning clinic in Brooklyn, New York,

COMSTOCK, ANTHONY (1844–1915)

Anthony Comstock was born in New Canaan, Connecticut. The roots of Comstock's social purity crusade, however, can be found within the social currents of post–Civil War New York City, where Comstock settled after serving as a Union soldier. The roots of Anthony Comstock's social purity crusade can be found within the social currents of post–Civil War New York City, where Comstock settled after his years as a Union soldier.

An early supporter of the notion that prostitution and obscenity presented a grave threat to America's youth, Comstock, along with other anti-vice campaigners, established a crusade to battle the sins of indulgence in alcohol, prostitution, and obscene materials—from pornography to information about birth control. Together, they organized various preventive societies, including the Society for the Suppression of Vice, which Comstock remained secretary of until his death in 1915.

While advocacy groups of the time debated the pros and cons of legalizing prostitution, Comstock aimed to shift American morals and values. Within Comstock's purview, any visual material or literature related to sexuality that was not observed in a museum was conflated with obscenity. His views also exemplified the connection many reformers saw between various vices. For Comstock, alcohol led to alcoholism, which combined with lust resulted in venereal disease, which in turn contributed to further corruption. In his major treatise *Traps for the Young* (1883), he equates lust with criminality.

According to Comstock, young males were more susceptible to the traps associated with the intoxicating matrix of prostitution, drink, and gambling than young women—whom he also considered more expendable. In Comstock's eyes, the very existence of prostitution and drink blighted American manhood, thus presenting a threat to the country's future.

Comstock authored the 1868 New York State statute forbidding immoral works. But he did not stop there. By 1873, Comstock had successfully lobbied for passage of federal anti-obscenity legislation—dubbed the "Comstock Law"—with the backing of the Young Men's Christian Association (YMCA). Subsequently, the postmaster general named Comstock a special agent charged with enforcement of this law, which prohibited the passage of sexually explicit matter through the U.S. postal system.

Over the next forty years, Comstock actively researched and condemned materials that he judged to be smut or filth. In addition to addressing more blatant examples of obscenity, Comstock's efforts targeted such writers as Ida Craddock, who wrote several books that dealt with issues of marital sex. Beyond his focus on examples of "sexual depravity" in print and the arts, Comstock also sought to eliminate live sexual performances of all kinds, as well as what he considered "lewd" dancing, repress all materials and efforts related to birth control, and expose various fraudulent practices and advertisements.

Over the years, Comstock's name became synonymous with the recurring American fixation on moral regulation and sexual suppression. In 1905, after Comstock denounced George Bernard Shaw for the play *Mrs. Warren's Profession*, Shaw termed his standards for decency in art and the distinctive national tendency they represented "Comstockery."

Benjamin Shepard

that year. Soon thereafter, Sanger and two colleagues were arrested under the same New York anti-obscenity law that had ensnared Craddock. Sanger's imprisonment brought greater attention to both contraception and anti-obscenity legislation.

CULTURAL ANXIETY

The subtext of much of the Comstock crusade and the anti-vice movement at large played on cultural anxieties about the growing political power of immigrants and broader threats to the social and political positions of the upper and middle classes. Contraception threatened social hierarchies by giving women the opportunity to leave the domestic sphere of the home and gain autonomy from men, and also aroused white Anglo-Saxon Protestant fears of being overwhelmed by immigrant populations that tended to have many children. The anti-vice movement was most successful when it linked fears about the moral corruption of youth to changes in gender roles and social and economic hierarchies. Often, repression of vice functioned as a cover for opposition to shifts in class and racial hierarchies.

Many of the early attacks on explicit materials, brothels, and other aspects of sexual commerce followed labor unrest in New York City. Sexual libertinism coincided with a burgeoning Anarchist and Socialist labor coalition driving for political and economic power in the city. Anti-vice campaigns closely matched attempts to break strikes and Socialist organizing efforts throughout the 1870s. However, all the while, each brothel that was closed seemed to reopen somewhere else, in another tenement within the city.

Comstock's core argument—that obscenity threatened children—was a powerful message. By claiming that children were endangered, the anti-vice movement gained legitimacy. These echoes continue to reverberate within current political discourse. Many of the rhetorical dynamics of Comstock's crusade against pornography, abortion, contraception, indecency in art and literature, and the corruption of children were a consistent theme throughout nineteenth- and twentieth-century moral crusades. The temperance movement of Comstock's era mobilized a powerful coalition against the use of alcohol by making the case that inebriated husbands were more likely to squander wages and to neglect and abuse their children. Later, anti-abortion activists deployed arguments about the protection of children in their campaign for parental consent laws that mandate control over teenage girls. Similarly, those opposed to gay rights have used arguments that gays, lesbians, bisexuals, and transgender people recruit children as a justification for turning back antidiscrimination laws.

RESISTANCE TO COMSTOCKERY

Yet from its earliest days, Comstockery was never without its opponents. Various freethinkers, Anarchists, Socialists, and utopians sought social reform, greater civil liberties, and increased freedom for women through the loosening of oppressive moral strictures. At the height of the nineteenth-century anti-vice campaign, radical author and lawyer Lysander Spooner, in *Vices Are Not Crimes* (1875), argued that the government had no right to make laws against consensual vices that harmed no one other than the person who committed them:

> Vices are simply the errors which a man makes in his search after his own happiness. Unlike crimes, they imply no malice toward others, and no interference with their persons or property. . . . Unless this clear distinction between vices and crimes be made and recognized by the laws, there can be on earth no such thing as individual right, liberty, or property, and the corresponding and coequal rights of another man to the control of his own person and property.

Spooner's successors would continue to battle the heirs of Comstock throughout the ensuing century, encompassing efforts such as the censorship of movies under the Hays Production Code in the 1930s, the prohibition of the homosexual Mattachine Society's *ONE* magazine in the 1950s, and the banning of purportedly obscene literature throughout the first half of the twentieth century. Although the last Comstock laws were repealed in the mid-1960s, the social purity impulse has lived on, as evidenced by the religious right's "traditional values" campaign of the 1980s and more recent attempts to control sexually explicit material on the Internet.

Benjamin Shepard and Liz Highleyman

BIBLIOGRAPHY

Beisel, Nicola. *Imperiled Innocents: Anthony Comstock and Family Reproduction in America.* Princeton, NJ: Princeton University Press, 1997.

Comstock, Anthony. *Traps for the Young.* Reprint, Cambridge, MA: Harvard University Press, Belknap, 1967.

Gilfoyle, Timothy J. *City of Eros: New York City, Prostitution, and the Commercialization of Sex, 1790–1920.* New York: W.W. Norton, 1992.

Goldman, Emma. "The Traffic of Women." In *Anarchism and Other Essays.* New York: Dover, 1917.

Kendrick, Walter. *The Secret Museum: Pornography in Modern Culture.* Berkeley: University of California Press, 1996.

Spooner, Lysander. *Vices Are Not Crimes: A Vindication of Moral Liberty,* 1875. http://www.druglibrary.org/schaffer/history/vices.htm.

PROHIBITION AND REPEAL

The use of alcohol in the United States dates to the founding of the country, and consumption of beer, wine, and distilled spirits was a prominent feature of colonial life. Yet since that time attempts have been made to regulate and control alcohol use. Many of the earliest efforts encouraged moderate use (the true meaning of "temperance") rather than outright prohibition and were often based on health concerns. While overt drunkenness was frowned upon, moderate consumption—especially of beer and wine—was widely regarded as acceptable, even salutary. Thus, early temperance advocates urged others to limit, or temper, their consumption of alcohol, not to necessarily abandon it altogether. Former Army Surgeon-General Dr. Benjamin Rush was one of the first to write about the harmful effects of alcohol in his 1785 *Inquiry into the Effects of Ardent Spirits Upon the Human Body and Mind.*

In the ensuing years, various Protestant religious groups—including Methodists, Presbyterians, Universalists, Baptists, and the Society of Friends—began to promote temperance, or even to demand that their members abstain entirely from alcohol. In contrast, Catholic and Jewish groups—the religions of many new immigrants—generally did not support alcohol prohibition. In part, Protestant religious groups were motivated by a general Puritan suspicion of pleasure, but in the years to come they would take up many of the societal harm arguments against alcohol put forth by feminist temperance activists and other social reformers.

In 1789, a group of farmers in Litchfield, Connecticut, formed what is thought to be the first U.S. temperance society. The Massachusetts Society for the Suppression of Intemperance, formed in 1813, agitated against gambling and "profaneness" as well as alcohol. In 1826, the American Society for the Promotion of Temperance was founded in Boston. By the 1830s, there were an estimated 6,000 temperance societies, with over one million members. Other groups included the Washingtonian Society in 1840—a group of reformed drinkers who had repudiated their old ways—the Sons of Temperance in 1842, and the Independent Order of Good Templars in 1852.

During the first half of the nineteenth century, temperance efforts often relied on moral suasion, including efforts to encourage people to sign voluntary abstinence pledges. In 1842, while he was a member of the Illinois General Assembly, Abraham Lincoln gave a speech supporting temperance and encouraging citizens to take such pledges. But as time went on, legal coercion came to replace persuasion.

Throughout the 1800s, various state laws were put in place to regulate the sale and consumption of alcohol. The Oregon territory—not yet a state—passed a prohibition law in 1843. The first state law was enacted in Maine in 1851. Many of these early efforts were short-lived; several were repealed after only a few years due to lack of popular support, lax enforcement, or judicial decisions against them. But as the century progressed, sentiment in favor of alcohol prohibition increased.

ALCOHOL AS SCAPEGOAT

During the latter half of the 1800s, concern grew about excessive alcohol consumption, saloon culture, and the purported detrimental societal effects of drink. Alcohol was seen as leading to moral decay, crime, poverty, insanity, divorce, violence against women, and neglect of children—the same themes that underlie social purity and anti-vice campaigns today. Alcohol—along with prostitution, obscenity, and drugs—became a scapegoat for concerns about family, societal, and demographic changes brought about by economic restructuring, industrialization, and urbanization. Indeed, the bleak conditions of factory workers and isolation from families as people moved to the cities no doubt encouraged many to seek comfort in the bottle.

In addition, as fears about immigration increased, alcohol control efforts were linked to opposition to the drinking habits of new arrivals, particularly Irish and Germans.

Although temperance was largely a middle-class phenomenon, segments of the early labor movement took up the cause. For example, the Knights of Labor prohibited those connected with the alcohol trade from becoming members. In 1908, the Socialist Party resolved that "any excessive indulgence in intoxicating liquors by members of the working class is a serious obstacle to the triumph of our cause since it impairs the vigor of the fighters in political and economic struggle." And in an unusual alliance, Unionists were joined by employers and business owners concerned that alcohol eroded productivity and led to workplace accidents. (Exceptions were those involved in the liquor trade, the brewing industry, saloon owners, and related industries.)

Physicians, troubled by the negative physical and mental health effects of excessive alcohol consumption, also lent their voices to the movement. In 1917, the American Medical Association (formed in 1847) came out in support of national prohibition, stating that controlling alcohol was a means of controlling syphilis. By the end of the nineteenth century, however, alcohol use had come to be seen primarily as a moral or criminal rather than a health problem.

Finally, some prominent antislavery and African-American leaders such as William Lloyd Garrison and Frederick Douglass spoke out in favor of temperance, and the temperance movement came to be associated with the movement for the abolition of slavery. Nevertheless, some prohibitionists were not above exploiting panic about sexual assaults on white women by black men under the influence of alcohol.

TEMPERANCE AND FEMINISM

The temperance movement was profoundly affected by the changing place of women in society, and the movement in turn impacted the social role of women. It is not a coincidence that the feminist movement—usually dated from the Seneca Falls, New York, convention in 1848—and the social purity movements against alcohol, prostitution, and obscenity arose during the same era.

As women left the home, they became increasingly involved in campaigns for social reform. Early efforts by women reflected traditional ideas about their roles as nurturers, caretakers, and guardians of virtue. In addition to mothering their own children, middle-class women began to play a maternal role in

In efforts to curtail the sale of alcohol, women led prayer vigils outside saloons in the nineteenth century. *(Brown Brothers)*

the larger social sphere, as illustrated by women's benevolent societies. The Washingtonian Society's women's auxiliary—the Martha Washingtonians—continued this tradition, collecting money and providing support for women and children adversely impacted by drink. Beyond such activities, women—lacking the vote—influenced public policy by such means as demonstrations, prayer vigils, petition campaigns, and in some cases direct action such as saloon destruction.

But women faced obstacles within the movement. At both the Sons of Temperance Convention in 1852 and the World's Temperance Convention in 1853, women were not allowed to speak. Early feminists did not take such affronts lightly, and women's role within the reform movement began to shift from maternal benevolence to demands for equality. Renowned suffragist Susan B. Anthony established the first women's temperance society, the Woman's State Temperance Society of New York, in 1852. Other early feminists such as Lucretia Mott and Elizabeth Cady Stanton also rallied to the cause.

With a Bible in one hand and a hatchet in the other, Carry Nation of the Woman's Christian Temperance Union smashed liquor bottles and furniture in bars throughout Kansas. Such acts of "smashing" and "hatchetation," as she called them, led a Topeka temperance convention to award her a gold medal inscribed, "To the Bravest Woman in Kansas." (Brown Brothers)

Alcohol use—and especially saloon culture—was seen as a problem of men. Some suffragists used claims of women's purported moral superiority as an argument for giving women the vote. Drunkenness was said to enflame lust, engender violence, and lead to economic ruin and family dissolution, thus endangering women and children. Among Stanton's demands were that no woman should remain the wife of a drunkard and that state marriage and custody laws should be modified so that drunkards would have no claim to their wives or children. By the time national prohibition was enacted in 1919, women had become a major force and the movement had become closely associated with early feminism. Along with suffrage and the abolition of slavery, temperance was among the first issues for which women agitated publicly and effected major social and legislative change.

THE TEMPERANCE MOVEMENT GAINS STRENGTH

As the nineteenth century drew to a close, anti-alcohol groups increased in number and strength, and tended to focus on the elimination of saloons and the outright prohibition of alcohol rather than on voluntary abstinence and moderate use. By this time, most reformers held that alcohol was almost always harmful and addictive, and that moderate users would inexorably be drawn to heavy use and its attendant social ills. Not until the early 1900s would the medical view emerge that alcoholism was a disease that affected some people while others could drink responsibly. The era's attitudes toward alcohol and its inevitable adverse effects were similar to beliefs about drug use that persist to this day.

In 1869, the National Prohibition Party was formed in Chicago as an alternative to the Republicans and Democrats, who many believed were not doing enough to promote temperance. The party gained strength on the local, state, and federal levels throughout the 1880s and 1890s, and was a major force in passing the national prohibition amendment. In the 1884 presidential election between Republican James Blaine and Democrat Grover Cleveland, Blaine supporters denounced the Democrats as the party of "Rum, Romanism, and Rebellion." In 1892, at the Prohibition Party's peak, its presidential candidate John Dedwell received over 270,000 votes.

TEMPERANCE ORGANIZATIONS

A leading organization in the campaign to suppress alcohol and vice was the Woman's Christian Temperance Union (WCTU). The WCTU was founded in Cleveland, Ohio, in 1874 as an outgrowth of the Woman's Temperance Crusade. Born of a moral crusade, the WCTU advocated for abstinence in its broadest terms—both from alcohol and from other vices. Its membership included hatchet-wielding vice crusader Carry Nation, who gained fame for destroying saloons. The WCTU was one of the era's many women's organizations that were responding directly to changes in the home and the social milieu. Under the leadership of its second president, Frances Willard, membership in the American WCTU swelled to a quarter of a million members.

Through a conservative/liberal collaboration, the WCTU organized middle-class and working-class

CARRY NATION (1846–1911)

Known as "Hatchet Nation" for her weapon of choice, Carry Nation is the most famous temperance advocate in American history. Moving beyond traditionally female techniques of peaceful petitioning and moral suasion, Nation took up hatchets, rocks, and crowbars in her campaign to banish alcohol from America. Nation considered alcoholic drinks the root of all evil, responsible for the social problems of her day.

Carry Amelia Moore was born on November 25, 1846, in Garrard County, Kentucky, to George Moore and Mary Campbell. Moore was at one time a successful plantation owner, but his fortunes failed while Carry was a child. The family moved to Grayson County, Texas, and then to Belton, Missouri, in 1862. Nation did not receive much formal education, was often sick, and spent much time alone reading the Bible. At the age of ten, she had a religious conversion.

At twenty years of age, Nation was briefly married to Charles Gloyd, a young doctor and a heavy drinker. Their only child, Charlien, was born with ailments Nation attributed to her husband's drinking. In 1877, Carry married David Nation, a lawyer and minister. While living in Texas, Nation decided to devote herself to God by waging war against tobacco and alcohol. At a time when neither the law nor the ministry was a field open to women, Nation used her husband's professional training to advance her own causes, making him her mouthpiece and deputy.

After David Nation became minister in Holton, Kansas, Carry chose his sermons and sometimes wrote them herself. She used his position particularly to speak out against tobacco and liquor.

The Nations moved to Medicine Lodge, Kansas, in 1890, where David Nation took up the practice of law. Again directing her husband's career into the channels of her own interest, Carry encouraged him to prosecute liquor interests in the town. In 1880, voters of Kansas approved an amendment to the state constitution prohibiting the production or use of alcohol except for medicinal purposes. Nonetheless, Kansans continued to drink, and saloons operated unmolested by the local police.

Nation started the Medicine Lodge chapter of the Women's Christian Temperance Union (WCTU) with her friend, Mrs. Wesley Cain, who was married to the local Baptist minister. Nation visited men in jail and urged them to stop drinking. She also spent time helping the poor and was known locally as "Mother Nation" for her benevolence.

In Medicine Lodge, Nation began standing up in church to name local saloonkeepers and to ask why antiliquor laws were not prosecuted. In June 1899, responding to an internal voice that told her to "go to Kiowa," Nation traveled to Kiowa, Kansas, with a wagonload of large stones. In Kiowa, she threw stones at saloons, claiming the illegality of the saloons made her actions legal and defying local officials to arrest her.

Nation and her followers—mostly women—then took their campaign to Wichita, seen as the center of the liquor distribution in Kansas. In Wichita, Nation smashed saloons with a cane, stones, and an iron rod, for which she was arrested and jailed. Nation was arrested another twenty-nine times throughout her life.

Nation first used the hatchet that became associated with her name in 1901 in James Burnes's saloon in Wichita. In 1901, Kansas temperance advocates held a conference in Topeka. Although they did not invite Nation, she attended anyway and organized several hundred people—again, mostly women—into Home Defender clubs, with the purpose of attacking saloons.

Letters from people across the country and around the world came to Nation, asking her to bring her campaign to their communities. She began to travel, lecturing and advocating saloon smashing in many places. She once said to an audience, "Oh, I tell you, ladies, you never know what joy it gives you to start out to smash a rumshop."

Home Defender groups attacked saloons throughout Kansas, and local leaders began to call for stricter enforcement of the 1880 amendment. Nation, an advocate of women's suffrage, told the state's lawmakers, "You refused me the vote and I had to use a rock," drawing a direct connection between her protest and suffrage. The Kansas state legislature responded to the wave of violent activism by passing significant new prohibition laws and by enforcing them more rigorously than before.

Nation also was opposed to tobacco use, snatching cigars out of the mouths of smokers and speaking out against cigarettes as unhealthy and part of saloon culture. She retired to a farm in Arkansas and died in 1911. According to her wishes, her tombstone reads "She hath done what she could." Although Nation made alcohol prohibition a national issue, she is not directly credited with helping to pass the Eighteenth Amendment because most of the advocates of the amendment did not support her violent activism.

Megan J. Elias

women to mobilize in support of social reform. As was the case with many of the social reformers of the day, it would be difficult to describe this organization as either "progressive" or "conservative" in today's terms. Although the WCTU itself did not endorse women's suffrage, Willard supported equality of the sexes and believed that "drink and tobacco are the great separatists between men and women." The WCTU enjoyed the support of church groups and industrialists, but also worked in coalition with labor, actively supporting efforts that had nothing to do with alcohol. Willard was an active member of the Knights of Labor, and the WCTU worked on issues ranging from workers' protection and the eight-hour day to age of consent laws and international peace. The WCTU also worked to support kindergartens and to establish schools for women. In addition, it succeeded in ensuring that children were taught about alcohol abstinence in schools—a harbinger of later attempts by conservative groups to demand abstinence-based sex education. By the early 1900s, every state had laws requiring temperance instruction.

Through its school programs and support of former alcoholics (whose testimonials presaged those of today's Alcoholics Anonymous meetings), the WCTU was able to articulate a moral rationale that inspired other reformers and captured the sympathies of a public swept up in the pro-reform sentiment of the era. But as was the case with later social change movements such as the gay liberation movement, there was a persistent tension between those who believed the WCTU should focus on the single issue of alcohol prohibition and those who favored a broader agenda of social reform. Despite the eventual defeat of national Prohibition, the WCTU is still in existence today.

The Anti-Saloon League (ASL) was founded in Oberlin, Ohio, in 1893 by Howard Hyde Russell, a Congregational minister and former lawyer. It is notable that much of the strength of the prohibition movement came from the Midwest and from rural areas rather than cities. Although the league was financially supported by industrialists such as John D. Rockefeller and Pierre DuPont, its major support came from Protestant churches. ASL had lawyers write anti-alcohol legislation that was put forward by politicians who supported the cause. The bipartisan organization backed both Democrats and Republicans who favored prohibition and lobbied for "dry" (total prohibition of alcohol) laws on both the local and national levels. The league organized a rally of some 4,000 people in Washington, D.C., in 1913 and was a major force in pushing the Prohibition amendment through Congress. The ASL later became the American Council on Alcohol Problems, which remains active today.

THE PASSAGE OF PROHIBITION

By the beginning of the twentieth century, many states had introduced their own anti-alcohol laws and over half the country and its territories were "dry." The advent of World War I ushered in an upsurge of patriotism, a growing call for national strength through purity, and intensified animosity toward ethnic and racial "others." The alcohol prohibition effort received a boost from anti-German sentiment, which engendered increased opposition to the largely German-American brewing industry. Prohibition failed to pass Congress in 1914, but the necessary two-thirds majority voted in favor of the Eighteenth Amendment to the Constitution in 1916. The necessary thirty-sixth state, Nebraska, ratified the amendment in 1919. In October 1919, the National Prohibition Enforcement Act—better known as the Volstead Act—went further, outlawing possession of alcoholic beverages. Prohibition—banning the manufacture, transportation, and sale of all alcoholic beverages—went into effect in January 1920.

REACTION TO PROHIBITION

With the passage of the Eighteenth Amendment and the Volstead Act, the stage was set for a new era in America's response to vice. Prohibition was widely flouted, and enforcement proved exceedingly difficult. Smuggling on a large scale could not be prevented, and the illicit manufacture of liquor sprang up with such rapidity that authorities were unable to suppress it. There followed a period of unparalleled illegal drinking and lawbreaking. Speakeasies cropped up everywhere, bootlegging and smuggling were rampant, and bribery and official corruption increased. For most Americans who enjoyed a drink from time to time, Prohibition was less an obstacle than a nuisance.

In the wake of the moral campaigns of the turn of the century, the "roaring twenties" was an era of cultural liberalization characterized by increased freedom for women, sexual license, erotic entertainment, jazz, the development of a youth subculture, and experimentation of all sorts. But the decade was also marked by considerable social anxiety. The fashion among young women for bobbed hair and clothing styles that emphasized a slender figure—rather than corsets that enhanced feminine curves—spurred criticisms about gender ambiguity that prefigured those leveled against men with long hair and beads in the 1960s. Young men and—most scandalously—young women drank alcohol and smoked tobacco (which was then banned in many states) in unprecedented numbers. The traditional small-town American way of life was challenged by exploding urbanization, increased social and occupational mobility, and economic restructuring. Anglo-Saxon Protestants began to lose their former hegemony over American life amid increasing immigration and foreign influence.

By the early 1930s, America was again ready for change. The national mood during the Great Depression was very different from that which prevailed during World War I, when heightened patriotism, xenophobia, and social anxiety had prompted moderates to temporarily side with extremist reformers to pass Prohibition. Many now came to believe that repeal of Prohibition would stimulate the economy and provide much-needed jobs. Others were concerned about the growing loss of respect for the law and hoped that legal availability of alcohol would improve working-class morale in an era of growing revolutionary sentiment. The Association Against the Prohibition Amendment was formed to lobby for repeal. The Women's Organization for National Prohibition Reform—a counterpart to the WCTU—was also established to fight Prohibition, decrying "the hypocrisy, the corruption, the tragic loss of life, and the appalling increase of crime which has attended the abortive attempt to enforce it." Some of the same elite players who once had supported national alcohol prohibition, including Pierre DuPont and John D. Rockefeller, came out against it. In the 1932 presidential election, both Republicans and Democrats supported repeal.

Prohibition had several unintended effects. By driving the alcohol industry underground, Prohibition encouraged criminal activity related to alcohol production and distribution. Organized crime burgeoned—as exemplified by Al Capone, who headed up the illegal alcohol racket in Chicago. The illegality of alcohol made it more profitable and a better risk to produce and transport high-proof distilled spirits compared to beer and wine. Since alcohol is relatively easy to make, production shifted from a few large manufacturers to multiple small-scale producers. And lack of regulation led to inferior, poor-quality alcohol that led to many poisoning deaths. The War on Drugs in the late twentieth century would lead to many of the same consequences.

THE END OF PROHIBITION

Congress passed the Twenty-first Amendment repealing Prohibition in February 1933. By the end of the year, the final necessary states had ratified it by 73 percent overall. The ease with which repeal passed demonstrated that the public sentiment underlying Prohibition was shallow. Although crusaders wanted to ban alcohol, mainstream Americans only wished to control the excesses of drunkenness and saloon culture—not to give up their own personal use. In the wake of repeal, the states instituted their own mechanisms for alcohol control. Laws were enacted governing the hours, days, and manner in which alcoholic beverages could be sold. Many state laws were based on the recommendations in a report commissioned by John D. Rockefeller and written by his adviser Raymond Fosdick. Some states mandated that alcohol could only be sold in state monopoly stores. Under religious pressure, many banned sale on Sundays. Today, no state has a blanket prohibition on alcohol but many towns—especially in the South—remain "dry."

LATE TWENTIETH-CENTURY ALCOHOL CONTROL EFFORTS

In more recent years, alcohol control efforts have focused on laws against drunk driving and raising the legal drinking age. After Congress passed the Twenty-sixth Amendment in 1970 lowering the voting age to eighteen, states began to extend other adult privileges to eighteen-year-olds. Many found it absurd that men in their late teens could be drafted to fight in Vietnam but could not legally consume a beer. Beginning in the late 1970s, this trend was reversed, in part due to concern about the high number of traffic fatalities involving this age group, but also reflecting an ongoing infantilization of young adults. In 1984, Congress passed the Minimum Drinking Age Law, requiring states to raise their legal drinking age to twenty-one or face the loss of federal highway funds; a majority of states complied by 1986. Today the debate continues. Mothers Against Drunk Driving (MADD) is one of the strongest voices lobbying against lowering the drinking age.

Benjamin Shepard and Liz Highleyman

BIBLIOGRAPHY

Cherrington, Ernest. *The Evolution of Prohibition in the United States of America.* Montclair, NJ: Patterson Smith, 1920.

Debler, Carl N. *Out of the Past: The Forces That Shaped Modern America.* New York: Harper & Row, 1984.

Dobyns, F. *The Amazing Story of Repeal*. Chicago: Willett, Clark, 1940.

Furnas, J.C. *The Life and Times of the Late Demon Rum*. New York: Putnam, 1965.

Gertzman, Jay A. *Bookleggers and Smuthounds: The Trade in Erotica, 1920–1940*. Philadelphia: University of Pennsylvania Press, 1999.

Gusfield, Joseph R. *Symbolic Crusade: Status Politics and the American Temperance Movement*. Urbana: University of Illinois Press, 1963.

Kobler, John. *Ardent Spirits: The Rise and Fall of Prohibition*. New York: Da Capo, 1973.

Levine, Harry G. "The Discovery of Addiction: Changing Conceptions of Habitual Drunkenness in America." *Journal of Studies on Alcohol* 15 (1979): 493–506.

———. "The Committee of Fifty and the Origins of Alcohol Control." *Journal of Drug Issues* (1983): 95–116.

———. "The Birth of American Alcohol Control: Prohibition, the Power Elite and the Problem of Lawlessness." *Contemporary Drug Problems* (1985): 63–115.

Rush, Benjamin. *Inquiry into the Effects of Ardent Spirits Upon the Human Body and Mind*. Philadelphia: Tract Association of Friends, 1943.

Sinclair, Andrew. *Prohibition: The Era of Excess*. Boston: Little, Brown, 1962.

Timberlake, James. *Prohibition and the Progressive Movement, 1900–1920*. Cambridge, MA: Harvard University Press, 1963.

Wechsler, H., and E.S. Sands. "Minimum-Age Laws and Youthful Drinking: An Introduction." In *Minimum Drinking Age Laws*, ed. H. Wechsler. Lexington, MA: Lexington Books, 1980.

ANTI-DRUG MOVEMENT

The nonmedical use of drugs in the United States extends back to colonial times. Cocaine, opium, and marijuana were not criminalized for much of the country's history. During the Civil War, the use of opium as a painkiller ushered in the birth of modern surgery but left many soldiers addicted. In the mid- to late nineteenth century, the unrestricted dispensing of drugs and the explosive growth of the patent medicine industry brought opiates and cocaine into American homes; even Coca-Cola contained cocaine until 1903. The popularity of such over-the-counter elixirs—which typically were not accurately labeled and were often advertised with extravagant cure-all claims—led to a dramatic increase in drug use and addiction, especially among middle-class white women. The rate of opiate addiction in this era was higher than at any time since.

Opium use was first restricted in the United States in the 1870s, beginning in San Francisco. In 1901, the Senate adopted a resolution prohibiting the sale of opium and alcohol to "aboriginal tribes and uncivilized races." By the early 1900s, several other states had enacted opium laws. Early laws tended to focus on opium dens and opium smoking, which was seen as a vice of Chinese immigrant workers such as those who built the railroad to the West Coast. Agitation for such laws was based to a large degree on antipathy toward the Chinese and fears about Asian men using opium to seduce and sexually corrupt white women.

Amid the growing climate of social reform at the turn of the century, Congress passed the Pure Food and Drug Act in 1906. Before this, various states had a patchwork of laws regulating the distribution and sale of narcotics and cocaine. The 1906 law created the Food and Drug Administration (FDA) and required that labels report the amount of alcohol, cocaine, opium, morphine, chloral hydrate, and marijuana contained in a product, as well as whether the product was potentially habit-forming. The act decimated the patent drug industry and greatly reduced the occur-

rence of accidental addiction. The Pure Food and Drug Act had a public health rather than a criminal focus; at the time, addicts were widely viewed as innocent victims. It is notable that this health-focused law was one of the most successful in curbing drug use and addiction. In contrast to the Pure Food and Drug Act—which addressed the problem of drug use among the middle class—subsequent drugs laws tended to emphasize criminal penalties and social control, especially of racial and ethnic minorities, working-class and poor people, and counterculture youth.

THE HARRISON NARCOTIC ACT

In 1909, Congress restricted the importation of opium. The next major federal drug legislation was the Harrison Narcotic Act of 1914. Dr. Hamilton Wright, a physician and the State Department's opium commissioner, was a major advocate for stronger narcotics laws. The Foster Bill, the predecessor to the Harrison Act, was opposed by the drug industry, which in 1913 established the National Drug Trade Conference to persuade Congress to enact a less strict law. The bill was also opposed by Southern Democrats who feared federal encroachment on states' rights, in part because they wished to retain their state laws enforcing racial segregation. To counter such opposition, Wright whipped up fears of cocaine use by African Americans, contending that black "cocaine fiends" were prone to commit violence against whites.

The Harrison Act imposed taxes and registration and recordkeeping requirements on anyone who imported, produced, sold, distributed, or gave away products containing opium or cocaine and their derivatives. (Marijuana was included in the original bill but was deleted before the law was passed.) Although the act did not ban the possession of opiates and cocaine outright, it imposed such high transaction costs that the drugs were effectively outlawed. Congress used a tax measure to implement a moral agenda that—in an era of strong states' rights—could not be imposed directly; for decades federal drug regulation remained under the purview of the Treasury Department.

The Harrison Act largely targeted physicians and pharmacists who dispensed narcotics, and did not penalize users directly. Initially, the law was not stringently enforced, and the Supreme Court ruled that physicians could prescribe opium and cocaine as they saw fit, including for the maintenance of addicts. In 1919, the Court reversed itself, ruling that addiction maintenance was not an appropriate use of narcotics. In the years that followed, narcotics clinics that maintained and attempted to gradually withdraw addicts—precursors to the modern harm reduction movement—were closed. By rendering opium and cocaine effectively illegal, the Harrison Act drove addicts underground and led to inflated drug prices and increased criminal activity, which in turn reinforced the public image of drug use as immoral and problematic.

PROHIBITION AND THE DRUG WAR

The temperance/prohibition movement and the beginnings of the anti-drug movement occurred during the same era and tapped into many of the same social reform sentiments. Both crusades took advantage of uneasiness about social and cultural change and played on fears of disease, crime, poverty, immigration, and family dissolution. But as explained by Richard Bonnie and Charles Whitebread in "The Forbidden Fruit and the Tree of Knowledge," there were also some important differences. The temperance/prohibition movement grew from the grassroots, with religious, feminist, labor, and business groups pressuring legislators to pass anti-alcohol legislation. The issue was a major topic of public debate, and by the turn of the century there was a strong lobby in favor of prohibition.

In contrast, the early anti-drug movement was largely the work of elites. There was no major grassroots push for anti-drug laws, and the drug issue was not particularly prominent in the public debate. The major temperance organizations, as well as feminist and religious leaders, seemed to have little to say about the use of narcotics, even though addictive patent medicines were widely used at the time. In this era, drug use was still seen mainly as a medical rather than a moral or criminal problem, largely because it was a middle-class phenomenon. Although exaggerated fears about Chinese opium smokers and black cocaine users gave an indication of what was to come, attempts to link drug use to anxieties about racial and ethnic minorities, the poor, and the youth counterculture did not really take hold until later in the twentieth century. It was only after the passage of legislation such as the Harrison Act that the public at large widely began to adopt anti-drug attitudes. Indeed, the very passage of such laws helped change the public image of drug use in America.

EARLY ANTI-DRUG CAMPAIGNS

With the repeal of the Prohibition amendment, social reformers increasingly turned their attention to drugs. Heroin, which by World War I had become a favorite recreational drug among certain urban subcultures, increasingly became associated with violence, crime, and foreign elements. In 1924, the United States banned the importation of opium for use in the manufacture of heroin.

Although hemp was a favored crop in colonial times, by the mid-1930s most states had passed criminal laws relating to marijuana, beginning with Utah in 1915. In the Southwestern states, early marijuana laws were motivated in large part by antipathy toward Mexican immigrants. Public authorities and the media linked use of cannabis to crime, violence, lowered sexual inhibitions, and insanity; one common image was Mexicans selling marijuana cigarettes to white schoolchildren. Although marijuana was beginning to make its way into the urban Bohemian and black jazz subcultures in cities such as New Orleans, New York City, and Chicago, during the 1920s and early 1930s cannabis use was not prevalent. Many middle-class Americans likely were not even aware of the drug's existence, and there certainly was no grassroots campaign to ban it.

In 1930, the United States established the Federal Bureau of Narcotics (FBN), which for its first three decades was headed by crusading Commissioner of Narcotics Harry J. Anslinger. In 1932, a federal commission developed the Uniform Narcotic Drug Act, which Anslinger successfully lobbied the states to pass. The act prohibited opiates and cocaine but left marijuana legislation up to the states. Later, under pressure from state politicians and law enforcement officials, the FBN decided to push for a national marijuana law. The FBN initiated a campaign to educate the public about the dangers of cannabis—as exemplified by the 1936 film *Reefer Madness*—using linkages to immigrants, racial minorities, the working class, and counterculture youth. The Marijuana Tax Act was passed in 1937 with minimal congressional debate. The act did not ban marijuana outright but, like the Harrison Act, imposed such high taxes and onerous regulation that the drug was effectively made illegal.

The 1951 Boggs Act and the 1956 Narcotic Control Act instituted harsher penalties and mandatory minimum prison sentences for narcotic and marijuana law violations. For the first time marijuana was classified with the most dangerous drugs, under the theory that cannabis use led inexorably to use of harder substances. In this atmosphere of general paranoia, drug warriors such as Anslinger raised fears of Communists distributing drugs to undermine American youth.

THE WAR ON DRUGS

The political and cultural ferment of the 1960s and 1970s prompted a shift in the targets of moral reformers. Despite leftist revolutions in the developing world, post-McCarthy America was more concerned with unrest at home. Federal Bureau of Investigation (FBI) statistics reported a nearly 50 percent increase in crime during the 1960s. There was renewed emphasis on law and order—and fighting crime often meant combating vice. Liberals were derided as being more concerned about the civil rights of criminals than about crime victims. Politicians set out to sanitize public spaces, and nowhere was the drive to "clean up" America as pronounced as in the realm of drugs.

Both Barry Goldwater in 1964 and Richard Nixon in 1968 used themes of crime and drugs in their presidential campaigns. Rhetoric about the danger to children and members of the middle class presented by escalating crime rates reflected a classic panic—mobilizing racial bias and scapegoating—coordinated by conservative legislators, a burgeoning crime-control industry, and the media. Although Goldwater's campaign was not successful, the panic over crime as a threat to social order played a major role in Nixon's election. In the decades that followed, government funding shifted from social programs toward crime control, police powers increased, and the prison population exploded.

During this era, drug use increased considerably and entered American consciousness as never before. A 1969 Gallup poll estimated that 10 million Americans (4 percent of adults) had smoked marijuana. Drug use was widespread among U.S. soldiers in Vietnam. Along with the established drugs—opiates, cocaine, and marijuana—other drugs, including LSD, speed, and exotic substances such as psilocybin, mescaline, and peyote also gained popularity. The government and the media spun scare stories about the dangers of drugs—including drug-addled youth leaping from windows believing they could fly, and the threat of LSD being introduced into the public water supply—making little distinction between the most harmful drugs and the most innocuous. Already inclined to distrust the establishment, young people who had pleasant experiences with marijuana tended to discount all official anti-drug propaganda.

Nixon's Anti-Drug Campaign

Nixon is often cited as the instigator of the modern War on Drugs. In September 1969, he implemented Operation Intercept, a plan to reduce the supply of marijuana and other drugs coming from Mexico by means of stepped-up searches at border crossings and increased surveillance of air and sea traffic. In 1970, Congress passed the Comprehensive Drug Abuse Prevention and Control Act, which replaced a host of existing drug laws. This legislation included the Controlled Substances Act, which established a system of schedules classifying drugs on the basis of medical use and potential for abuse; schedule one, the most restrictive, includes heroin, LSD, and marijuana. In June 1971, the president announced an all-out offensive against drugs, calling drug abuse "America's Public Enemy No. 1." Nixon created new drug control agencies, including the Office of Drug Abuse Law Enforcement and the Office of National Narcotics Intelligence. This era saw the expansion of law-enforcement tactics such as no-knock warrants and wiretaps that civil libertarians continue to fight today. Nixon appointed the first "drug czar," Myles Ambrose, who proposed the idea of an all-encompassing drug agency. In 1973, existing federal drug efforts were consolidated into the Drug Enforcement Administration (DEA), which remains the key agency in charge of domestic and international drug control.

The strategy used by Nixon and his law-and-order attorney general John Mitchell to associate drug use with criminal activity was similar to that of New York governor Nelson Rockefeller, who during these years instituted a set of draconian drug laws that remain among the strictest in the nation. Rockefeller played on fears about crime and public safety to gain the support of conservatives, while at the same time utilizing rhetoric about treatment (albeit forced) to blunt liberal opposition. Not only did heroin users harm themselves, the argument went, but their addiction led them to commit crimes such as mugging, robbery, and prostitution to fund their habits. Depending on their audience, both Nixon and Rockefeller spoke of drug addiction as either an invading army that must be stopped by militaristic means or a spreading

Seeking to rid their neighborhood of drug dealers, activist Jackie McCray leads a march through Marion, Indiana, on May 14, 1999, chanting, "Up with hope, down with dope." *(AP Wide World Photos)*

disease, cancer, or epidemic that must be stopped by quarantining addicts.

CONSTRUCTING A DRUG PANIC

Many of the policies implemented during the 1960s and 1970s appear quite liberal compared to what was to follow in the 1980s and 1990s. In the 1960s, drug addiction was increasingly seen as a medical problem, and several laws were passed to fund addiction treatment and to allow for treatment as an alternative to jail. In 1971, the National Commission on Marijuana and Drug Abuse was established, and its first report in 1972 recommended decriminalization of the drug— a recommendation Nixon ignored. In the years that followed, many states reduced penalties for posses-

sion of small amounts of cannabis, essentially decriminalizing personal use. As the 1970s drew to a close, the public had become increasingly tolerant of drug use. Although a 1973 Gallup poll found that 20 percent of respondents thought drugs were the most important problem facing the country, drugs were not even mentioned in the 1979 through 1984 surveys. And a growing number of Americans expressed support for loosening drug laws.

But in the next decade these attitudes began to shift. In the early 1980s, President Ronald Reagan renewed the War on Drugs, reflected in his wife Nancy's "Just Say No" campaign. The demonization of racial minorities and countercultural youth continued. Reformers, the media, legislators, and the public often focused on a specific drug or population as a stand-in for the drug problem as a whole and for wider social anxieties. The drug panic intensified, with public concern about drug use burgeoning in 1985 and 1986.

In the mid-1980s, drug use came to be seen as a—or even *the*—major American social problem. A *New York Times*/CBS News poll charted this shifting sentiment. While in April 1986 only 2 percent identified drug use as the country's main problem, this number grew steadily; by September 1989, a full 64 percent said drug abuse was the nation's most significant concern. Media attention to drugs exploded with the 1986 deaths of two prominent athletes, Len Bias and Don Rogers, due to cocaine use. Perhaps at no other time had the issue of drugs occupied such a large and troubling space in the public consciousness. The racial nature of the panic was exemplified by the "crack baby" scare, which targeted poor African-American women and played on popular fears about the abuse of children. Criminal prosecution was proposed for pregnant women who exposed their fetuses to drugs during pregnancy, tying the drug issue to the struggle over abortion and women's right to control their bodies. Penalties for crack—a cheap form of cocaine associated with poor urban blacks—were disproportionately increased relative to those for the powdered form of cocaine more popular with wealthier users.

In an escalating cycle, politicians both responded to and exacerbated public anti-drug sentiment. In 1981, Congress amended the 1878 Posse Comitatus Act to allow the armed forces to take part in drug control efforts. In 1986, Congress passed a nearly $2 billion federal drug bill that called for increased enforcement, the death penalty for "drug kingpins," more treatment funding, and sanctions against nations that were not sufficiently cooperative with U.S. drug eradication efforts. In addition, to thwart small producers who were creating drugs chemically similar to controlled substances, legislators passed the Controlled Substances Analogue Enforcement Act to ban so-called designer drugs. The year 1988 saw the passage of the Anti-Drug Abuse Act, which established the Office of National Drug Control Policy, the aim of which was to "restore order and security to American neighborhoods, to dismantle drug trafficking organizations, to help people break the habit of drug use, and to prevent those who have never used illegal drugs from starting." In these and later years, several laws were put into place allowing drug testing in workplaces and schools.

Growing Disenchantment

Ironically, as Erich Goode and Nachman Ben-Yehuda, co-authors of *Moral Panics: The Social Construction of Deviance* (1994), note, fewer people saw drugs as a problem in the late 1970s when actual drug use was quite prevalent than in the 1980s when actual use had substantially declined, exemplifying the "constructed" nature of social problems. Yet just as the social panic about drug use had skyrocketed in the late 1980s, it dissipated at the turn of the decade—demonstrating that social problems can also be "deconstructed." The *New York Times*/CBS News poll found that the proportion of the population identifying drugs as the country's top problem had fallen to 30 percent by April 1990, and by August 1990 it was down to 10 percent. Economic recession and the Persian Gulf War competed with drugs as a social concern, and the media stopped feeding the panic. The fact that moral panics tend to ebb when the country is facing other major problems was demonstrated yet again when the terrorist attacks of September 11, 2001, a new economic recession, and a second war in Iraq once again bumped drugs and sex off the front pages.

Indeed, by the late 1990s and early 2000s, segments of the media had done a turnaround and began to produce stories putting a negative spin on the War on Drugs. Advocacy and lobbying groups such as the National Organization for the Reform of Marijuana Laws (NORML), the Marijuana Policy Project, and Students for Sensible Drug Policy were born. Politicians such as Minnesota governor Jesse Ventura and New Mexico governor Gary Johnson began to speak in favor of drug law reform. Increasingly, drug law reform proponents called for an exploration of various proposals to legalize, regulate, and tax drugs—that is, to treat them like alcohol and tobacco—in order to reduce the negative effects of the underground drug economy. Beginning with California's Compassionate Use Act of 1996 (Proposition 215), a growing number of states passed laws, mostly by voter initiative, permitting the medicinal use of marijuana.

But even as public disenchantment with the War on Drugs grew, most politicians—seemingly failing to read the public mood—were not yet ready to let up. President Bill Clinton, haunted by his own admission of marijuana use, increased anti-drug funding and appointed a strict drug czar, General Barry McCaffrey. The drug war increasingly shaped U.S. foreign policy, especially in Latin America and central Asia. The United States pressured foreign governments to eradicate marijuana, coca, and opium crops, and provided funding and military assistance for anti-drug efforts. In 1998, Congress passed an amendment to the Higher Education Act denying financial aid to students convicted of drug offenses, and in 2001 it considered the Reducing Americans' Vulnerability to Ecstasy (RAVE) Act, which would penalize owners for any drug use occurring on their property, whether or not they condoned it—or were even aware of it. Although perhaps a majority of today's middle-aged adults—including politicians—have tried some illegal drug, many remain unwilling to challenge the prevailing drug war orthodoxy for fear of sending the "wrong message" to youth.

THE HARM REDUCTION MOVEMENT: OUTLAW PUBLIC HEALTH

The War on Drugs spawned many responses, one of which was the birth of the harm reduction movement. Harm reduction is the philosophy of helping drug users and others engaged in stigmatized behaviors to stay healthy and safe without insisting that they give up their behavior. Born of needle exchange and AIDS activism in the late 1980s, the harm reduction movement continues to grow, building a coalition of syringe exchange workers, AIDS activists, health and social service providers, drug policy reformers, researchers, women's rights advocates, local and state politicians, and advocates of progressive healthcare and criminal justice reform. At its core, it is a movement that promotes a more humanistic, less moralistic approach to individual and social problems.

The roots of the harm reduction movement can be traced to the early years of the century, when certain doctors and clinics provided morphine or heroin to prevent withdrawal in people who had become addicted to opiates. However, in 1919 the U.S. Supreme Court ruled that addiction maintenance was not an appropriate use of narcotics, and in the years that followed existing narcotics maintenance clinics were closed. In the 1960s and 1970s, addiction increasingly came to be seen as a medical problem. By this time, maintenance therapy with methadone—a long-lasting synthetic narcotic that staves off withdrawal symptoms and drug cravings—had become the accepted method for treating opiate addiction. Modern methadone maintenance therapy was pioneered in the 1960s in New York City by Drs. Vincent Dole and Maria Nyswander. Rather than using decreasing doses of methadone to wean addicts off drugs, long-term maintenance therapy was designed to stabilize drug users. By providing a safe and legal alternative

On March 27, 2001, demonstrators march to the Capitol Building in Albany, New York, demanding reform or repeal of the Rockefeller anti-drug laws. The laws, spearheaded by Governor Nelson Rockefeller in the 1970s, were among the harshest ever passed. *(AP Wide World Photos)*

to heroin, methadone maintenance is intended to help addicts stop committing drug-related crime, separate themselves from the drug subculture, and lead productive lives. Although officials generally have supported methadone maintenance as a way to reduce crime, some drug warriors, moral reformers, and public health professionals oppose methadone maintenance, contending that it simply substitutes one drug dependency for another.

The growing AIDS epidemic in the late 1980s spurred the development of the harm reduction movement in the United States. As a self-conscious approach and philosophy, harm reduction first emerged in the Netherlands in the early 1980s as a pragmatic partnership between drug users and city officials, who started a needle exchange program to tackle the growing problem of hepatitis B transmission. The first American needle exchange programs were set up by grassroots AIDS activists, front-line AIDS service workers, civil rights activists, and current and former drug users. Faced with official denial and hostility regarding AIDS, and recognizing the explosion of HIV in poor urban communities, activists took clean needles to the streets in direct acts of civil disobedience. Harm reduction programs such as syringe exchange were designed to be "low threshold" and able to meet drug users "where they're at," rather than demanding that they stop their use. Most early activists explicitly rejected the abstinence orthodoxy of the era, which held that drug users could be helped only by stopping drug use completely.

The earliest underground needle exchanges were established in 1986 in New Haven and Boston by Jon Parker. The Point Defiance program in Tacoma, Washington, organized by Dave Purchase, was perhaps the first to operate with the tacit approval of public officials. San Francisco's Prevention Point was established by activists in 1988 and operates today under a city-declared state of emergency. The New York City Health Department began an experimental syringe exchange in 1988, but the program was "high threshold," requiring that clients enter drug treatment, and was inconveniently located across the street from city hall. Members of ACT UP/New York began a "low-threshold" needle exchange on the Lower East Side of Manhattan soon thereafter. The operators of the needle exchange were arrested for providing syringes, but the charges were thrown out when they successfully argued that exchanging needles was a "medical necessity" to prevent the spread of HIV and therefore to save lives. According to the Centers for Disease Control and Prevention (CDC), by the end of the 1990s there were over 100 needle exchange programs in the United States exchanging nearly 20 million syringes per year.

Harm reduction in the United States has been an "outlaw" practice, in stark contrast to the experience in many other countries, including Australia, Canada, and several European nations. In such countries, the consensus is that AIDS constitutes a greater immediate threat to public health than drug use. No such consensus has been possible in the United States. No presidential administration has allowed federal funding of syringe exchanges. Public opposition came from moral crusaders who believed that the harm related to drug use should not be minimized, lest users be discouraged from quitting (although some reformers reluctantly supported needle exchange to protect the "innocent" sexual partners and babies of injection

drug users). Other objections came from law-and-order proponents and "NIMBY" community members who feared needle exchanges would contribute to crime. As a result, by 1996 the United States reported over 146,000 cases of drug-related HIV transmission.

Another current of opposition to needle exchange came from communities devastated by drug use and the drug economy. For many people in such communities, AIDS was not the priority. Drug dependency, drug-related violence and crime, and the resulting impacts on social and economic life were experienced as more serious problems. Far from being seen as a life-saving measure, syringe exchange and harm reduction more generally were resisted and denounced by leaders of communities of color as enabling the very behavior that was killing their people and damaging their neighborhoods. In order to work with and within the most affected communities, there was a need to take harm reduction beyond HIV prevention and toward an analysis of and response to the multiple harms related to drug use, drug sales, and anti-drug policy. The Harm Reduction Coalition, formed in 1993, remains a key player in expanding harm reduction efforts across the United States, guided by a broad vision of social change that includes community involvement, criminal justice reform, universal healthcare, reproductive rights, and civil liberties.

As the 1990s progressed, the magnitude of the AIDS epidemic and the demonstrated success of needle exchange programs began to turn the tide. By the late 1990s many public health officials and much of the populace accepted harm reduction as a strategy for reducing disease transmission. As harm reduction moved in from the outside, needle exchange and related programs were "professionalized," often leading to increased bureaucracy, regulation, and the exclusion of the grassroots activists who had pioneered the strategy. As harm reduction efforts have been mainstreamed, they have sometimes come to resemble technical interventions directed at "them" (drug users) for the sake of "us" (the public), rather than programs by and for affected communities.

Following the example of needle exchange programs, the harm reduction philosophy has been extended and applied to other types of socially stigmatized behavior. For example, sex worker activists have developed peer education programs to teach prostitutes how to work more safely and protect themselves from disease transmission. Drug user activists have advocated for education and self-administered medication (naloxone, or Narcan) to prevent deaths from heroin overdose. And ravers such as those who founded DanceSafe have begun programs to test the purity of ecstasy and other drugs used in dance clubs. Although official and public opposition to drug use remains strong, grassroots activists have increasingly taken public health into their own hands.

LESSONS FROM THE WAR ON DRUGS

Like Prohibition, the War on Drugs produced several unintended consequences, including the greater availability of harder substances, an increase in experimentation spurred by publicity about drugs, promotion of an underground market and its attendant crime and violence, and the development of an addict subculture. Although crime is unquestionably associated with drug use, advocates of drug law reform contend that it is not drugs themselves that cause crime, but rather their high price on the black market, which prompts many addicts to turn to crimes such as robbery and prostitution to support their habits. Based on its stated aims, the War on Drugs appears to be a failure. But as Erich Goode points out, proponents of the anti-drug crusade—like other anti-vice movements—do not measure its success by whether or not it is able to achieve its purported goal. Rather, the crusade serves an ideological agenda, allowing politicians to promote a law-and-order image. In addition, prohibitionist crusades provide a focus for social anxieties about political unrest, urbanization, economic restructuring, the changing place of youth in society, and, especially, race.

One of the most visible outcomes of the drug war has been the explosion in the prison population, in particular the incarceration of young men of color. Today, the "prison-industrial complex"—the network of judges, police, prison officials, and those who profit from building and operating prisons—is large and influential and plays a role in perpetuating the drug war out of economic self-interest. One of the downfalls of Prohibition was that it became obvious that laws against alcohol were unfairly enforced, falling heavily on the working class while the middle and upper classes were spared. Similarly, during the 1960s and 1970s, drug laws often were selectively enforced against hippies and student radicals by a government and police force trying to thwart challenges to their authority; despite "mandatory" sentences, children of the wealthy and powerful seldom paid a criminal price for their drug experimentation. In addition, drug law enforcement focused on African Americans and Latinos, whose involvement in civil rights pro-

tests and potential for social revolution offered the most serious threat to the American elite since the early 1930s. Although several studies have shown that drug use is not more common among blacks compared to whites, by the 1980s and 1990s African-American youth were the primary target of drug enforcement. Just as McCarthy in the 1950s spoke of Communists as an "internal enemy" that would undermine the country unless assiduously rooted out, in the latter half of the century the most feared "enemies within" were communities of color.

Although progressives tend to see social problems such as crime, drug use, and poverty as being grounded in social conditions, and therefore remediable by social solutions, conservatives tend to see them as individual moral failings that are best addressed by punitive measures. In the final decades of the twentieth century the conservative view held sway. As the emphasis on crime overshadowed issues such as civil rights and economic entitlement, government expenditures followed suit. Funding for public education declined as monies for the prison industry grew. The 1994 California "three strikes" law—which imposes life sentences for people convicted of three felonies—exemplified the increasingly harsh attitude toward lawbreakers. For young people of color, the policies of the 1980s and 1990s created a contentious society divided along class and race lines. Although the moral panic nominally focused on drugs, its result has been the control of racial and ethnic minorities and the poor.

Liz Highleyman and Benjamin Shepard

BIBLIOGRAPHY

Bonnie, Richard J., and Charles H. Whitebread. "The Forbidden Fruit and the Tree of Knowledge: An Inquiry into the Legal History of American Marijuana Prohibition." *Virginia Law Review* 56:6 (October 1970). http://www.druglibrary.org/schaffer/Library/studies/vlr/vlrtoc.htm.

Brecher, Edward M., and the Editors of *Consumer Reports* Magazine. *Licit and Illicit Drugs: The Consumers Union Report on Narcotics, Stimulants, Depressants, Inhalants, Hallucinogens, and Marijuana.* Boston: Little, Brown, 1972. http://www.druglibrary.org/schaffer/Library/studies/cu/cumenu.htm.

Chambliss, William J. "Control and Ethnic Minorities: Legitimizing Racial Oppression by Creating Moral Panics." In *Ethnicity, Race, and Crime: Perspectives Across Time and Place*, ed. Darnell F. Hawkins. Albany: State University of New York Press, 1995.

Epstein, Edward Jay. *Agency of Fear: Opiates and Political Power in America.* New York: Verso, 1990.

Goode, Erich. *Drugs in American Society*. New York: Alfred A. Knopf/McGraw-Hill, 1972.

Goode, Erich, and Nachman Ben-Yehuda. *Moral Panics: The Social Construction of Deviance*. Cambridge, MA: Blackwell, 1994.

Greig, Alan, and Sara Kershnar. "Harm Reduction in the USA: A Movement Toward Social Justice." In *From ACT UP to the WTO: Urban Protest and Community-Building in the Era of Globalization*, eds. Benjamin Shepard and Ron Hayduk. New York: Verso, 2002.

Lane, Sandra D., et al. *Needle Exchange: A Brief History*. The Henry J. Kaiser Family Foundation, 1993. http://www.aegis.com/law/journals/1993/HKFNE009.html.

Levine, Harry G., and Craig Reinarman. "From Prohibition to Regulation: Lessons from Alcohol Policy for Drug Policy." *Milbank Quarterly* 69:3 (Fall 1991). http://www.mega.nu:8080/ampp/drugtext/craig100.htm.

———. "The Politics of America's Latest Drug Scare." In *Freedom at Risk: Secrecy, Censorship, and Repression in the 1980s*, ed. Richard O. Curry. Philadelphia: Temple University Press, 1988.

Lurie, Peter, et al. *The Public Health Impact of Needle Exchange Programs in the United States and Abroad: Summary, Conclusions and Recommendations*, 1993. http://www.caps.ucsf.edu/publications/needlereport.html.

Musto, David F. "The History of the Marihuana Tax Act of 1937." *Archives of General Psychiatry* (February 1972). http://www.druglibrary.org/schaffer/hemp/history/mustomj1.html.

———. *The American Disease: Origins of Narcotic Control*. New Haven, CT: Yale University Press, 1973.

Nadelmann, Ethan A. "Drug Prohibition in the United States: Costs, Consequences, and Alternatives." *Science*, September 1989, pp. 939–947.

National Commission on Marihuana and Drug Abuse. *Marihuana: A Signal of Misunderstanding*, 1972. http://www.druglibrary.org/schaffer/Library/studies/nc/ncmenu.htm.

Shepard, Benjamin. "The AIDS Coalition to Unleash Power: A Brief Reconsideration." In *Teamsters and Turtles? U.S. Progressive Political Movements in the 21st Century*, ed. John C. Berg. New York: Rowman and Littlefield, 2002.

Shichor, David. "Three Strikes as a Public Policy: The Convergence of the New Penology and the McDonaldization of Punishment." *Crime-and-Delinquency* 43:4 (October 1997).

Sinclair, Andrew. *Prohibition: The Era of Excess*. Boston: Little, Brown, 1962.

White, William L. "Themes in Chemical Prohibition." In *Drugs in Perspective*. Rockville, MD: National Institute on Drug Abuse, 1979.

PROGRESSIVE MOVEMENT

Several generations of historians have agreed that there was a period of time—beginning in the late 1800s and ending sometime around World War I—when the majority of Americans were so immersed in the quest for "progress" and "reform" that those years could fairly be called "The Progressive Era." Yet, those same historians have generally disagreed—fundamentally and vociferously—over whether or not that era's myriad activities and achievements were the result of a definable "Progressive movement," energized by a reasonably coherent ideology worthy of the label "Progressivism."

THE HISTORICAL DEBATE

The existence of that debate dates at least from the publication of Benjamin Parke De Witt's *The Progressive Movement: A Non-Partisan, Comprehensive Discussion of Current Tendencies in American Politics.* In that pioneering work, De Witt acknowledged that the term *Progressive Movement* has "been so widely used, so much discussed, and so differently interpreted that any exposition of its meanings and principles, to be adequate, must be prefaced by careful definition." To some contemporaries, he said, the term merely "represents the efforts of a small body of self-seeking politicians to gain position and influence by making capital of a movement that is temporarily popular." To others, it "expresses the efforts of a few sincere but misguided enthusiasts to carry out an impossible and chimerical program of social reform through government and legislation."

Although some saw the Progressive movement as "new, fleeting, and evanescent," De Witt himself viewed it as "permanent, deep-seated, and fundamental, involving a modification and readjustment of our political theories and institutions." Although conceding that "this widespread political agitation" frequently seemed "incoherent and chaotic," De Witt nevertheless insisted that careful examination and analysis revealed three unifying "tendencies": (1) the insistence by the "best men in all political parties" that special interests be eliminated from government and politics; (2) the demand that the structure or machinery of government be controlled by the many instead of the few; and (3) the rapidly growing conviction that the functions of government must be increased and extended to relieve social and economic distress. It was these three "tendencies"—manifested in political platforms and programs and in reforms advocated and enacted in city, state, and nation—that "may be said to constitute the real progressive movement," because of their "universality and definiteness."

Over the ensuing half-century, numerous scholars attempted to distill the essence of what they conceived of as a generic progressive movement. For the most part, they sought to define that movement by applying one or more of three criteria: a common social type; a shared system of values; or a reasonably coherent program of "reform." The high-water mark of their efforts occurred during the 1950s and 1960s in the work of the "status revolution" and "organizational revolution" historians. The status revolution historians, led by Richard Hofstadter and George Mowry, utilized "collective biographies" of the period's intellectuals and activists to construct a "progressive profile" that almost exclusively contained people of British-American roots, middle- to upper-middle-class social status, above-average formal education, and "touched by the long religious hand of New England."

In their view, the Progressive movement was fundamentally "an expression of an older America objecting to the ideological and social drifts of the twentieth century," especially the rise of the monopolistic corporation, on the one hand, and organized labor and socialism, on the other. Their security and position thus threatened from above and below, the members of this gentry abandoned their customary distaste for organized intervention and political action in order to restore their vision of the pristine quality of an earlier American life. The founders of the status revolution school maintained that "progressive reform drew its greatest support from the more discontented of the native Americans, and on some issues from the rural and small town constituencies that surrounded the big cities."

Whereas the status revolution historians believed that the Progressive movement reflected the "complaint of the unorganized against the consequences of organization," the proponents of the organizational revolution interpretation turned that idea on its head. For Robert Wiebe, Samuel Hays, Louis Galambos, James Weinstein, and other noted scholars, that movement was centered in the activities of a "new middle class" engaged in a "search for order." It was a concerted effort by an emerging elite group of professionals, bureaucrats, administrators, intellectuals, and technicians to impose their vision, structure, and values upon a society and culture dangerously fragmented and disoriented by rapid and massive change. In short, the essential dynamic of progressivism was not "power to the people," but the flow of decision making of all sorts upward in an increasingly rigid hierarchy of authority.

Even during the heyday of the status revolution and organizational revolution schools, however, many other historians provided evidence of significant reformist activity among segments of the population that not even the most elastic interpretations of either could encompass: the urban, foreign-stock working class, midwestern German-American Catholics, Socialists, entrepreneurs, and agrarian radicals, to name only the most cited. "Movements with tolerable progressive credentials," historian Lewis Gould has written, "have been found in the agrarian South, among machine politicians in the city, within technical and professional groups, the military, the arts, as well as in the more familiar environs of middle-class America."

Some historians openly questioned whether the movements delineated by the status revolution and organizational revolution interpretations were really "progressive" in any meaningful sense, whereas others argued that the progressive profiles upon which these explanations were based failed to differentiate avowed "progressives" from admitted "conservatives." They pointed out that virtually every significant issue of the era drove deep fissures within the ranks of both "movements," and that the label "progressive" was frequently affixed by both contemporaries and historians to mutually contradictory ideas, goals, and programs.

By 1970, at least one historian proclaimed that the Progressive movement never existed. In a provocative article entitled "An Obituary for the Progressive Movement," Peter Filene charged that historians were "struggling desperately" to fit their concept of a progressive movement "onto data that stubbornly spill over the edges of that concept," largely because "they are dealing with an aggregative group as if it were a collective group." Starting with the observation that many early twentieth-century Americans were "reformers" or "progressives," he asserted, historians have leapt to the conclusion that Americans, therefore, joined together in a "reform" or "progressive movement," thus "slurring over the intermediate question of whether the reformers themselves felt a common identity and acted as a collective body." A "diffuse progressive 'era' may have existed," he argued, "but a progressive 'movement' did not."

Although there were plenty of "progressives," Filene continued, they were of "many types"—intellectuals, businessmen, farmers, labor unionists, white-collar professionals, politicians, lower, middle, and upper class, southerners, easterners, westerners, urban, and rural—and their differences were at least as significant as their similarities in explaining the nation's response to its profound transformation during those crucial years. Contending that "the evidence points away from convenient synthesis and toward multiplicity," Filene concluded that "the progressive era seems to be characterized by shifting coalitions around different issues, with the specific nature of these coalitions varying on federal, state, and local levels, from region to region, and from the first to the second decade of the century."

Although a few historians continue to acknowledge a single Progressive movement, most historians have conceded that there were—at the very least—a variety of Progressive *movements*, sometimes working in harmony, frequently acting at cross-purposes, and often having little in common save rhetoric and style. In his introduction to the reissue of De Witt's *The Progressive Movement*, Arthur Mann warned that, in assessing the validity of the earlier interpretation, "the whole should not blind us to its parts." The Progressive movement, he asserted, "is an umbrella term, an historical shorthand, that covers a variety of reform thrusts fifty and more years ago in the churches, the universities, social work, publishing, journalism, racial relations, and so on almost indefinitely." It was "in short, a many-sided affair."

In a perceptive article entitled "In Search of Progressivism," written in the early 1980s, Daniel T. Rodgers chided those fellow historians seeking to salvage the Progressive movement and Progressivism by engaging in a "rage for bifurcation": social vs. structural, insurgents vs. modernizers, urban vs. rural, or western vs. eastern—but "Progressives" all. If these contradictory lists proved anything, he argued, it is that "those who called themselves progressives did not share a common creed or a string of common values, however ingeniously or vaguely defined." At most, Rodgers asserted, those who called themselves Progressives drew upon "three distinct clusters of ideas—three distinct social languages—to articulate their discontents and their social visions": the rhetoric of antimonopolism, an emphasis upon social bonds and the social nature of human beings, and a language of social efficiency. Although Rodgers doubted that most historians would "call off the search for that great overarching thing called Progressivism," he concluded that their real task was to concern themselves "less about the internal coherence of the progressive 'movement' than about the structures of politics, power, and ideas within which the era's welter of tongues and efforts and 'reforms' took place."

THE GREAT TRANSFORMATION

The first step in performing that task is to recognize that the Progressive Era was a time of breathtaking metamorphosis. Those people whose minds "boggle" at the magnitude and velocity of the changes being brought about by the twenty-first century's electronic revolution should have little difficulty identifying with those who experienced that earlier transformation firsthand. Those growing up in the early twentieth century were every bit as awe-stricken by the introduction of electricity, steam turbines, internal combustion engines, skyscrapers, electrified street railways, elevators, and motion pictures as we are by personal computers, the Internet, cell phones, Palm Pilots, DVDs, and similar electronic wizardry. Looking back over his life of sixty-plus years from the vantage point of the 1920s, novelist Hamlin Garland proclaimed that he had "seen more of change in certain directions than all the men from Julius Caesar to Abraham Lincoln." He had, he marveled, witnessed "the reaping hook develop into the combined reaper and thresher, the ox-team give way to the automobile, the telegraph to the radio, and the balloon to the flying machine." Television, he fearlessly prophesied, "is certain to arrive tomorrow."

At least as bewildering was the rapid and drastic reconfiguration of the socioeconomic order resulting largely from the widespread diffusion of these technological marvels. Deliberately or uncannily using the age's high-speed, complex, precision machinery as metaphor and model, an emerging elite of entrepreneurs, financiers, intellectuals, professionals, technicians, managers, bureaucrats, and politicians strove to recast most facets of existence into large-scale, compartmentalized, impersonal systems made up of discrete, hierarchically arranged components. People—like machine parts—became increasingly interchangeable and disposable. Those on the "cutting edge" of this metamorphosis strove to drive into as many people as possible the discipline and worldview of the modern, urban, industrial order, which prized predictability, docility, standardization, and an insatiable appetite for consumption of mass-produced goods and services. Nearly everything from sports to entertainment to recreation to politics was increasingly "commodified": packaged, advertised, and sold to a nation of consumers and spectators. In virtually every line of human endeavor, productivity, efficiency, and expertise became the operant values cherished by those determined upon what historians Alan I. Marcus and Howard P. Segal have dubbed "systematizing the fabric of American life."

Driving this remarkable transformation were the "neotechnic revolution" and the "new industrialism." Whereas the first two stages of the industrial revolution had relied upon water, wind, and steam to energize its machinery, the neotechnic phase employed electricity and the internal combustion engine as its power sources. Whereas people of the earlier two phases had built their machinery and structures primarily out of wood, brick, stone, and iron, the people of the neotechnic revolution increasingly utilized steel and other fabricated metals. Significantly lighter, stronger, and more flexible than iron, steel provided the essential metal for massive, high-speed, precision machinery, high-rise construction, and modern transportation and communication media.

Steelmaking evolved during the late nineteenth century out of continuous improvements in the superheating of ores, culminating in the discovery of the open hearth process that allowed large quantities of scrap metal to be mixed with relatively small amounts of molten pig iron to produce ten times as much steel—of significantly greater tensile strength—than that yielded by the earlier Bessemer process. Between 1895 and 1900, the amount of steel produced nearly tripled—to almost 4 million tons per year. Similar developments also revolutionized the brass, bronze, and copper industries. This technological sea change permitted the construction and operation of gigantic, fast, precise machines capable of being run almost constantly in order to produce a seemingly infinite supply of goods.

To take the fullest possible advantage of these innovations, manufacturers expanded and redesigned their factories for mass production, eventually developing the assembly-line method. To raise the necessary capital, they eagerly embraced the corporate form of organization, which also provided them with limited legal and financial liability while virtually guaranteeing the immortality of the enterprise. These highly capitalized, large-scale, complex organizations rapidly came to dominate the vast majority of industries in the United States and to transform them through innovative strategies and techniques in production, distribution, and marketing. They also drastically redefined the nature of work, the workplace, and the workforce, transferring "skill" from the worker to the machine and decision making from the shop floor to the central office. The need for "skilled" artisans and craftsmen declined precipitously, while the demand for "unskilled" and "semiskilled" machine operatives expanded, substantially increasing the number of women, children, and recent immigrants in the industrial workforce.

At the same time, as economist Richard T. Ely observed in 1889, "Every new invention, every economic improvement, in short, nearly all industrial progress centralizes the population in cities." Between 1890 and 1920, the total urban population of the United States grew from 22,106,000 to 54,158,000; the percent urban from 35.1 to 51.2; the number of urban places from 1,348 to 2,722; and the number of cities of over 100,000 population from 28 to 68. Urban population grew nearly twice as fast as total population during those three decades. While the electric trolley and the automobile enabled cities to expand ever outward, the electric elevator, structural steel, and reinforced concrete allowed them to soar steadily upward. Increasingly, the burgeoning urban masses found themselves segregated and stratified according to a complex formula of socioeconomic and ethnocultural factors, while the mobility and instability of city life accelerated at a dizzying pace. Demands for an expanded range of municipal services from all quarters of the city escalated, giving rise to continuous conflicts over how, by whom, where, and in what order these would be provided, delivered, and financed.

"NATIVES" AND NEWCOMERS

Although this urban population explosion was fueled significantly by the "natural increase" of births over deaths—due primarily to remarkable improvements in medicine and public health—and by the movement of native-born Americans off the farms in search of a better life, an increasing proportion was provided by immigration from Europe, Asia, and the American South. After surging during the 1880s and declining during most of the depression-ridden decade of the 1890s, European immigration hit an all-time high between 1897 and 1914, averaging nearly 800,000 per year. Moreover, the bulk of these new arrivals came from southern and eastern Europe—from Italy and the Mediterranean and from the multiethnic empires of Austria-Hungary, Russia, and Turkey. Their clothing, language, customs, and religions seemed increasingly strange and threatening to old-stock Americans—even to the descendants of the Irish, German, and Scandinavian immigrants whose arrival had evoked similar reactions just a few decades earlier.

Even more unsettling to white America was the relatively minor influx of Chinese and Japanese immigrants to the West Coast that gave rise to fears of an irresistible "yellow peril." Driven by the same economic imperatives that impelled native-born Americans, European and Asian immigrants flocked primarily to the cities and factories of the Northeast, Great Lakes, and Pacific Coast, where they strove to survive and prosper while preserving as much as possible of their Old World identities and cultures. Although more often the primary victims of industrialization and urbanization, they frequently served as handy scapegoats for those seeking to assign blame for the nation's problems. Perhaps even more disturbing to white Americans was the "Great Migration" of southern "Negroes" to northern cities. Whites increasingly responded with de facto segregation of housing, schools, and public accommodations, job and wage discrimination, and violent "race riots." By the onset of World War I, almost every Northern city of any size had its "black ghetto," where living and working conditions were generally the worst in town.

From a national perspective, the Gilded Age and Progressive Era combined constituted a period that prominent historian Rayford W. Logan has labeled the "nadir of American Racism." With the end of Reconstruction, Southern states moved quickly to negate the Fourteenth and Fifteenth Amendments, instituting legal segregation in public facilities and disfranchising

Residents view the devastation in Chicago following the race riots in the summer of 1919, a year that witnessed some of the bloodiest and most destructive riots in American history. Despite many reforms instituted during the Progressive Era, race relations hit a nadir as segregation became widespread and entrenched in the early 1900s. *(Brown Brothers)*

virtually the entire African-American electorate. At the same time, lynching and other forms of violence against "Negroes" reached an all-time high. Responding to pressure from organized labor and West Coast populations in general, Congress moved to exclude virtually all Asian immigration. In 1911, the U.S. Immigration Commission issued a forty-two-volume report that blamed the "inferior races" from southern and eastern Europe for most of the nation's problems and pronounced them incapable of assimilation into American society. After World War I, its findings provided much of the documentation for the highly biased and restrictive National Origins Quota System

that virtually ended immigration from southern and eastern Europe and Asia.

Meanwhile, the General Allotment Act of 1886 broke up what remained of tribal lands and mandated the forced acculturation of Native Americans, while the U.S. Army callously suppressed any remaining armed resistance. By 1910, most scholars regarded them as a "vanishing race," a judgment seemingly documented by the census returns. Similarly, American incursions into Hawaii, Puerto Rico, the Philippines, Samoa, Guam, China, and other parts of Asia and Latin America were justified largely by a belief in the "racial inferiority" of their inhabitants and in the responsibility of the United States to "civilize" and "Christianize" them. Perhaps most telling of all was the fact that "experts" generally agreed upon the notion of a racial hierarchy with "white people" at its apex, a worldview that justified everything from segregation to immigration restriction and from forced acculturation to eugenics—the "science" of human breeding.

Americans adapted as best they could to the ongoing changes of the early twentieth century. Largely by trial and error, growing numbers hit upon a three-stage strategy. The first stage was to band together with others in similar situations or of compatible persuasions—whether as producers, consumers, taxpayers, citizens, professionals, or members of a particular ethnocultural group. The second step was to attempt to intervene purposefully and effectively into the process through which the fruits of the new socioeconomic order were distributed. The third phase was to call upon government—at all levels—to intervene in that process on behalf of those who felt aggrieved or injured.

EARLY REFORM MOVEMENTS

Prior to the severe economic depression of 1893–1897, most of these reform movements fit into three broad strains, each of which operated in effective isolation from—and often at cross-purposes to—one another. The first of these was the patrician strain, composed of middle- and upper-middle-class native-born Americans, who were inclined to place the blame for most of society's problems on the weaknesses and excesses of the social orders above and below them. Accordingly, they usually favored limited government, fiscal retrenchment, the elimination of patronage and political corruption, and anti-vice crusades. Regularly derided as "goo-goos" or "Mugwumps" by their opponents, they tended to feel that most of the world's problems could be solved by replacing "bad" men with "good."

At the other end of the spectrum were a variety of movements firmly rooted in the urban, industrial working class, such as the Union Labor Party, the Socialist Labor Party, and the Knights of Labor, which placed the onus for social ills primarily on the capitalist system and on the rapacity of the people who managed it. While the more radical members of this cohort boldly espoused collective ownership of property and the establishment of a cooperative commonwealth, the majority demanded more realizable goals, such as higher wages, shorter hours, and better working and living conditions.

Forming yet a third strain of Gilded Age reform movements were several predominantly agrarian associations and organizations, such as the Grange, Alliances, and Populists. Identifying their enemies primarily as the railroads, banks, grain elevator operators, and their political allies, agrarians combined to maximize their own economic power, while petitioning government to regulate the rates and services of those whom they perceived to be their oppressors. Although the 1892 Omaha Platform of the People's Party proclaimed that "the interests of rural and civil labor are the same; their enemies are identical," efforts to forge a working alliance between the two usually ended in mutual frustration. Also standing in the way of effective cooperation among the three strains were deep-seated ethnocultural and religious issues, and the persistence of a mutual urban-rural animus. Cooperation across all of these fissures was rarely, if ever, possible.

Reinforcing those boundaries were an interlocking set of beliefs and values that historian Eric Goldman has called "the Steel Chain of Ideas." Among its strongest links were a series of supposedly absolute and unchangeable "natural laws" and "natural rights": the law of supply and demand, the iron law of wages, the law of diminishing returns, governmental laissez-faire, and the inviolate right to private property. Conveniently ignoring the fact that the growing dominance of large corporations was due primarily to their ability to manipulate those very same "natural laws" to their own advantage, the nation's elite adamantly denied that same privilege to labor unions, producer and consumer cooperatives, government agencies, and lawmakers. For others to intervene—either to regulate or tax corporations and their owners or to provide assistance to other segments of society—would allegedly only make matters worse for everyone by undermining the self-regulating "natural order" of society.

Another strong link in the chain was provided by the advocates of Social Darwinism, an analogous concept to the theory of evolution which argued that the prime law of society—like the prime law of nature—was "survival of the fittest." Only the "fittest" prospered, and their prosperity was all the proof necessary of their "fitness." By the same token, failure was proof positive of "unfitness." In society, as in nature, aiding the unfit or restricting the fit jeopardized the chances of survival for the entire species. Yet another link was provided by the proponents of the "Gospel of Wealth," a takeoff on the Calvinist doctrine of predestination. In John Calvin's view, the "elect" predetermined by God for salvation gave testimony to their status by their piety and purity, while those predestined to eternal damnation betrayed their status by leading dissolute and sinful lives. According to the Gospel of Wealth, God rewarded the elect with material wealth in this life and punished the preternaturally damned with poverty and deprivation. Thus the sanction of theology was added to that of science and philosophy in order to justify the status quo and to stigmatize any attempt to alter it.

THE REFORM MOVEMENTS MATURE

Dissolving the Steel Chain of Ideas—and building organizational strength sufficient to provide even minimal challenges to corporate domination—was a slow and laborious process during the last quarter of the nineteenth century. Its biggest boost was provided by the depression of the mid-1890s, whose severity and duration starkly revealed many of the societal dislocations and inequities that were easily ignored during more prosperous times. The depression transmitted those disabilities to large numbers of people who had previously thought themselves to be invulnerable. Problems easily rationalized during good times demanded much more thorough examination now that they touched a significant portion of mainstream society and—as more astute observers noted—those problems did not disappear with the return of general prosperity. Such traumatic experiences also made it easier for people of backgrounds previously antagonistic to one another to realize their shared situations and concerns as taxpayers, consumers, and citizens and to unite in "common cause" on many issues.

This "Crisis of the 1890s" also accelerated the growth of three intellectual movements antithetical to the principles of the Steel Chain of Ideas: the social sciences, the ascendancy of professionalism and expertise, and the Social Gospel. Awed by the achievements and prestige of natural and physical scientists, economists, sociologists, psychologists, historians, and political scientists sought to adapt empirical, inductive methods to the study of human behavior. Rejecting a priori, deductive approaches to the acquisition of knowledge, they stressed the importance of intensive case studies and of the scrutiny of meticulously gathered evidence before forming any conclusions or proposing any remedies. They generally decided that the nation's social problems were the result of self-interested decisions made by powerful individuals and organizations. Many became social and political activists determined to intervene into those same processes on behalf of what they considered to be the general welfare.

Closely intertwined with rise of the social sciences was the growing professionalization of medicine, law, engineering, journalism, social work, education, and a variety of other occupations. Each of these professions developed a systematized and specialized body of knowledge, detailed rules of procedure, a technical vocabulary or "jargon," schools to train aspirants, sanctions and enforcement machinery to discipline those who violated professional norms, journals to communicate among themselves, and an espirit de corps that bound together its members and set them off from "amateurs." Collectively, social scientists and professionals constituted a burgeoning cadre of "experts," who alone possessed the specialized knowledge and methodology needed to solve complex social problems and to function effectively, efficiently, and justly in the modern world. Balancing the need for "efficiency" and "expertise" against the desire for more popular participation and influence rapidly became a classic question of the times.

Attacking the status quo from a different—but equally influential—perspective were the proponents of the Social Gospel, also referred to as the "New Religion" or the "Institutional Church." Its apostles insisted that the road to salvation and spirituality lay not in personal piety and was not signified either by upright behavior or by material prosperity, but rather in how one treated those less fortunate. True Christianity manifested itself "in ethical movements, in benevolence, in expressions of genuine brotherhood." Although Social Gospelers frequently disagreed with social scientists and professionals on a variety of specific issues, they joined with them in challenging the notion that society was a closed system governed by rigid and unchangeable natural laws that justified "what is," rather than finding ways to move toward "what should" or "what could" be.

THE "NEW INTERVENTIONISM"

Energized by the trauma of a severe, protracted depression and by these new intellectual currents, a large number of fin de siècle Americans began to engage in what historian John W. Chambers has called the "new interventionism." At the outset, most of them practiced "associationalism" or "voluntarism—organized action by nonstatutory institutions" in the private sector—a strategy that Alexis de Tocqueville had long before identified as the peculiar genius of Americans. Labor abided by the "pure and simple trade unionism" dictum of Samuel Gompers, prefer-

With its doctrine of "pure and simple trade unionism," the American Federation of Labor came to dominate the American labor movement in the early twentieth century. Its founder, Samuel Gompers, seated in the center with the executive council, led the organization for almost forty years. Following Gompers's death in 1924, William Green, standing second from left, became president. *(Brown Brothers)*

ring collective bargaining, strike, and boycotts to lobbying for legislation. The National Consumers Union granted its seal of approval to businesses that met its standards and placed noncompliers on its "blacklist." The Women's Trade Union League engaged in organizing drives, joined picket lines, and gave aid and comfort to strikers. Idealistic young women and men, imbued with a mixture of social science and the Social Gospel and funded by private philanthropy, founded social settlements where they lived among and ministered to the urban underclasses. Business associations embraced volume buying to compete with the economies of scale enjoyed by big corporations, while

the Immigrants' Protective League established waiting rooms, provided interpreters, procured transportation, jobs, and lodging, helped locate relatives, and screened employment agencies, banks, and night schools. The Country Life Movement sought to make the agrarian environment more attractive, to bring the benefits of urbanism to farmers, and to stem the tide of "rural drain" to the cities.

Many organizations turned to political action—if for no other reason than that their perceived enemies were doing the same thing. Many came to realize that only government possessed the leverage necessary to achieving their ends. Organized labor found its methods ineffectual as long as unions were regarded as "conspiracies," "yellow dog" contracts and labor spies were legal, and strikes and boycotts could be easily halted by injunctions. Trade associations and consumer organizations found fair trade laws and regulatory legislation effective weapons against "big business."

The National Consumers League, among others, concluded that political action was a necessary supplement to its efforts at propaganda and negotiation. The Country Life Movement evolved into the Country Life Commission in 1908, while agrarian groups lobbied for the county agent system, agricultural extension, and government subsidies to agricultural education. The Women's Trade Association found that "political action, then, was required along with trade union activities to secure better conditions, a decent wage, a limit on hours and the right to bargain and organize without harassment." The Immigrants Protective League "urged that local and national governments take over tasks begun by private organizations." Settlement workers increasingly found that political action was necessary because "to keep aloof from it might be to lose the one opportunity of sharing the life of the neighborhood" and because "private beneficence is totally inadequate to deal with the vast numbers of the city's disinherited." The largely unorganized urban masses, caught in the grip of impersonal economic forces and under increasing pressure from nativists and restrictionists, urged their elected representatives on to greater efforts on their behalf.

Gradually, a number of fairly stable "coalitions" or "movements" developed around broad categories of issues: welfare legislation, the recognition of organized labor, taxation, business regulation, political restructuring, and cultural conflicts.

LAUNCHING THE WELFARE STATE

The launching of the welfare state in the form of workmen's compensation, old age pensions, factory codes, housing regulations, standards for child and female labor, and the like was primarily the work of three segments of society. The first was a sizable portion of the native middle class, particularly social scientists, clergymen, social workers, artists, and intellectuals. Their training and occupational experiences made them acutely aware of the existence of social evils. What percentage of the native middle class was so disposed—and precisely what differentiated them from the rest of that class—are still subjects for research. These reformers formed the social justice organizations, sought to educate other com-

fortable Americans to the need for public action, drafted legislation, and lobbied for its passage. Many became advisers to influential politicians or served on newly created welfare agencies.

Joining them often was organized labor, although the leaders were not all of one mind about welfare legislation either. Samuel Gompers and many of his associates feared government intervention and preferred collective bargaining to establish standards of labor, feeling that the legal minimums would ipso facto become the going rates. They were not the entire labor movement, however, and the American Federation of Labor (AFL) was a federation. State and local affiliates, especially those in the most populous states, and non-AFL unions generally took a more favorable attitude, exerting pressure on the national organization to follow suit. So, too, did the growing number of Socialists and such radical labor groups as the Industrial Workers of the World. By 1915 there was a debate on the floor of the national AFL convention between the followers of Gompers and those of William Green of Ohio, who, as a state senator, had sponsored a variety of welfare measures. As a rule, organized labor favored government programs for women, children, and the unorganized, while preferring that unions rely primarily on collective bargaining. Pragmatically, unions supported government intervention where they were weak and opposed it where they were strong.

The third, and numerically largest, group in the pro-welfare coalition was the great mass of urban industrial workers who stood to benefit most by ameliorative legislation. Many had come from a European tradition where government, guilds, churches, and landlords had assumed some responsibility for the welfare of the less fortunate. Foreign-language newspapers, especially in the Far West, often bordered on socialism in their outlook. Most immigrants had also experienced firsthand the horrors of the sweatshop and the tenement and had survived them largely through the ministrations of priests, politicians, social workers, and fraternal societies.

"The evidence suggests," as Herbert Gutman pointed out, "that awareness of poverty did not await its discovery by sensitive members of the middle and upper classes." Unorganized economically, urban immigrants possessed considerable political leverage because political machines depended upon them for support. The most important steps in the adoption of welfare legislation generally came in such key industrial states as New York, New Jersey, Ohio, Illinois, and Massachusetts at a time when the representatives

Although the Knights of Labor had all but vanished by the early 1900s, workers' ideals and pride in their trade carried over into the Progressive Era. Note the tools held by these carpenters. *(Catholic University of America)*

of urban political machines were clearly in charge. In many cases, the more sophisticated elements in the business community sought to blunt the impact of welfare legislation by designing their own measures and forcing a compromise. The vast majority of small businesses, however, remained adamantly opposed. The interaction of these groups on behalf of welfare legislation fully justifies the conclusion of June Axinn and Herman Levin that "the reform activities of the Progressive Era were spearheaded by many groups, some working cooperatively as particular issues warranted cooperation, some working for individual aggrandizement, some working altruistically for the larger society."

ESTABLISHING THE LABOR MOVEMENT

The same three groups generally shared the most earnest desire for the recognition of organized labor, although the middle-class contingent was significantly smaller. Welfare measures involved a kind of paternalistic concern for the less fortunate; unions opened

the possibility that the lower classes could achieve enough power to plot their own destiny. Still, many native middle-class reformers did battle for labor in the difficult days of its infancy. Social worker Graham Taylor judged unions "the most practical bond of brotherhood next to the Christian Church," while Jane Addams insisted that unions were "the first real lesson of self-government—for the union alone has appealed to their necessities." Settlement workers usually hired only union labor, provided strikers with food and shelter, organized mass support for strikers, and often joined picket lines themselves. "At Hull-House," Alice Hamilton confessed, "one got into the labor movement as a matter of course, without realizing how or when." All factions of labor were, by definition, in favor of union recognition.

The urban political machines and their predominantly working-class constituencies were again the most politically effective segment of the pro-labor coalition. Most urban machine spokesmen had working-class backgrounds themselves and many union officials ran for the city council and state legislature with organization backing. Urban representatives who were attorneys often got their start as labor lawyers. The leadership and membership of the nation's unions were largely drawn from the same ethnic stocks as were the representatives and constituents of the political machine. By 1911, the New York Federation of Labor was heading its honor roll with Tammany Hall politicians, while Boston's ward bosses agreed that "any hint from organized labor was enough to cause an order requiring action." Together with sympathetic members of the old-stock middle class, machine politicians and organized labor sought to outlaw blacklists and yellow dog contracts, to provide for jury trials for violation of injunctions, to require companies to admit whether they were being struck when advertising for workers, to label convict-made goods, to use the union label in government-issued products, and, above all, to establish labor's right to organize, bargain collectively, and strike.

Business was generally opposed to such notions and resisted them ferociously, although the most sophisticated financial capitalists, recognizing that strikes interrupted profits, preferred cooptation to confrontation. The National Civic Federation generally had a more favorable attitude toward unionization, as opposed to the National Association of Manufacturers, which had greater support among businessmen. Farmers, as employers of labor, usually shared corporate antagonism toward labor organization.

A REVOLUTION IN TAXATION

Tax reform alignments depended largely upon the specifics of each proposal. Generally speaking, all social groups sought to throw the major share of the burden onto someone else. There was, however, a fairly general consensus that the wealthy holders of stocks and bonds were not paying their fair share because the existing structure relied upon real estate and excise taxes and customs duties. Revelations that the rich avoided taxes, coupled with the rising cost of living and increased governmental expenditures, aroused most segments of society to demand tariff revision and income and inheritance taxes.

Under the general slogan of taxes based on "the ability to pay," many diverse groups agreed on the broad outlines of "reform," while differing on the specifics. The urban middle class paid most of the property tax, consumed the lion's share of goods, and demanded better public services. They had the expertise and the erudition to popularize the need for change through tax reform associations. Farm spokesmen saw great advantages in shifting the burden from tangible property to intangible. The urban working class was also eager for better social services and happy to tax the rich. Professional politicians were anxious to supplement their extralegal sources of revenue—kickbacks, protection money, and assessment of payrollers—with more lucrative and predictable means. "The parties' assessment of jobholders and political candidates, the political levies against corporations and certain criminal businesses on the basis of their ability to pay," C.K. Yearley has concluded, "in effect, have been formally incorporated into state income taxes or into a variety of special taxes."

On the state level, tax struggles often took on an urban-rural cast, as the cities sought to stop the flow of money to the state capitol and increase their ability to tap their own wealth. On the national level, southerners and westerners were motivated by sectional feelings against the Northeast, even though the southerners and westerners wanted a "tariff for revenue only" and the Northeast a more equitable system of protection. The opposition to these changes was centered primarily in the 3 percent of upper income receivers who benefited by continuation of the existing tax structure; their ability to postpone and emasculate the new one is evidence of their political influence. The rich were often successful in obfuscating the issues by appeals to sectionalism and states' rights, by stigmatizing tax reformers as radicals, and by introducing such divisive issues as federal taxation of state and municipal bonds. Nearly every influential business journal in the nation was against the federal income tax, and business spokesmen who appeared before Congress were almost unanimous in their denunciation of both the tax and the Underwood-Simmons tariff, which provided for the reinstitution of a federal income tax.

TRUST-BUSTING OR BUSINESS REGULATION?

The regulation of business is much more difficult to unscramble. Virtually every politically active group in the nation favored some form of regulation. Agrarian demands even antedated the Grangers and the Populists, while small-town merchants and bankers had an equally important stake in controlling the activities of those on whom they were dependent for transportation, financing, and processing. The urban middle class also favored regulation as part of its demand for adequate transportation and communication facilities, as well as its desire to break up the graft-ridden connection between franchise holders and political machines. The foreign-stock working class in the nation's largest cities also pressed for better products and services at lower rates. Even big business developed a yen for regulation, especially by the federal government, in order to rationalize the system, and to eliminate uncertainty, competition, and the threat of state regulation.

The federal regulatory legislation of the Woodrow Wilson years may have been heavily influenced by those views, but pressures from other segments of the economy produced important compromises. State and local regulatory reformers could hardly have desired to nationalize markets. All of these groups disagreed over whether public ownership, regulation, or trust-busting was the best solution, as well as over specific provisions. The importance of any one social segment to the regulatory coalition varied over time and place. Regulatory laws resulted from the interaction of several or all of these groups, with business often diluting the provisions and "capturing" whatever commissions were established, such as the Interstate Commerce and Federal Trade Commissions.

NEW POLITICAL DIRECTIONS

Patterns of political reform coalitions are particularly difficult to discern because the measures being proposed did not all go in the same direction. Moreover, virtually everyone employed such reforms as "instruments of political warfare," hoping that new devices would help outmaneuver opponents. Many proposals designed to free cities from the domination of rural legislators provoked a fairly clear split between the metropolis and the countryside, but small-town business alliances often operated to defend the political status quo. These same social and business elites, joined by a large portion of the native middle class, consistently sponsored "structural reforms"—civil service, at-large and nonpartisan elections, city manager and commission forms of government—which were intended to vest political power in experts free from popular control.

Although couched in democratic rhetoric, these proposals sought to centralize the method of decision making, leaving out "undesirable elements" of the population. The rosters of the Civic Clubs, Voters Leagues, and Good Government Associations read like the city's social and financial registers. Their adherents generally believed that "a city is a business corporation," and aimed for a government that "gives us our money's worth." Referenda on structural re-

form issues almost always resulted in heavy support in upper-class areas and overwhelming opposition in working-class districts, with the middle-class neighborhoods holding the balance. The enactment of structural reforms usually altered the makeup of city councils, replacing lower- and lower middle-class aldermen with professionals and businessmen. State-wide, such measures generally received the added support of rural and small-town lawmakers.

Historians find it difficult to believe that the same groups that sponsored these structural measures could also have favored the period's celebrated democratic reforms, such as direct legislation, primaries, direct election of senators, reapportionment, and woman suffrage. Many elitists favored woman suffrage in order to enfranchise upper- and middle-class native white women as a further bulwark against lower-class power, but many of the most prominent opponents of woman suffrage feared the threat of working-class women. Many foreign-stock people were actively hostile toward woman suffrage on cultural grounds, but a large portion changed their position in time to support the Nineteenth Amendment, due partly to a moderation of position by the suffragists.

The other democratic reforms split the middle class into those who trusted in the ultimate good judgment of the lower classes—or in their own ability to channel it—and those who did not. The urban working class had a clear self-interest in joining this coalition, one that their political mentors were at first slow to recognize but then strongly advanced. Direct legislation and primaries required the gathering of signatures, and the urban machines were better equipped than anyone to do that. Pressed by precinct and block captains, their constituents could be turned out in greater numbers at primaries than could rural or independent voters. Direct election of senators enhanced the chance of electing urban candidates. Organized labor also generally supported democratic reform, calculating that it would augment the working-class voice in government. In the South, small farmer groups, such as the National Farmers Union, backed certain democratic reforms as a device against Bourbon rule but opposed others out of dislike of the city.

CULTURAL CONFLICTS

The alignment on cultural issues was primarily an ethnoreligious one. Protestant Americans, whether in the city or the countryside, were the main advocates of Prohibition, Sunday blue laws, immigration restriction, and drives against gambling and prostitution. Protestantism had freed the slaves and animated the Social Gospel, but it contained a darker side. Faced with the challenge of industrialization, urbanization, and immigration, many native Protestant Americans responded with campaigns to improve individual morality rather than confront broader social issues. For them the saloon, the gambler, the prostitute, and the foreigner replaced the sweatshop, the tenement, the trust, and the political machine as symbols of evil. It was that same outlook that caused Madison Grant to see in the new immigrant and the black man a common threat to Anglo-Saxon hegemony, causing many northerners to sympathize with the South's solutions of segregation and disfranchisement. Prohibition was largely an anti-immigrant movement in the North and an anti-Negro one in the South. In Oklahoma and the West, it was often aimed at the "red man" as well. Immigration restriction and forced Americanization were sponsored by a coalition of social workers, educators, superpatriots, and businessmen.

The coalitions that consistently opposed these efforts were a combination of the most traditional and liberal elements in society. The newer immigrant stocks, working with urban machine politicians, formed the largest segment of the coalition; their newspapers were as one in their denunciations of threats to personal liberty. Southern blacks were disfranchised first—then segregated and "reformed," so that they were able to offer little or no resistance. Many business leaders stood with the ethnic minorities on these issues because they saw the drives at liquor, gambling, and prostitution as illegal confiscations of property, and viewed free immigration as a source of cheap labor. Other businessmen, however, were enamored of Prohibition on the grounds of industrial efficiency and of immigration restriction when there was a surplus of unskilled labor. At the other end of the political spectrum were those academics and professionals whom education and experience had turned into hedonists or cultural liberals, uprooting them from the moralistic moorings of their youth. Although the national AFL did not openly condemn Prohibition until 1919, only 12 of its 186 city labor councils, 5 of its 46 state federations and 19 of its 111 craft unions ever endorsed the idea.

The evidence of referenda and legislative roll calls on cultural issues during the Progressive Era clearly mirrored these cultural divisions. In nearly all cases, they featured the upper and lower classes of the cities and some cultural liberals against the urban middle class and the rural populace. In most cases, these align-

ments cut across the socioeconomic and political reform coalitions that had been building and were a major factor in curtailing their effectiveness. A 1911 Prohibition vote in the California Senate split the normal reform coalition asunder, throwing many urban–labor–immigrant reformers into alliance with acknowledged pro-business conservatives. The coalitions that defeated an anti-saloon ordinance in Boston the same year consisted of the Back Bay and the Irish, Italian, Jewish, and black wards, predominating over the middle-class sections of the city. In a Chicago referendum on Prohibition, nearly all of the city's immigrant groups voted more than 80 percent against the measure, with only native Protestants, Swedes, and some blacks showing any real support. The only congressmen willing to stand against the final votes on Prohibition and the literacy test for immigrants were those with heavily new-stock constituencies.

CONSTRUCTING REFORM AGENDAS

It was out of their position in these various coalitions that individuals and organizations developed their reform agendas. Many eventually evolved formal programs, combining stands on several of these issues, while others simply responded to questions as they arose, leaving still others to discern meaningful patterns. Those who espoused structural political reform as a defense against the urban masses often coupled that with a proclivity for legislated cultural conformity, strongly opposed organized labor, and were lukewarm, at best, toward welfare measures. Those for whom welfare measures were the most pressing order of business often favored the recognition of labor and democratic political proposals, while fiercely opposing cultural uplift. The possible combinations and permutations were numerous; the likelihood of deviation from the general position because of the peculiarities of a single proposal clearly increased the complexity. Measuring individual reformers and groups against their usual positions on the broad categories discussed above, however, holds out the best possibility for determining what kind of "progressive" they were and what implications that term really had.

Individual politicians, contending factions, and political parties were thus faced with the task of constructing programs that appealed to members of several reform coalitions. Political platforms are notorious for being all things to all men, but there are certain reasonable limits. Even in the extravagant rhetoric of reform that characterized the day, it was difficult to appeal consistently to the proponents of both structural and democratic political change, to both the advocates and opponents of legislated conformity, to both the supporters and the antagonists of labor and welfare measures.

The successful candidate, faction, or party in any given locale had to develop a platform with enough internal consistency to appeal to the membership of several compatible reform coalitions. This orientation naturally served the needs of certain socioeconomic, ethnoreligious, and geographic segments better than others and allowed these groups, temporarily at least, to impose their worldview on the rest of society. Their very success, however, generally aroused those with different outlooks who intensified their political activity and constructed a competing coalition and program. Each party started with a hard core of voters committed to it through habit and ethnoreligious or sectional tradition; broadening its constituency by appealing to issue-oriented independents or party switchers ran the risk of alienating a segment of original partisans.

MUNICIPAL REFORM MOVEMENTS

Reformers entered the political arena on the municipal level during the 1870s; their descendants were still laboring there forty years later. Their numbers were legion; their backgrounds, motives, goals, programs, and results myriad—and frequently contradictory. Many pursued multiple avenues of reform and appealed to a variety of constituencies. Some reformers were elected officials, and others were appointed to administrative posts, but the majority exercised influence through organized lobbying and electioneering efforts.

A large number of affluent, respectable reformers sought to solve urban problems by restructuring municipal government through the adoption of a strong mayor–weak council, commission, and city manager forms. Many of the same people also backed significant alterations in the electoral system through at-large, nonpartisan elections held at a different time from state and national contests, the short and secret ballots, tighter voter registration requirements, and the disfranchisement of "ignorant" and "corrupt" lower-class voters. They and other like-minded people often spearheaded anti-vice crusades designed to eliminate or control gambling, drinking, prostitution, pornography, motion pictures, stage productions, professional athletics, and other forms of "lewd" entertainment and recreation. A growing number of municipal reformers embraced the burgeoning city planning and "city beautiful" movements, and sought to suppress omnipresent water, air, and noise pollu-

tion. Others concentrated on housing regulation, stringent public health measures, improved public education, playgrounds and other child-care innovations, and more effective police and fire protection. Nearly every city of any size during the period was energized by drives to regulate the service and rates of gas, electricity, water, transit, and other "public utilities." Reformers in a number of cities even seriously pushed for the municipal ownership of various utilities.

Not surprisingly, the results of more than four decades of agitation for municipal reform were inconsistent. Even where "reformers" were apparently successful, these triumphs were often compromised significantly by the give and take of the political process, the resiliency of their opponents, and the seemingly inevitable erosion of reformist zeal on the part of the general populace. Much of the reason for the mottled outcome of municipal reform during the era, however, lay with the fact that cities were literally "creatures of the state." Their ability to deal constructively with their own affairs was severely limited by charters issued by legislatures that were all too frequently dominated by indifferent or hostile rural lawmakers, in collaboration with the state's most powerful business interests. Restrictions on the city's taxing, borrowing, and regulatory authority severely curtailed reformist efforts.

By the last decade of the nineteenth century, municipal reformers increasingly recognized the need to involve themselves in state-level politics and to lobby state government for various forms of redress. Their insurgency coincided with similar movements by agrarian activists; the combination led to an exponential increase of demands on state governments and escalating pressures to revamp their structures and operations. As a result, the first two decades of the new century were characterized by an unprecedented flurry of reformist activity, with New York, New Jersey, Wisconsin, Minnesota, Kansas, North Carolina, Washington, Oregon, and California gaining reputations as Progressive models and "laboratories of democracy." Except for the brief disruption by the Progressive Party in 1912—and for the activities of Socialist lawmakers in Wisconsin and a few other commonwealths—statewide battles between "Progressives" and their opponents were waged within the confines of the existing two-party system.

STATES AS "LABORATORIES OF REFORM"

The most salient outcome of statewide Progressive reform was the tremendous expansion in the size, complexity, scope, and cost of state government. Almost equally significant and widespread was the shift in emphasis from the "distribution" or "allocation" of divisible benefits to specific constituencies to more generalized functions of administration, regulation, and planning—and the consequent transfer of power from the legislative to the executive branch. In almost every state, government assumed a far greater share of responsibility for education, the conservation of natural resources, agriculture, the regulation of public utilities and other businesses, and the licensing of professionals, to name only the most obvious.

Many state governments also began to assume some responsibility for the welfare of some of their citizens by enacting workmen's compensation, industrial health and safety laws, housing codes, public health measures, mothers' pensions, wages and hours legislation, and standards for child and female labor. Although most of these efforts were inadequate to the need, they did establish important precedents that would be built upon at a later date. Many states also pioneered a "revolution in taxation" by shifting at least some of the burden from real estate and excise levies to income and inheritance taxes, in an effort both to provide revenue adequate to their expanded size and functions and to promote "tax equity." A large number also experimented with "drastic" changes in their political systems by adopting such innovations as woman suffrage, direct primaries, the popular election of United States senators, the Australian ballot, nonpartisan local elections, and initiative, referendum, and recall.

While "Progressives" almost universally proclaimed the democratizing inclination of such reforms, some saw them as devices for shifting political power upward—from the "ignorant," "corrupt" lower classes to more affluent, respectable citizens. Some "reformers"—principally, though not exclusively, in southern states—openly promoted the disfranchisement of African Americans, immigrants, and other "undesirables" through literacy tests, poll taxes, and restrictive voter registration laws. Whether or not they were intentionally designed to do so, the net result of the drive to make the political system more inclusive, accessible, and responsive was a precipitate drop in voter participation—especially among the lower social orders—that has continued down to the present day.

THE NATIONAL ARENA

In most states, the Progressive Era reached its zenith between 1910 and 1914, about the same time that it peaked on the national level. Historians have traditionally begun discussions of the Progressive Era there with the elevation of Theodore Roosevelt to the presidency in 1901. Actually, Roosevelt dabbled in Progressive politics at all three levels of government, having served as police commissioner and reform mayoral candidate in New York City and as governor of New York State before being elected vice president in 1900. As president, he railed at the "malefactors of great wealth," promised a "square deal," cultivated his image as a "trust-buster," mandated arbitration in labor disputes, strengthened the Interstate Commerce Commission, helped enact the Pure Food and Drug Act, and set aside millions of acres of federal land for national parks.

Although he gave rhetorical support to tariff reduction, child labor legislation, and federal income and inheritance taxes, Roosevelt failed to follow through. Probably his greatest contribution to the cause of Progressive reform was his use of the presidency as a "bully pulpit" from which to make respectable measures formerly associated with Socialists, Populists, and other "radicals." As Roosevelt himself told a group of business leaders, his aim was to help "radicalism prosper under conservative leadership," so that "the progressive people will not part company with the bulk of the moderates."

Eschewing certain reelection in 1908, Roosevelt engineered the nomination of his friend William Howard Taft, who swept to an easy victory in the presidential race. More fundamentally conservative than Roosevelt—and far less politically astute—Taft had the misfortune of taking office at the precise moment when the long-simmering conflict between Progressive and "stalwart" Republicans was about to erupt into open warfare. The former, in the person of midwestern and western "Insurgents," challenged the eastern, business-oriented "Standpatters" on tariff reform, the enactment of an income tax, conservation of natural resources, and curtailing the power of the Speaker of the House of Representatives. When Taft sided with his party's eastern establishment on all of those issues, the Insurgents, led by Senator Robert M. La Follette Sr. of Wisconsin, formed the National Progressive Republican League in 1911, with an eye toward nominating a Progressive Republican for president the following year. With Taft clearly vulnerable and Roosevelt thoroughly disgusted with the performance of his hand-picked successor, the stage was set for Roosevelt to challenge for his party's nomination. When he failed to achieve that goal at the Republican Convention, Roosevelt bolted and orga-

As both governor and senator, Robert M. La Follette of Wisconsin advocated progressive reforms, such as primary elections, railroad regulation, and direct election of senators. Although he failed to get the Progressive Party's nomination for president in 1912, he won it in 1924 and captured almost 5 million votes. *(Images of American Political History)*

nized the Progressive Party, with himself as its presidential candidate. As one stalwart cynic observed, the only question left to be answered for the Republicans was "which corpse gets the most flowers."

The 1912 election was one of the most titanic in American history, and one in which the three "Progressive" candidates—Roosevelt, Democrat Woodrow Wilson, and Socialist Eugene Debs—garnered 77 percent of the popular vote and 523 out of a possible 531 electoral votes. The election supposedly turned primarily on the choice between two brands of Progressivism—Roosevelt's New Nationalism and Wilson's New Freedom—although the differences proved to be more rhetorical than substantive. The former president of Princeton University who had cultivated a reputation for Progressive reform as governor of New Jersey, Wilson was blessed—thanks to the Progressive–Republican split—with working majorities in both houses of Congress.

Directing the Democratic caucus with a firm hand, the first Wilson administration enacted an impressive array of "Progressive" legislation, including the Federal Reserve Act, the Federal Trade Commission, a federal income tax law, significant tariff reduction, the Federal Farm Loan Act, the Clayton Anti-Trust Act, the Keating-Owen Child Labor Act, the La Follette Seamen's Act, and the Adamson Act for railroad workers. Although few realized it at the time, Wilson's narrow reelection victory in 1916 proved to be the denouement of the Progressive Era nationally. Although his second administration produced the Eighteenth and Nineteenth Amendments, the energy that had sustained reformist efforts for over a quarter century was largely dissipated or displaced. In an almost complete reversal from the election of 1912, conservative Republican candidate Warren G. Harding—who promised to return the country to "normalcy"—received over 60 percent of the popular vote and three-fourths of the electoral vote.

DISINTEGRATION AND DECLINE

It was the fragile and transitory nature of coalition politics and the difficulty of sustaining a cooperative mood among different social groups that ultimately brought an end to the Progressive Era. Although they staked out broad areas of agreement and frequently cooperated on concrete reforms, any more permanent alliance between the old-stock, Protestant middle class and the new-stock, non-Protestant lower classes was foreclosed by a fatal inner tension. Distrust arose fundamentally because the middle-class reformers were engaged in uplifting others while the lower classes were concerned with self-improvement. The middle class held up its values and lifestyles as models to be emulated, while the lower classes wished to be highly selective about what they adopted. The exact date of the rupture varied from place to place; in several states, reformist momentum was spent as early as 1914.

Elsewhere, disintegration was triggered by World War I. The issue of American participation in the war drove deep fissures into the ranks of those who had cooperated on other issues. Even among middle-class social reformers there were some who continued to protest the war, while others gave their enthusiastic support. The antiwar Germans, Irish, and Scandinavians clashed sharply with the pro-war Poles, Czechs, and Slavs. Moreover, Wilson made the fatal, though understandable, mistake of couching the war in the rhetoric of Progressivism. When it failed to produce a safer or more just world, the result cast doubt upon domestic reform as well. "By pinning America's role in the war so exclusively to high moral considerations and to altruism and self-sacrifice," Richard Hofstadter insisted, "by linking the foreign crusade as intimately as possible to the Progressive values and the Progressive language, he was unintentionally insuring that the reaction against Progressivism and moral idealism would be as intense as it was."

The greatest disillusionment came among the professionals and intellectuals who shared Wilson's aspirations. Shocked by the horrors of war and the failures of the peace conference, many of them took refuge in elitism and campaigns for personal betterment. For many, the war unleashed an irrational fear of radicalism and social protest. The atmosphere that had made the muckrakers' attacks seem so exhilarating disappeared under the watchful eye of the Committee on Public Information and the Red Scare. The Wilson administration's shoddy record on civil liberties disaffected the major libertarian organizations, further disintegrating the coalition that had upheld the New Freedom. It also alienated untold numbers of ethnic minorities who had traditionally supported the Democratic Party, laying the groundwork for the electoral disasters of 1920 and 1924.

More comfortable Americans also developed a growing fear of the potential economic and political power of the urban working class. Even those middle-class reformers who had backed labor and welfare measures earlier harbored doubts about the goals of the labor movement. Settlement workers wanted social justice for the working class, but not at the expense of the violence and disturbance of the peace that often accompanied strikes. "It is only occasionally that I get a glimpse of the chivalry of labor," Jane Addams remarked to a friend; "so much of the time it seems so sordid."

The rash of strikes that followed the end of the war frightened all but the most diehard middle-class supporters of unions. "Everywhere," a contemporary student of the Wilson administration's labor policies noted in 1920, "labor representatives are presenting new and greater demands and many defenders of the status quo fear the unleashing of disintegrating forces." The government's National Industrial Conference to promote business–labor cooperation in 1919 broke up in mutual animosity over compulsory arbitration, the prohibition of strikes, and other issues. Agrarian reformers grew similarly fearful, with some charging that "farmers are suffering more now from the leaders of labor than from the leaders of industry or finance." Many middle-class reformers also grew uneasy as the lower classes pressed for more sweep-

ing welfare measures, such as health and unemployment insurance.

Mostly, though, coalition politics perished on the shoals of cultural reform. As urban and rural old-stock Protestants devoted more attention to legislated morality, the gap between them and the new-stock working class grew greater. The reform coalitions eventually conceded to the issues of Prohibition, immigration restriction, and Sunday blue laws: The National Conference of Social Work endorsed Prohibition by 1917, hailing it as the ultimate solution to poverty, prostitution, crime, and industrial inefficiency. When Congress passed the literacy test over Wilson's veto in 1917, not even the Immigrants' Protective League raised much protest. The foreign-stock working class was forced into a necessary alliance with business-oriented conservatives who opposed Prohibition and immigration restriction on economic grounds. Prohibition helped destroy previously effective reform coalitions in Kansas, California, and Colorado, while immigration restriction and Americanization became increasingly attractive to many native middle-class reformers. Many made the journey from reformers to militant Americanizers and spokesmen for the "welfare capitalism." Some new-stock reformers became so distrustful of government intervention into their lives that they even temporarily lost their enthusiasm for welfare measures and opposed the national child labor amendment and federal aid to education. These cultural issues destroyed the socioeconomic and political coalitions that had been so carefully constructed in earlier years.

THE LEGACY OF PROGRESSIVE REFORM MOVEMENTS

The Progressive Era was a seminal period in its attempts to cope with the implications of living in an urban, industrial, multicultural society. Would-be reformers from many walks of life advanced solutions to the nation's problems that—first and foremost—served the particularistic needs of the members of that movement. Although many sought redress through private action, nearly all eventually turned to political action. This widespread consensus that the state should actively promote social justice clearly marked the period off from earlier ones and established a precedent for future reformers. Under the pressures of political necessity, reform movements of all sorts were forced to compromise, coalesce, and cooperate to achieve positive legislative results. By this process they established a framework in which profound social change in a pluralistic society could be assimilated.

The very nature of that process has undoubtedly inhibited the nation's response to modernization down to the present day, by placing a premium on compromise, conciliation, and consensus. It has necessitated an emphasis on "incremental adjustments" rather than sweeping or comprehensive change, generating politicians "who learn to deal gently with opponents, who struggle endlessly in building and holding coalitions together, who doubt the possibilities of great change, who seek compromises." Whether a nation as large and diverse as the United States could have responded to the massive social transformations of the late nineteenth century in any more radical manner without major alterations in its political system is certainly open to serious question. Whether any more fundamental alterations were possible in a society so socially and culturally fragmented—lacking a genuine national identity and culture—is even more questionable. It is that process—rather than any specific reform measures—that constitutes the most important legacy of the Progressive Era.

John D. Buenker

BIBLIOGRAPHY

Axinn, June, and Herman Levin. *Social Welfare: A History of the American Response to Need.* New York: Dodd, Mead, 1975.

Buenker, John D. "The Progressive Era: A Search for a Synthesis," *Mid-America* 51 (1959): 175–193.

Buenker, John D., John C. Burnham, and Robert M. Crunden. *Progressivism.* Boston: Schenkman, 1977.

Chambers, John W. *The Tyranny of Change: America in the Progressive Era, 1890–1920.* New Brunswick, NJ: Rutgers University Press, 2002.

Cohen, Nancy. *The Reconstruction of American Liberalism, 1865–1914.* Chapel Hill: University of North Carolina Press, 2002.

Crunden, Robert M. *Ministers of Reform: The Progressives' Achievements in American Civilization 1889–1920.* New York: Macmillan, 1882.

Danbom, David. *The World of Hope: Progressives and the Struggle for an Ethical Political Life.* Philadelphia: Temple University Press, 1987.

Dawley, Alan. *Struggles for Justice: Social Responsibility and the Liberal State.* Cambridge, MA: Harvard University Press, 1991.

De Witt, Benjamin Parke. The *Progressive Movement: A Non-Partisan, Comprehensive Discussion of Current Tendencies in American Politics.* New York: Macmillan, 1915.

————. *The Progressive Movement.* Seattle: University of Washington Press, 1968.

Diner, Steven J. *A Very Different Age: Americans of the Progressive Era.* New York: Hill and Wang, 1998.

Ely, Richard T. "The Needs of the City: An Address Delivered Before the Boston Conference of Evangelical Alliance." December 4, 1889.

Filene, Peter. "An Obituary for the Progressive Movement." *American Quarterly* 22 (1970): 20–34.

Garland, Hamlin. *Backtrailers from the Middle Border.* New York: Macmillan, 1928.

Goldman, Eric. *Rendezvous with Destiny: A History of Modern American Reform.* New York: Alfred A. Knopf, 1952.

Gould, Lewis. *The Progressive Era.* Syracuse, NY: Syracuse University Press, 1974.

Grant, Madison. *The Passing of the Great Race.* New York: Scribner's, 1918.

Gutman, Herbert, and Gregory S. Kealy, eds. *Many Pasts: Readings in American Social History.* Englewood Cliffs, NJ: Prentice Hall, 1973.

Hays, Samuel P. *Response to Industrialism, 1885–1914.* Chicago: University of Chicago Press, 1957.

Hofstadter, Richard. *The Age of Reform: From Bryan to F.D.R.* New York: Alfred A. Knopf, 1956.

Klein, Maury. *The Flowering of the Third America: The Making of an Organizational Society, 1850–1920.* Chicago: Ivan R. Dees, 1993.

Link, Arthur S., and Richard L. McCormick. *Progressivism.* Arlington Heights, IL: Harlan Davidson, 1983.

Logan, Rayford W. *The Betrayal of the Negro, from Rutherford B. Hayes to Woodrow Wilson.* New York: Collier Books, 1965.

Marcus, Alan I., and Howard P. Segal. *Technology in America: A Brief History.* San Diego: Wadsworth, 1989.

Mowry, George E. *The Era of Theodore Roosevelt and the Birth of Modern America.* New York: Harper & Row, 1959.

Painter, Nell Irvin. *Standing at Armageddon: The United States, 1877–1919.* New York: W.W. Norton, 1987.

Rodgers, Daniel T. "In Search of Progressivism." In *The Promise of American History: Progress and Prospects,* ed. Stanley I. Kutler and Stanely N. Katz, 113–132. Baltimore, MD: Johns Hopkins University Press, 1982.

Rodgers, Daniel T. *Atlantic Crossings: Social Politics in a Progressive Age.* Cambridge, MA: Belknap Press of Harvard University Press, 1998.

Thelen, David P. *The New Citizenship: Origins of Progressivism in Wisconsin, 1885–1900.* Columbia: University of Missouri Press, 1972.

Wiebe, Robert H. *The Search for Order, 1877–1920.* New York: Hill and Wang, 1995.

Yearley, C.K. *The Money Machines: The Breakdown and Reform of Governmental and Party Finance in the North, 1860–1920.* Albany: State University of New York Press, 1970.

EUGENICS MOVEMENT

The American eugenics movement, along with its counterparts in European as well as Asian nations, sought to engineer a "better" population through the science of human heredity. Eugenicists correlated biology with social fate: they assumed that a hierarchy of ethnic groups existed and that mental, physical, and behavioral characteristics were primarily hereditary, rather than environmental, in cause. Fearful that the "quality" of the population was declining because the genetically "unfit" were having more children than the "fit," the movement's advocates encouraged procreation among the fit (positive eugenics) and discouraged procreation, sometimes forcefully, among the unfit (negative eugenics).

American eugenicists did gradually come to realize that individuals with "good" traits were spread throughout society, but they predominantly focused on the group, not the individual, and their definitions of quality were determined by the norms of their upper-class society. "Fit," in other words, was largely a corollary for the fair-skinned middle and upper classes.

The movement was never popular among the larger public, though its central idea—the concern with differential fertility among ethnicities and social classes—was at least casually supported by many educated, white Americans. The organized movement declined in the 1930s, despite efforts to tame its doctrine to allow a role for nurture as well as nature, and was then nearly killed off by the public's recognition of the links between Nazism and eugenics. A sanitized eugenic ideology lingered into the postwar United States, and the revolution in human genetics revived eugenic goals of manipulating the population that still echo today, but the American eugenics movement must ultimately be labeled a failure.

HISTORICAL ROOTS

Charles Darwin's theory of evolution was the intellectual cornerstone of the trans-Atlantic eugenics movement. In *The Origins of the Species* (1859), Darwin argued that species evolve through "natural selection," a "struggle for existence" in which reproductive success is determined by heritable differences. Eugenics was born in 1860s England when Sir Francis Galton, a cousin of Darwin concerned with the declining birth rate of the upper classes, applied statistical methods to the study of heredity to create what he hoped would become a new secular religion of scientific breeding. (He later coined the term "eugenics" from the Greek word for "good in birth.") Eugenic thought grew in the last third of the nineteenth century with Social Darwinism, the intellectual movement that sought to apply Darwin's model of natural selection to human society.

Eugenics and Social Darwinism shared a basic evolutionary outlook. Yet while Social Darwinists argued that society should not interfere with the struggle among social groups, eugenicists hoped to "speed up" and improve upon natural selection by influencing who gave birth. Unimpeded natural selection implied chaotic breeding followed by destruction, but eugenics promised to bring into the world only superior individuals. "If farmers could breed better plants," Galton wondered, "Could not the race of men be similarly improved? Could not the undesirables be got rid of and the desirables multiplied?" His *Hereditary Genius: An Inquiry into Its Laws and Consequences* (1869) argued that the superior came from only a few families and previewed his Law of Ancestral Heredity, which held that characteristics (ranging from eye color to intelligence) were inherited in an orderly, linear fashion. Karl Pearson, Galton's principal successor, preferred science to action, but the two jointly advanced and promoted the infant science of "biometrics," the statistical study of human characteristics and inheritance.

Galton and Pearson's work and prescriptions gained a smattering of acceptance among American scientists and philanthropists, but two major preconditions were required before eugenic thought would gain momentum during the first decade of the twentieth century. The first was the development of a new evolutionary paradigm, which, unlike Darwin's theory of natural selection, greatly privileged heredity over environment and hence forged a temporary alliance between science and eugenics. The triumph of hereditarianism was a multistep process. Galton's theories of inheritability had actually been out of step with the ruling theory of evolution in the late nineteenth century neo-Lamarckism, which held that evolution involved the adaptation of organisms to their environment and that characteristics acquired during the lifetime of an organism could be passed on.

By insisting on the biological transmission of acquired characteristics, neo-Lamarckism blurred the distinction between heredity and environment and laid the groundwork for the triumph of heredity. The next major development in the theory of evolution, the German scientist August Weismann's overturning of neo-Lamarckism in the 1880s and 1890s, continued the trend toward hereditarianism. Weismann's germ plasm theory divided the body into germ cells, which transmitted hereditary information, and somatic cells, which did not. His work thus suggested that many traits were not inherited, but his discovery that changes accumulated during the lifetime of an individual organism were not passed on to the germ cells of the next generation was taken by many as endorsement of the ultra-hereditarian position.

Finally, around the turn of the twentieth century, American and European scientists rediscovered the forty-year-old experiments with the breeding of peas by Gregor Mendel, an Austrian monk. Mendel had identified dominant and recessive genes (what he called "unit characters") and argued that traits either appeared or did not appear; and the new Mendelians demonstrated that some human traits (e.g., color-blindness) indeed worked according to Mendel's binary model. They forged a consensus that the mechanism of evolution was mutation rather than natural selection, or the ability of organisms to pass on acquired characteristics. American eugenicists not trained as biologists may not have understood the finer points of Mendel's work—indeed, his theories allowed for a complex relationship between environment and heredity—but they seized on the notion that traits could be reduced to a single gene. For the first third of the twentieth century, American eugenicists would largely ignore advances in genetics in favor of a biological determinism that explained nearly all human actions and characteristics in terms of simple Mendelian unit characters—and which therefore held that only biological manipulation, not environmental reforms, could enhance the "quality" of the population.

RACE, ETHNICITY, AND EUGENICS

The second precondition was the tumultuous transformation of American society in the years surrounding the turn of the century—and the perception that deficiencies in groups rather than individuals accounted for many social ills. American eugenic ideology was shaped by concerns surrounding race, gender, and class; and the rise of mass immigration, urbanization, and industrialization reinforced anxieties in each of these three areas. The science of identifying "races" (which claimed the superiority of the "white race") had been popularized in the years following Darwin and reinforced traditional American racism. Confronted with a falling birthrate among native-born, "white," middle-class Americans (the result, many argued, of the selfish attitudes of the city-dwelling "New Woman") and higher birthrates among the newer immigrants from Southern and Eastern Europe, many elite individuals, including Theodore Roosevelt, warned of a pending "race suicide." In a society with increasing ethnic and economic divisions, eugenics also provided members of the upper classes a biological justification of their status. It was a social ideology with (supposed) scientific support.

Eugenics was also a multidisciplinary enterprise. The natural sciences led the way—a committee of the American Breeding Association became the first eugenics organization in the nation—but scholars in several fields contributed to the vogue. Eugenic explanations appealed to some psychologists and psychiatrists seeking to find the roots of deviance. For example, the psychologist Henry Goddard, who ran a school for the "feebleminded" in New Jersey, published a flawed but influential study of the offspring of one man called *The Kallikak Family: A Study in the Heredity of Feeble-Mindedness* (1912). It assumed that mental capacity was a single genetic trait, and it purported to show how the nation could be swamped with degenerates and "morons" (he coined the term) within a few generations. Eugenic research institutions grew as well.

The leading early American eugenicist was the biologist Charles B. Davenport, who with support from the Carnegie Institution founded a research station in 1904 at Cold Spring Harbor, Long Island. In 1910, the Harriman railroad fortune bankrolled the creation of the nearby Eugenics Record Office, which served as a clearinghouse for genetic information via the thousands of family-trait histories mailed to it. Still, one must be careful not to exaggerate the reach of the eugenics movement. Without contemporary polling data, the exact amount of support for the movement in any segment of society cannot be precisely gauged, but it is safe to assume that, although only a small minority of American natural and social scientists was in vocal opposition, an even smaller minority was in active support. Most professionals were either indifferent or bound by a code of professional ethics not to criticize colleagues. And many geneticists shied away from the eugenic debate because eugenic organizations were a source of grant money.

AMERICAN EUGENICS SOCIETY

Hereditary organizations, with membership based on genealogical purity, had existed since the late nineteenth century, and now more explicitly eugenic societies sprang up in dozens of cities. The first incarnation of the national American Eugenics Society was founded in 1910. Membership never exceeded 1,200—a small number by any measure—but its membership of elite businesspeople, social activists, philanthropists, and scientists did afford it, for a time, a modest amount more influence than its size suggested.

Among the movement's first generation of leaders was David Starr Jordan, the first president of Stanford University, and luminaries such as John D. Rockefeller Jr. and George Eastman provided financial aid. Eugenic groups sought to make the public "eugenic-minded" by sponsoring "fittest family" contests at state fairs, successfully lobbying for the addition of eugenics into college curriculums, canvassing the lecture circuit, and participating in international eugenic conferences. World War I also buttressed the movement. Concerns with the quality of the population grew when childless youth in their prime went to fight; and eugenicists, including Goddard, aided the army in developing intelligence tests for soldiers, the results of which further reinforced the eugenic belief in the dominance of nature and the inferiority of nonwhites.

THE MOVEMENT'S DIVERSE STRANDS

The majority of Americans had little knowledge of the eugenics movement, though many nonwhites knew that it constituted a threat. For a time many elite Americans did consider eugenics a reputable, if somewhat odd, reform movement, in large measure because the movement's unifying ideas of evaluating social problems in biological terms and reforming society by modernizing procreation were malleable enough to attract support from a variety of constituents. The outlook of eugenicists ranged from the utopian to the reactionary.

Radicals did not generally support the movement because of its early insistence that women adhere to traditional roles of childbirth and mothering (that is, serve as "race mothers"). However, some did find common ground in the movement's lack of religiosity and in its assertion that unregulated capitalism made the cost of children prohibitive to the middle classes and hence damaged the gene pool. Whereas mainstream eugenicists before the 1930s tended to be anti–birth control, advocates for legalized contraception, including Margaret Sanger, used the eugenic argument that spreading access to birth control to the lower classes would improve the quality of the population.

Eugenics was also popular in the conservative, racist wing of the Progressive movement, the umbrella term for the diverse efforts to tame industrial capitalism in early twentieth-century America. Progressives and eugenics overlapped in their calls for the scientific management of society, their desire for efficiency (eugenics would reduce the taxpayers' bill of caring for the poor and disabled), and their belief that individual decisions (e.g. childbearing) should be subordinated to the needs of the greater society. Finally, racist conservatives such as Madison Grant, author of the influential *The Passing of the Great Race; or, The Racial Basis of European History* (1916), hoped above all that eugenic measures would preserve America as a "Nordic" nation. Despite the diversity of political opinion, the vast majority of eugenicists were middle- to upper-class European-American Protestants who tended to equate "good traits" with those of their dominant group.

TARGET POPULATIONS

Beyond increasing societal concern with the "quality" of the population, the American eugenics movement achieved specific success in two major policy areas: sterilization and immigration restriction. Most eugenicists believed in the basic preservation of voluntary decisions surrounding marriage and childbirth and hence merely urged people to think eugenically. Even the most fervent realized that revolutionary selective-breeding policies, for example, requiring a license to give birth, were unlikely to emerge. However, in the case of those they deemed severely disabled or "fee-

On March 10, 2000, Sarah Jane Wiley stands in the operating room in which she was sterilized forty-one years earlier in the Virginia Colony for the Epileptic and Feebleminded in Lynchburg. Wiley and her brother were among the thousands of Americans sterilized without their consent in the name of eugenics. *(AP Wide World Photos)*

bleminded," which they considered a genetic trait, they sought to actively prevent procreation through involuntary sterilization. As a result of eugenicists' lobbying as well as a broad societal consensus, between 1907 and World War II more than half the states enacted laws permitting the involuntary sterilization of the "feebleminded."

The targets of sterilization were generally the mentally ill, but "feeblemindedness" was a flexible category; thus, sexual promiscuity and other forms of "immorality" were often grounds for sterilization. The belief in the biological origins of social behavior sometimes made criminals targets, too. The vast majority of those sterilized were poor, and in at least one state (Virginia) nearly half were African American. In *Buck v. Bell* (1927), the U.S. Supreme Court upheld Virginia's sterilization law, Justice Oliver Wendell Holmes declaring, "three generations of imbeciles are

enough." Separately, the eugenics movement contributed to passage of the 1924 Johnson-Reed Act, which adopted racial quotas for immigrants that largely closed America's borders. The Congressional Dillingham Commission on Immigration, which reported in 1910–1911, used eugenic research to report that immigrants were less intelligent than the native-born, and Harry H. Laughlin, Davenport's assistant at Cold Spring Harbor, made similar arguments while serving as "Expert Eugenical Agent" to Congress in the early 1920s.

OPPOSITION AND THE MOVEMENT'S DECLINE

Criticism of the movement widened in the 1920s and into the 1930s as the temporary triumph of nature over nurture crumbled on many fronts. The vast majority of a new generation of geneticists, led by Herbert Jennings, rejected the movement's spurious biology—its simple, like-produces-like model of inheritance as well as the racism embedded in eugenic research. They noted that given the nature of recessive genes, meaningfully reducing the occurrence of any physical or mental deficiency (even the few that could be definitively identified as solely genetic in cause) would take hundreds of years.

Further developments in population genetics in the late 1930s and 1940s, particularly recognition that a species displayed a range of characteristics, cemented the break between eugenics and science. In addition, the fields of anthropology and psychology, which had adopted the stress on nurture in the early twentieth century, turned toward an environmentalist approach and further eroded acceptance of biological determinism. The major foundations eliminated their support for eugenic projects, and, in 1935, the American Neurological Association issued a report rejecting the genetic rationale for sterilizations. Religious groups stepped up their campaign against the assumption that some individuals were superior to others. As the 1930s progressed and a better understanding of the Nazi regime emerged, American eugenicists' links to the regime (indeed, parts of the 1933 Nazi eugenic law were modeled after California's sterilization law) significantly tarnished public opinion of the movement. Eugenics had become both a flawed moral endeavor and a stigmatized science.

In response to declining institutional strength and legitimacy, the eugenics movement tried to save itself in the 1930s by softening its rhetoric. Leadership shifted to a loose coalition of "reform" eugenicists, led by Frederick Osborn, a retired financier who broke with his uncle, a paleontologist at the New York Museum of Natural History and virulently racist eugenicist. Reform eugenicists maintained the desire to use the science of heredity to improve the quality of the population, but they at least claimed to recognize a role for nurture as well as nature and to emphasize differences among individuals rather than between groups. Rejecting many eugenicists' earlier preference for pure science over propaganda, they also articulated lofty social reform goals.

Osborn believed that the goal of the eugenics movement was to maintain a sufficient quantity of men of sufficient quality as a means of improving civilization. Women were still expected to perform traditional roles, but support for birth control and the right to sexual satisfaction grew. (Indeed, eugenicists

now assured leery doctors that sterilizations were not "unsexing.") In short, the movement now tried to create a democratic eugenics far removed from totalitarian racial science.

The reform-eugenic project transformed and simultaneously ensured the survival of the core concerns of the movement, but it was ultimately both a hollow intellectual endeavor and ineffectual in influencing social policy. Eugenicists had blended into the maturing American demography profession, which thus declared its intentions to research both the qualitative and empirical components of the population even as it strove to remove the taint of eugenics from population science. When in the 1930s eugenic-demographers and other social scientists instigated an unsuccessful campaign for a comprehensive American "population policy," the concern with quality remained alongside the concern with quantity (demographers now falsely predicted a future decline in the aggregate population) and the concern with the geographical imbalance between people and industry.

Many planks of the ideal population policy, such as improved public health and a downward redistribution of income through tax and spending measures, were nearly indistinguishable from other New Deal–inspired blueprints for social reform. "Quality" no longer connoted the germ pool so much as the health and welfare of the population. Still, the drive for population policy was very much a positive-eugenics campaign. The hope was that equalizing environmental conditions would make children more affordable for the "better" families in the middle classes. In addition, although there was a new recognition of the effect of social inequalities on "quality"—some even stressed that economic redistribution would prove that the genetically superior could be found in all socioeconomic groups—many eugenicists remained unable to shed the idea that class and ethnicity were reasonably accurate predictors of biological quality. Finally, while eugenicists publicly emphasized the campaign to extol the virtues of motherhood and large families, negative eugenics actually thrived. About 9,000 Americans had been sterilized between 1907 and 1928; by 1941, the number had reached 36,000.

SURVIVAL OF EUGENICS

Full revelation of the horrors of Nazism discredited eugenics in postwar America. Sterilizations sharply decreased, and the organized movement dwindled to almost nothing, despite its promise to seek improvement of only the human race as a whole. Nonetheless, eugenic ideas did not disappear in postwar America. Concerns with the quality of the population were embedded in the 1950s vogue for family values and child rearing; and eugenicists from the 1930s reemerged as leading figures in the marriage counseling movement. A eugenic discourse of quality was also present in the development of family-planning programs in the Third World designed to address the population explosion.

Although the field of human genetics made every effort to separate itself from its eugenic heritage, the discovery of DNA, better identification of genetic disorders, and the concomitant promise of "genetic engineering" through prenatal screening and later artificial insemination also fostered a revival of eugenic goals. Herman Muller, a geneticist who had advocated a socialist eugenics in the 1930s, led the new movement for "germinal choice"—artificial insemination after freezing the sperm for a long period of time so that the quality of the donor could be properly measured. After his death in 1967, a sperm bank with his name was established that initially accepted only the sperm of Nobel laureates. Finally, the "white backlash" that emerged in the late 1960s in response to the civil rights movement and the rise of Affirmative Action also permitted a brief revival of neo-eugenic ideas in educated circles. Most famously, a 1969 *Harvard Educational Review* article by Arthur Jensen suggested that genetic differences were perhaps a contributing factor in the gap between African-American and white test scores.

Yet social critics and historians have perhaps been too eager to find the contemporary "legacy" or "survival" of the eugenics movement. The germinal choice movement was inconsequential, and the current fear over the cloning of humans seems to indicate that serious efforts at eugenic reproduction are highly unlikely. True, many Americans continue to fear that certain groups will have more babies than others; and some social scientists occasionally resort to crude biological determinism. For example, the widely debated and refuted book *The Bell Curve: Intelligence and Class Structure in American Life* (1994) by Herrnstein and Murray argued that success in America is largely determined by supposed innate differences in intelligence among social classes and ethnicities. In addition to using spurious research funded by racist organizations, the book contained several methodological errors, including falsely assuming that intelligence is reducible to a single number and is un-

responsive to environmental shifts. Still, garden-variety American racism preceded the eugenics movement, and the continued strength of racism should not be seen as evidence of the residual strength of the eugenics movement. Even during the movement's heyday in the early twentieth century, eugenic ideas were just one element of a larger concern with social, mental, and racial hygiene, and by the third decade of the twentieth century they were already in decline.

Today eugenics is important not as an ideology or as a movement but as a weapon—a tool to stigmatize certain groups and ideas that, according to their critics, have overreached in their pursuit of manipulating the population. For example, advocates of stringent birth control measures (such as paying young women not to have children) have been called eugenic by minority groups. To be sure, echoes of eugenics can be found in several social policy debates, such as those related to social benefits. (The image of the "welfare mom" incorporated fears that the poor were outbreeding the nonpoor.) Eugenic ideas, grounded in traditional bias and tantalized by the coming mastery of the human genome (misunderstood by many as the promise of once again discovering single genes that account for complex traits), seem unlikely to fade away entirely. However, given America's almost universal acceptance of at least formal racial equality, the rise of individual civil liberties, and widespread fears of genetic experimentation, a new eugenics movement seems unlikely.

Derek Hoff

BIBLIOGRAPHY

Cravens, Hamilton. *The Triumph of Evolution: American Scientists and the Heredity-Environment Controversy, 1900–1941.* Philadelphia: University of Pennsylvania Press, 1978.

Darwin, Charles. *On the Origin of Species by Means of Natural Selection.* London: J. Murray, 1859.

Dikotter, Frank. "Race Culture: Recent Perspectives on the History of Eugenics." *The American Historical Review* 103 (April 1998): 467–478.

Galton, Francis. *Hereditary Genius: An Inquiry into Its Laws and Consequences.* London: Macmillan, 1869.

Goddard, Henry Herbert. *The Kallikak Family: A Study in the Heredity of Feeble-Mindedness.* New York: Macmillan, 1912.

Grant, Madison. *The Passing of the Great Race; or, The Racial Basis of European History.* New York: Charles Scribner's Sons, 1916.

Haller, Mark H. *Eugenics: Hereditarian Attitudes in American Thought.* New Brunswick, NJ: Rutgers University Press, 1963.

Hansen, Randall, and Desmond King. "Eugenic Ideas, Political Interests, and Policy Variance: Immigration and Sterilization Policy in Britain and the U.S." *World Politics* 53 (January 2001): 237–264.

Herrnstein, Richard J., and Charles Murray. *The Bell Curve: Intelligence and Class Structure in American Life.* New York: Free Press, 1994.

Jacoby, Russell, and Naomi Glauberman, eds. *The Bell Curve Debate: History, Documents, Opinions.* New York: Times Books, 1995.

Jensen, Arthur. "How Much Can We Boost IQ and Scholastic Achievement?" *Harvard Educational Review* 39 (Winter 1969): 1–123.

Kevles, Daniel J. *In the Name of Eugenics: Genetics and the Uses of Human Heredity.* New York: Knopf, 1985.

Kline, Wendy. *Building a Better Race: Gender, Sexuality, and Eugenics from the Turn of the Century to the Baby Boom.* Berkeley: University of California Press, 2001.

Ladd-Taylor, Molly. "Eugenics, Sterilisation and Modern Marriage in the USA: The Strange Career of Paul Popenoe." *Gender and History* 13 (August 2001): 298–327.

Mehler, Barry Alan. "A History of the American Eugenics Society, 1921–1940." Ph.D. diss., University of Illinois at Urbana-Champaign, 1988.

Pickens, Donald K. *Eugenics and the Progressives.* Nashville, TN: Vanderbilt University Press, 1968.

Soloway, Richard A. *Demography and Degeneration: Eugenics and the Declining Birthrate in Twentieth-century Britain.* Chapel Hill: University of North Carolina Press, 1990.

ALCOHOLICS ANONYMOUS

Alcoholics Anonymous (AA) is a voluntary, mutual-help movement comprised of recovering alcoholics devoted to aiding still suffering alcoholics overcome alcohol addiction. Since its formation in 1935, few organizations, public or private, have rivaled AA's impact on prevailing conceptions of alcoholism and addiction treatment. During its history, AA has grown from a fledgling movement of 100 to 1 million members in the United States and over 2 million members worldwide. With its success in helping alcoholics, AA's conception of alcoholism and addiction treatment has become the predominant model of professional treatment in the United States. As early as 1939, AA members were actively aiding hospitals in the treatment of alcoholics. By 1957, AA members were present in over 250 hospitals nationwide. Today, there are few treatment programs that do not treat alcoholism as a disease and employ some part, if not all, of AA's Twelve Step practices in their treatment program. Besides alcoholism treatment, the Twelve Step approach to life change has been adopted by numerous mutual-help groups to address problems ranging from gambling and sex to overeating and emotions. Underlying each of these movements is a practice of mutual help where members help themselves recover by helping others do the same.

Despite its widely recognized impact on conceptions of alcohol addiction and treatment, AA is not often considered as a social movement because it defies ordinary divisions, classifications, and distinctions within social movement theory. In part, the classificatory difficulties are created by AA's self-described relation to wider social practices. Unlike social movements that explicitly or implicitly identify their aims with socioeconomic or political change, AA recognizes only one purpose for its membership: to aid other alcoholics in abstinence. Some scholars classify AA as a self-help movement to highlight the fact that members seek help for addiction problems that they believe cannot be cured through existing social institutions. According to this view, members seek help from others with similar difficulties rather than professionals who specialize in aiding them. Other scholars classify AA as a mutual-help movement to stress the ways that members cooperatively aid one another and engage in a practice of helping themselves through helping others. Each of these classifications adds a dimension to understanding AA as a social movement, but difficulties remain. Since official AA literature endorses strict rules of nonaffiliation, organizational autonomy, and the singular purpose of helping alcoholics, there is little explicit clarification of AA's social aims in its official self-descriptions.

The most substantial effort to understand AA as a social movement is Robin Room's article entitled "Alcoholics Anonymous as a Social Movement," which suggests that AA is a mutual-help movement aimed at personal rather than social transformation. Drawing on AA's organizational principles, commonly known by members as the Twelve Traditions, Room interprets AA as a social movement by focusing on AA's self-described organizational structure and complex pattern of relating to wider social practices. Unlike the Twelve Steps that guide members in overcoming their addiction to alcohol, the Twelve Traditions guide AA groups on internal policies and external relations. For example, AA promotes an open membership policy as expressed in tradition three, which states that "the only requirement for AA membership is a desire to stop drinking." Membership requirements in the traditions correlate with AA's primary mission to help suffering alcoholics. In addition to open membership policies, AA traditions also stress the primacy of group independence and financial self-sufficiency, prohibitions against external affiliations or property ownership, and external anonymity. Each of the aforementioned policies is a distinctive feature of AA and provides a helpful lens by

TWELVE STEPS

1. We admitted we were powerless over alcohol—that our lives had become unmanageable.
2. Came to believe that a Power greater than ourselves could restore us to sanity.
3. Made a decision to turn our will and our lives over to the care of God as we understood Him.
4. Made a searching and fearless moral inventory of ourselves.
5. Admitted to God, to ourselves and to another human being the exact nature of our wrongs.
6. Were entirely ready to have God remove all these defects of character.
7. Humbly asked Him to remove our shortcomings.
8. Made a list of all persons we had harmed, and became willing to make amends to them all.
9. Made direct amends to such people wherever possible, except when to do so would injure them or others.
10. Continued to take personal inventory and when we were wrong promptly admitted it.
11. Sought through prayer and meditation to improve our conscious contact with God as we understood Him, praying only for knowledge of His will for us and the power to carry that out.
12. Having had a spiritual awakening as the result of these steps, we tried to carry this message to alcoholics and to practice these principles in all our affairs.

Source: Alcoholics Anonymous. 4th ed. (Alcoholics Anonymous World Services, 2000).

which to understand AA's relation to wider social norms. For instance, early AA members realized the importance of anonymity for individual members and AA as an organization. Thus, in press reports, members went by first name and last initial in their self-identifications. In film, members covered their faces with a mask or some other way to conceal their identities. Early experiences taught members that anonymity secured the trust of new recruits, insured member confidentiality and avoided the negative impact of members who might fall off the wagon and damage the AA name.

Analysis of the traditions reveals much about AA as a social movement, but Room's approach leaves a crucial tension between AA's helping-others practices and its organizational principles unexplored. Al-

though it is true that the Twelve Traditions are a barometer for assessing AA's internal policies and its relationship to wider networks, focusing on the Twelve Traditions misses fundamental points of contact between central AA practices and wider social practices. Most notably, a central feature of AA membership is the practice of helping-others or what is referred to as "Twelve Step work." Practices aimed at helping-others often include hospital visits to alcoholics in rehabilitation clinics, meetings at prisons or detoxification centers, and promoting the abstinence practices of AA. Attempts to understand AA as a social movement apart from this "Twelve Step work," obscures the significant degree of interaction between AA members and wider social practices and networks of alcohol treatment activities. By limiting his analysis to the traditions, fundamental practices and sources of AA's development and character as a movement are minimized.

CONTEXT OF AA'S BEGINNINGS

Pre-AA Treatment for Alcoholics

Pre-AA approaches to aiding alcoholics vary widely over the 220-year history of helping alcoholics in the United States. Undoubtedly, a careful study would elaborate the varying conceptions of alcoholism and sources, whether moral, religious, or medical, that contributed to these conceptions. Although aid to alcoholics has taken different guises, the advocates of helping alcoholics have all shared some basic ideas and aims. Most notably, helpers view alcoholics as powerless over alcohol in such a way that requires some sort of intervention (whether religious, moral, medical, or political) to cure their alcoholism. In this respect, the conception of alcohol and alcoholism presented by AA is unique in its approach to alcoholism, but shares significant affinities with previous notions of helping alcoholics. Dr. Benjamin Rush, a signer of the Declaration of Independence, was among the early advocates of helping and aiding alcoholics. Unlike many of his contemporaries, Rush forwarded the idea that alcoholics were powerless over their drinking habits and needed help in overcoming their drinking as early as 1774. In response to the problems of alcoholism, Rush proposed the establishment of a "sober house" where alcoholics would be rehabilitated through religious and moral education.

In addition to professional helpers, attempts to aid alcoholics also emerged in the temperance movements, which aimed to help alcoholics by requiring their members to pledge to refrain from drinking distilled spirits and attend temperance gatherings. In addition, the temperance societies often provided public information regarding alcohol and its impact on health. Initially, temperance supporters advocated pledges to moderate drinking; but by the middle of the nineteenth century, temperance supporters began to advocate total abstinence either through an individual's pledge or government-backed prohibition. The shift in policy resulted from numerous causes, including the rising number of alcohol-related difficulties facing the early republic and the general sense among temperance advocates that alcoholics could only overcome drunkenness through total abstinence.

A temperance movement of particular significance to AA's historical consciousness is the Washingtonian movement. The Washingtonians advocated total abstinence, held regular meetings where members shared their experiences with drinking and abstinence, and provided service to others. By 1842, when the Washingtonians were at their peak, over 600,000 pledges had been signed and its speakers lectured across the country. In addition, the Washingtonians engaged in political action and aimed at social change. Early members of AA suggested that the Washingtonians splintered and failed when they directed their energies toward the social and political features of the temperance movement and lost their singleness of purpose. Although the AA founders often looked to the Washingtonians for lessons, it is likely that other mutual-aid groups devoted to alcoholism influenced early AA members, including the Emmanuel Movement and the Jacoby Club, which described itself as "A club for men to help themselves by helping others."

Oxford Group Movement: Beliefs and Practices

The Oxford Group Movement (OGM) was one of the most significant influences in shaping AA's approach to aiding problem drinkers. Unlike temperance movements and other alcoholic help strategies, the OGM never focused on the problem of alcoholism. Instead, they focused on the problems of sin and viewed alcoholism as an effect of an underlying sinful condition. Early members of AA, including both co-founders, attended OGM meetings in their efforts to quit drinking.

Founded by Frank Buchman in 1908 as a Christian revival movement, the OGM employed personal evangelism practices or what adherents sometimes called soul surgery. Personal evangelism aimed to induce a conversion experience sufficient to overcome an individual's struggle with sin. Through personal

evangelism, OGM adherents believed that they were aiding others in living a Christian life by overcoming sinful living. Personal evangelism practices were not unique to Buchman and his followers. Henry Drummond, Dwight L. Moody, and John Mott employed similar methods in their revival efforts. In fact, Buchman most likely developed many of his techniques through the guidance of Henry B. Wright of Yale University, who wrote manuals explaining personal evangelism practices and techniques. According to Wright, the task of personal evangelism was a persuasive appeal that introduces a person to Christ through the evangelist's example and labors. The techniques employed by personal evangelists focused on personal interactions and trust building. Wright's "expert friendship" model required evangelists to befriend others to provide a living example of Christ's effects in one's life. Practically speaking, Wright believed personal evangelism was best done within specialized groups such that students worked with students, soldiers with soldiers, and so on. Although rarely noted, the practice of expert friendship as expounded by Henry Wright bears significant resemblance to the early practices of helping others and what has since become standardized in AA under the practice of sponsorship where one alcoholic mentors another into the AA program.

In turn, Buchman summarized Wright's tasks and techniques under the label of the "Five C's" of confidence, confession, conviction, conversion, and continuance. Thus, members were to gain the confidence of a new recruit, witness to the recruit to bring to awareness how his anxiety was a sign of sin (conviction), and thereby induce a conversion. Conversion was followed by a sustained attempt to live a life free of sin, governed by God's will and guidance. To this end, the OGM members promoted the four absolutes of honesty, purity, unselfishness, and love as the guides to action that cleansed the heart and mind so that God's guidance could be received. As a group, members would sit silently and await God's guidance in "quiet time." When a member received guidance on a particular problem or question, he or she would share it with the group to assess whether the guidance in question was reliable.

The OGM often claimed greater revival successes than could ever be verified. In part, the OGM leadership believed that publicity was an excellent form of evangelization. Although its critics accused OGM leadership of publicity seeking, the movement was still visible across the United States by 1932. Regardless of its actual impact, it actively began operations in 1930 at Calvary Church in New York under the American leadership of Reverend Samuel Shoemaker. Between 1930 and 1936, the OGM gathered frequently at Calvary Church. Although they did not seek out drunks, some alcoholics were attracted to their membership. Among these was Rowland Hazard. During his brief association with the OGM, Hazard learned that a friend, Ebby Thatcher, faced commitment for alcoholic insanity. Hazard visited Thatcher with an OGM team, and Thatcher responded by attending the OGM meetings at Calvary Church in New York. Thatcher would later become the connection between the OGM and AA cofounder William Wilson.

AA Founders

The AA literature identifies AA beginnings with the initial encounter and subsequent collaborations of cofounders William G. Wilson and Dr. Robert H. Smith, later known as Bill W. and Dr. Bob, respectively. Both men suffered years of heavy drinking and hospitalizations, and eventually sought help for their drinking problems in the OGM.

Wilson was born to Gilman and Emily Wilson in East Dorset, Vermont, in 1895. His childhood and adolescence were marked by two traumatic events. When Wilson was ten, his parents divorced. Shortly afterward, his mother went to Boston to pursue a career as an osteopath, leaving Wilson and his younger sister in the care of her parents. Later in life, Wilson recalled his deep sense of rejection and abandonment resulting from the absence of his parents. During his adolescence, Wilson's grandparents sent him to Burr and Burton Academy. While at the Academy, Wilson became head of a Young Men's Christian Association (YMCA) chapter, excelled in school, and fell in love with a classmate, Bertha Branford. During chapel one morning, Wilson was devastated to learn that Bertha had died suddenly while traveling in New York with her parents. Later in life, Wilson acknowledged that Bertha's death began a cycle of depression that lasted nearly three years. Despite these early traumas, it was not until shortly after Wilson was commissioned as a second lieutenant in 1917 that he had his first drink while attending a social function supporting servicemen and the American war effort in Europe. Most notably, Wilson experienced a subtle shift in his disposition from a sense of awkwardness to social ease.

Between 1918, when Wilson married Lois Burnham, and 1923, there is little evidence that Wilson's drinking was a problem. In fact, during that period Wilson completed a year-long tour of duty in Europe, finished law school, and became a stock company re-

searcher. Little by little, however, Wilson's drinking escalated to troubling proportions. Despite significant success as a stock investigator on Wall Street, Wilson recorded a written pledge in the family Bible to abstain from drinking for one year in 1923. His pledge lasted only two months. In 1927, he made another pledge with similar results. With the stock market crash in 1929, Wilson's financial future looked bleak. Through an associate, he was able to find good paying work in Canada, but this opportunity ended with a drinking-related conflict. For the next several years, Wilson struggled with his alcoholism and found keeping a job difficult. By 1933, he was admitted to Charles Townes Hospital in the first of several efforts to cure him of his alcoholism.

Wilson was aided in these early efforts at abstinence through his association with the OGM. Wilson's acquaintance with the OGM and its practices began when Ebby Thatcher, an old school friend and known drunkard, visited Wilson in November 1934. Unlike previous visits, Thatcher was clear eyed, sober, and eager to discuss his newfound sobriety with Wilson. Crediting the OGM brand of "religion" and "life-changing" for his newly acquired self-control and abstinence, Thatcher encouraged Wilson to attend the OGM. Although religion did not appeal to Wilson, four alcohol-related visits to the Charles Townes Hospital between 1933 and 1934 left him open to his school friend's suggestions. Wilson attended his first OGM meeting at Calvary Church mission in New York. Drunk on arrival, he was allowed to participate after eating a meal and drinking some coffee. After the meeting, Wilson returned home without stopping at a bar. A few days later, he checked himself into the Townes Hospital one last time. While at the hospital, he had a spiritual experience. Filled with feelings of desperation and hopelessness, he found himself asking God to help him. Then Wilson felt an assuring presence he believed to be God.

Upon leaving Townes Hospital in late December of 1934, Wilson began to associate with the OGM and to focus his efforts on evangelizing to other alcoholics. His brief experience with OGM, his twelve years of excessive drinking, and his trips to the Townes Hospital convinced him of two basic ideas that shaped his message. First, alcoholics are powerless over their desires to drink, and a self-conscious recognition of this powerlessness was essential to an alcoholic's recovery. Second, recognition of one's powerlessness must be accompanied by the recognition that the only remedy for alcoholism is a spiritual experience. Through his association with the OGM, Wilson learned the personal value of sharing his experience with other alcoholics, and to his own surprise he found that sharing his story with other alcoholics was helping him stay sober. Although he was ineffective in persuading alcoholics to adopt a life design consistent with OGM, Wilson still persisted in efforts to help other alcoholics.

Wilson's cofounder, Dr. Robert Smith, followed a slightly different path to alcoholic desperation. At age nine, Smith had his first drinking experience. Throughout his education, especially his college years at Dartmouth, Smith was regarded as a heavy drinker, but it was not until medical school at the University of Michigan that he began to suffer alcohol-related problems. Unlike his college years where he could drink without consequences, he now began to engage in heavy binge drinking that interfered with his studies. Shortly before his dismissal from the University of Michigan in 1907, Smith transferred to Rush Medical School in Chicago where he was able to finish his degree only after swearing off drinking for two semesters. After completing medical school, Smith moved to Akron, Ohio, and opened a medical practice. There his drinking continued to intensify, regularly landing him in sanitariums. In 1914, Smith's father brought him back to Vermont to sober up. Smith stayed sober and married Anne Ripley in 1914. His sobriety lasted until just before passage of the Volstead Act. After the passage of Prohibition, Smith continued to drink by forging alcohol prescriptions for himself and, later, sedatives as well. During his sixteen years of heavy drinking, he placed himself under medical care on no fewer than one dozen occasions. By 1933, his medical practice was nearly destroyed. Guilt-ridden and ashamed by the impact of his drinking on his family, Smith agreed to attend meetings of the OGM in Akron with his wife, Anne Smith. Beginning in 1933, he began regularly attending OGM meetings but with little impact on his drinking.

Wilson/Smith: First Meeting

In May of 1935, Wilson found himself alone in the Mayflower Hotel in Akron, Ohio, after a failed business venture. While puzzling over his next move, he began calling local ministers in search of another alcoholic with whom he could share his story. Through a clergy contact, Wilson was put in touch with an OGM member who had been working with Dr. Robert Smith.

Wilson and Smith met on Mother's Day in 1935 at the Akron home of an OGM member. In his message to Smith, Wilson emphasized that alcoholism was a disease of mind, body, and spirit. Like his friend Ebby before him, Wilson shared his observations on how drinking had destroyed his life and how his continued abstinence depended on helping others through sharing his story. The conversation was by no means novel to either man. Wilson had been attempting to help other alcoholics for months through his association with the OGM. Smith had spoken with medical experts, clergy, and friends about his drinking, and none of these previous discussions had proven effective. Yet, both men were changed by their meeting. Years later, Wilson reported that his initial encounter with Smith was marked by an altogether different attitude and approach. Unlike previous attempts, Wilson did not preach or try to convert. Moreover, as he spoke with Smith, he began to realize that he needed Smith as much and possibly more than Smith needed him. Similarly, Smith later reported that his exchange with Wilson was reciprocal and mutual. In Wilson, Smith found a man who shared a similar struggle with alcohol and was cured by the same spiritual practices he was pursuing.

Encouraged and moved by Wilson's message, Smith invited Wilson to stay that evening at his home. Wilson remained with the Smith family for the next several weeks while Wilson and the Smiths tried to apply OGM practices to their lives in an attempt to stay sober. Smith remained sober for three weeks, at which time he was called away from home for a few days to attend an annual medical convention. When he returned, he was drunk. Wilson and Anne Smith tended to Smith as he tried to sober up. Only three days later, Wilson drove Smith to the hospital to perform surgery. Before the surgery, Wilson gave Smith a beer to calm Smith's jitters. After the surgery, Smith committed to the project of sobriety and suggested to Wilson that they ought to start something to help other alcoholics. Smith claimed his first date of sobriety as June 10, 1935.

Together, Wilson and Smith began their mission of helping other alcoholics within the context of the OGM. They began their project by seeking out alcoholics at the Akron City Hospital. Within a few weeks, Wilson and Smith had recruited a third member to their fledging group of sober alcoholics. By the end of the summer when Wilson returned to New York, he and Smith had increased their number to six. In these very early efforts, Wilson and Smith searched out other alcoholics in an effort to share their experiences with alcohol and abstinence. Moreover, Wilson and Smith continued to employ OGM practices in working with alcoholics by stressing powerlessness over alcohol to new recruits and instructing them to follow policies of rigorous honesty, restitution, and unselfishness through unpaid aid to other alcoholics. Although the self-conscious identification of AA would not be complete for another four years, the basic practices were now in place.

STEPS TOWARD INDEPENDENCE AND GROUP IDENTITY

Wilson/Smith Difference with OGM

As their numbers increased, the presence of alcoholics focused primarily on helping other alcoholics began to strain relations between the alcoholic and nonalcoholic members of OGM. The most prominent strain in the New York branch of the OGM centered on an insistence by more senior OGM members that Wilson and his fellow alcoholics should evangelize to any, and all, sinners and not limit their efforts to alcoholics. But within only a few months, Wilson and his small group within the OGM had shifted its focus from saving sinners to saving alcoholics. Moreover, whereas the OGM focused its efforts around its motto, "Nation changing through life changing," the alcoholic members focused solely on life changing without regard to social and political transformation.

This fundamental difference was not the only one. Certain OGM practices, including the four absolutes, guidance, and quiet time, were either too explicitly religious or counterintuitive to working with down-and-out drunks. These practices found little support among the alcoholic members of OGM. In addition, OGM public relations were seriously jeopardized by Frank Buchman's favorable comments about the Nationalist Socialist Party in Germany and the impending condemnation of the OGM by the Roman Catholic Church. By 1937, the differences were too difficult to bear, and Wilson and his drunks left the OGM and began meeting independently. The split in Akron occurred in 1939 but was less contentious.

Clarifying the Alcoholics Anonymous Identity

Several important events transpired during the years between the initial Wilson/Smith encounter and the publication of the AA "Big Book" that contributed to solidifying group identity. In 1936, Charles Townes offered Wilson a paid position as lay therapist and asked him to transport his practice of helping others into the Townes Hospital. Enthusiastically, Wilson brought the proposal to his alcoholic colleagues, who openly worried that involvement with for-profit enterprises might undermine the efforts and successes they were experiencing with helping others. Wilson rejected Townes's offer on recommendation from the members of the new fledgling and unnamed society of alcoholics helping other alcoholics. Later, Wilson's decision would be formalized in Tradition Eight which reads: "Alcoholics Anonymous should remain forever nonprofessional, but our service centers may employ special workers."

Shortly thereafter, through family connections, Wilson was given a meeting with John D. Rockefeller's charitable foundation. Wilson requested $50,000 to continue their work and build a hospital. Rockefeller declined but put a small sum in trust to support Smith and Wilson while they continued their efforts to help alcoholics. Rockefeller reasoned that early AA members were better off working without the aid of these funds. The experience with Rockefeller would later be institutionalized as the seventh tradition, which states: "Every AA group ought to be fully self-supporting, declining outside contributions." In order to oversee the funds donated by the Rockefeller Foundation, the Alcoholic Foundation was established in 1938.

A crucial component of the articulation and evolution of group identity was the production of what would later become *Alcoholics Anonymous: The Story of How Many Thousands of Men and Women Have Recovered from Alcoholism* (1939). In May 1938, Wilson began drafting an outline of practices he and his new colleagues found successful in helping other alcoholics. The book is divided into two parts. The first part is devoted to outlining the practices early members followed in successful abstinence. Wilson began by outlining the six steps he and others were employing in helping others: a recognition of powerlessness, honest self-appraisal, shared honesty with another, amends and restitution to persons harmed by alcoholic drinking, help to other alcoholics without compensation, and reliance upon God. Wilson later expanded these six steps to the Twelve Steps. The second part of the book consists of forty-four similarly structured personal stories, averaging between 1,500 and 2,000 words, that narrate experiences of the founding members. Wilson's draft was carefully edited by other sober alcoholics in New York and Akron. The book was later called "The Big Book" in reference to its large dimensions and thick paper. Later, this moniker would take on additional connotations and has since been referred to by scholars as the AA Bible, which references how the book has come to be the object of special reverence by some of the AA membership.

By 1939, AA membership had reached 100, *Alcoholics Anonymous* was published, and groups were located in several cities. Among the contributions to AA's early growth was the positive press received by the group. Articles in *Liberty Magazine* and the *Cleveland Plain Dealer* generated over 1,000 calls for help. In 1941, an established reporter, Jack Alexander, wrote an article on AA for the *Saturday Evening Post* that resulted in 6,000 new members in a ten-month period. In 1944, members of AA began a "meeting in print" entitled the *AA Grapevine*, which quickly became a national newsletter and source of exchange between AA members throughout the United States. Even with the aid of the newsletter, small groups across the United States looked to AA's central office in New York for guidance and instruction. With its rapid expansion, the AA membership began facing important issues of group governance, organization, and authority. In some cases, disputes emerged over internal policies and relations to the wider public.

During its first decade, the AA members accumulated substantial experience indicating that certain group attitudes and principles were particularly valuable in assuring the survival of the informal structure of the "fellowship." In 1946, the fellowship's international journal, the *AA Grapevine*, published these principles as the Twelve Traditions of Alcoholics Anonymous. They were accepted and endorsed by the membership as a whole at AA's first international convention in Cleveland, Ohio, in 1950.

AA as a Social Force for Treating Alcoholics

As AA became a recognized source of aid for problem drinkers, local groups were deluged with calls for help. In an effort to field these calls and facilitate communication within groups, local groups formed central offices and intergroup associations designed to keep updated lists of meeting times and locations, distribute AA literature, and provide a clearinghouse for service opportunities. By the twentieth anniversary of AA beginnings, the original Alcoholic Foundation had been renamed the General Service Board and the office in New York renamed it the General Service Office, which began its services as the basic support structure for group activities throughout the United States. Recent studies of AA suggest that its unique structure forms an upside-down pyramid, with the central structure serving as a base to local activities rather than the reverse. Through this process of adaptation, AA built an administrative structure that enabled new groups to develop their own constituencies and form networks at the local levels while providing

TWELVE TRADITIONS

1. Our common welfare should come first; personal recovery depends upon AA unity.
2. For our group purpose there is but one ultimate authority—a loving God as He may express Himself in our group conscience. Our leaders are but trusted servants; they do not govern.
3. The only requirement for AA membership is a desire to stop drinking.
4. Each group should be autonomous except in matters affecting other groups or AA as a whole.
5. Each group has but one primary purpose—to carry its message to the alcoholic who still suffers.
6. An AA group ought never endorse, finance or lend the AA name to any related facility or outside enterprise, lest problems of money, property and prestige divert us from our primary purpose.
7. Every AA group ought to be fully self-supporting, declining outside contributions.
8. Alcoholics Anonymous should remain forever non-professional, but our service centers may employ special workers.
9. AA, as such, ought never be organized; but we may create service boards or committees directly responsible to those they serve.
10. Alcoholics Anonymous has no opinion on outside issues; hence the AA name ought never be drawn into public controversy.
11. Our public relations policy is based on attraction rather than promotion; we need always maintain personal anonymity at the level of press, radio and films.
12. Anonymity is the spiritual foundation of all our traditions, ever reminding us to place principles before personalities.

Source: Alcoholics Anonymous. 4th ed. (Alcoholics Anonymous World Services, 2000).

the local groups with the necessary communication and support.

The AA Program: The Twelve Step Practices

The Twelve Steps are offered as suggestions in both *Alcoholics Anonymous* and a later exposition written by Wilson entitled "Twelve Steps and Twelve Traditions." Unaltered since their initial presentation in print form, the steps represent the collective experience of AA's founding members itemized into the most basic components of a turn from a life of active alcoholism to a life guided by AA principles and practices. In this respect, the steps refer to shifts in beliefs, actions, and attitudes of alcoholics and their relations to alcohol, self, God, and others.

Many scholars divide the Twelve Steps into three categories: decision, action, and maintenance steps. The decision steps (1–3) are classified as decision because members make significant and life-altering decisions with respect to their own beliefs, attitudes, and actions. These life changes refer specifically to an alcoholic's recognition of powerlessness, belief in a higher power, and a choice to surrender to that higher power.

The action steps (4–9) refer almost explicitly to repairing relations with others by changing the beliefs, attitudes, and practices that figure into one's relations with others. Underlying these action steps is the idea that certain beliefs, attitudes, and actions become mechanisms in one's ordinary life. When the mechanisms are organized around self-will and self-reliance, the results are invariably dangerous for alcoholics since poor relations with others hinders sobriety. Thus, the steps are guides to rooting out these deleterious mechanisms. Two such mechanisms, fear and resentment, are cited as the kinds of mechanisms targeted by Steps 4 through 9. For example, fear is described as a pervasive force extending to every area of life. According AA literature, alcoholics have a special tendency to allow fear to motivate their life choices. The mechanisms connected to fear vary but tend to connect fear to excessive self-reliance, which produces dishonesty, manipulation, and other vices. What is crucial, however, is to realize that the inventory and admission steps (4 and 5) identify these mechanisms as they play out in an individual's life as well as the subsequent steps that aid in ridding persons of those mechanisms and replacing them with alternative mechanisms based in reliance upon God.

The maintenance steps (10–12) refer to maintaining sobriety through continued efforts to keep right relations with others (Step 10), God (Step 11) and sobriety through the practice of helping others (Step 12). Step 12 reads: "Having had a spiritual awakening as the result of these steps [steps 1–11], we tried to carry this message to alcoholics and to practice these principles in all our affairs." Carrying the message to alcoholics is practiced communally and individually. Group activities identified as carrying the message include AA meetings, group commitments to set up AA meetings for alcoholics in rehabilitation or detoxification centers, and other forms of outreach. In-dividually, helping others involves participation in meetings through sharing one's story, service activities for the meeting (e.g., making coffee or setting up chairs for the meeting), outreach to the still suffering alcoholic, and sponsorship (working one-on-one with another alcoholic).

Helping Individual Alcoholics

The seventh chapter of the Big Book, "Working with Others," identifies further techniques and guides for helping others. In short, these techniques emphasize a regard for the still suffering alcoholic. In helping others, members are directed to search out alcoholics who are ready for change in their drinking practices and express their readiness through a desire to stop drinking. AA members are advised to refrain from approaching drinkers who have not solicited their help or advice. This "readiness requirement" even suggests that members might find it necessary to wait for a potential recruit to go on an alcoholic binge before approaching him or her, because it is after a binge that the alcoholic is most remorseful and ready for the AA message. A second requirement for helping the prospective candidate is sharing one's own experience. This sharing must follow the storytelling formula and must therefore emphasize that recovery from alcoholism depends on shifting from a life based on self-will to a life based in God's will or the will of a higher power. The only restriction on this technique is that members are advised against imposing a conception of God or spirituality on a recruit. A related requirement is to never let the alcoholic believe that his or her recovery depends on something other than God's will because it is just such a belief that promotes self-will. Thus, those who would make recovery contingent upon the restoration of family or career are informed that this basis is insufficient. The aim of this emphasis is to ensure that the prospective member possesses the appropriate reasons for embarking on the new pattern of life.

The rule of helping others is balanced with special relations besides membership, such as self, family, and employers. A member may go to great lengths to help a prospective candidate, provided that the prospective member is not using the member's generosity as a "blank check" for motives other than reassembling a life according to spiritual principles. Whether providing money, shelter, or other assistance that is required, helping others should never deprive the family, creditors, or employer of their due. This balance is justified by the experience of complimenting self and others. Helping others should not empty one of the

After years of excessive drinking, William G. Wilson cofounded Alcoholics Anonymous in the 1930s. The group's "Twelve Step" program, which Wilson largely created, has helped millions of people worldwide to overcome their addiction to alcohol. *(AP Wide World Photos)*

capacity to meet special commitments necessary to human flourishing.

A 12th Step Call is an occasion where a member shares his or her story with the "still suffering alcoholic." This may involve meeting the prospective member at his or her home, a detoxification center, hospital, or AA meeting. Members make Twelve Step calls only when requested by an alcoholic. Thus, the 12th Step Call is a venue where the existing member and prospective share a similar struggle with self-will. In this sense, the 12th Step Calls, however anonymous, involve a relationship based in mutuality. The

paradigmatic story against which all other stories are measured is the encounter between cofounders Bill Wilson and Dr. Bob Smith.

Meetings

Meetings serve as the primary medium for AA practice and are crucial to AA's success as a social movement. Meeting locations vary significantly from church basements to community halls, but meeting participants occupy space in predictable patterns. Typically, important features of AA practices such as the Twelve Steps and Twelve Traditions are posted in prominent places. Similarly, pictures of AA cofounders Wilson and Smith, important slogans, and the Serenity Prayer are posted. Finally, a literature table with AA literature as well as a list of meetings in the local area is usually found at the entrance. Meeting participants will vary their seating arrangement according to meeting sizes, with larger meetings in audience style and smaller meetings arranged in a circle of chairs. Practically speaking, meetings are the social sites where members acquire the skills, relationships, and motivation to sustain abstinence. When new members express concern over success in their new endeavor, older members will reassure new members by saying, "Read the Big Book, Go to Meetings and Listen to Your Sponsor."

Ordinarily, AA meetings are divided into closed and open meetings. Closed meetings are restricted to members only, while open meetings allow family and friends of alcoholics as well as interested outsiders. Although open meetings typically present a speaker with a minimum amount of sobriety to share his or her story, closed meetings follow a variety of formats designed to focus on particular elements of the program.

Meeting formats do vary, but a typical meeting is opened by a group member who welcomes regular attendees, guests, and newcomers. Participants are then prompted to introduce themselves by saying, "My name is _____, and I am an alcoholic." Not all participants are required to add "alcoholic" to their introductions as visitors may indicate their indecisiveness. After introductions, a member will review announcements for the group and then read, or request a volunteer to read, from foundational texts within the group. Often a member reads aloud Chapter 5 from *Alcoholics Anonymous*, entitled "How It Works," which contains a description of the alcoholic dilemma and the Twelve Steps. Some meetings select additional readings, but these choices are left to group discretion per traditions of meeting autonomy. Concurrent with the readings, members will pass a hat to honor the fifth tradition, which states that each AA group is fully self-supporting. The money collected is used to pay for meeting expenses and AA literature, and a small amount is sent to the General Service Office in New York. Afterward, members will often set aside time to recognize sobriety anniversaries ranging from twenty-four hours to many years. Depending on meeting type, the remainder of the typical meeting varies. For instance, speaker meetings will devote the remaining time to a speaker or speakers who share their stories, which follow the standard pattern established in the Big Book. Speakers share "what it [their drinking experience] was like, what happened [the intervening experiences that led to AA membership], and what it is like now [life since the beginning of sobriety]." In discussion meetings, a more experienced member will raise a topic for discussion through a five- to ten-minute talk, and then each member is given time to discuss the topic as it relates to his or her experience. In larger groups, there is a short break to reconfigure into smaller discussion groups, where each member is given an opportunity to share. Meetings may also have a special agenda. For example, in step meetings speakers discuss one of the twelve steps rather than a topic, and in Big Book meetings a sustained study of the Big Book is usually involved. Almost all meetings close with a prayer ritual that in many groups still reflects the influence of the OGM. Members will sometimes join hands to close the meeting with a prayer, which could be the serenity prayer or what is known as the Lord's Prayer in the Christian tradition.

Alternative Alcohol Recovery Movements

The diffusion of AA and the Twelve Steps as the predominant treatment modality has spawned several alternative alcohol recovery movements such as Synanon, Women for Sobriety (WFS), Secular Organizations for Sobriety (SOS), and Rational Recovery (RR), to name only a few. In each of these cases, these movements were self-conscious departures from AA practices emerging from ideological differences with AA. For example, Jean Kirkpatrick, Ph.D., founded WFS in 1976 to aid women in recovery from alcoholism. Drawing on her experiences with AA recovery practices, Kirkpatrick concluded that the masculine bias in AA could never successfully aid women in their recovery efforts because AA practices failed to account for significant gender differences contributing to alcoholic behaviors and recovery. From sexist

discourse at meetings to a male-oriented approach to recovery that begins with powerlessness, Kirkpatrick concluded that women alcoholics were ordinarily saddled with subordinate roles that led them to experience a feeling of dependence. Instead of focusing on powerlessness, Kirkpatrick suggested that women alcoholics need to focus on recognizing alcoholism as a physical disease and to assume responsibility for their bodies and the illness from which they suffer. In keeping with these differences, WFS employs alternative recovery techniques such as the thirteen affirmations that emphasize the power of positive thinking rather than AA's Twelve Steps. Members introduce themselves by saying: "My name is _____ and I'm a competent woman" rather than "My name is _____ and I am an alcoholic." Organizationally, groups are limited to ten members who meet weekly for ninety minutes under the direction of a Certified Moderator.

Both SOS and RR describe their organization as an alternative model of recovery based on a secular approach and view addiction recovery as independent of religious or spiritual endeavors and projects. For instance, SOS views alcoholism as a disease requiring total abstinence, but total abstinence does not require spiritual experiences or religious ideology. Instead, the SOS program of recovery stresses substituting cycles of addiction with cycles of sobriety. According to this view, addiction begins with a physiological need habitually satisfied until addiction satisfaction becomes a fundamental priority. The addict simultaneously suffers from denial of this very problem. In response to the cycle of addiction, SOS recommends a cognitive therapy based on individual acknowledgment of one's addiction, acceptance of one's disease, and emphasis on sobriety as one's number one priority. The cycle of sobriety remains unless the addict chooses to abandon it.

Understanding AA's Impact as a Social Movement

Most scholars agree that researchers are years away from calculating AA's impact on treating alcoholics, but two sites of activity express and signify AA's impact as a social movement: alcohol treatment practices and attempts by U.S. courts to evaluate the constitutionality of Twelve Step practices in criminal rehabilitative efforts.

Almost since its inception, AA practices have been adapted to professional treatment settings in varying degrees. William White's authoritative history of alcohol treatment in the United States chronicles AA's influence in shaping models of alcohol treatment. Beginning with Dr. Bob's efforts at St. Thomas's Hospital in Akron, the practice of hospitals employing a Twelve Step philosophy and relying on unpaid members of AA to help treat alcoholics is the dominant treatment model. The St. Thomas model emphasized sponsorship of patients by members of AA, employed the Twelve Steps in treating alcoholics, and stressed mutual-help strategies, with clients helping clients. Similar strategies and arrangements emerged simultaneously within prison and correctional facilities to treat alcoholics.

In recent years, rehabilitation programs that draw on the Twelve Steps, or require AA attendance, have been challenged in U.S. courts on the basis that mandated and compulsory attendance at AA meetings violates the establishment clause. In almost all cases heard before the courts, the questions have emerged from the presence of Twelve Step practices in the criminal rehabilitation process. In the earliest cases before the courts, the role of Twelve Step practices as a part of sentence fulfillment was ruled as constitutional. According to these early cases, the courts found that correctional authorities who employed Twelve Step practices and mandated AA meetings were in fact neutral on questions of religion and that whatever religious encouragement an inmate might endure at a Twelve Step meeting was secondary to the state's interest in treating an inmate's substance abuse problems. In short, the earliest cases followed a fairly strict application of the traditional "Lemon Test" the courts employed to verify establishment clause violations (*O'Connor v. California* [1993], *Stafford v. Harrison* [1991], and *Jones v. Smid* [1993]).

The courts have not been uniform in viewing the religious features and effects of AA and Twelve Step practices as secondary. For instance, in 1996, the New York Court of Appeals decided in favor of David Griffin, an inmate at New York State Shawangunk Correctional Facility, who petitioned the court to excuse him from taking part in the Alcohol and Substance Abuse Treatment Program (ASAT). ASAT provided treatment services for corrections inmates suffering from alcoholism and chemical dependency. Griffin sought relief from participating in ASAT because the program involved attendance at AA meetings, which based some of its therapeutic techniques on religious principles. Griffin's attorney argued that compelling attendance at AA meetings violated inmate rights to religious freedom.

The court ruled that the nature of the ASAT program and Griffin's participation in it violated the es-

tablishment clause and was unconstitutional. Griffin's involvement in ASAT and the resulting expectation of attendance at AA meetings were predicated on his participation in the Shawangunk Family Reunion Program, which placed three conditions on participating inmates. First, inmates must have served a minimum length of their sentence, and, second, inmates must be free of disciplinary probation for prison rule violations. The last condition, and the most contentious one, required inmates with histories of substance abuse to participate in ASAT as a condition of participation in the Family Reunion Program. Because Griffin met each of these conditions (including sustained heroine abuse from 1955 to 1968), his participation in Family Reunion required his attendance at ASAT and AA meetings. In the court's view, the connection between AA and sentence requirements created the primary effect of advancing religion.

Finally, what the sites of treatment practices and the court rulings direct our attention to is the range and impact AA has had on practices of helping alcoholics, the difficulties of measuring AA's impact, and the contested territories in which AA operates. In focusing on the practice of helping others, the present article has traced but one genealogy in a complex web of untold stories. To fully appreciate the movement, further analysis focused on AA practices as they relate to race, gender, disability, and class is needed.

James Swan Tuite

BIBLIOGRAPHY

Clark, Walter H. *The Oxford Groups: Its History and Significance.* New York: Bookman, 1951.

Colon, Leon S. "*Griffin v. Coughlin*: Mandated AA Meetings and the Establishment Clause." *Journal of Church and State* (Summer 1997): 427–454.

Eister, Allen. *Drawing-Room Conversions: A Sociological Account of the Oxford Group Movement.* Durham, NC: Duke University Press, 1950.

Kaskutas, Lee. "Women for Sobriety: A Qualitative Analysis." *Contemporary Drug Problems* (Summer 1990): 177–200.

"Kirk Collected Papers." John Hay Library, Brown University Rare Books Library. Various years.

Kurtz, Ernest. *Not-God: A History of Alcoholics Anonymous.* Center City, MN: Hazelden, 1991.

Levine, Harry G. "The Alcohol Problem in America: From Temperance to Alcoholism." *British Journal of Addiction* (1984): 109–119.

Makela, Klaus, ed. *Alcoholics Anonymous as a Mutual-Help Movement:*

A Study in Eight Societies. Madison: University of Wisconsin Press, 1996.

Room, Robin. "Alcoholics Anonymous as a Social Movement." In *Research on Alcoholics Anonymous: Opportunities and Alternatives*, ed. Barbara McCrady and William R. Miller, pp. 167–187. New Brunswick, NJ: Rutgers Center of Alcohol Studies, 1993.

White, William. *Slaying the Dragon: The History of Addiction Treatment and Recovery in America.* Bloomington, IN: Chestnut Health Systems, 1998.

8

RELIGIOUS, UTOPIAN, AND
HEALTH MOVEMENTS

INTRODUCTION

The explosive combination of America's radical religious and cultural diversity within a hegemonic, entrenched Protestantism has served as the catalyst for some of the most powerful social movements in U.S. history. Pre-contact Native Americans practiced many different beliefs whose multiplicity was only enhanced by the post-Columbian immigration of Europeans and Africans with their own myriad systems of belief and practice. The U.S. Constitution's prohibition against establishing a single national religion further set the foundation for a plurality of religions to flourish. Without the state to regulate orthodoxy, Americans were free to believe as they chose and to start new movements when they became dissatisfied with existing religions. Substantial immigration added to America's religious diversity. Men and women from all over the globe brought their cultures to the North American soil. Yet immigrant and Native religions never remained static, but in different regions around the country evolved in particular and distinct ways, lending local flair to adherents' spiritual lives. At the same time, Protestant Christianity has left an indelible imprint on the major institutions, creeds, and belief systems that shape civic life. But like every other American religion, Protestantism has changed over time, influencing other religions as they influence it. American religions are in a constant state of evolution resulting from centuries of contact between competing groups of religious people. This contact and combination between the dominant culture and the nation's many subcultures has been the definitive characteristic of American religion and has inspired complex social movements.

Colonists raced to the Americas in the seventeenth and eighteenth centuries for a variety of reasons, including reaping profit, proselytizing, and building a new way of life. On the East Coast, pluralism flourished as New England Puritans sought to define the trajectory of North American life, while Quakers, Natives, and a host of other religious groups served as constant reminders that the American story was much more than one of Protestant triumphalism. On the West Coast, Father Junipero Serra and his allies struggled to bring Roman Catholicism to the indigenous people of California. Within a couple of centuries, revivals broke out on the Eastern Seaboard, which helped set the stage for the American Revolution.

After the war, multiple major religious movements emerged. One of these movements, "civil religion," was initiated primarily by elites who sought to give religious meaning to their new nation. Other movements emerged from a series of Protestant-initiated revivals that fit the character of the times. They were more democratic and egalitarian than the revivals of the prewar era, and they spawned unique social movements affecting Anglos, African Americans, and Native Americans, among others, in different ways. Visionaries, unencumbered by the restrictions of previous generations, built utopian communities, while prophets looking heavenward foretold the end of the world.

After the Civil War, the United States' immigration patterns shifted. More and more people began arriving from Central, Eastern, and Southern Europe in contrast to the previous generations which had more often originated from Western Europe. And on the West Coast, Asians arrived in great numbers, answering American business's call for inexpensive labor. With the evolving immigration came new religious trends. The country's Jewish and Catholic populations, which were already sizable, surged. At the same time, new religions from other parts of the globe appeared for the World's Parliament of Religions, a conference of leaders from major world religious groups held in Chicago in 1893. Out of this increasingly pluralistic context and fueled by continuing heavy immigration, many new social movements emerged, which only multiplied after World War II. In the 1960s, Congress passed legislation that reformed America's immigration laws. Nonwhite, non-Protestant religions flourished as quotas favoring the immigration of Europeans and restricting the immigration of Asians and other national groups came to an end. The result has been a revolution in religious diversity in which America's pluralism has emerged from back alleys and moved to Main Street. Islam, Hinduism, and Buddhism are among the groups that illustrate this change, while other Americans have reached out to the New Age movement.

Religiously based social movements have defined America. Thousands of pioneers have emerged, some manipulating historic faiths and others building entirely new movements. Some have enjoyed tremendous success, while others have faded into oblivion. Heavy immigration, charismatic individuals, strong organizations, and protection against the establishment of a single religion have allowed thousands of religious movements to thrive in North America.

UTOPIAN AND HEALTH MOVEMENTS

This section also includes entries documenting the unique phenomenon of utopian communities that have been integral to American society from the origins of European colonization. From the earliest days of settlement to the contemporary era, utopian and communal communities remained pivotal to understanding the distinctive American culture and society built on the yearning to build a better society. From the earliest days of settlement in North America, utopian sentiment proliferated, as people with idiosyncratic ideologies and religious feeling, estranged in their homelands abroad or alienated within the broader American society, sought out a more meaningful life. Throughout the nation's history, utopian communities have held a broad range of beliefs and ideologies, ranging from fundamentalist religion to ideological principles on building egalitarian communities.

Although many held distinctive and contradictory ideas and practices, they all shared dissatisfaction with mainstream society, whether they were European Christians migrating to the nation to establish religious communities that more specifically adhered to their sometimes fundamentalist beliefs and ascetic lifestyles or utopian socialists seeking to establish collectivist communities. Utopian communities established settlements that put their sometimes abstract philosophical beliefs into active practice. Another feature of utopian communities was their lack of continuity. Again and again, utopian societies have been established, expanded, and then usually declined as the most extreme advocates lost their passion or could not convince their descendants to stay on and carry out their missions. Still, some older utopian communities remain to this day, though on a smaller scale, and new models that attract new generations of adherents gain power. Throughout U.S. history, communities establishing communal forms of organization have predominated, starting with the early colonists who escaped established European religions and extending much later to the Buddhist retreats and Hindu ashrams that have gained sway in the contemporary era.

Religious fervor or alienation from the dominant community has always been a central feature of utopian communities. Perhaps the most well-known such communities were the Shakers—formally, members of the United Society of Believers in Christ's Second Appearing—who migrated from England in the late eighteenth century and established a community based on ascetic ideals of repentance and denial of what they considered to be gluttonous and worldly lifestyles based on the pleasures of life. A distinctive feature of the Shakers was their demand that all members remain celibate. Ironically, the Shakers became known for their handiwork and their production of craftworks that were demanded outside their communities. Later the Shakers became known for their innovations—including the circular saw, the clothespin, and flat broom—and were keen on new technological advances, including the automobile. Still, at the core of the Shakers' religious belief was their strong belief in monastic, simple lives unencumbered by possessions and human desire. At their height in the early nineteenth century, the Shakers had several thousand members in twenty community villages. But the membership began to decline at the end of the nineteenth century as communal villages closed. Today only one Shaker community remains— Sabbathday Lake, Maine, and the sect's future is tenuous and uncertain.

As new immigrants arrived on American shores, fervent religious believers among them established new utopian communities. In the nineteenth century, religious German communities were established in the Northeast and Midwest, including the Harmonists and the Rappites, Inspirationists, Amana, Noyes, and the Oneidans. But religion was not the only basis for the formation of communal societies. Some communities were established on the basis of cooperatives and the sharing of all resources. Perhaps the best known was Harmony Society established in New Harmony, Indiana, in early 1825. Utopian communities frequently failed to establish enduring communities, primarily because they were open to all and because of difficulty in encouraging all to participate on an equal basis, as was the case in New Harmony, two years after its formation. Although utopian communities frequently did not flourish, as was the case in New Harmony, they attracted academics, scholars, and scientists, and became models for progressive educational reform.

Brook Farm, a community formed in 1841 in West Roxbury, Massachusetts, by New England transcendentalists, including Ralph Waldo Emerson, pursued free mental exploration and direct experience of the material world in rural areas in the early nineteenth century. The community engaged in manual labor and thoughtful interchange, education, and socializing, which helped them gain adherents throughout the country. Subsequent communities based on the Brook Farm model, most notably Charles Fourier's phalanx community, were specifically designed according to plans intended for communal participation. Still, most were short lived. Subsequent secular communities were established throughout the late nineteenth century as European settlement moved West. Traditions ranged far and wide, from communal sectarianism, economic reform to socialism and anarchism.

The formation of communal settlements by immigrants and by those alienated by the big cities expanded throughout the nineteenth century as Americans searched for spiritual nourishment and uplift. Perhaps the most well known were the Mormons—a sect that, although essentially jettisoning the communal experiment, expanded into major religious social forces to this day. Members were attracted to the religious fervor and to the social and economic supports such communities provided. During the war years, from 1914 to 1945, German pacifists facing discrimination formed the Hutterite community, which grew to over 40,000 members in 400 colonies, declining to about 2,000 members by the early 2000s.

New Age religions, whose roots are largely in Eastern philosophy, became popular in the early twentieth century but exploded after the 1960s. Each

community, even those based on common religious philosophy, maintained distinctive ideas. Communal Hindu ashrams and Buddhist monastic communes of all types proliferated throughout the country from the 1960s to this day, each with a distinctive sectarian twist. In the 1960s and 1970s, communes were established in the wake of the social movements of the era, including Anarchists, groups espousing music and the arts, and those promoting psychedelic drugs.

Religious fervor has been an enduring theme in American culture, and sectarian utopian societies continue to form on the basis of fervent belief even in the age of enlightenment, the development of scientific discoveries disproving religions, and rational thought. Indeed, after the 1970s, religious fervor spurred the formation of religious communities embracing radical millennial philosophies of Armageddon, the second coming of Christ, and the coming of the Messiah. Frequently, the leaders of communities were self-styled messiahs, charismatic figures such as James Jones and David Koresh, who were able to sway typically down-and-out and weak people to embrace them as the saviors. Engaging in some of the very same practices as communal societies of generations past—hard work and denial of human urges (except for leaders)—the communities nonetheless became emblematic of the search for meaning and the singular importance of their cause. These sects went so far as to engage in ritual mass suicide, as for instance, the Hale-Bopp Cult that believed they would be chosen for space travel by aliens. Each group had a distinctive character—vegetarianism, gun ownership, drug use, rock and roll, sex, science fiction, and popular culture.

Communes and utopian communities in the United States have both reflected the alienation felt by many in American society and revealed the continual desire of the alienated to create meaning in their lives beyond the culture of consumerism through sharing and visualizing a better future for themselves.

This section also examines the health food movement, comprised of a diverse, disparate effort among many Americans to make food an integral part of their daily living. The health food movement extends well beyond consumer choice and represents an integral part of a long tradition of adherents with a strong belief system. One's choice in food was an ethical consideration on which the fate of the larger community, the nation, and the world depended. Like the utopian communities, the health food movement had no central core belief, but was comprised of many followers with a diversity of beliefs and ideologies about how food connected to their lives. The movement was led by religious groups, scientists, and ethical organizations committed to the ethical treatment of animals, the environment, politics, and nutrition. For the movement to operate practically, it was connected to food producers, marketers, and distributors that profited from those committed to the movement. The health food movement has remained firmly grounded in American tradition from the nineteenth century to the current era.

Matthew A. Sutton and Immanuel Ness

RELIGIOUS MOVEMENTS: OVERVIEW

From pre-Columbian indigenous rituals to modern mass market, technologically savvy faiths, religion has served as a catalyst for social engagement. Steady immigration, revitalization movements, charismatic leaders, and strong institutions have transformed the ideas of a few pioneers into powerful religious movements, reshaping American culture.

Religion in America is distinguished by the combination of a radical religious and cultural diversity with a hegemonic, entrenched Protestantism. Native American groups practiced many different beliefs whose multiplicity was only enhanced by the post-Columbian immigration of Europeans and Africans with their own myriad systems of belief and practice. The U.S. Constitution's prohibition against establishing a single national religion further set the foundation for a plurality of religions to flourish. Without the state to regulate orthodoxy, Americans were free to believe as they chose and to start new movements when they became dissatisfied with existing religions. Substantial immigration has also bolstered America's religious diversity. Men and women from all over the globe have brought their cultures to the North American soil. Yet immigrant and native religions never remained static, but in different regions around the country they evolved in particular and distinct ways, lending local flair to adherents' spiritual lives. At the same time, Protestant Christianity has defined the major institutions, creeds, and belief systems that a broad selection of the American public accepts. This influence is evident in the nation's holidays, songs, political activities, and popular culture. But like every other American religion, Protestantism has evolved over time, influencing other religions as they have influenced it. Historian Catherine L. Albanese argues that American religious life is best described by religious combination. Rather than treating religious systems as relics that resist change and transformation, American religions are in a constant state of evolution

resulting from centuries of contact between competing groups of religious people. This contact and combination between the dominant culture and the nation's many subcultures has been the definitive characteristic of American religion and has inspired complex social movements.

COLONIAL RELIGION

Colonists raced to the Americas in the seventeenth and eighteenth centuries for a variety of reasons, including profit-making, proselytizing, and building a new way of life. On the East Coast, pluralism flourished as New England Puritans sought to define the trajectory of North American life, while Quakers, Native Americans, and a host of other religious groups served as constant reminders that the American story was much more than one of Protestant triumphalism. Meanwhile, on the West Coast, Father Junipero Serra and his allies struggled to bring Roman Catholicism to the indigenous people of California. As each of these groups labored across generations to advance their religions, a revival broke out on the Eastern seaboard. Known as the Great Awakening, these meetings revitalized colonial Protestantism in the 1730s and 1740s.

England's efforts to expand its empire in the 1600s led to the creation of American Puritanism, one of the continent's most distinctive and formative social movements. Frustrated with the state of the Church of England in the sixteenth century, British Puritans abandoned their homes in search of a place where they could isolate themselves from England's supposed moral degradation and where they might raise their children in the faith. The Puritans believed that in coming to America, they were establishing an unbreakable covenant with God, which was chronicled by Plymouth, Massachusetts, governor William Bradford. Another group of Puritans, who settled a decade later on Massachusetts Bay, had a slightly different goal in mind. They had embarked on an "errand into the wilderness" to build a holy city, which they hoped would provide a model for governing back in England.

As their leader John Winthrop articulated their goal, they sought to establish a godly, utopian society in the New World that would demonstrate the legitimacy of the Puritan faith to the English. The Puritans ultimately expected to be welcomed back to their homeland where they could lead a religious and political reformation, but this wish never materialized. Puritanism's success derived from its integration of religious ideology with all other aspects of life and society. Government, church, and community were seamlessly entwined, establishing a powerful foundation for the movement to flourish. Puritans were committed to education and built strong schools in North America. They also left little room for dissent. Mavericks who challenged colonial authorities were quickly and severely punished. The two original groups of Puritans eventually merged and together, with new immigrants from England, articulated one of the major religious themes in U.S. history, that of Protestant triumphalism. The Puritans believed that they were God's chosen people for his chosen land, an idea that has resonated with generations of American Protestants.

Although the Puritans have received the most scholarly attention, they were not the only European colonists building religious movements in early America. The Society of Friends, or Quakers, were influential religious pioneers who constantly and intentionally antagonized the Puritans. They built successful communities in New England and in the middle colonies as well. The largest Quaker settlement was in Pennsylvania, a colony established by William Penn as a refuge for his co-religionists. Quakers tended to be more egalitarian than other Protestants and were tied together by their strong communal emphasis. They dressed simply, they rejected social distinctions, and they attempted to live humbly. Theologically, they emphasized all people's ability to find the light of Christ within them, which they believed was a means by which God communicated. This radical idea empowered individuals and shattered religious hierarchies—God could speak through anyone, regardless of age, race, or gender. Unlike most of the Puritans who insisted on keeping their colony religiously "pure," Penn promoted toleration of other groups, including different Protestant sects, Catholics, and Native Americans. Quakers dominated Philadelphia's politics, and as slavery in-

creased in North America they became leading abolitionists. In the nineteenth century, Quakers helped direct the fight for women's equality.

Religious movements were developing on the West Coast as well. In the mid-1700s, Franciscan Father Junipero Serra established an impressive line of mission stations along the California coast from San Diego to San Francisco where Native converts lived with Spanish missionaries. Indians were required to adopt European cultural norms, but in subtle ways they helped the Catholic fathers apply their faith in a context quite different from their homeland. The missions offered Indians tools, trade goods, and food and became a means of social advancement for some. The religious life of the missions became a hybrid of European and native North American customs that were actively negotiated by the two people groups. Well after the missions secularized, local Natives continued practicing an integrated religion that drew from both Catholicism and the traditions of their tribes, which permanently influenced religion in the Southwest.

Over the course of American history, revivals of faith were common. They often arose when religious men and women, dissatisfied with the state of their religious lives and institutions, looked back to previous generations for inspiration. In their predecessors, they discovered what they believed was a higher level of commitment and authenticity than that characterizing their own generation. As a result, they would demand a return to the old-time faith of their forebearers, which led to a renewal of religious vigor and a revitalization of faith. This occurred in the mid-eighteenth century and has occurred repeatedly among people of different ethnicities and faiths ever since.

In the mid-1700s, the colonies experienced a tremendous revival called the "Great Awakening," which eventually influenced the entire Eastern seaboard. Led by charismatic men and women, the revival stemmed from the growing discouragement of a handful of preachers over what they thought was rampant impiety. The faith of their Puritan forebearers had been diluted over time. They believed that even other clergy lacked the proper spiritual credentials to be leading parishioners. Therefore, a group of men and a few women, starting in the middle colonies and New England and progressing to the Southern colonies, began traveling from town-to-town calling for revival. They were controversial, and their ideas eventually caused many churches to split between loyalty to traditional leaders and allegiance to the revivalists. Among the many factors contributing to the Awak-

JUNÍPERO SERRA (1713–1784)

Junípero Serra was born Miguel José Serra in Majorca, Spain, on November 24, 1713. On September 14, 1730, he entered the Franciscan Order and took Junípero as his name. For his proficiency in studies, he was appointed lector of philosophy before his ordination to the priesthood. Later he received the degree of doctor of theology from the Lullian University at Palma, where he also taught philosophy for fifteen years. He occupied the Duns Scotus chair of philosophy until he traveled to Mexico in 1749.

In 1749, Serra was sent to Mexico with Francisco Palou, his lifelong friend and biographer, and proceeded to Mexico City, where he taught briefly at the College of San Fernando. For three years he worked successfully among the Native Americans of the Sierra Gorda and then returned to Mexico City for seven more years, working half of each year in the surrounding villages. A strenuous defender of Indians, he learned the language of the Pame Indians, and translated the catechism into their language. He became famous as a most fervent and effective preacher of missions. His zeal frequently led him to employ extraordinary means in order to move the people to penance. He would pound his breast with a stone while in the pulpit, scourge himself, or apply a lighted torch to his bare chest.

In 1769, Serra went with the second expedition to California, which was commanded by Gaspar de Por-tolá. When the party reached San Diego, Serra remained to found the mission there, while most of the rest of the party went on in search of the harbor of Monterey. It was the first of the twenty-one California missions (he established nine himself) which converted all the natives on the coast as far as Sonoma in the north and marked the beginning of the European settlement of California. When they returned unsuccessful from the expedition, Serra urged the sending of another, which he accompanied. After they reached Monterey and founded the mission San Carlos de Monterey (1770), Serra remained there as president of Alta California missions; in 1771, because the soldiers were not friendly to the Indians, he moved the mission to Carmel-by-the-Sea and renamed it San Carlos Barromeo de Carmelo, which became his headquarters for the rest of his life. He died at Monterey, California, on August 28, 1784.

Serra is considered by many to be the founder and the pioneer of California. The esteem in which his memory is held by all classes in California is reflected in the fact that a non-Catholic had a granite monument erected to him at Monterey. A bronze statue of heroic size represents him as the apostolic preacher in Golden Gate Park, San Francisco. In 1884, the California legislature passed a concurrent resolution making August 29 of that year, the centennial of Father Serra's burial, a legal holiday.

James G. Lewis

ening's success were charismatic leaders, a well-developed intellectual foundation, and changes in technology and communications.

The Great Awakening's most important and successful revivalist was Englishman George Whitefield, who tied together the many strands of revival into a somewhat distinct social movement. Known as the "great itinerant," he was not confined to one particular church and pulpit, but proclaimed his message wherever he could find listeners. He first came to America in 1739 (at age twenty-five) and eventually made seven trips to the United States, touring all over the colonies. He regularly spoke outdoors to accommodate large crowds, and he preached without notes, in stark contrast to the traditional written sermons of the Puritans. Whitefield's style reduced the physical and social distance between preacher and listener, making him seem accessible to common people. He became America's first intercolonial hero, a celebrity superstar, which was an image he cultivated. His appeal lay in his powerful voice, his theatrical panache, his unique looks—he had a wandering eye—and his masterful rhetorical skill.

The primary philosopher and theologian of the Great Awakening, and one of America's most brilliant minds, was Jonathan Edwards, the pastor of a Congregational Church in Northampton, Massachusetts. In the mid-1730s, Edwards began to preach on the importance of justification by faith, which caused a revival in his church. Congregants experiencing conversion expressed themselves in a variety of ways ranging from weeping to convulsing, to falling prostrate onto the ground, to producing strange verbal sounds. Seeking to build the movement, Edwards began working with other preachers in the region, triggering a widespread revival across the Connecticut Valley. He combined Puritan theology with Enlightenment philosophy, reading heavily in John Locke and Isaac Newton. His intention was not to teach static doctrine, but to bring about a change of consciousness in listeners. He did this by appealing to their "affections," or emotions, with vivid sensational images. He also served as the Great Awakening's foremost promoter, publicist, defender, and interpreter.

Another element of the Great Awakening's success was its inclusive nature. The revival affected more than just Anglo Americans. David Brainerd, Edwards' son-in-law, became a "missionary to the Indians," taking Edwards' ideas to Native Americans. He led a revival among a band of Delaware Indians, baptized thirty-eight of them, and formed a church. When Brainerd died prematurely, Edwards fashioned the revivalist's diary into a heroic book that popularized Brainerd's work, which was read all over the colonies. On Whitefield's tours to the South, many African Americans converted, marking the beginning of Christianity's integration into slave culture. Women were also key players in the movement. A few, the most famous of whom was Bathsheba Kingsley, actually went from church to church preaching and exhorting audiences and even ministers to experience conversion. Although male leaders were never entirely comfortable with women preaching, some like Edwards acknowledged the women's contributions. The revivals ultimately challenged traditional gender roles, providing opportunities for women to speak in public and to teach the scriptures.

The Great Awakening emerged at a time when important new innovations in communication were developing, which was most obvious in the distribution of newspapers. Colonists in both North and South could read about the tremendous crowds and the amazing spectacles of Whitefield's meetings. These reports helped build momentum behind the revivalists and aroused the interest of common people and elites, from poor farmers to Benjamin Franklin. In addition to its formative influence on American Protestantism, the Awakening also had a decisive effect on the colonists' move toward revolution in that it provided one of the first unifying experiences of the eighteenth century. As a result of the widespread popularity of people like Whitefield, colonists began thinking of themselves as distinctly American rather than English or "Virginian." More important, revivalists infused in their audiences a belief that the common person could trust his or her own instincts. No longer did established authorities have to be deferred to, but the religious impulses of regular people were valued. A new national identity, a communications revolution, and the fracturing of traditional authorities spawned by the Awakening helped the colonies unite against England during the Revolution.

THE REVOLUTION AND EARLY REPUBLIC

In the wake of the American Revolution, two major religious movements developed. The first was civil religion, a movement initiated primarily by elites who sought to give religious meaning to their new nation. The second was a series of revivals called the Second Great Awakening. These revivals fit the character of the times. They were more democratic and egalitarian than the revivals of the previous centuries, and they spawned a number of unique social movements affecting whites, African Americans, and Native Americans in different ways.

One of the most important and distinctively American belief systems is "civil religion," which emerged around the time of the American Revolution. First and foremost, civil religion stemmed from the patriots' efforts to give religious significance to their new nation. The religion of most of the Revolutionary leaders was not the evangelical faith of Jonathan Edwards or George Whitefield but a synthesis of Puritan ideas and humanist philosophy. Like their Puritan predecessors, the patriots believed that America occupied a unique position in God's unfolding plan for history. The result was a combination of religious and political language that put the Revolution on a par with biblical epics. Their belief in a dualistic world with good battling evil, an unrelenting sense of the providence of God, and melodramatic interpretations of international events also had Puritan roots.

These ideas were tempered by the patriots' confidence in humans' ability to make the world a better place and assumptions about God's transcendence from His creation, which derived from European philosophy. Revolutionary leaders, under the spell of the Enlightenment, replaced the active deity of Whitefield with the God of reason, natural law, and natural rights. The Bible inspired much of the rhetoric of the war, but it was a deistic God who had set the universe in motion with specific laws whom they honored. George Washington, after his death, became the ultimate symbol of civil religion. He acquired an almost divine status, recognized as the messiah of the new nation. In America's national songs, on the walls of its shrines, on its money, and in its holiday celebrations, religion and patriotism merged.

While civil religion influenced the national life of the United States, the early Republic proved to be fertile ground for the birth of new social movements. Protestants, who remained the dominant religious group, reshaped their faith in ways that ultimately accommodated the growth of new sects. A few sweeping trends made this possible. First, conversion was simplified. Rather than having to make public and arduous demonstration of their faith, people were able to make an immediate and inward decision to convert. This individualistic accentuation of Christianity appealed to the illiterate and poorly educated, including slaves, rural settlers, and newer immigrants. Second, the role of the preacher evolved. One's authority was justified on the basis of his or her individual conversion experience and his or her ability to attract followers; many Protestants rejected the traditional requirement of a "proper" education for their leaders. Third, religious outsiders faced few restrictions. They encountered a world turned upside down by the Revolution where anything was possible. Traditional authorities had been subverted, leaving insurgents free to shape their faith as they chose.

Out of this context burst the Second Great Awakening. In the last decade of the eighteenth century and in the first of the nineteenth, the colonies experienced a tremendous revival of Christianity, both in the East and among settlers expanding into the Western United States. Among the most famous and important of these revivals were the Cane Ridge camp meetings of 1801. Seeking to influence the spiritual lives of the thousands of people heading westward, local clergy around rural Bourbon County, Kentucky, sent off invitations for a nationwide revival. Between 10,000 and 25,000 people responded, arriving in wagons for this unprecedented opportunity to socialize, to catch up on news and gossip, and to gain valuable information about the West. The result was a sudden and temporary urban setting springing up for a week in the wilderness. Religious meetings were organized around crude, mostly outdoor, preaching platforms, which were shared by a potpourri of speakers, including black and white Methodists, Baptists, and Presbyterians. Parishioners responded physically to the revival services by falling, experiencing the "jerks," dancing, barking, running, and singing when they came under the "power of the Spirit." So many people fell to the earth that parts of the revival grounds appeared to be strewn like a battlefield, bodies shook and convulsed, and some enthusiasts babbled incoherent speech. Skeptics, however, noted that more souls might have been conceived at Cane Ridge than saved. Each of the major denominations represented at Cane Ridge continued to organize similar meetings in the following years. As a result, thousands of Americans converted to the evangelical Protestant faith and many new churches were established, fueling the growth of Pres-

byterianism in the South and the explosion of the Methodist and Baptist denominations in the West.

Cane Ridge occurred as a semispontaneous, enthused event that represented church leaders' growing concern about the souls of their peers and Americans' increasing appetite for religion as they built a new nation. The Methodists made the most of this opportunity, creating an enormous network of churches through their brilliant organizational skill. Like the itinerants of the Great Awakening, Methodist preachers traveled from region to region spreading the gospel. However, rather than focusing on the spiritual state of the churched as had Edwards and Whitefield, Methodists worked hard at organizing the unchurched. As the American population sprawled westward, Methodist preachers called circuit riders took it upon themselves to ensure that the influence of the Christian gospel did the same. Their goal was to restore the "primitive church," freeing religion from the encumbrances of tradition and shaping it for the needs of the changing nation. The circuit riders divided up regions between them, overseeing multiple congregations at the same time since there were not enough ministers to match the nation's expansion. They traveled from church to church, stopping to preach whenever a crowd gathered. Between visits by the circuit rider, Methodist congregations met on their own for prayer and worship. If they had a skilled lay exhorter, he or she might occasionally preach. As a result of its democratic tendencies and its strong organizational efforts, Methodism appealed to Americans of all races and classes, becoming the largest American religious movement in the nineteenth century.

While Methodists built churches around the country, Charles Grandison Finney attempted to fuel the revival fires in the Northeast in the 1820s and 1830s. A lawyer by trade, Finney had a radical conversion experience. He then began preaching, leading a large revival in the boom town of Rochester, New York, where the Erie Canal had opened the way for rapid growth. Finney was an innovator; he encouraged women to testify in public, and he pioneered the use of the anxious bench—a bench placed at the front of the church where suppliants could contemplate their sinfulness and seek conversion. Finney's success may be partially attributable to the support of capitalists leading the market revolution engulfing Rochester. As workers gained more autonomy over their private lives, business leaders benefited from churches that taught workers to be temperate and reliable. However, religion seems to have been much more than an opiate for the masses. Workers used religion as a liberating force in their lives and for opportunities to build relationships in their community. Finney later moved to Ohio where he became president of the new Oberlin College, a school that admitted men and women, whites and blacks. The college was also one of the nation's leading voices for social reform.

Revival affected the South as well as the West, transforming life in slave communities. Little noticed by whites, slaves responded to the democratic, egalitarian message of the Second Great Awakening in radical ways. Not content worshiping in the prescribed manner of their masters, slaves crafted their own network of churches and anointed their own religious authorities. They met secretly, often after dark, in shanties far from masters' homes where they were free to worship, to pray, to share news, and to testify. The religion slaves followed merged West African practices and beliefs with evangelical Christianity, which provided a framework for analyzing the hardships they faced and allowed them to take solace in each other and in their creator. The church inspired many of their most fervent calls for freedom and cultivated the leadership skills of men and women who orchestrated revolts. Throughout the nineteenth- and twentieth-century South, the black church served as the centerpiece of the African-American community. African Americans took the religious ideas and practices of their homeland and of the Second Great Awakening, blended them, and created their own religious movement that provided much of the basis for their economic, political, and social life.

Large numbers of African Americans in the North also found religion to be an empowering force. Independent black churches arose in part out of African Americans' growing impatience with racist church policies. One influential early leader was Richard Allen, who was born into slavery in Philadelphia. He was converted by Methodists and began preaching, eventually converting his own master who responded by allowing Allen to purchase freedom. He became a circuit rider after the war, and then returned to Philadelphia where he led prayer services at the biracial St. George's Methodist Church. As the congregation's black population increased, so did the racial animosity of the whites. Ultimately, the white church leadership began segregating the pews and altar areas. In 1787, Richard Allen and a number of his friends left St. George's in protest of its racial discrimination and started a church in a blacksmith shop. It led to the creation of the African Methodist Episcopal Church, which focused on both the spiritual and economic well-being of African Americans. The denomination became an important center of political and social support for the black community in America.

Women were also involved in the development of the black church. Jarena Lee, a member of Richard Allen's congregation, believed that God had called her to preach. Although Allen originally forbade it because of her gender, Lee spontaneously arose during a service and began preaching extemporaneously. Allen stood and told the congregation that Lee was as qualified as any of the men to speak. She then became an itinerant preacher, traveling with a message of revival. She wrote and published an autobiography, an unprecedented action for a black woman in this era.

Methodists were not the only people in North America attempting to elicit religious revival. When Europeans first landed on the shores of North America, they encountered a diverse set of cultures. American Indians lived in hundreds of different societies with distinct languages, cultures, and religions, sharing little in common. Over the centuries, however, they occasionally began to work together, creating new alliances in the face of their common threat. A consequence was Native American religious revitalization movements. One of the most famous began in the early nineteenth century when a Shawnee named Tenskwatawa started having visions. He claimed to know the key to Native survival: Indians must completely reject all of the cultural practices that they had inherited from Europeans. Dress, tools, dietary and religious practices were all to return to traditional Native ways if they wanted to protect their land. Tenskwatawa was aided by his bother Tecumseh, a powerful chief who had built a confederacy of tribes in Michigan, Ohio, and Indiana. Together the chief and the prophet organized a large coalition of Indians against whites in a political and religious alliance. Ultimately, however, they were defeated at the hands of the American military under the command of William Henry Harrison. U.S. soldiers decimated one of Tenskwatawa's critical towns, forcing the Natives to retreat. As a result, Tenskwatawa's power quickly declined, extinguishing the movement. Despite its political failure, this revitalization movement evidenced the Natives' growing frustration with white encroachment on their land and their savvy at organizing powerful religious and political alliances that unified quite diverse people groups.

THE NINETEENTH CENTURY

The revivals of the early nineteenth century spawned many more unique religious movements. Visionaries, unencumbered by the restrictions of previous generations, built utopian communities. Prophets looking to the sky were sure that the end of the world was near. In the mid-nineteenth century, despite growing tension and ultimately war, men and women adapted their faiths in unique ways, finding refuge from their surroundings in new expressions of religion.

One of the most original and distinctively American religions is the Church of Jesus Christ of Latter-day Saints, whose adherents are more commonly known as Mormons. Joseph Smith, Jr., a poor teenager from upstate New York's "burnt-over-district"—named for the many revivals that passed through it—started the movement early- to mid-nineteenth century when he claimed to have received new revelations from God. Smith had been distressed by the competing and seemingly contradictory messages of local preachers as well as the social turmoil rural Americans faced as a result of the Revolution. He claimed to have seen a great light in the woods and later to have been visited by an angel named Moroni, who directed Smith to a secret location where golden tablets were buried. These tablets purportedly revealed the history of early America. Smith eventually translated the plates with magic stones, which became the basis for the *Book of Mormon*, a foundational text of his movement.

The *Book of Mormon* is a uniquely American work that blends civil religion and biblical themes with a few unique innovations. It teaches that Native Americans descended from members of the twelve Hebrew tribes of the Old Testament, some of whom traveled to America around 600 B.C.E. According to this book, the United States was therefore not a new Israel as the Puritans had asserted but was actually linked with God's original chosen people. America was a sacred place unlike any other in which the Almighty had revealed His new gospel. The *Book of Mormon* also contained an element of social protest. It attacked the class distinctions of the era and took organized religion to task for perpetuating and reifying inequalities.

Smith's ideas provoked a lot of opposition since most Americans believed that it was heretical to supplement the "divine revelation" of the Bible with new revelation, and since the Mormons engaged in controversial social practices. As a result, Smith was forced to lead his band of followers from place to place, seeking refuge and a peaceful region where the movement could blossom. In the 1840s, with over 10,000 followers, Smith was jailed and then killed by a lynch mob. Brigham Young, who replaced Smith as the Saints' leader, took the group to Utah where they established a permanent Mormon empire. In Utah the movement's growth exploded. The Mormons' commitment to hard work, a centrally planned economy, strong families, and a belief in their potential divinity led to their success. A religious group that was once on the outskirts of American culture, the Latter-day Saints are now as American as apple pie.

Although Smith achieved the greatest following, many other visionary leaders built social movements in the nineteenth century; among them were William Miller, Ann Lee, and John Humphrey Noyes. William Miller was a self-educated religious innovator. The strength behind his movement derived from his marketing skills and the scientific appeal of his ideas. A Baptist and a New York farmer, in the 1830s, Miller abandoned his land to become a lay exhorter. He traveled from church to church, proclaiming the imminent return of Christ. Crowds followed, generating excitement that was stimulated by the work of his publicist, Joshua Himes, who created elaborate charts detailing Miller's calculations for determining the date of Christ's return. These charts fed Americans' fascination with things that appeared "scientific." Using a rigid interpretation of the Bible as his guide, Miller calculated and publicized the day of Jesus's reappearance: March 21, 1843. When Christ didn't return as expected, Miller adjusted his calculations and placed the new date in 1844, but was again disappointed. Members of his Millerite group later reorganized themselves as the Seventh-day Adventists. Over the course of his life, Miller published over 5 million pieces of literature, including numerous religious tracts and a magazine.

Yet another visionary dedicated to Christ's imminent return was Ann Lee, who built a small following. Lee was illiterate and worked as a domestic servant. She lost four children during infancy, which caused her to question the appropriateness of sexual activity. Consequently, she began advocating total abstinence, both within and outside of marriage, and she also taught strict equality between the sexes. For a while she worked with a band of Quakers, whose trembling (or "shaking") during worship influenced her religious style. She later ventured out on her own, building a movement officially called the United Society of Believers in Christ's Second Appearance, but more often referred to as the Shakers because of their distinctive worship practices and stylized dance. The group lived communally and simply, holding almost everything in common. They led demanding lives, working hard and sacrificing much to support the community. Unlike groups such as the Latter-day Saints who gave birth to many children, the abstinent

TARRING AND FEATHERING OF JOSEPH SMITH.

An angry mob tars and feathers Joseph Smith, founder of the Church of Jesus Christ of Latter-day Saints, popularly known as the Mormons. Smith claimed as a child to have had revelations from God and been visited by an angel. Mormons were attacked everywhere they settled, and Smith was murdered by a mob in Carthage, Illinois, in 1844. *(Brown Brothers)*

Shakers adopted children in an effort to perpetuate the movement, but their growth was limited. The community eventually came to regard Lee as the incarnate Christ.

Similar to the Shakers in their communitarian emphasis was another nineteenth-century group, the Oneida Perfectionists, who sought to build an enduring religious movement. Led by John Humphrey Noyes, this group believed that people could live sinless lives, they practiced economic cooperation, and

they sought divine healing. Noyes, like other religious leaders of the era, had a unique interpretation of Christ's second coming. He believed that Jesus had returned to earth in C.E. 70, which was the basis for his commitment to the attainability of perfection. More controversially, Noyes and his community also practiced "complex marriages" in which wives and husbands rotated between one another in the community. Opposed by their neighbors, they relocated to Oneida, New York, in 1848, where, in contrast to many of the century's other utopian communities, the faithful at Oneida enjoyed economic prosperity for a time. They built steel traps and the still popular Oneida silverware. However, by the end of the century, the movement had mostly dissolved.

As pioneers ventured out on their own, others sought to reform more mainstream religions. One of the central strands of the era, human perfectionism, had a tremendous impact on men and women like Noyes as well as on American Methodists. John Wesley, the founder of Methodism in Europe, encouraged Christians to strive for perfection in their lives. As a result, Wesleyans emphasized the sanctifying work of the Holy Spirit after conversion and attempted to embody absolute love for God and one's fellow human beings. Combining the century's optimism with its religious creativity, the holiness movement emerged from this strain of Methodism. Holiness's most popular teacher was Phoebe Palmer, a woman who had a postconversion experience in which she claimed to feel the Holy Spirit's power. She then began teaching other women about her experience and eventually taught men too, inciting a renewed effort toward perfect living. A popular lecturer, she went on numerous tours around America and published many books. Among her lasting contributions to the nation's religion was a biblically based defense of women's right to preach. Holiness advocates like Palmer also believed strongly in missionary work, and they engaged in many of the moral reform movements of the era.

THE PROGRESSIVE ERA

After the Civil War, the United States' immigration patterns shifted. More and more people began arriving from Central, Eastern, and Southern Europe in contrast to the previous generations of newcomers who had more often originated from Western Europe. On the West Coast, Asians arrived in great numbers, answering American business's call for inexpensive laborers. With the evolving immigration came new religious trends. The country's Jewish and Catholic populations, which were already sizable, surged. At the same time, new religions from other parts of the globe arrived for the landmark 1893 World's Parliament of Religions, held in Chicago. Out of this increasingly pluralistic context and fueled by continuing heavy immigration, many new social movements emerged.

Jews were among the major groups benefiting from the new immigration. They had been on American soil since the seventeenth century, migrating like many other groups in hopes of practicing their religion freely. In the mid-nineteenth century, a new,

distinctively American, movement called Reform Judaism developed. Proponents of Reform Judaism sought to make the ancient faith more compatible with modern American life through numerous changes. They used English rather than Hebrew for their services, they initiated mixed-gender seating, and most controversially they denied the actual personhood of the Messiah. Instead, Reform Jews believed that the Messiah was the religion itself. A leading advocate of these alterations was Isaac Mayer Wise, who founded Hebrew Union College in Cincinnati to shape and perpetuate Reform Judaism. The movement appealed to many older generation Jewish Americans who sought to integrate their beliefs more thoroughly with American culture. Through Reform Judaism, they were able to practice their historic faith without isolating themselves from the surrounding society.

Not all Jews, however, found this movement appealing. Reform Judaism was especially problematic among the newer immigrants arriving from poorer parts of Europe. They were troubled by the Americanized changes and believed that such "reforms" did little more than dilute the faith. These religionists insisted on keeping the genders segregated during worship, on obeying all 613 laws prescribed in the Torah, and on using Hebrew for worship services. To distinguish themselves from Reform Judaism, they began calling themselves Orthodox Jews. They settled primarily in the nation's major cities, forming close-knit communities where they could protect their religious traditions. A third group, called Conservative Jews, embodied a sort of synthesis between Reform and Orthodox. Also emerging during the late nineteenth century, they interpreted the Torah more loosely than their Orthodox brethren, and they placed significant value on the nonreligious elements of Jewish culture.

As the Jewish population in the United States increased, so too did the size and power of the Roman Catholic Church. Between 1870 and 1910, it quadrupled. Because the Catholic Church had historically penetrated so many different cultures, it found a variety of expressions in America. As Catholic Europeans poured into the country, they developed their own national churches based on ethnicity, which functioned as religious, as well as social, political, and economic strongholds for the local community. Diverse groups of Poles, Irish, and Italians all maintained their autonomy and yet struggled together to defend their faith in the face of the dominant, sometimes hostile, Protestant culture. Meanwhile, turmoil and revolution in Mexico pushed Catholic Latinos into the Southwestern United States, where they practiced their own culturally distinctive form of the faith. Each of the various Catholic ethnic groups sought to promote their beliefs among younger generations in America and, at times, battled each other for control of the Church in the United States. They built shrines, celebrated holidays, and organized parades to demonstrate their religious devotion and to honor their local traditions. They also proved to be capable institution builders, establishing thousands of parochial schools and a number of colleges to raise their children in the faith.

As Catholic immigrant groups adjusted their religion for a new context, so too did America's Natives look for creative ways to build and sustain their religious lives. In the late 1800s, a widespread social movement similar to the revitalization movement earlier in the century linked religious ideas with a political agenda. The movement began when a Nevada Paiute named Wovoka had a series of dreams in which he traveled to a utopian land full of wild game and resurrected Indian ancestors. He returned from this paradise with an edict for his fellow Indians. They were to stop fighting with each other and with whites. Instead, Wovoka taught them a sacred practice, called the Ghost Dance, which was supposed to drive the whites away, to restore the land, and to reunite the Indians with their ancestors. The Ghost Dance spread, bringing political ramifications. The Sioux believed that through their practice of the Ghost Dance, they would be invincible in battle. As a result, they engaged in bloody confrontations with the American military, which concluded in a massacre of Natives at Wounded Knee, South Dakota. The Ghost Dance, like many of the other utopian movements of the nineteenth century, left its adherents disappointed.

Similar to Native Americans and Jewish and Catholic immigrants who modified their faiths to fit their particular social circumstances, a group of white, somewhat elite Protestants, did the same. In the Progressive Era, good physical health was a highly prized commodity, and in every newspaper and on every street corner thousands of people offered myriad cures, remedies, and practices for attaining it. Christian Science, developed by Mary Baker Eddy, became a popular religious movement driven by Americans' concern with their well being. As a child Eddy struggled with poor health and found few answers in mainstream American religion or in medicine. She eventually met Phineas P. Quimby, a folk healer who believed that reality was no more than an idea pervading from God's mind. He also reasoned that God

was absolutely incapable of error, suffering, or death. Taking Quimby's ideas to their logical conclusion, Eddy believed that suffering was therefore just an illusion. She articulated a corresponding interpretation of Jesus. He was not God incarnate, but the model human who understood such ideas. She published her teachings in a series of books, the most important of which was called *Science and Health, with Key to the Scriptures* (1875). Although the Christian Science movement spread around the nation, Eddy was most popular in the Northeast, especially among the wealthier classes. Christian Science appealed to the many men and women hoping to recover from the ailments of the era.

Confronted with the rapid growth of other religions and new sects, traditional American Protestants, whose constituencies were declining, faced an identity crisis. Theological and philosophical trends sweeping the nation further contributed to their identity crisis. The growing popularity of Darwinian evolution and the application of literary criticism to the Bible became divisive issues that would eventually sever many churches and even some denominations. On the one side were the fundamentalists, who rejected contemporary trends and maintained a literal approach to the Bible. They were willing to fight for their beliefs, refusing to let modernism seep into their churches, schools, or homes. On the other side of the debate were the liberal Protestants, or modernists, who were broadly characterized by their efforts to keep their faith up-to-date with the latest scientific and philosophical movements. Like Reform Jews, they wanted to contemporize and apply their faith to the modern world. Ascribing generally to either the modernist or the fundamentalist movements, dozens of smaller Protestant submovements emerged. Two of the most influential were the Social Gospel and Pentecostalism.

The Social Gospel was a revival of sorts that developed out of mainstream Protestants' efforts to meet the demands of a changing nation. The United States, like Europe, faced increasing economic inequality, abysmal healthcare, dangerous working conditions, exploitation of workers, and unrestrained, rapid urban growth, triggering clerics' movement out of their church and onto the street. The Christian gospel, they believed, was not just about a person's relationship with God but also about his or her social relationships. These men and women taught Christians to engage their faith with culture and to think about the social message of the scriptures. The Social Gospel influenced many of the classic Protestant denominations, but its most obvious expressions surfaced through interdenominational organizations. The Men and Religion Forward Movement of 1911–1912 (which linked a form of "muscular Christianity" that emphasized the strength and virility of Jesus with the Social Gospel) and the Federal Council of the Churches were two leading organizations with strong Social Gospel components. Through such interdenominational agencies, the movement accomplished many things. It revived Protestant liberalism and reshaped the role of the church in society. Religiously inspired men and women established schools for all ages to educate the new urban public, while settlement houses were built for the poor. Northern churches created schools in the South for African Americans who otherwise received little help. Some leaders immersed their churches in political issues like suffrage, prohibition, and expansionism, while others were more subtle about their politics. Social action groups, missionary societies, and student organizations were established or expanded under the auspices of the movement. From church pulpits, seminaries, street corners, and the academy, Social Gospel leaders attempted to convert all who would listen to a new way of life.

Pentecostals, on the other hand, were linked to both the emerging fundamentalist movement and the Holiness movement. They subscribed to most of the same beliefs about the Bible's inerrancy as fundamentalists; they too claimed to interpret it literally, and they rejected many of the intellectual and cultural trends of the era. Their distinguishing feature was an emphasis on what they called the Baptism of the Holy Spirit. Like Holiness folks, Pentecostals believed that after conversion, a person gained a sense of empowerment derived from the Holy Spirit. They were subsequently able to exercise the spiritual gifts listed in the New Testament, the most prominent of which was speaking in tongues. With strong organizations, charismatic leaders, a somewhat more racially inclusive attitude than many other Protestants, and the appropriation of new technologies, Pentecostalism became one of the most vibrant social movements in the twentieth century.

MODERN AMERICAN RELIGIOUS MOVEMENTS

After World War II, many of the religious movements developing in the Progressive Era continued to expand. In the mid-1950s, sociologist Will Herberg published *Protestant, Catholic, Jew: An Essay in American Religious Sociology* (1956), which argued that America was no longer a religiously monolithic nation, but a pluralistic country composed primarily of the three major faiths constituting his title. However, little did Herberg know that America was on the verge of a new explosion of religious diversity. In the 1960s, Congress passed legislation that reformed America's immigration laws. Nonwhite, non-Protestant religions flourished as quotas favoring the immigration of Europeans and restricting the immigration of Asians and other national groups came to an end. The result has been a revolution in religious diversity in which America's pluralism has emerged from back alleys and moved to Main Street. Islam, Hinduism, and Buddhism are three groups that illustrate this change, while other Americans have reached out to the New Age movement for answers.

Islam is one of the fastest growing of America's "new" religions. Muslims have been on North American soil for hundreds of years, but their numbers remained small until Progressive Era immigration brought additional Muslims from around the world to America. Most settled in the urban cities of the North and in California. For centuries they remained primarily in the shadows, living in close-knit communities where they tried not to draw attention to themselves. In recent decades, this pattern has reversed itself. Muslims have erected thousands of mosques, developed thriving student movements, and established influential community organizations. As it has integrated into American society, Islam has evolved in particularly American ways. Muslim women participate more in public life than they do in traditional Muslim countries and worship centers, and services have taken distinctly American tones. Muslims have reconceptualized their faith to make it relevant for a generation of children born and raised in the United States.

One offshoot of historic Islam is the American-based Nation of Islam. This movement appeals primarily to urban African Americans who have rejected more mainstream American traditions. Although Islam has prospered among Africans and African Americans for centuries, it experienced a significant revival during mid-century under the mysterious Wallace Fard and his successor Elijah Muhammad. In 1930s Detroit, Fard established a Temple of Islam, which drew parishioners from the city's working-class black population. Fard taught that blacks were God's highest creation, whereas whites were an inferior off-shoot. The movement capitalized on widespread black identity movements, which critiqued mainstream American religion for its pervasive racism. Under Elijah Muhammad, the Nation of Islam established a new headquarters in Chicago. A brilliant leader and organizer, Muhammad integrated the Qur'an with the Bible and reshaped some of the major creeds and holidays of the faith to mold them for an American population. Malcolm X became one of the Nation's most popular spokespeople. The movement's success lay foremost in its practicality. Muhammad taught his followers the values of hard work, economic independence, and a strict moral code. Although controversial, the Nation of Islam has subsequently transformed many inner-city areas, helping the black community defend itself against the hegemony of the dominant culture.

Like the world's other major religions, Hinduism has been present on American soil for generations. In the nineteenth century, Transcendentalists like Ralph Waldo Emerson were influenced by classic Hindu texts; however, there were few practicing Hindus in the United States until Indians began migrating to North America in the Progressive Era. Hindu Swami Vivekananda came to the United States for the 1893 World's Parliament of Religions, where he was well received. Sensing unparalleled opportunity, he established the Vendanta Society in America, which sought to influence the West with his ideas that emphasized the ultimate unity and peace of all things. He taught religious practices including yoga, which has found widespread popularity in the United States. Yoga consists of physical and breathing exercises that are designed to relax the body and to bring about a state of total concentration. Since the immigration reforms of the 1960s, numerous other gurus, or religious leaders, have arrived in the United States where they have built small followings. Although many immigrants practice Hinduism, the religion has also appealed to white Americans who reject Christianity for what they find to be a more peaceful, holistic religion from the other side of the globe.

Adding to America's religious diversity is Buddhism, whose adherents first arrived in significant numbers in America during the eighteenth century. Chinese immigrants entering California and Japanese laborers seeking work in Hawaii continued their religious traditions in the new land, adapting as had just about everyone else to novel social circumstance. Temples were erected in places like San Francisco where Buddhism blended with other traditional Asian religions. Missionaries also arrived from the East, hoping to convert Americans to their faith. Over time, Buddhist immigrants reshaped their religion in America in traditionally "Christian" ways, building "churches," anointing "bishops," and holding Sunday services complete with Sunday schools.

One of the more popular and elite social movements emerging from Buddhism was the Zen movement. Zen had been represented at the World's Parliament of Religions in Chicago, and over the coming decades a few pioneers worked to popularize it in the United States. The foremost leader was Daisetz Teitaro Suzuki, who wrote many books in English about Zen and lectured in major universities. San Francisco "beat poets" of the 1950s such as Allen Ginsberg and Jack Kerouac began practicing and popularizing a form of Zen. Shunryu Suzuki, a Japanese religious teacher, established one of America's first Zen religious centers in San Francisco in the 1960s where practitioners would sit and meditate in traditional postures, seeking to clear their minds and to achieve enlightenment. The movement places little emphasis on religious texts or artifacts but is instead based on concentrated meditation, often on a paradoxical question. As Zen's popularity grew among educated, young, white Americans, the movement engaged in social issues such as the AIDS crisis and the environmental movement.

Among the most influential religious movements in the last part of the twentieth century was the New Age movement. Although it has roots in America's long-standing metaphysical tradition, the modern New Age movement began in the late 1960s and early 1970s, a period when many Americans were being challenged to rethink their traditional religious beliefs. Frustrated with mainstream religions, they reached out for something that seemed more authentically "spiritual." The New Age movement evades definition and consists of countless religious ideas and practices that adherents appropriate selectively. Some New Agers express their beliefs through environmental activism or holistic health practices, whereas others look to channeling or astrology. Many practitioners emphasize positive thinking and look within themselves for transformation rather than to a religious community. Although they usually deny the supernatural worlds of more traditional religions, New Agers commonly believe in a different type of transcendent, extraordinary dimension of entities—for example, many believe in the existence of life on other planets and UFOs. The immigration of religious teachers from all over the world, the revitalization of

Native American spirituality, and the rise of the holistic health movement opened many people's minds to new ideas, fueling the birth and growth of the New Age movement.

Social movements based on religion have defined America. Thousands of pioneers have emerged, some manipulating historic faiths, while others built entirely new movements. Some have enjoyed tremendous success, while others have faded into oblivion. Heavy immigration, charismatic individuals, strong organizations, and protection against the establishment of a single religion have allowed thousands of religious movements to thrive in North America.

Matthew A. Sutton

BIBLIOGRAPHY

Albanese, Catherine L. *America, Religions and Religion*, 3d ed. New York: Wadsworth, 1999.

Brekus, Catherine A. *Strangers and Pilgrims: Female Preaching in America, 1740–1845*. Chapel Hill: University of North Carolina Press, 1998.

Butler, Jon. *Awash in a Sea of Faith: Christianizing the American People*. Cambridge, MA: Harvard University Press, 1990.

Eck, Diana. *A New Religious America: How a "Christian Country" Has Now Become the World's Most Religiously Diverse Nation*. San Francisco: HarperCollins, 2001.

Hatch, Nathan O. *The Democratization of American Christianity*. New Haven, CT: Yale University Press, 1989.

Herberg, Will. *Protestant, Catholic, Jew: An Essay in American Religious Sociology*. New York: Doubleday, 1955.

Noll, Mark. *A History of Christianity in the United States and Canada*. Grand Rapids, MI: Williams B. Eerdmans, 1992.

Raboteau, Albert J. *Slave Religion: The "Invisible" Institution in the Antebellum South*. New York: Oxford University Press, 1978.

Roark, James, et al. *The American Promise: A History of the United States*. Boston: Bedford Books, 1998.

Tweed, Thomas, ed. *Retelling U.S. Religious History*. Los Angeles: University of California Press, 1997.

Wacker, Grant. *Religion in Nineteenth Century America*. New York: Oxford University Press, 2000.

Williams, Peter. *America's Religions: Traditions and Cultures*. New York: Macmillan, 1990.

RELIGIOUS MOVEMENTS 1730s–1830s

The eighteenth century in America was a time of awakening from the slumber of the past. Light was shed on the darkness of superstition, irrationality, autocracy, aristocratic privilege, and dogma. The individual, weighed down by the chains of time, institutions, thought, and traditions, became unencumbered and liberated. The new science taught Americans the value of reason, the laws of motion, and the tools of empiricism. Political and social philosophers on both sides of the Atlantic discovered the laws of nature that applied to society and government. Religious thinkers broke from the constraints of orthodoxy, presenting Christians with the gift of choosing how best to recognize, worship, and serve God. The Great Awakening, beginning in the 1730s, was a reaction to the limits of the past and to the social and economic constraints of the present. The awakeners shared a vision of a society based on the recognition that God's will was the basis for human actions, thought, institutions, history, and existence.

CALVINISTS AND PURITANS

American history seemed indeed to be shaped by the will of God. So argued seventeenth-century New England Puritans such as William Bradford (in *Of Plymouth Plantation,* completed in 1651, though not published in full until 1856) and Cotton Mather (in *Magnalia Christi Americana,* 1702), who believed that divine providence led religious reformers to America to fulfill the visions of the first Protestant reformers, in particular John Calvin. As Jeremy Belknap wrote in his *History of New Hampshire* (1784), "It is happy for America that its discovery and settlement by the Europeans happened at a time, when they were emerging from a long period of ignorance and darkness. The discovery of the magnetic needle, the invention of printing, the revival of literature and the reformation of religion, had caused a vast alteration in their views,

and taught them the true use of their rational and active powers." Similarly, Calvin believed that God shed light upon His will and His works for those who could discern it and act upon such knowledge for the sake of His kingdom. Calvin thought that the cornerstone of the Protestant Reformation was the individual examination of God's holy word in Scripture and in nature. The awareness of what is the true and original expression of Christianity would lead to active reformation of those abuses in contemporary Christianity that were inconsistent with God's will and word. Calvin, educated in French legal scholarship and the texts and assumptions of the Renaissance, envisioned congregations of devout Christians working in concert to achieve virtue in civil society that was never accomplished by secular governments. These saintly citizens of the "Bible commonwealth" were to reform the world according to the model of the heavenly city of God found in the Old Testament and New Testament. Calvin and his followers organized these self-perceived Christian "saints" (those bound for heaven) into active soldiers fighting for the word of God. This joining of political and social concerns and actions with deeply held religious beliefs had a revolutionary impact on Europe, England, and America.

Calvin's followers in England, for example, sought to purify not only the Roman Catholic Church but the Church of England (the Anglican Church) as well. Each congregation of these "Puritans" performed illegal, treasonous actions in refusing to abide by all of the requirements of the Church of England, which included use of the Book of Common Prayer and obedience to the hierarchy of church authorities, culminating in the Archbishop of Canterbury and the Crown. Puritans believed in action to accomplish God's will. Their singular devotion to a perceived divine cause resulted in dramatic consequences, the two most important of which were the English Civil War and the Puritan migration to North America.

American Calvinists such as John Winthrop saw in the examples of the Old Testament patriarchs and the teachings of the New Testament apostles models for uniting political and religious order under one system of government. The "New England Way" was very close to a theocracy, basing governing on religious belief and participation in religious activities. These first New England Puritans perceived themselves engaged in an "errand into the wilderness," a notion that continued to guide religious and secular thinkers alike in coming centuries. The errand was to create a religious commonwealth, to civilize and hence Christianize the wilderness and its native peoples, to stay true to the covenant that united themselves to God, to exercise constant restraint in material and secular matters, and to reform as much as possible human institutions.

As the decades passed, however, the errand into the wilderness was forgotten and ignored, its institutions altered, its ideals trod upon. Some Puritan ministers called upon the flock to repent and to form a new covenant with God, but in vain. Change forever has an impact on religious beliefs and institutions. The anxiety and uncertainty of sixteenth-century Europe brought about a religious response, the Protestant Reformation. Likewise, social, economic, political, and intellectual changes in America during the late seventeenth and early eighteenth centuries brought about varying religious consequences. Trade grew, particularly with England. Merchants became wealthy, inspiring in others the same goal. Population expanded because of immigration, better diet, and growing medical knowledge. As a consequence, cities emerged from the wilderness.

Success breeds jealousy and aggression among contestants for land and wealth. British Americans contested with Native Americans and French Americans over the rich frontier and important waterways of the Piedmont and lands west of the Appalachian Mountains. Wars in Europe yielded wars in America. The expanding frontier brought with it a host of political problems. Meanwhile, Americans became aware of new ideas in science about the universe and its governing laws; in the philosophy of science and government; and in the origins, progress, and significance of Christianity. Bombarded by the new and unknown, uncertain as to what were right and wrong, good and bad, some Americans rejected Christianity as untenable; others embraced it all the more. Such was the setting for the Great Awakening of the 1730s and 1740s.

OLD LIGHTS AND NEW LIGHTS

George Whitefield, an itinerant preacher from England, personified the uncertainty and restlessness that resulted in the Great Awakening. A man without a parish in America, a wanderer intent on attracting notice by dramatic speeches rather than solid theology, Whitefield caught the attention of masses of men and women, young and old, seeking release from life's daily drudgery, searching for alternatives to the sermons of college-educated clergy who always had the same message. Whitefield was different. Theology meant little to him. Denominational distinctions, the intricate variations of the sacraments, the learned discourses of the educated, were meaningless next to the horror of the dread consequence of sin and the joy of salvation through Christ. Whitefield's appeal to the emotions fit well the character of a people devoted to the practical and commonplace who eschewed thought for action, who were experiential and intuitive rather than logical and sophisticated. Whitefield tapped into common American qualities that transcended the individualism of a capitalist, frontier society.

Imitating Christ in his choice of venue, Whitefield preached in open spaces, fields, and meadows. Farmers journeyed from far and wide in response. Whitefield's discourse, filled with imagery and drama yet void of doctrinal intricacy, fit well in such unpretentious, familiar surroundings. People listened in common and responded en masse. The old ways of religious habit and perfunctory faith, a nod to God on Sunday and a return to sin on Monday, vanished as the multitude felt anew the presence of a Redeemer disgusted with the sinful neglect of His people, demanding wholehearted repentance and complete abandonment to His will.

Some forms of Christianity have thrived on fear, guilt, loneliness, and despair. The Great Awakening brought such suffering, an awareness of its causes and consequences, to the surface, where it lost its illusory singularity and achieved common recognition. Personal anxiety, fear, suffering, and pain were revealed as universal human experiences. One could sob and wail in the open, surrounded by strangers, and yet feel the comfort of releasing a burden to one's intimate friends. Surprised by joy amid suffering, one could laugh and shed tears of happiness without embarrassment. Religious affectations became emotions to share with others rather than to experience in private. This was an "awakening" of fundamental hu-

later does the mind acquire recognition. Edwards's *Personal Narrative* (1765) provides wonderful insights into his own religious journey, his abandonment of reason and thought to his base feelings of sin and depravity, and his joyful emotions of healing and redemption through Christ, not self. Yet Edwards's *A Faithful Narrative of the Surprising Work of God* (1737), which focuses on the revival in Northampton, describes the Great Awakening as a group rather than an individual phenomenon.

For some clergy, the emotional response of tears and wailing and writhing on the floor of the New Lights did not fit at all the decorum, piety, and restraint required of the pilgrim when worshipping in the house of the Lord. The Boston clergyman and theologian Charles Chauncy responded to Edwards's joyful tracts with literary attacks on the enthusiasm, spontaneity, and emotions of the masses. The uneducated common herd of humankind could hardly know how best to worship God. Emotion is not an adequate tool to measure God's will and ways. Christ requires piety, forbearance, silence, reason, order in His worship, he stated. Chauncy's *Enthusiasm Described and Caution'd Against*, published in 1742, was welcomed by the solid middle and upper classes, the well educated and professionals, who were suspicious of the immediacy of New Light religious conversion. Their experience taught them that God revealed Himself to the intellect, not the emotions. Conversion took time; it was a subtle occurrence rarely recognized until by learned hindsight one could trace it and accept it. Chauncy and other Old Lights, content with the ways of their fathers, could hardly accept Edwards's description of hell in *Sinners in the Hands of an Angry God* (1741), which was graphic, horrifying, and intent on eliciting the most emotional response. The uneducated lacked the intellectual resources to decide such matters of God's benevolence, justice, and love for themselves. The Old Lights refused to accept the logical contradiction of a just and loving God who condemns His children to unending torment in Hell. New Light arguments—that human sin is universal, inherited from the first man and woman, Adam and Eve; that all humans deserve condemnation; that God for unknown reasons mercifully saves some from hellfire; that humans do not have the free will to determine their own eternal fate—did not accord with a rational God currently being fashioned in Europe and America by Arminians and Deists. Chauncy and the Old Lights, raised in the Calvinist theological environment of Congregationalism, slowly rejected Calvin's claims

Speaking up and down the colonies in open fields and meadows, George Whitefield drew large, enthusiastic crowds in the late 1730s and 1740s. His emotional sermons—filled with imagery and drama and void of distinctions based on class and wealth—fueled a religious revival known as the Great Awakening. *(Brown Brothers)*

manness. New light was shed upon the darkness of the soul.

Jonathan Edwards, the Yale-educated pastor of Northampton, Massachusetts, understood these feelings of loss and hope, repentance and redemption, the abandonment of self to God, that were products of the "New Light" experience of the Great Awakening. In *A Treatise Concerning Religious Affectations* (1746), Edwards argued that the emotions rather than the intellect were the true foundation and expression of religious belief. Who can have an intellectual understanding of the Incarnation or the Resurrection? One can only feel Christ's sacrifice, empathize with it, and make the experience one's own. In *A Divine and Supernatural Light* (1734), Edwards showed that reason relies on intuition, that thought is dependent on emotion. Knowledge of God comes from God, who makes Himself known in the human heart and soul; only

and the revolutionary consequences of Calvinist social thought.

RELIGION AND REVOLUTION

Indeed, it is not surprising to learn that as the eighteenth century progressed, the Old Lights were less apt to embrace the revolutionary political arguments of Whig statesmen. In contrast, the New Lights could accept the paradoxes and dangers of the American Revolution simply because their theology taught them that life is full of paradox, that human reason is limited, that God Himself threatens all of His sinful children with eternal damnation, that security in mind, body, society, and institutions is illusory. The Great Awakening taught its adherents that God does not respect class, inheritance, fame, and power. All humans are equal in respect to God, who alone is separate, elevated beyond all others. New Light religious beliefs did not allow them to accept the pretensions to power and rank of the British aristocracy, the House of Lords and House of Commons, and the King. Politics made little sense without religion, and if religion taught equality among all men and women, politics must follow. The revolutionary tendencies of the Great Awakening spilled over into the revolution against Great Britain.

Neither theology nor politics is black and white—and sensitive eighteenth-century Americans often found themselves caught between the Old Light/New Light debate as well as the struggle between Loyalists and Patriots. It was difficult to reconcile the order and decorum at the meetinghouse on Sunday and the disorder and chaos of town meetings on Monday. Some Old Lights such as the Boston clergyman Mather Byles, refusing such contradiction, became notorious (if consistent) Tories. Others, such as the New Hampshire pastor Jeremy Belknap, sought ways to avoid the confrontation of religion and politics by questioning the traditional beliefs of their fathers. Belknap was raised in the still Calvinist environment of mid-eighteenth-century Boston. He was descended from Increase and Cotton Mather on his mother's side. As a communicant of South Parish, he found a mentor in the Reverend Thomas Prince, a clergyman interested in science and history. At Harvard College Belknap discovered the writings of Jonathan Edwards, which inspired in him a search for God's saving grace. His great uncle Mather Byles counseled the young pilgrim not to seek the type of emotional conversion described by Edwards. But Belknap was dissatisfied with a rational approach to God. He refused to consider the ministry until he experienced the saving change of God's grace, which occurred during the long New England winter days of 1766. Belknap became the pastor of the First Parish of Dover, New Hampshire, in 1767 and proceeded to try to inaugurate an awakening among his parishioners. But Dover was not Northampton. Belknap found a few close associates willing to allow emotion and intuition to guide them; but his religious zeal alienated many others.

Eventually, Belknap, like many clergymen, turned his religious zeal toward political issues. Like many of his colleagues of the cloth who were alumni of Harvard or Yale, he became a firm, if conservative, patriot. The pastor and his family suffered economic privation during the war and rarely were free from the dismal feeling of possible doom should the British gain the upper hand in the war. Belknap's solace was his historical and scientific studies. But as a clergyman he was called to study the Scriptures as well. One bleak day in 1778 Belknap experienced a revelation while reading the book of Daniel in the Old Testament. He felt sure that Daniel prophesized the eventual defeat of Britain and American independence. In other words, it was God's will that America become free. Excited and astonished, Belknap preached a sermon and told his friends and family about his insight. For the remainder of his life, twenty years, he lived according to this revelation of the divine will.

That the divine will might enter into and direct society and government was not a new idea. Pagans and Christians, Muslims and Jews, if devout, rarely purposefully act in contradiction to what they perceive to be God's will. The uniqueness of the Protestant Reformation was the range of interpretation of God's will. Calvin channeled the perception of God's grace that he and his fellow "saints" had purportedly experienced into an active crusade to spread Christianity and the awareness of God's will on earth. It is slightly absurd, of course, to proclaim the omniscience and omnipotence of God and in the same breath proclaim that notwithstanding the limited perspective, clouded by time and sin, of one's life one still knows God's will. Some Christians, both New Light and Old Light, turned their freedom of the will into God's will, and vice versa.

Jonathan Edwards, in his essay *Freedom of the Will* (1754), argued that free will, which obviously exists, is not "will" itself, just as human goodness is not "good" itself. These were not new ideas. What was new was the unique situation of eighteenth-century America. Edwards and his parishioners felt the presence of the Holy Spirit, God's overwhelming will, even as they felt called upon to exercise their respective freedom to choose. This differed from John Calvin. One senses from Calvin's *Institutes* a sense of the inexorable will of God that no human can reject. Calvin needed the help of the community of believers to substantiate this feeling that he was chosen, against his will, but according to God's will, to act for the sake of God and His kingdom. Calvin manufactured a kind of certainty amid all the overwhelming uncertainties of life. And yet he still felt a terrible anxiety knowing that his will was never perfectly free, yet bound to another.

Uncertainty and consequent anxiety are the sine qua non of life. Some respond in silence and humility, becoming a monastic in theory or in fact. Others give voice to their fears in writings and confessions, hoping to solicit a silent empathy from listeners and readers. Still others are driven by anxiety to join in common with others equally in despair, where numbers and a collective voice drown out solitary cries, giving energy, even if elusive and fleeting, to one's individual impulses. When one is afraid, it feels so much better to act when others are acting as well. Collective action gives legitimacy to individual actions. One person might not challenge the world, but a host can; one person might not challenge authority unless joined by countless others; one person might not speak in tongues, or scream and faint in the presence of the congregation, unless others have removed its singularity.

To do something strange or untraditional requires a certain anonymity, which the collective provides. If the Great Awakening had been the awakening of one soul to God, it would be a footnote, not a chapter, in the pages of history. Social, religious, and political movements require the subjugation of the individual self to the collective self, which ironically legitimizes and strengthens individual self-perception. Scores of people believing and acting give credence to the claim that it is God's will that drives such actions.

It felt good to Edwards to reduce his freedom to a single spark in the light of freedom. In a similar way, it felt good to Thomas Paine and Thomas Jefferson, and all the other patriots who rejected tyranny for freedom, to universalize their feelings, to make their cause *the* cause, to make their perceptions self-evident to all humans. Jefferson's Declaration of Independence reads like a religious tract in its focus on the will of the people, the necessity of history, the laws of nature and God. Some patriots, like Jeremy Belknap, applied Jefferson's secular, deist tone to a religious format. But clearly Jefferson's vague allusions to the divine and concrete images of human experience and

action struck a chord with the mass of Americans, who by 1776 had been awakened to a recognition of God's will, no matter what form it might take.

Hence, the Great Awakening succeeded, but only through transformation, adjustment to the perceived realities of the Enlightenment. The enlightened thinker of the middle to late eighteenth century had come to realize the power of human reason. Yes, there might be this vague universal force, Reason, but it was distant, growing more anonymous, giving a perfunctory nod to Reformation and Revolution. Freedom of the will grew in stature before, during, and after the American Revolution. There might be a transcending Will, as the French believed in their Declaration of the Rights of Man and Citizen, which legitimized the violence of the French Revolution, but even this transcendent force was the general will of the people rather than the universal will of God.

Social and political movements still sought St. Augustine's *City of God* but with a secular twist. Theirs was a heavenly city, a utopia, on earth, where all humans would find happiness; disease, starvation, poverty, ignorance, would be eliminated. The millennium still beckoned; it could still be inaugurated on earth. The millennium of the enlightened philosopher of the eighteenth century, of the utopian thinker of the nineteenth century, was still eschatological, still divinely sanctioned, however vaguely. Yet this millennium lacked Christ. It lacked the Second Coming, the sound of trumpets, Armageddon, Judgment. It was a secular millennium that the philosophers and quasi-religious called for and expected.

THE SELF-RELIANT BELIEVER

Social and ideological movements of the late eighteenth and early nineteenth centuries were still caused by uncertainty about life, anxiety brought about by the fear of change and death, and the manifold wars, epidemics, famines, and the like of the times. The mind struggles to make sense out of disaster, mortality, and suffering, and it finds answers to fit the times. The answers of the early nineteenth century were of an astonishing variety: Deism, Universalism, Unitarianism, Transcendentalism, Millennialism, Mormonism.

The apparent diversity of these responses to the uncertainty and anguish of war, revolution, and industrialization should not blind us to their similarities. The groups who take political and social matters into their own hands, who rise up and revolt and realize their power, understand sovereignty not according to the exclusive right of kings and aristocrats but according to the inclusive right of all people. They experience power as a possession, an expectation, a fundamental right. Having experienced such power, they will hardly relinquish it to others, human or divine.

The years before and after the American Revolution, then, hosted the unabashed awareness of the power of the human mind. Deists allowed human reason to penetrate all facets of the human and natural past. Thomas Paine referred to his time as *The Age of Reason* (1794), where superstition and the supernatural took a back seat to science, mathematics, historicism, and empiricism. "My own mind is my own church," he proclaimed. Unitarians used logic and experience to proclaim that God is a Unity rather than a Trinity. Universalists assumed that their kind of God would not contradict human expectations of goodness and justice in condemning humans, both guilty and not guilty, to eternal torment in hell. Unitarians and Universalists, like Transcendentalists, ignored revelation, sources of truth and inspiration such as the Old Testament and New Testament, preferring instead their own reason and experiences to gauge what is truth and what is falsehood, what is divine and what is not. Taking a page from the Old Lights, the Unitarians and Universalists could not countenance beliefs and institutions based on the fundamental assumption of human sinfulness, for humans are inherently good, and Adam's fall has no bearing on the present.

A good example of the movement toward a less rigorous Christianity, a more accommodating spirituality of love, goodness, and peace, was the Transcendentalist Henry David Thoreau. Thoreau and his friends and associates, such as Ralph Waldo Emerson, believed that the route to truth lay within the human heart. Intuition, not reason, not revelation, not tradition, taught the individual self what to believe and how to act. Self-reliance, independent thought, personal authority, personal knowledge: these were the credos of the early-nineteenth-century Romantic. Thoreau and his associates rejected the rationalism and empiricism of the Enlightenment thinkers and Old Lights as well as the energetic acceptance of God's will of the awakened New Light for the self in search of meaningful human experience. The only authority was the scripture of self, searching for and finding God within oneself via the conduit of nature. Emerson felt "perpetual youth" in nature and childlike innocence as well. Sacrifice, suffering, atonement, redemption, crucifixion, and resurrection blend in and become lost in the untold variety and plenty of nature, where all is good and life is peace. The phenomenon of social movement—the idea of a Great Awakening—was ignored and became inconsequential to Transcendentalists such as Thoreau and Emerson.

Self-reliant philosophies such as Unitarianism, Universalism, Deism, and Transcendentalism could hardly sponsor—rather, they could only eschew—the religious concerns of the mass of people. In retrospect, a Second Great Awakening was inevitable given the confident, passive tone of early nineteenth-century religion and philosophy and at the same time the overwhelming anxiety caused by modernization. Americans, particularly in the northern states and especially the growing middle class, were going through a dramatic period of questioning and seeking answers. Independence brought with it a host of concerns. How could a society based on the Declaration of Independence, the Constitution, and the Bill of Rights sponsor such glaring abuse to people of color, slave and free? How could the factories of the North continue to rely on the raw materials of the South grown through human suffering and despair? What would be the price of the coming Industrial Revolution? How could Americans avoid unstoppable growth, urban blight, increasing poverty, and inequality? How best could ambitious young people best utilize their talents and energies in a society and economy exploding to the west, up rivers and canals, over the Appalachians, down the Ohio and Mississippi, up the Missouri, across the Rockies? The decade of the 1830s repeated the experiences of the 1730s—the change, the anxiety, the search, the discovery, the "answer."

NEW RELIGIOUS STIRRINGS AND THE SECOND GREAT AWAKENING

For some Americans, the answer to economic and social change was religious change—a new ideology, new scripture, new church, new life. John Humphrey Noyes at Oneida, New York, headed a community of believers who reveled in their perfection—and their sexuality. Shaker communities in New England practiced celibacy and awaited Christ's imminent return. Joseph Smith proclaimed his revelation that Christ had all along picked America as His chosen land, the place where He would return to reign for a thousand years, a millennium.

Indeed, millennialism was on the minds of quite a few people during the first half of the nineteenth century. The Second Great Awakening of the 1830s resulted from new ideas about Christianity, the sinner's relation to God, Christ's role in redemption, and the millennium. The great spokesman of the Second

sinner, having made the conscious decision to reject sin for salvation, will enjoy signs of heaven on earth. Material prosperity awaits the person who chooses to be saved. Gone from Finney's sermons were God's anger and the damnation of sinful souls, born in sin, predestined for hell.

The preceding century had taught rational Americans that God left the choice of salvation entirely in each person's hands. Self-reliant, independent, freedom-loving Americans could experience do-it-yourself salvation. Conversion does not come from some hidden, unexpected source in response to one's appeal to God for help. Conversion is a conscious decision to succeed, rather like the choice to go into business.

One can imagine the enthusiastic response to such a doctrine of salvation and success open to all with very little inconvenience. The people of the industrializing North, the people of Rochester, embraced such ideas and put their hearts to the grindstone to learn to be "perfect, as Christ is perfect." Christ's perfection, of course, resulted in terrible suffering and death. But the atmosphere of business, materialism, success, Americanism, and free will of the 1830s would hardly accommodate such a negative theology. Life had changed during eighteen hundred years, and so too had the church, the elect, sin, and salvation. Gone were the days of priests, confessions, the damned, God's wrath, suffering, and the cross. The Second Great Awakening and consequent evangelical movements gave the American in approaching the afterlife what he had always had in life: free choice, self-reliance, independence.

Religious social movements in America from the 1730s to the 1830s possessed a peculiar irony. Americans responded to anxiety and uncertainty by allowing themselves to be caught up in a movement involving large groups of people who conformed to the requirements of the majority, and who accepted the teachings of the religious spokesman. Yet these teachings tended to contradict the nature and function of the revival itself. Social movements sweep up the individual, make him a part of a whole, force him to relinquish some of his freedom, demand the merging of his identity with that of the group. The sacrifice of the individual earns rich dividends in return. By becoming a part of the group, one feels more an individual. By giving up freedom to act on one's own, one achieves the freedom of salvation. Free will is elusive in theory, yet in practice one can revel in it. And best of all, one can agree that the teachings of Christ—

Preaching that personal redemption and individual salvation were attainable by all, the evangelical Charles Grandison Finney led a religious revival in the Northeast in the 1820s and 1830s. The Second Great Awakening, as this revival was called, helped spark the abolitionist and social reform movements of the nineteenth century. *(Brown Brothers)*

Great Awakening was Charles Grandison Finney, who preached to the farmers and shopkeepers of New York, particularly upstate New York along the Erie Canal. Here were towns and cities undergoing tremendous change. Rochester, for example, experienced a population explosion, new trade, and business; it was a bustling atmosphere with young people willing to work hard, intent on achieving material success.

Finney, like Edwards and Whitefield of a century earlier, was a grand orator who could hold the audience of the hopeful in the palms of his oratorical hands as he re-created hell and suffering for sin, then painted a picture of redemption and heavenly success. For Finney, the sinner can achieve salvation completely by his or her own means. Just as the businessman needs to change his lifestyle to succeed, so the sinner needs to change her lifestyle to reach heaven. But before death bids us to such joy, the redeemed

humility, peace, acceptance, poverty—are best realized in the pride of conversion, the violence of reform, the pursuit of progress, and the rich signs of salvation.

Russell M. Lawson

BIBLIOGRAPHY

Belknap, Jeremy. *The History of New Hampshire.* Philadelphia, PA: R. Aitken, 1784.

Chauncy, Charles. *Enthusiasm Described and Caution'd Against.* Boston, MA: J. Draper, 1742.

Conkin, Paul Keith. *Puritans and Pragmatists: Eight Eminent American Thinkers.* Bloomington: Indiana University Press, 1976.

Edwards, Jonathan. *Basic Writings.* Edited by Ola Winslow. New York: New American Library, 1978.

Johnson, Paul. *A Shopkeeper's Millennium: Society and Revivals in Rochester, New York, 1815–1837.* New York: Hill and Wang, 1985.

Kelley, Donald. *The Beginning of Ideology: Consciousness and Society in the French Reformation.* Cambridge, England: Cambridge University Press, 1981.

McNeill, John. *The History and Character of Calvinism.* Oxford, England: Oxford University Press, 1954.

Paine, Thomas. *The Age of Reason: Being an Investigation of True and of Fabulous Theology.* New York: J. Fellows, 1794.

Persons, Stow. *American Minds: A History of Ideas.* Melbourne, FL: Kreiger, 1975.

Walzer, Michael. *The Revolution of the Saints: A Study in the Origins of Radical Politics.* Cambridge, MA: Harvard University Press, 1965.

RELIGIOUS MOVEMENTS 1830s–1870

Following the Second Great Awakening, the religious movements of the antebellum period through the Civil War focused much of their energies on moral and religious reform. Although they may have differed over approach to reform, there was little difference in general objectives: moral reform. Moral reform meant social reform, and social reform meant a moral *reformation* of American society. It did not matter that moral reform might lead to armed conflict or that women remained disenfranchised and without direct political power. Abolition, temperance, and other moral reforms were part of the broader effort to attain Christ-like perfection, the final goal of moral reform.

A national reform impulse did not suddenly appear in 1830. Reform efforts had been ongoing for decades, but beginning in the 1830s reform took on newer approaches, emphases, techniques, and ideas. The numerous immediate antecedents of the antebellum reforms can be found in the Second Great Awakening, that period of early-nineteenth-century American history characterized by revivals as the primary means of Christianizing the growing U.S. population. By the 1830s, reform had assumed the characteristics that would distinguish it for the next several decades. Whereas most of the revivals and campaigns of the Second Great Awakening began locally and did not expand to become a coherent national movement, the antebellum and post–Civil War reforms became national—national in vision, national in goals, and national in operations. Most important, they had national implications.

ABOLITION OF SLAVERY

Abolitionism provides an excellent example of how a regional idea became a national reform crusade and changed American society. Although the Religious Society of Friends, or Quakers, had long opposed slavery, the religious revivals of the 1820s inspired many

new followers, including Theodore Dwight Weld, William Lloyd Garrison, and Arthur and Lewis Tappan, to take up the cause of "immediate emancipation." Garrison, the Tappan brothers, and sixty others gathered in Philadelphia to found the American Anti-Slavery Society in December 1833. The abolitionists wanted to expunge the entire nation of evil in hopes of redeeming and saving the nation. Although by the 1830s slavery was restricted to Southern states, Northern abolitionists argued that the guilt for slavery was nationwide. Since guilt was national, repentance should also be national. "The highest obligations [are] resting upon the people of the free States to remove slavery by moral and political action," the American Anti-Slavery Society declared at its founding, "as prescribed in the Constitution of the United States."

To aid the cause, leading reformers sought the support of others around the country through various publications such as Garrison's newspaper, *The Liberator*, or in political tracts, and through state antislavery societies. The American Anti-Slavery Society received significant moral and financial support from African-American communities in the North and set up hundreds of branches throughout the free states. But Garrison's provocative call to discard the Constitution because it sanctioned slavery and his support of women's rights alienated the more conservative members of the movement, leading to harmful factionalism over the means to ending slavery.

Another abolitionist, Theodore Weld, promoted the "perfectionist" wing of the revival movement in a much different fashion than Garrison. Weld, a follower of the American clergyman-educator Charles Grandison Finney, left a career as a revivalist and temperance advocate and in 1832 enrolled at Lane Seminary in Cincinnati, Ohio, for more formal ministerial training. Most of the student body followed Weld's

IMPACT OF SLAVERY ON ORGANIZED RELIGION

Slavery opened the rift between Northern and Southern Christians very slowly at first. In 1852, it was ripped asunder with the publication of Harriet Beecher Stowe's book *Uncle Tom's Cabin* in which she indicted organized Christianity for its failure to overthrow the "injustice and cruelty" of slavery. The use of biblical language and references in discussions of slavery soon became common ideological currency. It was therefore not surprising that Americans often described the Civil War in biblical terms or viewed it as a religious event, or at least one with religious overtones.

Antislavery sentiment was either localized or regional, or did not cause lasting schisms among the "liturgical churches"—the Roman Catholic, Lutheran, and Episcopalian churches. Congregationalist and Unitarian churches were scarce in the South and remained largely unaffected as a result. But the three large national evangelical denominations—the Baptist, Methodist, and Presbyterian churches—all split over the issue. The formation of the Southern Baptist Convention in 1845 created little stir, in part because it was a decentralized denomination from the outset, and the split occurred rather quietly. The Methodists, who initially followed English religious leader John Wesley's antislavery teachings, tolerated slaveholding bishops when they first came on the scene in the 1830s, but the denomination finally split over that particular issue in 1845.

The Presbyterians faced a more complicated problem. By the 1830s, the denomination had begun to splinter into two factions over the issues regarding missionary work and doctrinal matters. The "liberal" ideas, given shape by American theologian Nathaniel William Taylor, led to the formation of a "New School" theological stance compatible with the activist spirit of revivalism. The liberal New School favored interdenominational benevolent societies aimed at reform, while the conservative "Old School" followers favored tradition, including keeping women from holding power in the church and the idea of predestination. The Old School followers gained control of the church's General Assembly in 1837 and ousted four New School synods, which immediately held their own assembly, leaving the church split along these ideological lines.

The Northern and Southern wings each split over slavery. The New School, mostly rooted in the North, divided in 1857 after some leaders took a series of

Founder of the antislavery newspaper *The Liberator* in 1831, William Lloyd Garrison was one of the nation's foremost abolitionists. *(Brown Brothers)*

lead by converting to his abolitionist principles and, together, began working with the city's black community. When the trustees of the school ordered Weld and his followers to cease their activism, they refused and instead moved to Oberlin College, where Finney was teaching theology. Founded in 1833 by New England Congregationalists, the college had already gained a reputation as the center for social radicalism and soon became the first coeducational and interracial American institution of higher learning. (Ohio saw the establishment of over a dozen colleges by evangelical churches in the first half of the nineteenth century.) Weld became a widely known organizer and publicist for the antislavery cause in the Ohio and New York region, helping to bring pressure to bear on the federal government and Northern opinion about slavery.

increasingly stronger antislavery positions. The Old School, more Southern-based and conservative, split in 1861, leaving the Presbyterian denomination divided into four different assemblies. After the Civil War, the various factions reformed along sectional lines, creating Northern and Southern Presbyterian churches that finally reconciled and merged in 1984.

"RUM AND ROMANISM"

Although the Protestants may have turned against one another over slavery, they did unite during the 1830s over one issue: their stand against Catholicism. In the early days of the Republic, Catholicism presented little problem because there were so few Catholics in the United States. Yet to be a good Protestant in the colonial and early Republic periods meant a person had to be something of an anti-Catholic. Protestantism, after all, came into being as a protest against the alleged corruption and evil of the Roman Catholic Church. Beginning in the 1830s, as the number of Catholics, particularly Irish Catholics, increased in large part because of immigration, anti-Catholicism, and with it antiliquor sentiment, grew in response. To American Protestants and nativists (those opposed to immigrants), the evils of alcohol and Catholicism—"rum and Romanism," as they were derisively called—went hand in hand.

Protestants responded with a combination of evangelism and temperance. Reverend Lyman Beecher, pastor of the Congregational Church in Litchfield, Connecticut, and one of the most eminent preachers of his day, launched one of the first attacks of this reform era on intemperance in 1825 by calling for total abstinence as the only solution to drinking and drunkenness. His six sermons on intemperance were printed and widely distributed over the next several years. After that, it was only a short step from the arguments for abstinence to the demands for prohibition as the best means of saving the American family in particular and American society as a whole. The rise of abolitionism in the 1830s and 1840s and the need to court the immigrant vote in the 1850s overtook the temperance movement and pushed it to the background until after the Civil War.

PROTECTING THE HOME AND FAMILY

As many as two-thirds of those converted during the Second Great Awakening were women. But just as quickly as their membership numbers rose, their power in public arenas eroded. By the time of the Civil War, public forums for women were all but eliminated and their sphere of influence had been largely reduced to the immediate household and issues directly affecting it. Through their participation in Sunday schools, missionary alliances, and benevolent societies, women frequently exercised powers denied to them in other public forums. At a time when they could not openly protest their subjugation and were denied the right to vote, involvement in evangelical reform movements provided a means of asserting their autonomy. It was not until after the Civil War that women would regroup and demand rights for themselves.

Although the majority of church members were women, paradoxically the church disenfranchised women and stripped them of power. But that did not drive women away. They stayed because they shared the church's perceived role of transmitting republican and moral values to the next generation and because it offered them moral support as they coped with the great difficulties associated with motherhood. Their influence was felt in the message from the pulpit. The portrayals of Jesus and God evolved from one of Christ as king and magistrate to one of a gentle Jesus and a loving and forgiving God.

As the economy industrialized and society urbanized, married middle-class women found they had fewer opportunities to exert themselves than their single counterparts and increasingly became relegated to nonincome-generating work. They embraced their new roles as provider and protector for piety and domestic purity. Their evangelical values made it possible for them to better serve as guardians of morality, purity, culture, and patriotism, collectively known as "domestic feminism." As they lost power in the public sphere, they embraced their role as "great sufferers," which allowed them to invoke the suffering of Christ on the cross and the grievous loss and sacrifice of his mother to their benefit. They took advantage of the tradeoff to exert tighter control over household activities and assert themselves in sexual matters, such as having a say in the number of children they had.

Domestic feminism extended to the schoolroom and benevolent societies. Catherine Beecher, daughter of Lyman Beecher, argued that Christian perfectionism could be attained when children received the benefits of a sound Christian education. Although she was instrumental in opening the teaching profession to women, she also supported the notion of less compensation for women than men received. Mary Lyon founded Mount Holyoke Female Seminary in 1837 as a school for women and preached revivals on religious subjects. Mount Holyoke trained hundreds of missionaries and teachers who fanned out across the country, carrying forth the values instilled in them at the school.

With few other outlets for their energy available to them, middle-class women became deeply involved in benevolent reform. As part of their work to eliminate prostitution, alcoholism, and other threats to their men and society, they acquired political and organizational skills and handled money and property on behalf of their societies. Some published stories about their evangelical experiences, while others hit the revival circuit to speak. In the home and at public meetings, they discussed issues such as slavery or closing businesses on Sunday. Many men initially accepted the idea that women should have strong opinions on some public questions because women were long considered the guardians of Christian and republican ideas.

Abolitionism proved the first great forum for women to accumulate and exercise power. The American Anti-Slavery Society attracted a great deal of participation by women. Women organized local and state-level Female Anti-Slavery Societies, which gave them opportunities to organize and lead. The abolition movement provided the first taste of autonomy for many of them. Feminists and women's rights leaders such as Sarah and Angelina Grimké, Margaret Fuller, Lucretia Mott, and Lucy Stone all began their women's rights work while campaigning for abolition. But William Lloyd Garrison's support of women's rights and his confrontational manner led to a falling-out within the American Anti-Slavery Society in 1840 that hurt the feminist cause. The American Anti-Slavery Society split over whether it was proper for women to speak publicly to audiences containing both men and women. The more conservative members, including many clergy, withdrew and formed the American and Foreign Anti-Slavery Society, in which the role of women was more restricted. Despite this setback, participation in abolitionism and other reform efforts nonetheless increased female empowerment.

With the ending of the Civil War and slavery, temperance reemerged as the most pressing reform issue. This gave women a new opportunity to assert themselves as never before by expanding the focus of their benevolent societies. The Woman's Christian Temperance Union (WCTU), formed in 1874, initially concerned itself only with eliminating alcohol but became a leader and supporter of women's suffrage and other reform efforts. Several of its members took the energy they had poured into abolitionism and focused it on gaining a political voice in hopes of protecting immigrants and lower-class women and children being exploited by the industrial revolution. Their work and that of others laid the groundwork for the Progressive reformers, who shared many of the same Protestant values and employed the techniques pioneered by the mid-nineteenth-century reformers.

James G. Lewis

BIBLIOGRAPHY

Bartlett, Irving H. *The American Mind in the Mid-Nineteenth Century.* Arlington Heights, IL: Harlan Davidson, 1982.

Bendroth, Margaret L. "Rum, Romanism, and Evangelicalism: Protestants and Catholics in Late-Nineteenth-Century Boston." *Church History: Studies in Christianity and Culture* 68 (1999): 627–647.

Griffin, C.S. *The Ferment of Reform, 1830–1860.* Arlington Heights, IL: Harlan Davidson, 1967.

Hood, Fred J. *Reformed America: The Middle and Southern States, 1783–1837.* Tuscaloosa: University of Alabama Press, 1980.

Mead, Frank S., and Samuel S. Hill. *Handbook of Denominations in the United States.* 10th ed. Nashville, TN: Abingdon, 1995.

Swift, Donald C. *Religion and the American Experience: A Social and Cultural History, 1765–1997.* Armonk, NY: M.E. Sharpe, 1998.

Williams, Peter W. *America's Religions: From Their Origins to the Twenty-first Century.* Urbana: University of Illinois Press, 2002.

RELIGIOUS MOVEMENTS

After the Civil War, the dominant social groups in the United States were primarily white, native-born, and small-town or rural. Imbued with an aura of respectability, they were institutionalized to such an extent that regular attendance in a moderate Protestant denomination—Methodist, Presbyterian, Congregational, and in some regions Lutheran or Baptist—signified not only religious devotion but also an opportunity to establish social networks and demonstrate civic involvement, which was so essential for those aspiring to positions of authority in business or public life. Other Protestant sects, practiced primarily by the rural poor and people of color, and Roman Catholicism, practiced primarily by the urban working class, were variously marginalized or suppressed. Non-Christian religious traditions were ignored. During the twentieth century, however, a number of social movements mobilized, with little denominational support, to challenge the hegemonic status of moderate Protestantism and champion the religious traditions of the disenfranchised.

CONSERVATIVE CHRISTIAN MOVEMENTS

The Fundamentalist Movement

During the 1880s and 1890s, many working-class, poor, and rural believers separated from the Methodist-Presbyterian-Congregational mainstream of American Protestantism, believing that their increasing attention to liberalism and commitment to social justice hindered or even perverted the true goals of Christianity: "evangelizing," or converting non-believers, and attaining "holiness," or spiritual perfection. In 1895, Phineas F. Bresee consolidated several such groups into the Church of the Nazarene, the most prominent of the new Holiness denominations.

During the 1910s and 1920s, concerns over the increasing encroachment of modernism led many Protestants, mostly from evangelical and Holiness

denominations, to affirm that they were "fundamentalists," aggressively adhering to "fundamentals" of the Christian faith that soon expanded from a short list of doctrinal positions (the Virgin Birth, the Blood Atonement, and so on) to disdain textual criticism of biblical texts and embrace a more or less rigid interpretation of the Bible as the literal Word of God. During the first twenty years of the century, they mobilized against all sorts of developments they deemed public ills, from alcohol consumption to the cinema, but especially against the theory of evolution, which they condemned as atheistic and subversive. The trial of John Scopes in 1925, in which a Tennessee schoolteacher was arrested for teaching evolution, gained national recognition for the fundamentalist movement, but cast it as backward, superstitious, and rigid, causing fundamentalists to shy away from political activism for the next half-century. There were only a few fundamentalist groups with much impact outside their own denominations until the Cold War, when the association of Communism and the forces of Satan made a new mobilization imperative.

During the 1950s, mobilization occurred most frequently in high schools and colleges. The Intervarsity Christian Fellowship, a fundamentalist collegiate group founded in England in 1877, entered the United States in 1941 and by 1950 had chapters on nearly 500 college campuses. Campus Crusade for Christ, founded by Bill Bright in 1951, brought the twin principles of evangelization and spiritual perfection to almost every college campus in the United States through small peer-led Bible studies and "witnessing," or one-on-one proselytization. Meanwhile, Youth for Christ, founded in 1944, virtually abandoned its early outreach to soldiers stationed overseas to form "Campus Life" groups at thousands of high schools and junior highs. Adult men could join the Christian Businessman's Committee, founded in 1938,

Rev. Billy Graham applauds with his son Franklin Graham during a religious crusade in North Carolina in 1996. The elder Graham was the nation's most prominent evangelist for more than half a century. *(AP Wide World Photos)*

and the Full Gospel Business Men's Fellowship, founded in 1952, which provided not only evangelization and the quest for Christian perfection, but also social networking that mirrored the Chambers of Congress and Toastmasters popular in mainstream society, and the assurance that God was a capitalist.

Although fundamentalist churches remained small and deeply suspicious of the "world," with outreach mostly to the disenfranchised, dozens of parachurch organizations, beginning in 1950 with the Billy Graham Evangelistic Association, introduced the twin goals of evangelization and Christian perfection to a huge mainstream audience. They even managed to redefine "Christian" to refer only to those who have been "born again"—that is, experienced a spiritual transformation through a personal relationship with Jesus. Intimate of movie stars and presidents, Billy Graham had the uncanny ability to popularize his

moderate evangelical message through television and radio appearances, a series of well-received evangelistic films, and many local, stadium-filling crusades. He was followed by dozens of evangelists working primarily through the new medium of television; only Robert Schuller matched his charisma and moderate message, but Kenneth Copeland, Jimmy Swaggart, Benny Hinn, John Hagee, Ron Parsley, and Pat Robertson all drew adherents. The excesses of the 1970s and 1980s, ranging from sexual improprieties to money laundering to extreme claims (such as Oral Roberts' threat that God would kill him unless he raised $8 million) sent televangelism into a decline survived by only the most tenacious. Yet televangelists still managed to imbue local fundamentalist Christians with a sense of community that transcended denominational and doctrinal differences, mobilizing them into a formidable social force that has endured into the twenty-first century.

The Charismatic Movement

Glossolalia, or speaking in unknown tongues during spiritual ecstasy, is common to many religious traditions, but prior to the twentieth century it occurred only rarely in Christianity. The modern charismatic movement associates speaking in tongues and other spiritual gifts (interpreting tongues, prophecy, and so on) with baptism in the Holy Ghost, the second work of grace in the Holiness tradition and either a requirement for salvation or a sign of Christian perfection. It began in January 1901, when several students at Charles Parham's Bethel Bible School in Topeka, Kansas, began speaking in tongues. Lauding the event as evidence of the restoration of the true Christianity practiced by the Apostles, Parham closed his school and began amassing followers in the Apostolic Faith Missions, mostly among the disenfranchised poor and nonwhite in the southern United States. Little glossolalia recurred until 1906, when one such mission on Azusa Street in Los Angeles experienced the "new Pentecost" under the direction of William J. Seymour, and the signs and wonders continued for three years. In the wake of Azusa Street, many new "Pentecostal" denominations were founded, including the Church of God in Christ, the International Church of the Foursquare Gospel, and the Assemblies of God, but just as often adherents remained within their own Holiness or Baptist denominations and sought baptism in the Holy Ghost at camp meetings and revivals. Today the various Pentecostal denominations and parachurch organizations have between 100 million and 400 million adherents worldwide; they have seen considerable success in Europe, sub-Saharan Africa, and especially in Latin America, where Brazil may reach a Pentecostal majority within the next decade.

In beliefs and practices, Pentecostalism rarely strayed far from its Holiness roots and rarely attracted the attention of mainstream Christianity, but in 1967 faculty and students of Duquesne University established the Catholic Charismatic Movement, incorporating glossolalia, and its attendant signs and wonders, into traditional Roman Catholic devotions. Small groups of Lutherans, Presbyterians, and others followed, until today an estimated 55 million members of mainstream Protestant denominations belong to the Charismatic Revival.

The Religious Right

The Religious Right of the contemporary United States grew out of the fundamentalist movement in several denominational families, especially Holiness, Baptist, and Pentecostal, mobilized through televangelism and a number of parachurch groups of the 1980s, notably Jerry Falwell's Moral Majority, Pat Robertson's Christian Coalition, and James Dobson's Focus on the Family. It combined fundamentalist beliefs with a hitherto uncommon commitment to political activism, and it used state-of-the-art media saturation to mobilize Christians into an apocalyptic struggle between God and Satan. The goal of the Religious Right was to "take back America" through specific political action: defeating or repelling gay rights and pro-choice legislation, forbidding the teaching of evolution and sex education, and legislating fundamentalist Christianity as the official religion of the United States. In the twenty-first century, the Religious Right continues to play a role in politics, lobbying for conservative candidates and legislation and fighting to overturn Supreme Court decisions that allow abortion and ban prayer in public schools.

The Traditional Catholic Movement

Although individual Catholics have become involved in many social movements, both religious and secular, few such movements have been associated with the Roman Catholic Church itself; even the pro-life movement mobilizes primarily through Protestant fundamentalists. A notable exception can be found in the various quasi-denominations, individual churches, and parachurch organizations that grew up to protest the modernization of the Church after Vatican I (1869), and especially after the modernization of the Mass in

Vatican II (1962–1965). Objecting to the increased participation of the congregation, the new accessibility of the priesthood, the increased fellowship with Protestants and members of non-Christian religions, and especially the institutionalization of a vernacular Mass, "traditional Catholics" are small in numbers but extremely media-savvy, utilizing not only television and radio but the Internet, and they are highly influential, especially among their conservative brethren. They vary in their attitudes toward the Vatican, from sadly concluding that the current papacy is misguided to asserting that the last true Pope was Pius XII, and that the Antichrist is sitting on the throne. One group even has its own College of Cardinals, which has elected a Pius XIII.

ECUMENICAL CHRISTIAN MOVEMENTS

During the last half of the twentieth century, religious observation ceased to play its earlier role in fostering social relations in the community: one's social prestige or network of contacts did not increase as a result of attendance. Conservative Protestants attended anyway, as they had an apocalyptic enemy to fight, but mainstream Protestants, Methodists, Presbyterians, Congregationalists, and some Baptists and Lutherans faced a staggering loss of numbers. They founded several ecumenical groups, including National Council of Churches and the World Council of Churches, to encourage fraternity among their remaining members and asserted that denominations were divided more by tradition than by beliefs and practices. Many such groups, such as Bread for the World, Habitat for Humanity, World Vision International, and Faith in Practice, replicate moderate Protestantism's commitment to social activism, fighting poverty, hunger, and homelessness with often the same degree of media savvy that characterizes fundamentalist televangelism. Only a few, such as the Taizé Community in France, are primarily concerned with spiritual development.

EASTERN RELIGIONS

Hinduism and Hinduism-Based Movements

In 2000, there were 1.2 million practicing Hindus in the United States; before 1965, when strict immigration laws limited Asian immigration, there were perhaps 100,000. Nevertheless, social movements based on Hindu beliefs and practices have been mobilizing Americans for over a century, since Swami Vivekananda founded the Vedanta Society in 1894. In 1920, Paramahansa Yogananda founded the Self-Realization

Fellowship in Los Angeles. Perhaps the most successful of all the Hindu-based movements, the Self-Realization Fellowship combined traditional krija yoga with jazz-age mental science to reach middle-class drawing rooms across the United States and Europe. After the immigration quotas were eliminated in 1965, many South Asian *gurus,* or independent religious leaders, saddened by what they considered the deplorable spiritual health of the West, felt called by God to reach out to His children in the New World; among the most famous were Haidakhan Samaj, Sri Satchinanda, Yogi Amrit Desai, and Gurudeva Sivaija Subramaniyaswami. Soon many groups, based in Hinduism but also including elements from other religions, Western parapsychology and mind science, and the 1970s New Age, were founded, drawing followers from among not only white middle-class intellectuals but also the disenfranchised.

The most controversial of the Hindu-based movements, the International Society for Krishna Consciousness (ISKCON), was founded in 1966 when Swami Srila Prabhupada came to America to win followers for the God Krishna. While thoroughly conventional in India, his practices of chanting, communal living, and aggressive begging were foreign to the West, and though its adherents, known as "Hare Krishnas," never numbered more than a few thousand, they became a primary target of the anti-cult movement of the 1970s. In 1988, when a scurrilous expose by John Hubner and Lindsey Gruson, *Monkey on a Stick: Murder, Madness, and the Hare Krishnas,* hit best-seller lists, parents hired cult deprogrammers to "rescue" young converts, and followers were accused of a variety of abuses, including brainwashing.

Buddhism and Buddhism-Based Movements

The many varieties of Buddhism have between 3 million and 6 million adherents in the United States, but again, a much larger number of persons have been influenced by social movements based on Buddhist teachings. In the 1950s, members of the influential Beat Generation began examining Zen and Tibetan Buddhist texts, either in translation or through the popularizations of Alan Watts and D.T. Suzuki, until a passing acquaintance with Buddhism became mandatory in artistic and literary circles. Since Buddhism has always been propagated through family and monastic devotion rather than a hierarchical ministry, it was amenable to those who wished to explore more deeply through individual reading or association with a local spiritual group. By the 1970s, Tibetan and Zen Buddhism were flourishing, and other Mahayana

sects that were obscure in Asia, such as Reiyukai, enjoyed an enormous popularity.

As with Hinduism, some of the Buddhist-based movements have been subject to controversy, especially Nichiren Shoshu, which was originally practiced by Japanese immigrants. It became "Americanized" through missionary activity in 1966 and had as many as 200,000 followers by the 1970s.

ALTERNATIVE MOVEMENTS

African-American Religious Movements

Immediately after World War I and extending through the Depression, African Americans who had recently immigrated from the South to the urban centers of the North, especially New York, Philadelphia, Detroit, Chicago, and also to Los Angeles, often abandoned or decreased their affiliation with their home Baptist, Methodist, and Holiness to embrace a wide variety of alternative religious movements. Although some, such as the various Afro-Israelite and black Muslim groups, rejected Christian tenets altogether in favor of a nominal affiliation with Judaism or Islam, and others, such as vodoun, worked within and around elements of folk Catholicism, most maintained the belief system and practices of traditional African-American Protestantism, merely adducing that their idiosyncrasies were the fulfillment of Scripture

Perhaps we can explain the sudden availability of alternative religious movements, and their sudden popularity, through the disillusionment that set in after the migration northward failed to alleviate institutionalized racism or significantly increase economic prosperity. The alternative movements offered a Promised Land that was not some distant heaven, but literally, physically on earth. Marcus Garvey's Universal Negro Improvement Association (UNIA) found it in Africa and sought mass repatriation for all Africans exiled in the Americas. The Rastafarians specified Ethiopia and petitioned the Messiah, Emperor Haile Selasse, to admit them into Paradise. Similarly, alternative religious movements offered a God who was not distant, but immediate, accessible, flesh and blood: Father Hurley in Tennessee, Bishop St. John the Vine in Baltimore, John the Revelator in New York, and Sweet Daddy Grace in Oakland all assured believers that they were literally Jesus Christ, God the Father, or both. The most successful, Father Divine, "God visibilated," established the literal Heaven in Sayville, Long Island, as well as many subsidiary heavens in urban centers across the United States. By 1935, he had gathered perhaps a million literal, physical angels, both black and white, to practice celibacy and entrepreneurship, and to greet each other with what would become a catchphrase of the day, "Peace—it's wonderful."

The rage for alternative African-American religious movements did not survive the Depression; Father Divine's Peace Mission Movement endures, but barely, under the leadership of the aging Mother Divine. Several sects of Afro-Israelites and black Muslims remain, but in idiosyncratic, racist configurations unlikely to win many followers.

Cults and New Religions

New religious groups, based on the dominant Christianity, on some other religion, or on the vision of a single iconoclast, are constantly springing up in the Western world. A few, such as the Jehovah's Witnesses, the Church of Christ, Scientist, and the Church of Jesus Christ of Latter-day Saints, have experienced a numerical success rivaling mainstream denominations. Most of them, however, never attract more than a few hundred members; at best they form fascinating but idiosyncratic byways in American religious history. During the early 1970s, some of these groups attracted the attention of the mainstream media, initiating a moral panic to rival the Satanic ritual abuse scare of the 1980s. Called "cults" not out of any definitional integrity but to underscore their aura of secrecy and threat, they were subject to a multitude of lurid tell-all books, endless discussion in the tabloids and on the talk-show circuit, police alerts and task forces, and eventually an army of professional anti-cult activists, including deprogrammers who abducted converts and attempted to restore them to "sanity." During the middle and late 1970s, the federal and local government often stepped in with lawsuits, punitive legislation, and even armed intervention.

Although the new religions were subject to abuses, like all religious groups, and emotionally damaged and unstable persons did form a percentage of the leadership, the tales of brainwashing, intimidation, physical and sexual abuse, and violence were vastly exaggerated. Among the most often excoriated groups were the Children of God; the Church of Scientology; the Unification Church of Reverend Sun Myung Moon; Nichiren Shoshu; and the International Society for Krishna Consciousness (1959). But guidebooks enumerated hundreds of "cults," including extremely obscure mental science organizations that had

been plodding along with a few dozen members for over a century. Even mainstream Christian denominations got into the act, with Protestant fundamentalists and Roman Catholics defining each other as mind-control cults and attempting to deprogram each other's converts.

The reasons for the sudden mania are obscure, but one might suggest the strategic appearance of many new alternative religious movements on college campuses, which attempted to emulate the success of Campus Crusade for Christ and the Intervarsity Christian Fellowship (as well as Newman Centers and Hillel), in the early 1970s, just as the last of the baby boomers began college. Parents who had already experienced the disenfranchisement of the hippie generation might be aghast at tales of innocuous religious exploration and sensitive to any attempt to foster a communal identity.

The mass suicide of the People's Temple in 1978, a utopian commune founded by the Reverend Jim Jones, effectively ended the wide-scale proselytization efforts of the new religions, especially on college campuses. A few new religions, such as David Koresh's Branch Davidians and Heaven's Gate, would continue to make the news if they went terribly wrong, but the anti-cult mania was over.

The New Age

The New Age refers to a vast number of groups and individuals with syncretic interest in a wide range of religious experience, including Christian and Jewish mysticism, Buddhist and Hindu practices, Sufism, shamanism, and global mythology, as well as many interests that are not religious or necessarily even spiritual, such as vegetarianism, meditation, holistic healing, astrology, environmentalism, UFOs, New Age music, reincarnation, parapsychology, and political activism. Even the movement to "free Tibet"—that is, to restore Tibet as a politically autonomous entity distinct from China—is often labeled New Age. Practitioners often belong to mainstream Christian denominations, but they combine a wide and eclectic reading in various forms of mysticism, Eastern religions, books by New Age professionals, and the American mental science tradition. They may be concerned almost exclusively in increasing their individual spiritual awareness, or they may be thoroughly committed to the spiritual transformation of global society. Although there are a few organizations, such as the Aetherius Society and est, most New Age activity occurs through loose confederations of associates who gather at New Age bookstores, concerts, or holistic healing centers.

Neopaganism

Though often labeled New Age, and complicit with its expansive and eclectic orientation, neopagans practice specific religious traditions. They may call themselves Wiccans, witches, or simply pagans. There are several distinctive branches, but most trace their lineage to Gerald Gardner, who in the 1930s claimed to have discovered and restored the pre-Christian earth-based religion of England. Although theoretically any neopagan religion is open to anyone, a great emphasis is placed on ancestral practices. Thus, Celtic, Norse, or Slavic traditions draw members primarily from individuals of those ethnic backgrounds, whereas persons of African ancestry are drawn primarily to the Afro-Caribbean syncretic religions of vodoun and Santeria.

Jeffery P. Dennis

BIBLIOGRAPHY

Bruce, Steve. *Pray TV: Televangelism in America.* New York: Routledge, 1990.

Cox, Harvey. *Fire from Heaven: The Rise of Pentecostal Spirituality and the Reshaping of Religion in the Twenty-first Century.* New York: Addison-Wesley, 1994.

Eck, Diana. *A New Religious America: How a "Christian Country" Has Become the World's Most Religiously Diverse Nation.* San Francisco: Harper, 2001.

Ellwood, Robert S. *Alternative Altars: Unconventional and Eastern Spirituality in America.* Chicago: University of Chicago Press, 1979.

Fauset, Arthur H. *Black Gods of the Metropolis: Negro Religious Cults of the Urban North.* Philadelphia: University of Pennsylvania Press, 1971.

Fields, Rick. *How the Swan Came to the Lake: A Narrative History of Buddhism in America.* Rev. ed. Boston: Shambhalla, 1986.

Hubner, John, and Lindsey Gruson. *Monkey on a Stick: Murder, Madness, and the Hare Krishnas.* San Diego: Harcourt Brace Jovanovich, 1988.

Hutton, Ronald. *The Triumph of the Moon: A History of Modern Pagan Witchcraft.* Oxford, UK: Oxford University Press, 1999.

Jenkins, Philip. *Mystics and Messiahs: Cults and New Religions in American History.* Oxford, UK: Oxford University Press, 2000.

Marsden, George. *Evangelicalism and Modern America.* Grand Rapids, MI: Eerdmans, 1984.

Melling, Phillip. *Fundamentalism in America.* New York: Columbia University Press, 2001.

Melton, J. Gordon. *New Age Encyclopedia.* Detroit: Gale Research, 1989.

Rosenberg, Ellen M. *The Southern Baptists: A Subculture in Transition.* Knoxville: University of Tennessee Press, 1989.

Synan, Vinson. *The Holiness-Pentecostal Movement in the United States.* Grand Rapids, MI: Eerdmans, 1972.

Social Gospel Movement

The Social Gospel movement, also known as Christian socialism until after 1907, was a moral reform movement of the late nineteenth and early twentieth centuries that provided the moral underpinnings for the Progressive movement. Social Gospel represented the intersection of Christian activism and social reform with economic theory. The Social Gospel movement was initiated informally by several inner-city clergymen in the Gilded Age who were attempting to draw the working class into their middle-class congregations. The effort spread to secular reform leaders interested in securing social justice for the poor by applying the Gospel to their social and economic problems.

The Roots of the Movement

The roots of the Social Gospel movement are diverse. Similar efforts at aiding the working class had been underway for some time in Victorian England and in Germany. The Social Gospel movement drew heavily upon European ideas, most especially the British strain of Christian socialism and also the Fabian movement, which called for gradual rather than revolutionary and violent means for spreading Socialist principles. Europeans themselves delved into the past for ideas. The medieval principle that social, economic, and political theory comprised Christian ethics enlightened Christian socialism reform efforts.

From Germany the Americans borrowed nearly its entire biblical and theological foundation as well as the historical view of economic theory, especially from Marxism. The writings of Albrecht Ritschl and Adolph von Harnack gave the rising Social Christian movement and its advanced social legislation in Germany and Switzerland its intellectual heft. Ritschl provided the overarching idea for the movement with his Jesus-centered, anti-metaphysical theology of the Kingdom of God. His theology stressed ethics and the community of man. A leading student of Ritschl's ideas, von Harnack articulated many of these ideas more clearly by attacking esoteric intellectual exercises and other shortcomings of the church leaders.

Although its European roots were substantial and vital, its American ones were even more so. The Social Gospel movement was part of a larger religious reform movement in the United States that predated the Civil War. It had its foundation in American Puritanism and its powerful drive to shape and possibly remake society. The Second Great Awakening and the antislavery movements of the antebellum period present clear evidence of these tendencies. Abolitionism had harnessed the energy and resources of the church and asked its followers to subordinate other interests to address the great moral question of the day, slavery. The Social Gospel movement would ask the same of its adherents.

The Social Gospel movement sought to overcome the attitudes created by laissez-faire economics of the period and Social Darwinism. The Social Gospel movement emerged during the Gilded Age, when a handful of men like John D. Rockefeller and Andrew Carnegie amassed great sums of wealth from the labor of others. Many preachers praised the acquisition of wealth from the pulpit, or like Henry Ward Beecher, pointed out that it demonstrated their high moral standing, whereas poverty was equated with sin. This view of wealth and poverty gained "scientific" credence with the emergence of the theory of Social Darwinism. Herbert Spencer in Britain and William Graham Sumner in the United States applied Charles Darwin's scientific theories of evolution through struggle and natural selection of the fittest to human societies. Sumner, a Yale sociologist and former minister, developed arguments about evolutionary determinism used by politicians in their debate against social reform and governmental intervention on behalf of the poor. Instead, he argued that a work-oriented moralism and the evolutionary process offered the only hope for society.

Henry Ward Beecher spoke favorably of the theory of evolution and Social Darwinism from his influential pulpit at Plymouth Church (Congregational) in Brooklyn, New York. Beecher, along with other preachers who shared his conservative values, defended the truth of the Gospel from attack by Darwinists by assimilating evolutionary views without harming or undermining Christian faith. Beecher and other conservatives linked creation as described in Genesis to Darwin's developmental theories, and sought to make the Bible more relevant to current conditions. Ironically, by doing so the conservatives helped to liberate organized religion from its constrictive past and paved the way for the liberal Social Gospel.

SOCIALISM AND NEW THEOLOGY

In the decades following the Civil War, some ministers and other Christian spokesmen around the country began to question whether the free enterprise system would automatically solve the nation's problems. Christianity and the church also came under some criticism for its failure to understand and defend the working class. Professor John Bascom of Williams College, who, like many contemporaries, held the poor in equal contempt, nonetheless criticized the conservatism of the Protestant pulpit and questioned the effect of the free competition on the workers. While at Williams, Bascom taught Washington Gladden, "the father of the American Social Gospel." Bascom's position evolved, and he later embraced the "Kingdom theology" of the Social Gospel movement first put forth by the Reverend Jesse Henry Jones, a Boston Congregationalist.

Jones blended Christianity with socialism. He founded the Christian Labor Union in 1872 and was editor of its journal, *Equality*, which advocated socialism until its dissolution a few years later in 1878. He attacked Beecher's positions and defended a labor theory of value. He also called for an eight-hour workday at a time when most laborers worked twelve to fourteen hours a day. In his book *The Kingdom of Heaven* (1871), Jones discussed a perfect Christian society on earth made up of independent socialistic communities. Other ministers like William Dwight Porter Bliss and George Herron went further still by leaving the pulpit and becoming Socialists.

In contrast to Christian socialism, another Congregationalist, Theodore Munger, developed the "New Theology" as the basis for a non-Socialist approach to the Social Gospel. Munger drew upon the writings of Horace Bushnell, who directly influenced several fellow American thinkers. Bushnell, who wrote and ministered in the North Congregational Church in Hartford, Connecticut, from the 1830s to the 1870s, bridged the gap from the old to the new theology and from the Second Great Awakening to the Social Gospel. He fashioned a theology based on Christian experience rather than on any doctrine. The Bible was a historical document, Bushnell said, that offered recorded experiences to be reproduced and emulated. Munger elaborated on these ideas, declaring that Christianity was not a theory but a life and a living process, one centered on Christ. He gave shape to his theory in *The Freedom of Faith* (1883), which acknowledged the rights of the individual but insisted that each person must accomplish his goals within a system that incorporates the good of the family and the nation.

Three American writers in politico-economic theory need to be mentioned along with Jones and Munger. Edward Bellamy, with his utopian novel, *Looking Backward, 2000–1887* (1888), a romance set in a Socialist United States in the year 2000, helped inspire the optimism of the Social Gospel. Henry George started a political movement for a single-tax system with *Progress and Poverty* (1879), his indictment of the American social system. George ran for mayor of New York City in 1886 as an independent candidate and finished second to Democrat Abram Hewitt, outpolling the young Republican candidate, Theodore Roosevelt. Lester Ward, though decidedly too secular in his writings to directly affect the Social Gospel, contributed to the movement by offering sociological arguments against Social Darwinism. He supported state intervention, charity, and other "artificial" devices to deal with the "natural" process that created poverty.

SOCIAL GOSPEL MOVEMENT LEADERS

A major proponent of the New Theology, Washington Gladden served as pastor of the First Congregational Church of Columbus, Ohio, from 1882 to 1914. His seven years as minister in the industrial city of Springfield, Massachusetts, from 1875 to 1882, where he dealt extensively with the unemployed, had done much to shape his views, but not as much as the Hocking Valley coal strike of 1884 in Ohio. Gladden knew the lengths to which the mine operators were going to break the strike and the union because many of them were in his congregation. They ended the strike only to face another one year later. When the miners won, the manager of the company admitted

OBITUARIES OF
WASHINGTON GLADDEN AND
BENJAMIN TILLMAN   1918

*The obituaries of white minister Dr. Washington Gladden
and South Carolina senator Benjamin Tillman were published jointly in the* Cleveland Advocate *on July 13, 1918.
The newspaper praised Gladden for his belief in racial equality and assailed Tillman for his relentless racism, silenced
only by his death.*

There died last week, within twenty-four hours of each
other, two men both of whom were known, at least by
name, throughout the country. The first to die was Dr.
Washington Gladden, the great Congregational minister, author and philosopher, who died at Columbus,
Ohio. The second to die was Benjamin R. Tillman,
United States Senator from South Carolina. Each had
passed the allotted three score and ten.

At one time, when a group of Colored people in
Columbus, Ohio, desired to establish a Colored Congregational church they sought Dr. Gladden, pastor of
the largest and most notable white Congregational
church in Ohio, for encouragement. His reply was this
terse sentence: "So long as there are vacant pews in my
church I will not favor a separate church for Colored."

Dr. Gladden was never one of those super-
enthusiastic agitators for equal rights and privileges for
the race, but he was a staunch believer in the Constitution, and regarded that instrument as one which conferred EQUAL RIGHTS upon ALL American citizens,
without reference to color or race, and he never, during
his eighty-two years of living gave utterance to a single
sentence designed to be hurtful to our race. To him the
color of a man's skin was simply the design of the
same God who gave to him his white skin, and it neither gave to the man special privileges or denied to
him equal privileges.

Senator Tillman never lost an opportunity to assail
the race; to discredit it in the eyes of the world, until
God, in His "mysterious way his wonders to perform,"
paralyzed the tongue that had denounced a struggling
race. For we had done naught to Senator Tillman save
to till his soil, and make it possible for him to represent
his state in the United States Senate by denial of suffrage. From the far South to the far North, he bitterly
traduced us—and for pay. When that vile tongue was
touched with paralysis, it was stilled for a while. But
when he had partially recovered from his first paralytic
stroke, he again resorted to bitter denunciation of a patient, long-suffering, loyal people.

Dr. Washington Gladden, perhaps the most famous

and most widely known of ministers, always spoke en-
couragingly of, and for our race. Although a cold, calculating, analytical student, he never designedly
erected a single bar to race advancement; he rather
pulled down bars which hedged it in.

Benjamin R. Tillman, perhaps as superficial a man
as ever represented a sovereign state in the United
States Senate, always spoke discouragingly of, and for
the race—never opened his mouth to discuss the race
but he denounced it in bitterest terms, merely for
cheap notoriety, and to satisfy and promote his political
ambitions. He piled high the very bars which Dr. Gladden would have leveled down.

When Death paused at the bedside of Dr. Gladden
to seal lips which had never uttered a single hurtful
word against our race, the smile which covered his vis-
age told how sweet to him had been the satisfaction of
living a life of helpfulness to ALL mankind, and when
life had left that body—weighed down with eighty-two
years—a voice must have murmured: "Well done, My
good and faithful servant"—and a suffering race wept
o'er his parting.

When Death paused at the bedside of Benjamin R.
Tillman to forever silence the tongue which had for
years, without reason—without cause—assailed our
race from the lakes to the gulf; which had espoused
legislation designed to turn back the hands on the
clock for us, there was NOT A SINGLE moist eye in
any of the three million Colored homes in this broad
land. On the contrary, every Colored person—when
Senator Tillman's death was announced—believed,
more than ever, that God does answer prayers.

Because of his goodness of heart; his calm, long,
helpful life; recognizing men for their worth and merit,
despite the color of their skin, and believing justice had
been designed as a legacy for ALL MEN, the late Dr.
Washington Gladden was the antithesis of Benjamin R.
Tillman.

Because in his heart there was no place—no sympathy for such as whom God had created with darker
skin; because he used his position and prestige to
dethrone justice for a race which had earned it, by
faithful allegiance to country and state; by fighting for
it on an hundred battle fields, Benjamin R. Tillman,
was the antithesis of Dr. Washington Gladden.

For the one for whom we have tears, and for the
one for whom we HAVE NO TEARS to shed, we can,
at least say Rest in Peace—God's will be done.

*Source: Cleveland Advocate 5:10 (July 13, 1918). Available
at dbs.ohiohistory.org/africanam/page1.cfm?ItemID=
7366&Current=08_03A.*

to Gladden that it was easier to bargain with the union at the table than with a mob at the picket lines.

Gladden first made a name for himself with his controversial book, *Being a Christian: What It Means and How to Begin* (1876), and eventually published over three dozen books that helped awaken the American Protestant social conscience. His widely read books dealt with New Theology, but it was his theology of social action that brought him the title of "the father of the American Social Gospel." His was a pragmatic, activist approach to Christianity. He demanded that the churches concern themselves with social injustice and that they help bring the economic features of American life under the laws of God's kingdom by example and by advocacy.

Gladden declared that it was the duty of a Christian to love his neighbor as himself, that society must be reformed along Christian lines, and that this was as important as saving individual souls. He even sought equality for blacks. He took the workingmen's view and argued on their behalf while he urged them to seek unity in Christianity. He rejected socialism as well as laissez-faire economics and declared that workers had the right to collective bargaining and to organize and strike. Gladden's criticism of the free enterprise system sharpened over the years. Although he never became a Socialist, he advocated municipal ownership of public utilities and cooperative management of many industries along with other economic reforms.

Josiah Strong, another follower of Bushnell, provided much of the revivalist and organizing spirit of the movement. Strong regarded the new industrial city as the major crisis for the nation and the church. He spelled out his concerns in the most influential book of the movement, *Our Country: Its Possible Future and Its Present Crisis* (1885). It made him a national figure along with his work with the Interdenominational Congress and as general secretary of the Evangelical Alliance. Both organizations gave him an opportunity to push his agenda of interchurch action as a response to economic conditions and to take the Social Gospel movement national in its scope. His use of social research and public education on social issues served the movement well. However, his anti-Catholic stance and his espousal of American imperialism, both of which had wide support, also influenced the movement. Both of these issues—the establishment of national organizations and a firm belief in Anglo-Saxon superiority—paralleled those of the political Progressives.

Walter Rauschenbusch, a Baptist minister who

Father of the American Social Gospel movement, Washington Gladden preached a pragmatic, activist, and socially conscious approach to Christianity. He supported workers' right to form unions, and he urged fellow ministers to fight for social justice, racial equality, and economic reform. *(Brown Brothers)*

served in New York City's infamous neighborhood known as Hell's Kitchen for eleven years until 1897 before becoming a faculty member of the Rochester Theological Seminary, embraced the Social Gospel immediately and became its most articulate and popular spokesman in America. He supported Henry George's mayoral campaign in 1886, and worked with Jacob Riis for playgrounds and better housing for immigrants. He emerged as a leading spokesman with the publication of *Christianity and the Social Crisis* in 1907. It laid out the entire Social Gospel in seven short chapters. He dealt with pragmatic solutions and reforms for the capitalist system and discussed his long-held vision for the Kingdom of God on earth. His beliefs survived the tumult and chaos caused by World War I in part because it did not dwell on utopian outcomes. Instead, he shifted his focus from the Kingdom of God to the "Kingdom of Evil" to help explain the cataclysmic war then raging in Europe. In *A Theology for the Social Gospel* (1917), written during World War I, he blamed the war not on Germany exclusively but on the lust for power and money by all colonial powers. He called for a democratic cooperative society to be achieved by nonviolent means.

Besides seminaries and pulpits, the social sciences produced its share of Social Gospel supporters and writers as well as activists. Richard Ely, an economist, and Albion W. Small, a sociologist, were the social science counterparts to Rauschenbusch and Gladden. Both men had a comprehensive understanding of social science and exhibited an intense concern for its philosophical background and its ethical implications. They and other social scientists asked the empirical questions necessary to challenge the status quo and support reform legislation. Each infused his work and teachings with the notion that Christian ethics should be applied to answering social questions. Other social scientists and middle-class reformers shared this approach and applied it in various ways and places, like in the settlement house movement, for example.

WHAT THE SOCIAL GOSPEL ACCOMPLISHED

The academic lectern and the ecclesiastic pulpit focused all of this energy and thought on overcoming an assumed alienation of the working class from Protestant churches. Washington Gladden noted that only one-tenth of his congregation was from the working class, but the census reported that nearly one-fourth of the population were wage earners. He and others assumed that meant the churches had failed to reach them and that an active interest in their plight might bring them into the fold. But middle-class Protestants overlooked one basic truth: the working class simply did not belong to middle-class churches. They ignored the existence of a parallel working-class social Christianity movement underway at the same time as the more widely known Social Gospel movement. In fact, labor periodicals used much of the same imagery, rhetoric, and motivation for supporting union causes and labor's discontent. The effort to lure workers into middle-class churches by showing concern and sympathy largely failed because it usually did not have a direct impact on their lives. It also failed to win over many urban immigrants because they were predominantly Catholic and it proposed few lasting solutions to urban problems.

The movement also did little to alleviate the dire situation faced by minorities, including Native Americans, Asians, and African Americans. Many believed minorities to be inferior and incapable of self-government. Women's suffrage faced the same condescending attitude. The typical Victorian family served as the model for the organization of society, even though this denied women many opportunities. Most of the movement's leaders did not involve themselves in the suffrage movement, and some, including Rauschenbusch, opposed suffrage completely.

What the Social Gospel movement did succeed in doing is to provide the political Progressive movement and the Progressive Party itself with ideas for reform, organizational models, national focus, and missionary zeal. The Progressives adopted ideas first embraced by ministers like Washington Gladden, including demands by unions for an eight-hour workday and Socialist ideas such as municipal ownership of public utilities. Without the exposure to Socialist ideas and the problems faced by wage earners, immigrants, and urban dwellers, the Progressive movement would not have been much of a national movement at all.

In the end, the Social Gospel movement had mixed results. It attracted a number of followers and helped liberalize organized religion from its doctrinaire past. It also linked Christianity with progressivism. But it largely failed those it intended to help—those in the inner city and the working class.

James G. Lewis

BIBLIOGRAPHY

Ahlstrom, Sydney E. *A Religious History of the American People.* New Haven, CT: Yale University Press, 1972.

Dorrien, Gary. *Imagining Progressive Religion, 1805–1900.* Louisville, KY: Westminister John Knox, 2001.

Hudson, Winthrop Still, and John Corrigan. *Religion in America: An Historical Account of the Development of American Religious Life.* 5th ed. New York: Macmillan, 1992.

Swift, Donald Charles. *Religion and the American Experience: A Social and Cultural History, 1765–1997.* Armonk, NY: M.E. Sharpe, 1998.

MISSIONARY MOVEMENTS

The American mission movement from the early 1800s through World War II, carried out by the mainline evangelistic Protestant churches, had its roots in colonial New England and preached a mission of Christ and culture: to spread the word of God according to Protestant Christian theology as well as an Anglo-American culture of democracy, efficiency, and technology to the far corners of the earth. Indeed, American national identity has historically been grounded in a faith in America's manifest destiny to establish a civil and moral society so exceptionally favored by God that it would serve as an archetype for all other nations of the world to emulate.

In 1630, Puritan founding father John Winthrop inspired the Massachusetts Bay colonists with the vision that they were creating "a city upon the hill" without precedent on earth, but that nevertheless would become a beacon guiding all humanity. His fellow Anglo-American Puritan missionaries, most notably John Eliot, active from the 1640s to the 1680s, first spread their religious beliefs as well as their model for "civilized society," among the Native American populations they encountered on the North Atlantic coastline, establishing praying towns to convert the natives to a way of life, as well as a way of worship. Thus, they set the pattern for Anglo-American Protestant Christian missionizing, adapted from the Spanish, Portuguese, and French Catholic missionaries and colonizers who preceded them into the "new" worlds outside Europe. The Anglo-American tendency to denigrate the "heathen," "barbaric," "child-like," and "savage" non-European Protestant cultures they encountered, however, was greater in degree than their European Catholic counterparts and increased as Anglo-American settlers pushed westward into the North American continent and, by the early 1800s, beyond the continental borders.

Although mission theorists and missionaries in the field may have debated whether "civilization" (i.e., the American social, political, and economic model) should accompany evangelization (proclaiming forgiveness of universal sin and salvation through Christ to all confessed believers), in practice American missionaries found them linked in intricate and seemingly unavoidable ways. "Christian obligation and American obligation," William R. Hutchinson in *Errand to the World: Protestant Thought and Foreign Missions* (1987) has explained, "were fundamentally harmonious."

LINKS TO AMERICAN GLOBAL EXPANSION

Outside America's borders, this potent blend of national and Christian identity has led to stereotyping of all Americans as missionaries, crusaders, and cultural imperialists, who assume that progressive culture flows outward only from western Christian civilizations. With American continental expansion complete and industrialization of the economy achieved through technological advances borrowed from England and improved upon with American ingenuity, a more energetic global expansion agenda dominated national policy by the late 1800s and the United States staked its claim to world power status. Territorial acquisitions achieved through purchase, treaty, or war transformed America's self-image as well as how Americans thought about other cultures and peoples.

The idea that America's nineteenth-century experience could serve as a "template" for other less developed, less fortunate peoples, Michael Adas has elucidated in "From Settler Colony to Global Hegemon," led, at the turn of the century to even greater intervention in the outside world, further denigration of other cultures, and a firm conviction that other cultures would welcome American values and institutions. Misapplications of Charles Darwin's biological evolutionary theory to the social realm led Anglo-Americans to believe that people who failed to progress technologically and politically as Western

European and American societies had progressed (and who failed to believe in the Christian God) were destined to disappear or be absorbed into the western world order.

Yet among the many varieties of nineteenth- and twentieth-century American expansionists, those relative few who formally adopted the American Protestant missionary mantle felt most keenly and urgently their Christian and American obligations to create God's Kingdom on earth. Of these few, numbering at the zenith of the mainline Protestant Mission movement in the early 1920s, only some 13,000, embraced in the most literal sense Christ's biblical instruction to "go and make disciples of all nations" (Matthew 28: 18–20). And while the American missionary movement can certainly be viewed as the religious arm of a global movement of western, Anglo-American expansion, the missionaries' motives and influence on the cultures they encountered were complex and ambiguous. To a greater degree than most Anglo-American military, diplomats, or businessmen, missionaries interacted with native cultures in intimate ways. Missionaries became "cultural brokers [mediating] between their home societies and the peoples among whom they worked," according to Charles R. Taber in *The World Is Too Much with Us: "Culture" in Modern Protestant Missions* (1991). In some instances, noted Dana L. Robert in *American Women in Mission: A Social History of Their Thought and Practice* (1996), true cultural collaborations between American missionaries and native peoples "fundamentally changed Christian identity," making Christian identity among the newly converted at the same time less American or western, more culturally specific, and more universally relevant.

GENDERED ASPECTS OF THE MISSION ENTERPRISE

Men in American Mission

The American missionary movement involved men and women in distinctly gendered ways. Male missionaries served first and foremost as evangelical ordained Protestant ministers or lay preachers and secondarily as medical doctors, teachers, and social and industrial reformers. Male clergy and laymen ran the interdenominational American Board of Commissioners for Foreign Missions as well as the denominational Protestant mission boards and determined which fields would be open to the American mission enterprise and who would be sent forth as Chris-

tian agents. Male missionaries brought the rhetoric of global conquest to their evangelistic endeavors, proclaiming their goal: "evangelization of the world in this generation" by the 1880s.

John R. Mott, at the forefront of the American missionary movement in its heyday, met regularly with western diplomats and heads of state. And it was Baptist layman John D. Rockefeller, Jr., who, in 1930, launched an interdenominational inquiry into the historic record of the mainline Protestant missions to India, Burma, China, and Japan, and proposed new directions in mission policy based on the nearly two-year-long field investigation. Advancing a decidedly liberal Protestant view, the "Laymen's Inquiry," published as *Re-Thinking Missions* in 1932, proposed that the (male) missionaries' role was to act as ambassadors for Christianity rather than soldiers or salesmen, expert at addressing the social needs of the native populations. Throughout the duration of the American mission movement, men held the visible leadership and policymaking positions in spite of the fact that, by 1910, women accounted for 55 percent of the mission force.

Women in American Missions

Female missionaries served first as mission wives and models of pious Christian homemakers. Later, after the first generation of mostly married women in the mission field, single women missionaries served foremost as teachers, social reformers, doctors, and nurses. All missionaries felt called to the mission field to "save" heathen souls for Christ. But female and male missionaries alike believed that female missionaries had a special call to uplift the lives of their "degraded" nonwestern "sisters" living in non-Christian societies where women's oppression was judged to be more cruel and intense that that of men. Perhaps because their own Protestant churches denied them a formal ministerial role and relegated them to a separate, auxiliary role on church mission boards, female missionaries devised a mission theology that was active, practical, and holistic, with set goals to meet the native societies' material, intellectual, and spiritual needs. First promoted energetically by Mary Lyon at her Mount Holyoke Female Seminary in the mid-1800s, what became known as the "Woman's Work for Woman" missiology after the American Civil War was grounded in the belief that higher education was necessary for American women to become fully useful, well-trained teachers and thereby play a larger role in the public realm of society—even if that public realm was overseas. The profession of missionary became particularly attractive to many American women in the late nineteenth and early twentieth centuries because it provided one of the few socially accepted professional avenues for the increasing number of college-educated, single women.

American women missionaries, while undeniably colonial women who shared a crusading sense of cultural superiority with their male counterparts, nonetheless brought education and awareness of national and global, social, and political issues to the lives of colonized women and children that fostered distinctly subversive, anti-imperialist consequences. Dana L. Roberts has asserted that the American women's mission movement, intentionally or not, "with its goals of evangelizing and emancipating non-Christian peoples through education . . . gave non-western women the tools with which to shape their own destinies." After World War I, shaken as male missionaries were by the disillusioning specter of Christian nations at war, the Anglo-American women's mission movement adopted a new foundational watchword, "World Friendship," which displayed more cultural sensitivity and a conviction that nonwestern peoples would forge their own paths to Christianity. Within the women's realm of mission work, native women assumed leadership positions in schools, churches, and other religious organizations. Anglo-American women retreated to advisory roles in the mission fields, continuing to serve only at the specific request of native women and devoting their energies to promoting peace and internationalism in an increasingly violent and nationalistic era. Failing to avert World War II, the American women's mission movement as it had developed within the mainline Protestant churches, declined in number, and ceded its predominant position to faith-based evangelicals and Roman Catholic missions in traditional nonwestern mission fields as well as in European nations, and, in the 1990s, in states that had been part of the Soviet Union.

OVERSEAS MISSION 1870–1930

By the late nineteenth century, the emergence of the Social Gospel within American Protestant churches demanded Christian ministry to all human needs, physical and intellectual as well as spiritual, in order to perfect human society on earth. The rise of an expansionist ethos in mainstream American politics accompanied this growing adherence to the tenets of the Social Gospel among the middle class. These two concurrent developments fueled an outward-looking reforming zeal within mainline Protestant church

congregations, and the American mission movement flourished between 1870 and 1930. During these years, mainline Protestant theology shifted from a premillennial focus whereby American Protestant Christians sought to prepare the world for the imminent return of Christ to a postmillennial vision, in which American Protestants believed they were extending the Kingdom of God on earth by spreading Christian values through American cultural and political institutions. Firm belief in America's special covenant with God inspired a new wave of missionaries to go forth to nonwestern nations in order to advance Christian (and American) civilization. From 1860 to 1890, the number of Protestant missionary societies sending Christian emissaries into the foreign fields increased from sixteen to ninety.

THE YOUTHFUL CHARACTER OF THE NEW MISSION ERA

This more confident, energetic, and self-conscious national pride that permeated the American mission movement in these decades attracted young college students in increasingly larger numbers to the foreign fields. The movement was inspired by mission promoters like the Reverend Arthur T. Pierson who edited the *Missionary Review of the World* journal in 1886 and who insisted that new technological and political advances in American civilization had created the most opportune moment for expansion in Christian history. Fired by Pierson's charge that "all should go, and go to all," these young missionaries believed they could bring about "the evangelization of the world in this generation."

A newly organized interdenominational Student Volunteer Movement (1886–1946)—initially an outgrowth of the Young Men's Christian Association (YMCA)—took up the world evangelization "watchword" and defined the zealous, optimistic faith of this new mission era. YMCA activists like Dwight L. Moody, John R. Mott, and Luther Wishard inspired nearly 10,000 college students to volunteer for mission service by the turn of the century. Among them was a growing contingent of American women, who joined the Young Women's Christian Association (YWCA) and made up 55 percent of the mission force by 1910. During the American Woman's Missionary Jubilee celebrations held in forty-eight cities across the nation during 1910 and 1911, thousands of women regaled the accomplishments of fifty years of the Woman's Work for Woman global ministry and looked forward to a bright future for an ecumenical church women's movement in the overseas missions.

CONFRONTING NATIONALISM IN FOREIGN MISSION FIELDS

The mission experience challenged some American missionaries in ways they had not anticipated. American missionaries worked closely with native Christians in the foreign fields in the late nineteenth and early twentieth centuries, and they were forced to respond to nationalist aspirations among the populations they sought to convert and westernize. As American missionaries opened new mission fields in Latin America after 1870, some Latin American progressives welcomed their presence. Ministering to the masses of indigenous poor rather than to the landed rich and those of European origins, American Protestant missionaries distinguished themselves from the long established Roman Catholic missions and churches in the region. American Protestants brought their late-nineteenth-century progressive and democratic values with them to Latin American mission fields, and these ideas were well-received by some segments of the Latin American populations.

Yet they also brought their expansionist faith in America's manifest destiny and sometimes shared their government's political goals, which undercut their legitimacy with the Latin American nationalists they sought to convert. At the same time, some American missionaries struggled to define a "Christian imperialism" motivated by altruism and a desire to improve the lives of native populations less fortunate than their own and tried to distance their civilizing mission from the self-serving and acquisitive imperialism of their nation's businessmen and politicians who aimed to build an overseas empire.

In established mission fields in Asia and Africa, the new generation of American Protestant missionaries discovered changes among native populations, too. Although native populations in these fields were still reluctant to convert to a "foreign" religion, they were far more eager to acquire a western education from the missionaries than earlier generations had been. From the perspective of native nationalists in China, or Japan, or India, discovering the secrets of western wealth and power through a western education might reveal the keys to resisting western imperialism and "liberation" from western colonial control might be more meaningful than Christian "salvation" from original sin. Asian natives who did convert to Christianity were often motivated by certain aspects of Christian teachings that spoke to what they perceived to be the weaknesses or needs of their own societies.

Many Japanese Christians, for example, were inspired by the Christian ethic of social service in a time of transition among their national leadership. As a new constitutionally based Japanese government led by the Meiji emperor stripped the samurai warrior class of its hereditary role to serve the feudal shogunate, many former samurai families converted to Christianity and acquired western educations. They found a new moral foundation for their lives and new avenues to serve the Japanese nation in its modernizing project.

EVALUATING THE AMERICAN MISSION MOVEMENT

Young Men's Christian Association leader and mission enthusiast Robert Speer estimated that by 1950, western missionaries had converted 1.5 million non-western natives to Protestant Christianity, and in 1910, estimated that nearly 800,000 new converts had been added to the Christian fold. These numbers seemed impressive but represented only a fraction of the non-western populations in the mission fields. Far more successful were the number of schools and medical facilities that resulted from the missionaries' civilizing activities. These endeavors improved health conditions and spread literacy among native populations. In part, these results were the consequence of an increasing proportional number of laypersons among the missionaries' ranks. By 1910, nearly 70 percent of the American mission force was made up of laypersons, up from 52 percent in 1868.

Laypersons in the field tended to hold liberal Protestant beliefs. They deemphasized denominationalism and doctrinal differences among Protestant churches. The holistic Social Gospel, rather than engaging in pure evangelism, guided their mission activities. Nonetheless, many continued to adhere to the ultimate goal of the American mission movement, world evangelization. When in 1932 the ultraliberal "Laymen's Inquiry" financed by John D. Rockefeller, Jr. and compiled by William Ernest Hocking evaluated the historic record of over 100 years of the American Protestant mission enterprise and recommended new mission policies, many liberal missionaries in the field disavowed its conclusions. Hocking's report on the Laymen's Inquiry, or *Re-Thinking Missions*, advised Protestant missionaries to promote the expansion of world spirituality and to collaborate with other world religions rather than seek to convert all to Protestant Christianity.

The mainline Protestant American mission movement declined after 1930. Its strength and confidence were undercut by widening rifts between fundamentalists and liberal Protestants who disagreed about the nature and purpose of the foreign missions. Moreover, mainline Protestant churches struggled to meet the needs of congregations in the United States during the Great Depression, and deep cuts in church and mission board budgets reduced funding to send missionaries abroad. Separate auxiliary women's mission boards were merged into Protestant denominational boards, and the distinctiveness enjoyed by the American women's mission movement disappeared as its already limited institutional autonomy disappeared. In addition, as more professional opportunities opened to women in the United States, the number of women who pursued a mission career through traditional Protestant church mission channels decreased. After 1930, faith-based missionaries, who operated outside the bounds of institutional churches and raised their own funds for evangelical ministries to the "unsaved" populations, supplanted the mainline Protestant church missionaries in the field.

Karen Garner

BIBLIOGRAPHY

Adas, Michael. "From Settler Colony to Global Hegemon: Integrating the Exceptionalist Narrative of the American Experience into World History." *American Historical Review* 106:5 (December 2001): 1692–1720.

Davidann, Jon Thares. *A World of Crisis and Progress: The American YMCA in Japan, 1890–1930.* London: Associated University Presses, 1998.

Hutchinson, William R. *Errand to the World: American Protestant Thought and Foreign Missions.* Chicago: University of Chicago Press, 1987.

Robert, Dana L. *American Women in Mission: A Social History of Their Thought and Practice.* Macon, GA: Mercer University Press, 1996.

Taber, Charles R. *The World Is Too Much with Us: "Culture" in Modern Protestant Missions.* Macon, GA: Mercer University Press, 1991.

YMCA-YWCA

The Young Men's Christian Association (YMCA) and Young Women's Christian Association (YWCA) were Protestant Christian social service organizations founded by middle-class professionals in England in the 1840s (YMCA) and 1850s (YWCA). Initially, these gender-based organizations provided Bible study, and soon afterward recreational programs, for men and women working in industrial factories. Seeking to fill a perceived void in spirituality and to instill Christian values among the working classes, Christian laypersons in evangelical Protestant denominations formed the YMCA and YWCA to provide a "useful" and holistic ministry to needy populations. YMCAs and YWCAs were led by boards of directors; male businessmen served on YMCA boards and women of the leisured middle class served on YWCA boards. They employed professional teachers and social workers, or "secretaries," to carry out programs and services. This YMCA-YWCA organizational model soon spread to other countries in Western Europe and to North America.

THE AMERICAN ASSOCIATIONS

Zealous American middle-class reformers embraced the YMCA-YWCA activist "fourfold" philosophy to minister to the spiritual, intellectual, social, and physical needs of young American workers in New England's industrial towns, and Southern and Eastern European immigrants who settled in cities on the East Coast and in the Midwest. Evangelical preacher Dwight L. Moody preached the message that God's salvation was available to all who sought it sincerely, and began to campaign for YMCA recruits to help spread the "good news" on college campuses in the 1860s. By the 1880s, YMCA and YWCA chapters were thriving institutions on many college campuses, involving students in community service projects, recruiting them for professional social service careers when they graduated. Inspired by Moody and by ambitions to become a foreign missionary, Luther Wishard, a YMCA secretary at Princeton, decided to take the American YMCA idea to the foreign mission fields.

The YMCA (and soon, the YWCA) foreign mission message was salvation and social service; the medium was American college students. In summer 1886, Wishard and Moody hosted a student conference on Moody's Northfield, Massachusetts, Seminary campus. Reverend Arthur T. Pierson preached a rousing call to mission to the assembled students and, by the conclusion of the conference, one hundred college men had pledged themselves to mission service and the Student Volunteer Movement was born. Through Wishard's fierce campaigning and the support of YMCA leader John R. Mott who shared his vision of the YMCA's foreign mission potential, the American YMCA national board was persuaded to begin, in 1891, to support a few "foreign secretaries," who would develop YMCA organizations in India, China, and Japan along American organizational lines. American missionaries in foreign fields supported the expansion of the YMCAs and requested more secretaries, male and female, to serve the needs of youths in their mission districts. By 1895, the American YWCA, too, joined in the mission movement.

CHARACTERISTICS OF AMERICAN YMCA AND YWCA FOREIGN WORK

From the inception of their overseas mission work, American YMCA and YWCA foreign secretaries tried to follow the guiding precept to plant the "association idea," organizing young native mission school students or college men and women in Bible study, community service projects, and recreational programming to discipline their spirits, minds, and bodies in conjunction with Christian teachings and American pluralistic principles. American foreign sec-

Members of the Young Men's Christian Association, or YMCA, attend a Christmas party in Harlem, New York, in the early 1920s. The YMCA—along with the Young Women's Christian Association, or YWCA—began in the mid-nineteenth century as a religious institution to promote Bible study and spiritual growth. The organizations gradually evolved into community-based institutions that offered a wide range of social, recreational, and intellectual activities. *(Brown Brothers)*

retaries cultivated native youths to become leaders within their own national YMCA and YWCA organizations. But both American YMCA and YWCA secretaries encountered obstacles in the foreign fields. American foreign secretaries professed to find it difficult to train YMCA and YWCA members who displayed the leadership qualities that the Americans could recognize and appreciate. YMCA or YWCA leaders took programming in nationalist directions that alarmed some American foreign secretaries who considered foreign nationalism divisive, failing to recognize that their own American value-laden Christian

message was far from the "universal" message they claimed it to be.

Some American YMCA and YWCA secretaries, however, developed a deep understanding and sympathy for the nationalist views of their co-workers and constituents in the foreign fields. Beginning in the 1910s, the YWCA, and, in the 1920s, the YMCA, adopted the Social Gospel creed, and their interactions with the poorest and most exploited workers and peasants in foreign societies forced them to confront the legacies of Western European and American colonialism, and to recognize their own complicity in the Western imperialist enterprise. Beginning with the Spanish-American War in 1898, YMCA secretaries had accompanied American soldiers to fields of war in Cuba and the Philippines. During World War I, YMCA and YWCA secretaries served the Allied Western forces in Europe; in World War II, they served in Europe and Asia. Some American foreign secretaries realized that their social service had political ramifications.

THE TRANSFORMATION OF AMERICAN YMCA AND YWCA FOREIGN WORK

As with the mainline Protestant missions, the American YMCA and YWCA foreign secretary presence reached its peak in foreign mission fields in the 1920s. The Great Depression forced the American YMCA and YWCA to reduce the number of secretaries they sent abroad, and to limit funding for foreign building projects. After the 1930s, men and women assumed leadership of their own national YMCAs and YWCAs, and a few American foreign secretaries served in advisory roles when invited by national associations.

For both the YMCA and YWCA, international relationships were transformed in the post–World War II period. The Cold War divided the Communist and non-Communist world, and led to the restriction of the American YMCA and YWCA to non-Communist nations allied to the West. The YMCA and YWCA supported demands for decolonization and independence within the non-Western world with increasingly culturally sensitive policies and services. The American YMCA "Foreign Service" Division changed its name to "World Service." It has continued to promote mutual understanding of cultural differences among YMCAs globally and to offer funding, personnel, and other resources to independent YMCAs in other nations to meet self-defined local needs. The U.S. government's Peace Corps program, established in 1961, followed the YMCA "World Service" Division model. The American YWCA also changed the name of its "Foreign Division" to the "International Division" in 1961 and since the end of World War II has gradually deferred control over funds and personnel devoted to international initiatives. The World YWCA, based in Geneva, participates in a global women's movement as a leading women's international Non-Government Organization (NGO) that interacts with the United Nations and other global agencies and supports feminist, antiracist, human rights and social justice campaigns worldwide.

Karen Garner

BIBLIOGRAPHY

Boyd, Nancy. *Emissaries: The Overseas Work of the American YWCA, 1895–1970.* New York: Woman's Press, 1986.

Davidann, Jon Thares. *A World of Crisis and Progress: The American YMCA in Japan, 1890–1930.* London: Associated University Presses, 1998.

Fleming, Daniel J. *International Survey of the Young Men's and Young Women's Christian Associations.* New York: International Survey Committee, 1932.

Garrett, Shirley S. *Social Reformers in Urban China: The Chinese YMCA, 1895–1926.* Cambridge, MA: Harvard University Press, 1970.

Hopkins, C. Howard. *History of the Y.M.C.A. in North America.* New York: Association Press, 1951.

RURAL UTOPIAN MOVEMENTS
1820s–1850s

Since European settlement began, North America has proved a rich breeding ground for communal, cooperative, and collaborative settlements and communities. One recent study has enumerated over 900 such settlements founded up to 1965 in the territory of the United States alone, not counting monastic communities of the Catholic and other mainstream churches. Of this total, almost 250 were formed before 1860, and of those in turn the majority existed during the forty years or so leading up to the American Civil War. Their formation and respective fates were emblematic of major themes in this period's social history: the intersection of religious and secular impulses; the influence of European ideas on American movements; and a deep interest in experimentation in pursuit of social reform. The antebellum period was not unique in producing communal and cooperative utopias: there were comparable episodes in the 1890s and again in the 1960s. But some historians have suggested that at no other time in American history were such movements so closely linked to mainstream political and cultural developments, or so close to influencing patterns of change in society at large.

GERMAN PIETISM

Communal ventures of various kinds had accompanied early English settlements in North America, but few had lasted long. During the eighteenth century, however, German pietist groups had established settlements that operated temporarily or permanently on communal lines. Moravian missionaries had for a time conducted communal arrangements in their settlements at Bethlehem, Pennsylvania, and elsewhere. Significant numbers of Anabaptists, including Swiss Mennonites and Alsatian Amish, whose core American settlements also lay in Pennsylvania, maintained close-knit communities of mutual support even while retaining private property and individual family households. Amish settlements in Lancaster County,

Pennsylvania, founded in the 1730s, remained small until the later nineteenth century, but were expanding and adding congregations during the antebellum period. But some early nineteenth-century pietist groups adopted communal arrangements. The Harmonists, led by George Rapp, lived at a sequence of successful communal settlements in Pennsylvania and Indiana from 1805 to 1905; the similar Society of Separatists of Zoar, founded in Ohio in 1817, retained its communal organization until 1898. The Rappites' and Zoarists' success pointed the way for pietist settlements at Ebenezer, New York, in the 1840s and Amana, Iowa, in 1854, as well as for the large post–Civil War colonies of Hutterites in the Great Plains region that would become the most extensive and stable of all communal settlements in North America.

Significant as all these groups were, however, their religious and ethnic characteristics limited their wider impact on American society. They were divisions of or reactions to German Lutheranism and its European offshoots. They recruited almost exclusively from among German populations and retained German-language and religious practices. Although some originated in missionary efforts, the communities remained largely self-contained. North America provided a shelter for religious practices that was difficult to sustain elsewhere, and their emphasis lay in withdrawal from society and the preservation of pure religious observance. Zoar, for instance, was named for the place to which, in the book of Genesis, Lot fled to escape the evils of Sodom.

MILLENNIALISM AND REFORM

The communal dimensions of English-speaking religious movements, however, did have wider links with the American social reform movements of the antebellum period. A common characteristic of Anglo-American Protestantism in this period was its millennialism, the confidence that at some point

Christ would return to rule on earth. This belief had two kinds of influence on communalism. Some groups, holding that the millennium had already occurred, sought to build perfect societies that would express the rule of heaven on earth. Others, religious and secular, were profoundly influenced by the concept of "postmillennialism," the idea that Christ would only return to a world made ready for him—a spur to social action and to campaigns for social reform.

Prominent among groups of the first kind were the United Society of Believers in Christ's Second Appearing, popularly known as the Shakers for their dance-like form of worship. Originating in a small group of English believers who migrated to America in the 1770s with their leader Ann Lee, Shakerism crystallized in the 1790s into a significant communal movement which in due course built twenty-two village settlements from southern Maine to central Kentucky and had, at its peak around 1850, almost 4,000 adherents. Lee had died in 1784, but her successors, particularly Joseph Meacham and Lucy Wright, forged a set of communal arrangements based on the surrender of private property, the abolition of marriage, and strict celibacy. Shakers believe that God has both male and female components, and that Ann Lee had been Christ's female counterpart. Because they were living in the millennium, Shaker communities were therefore miniature heavens on earth, led by a hierarchy of male and female ministers and deacons. Centers of agricultural and craft production, most Shaker villages achieved considerable economic efficiency and prosperity in the first half of the nineteenth century.

Though enjoying brief revivals, however, Shakerism entered a long period of decline in the 1850s as its social and religious arrangements marked it out clearly from mainstream society and it lost most of its impulse for missionary work. It has never died out (one community still operates today), but most of its villages were abandoned or sold between 1875 and the 1920s. Shaker communities and economic arrangements, rather than their beliefs or celibate practices, nevertheless influenced other reformers. Members of subsequent communities sometimes studied Shakerism for the lessons it might provide. Friedrich Engels later proclaimed it to be a successful model for a Communist society.

In the 1820s and 1840s, events in Europe and the United States combined to produce further efforts at creating communal settlements in America. The Welsh-born reformer Robert Owen, having developed a model factory community in Scotland, and frus-

trated at Parliament's obstruction of necessary social reforms, inspired several communal settlements, including that at New Harmony, Indiana, which Owen himself founded in 1825 on a site purchased from the Rappites. Optimistic to a fault, Owen at first proclaimed rapid progress at New Harmony toward his goal of achieving a community without private property, but by 1827 disputes and divisions had so disheartened him that he backed away from this intention and the community dissolved. Owen held that social ills derived from circumstances and that reform would follow from the creation of an ideal form of society. This inspired the recruitment of a wide range of members, from intellectuals to prairie farmers, but many failed to meet Owen's expectation that they would see the reason of his prescriptions and fall into a new way of life. Owen covered his retreat from New Harmony with the accusation that his followers had not been worthy of the experiment. Meanwhile, his public pronouncements on marriage, property, and religion had incurred the wrath of the conventional churches. Owen also inspired the effort of the English radical Frances Wright to establish a community for freed slaves at Nashoba in Tennessee in 1826, but this also failed on Wright's patronizing assumptions and poor organizing ability. Publications on birth control by Owen's son, Robert Dale Owen, and Wright's self-description as a "free enquirer" added to the furor over Robert Owen's own radicalism and helped shape the ideological climate into which subsequent communal movements emerged.

Although Owen is best understood as a pioneer Socialist, cooperator, and secular reformer, the confident, almost messianic tone of his pronouncements gave his movement many parallels with contemporary millennial thought. And it was the climate of postmillennialist reform movements, coupled with economic distress, which gave rise to the next and greatest antebellum surge in community founding. During the early-to-mid-1840s, over sixty communities were established in the United States. Although they had varied roots, they shared a set of overlapping contacts with the broader stream of social reform movements that had been gathering weight over several years.

COMMUNITIES OF THE 1840S

A financial panic in 1837 led to a severe economic downturn that particularly affected the Northeast, the region most touched by the growth of capitalist industry and commerce. Coincidentally, movements in the same region to campaign for the abolition of

One of the most successful and long-lasting of the nineteenth-century utopian societies, the Oneida Community in upstate New York manufactured silverware, steel traps, and embroidered silks. The group was best known for its practice of "complex marriage," by which members had multiple sexual partners and children were raised communally. *(Brown Brothers)*

Southern slavery and other reforms also ran into difficulties. Economic depression fostered discussions in urban, intellectual circles about the ideals of rural life, and a "back to the land" movement began to ripen. Discussions among reformers about the problems they faced reinforced this trend with interest in communities as an ideal form of social organization. Publicity for these discussions was provided not only in specialist reform periodicals and newspapers, but also in the wider press, particularly the newly founded New York *Tribune*, edited by Horace Greeley.

In Massachusetts, debates among Unitarians about the church's role in social reform, and among the Boston transcendentalists, led to the establishment of a community at Brook Farm, a rural site just outside Boston, in 1841, led by the former Unitarian minister George Ripley. The same year, a group of "Practical Christians" under the Universalist minister

Adin Ballou, set up what they called Fraternal Community Number One not far away, at Hopedale, Massachusetts, in what they expected to be a model for the establishment of ideal Christian societies across the land. The following year a group of radical abolitionists founded a cooperative community at Northampton, in western Massachusetts, in the hope of establishing a model of industrial, agrarian, and educational work in a rural environment, free from the strictures and practices of conventional churches. Abolitionists were also instrumental in founding, subsequently, a number of communities in Ohio and Indiana. In all of these cases, secular and religious ideals were closely intermixed.

Also growing out of this reform environment, though with a strong and distinctive religious dimension, was a community first founded in the early 1840s at Putney, Vermont, that moved to Oneida, New

Reacting to the growing materialism, acquisitiveness, and competitiveness of industrial capitalism, French social theorist Charles Fourier advocated small cooperative communities called "phalanxes," based on handicrafts and agriculture. Americans organized phalanxes in the mid-1840s from Massachusetts to Wisconsin. *(Brown Brothers)*

York, in 1848. Led by its religious head, John Humphrey Noyes, Oneida was truly communal in the sense that private property was abolished, members participated in a regulated system of group marriage tempered for two decades by what Noyes called "male continence," or self-restraint to prevent ejaculation during intercourse. After the Civil War, Noyes modified this "complex marriage" regime into an early eugenic experiment, in which couples selected by him for their superior spiritual attributes were permitted to conceive children, to be raised by the community. Oneida continued as a communal group until 1881.

But these religious-based communities formed part of a wider movement that had, once again, secular and European origins. Owenism revived briefly in the 1840s and some new settlements were founded, but the greatest impetus came from American followers of the French social theorist Charles Fourier (1772–1837). Inspired by the writings of the chief American

Fourierist, Albert Brisbane, and supported by Horace Greeley and others, several thousand American artisans, workers, and professionals acted to form new communities in the mid-1840s. Only about one in ten of the members of Fourierist groups were farmers, but most communities were founded in rural locations accessible to urban markets.

Fourier's own writings centered on the perception that social harmony could be secured by building societies capable of permitting humans' built-in predispositions, which Fourier called "passions," to function. His calculations indicated that ideal communities, which he called "phalanxes," would consist of 1,600 to 1,800 men and women who would share the full range of available attributes in combination. Brisbane and other American interpreters stepped around the more fanciful of Fourier's visions and focused on his prescriptions for the organization of property and work, a combination of private ownership and cooperation that they called "Associationism." They offered life in communities as a preferable alternative to the drudgery, competitiveness, and waste of capitalism. Cooperation would, above all, permit men and women to exploit their talents and desires by applying Fourier's doctrine of "attractive industry," in which work was organized and individuals' tasks varied frequently so as best to match their natural inclinations. Associationists took pains to distance themselves from Owen's critiques of existing society. Fourier's theories, they insisted, would not abolish property, but would merely pool its uses for mutual advantage. Fourierist phalanxes would promote religious freedom and uphold the principles of monogamous marriage and family life.

Greeley, Brisbane, and other leaders had advocated a concerted effort to raise funds to build a full-scale version of a Fourierist phalanx, but in practice some thirty smaller communities were established in the mid-1840s, at sites from New Jersey to Wisconsin. Most were short-lived; twelve lasted a year or less. Still, a handful, like the Wisconsin Phalanx at Ceresco (later Ripon) showed signs of prosperity, and one, the North American Phalanx at Red Bank, New Jersey, lasted twelve years. The Associationists' greatest triumph was to convert George Ripley and his followers at Brook Farm to the virtues of Fourierism early in 1844. Brook Farm not only became the intellectual heart of the movement, publishing its chief periodical, the *Harbinger*, but it adopted organizational changes to accommodate Fourier's theories of attractive labor.

Associationism faced a serious dilemma. On one hand, the failure to concentrate efforts prevented the investment of sufficient capital on a single site and made most communities prey to financial weakness and failure. On the other hand, dispersed communities offered opportunities for participation to supporters across the Northeast and Midwest, and, by avoiding the rigidity of following a single prescribed community pattern, may well have fostered the movement's survival into the 1850s. Nevertheless, most of the communities did not survive the 1840s; two founded in the 1850s, at Raritan Bay, New Jersey, and La Reunion (near Dallas), Texas, were short-lived.

Comparison of Fourierism in America with another French-inspired communal movement of the period illustrates some of the complexities entailed in introducing communalism to an existing American population. The French theorist Etienne Cabet, having published in 1839 a novel, *Voyage en Icarie* (Journey to Icaria), describing an imaginary community, found himself heading a movement to enact this in reality. Thus, in 1849 he set out in advance of several hundred followers to establish a settlement, first in Texas, then in Illinois. By the time of Cabet's death in 1856, the movement had split, but small Icarian communities continued near St. Louis, Missouri, in Iowa, and in California until the 1890s. Unlike the Fourierist phalanxes, these had adopted communal property; unlike them, too, they had remained almost entirely French, and French-speaking, in their membership. Though secular in character, the Icarian communities shared the communalism and cultural uniformity of some of the German pietist groups, and this may have contributed to their relative longevity.

EVALUATING ANTEBELLUM COMMUNITIES

Communities founded during the 1840s lasted, on average, less than two-and-a-half years. By the end of the antebellum period, with the exception of Oneida and the Icarian communities, few new communal groups survived, while the preexisting Shakers and various German groups continued. Scholars have debated the significance and implications of this pattern. Conventionally, historians dismissed antebellum communalism as marginal, ephemeral, or irrelevant to major issues. Recent studies have taken a different perspective, indicating the role of community-founding in the wider context of social reform movements, and tracing the influence of movements like Fourierism on other activities, such as land reform, the labor movement,

and health reform, that long survived them. Paradoxically, community efforts also fostered ideas about individualism. The strong individualist current that emerged in Transcendentalist writing, especially that of Ralph Waldo Emerson, was in part a response to the formation of Brook Farm. Among Robert Owen's members at New Harmony in the 1820s were Josiah Warren, who later emerged as the pioneer American Anarchist, who formed two communities in Ohio in the 1830s and 1840s before establishing, with Stephen Pearl Andrews, the Modern Times community on Long Island (1851–1863) dedicated to the principle of "individual sovereignty."

Scholars have also considered the factors that can help explain why some communities lasted longer than others. Rosabeth Moss Kanter, in an influential study in the 1970s, suggested that engagement of members in a series of "commitment mechanisms" that bound them to one another and separated them from wider society, was a key feature of groups that lasted significant periods of time. Shakers, German pietists, the Oneidans, and Icarians all adopted communal property and sets of religious and social practices (such as celibacy and "complex marriage") that demanded personal sacrifice or set members off from the rest of society. Fourierists and others who attempted to gain the benefits of communal living without entirely altering their social or economic arrangements often found it harder to sustain their communities. Financial problems, common to small groups in their early years, were more likely to drive members away than they were in religious communes. Above all, perhaps, the lure of communal living and the advantages that it could manifestly offer were only competitive with conditions in the surrounding society when general economic circumstances were hard. As opportunities for employment or profit improved with the economic revival of the late 1840s, inducements to stay in communities that did not entail "commitment mechanisms" were relatively weak. And to the extent that Fourierists and others had conjured up visions of prosperous abundance in their communities, they were exposed to the harsh competition of a thriving and expanding national economy with the limited resources and short-term prospects of dozens of struggling nascent communes.

Christopher Clark

BIBLIOGRAPHY

Berry, Brian J.L. *America's Utopian Experiments: Communal Havens from Long-Wave Crises*. Hanover, NH: University Press of New England, 1992.

Brewer, Priscilla J. *Shaker Communities, Shaker Lives*. Hanover, NH: University Press of New England, 1986.

Clark, Christopher. *The Communitarian Moment: The Radical Challenge of the Northampton Association*. Ithaca, NY: Cornell University Press, 1995.

Guarneri, Carl J. *The Utopian Alternative: Fourierism in Nineteenth-Century America*. Ithaca, NY: Cornell University Press, 1991.

Kanter, Rosabeth Moss. *Commitment and Community: Communes and Utopias in Sociological Perspective*. Cambridge, MA: Harvard University Press, 1972.

Pitzer, Donald E., ed. *America's Communal Utopias*. Chapel Hill: University of North Carolina Press, 1997.

Stein, Steven J. *The Shaker Experience in America: A History of the United Society of Believers*. New Haven, CT: Yale University Press, 1992.

Sutton, Robert P. *Les Icariens: The Utopian Dream in Europe and America*. Urbana: University of Illinois Press, 1994.

New Harmony Movement

The early 1800s in Great Britain, with the onset of the industrial revolution, was a time of social upheaval. The poor and underprivileged flocked to employment in the manufacturing industry, which gave rise to the factory town. A cruel and unyielding environment often faced these families, who lived in crowded slums with poor sanitation and bad food, and who suffered long, harsh working conditions. It was not uncommon for children as young as five or six to work ten-hour shifts. High unemployment made families desperate, while investors and other capitalists reaped unheard of and often obscene profits from the labors of the lower class. Into this maelstrom of change stepped philanthropist, manufacturer, and social reformer Robert Owen.

Like his competitors, Owen reaped the benefits from the system, but unlike them, he did not seek to squeeze more profit from the laborers who produced the wealth. After purchasing the textile mill and its factory town of New Lanark, Scotland, Owen began experimenting with ways to improve the working and living conditions of his employees, and he began to observe that his changes resulted in increased productivity and happiness. Through these observations, Robert Owen developed his theory of character formation and education—that man's character is formed for him, not by him—which ultimately led him to establish the first secular utopian community in the Americas.

Utopian Dream

On October 2, 1824, Owen set sail from Liverpool with his youngest son William and Owenite disciple Captain Donald MacDonald to visit the Rappite settlement at Harmonie, Indiana, which was up for sale. Owen and his party arrived at Harmonie on December 16, accompanied by Frederich Rapp, the adopted son of "Father" George Rapp, a German religious leader who believed in the Second Coming of Christ.

On January 1, 1825, Robert Owen purchased the village of Harmonie from Father Rapp for $125,000 of his own money. He renamed the village New Harmony and took ownership of 20,000 acres that contained 180 log, frame, and brick structures, public buildings, manufacturing establishments, shops, and housing for 700. Owen left his son William and Captain MacDonald at New Harmony and set off to return to New Lanark.

Before embarking for Scotland, Owen, who had achieved some celebrity, as well as some notoriety about his social theories, spoke twice at the U.S. House of Representatives, met with incoming president John Quincy Adams and current president James Monroe, and stayed overnight with former president Thomas Jefferson. Perhaps Owen was swept away by his reception on the continent, or perhaps he was just anxious to start on his dream, but for some unknown reason, he did not formulate any plans to administer his new community. In spite of his reputation as an effective manager, Owen ignored his son William's advice to exercise caution in admitting persons to the Indiana community. While in the East, Owen "issued a manifesto inviting all who were in sympathy with his aims to proceed to New Harmony to join the New Community." Hundreds responded to the invitation and quickly descended upon New Harmony, overwhelming young William Owen in the absence of his father. William later confided in his journal, "The enjoyment of a reformer is much more in the contemplation than in the reality."

The Preliminary Society

Robert Owen returned to New Harmony on April 13, 1825, to find the village in chaos. A collection of 700 to 800 individuals, a mix of freethinkers and freeloaders, had already moved to the community, and more people arrived every day. On April 27, 1825, just two weeks after his arrival, Owen addressed the community membership in the old Rappite church: "I am come to this country to introduce an entire new state of society." On May 1, 1825, the Preliminary Society of New Harmony was formed. Members adopted for their community the constitution that Owen had proposed. It was preceded by this statement:

> The Society is instituted generally to promote the happiness of the world. This Preliminary Society is particularly formed to improve the character and conditions of its own members, and to prepare them to become associates in independent communities, having common property.

The constitution called for what Owen described as a "halfway house" that would help members make the transition from the old system to the new.

SEVEN MONTH ABSENCE

After the Preliminary Society's adoption of the constitution, Owen remained in New Harmony for a little more than one month before returning to New Lanark in June 1825. The purpose of this trip was to settle his affairs, which included providing for his wife and two of their daughters, Ann and Mary, who had decided to remain in Europe. Their third daughter, Jane Dale, along with her four brothers Robert Dale, William, David Dale, and Richard, all chose to settle in New Harmony. (By 1832, Mrs. Owen, Ann, and Mary had all died.) The senior Owen did not return to New Harmony until January 12, 1826. During his seven-month absence, the chaos in the New Harmony community had progressed, and the Harmonists looked forward to Owen's return to solve the problems. They expected that under Robert Owen's practiced hand, the community's idle factories would soon be in full operation and all the founder's projected plans, including building a new village of unity and cooperation, would be undertaken.

THE BOATLOAD OF KNOWLEDGE

To help fulfill the promise of New Harmony, Owen had vowed to bring to the community a boatful of the finest minds of the time. The keelboat, *The Philanthropist*, subsequently dubbed the "Boatload of Knowledge," arrived in New Harmony on January 18, 1826. Its passengers helped cement New Harmony's place in history. Included in the impressive collection of teachers, thinkers, and scientists were Thomas Say and William Maclure. Naturalist, entomologist, and esteemed conchologist, Thomas Say later became known as "The Father of American Zoology." Say was

also curator of the American Philosophical Society after 1821, and he served as professor of natural history at the University of Pennsylvania.

Robert Owen's partner, William Maclure, was a scientist and social/educational reformer with two passions, which ultimately outshone and outlasted those of Robert Owen. Born in Ayr, Scotland, in 1763, Maclure's life paralleled Owen's in several respects. Both were self-made men interested in social reform and the improvement of society, and both were willing to risk their own fortunes and reputations to prove their theories. Maclure's passion for geology led to his founding the American Geological Society, as well as to his being named "The Father of American Geology." His passion for learning changed the face of American education. Maclure had become an ardent advocate of the teaching methods of Swiss educator Johann Heinrich Pestalozzi, and he had sponsored schools in France and in Spain based on the Pestalozzian method.

Maclure had visited Owen's model factory town at New Lanark in 1824, after which, Owen invited Maclure to become a partner in the New Harmony venture. He asked Maclure to set up the Center for Education and Scientific Study in New Harmony. Maclure recruited all the passengers who ultimately embarked on the Boatload of Knowledge, and he instituted the Pestalozzian teaching method at New Harmony, which became the model for America's public school system. Maclure opened the first School of Industry in the United States at New Harmony, and he pioneered the trade school concept.

COMMUNITY OF EQUALITY

Shortly after returning to New Harmony in 1826, Owen was excited by what he perceived to have been accomplished in his absence, despite all the evidence to the contrary. The Preliminary Society had been created to allow members to convert to the Owenite system and to allow enough time to pass so they might learn to trust each other. Many felt nothing had been accomplished and based all hope of success on Owen's return. Owen however, was so carried away by his own optimistic perceptions that he decided to end the transitional Preliminary Society two years before it was due to expire. Perhaps Owen moved too quickly to form its successor, the Community of Equality. A committee of seven was chosen to draft a constitution, which was adopted on February 5, 1826. Equality's constitution began with this declaration:

When a number of the human family associate in principles which do not influence the rest of the world, a due record to the opinions of others requires a public declaration of the object of their association, of their principles and their intentions. Our object is that of all sentient beings, happiness.

It was followed by these Owenite Principles:

Equality of rights, uninfluenced by sex or condition, in all adults.

Equality of duties, modified by physical and mental conformation.

Cooperative union, in the business and amusements of life.

Community of property.

Freedom of speech and action.

Sincerity in all our proceedings.

Kindness in all our actions.

Courtesy in all our intercourse.

Order in all our arrangements.

Preservation of health.

Acquisition of knowledge.

The practice of economy, or of producing and using the best of everything in the most beneficial manner.

Obedience to the laws of the country in which we live.

The constitution outlining Robert Owen's philosophy included the following:

We hold it to be self evident:

That man is uniformly actuated by the desire of happiness.

That no member of the human family is born with rights either of possession or exemption superior to those of his fellows.

That freedom is the sincere expression of every sentiment and opinion, and in the direction of every action, is the inalienable right of each human being, and can not be limited except by his own consent.

That the preservation of life, in its most perfect state, is the first of all practical considerations.

And that, as we live in the state of Indiana, submission to its laws and to those of the general government is necessary.

Experience has taught us:

That man's character, mental, moral and physical, is the result of his formation, his location, and of the circumstances within which he exists.

And that man, at birth, is formed unconsciously to himself, is located without his consent, and circumstanced without his control.

Therefore, man's character is not of his own formation, and reason teaches us to a being of such nature, artificial rewards and punishments are equally inapplicable; kindness is the only consistent mode of treatment, and courtesy the only rational species of deportment.

We have observed, in the affairs of the world, that man is powerful in action, efficient in production, and happy in social life, only as he acts cooperatively and unitedly.

Cooperative union, therefore, we consider indispensable to the obtainment of our object.

According to Owen, the hasty transformation from the Preliminary Society to the Community of Equality was a contributing factor in the experiment's failure. The services of members were no longer paid in proportion to their value to the community, but equal payment was made to all members based solely on age, rather than by contribution. In *Threading My Way; An Autobiography* (1874), Robert Owen's son, Robert Dale Owen, indicated that he regretted letting this event transpire. "I had too much of my father's all-believing disposition to anticipate results which any shrewd, cool-headed business man might have predicted. How rapidly they came upon us!"

DISSENSION

A group of dissidents who disagreed with the new Community of Equality on religious grounds soon branched off to form a separate community, which they named Macluria (although William Maclure had nothing to do with this community). Macluria's members were mainly English farmers who were not happy with what they perceived as Owen's atheistic views. They kept most of the ideals and structure of the parent community (Equality), except they withdrew the right of women to vote in the assembly.

In mid-February 1826, superintendents were elected to oversee the various elements of the Harmonists' activities in the Community of Equality; these activities included agriculture; manufactures and mechanics; literature, science, and education; general economy; and commerce. The voices of dissension grew louder. Many people were unhappy with how the elected council was running community affairs, and Robert Owen was asked to take stewardship of the community while leaving the new constitution in force. In early March, yet another offshoot community formed. This one took its name, Feiba Peveli, from a grid system based on latitude, longitude, and the alphabet, which had been invented by resident social reformer Stedman Whitwell. Feiba Peveli aligned itself philosophically with its parent Equality community, but its plan of government was based more closely on that of Macluria, with its power in the male members over the age of twenty-one. Both Feiba Peveli and Macluria were given property and the right to purchase said property under these specific conditions:

> That they should always remain communities of equality and cooperation in rights and property, and should not be divided into individual shares or separate interests. That any surplus property their industry might acquire must not be divided but used to found similar communities. And, that there should be no whiskey, or other distilled liquors made in the communities.

New Harmony's official organ, the *New Harmony Gazette,* reported on Robert Owen's reaction to the splinter communities: "The formation of communities is now pretty generally understood among us, and is entered upon like a matter of ordinary business. The same thing will probably occur throughout the country."

New Harmony in general and Robert Owen in particular—with his purported atheistic views—had become a favorite target of the clergy on both sides of the Atlantic. From every pulpit, the clergy continuously assaulted New Harmony's social system, inspiring one Duke of Weimar to visit New Harmony in April of 1826. The Duke was curious about the increasing unpopularity of Owen's ideas in the eastern United States. He spent enough time in New Harmony to realize that Owen's perceptions differed considerably from the perceptions of the community's rank-and-file members.

Robert Owen was convinced that all was proceeding according to plan and that his experiment would reform the whole world. In contrast, almost every community member with whom the Duke talked felt he had been deceived in his expectations. The Duke found that social classes were not mingling but, contrary to the egalitarian rhetoric, were remaining distinct. The Duke observed that those who considered themselves well-born resented the common labor they were required to do, and that the better-educated

men fraternized together but did not mingle with those less educated.

Inside the community, the more vocal critics came from the working classes, while the upper classes enjoyed the novelty of association with others free from the conventions of society. For the young men of gentry, the informal access to the ladies of the community had its appeal. Robert Dale Owen commented,

> On the whole, my life in Harmony, for many months, was happy and satisfying. To this the free and simple relation there existing between youth and maiden much contributed. We called each other by our Christian names only, spoke and acted as brothers and sisters might; often strolled out by moonlight in groups, sometimes in single pairs; yet, withal, no scandal or other harm came from it. . . . I met almost daily, handsome, interesting warm-hearted girls; bright, merry, and unsophisticated; charming partners at ball or picnic.

MENTAL INDEPENDENCE

In spite of all the evidence to the contrary, Robert Owen continued to view the community with the rosiest perspective. July 4, 1826, marked the fiftieth anniversary of the signing of the *Declaration of Independence*, and on this date, Robert Owen delivered what he called the Declaration of Mental Independence in which he stated that man had been the slave to a trinity of evils: individual property, irrational systems of religion, and marriage founded on individual property. He followed this with a reiteration of the Principles set forth in his treatise, the *New Moral World*.

Members continued to become disenchanted, and other splinter groups continued to form. On July 30, 1826, a group by the name of the New Harmony Agricultural and Pastoral Society adopted a constitution modeled after those of previous splinter communities. Although Owen remained optimistic and willing to work with any and all groups that would form under his Principles, the New Harmony community continued to slide further into discord. After losing members to Macluria, to Feiba Peveli, and to the Pastoral Society, the Community of Equality had decreased to only about 800 members. Squabbles broke out between the different communities, who spent much time and energy wrangling with each other over boundaries and crop ownerships.

In May, William Maclure suggested that New Harmony be divided "into separate autonomous units according to the occupation of its members." Owen agreed, and the society voted itself into three separate groups—the Mechanic and Manufacture Society, the Agricultural and Pastoral Society, and the Education Society. A lease was drawn that granted to William Maclure about 900 acres of land for the Education Society, which included the Hall of New Harmony, the steeple house, Community House No. 2, the Granary, and the Rapp mansion. Maclure had been the driving force in the educational movement in New Harmony, but differences were beginning to emerge between his vision and Owen's.

MACLURE VS. OWEN

Robert Owen believed that he and Maclure were partners, a position Maclure did not share. Maclure believed himself to be obligated only to the society's lease and an additional $10,000. During travels away from New Harmony for his health, Maclure wrote letters to New Harmony's teacher, Madame Fretageot, which indicated he was losing confidence in the Owen enterprise: "My experience at New Harmony has given me such horror for the reformation of grown persons that I shudder when I reflect having so many of my friends near such a desperate undertaking."

When Maclure returned to New Harmony in April 1827, Frederick Rapp was there to collect a $20,000 installment due on the property and to request the entire remaining balance of an additional $20,000, though it was not due for another year. Owen agreed, and he asked Maclure to pay his partnership share of $128,000, telling him that the balance of his [Maclure's] share of the indebtedness amounted to an additional $90,000. Maclure vehemently disputed this claim, but in the end, he agreed to pay Rapp the $40,000 in return for the bonds Rapp held against Owen, which made Maclure Owen's creditor.

Maclure posted signs around the area declaring he was not responsible for Owen's debts, and he filed suit in the circuit court to collect the money he had paid to Rapp. Caught by surprise, Owen posted his own notices declaring the partnership to be in full force, and then he, too, filed suit in the amount of $90,000. Arbitration led to a compromise wherein Maclure paid Owen $5,000, and Owen gave Maclure an unrestricted deed to the 490 acres operated by the Education Society for an additional $44,000.

Robert Owen had said he would sell land to anyone willing to live by his Principles, and more of the property began to fall into private hands as he sold parcels of land to those who promised to continue the experiment. According to Paul Brown, the resident dissident who exposed the shortcomings of Owen and his views in his pamphlet, "Twelve Months in New Harmony," the community was in a state of disarray with fences torn down, animals roaming loose, and tempers flaring everywhere, including a fist fight among the women. Owen fell victim to a swindle by a member, William Taylor, who pretended to be a disciple. As such, he was entitled by contract to 1,500 acres "with all thereon." The night before the contract went into effect, Taylor moved all the livestock and equipment he could find onto the property he was about to acquire. Against Owen's wishes, Taylor then set up a distillery. He also established a tannery to compete directly with the one in New Harmony.

On February 1, a day that Paul Brown called "Doomsday," a vote of the assembly expelled many members of the Community of Equality. On March 28, 1827, a *Gazette* editorial written by Robert Dale Owen and William Owen acknowledged the defeat of the experiment, while still affirming the principles of the general plan: "Our opinion is that Robert Owen ascribed too little influence to the early anti-social circumstances that surrounded many of the quickly collected inhabitants. . . . New Harmony therefore is not now a community." Writing in his autobiography, Robert Dale Owen closed the chapter on New Harmony.

> Thenceforth, of course, the inhabitants had to either support themselves or leave town. But my father offered land on the Harmony estate to those who desired to try smaller community experiments, on an agricultural basis. Several were formed, some by honest, industrious workers, to whom land was leased at very low rates; while other leases were obtained by unprincipled speculators who cared not a whit for cooperative principles, but sought private gain by the operation. All finally failed as social experiments.

CONCLUSION

Prolonged study of Robert Owen, the "Father of Cooperationism" and the New Harmony community leads us to the conclusion that Owen's failure at New Harmony perhaps lay in the very thing that brought him to America in the first place. Owen had hoped his ideas would flourish in America's environment of free thinkers and independent-minded people. However, the people on the American frontier in the 1820s did not take to the yoke so easily. They did not resemble the working poor of the British slums who were already laboring sixteen hours a day for subsistence pay when Owen found them. Those workers developed gratitude and a loyalty for the changes he made to improve their lives.

On the American frontier, however, the true believers moved with the ne'er-do-wells, the misanthropes, the intellectual idealists, and the merely curious. It may have been that very independent, rugged individualism, so eloquently described by Alexis de Tocqueville, which contributed to Owen's failure. That, combined with Owen's apparent lack of interest in hands-on involvement in the community, leads one to wonder how it could not have failed.

Looking back more than 175 years, we can see that, in spite of the apparent failure of New Harmony, Owen's desire to create a new society was partially realized, as free, universal, and equal education was gradually institutionalized. Though change did not occur in the manner Owen intended, he might view these as partial successes and take pride in them.

Michael Clark

BIBLIOGRAPHY

Bestor, A.E., Jr., ed. *Education and Reform at New Harmony: Correspondence of William Maclure and Marie Duclos Fretageot, 1920 to 1833.* 1948. Reprint, Clifton, NJ: August M. Kelly, 1973.

Brown, P. *Twelve Months in New Harmony; Presenting a Faithful Account of the Principal Occurrences Which Have Taken Place There Within That Period; Interspersed with Remarks.* 1827. Reprint, Philadelphia: Porcupine, 1972.

Carmony, D., and J. Elliott. "New Harmony, Indiana, Seedbed for Utopia." *Indiana Magazine of History* 76 (September 1980): 161–261.

Lockwood, G.B. *The New Harmony Movement.* 1905. Reprint, New York: AMS, 1971.

New Harmony Gazette. University of Wyoming. Microfiche HN 64N4.

Owen, R. *The Life of Robert Owen.* Vol. 1. London: Effingham Wilson, 1857.

Owen, R.D. *Threading My Way; An Autobiography.* 1874. Reprint, New York: Augustus M. Kelley, 1957.

Owen, W. *Diary of William Owen from November 10, 1824 to April 20, 1825.* 1906. Reprint, Clifton, NJ: August M. Kelley, 1973.

Wilson, W.E. *The Angel and the Serpent: The Story of New Harmony.* Bloomington and Indianapolis: Indiana University Press, 1964.

PENTECOSTAL MOVEMENT

One of the most dynamic and explosive religious movements in the twentieth century, Pentecostalism has revolutionized American religion. Pentecostalism, a form of Christianity, is typified by an excited worship style and experience, including speaking in tongues. The "baptism in the Holy Spirit"—an emotional experience that occurs after conversion often associated with speaking in tongues—distinguishes the faith of Pentecostals from that of other Christians. The movement has attracted followers from all races and classes, and appeals primarily to the middle and lower middle classes. From its beginnings with a few disillusioned evangelicals, Pentecostalism has spread into all branches of Christendom—only the Roman Catholic Church has more worldwide adherents.

The Pentecostal movement began during the late 1800s, a time of dramatic change in American religion. Traditional mainline churches were declining in number and influence while evangelical groups were on the rise. The radical evangelicals who would eventually launch Pentecostalism had four primary traits: they emphasized personal salvation experiences, they believed in the imminent second coming of Christ, they often sought and practiced divine healing, and they expected to have an emotionally charged, post-conversion experience called the baptism of the Holy Spirit. In Topeka, Kansas, one group of these evangelicals led by Charles Fox Parham believed that speaking in tongues, a gift that had appeared minimally throughout Christian history, was evidence of Spirit baptism. Accordingly, the group began to seek it. Parham claimed that on January 1, 1901, a woman began speaking in an unknown language after he had laid hands on her, an event that began the modern tongues movement and marks the origins of Pentecostalism.

A few years later, African-American preacher William J. Seymour, a convert to Pentecostalism and disciple of Parham, helped initiate the Azusa Street revivals in Los Angeles. These meetings, led and supported by an interracial group of blacks, whites, Asians, European immigrants, and Latinos, lasted almost three years and attracted Christians and curiosity seekers from around the country, many of whom experienced their own baptism in the Holy Spirit. Meetings were held in a decrepit old building that lacked the pretension of established churches while news of the revival was printed in the *Los Angeles Times* and in numerous small religious periodicals, including Seymour's *The Apostolic Faith*. Services were chaotic. Pentecostals believed that the Holy Spirit should control the direction of the meetings; therefore, they had no formal, organized service order or explicit leadership. Men and women prayed, preached, exhorted, spoke in tongues, wept, trembled, and convulsed as they believed that the Spirit dictated. Azusa Street converts returned to churches located around the country to initiate new Pentecostal meetings.

Powerful charismatic leaders, who often had little formal education, popularized the movement. Following his return from the Azusa Revival, African-American Holiness preacher Charles H. Mason gave the newly established Church of God in Christ (COGIC) a Pentecostal emphasis. A popular leader among whites and blacks, he built COGIC into the nation's largest Pentecostal denomination. COGIC's emphasis on gospel music, and its many talented artists, helped Pentecostalism engage with the broader American culture and contributed to its growth. The most famous Latino Pentecostal preacher and faith healer, Francisco Olazabál, worked within a number of established denominations and also contributed to the birth of at least ten Pentecostal denominations. In Texas, California, Puerto Rico, and around North America, he converted tens of thousands of Latinos to the Pentecostal faith, helping spark the tremendous expansion of Latino Pentecostalism. But no individual leader had as significant an influence as Aimee Semple McPherson. Joining the movement in 1907, by the late 1910s McPherson was traveling the country spreading the message of Pentecostalism. Young, intelligent, and a gifted speaker, McPherson became a popular figure both in small towns and in the nation's burgeoning metropolises among all races, ethnicities, and classes. Her theatrical panache and dramatic sermons drew tremendous crowds. She encouraged her many converts to share their Pentecostal experiences with their local churches, regardless of denomination. When she decided to settle down in Los Angeles in the 1920s, McPherson did not build a traditional church but instead erected a theater-like building, the Angelus Temple, in which she staged elaborate productions, with ornate sets, live animals, and full orchestration to illustrate her sermons. She also built her own radio station, which became one of the most popular in the city. Despite these accomplishments, McPherson is probably best known as the founder of the International Church of the Foursquare Gospel. Following McPherson's lead, Pentecostals have often appropriated new technologies, such as television stations and broadcasting satellites, to proselytize.

In 1914, Pentecostal leaders from all over the nation gathered in Hot Springs, Arkansas. They did not intend to start a denomination, but hoped to develop Pentecostal schools and to solidify their evangelistic programs in order to keep the movement growing. This meeting resulted in the creation of the Assemblies of God, the denomination currently with the largest worldwide membership. One of the keys to their growth, as was the case in many other Pentecostal sects, was the institution of a successful publishing house that advertised meetings, publicized the movement's success, and inculcated followers with Pentecostal theology. The Assemblies' missionary work has also been crucial to their growth. Churches sponsor representatives who travel overseas to share the Pentecostal faith in new cultures, while preachers strongly encourage their parishioners to engage in personal evangelism with their acquaintances.

Pentecostalism did not grow as rapidly between the 1920s and 1950s as it did in previous decades. The movement experienced a rebirth and dramatic expansion in the 1960s, called the "Charismatic Renewal." Although Pentecostals always sought inroads into established denominations, in 1960 Dennis Bennett of St. Mark's Episcopal Parish, in Van Nuys, California, informed his "respectable" congregation that he had spoken in tongues and believed that other Christians should seek a similar experience. Bennett eventually resigned, but his confession symbolized the start of a wave of Pentecostal activity in older, more traditional Protestant churches as well as in Catholic circles around the country. Pentecostal practices and beliefs were no longer a monopoly held by radical evangelicals, but penetrated Christian institutions everywhere.

Pentecostalism is a social movement organized around intense religious commitment. Adherents have relatively unique spiritual practices and a dedication to a particular, somewhat narrow, creedal ideology. Charismatic leaders, strong institutions, the appropriation of modern technologies, and fervent proselytization has made the Pentecostal movement one of the most important of the twentieth century.

Matthew Sutton

BIBLIOGRAPHY

Anderson, Robert. *Vision of the Disinherited: The Making of American Pentecostalism.* Peabody, MA: Hendrickson, 1979.

Blumhofer, Edith L., Russell P. Spittler, and Grant A. Wacker, eds. *Pentecostal Currents in American Protestantism.* Urbana: University of Illinois Press, 1999.

Synan, Vinson. *The Holiness-Pentecostal Tradition: Charismatic Movements in the Twentieth Century.* 2d ed. Grand Rapids, MI: William B. Eerdmans, 1997.

Wacker, Grant. *Heaven Below: Early Pentecostals and American Culture.* Cambridge, MA: Harvard University Press, 2001.

Colorado Cooperative Colony Movement

Following the Civil War, a combination of social, economic, and legislative forces gave renewed impetus to the colonization movement in the United States. The industrial revolution and the unregulated capitalism that accompanied it produced cities that many pronounced increasingly unfit for human life, but in the steel tracks and the steam locomotion of the railroad, industry also produced the means for escape. Wars, treaties, and a subsequent series of legislative acts made Western lands more accessible and able to be irrigated. Digging an irrigation canal was not a task a person could accomplish individually, so many of these post–Civil War colonies were founded on cooperative or socialistic principles. Not only practical, cooperative/socialistic colonies also offered alternatives to greed, poverty, and other social problems believed to have been created by industrial capitalism. To fund their ventures, the founders of these colonies often organized as joint-stock companies. Several such colonies appeared throughout the West, in Utah, California, Washington State, and Colorado.

Similar to many of the colonies established during the latter half of the nineteenth century, one in Colorado began as the idealistic dream of a few people. These people desired to create a community where, according to their Declaration of Principles, "Man's first and greatest duty, care and thought should be to advance the common interests of the community." This colony organized, as did others of the period, as a joint stock venture. Its name was the Colorado Cooperative Company, and its primary task was to construct an irrigation ditch. Nearly every day for ten years, the courageous colonists of the Colorado Cooperative Company labored to build their thirteen-mile ditch, erecting an 840-foot-high trestle (the world's highest at the time) in the process, while struggling to hold their socialistic community together in the Colorado Rockies.

FORMATION

Neither wealthy nor destitute, members of the Colorado Cooperative Colony described themselves as eclectic and intelligent. Without a doubt, they were reflective thinkers who sympathized with social reformers and were not afraid to criticize the status quo. Early in their community life, they established a library, and, after ten hours of heavy labor on the ditch, their favorite evening activity was to perch on hard benches and read by flickering oil lamp. They formed a literary club and a drama club, and no community celebration was complete without readings, performances, music, and dancing. Above all else, they shared a passion in the belief that cooperative living would solve the ills of society, a belief to which they were so committed that they were willing to uproot their families and sacrifice comfort and even food to pursue it in an isolated spot in the mountains of Colorado.

On February 16, 1894, the Colorado Cooperative Company (CCC) incorporated with a capital stock of $100,000—1,000 shares with a par value of $100 each. Five of the seven members/stockholders who signed the Articles of Incorporation on that day were Colorado State Senator B. (Benjamin) L. Smith; Colorado State Farmers' Alliance organizer and former president of that group, J. (Jake) H. Brammeier; soon-to-be elected Colorado State Senator F. (Frank) E. Moody; Colorado State Fish Commissioner W. (William) R. Callicotte; and Judge P.A. Simmons.

Article V of the Articles of Incorporation designated the first board of directors of the CCC as the seven people who signed the articles, plus two others—J.S. (Joe) Bartow of Denver and Colorado State Engineer C.B. Cramer. The articles charged these nine people with responsibility for managing company affairs for the first year of its existence. Although they did not sign the Articles of Incorporation, nor were they listed among the first board of directors, four other names should be included among those of the founding members: T. (Truman) O. Smith, C. (Charles) E. Smith, F.H. Nye, and Ezra Simmons.

Born in Canada, B.L. Smith attended public schools in Michigan. He worked in the mining business in Idaho before being elected a senator of Colorado in 1890 on the Independent-Populist ticket. Smith's term as senator expired in 1894, about the same time he became the first CCC member to move with his family to Naturita, Colorado. His brother, T.O. Smith, was the second resident of the colony. They were soon joined by colonists arriving from Denver, Iowa, Kansas, New York, Minnesota, and a colony in Topolobambo, Mexico. By March 1895, forty-one people lived "on the ground," as colonists termed it, at the colony site in or near Pinon, Colorado; by November 1896, that number had more than doubled to eighty-six.

PRINCIPLES OF THE COLONY

The Articles of Incorporation stated the purposes of the company, which, along with constructing ditches, included sanitation, education, and entertainment. They determined the number of shares and the value of each, and, in accordance with the founding members' belief in cooperation, they dictated that every member, regardless of the number of shares of stock owned, was entitled to one and only one vote.

It is clear from the Articles of Incorporation that the founders knew what they wanted. They also knew what they did not want. Shortly before they incorporated, a lengthy and detailed article about Colorado appeared in the *Harper's New Monthly Magazine*. The author, Julian Ralph, described another Colorado colony, that of Greeley (founded by newspaperman and social reformer Horace Greeley), as ideal because the colonists themselves owned both the land and the means to irrigate it. This was not the case everywhere. In some colonies, the colonists were at the mercy of corporations and speculators who charged increasingly higher prices for water and canal maintenance. The founders of the Colorado Cooperative Company were determined to keep their community out of corporate clutches. Favoring ideals of cooperation and fervently opposing the mercenary aims of large corporations, they established a structure by which members, not an outside corporation, would build the ditch; they would pay for it with their labor, and they would own the ditch and the water it carried into perpetuity.

LOCATING THE COLONY IN COLORADO

After incorporating, the company sent one founding member—B.L. Smith—to find the ideal location for the cooperative colony. Prospective colonists could file for their land under either the Preemption Act or the Desert Land Act. Because the Desert Land Act required that land be irrigated before homesteaders could receive a patent, the CCC site would have to be fairly level and lie near a water source that would provide water year round. Article XII of Colorado Cooperative Company by-laws allowed members enough water for up to 40 acres each. To accommodate a town site and 40 acres for 1,000 members, the site would have to encompass approximately 40,000 acres.

Colorado was already becoming famous for its fruit, and the CCC founders planned orchards for their own use, as well as for export. Therefore, the colony site could not be too isolated—no more than a couple days' travel from a railroad. If they were to grow fruit, the climate had to provide an early frost-free date, plenty of sunshine, and a long growing season. And the soil, of course, had to be fertile once it was watered—not alkaline, nor too sandy, nor full of clay. Ideally, they should locate near some mining operations so that they would have a ready market for their agricultural products. The site had to possess ample stone and timber for building, and plenty of coal for fuel. Finally, if people were going to live out their days in this place and then leave it to their children and perhaps to their children's children, it had to be beautiful.

While recuperating in Placerville, Colorado, from an illness contracted during his travels, Smith heard of a mesa along the San Miguel River. Smith found this mesa, called Tabeguache Park, 50 miles from the Denver and Rio Grande station branch of Placerville. Situated on the western slope of the San Juan Mountains, it appeared fairly flat. The first issue of the company/colony newspaper, the *Altrurian,* described the site as possessing "rich land, ample water for irrigation and domestic purposes. The finest building stone in the world lying in strata from one inch to two feet in thickness . . . also coal not far away, and timber for fuel for an age." Smith determined that the climate would be conducive to the agricultural and fruit-growing endeavors the company planned.

Such a majestic land inspired grandiose dreams. The second issue of the *Altrurian* claimed: "We sincerely believe that there will yet spring up in some valley of the west a grander civilization than this world has ever known. Who will say that the Colorado Cooperative Colony is not the nucleus of such." They had found their Eden, but to make it bloom, they had to get water to it.

MEANS OF FORMATION

Build a Ditch

The mesa, where they planned to build their homes, lay 300 feet above the San Miguel River. Getting water to the mesa would require building a ditch approximately 13 miles in length. The founders knew that building this ditch would not be easy. They recognized the need for manpower, surveyors, and a ditch engineer. They recruited assistance from W.H. Porter, the man who superintended the construction of the cooperative ditch in Sinaloa, Mexico (Topolobampo Colony under Albert. K. Owen, 1871). Porter was asked by CCC founder and Superintendent B.L. Smith to share his ideas on cooperative ditch work. In the second issue of the *Altrurian,* Porter advised the CCC to follow sound business principles:

> All members should be stockholders with equal voice in the selection of a board of directors who should have the full power of authority to carry out the line of work agreed upon to be done. . . . The membership should always retain the right to recall (imperative mandate) the board management . . . but the membership should render obedience to said management until it was recalled.

Porter lauded the ideals of cooperation, but his experiences with A.K. Owen's colony in Mexico had made a realist of him, and he cautioned the CCC that humankind might not be ready for cooperation.

Cooperation

Membership in the CCC required a minimum deposit of $10 and payments of at least $5 per month until the $100 for the share of stock had been paid in full. Similar to the Anaheim Colony in California, some of the CCC members would live on-site to construct the ditch. Their labor would purchase their stock shares and their water rights. The rest of the members, residing outside the colony, would continue making monthly cash payments for their stock and water rights.

The first estimate of the cost of the ditch was $100,000 in labor and materials. Although the labor did not require cash, the equipment and supplies did. The plan depended on selling 1,000 shares of stock for $100 each, and that required members. Two main

strategies were employed to recruit these members. One was the publication and national circulation of the company/colony newspaper, the *Altrurian.* The other was the establishment of at least five CCC clubs around the country. Members of these clubs were CCC stockholders, and they had a single purpose— to recruit more members. As stated in the Declaration of Principles, cooperation of all the members would bring success:

> We affirm that only by and through co-operation, viewed from a social and business standpoint, can we reach the highest condition of social and intellectual attainment, and material equality.

As events unfolded over the next seven years, the CCC encountered many problems that W.H. Porter had warned them of. In particular, a few members refusing to "render obedience to management" threatened the colony's founding values; not instituting the "imperative mandate" from the beginning resulted in dissension; and failure to "act as one body or organism" practically destroyed the colony.

GOALS AND PURPOSES OF THE CCC

Conforming

In the addenda to the Declaration of Principles, the founders of the CCC summarized what they wanted to do and how they planned to accomplish it. These people were not Luddites opposed to technology; rather they welcomed technology for its labor-saving potential. However, they considered debt, interest, and rent the special evils of capitalism and so resisted them as means to build their ditch. The CCC founders believed in cooperation, but not to the exclusion of all individual rights; that is, they distinguished between democratic cooperation, or democratic socialism, and communism, and this distinction created problems when some communistic members attempted to gain control of the company.

During the months following the signing of the Articles of Incorporation, the original founders drafted a constitution and by-laws for the Colorado Cooperative Company. The by-laws were first published in January 1895 in Volume I, No. 1 of the *Altrurian* with this claim, "when experience proves them impractical they will be changed."

As reported in the March 1895 issue of the *Altrurian,* the new board of directors reported the first year's accomplishments, which included increased membership from twelve persons to forty-one; an in-

A team of surveyors belonging to the Colorado Cooperative Colony takes a break from their efforts to construct a thirteen-mile irrigation ditch in the 1890s. The colonists' goal was to bring water to a mesa called Tabeguache Park, where they hoped to establish a socialistic utopian community. *(Courtesy, Rimrocker Historical Society)*

vestment of over $1,000 in cash, livestock, and tools; and 203 days' labor in hauling lumber, building cabins and stables, and temporary ditch work. During their second year, the CCC conducted surveys on the ditch, purchased equipment for and began a sawmill, planted crops, built roads, completed a small ditch to water annual crops, built houses, and continued to recruit and gain additional members—including two babies born to colony members.

By the end of year two, the leadership planned to relocate the *Altrurian* from Denver to Naturita and to publish weekly rather than monthly. A total of eighty-six members voted at the annual meeting held in Naturita in January 1896. All eighty-six had signed the Articles of Agreement, which bound them to abide by the constitution and by-laws and to "respect the orders and instructions of all lawfully elected or appointed officers . . . while in the discharge of any . . . business or government of the affairs of said Company."

DIFFERENCE OF OPINION

B.L. Smith addressed the stockholders at the annual meeting of 1896. In this address, Smith referred to some grievances "born of jealousy," and he warned the body to "proceed carefully with consideration." An article in the February 1896 edition of the *Altrurian* entitled "Lessons on Keweah" provided a thinly disguised warning to some CCC members when it listed several of the Keweah Colony's problems, which editors identified as "unequal yoking," internal discord, and acceptance into the colony of members who were incompetent or unfit. The trouble at Keweah, according to this article, was "not in the system or ideas, but in the people . . . the struggle is not chiefly economic, but essentially moral." The April issue quoted CCC member C.E. Smith as saying, "If there are members who cannot subject themselves to the directions of the manager then they have made a mistake joining the Colony, for it is to be managed by one man."

The difference of opinion erupted in April 1896

and resulted in the expulsion of ten members. Resident members approved this action on May 2 by a vote of 24 to 2. Comments in the May issue of the company organ revealed that expelled members had preferred communism over cooperation and had threatened CCC management and by-laws:

> The Colorado Cooperative Company is a corporation chartered under the laws of Colorado. It is not communistic as the term is understood—nine-tenths of the stockholders believe in the private ownership of a limited amount of land. They believe that those who cultivate the soil should own it. They don't believe the people are ready to own land in common if they ever will be.

The CCC had survived its first internal threat and had emerged with its founding values not only intact but strengthened.

ONWARD

Now that the threat was behind them, CCC members could afford the luxury of turning some of their attention outward, toward the presidential campaign, for example. William Jennings Bryan was running for president of the United States on the Populist ticket. With their founders involved in the Farmers' Alliance, and with a collective belief in the advantages of cooperation over the "evils" of capitalism, it is not surprising that they favored Bryan. The CCC made their opinions known through the *Altrurian*, referring to Bryan as "champion of the common people, that intrepid foe of corporation greed, that splendid young statesman." The paper told its readers that choosing Bryan over McKinley was choosing the common people over the wealthy.

CCC members also turned their attention to the future, to their ideal community, which some were now calling "Ingleside." Plans included a CCC university that would provide summer study of the geology and the flora and fauna of the western slope of Colorado, as well as anthropological studies, as described in the colony paper, "homes of a vanished nation . . . the cliff dwellings of Mancos." The community would provide "fair labor for all, drudgery for none, healthful recreation, good fellowship, kindliness, charity, and friendship." A jointly owned and operated electric rail, along with no horses, no coal, no ashes, and no factory or kitchen fires would assure clean streets and clean air. In anticipation of a library, they established a reading room and requested outside members to send books and magazines.

In October 1896, the *Altrurian* moved its operations from Denver to Naturita, and in November it published a census of on-site members that revealed a total of eighty-six persons—forty men, eighteen women, and twenty-eight children—residing at Naturita, Pinon, or one of the temporary camps of Sawmill, Cottonwood, or Riverside. By the annual meeting in January 1897, there were a total of 197 members in good standing; the company was out of debt, with $250 after all bills had been paid, and there was "enough flour on hand to last half a year, [and] beef and pork to last two weeks."

STORMING THE SEAT OF POWER

Subscribing to a common philosophy of cooperationism was no guarantee that all CCC members would agree with everything other members or management did. Intelligent, well read, and opinionated, they had accurately characterized themselves as "eclectic" in the addenda to their Declaration of Principles. The annual meeting provided a time and place where members could make their grievances and arguments known by amending the by-laws and by electing new officers.

On January 3, 1897, shareholders voted on changes that nudged the seat of power further from the board and closer to the members. The original addenda was replaced by a completely new one, which pinpointed the crux of the problem that was to plague the CCC for the rest of its existence. Ironically, for a group of people who hated capitalism and who committed themselves to the ideals of cooperation, their major problem was money, as indicated by the new addenda:

> The number of men, who can be profitably employed by the Company is limited by the amount of money coming in from outside members. No cash is paid for work, but cash must be paid for food, tools, etc. What is most needed now is a large outside membership of self-sustaining workers who will send in regular monthly payments. . . .

The Colorado Cooperative Company/Colony began its fourth year of incorporation in January 1897. A special meeting that year, held in Pinon on May 1, finally resolved the issue, outlining a procedure of removing members of the board of directors under terms of the Imperative Mandate, a state constitutional amendment directing the state legislature to enact an eight-hour law for workers employed in mines, mills, smelters, and blast furnaces.

Money Problems

Although resident members were dependent on outside members for the cash they needed for supplies and equipment, the outside members did not feel the same dependence on the colony residents for attaining their mutual goal, and they did not send the needed cash to support the workers and their efforts on-site. The *Altrurian* published numerous pleas to outside members to make their promised cash contributions, including one by newly elected President T. O. Smith, in which he explained the difficulty of operating with an unpredictable cash flow. Smith reminded members of a new by-law, adopted at the previous annual meeting, that permitted the CCC to sell shares of stock when payments were not made, and he appealed to their desire for irrigated home sites to induce them to honor their financial commitments to the colony.

Unsure of the cash contributions from outside members, the board called for a year-long halt to any more families moving to the colony. In late August 1898, the board began issuing coupon books to families to use when purchasing supplies from the store or other departments. The system was designed to save time, thus cost, involved in keeping track of purchases.

Faced with increased debt and decreased supplies, continued hard work, and insufficient support from the outside, members began to find fault in several areas, including the board of directors, leveling criticisms at them for costing the company nearly $2 per hour to meet every week for what some considered to be trivial matters. In February 1899, former CCC president C.H. Robinson observed that the 28 percent of the membership who lived on-site had contributed 85 percent toward the completion of the ditch, while the 72 percent of the membership who lived outside the colony had contributed only 15 percent toward their mutual goal. By March, Robinson proposed the unthinkable—bonding the ditch.

CONTROVERSY

Controversy over two issues—bonding the ditch and implementing a self-sufficiency plan—eventually resulted in half of the board members submitting their resignations in April 1899. When he tendered his resignation, President T.O. Smith said he hoped this action would "unify the Stockholders of the company and promote harmonious action among the workers on the ground and the paying members on the outside."

Notice of the annual meeting of 1899 appeared in the June 7 *Altrurian*, and as had been characteristic of every other annual meeting, trouble was brewing. Twelve members of the Denver Club had sent a letter to the board of directors notifying them that, according to the Articles of Incorporation, the annual meeting should be held in Denver, not in Pinon, where it had been held since January of 1896. In response, the board decided to amend the Articles of Incorporation, an action that would require a two-thirds vote of the stockholders to ratify.

Before the Fourth of July celebration, the issue of where to hold the annual meeting landed in the hands of attorneys. Plaintiffs Charles E. Smith, George E. Wright, and George B. Ruggles sued on behalf of themselves and all other stockholders of the Colorado Cooperative Company. They claimed that the Articles of Incorporation did not provide for any location for the annual meeting except Denver, and they requested an injunction to prevent holding it anywhere except Denver. The *Altrurian* accused the Denver members of scheming to disenfranchise on-site members by forcing them to vote only in Denver, a trip most workers could not afford to make. On July 7, 1899, in District Court of Arapahoe County in the State of Colorado, Judge Frank T. Johnson refused to grant the injunction and ruled that the board of directors could decide where the annual meetings should be held. He told them to "go to the annual meeting at Pinon and fight for their alleged rights there."

Not enough votes were cast at the annual meeting held at Pinon on July 22, 1899, to decide the location of the company headquarters. It was not until three additional votes had transpired that the annual meeting of July 4, 1900, determined, with 192 voting for and 76 against, that "the principal office of the company within said state of Colorado, shall be located in Pinon, Montrose County. Other offices may be established elsewhere, where the Company may have interests as may be provided by the By-Laws."

Water Rights

For the next several months, articles and letters in the *Altrurian* reflected concern over water rights. The cost of a water right would equal the cost of the ditch divided by the number of members who had paid for the water, which made estimating the cost per member difficult. Members were warned repeatedly that water rights could be purchased only before the ditch was complete; after the water was on the land, no water rights could be purchased at any price. Outside members were encouraged to send payment for their water rights—$5 per month from each outside member would support more workers to complete the ditch.

Though expert opinion indicated that the Colorado land with water rights attached would be worth as much as $900 per acre, the appeals for payment were ignored. By January 1901, B.L. Smith reported that only eighteen outside members had paid anything on their water rights, averaging only $3.99 per month, and at that rate, it would take over nine years to pay for enough water for 40 acres. He made a last appeal to outside members to make regular and sufficient payments on water rights. Smith also proposed borrowing $10,000 at 6 percent for five years to complete the ditch, and the board further proposed creating a separate ditch company.

Reforming

June 6, 1901, marked the last publication date for the *Altrurian*. That issue began with a notice to stockholders that outlined the options to be voted on at the July 4 annual meeting. Members' options included reorganization or dissolution of the Colorado Cooperative Company, or segregation of the company's ditch and water rights. The second option provided for the organization of a new and independent company to construct and operate the ditch. At the annual meeting, members ultimately decided on two major changes in policy. First, they would convert all water credits into common stock at par, which necessitated increasing capital from $100,000 to $150,000. Each share would be entitled to a pro rata share of water in the ditch, as well as to a vote in the proceedings of the company. Second, they decided to contract the remaining ditch construction, with qualified CCC members to be considered for these contracts.

So, work on the ditch continued, though not under the same cooperative structure envisioned by the founders over six years before. The egalitarian spirit behind the "one man, one vote" principle faded, along with the publication of the *Altrurian*.

More colonists, including many former nonresident members, arrived in Pinon between 1902 and 1904, making it the second largest town in Montrose County. After six and one-half years of discussion about the town plan and what its name should be, residents decided on the name Nucla, from the Latin word for nucleus, because they hoped it would become the "center of Socialistic government for the world." They formed the Town of Nucla Improvement Company with a capital stock of $50,000 divided into 5,000 shares with a par value of $10 per share. Each share of stock entitled the owner to a "99-year lease to one business lot or two residential lots, 42 by 200 feet, no person to hold more than one block or twenty lots."

The 1901 annual meeting also established May 1904 as the deadline for completing the ditch. Workers came within thirty days of meeting this deadline, and water flowed through the ditch on June 4, 1904. Colonists celebrated the feat on July 4 by caravanning from Pinon along the ditchline road in company wagons, on horseback, and on foot to a picnic at the town site on the mesa. While colonists had reason to be joyous, they celebrated without their original founders. Only one of the charter members of the CCC stayed to see the completion of the ditch and to build a home on the park. That was Ada McElroy, of Denver, who had taught at the Pinon school for a while. Before that, in the summer 1895, she and her brothers H.E. Robinson and T. (Tom) W. McElroy exhibited their adventurous spirits by bicycling from Montrose, Colorado, over the Uncompahgre Divide to the Pinon Camp. This bicycle ride may have embodied the spirit of all the CCC founders, but for a variety of reasons, including discouragement, changes in policy, and irresolvable differences of opinion, one by one, they each decided to pursue different dreams.

With the founders went the original cooperative principles, and Nucla gradually evolved into the quiet, rural town it is today. The reformed Colorado Cooperative Ditch Company accomplished what it had intended to do: it brought the water that was needed to create a community. It continues to supply water to Tabeguache Mesa into the twenty-first century.

Pamela Clark

BIBLIOGRAPHY

Altrurian newspaper. Colorado Historical Society and Kansas State Historical Society. Microfilm.

Croke, F. "A History of the Colorado Co-operative Colony, and the Town of Nucla." Naturita, CO: Rimrocker Historical Society, n.d.

Peterson, E. *The Spell of the Tabeguache*. Naturita, CO: Rimrocker Historical Society, 1957.

Ralph, J. "Colorado and Its Capital." *Harper's New Monthly Magazine* 87 (December 1892–May 1893).

Swords, C., and W.C. Edwards. *Sketches and Portraitures of the State Officers and Members of the Ninth General Assembly of Colorado*. Denver, CO: Carson, Hurst & Harper Printers and Engravers, 1893.

Templeton, M. *The Visionaries: First and Second Generation Pioneers of the Pinon, Ute, and Nucla Areas*. Naturita, CO: Rimrocker Historical Society, 1998.

HOMEOPATHY MOVEMENT
1870–PRESENT

The initial growth of homeopathy coincided with the decline of the well-established professional class of "regular" physicians in the 1830s. As the public demanded that anyone be allowed to work as a healer, orthodox practitioners lost their privileged position and political power. Advocates of homeopathy became part of a group of dissident medical practitioners, referred to as "sectarians" by their orthodox counterparts. The sectarian challenge, reflecting public appeals for alternatives to an overly invasive and increasingly monopolistic orthodoxy, subsequently shaped both the structure of the profession and the approach to medical practice throughout the nineteenth century.

The Danish physician Hans Gram first brought homeopathy to the United States in 1825. Rising to the position of president of the Medical and Philosophical Society of New York in the early 1830s, he converted a group of prominent practitioners, who then spread homeopathy throughout neighboring states. By 1835, the Swiss physician Henry Detwiller and German physician Constantine Hering established the first homeopathic academy in Allentown, Pennsylvania. Hering, known as the father of American homeopathy, was instrumental in creating America's first national medical society in 1844, the American Institute of Homeopathy. By the time Hering obtained a charter for the Homeopathic Medical College of Pennsylvania in 1848, homeopathy represented a major source of competition for orthodox medical practitioners.

American medical orthodoxy emerged from the Enlightenment quest for a rational medical science. The orthodox approach, however, was largely empirical and based on counteracting the forces of nature. Their vehement opposition to the idea that nature had its own healing powers often distinguished practitioners of regular medicine. Prominent physicians like Philadelphia's Benjamin Rush were committed to direct and drastic interference in the patient's system. Believing that health is a function of the interaction between a person's constitution and the physical environment, physicians made dramatic efforts to stimulate and reinvigorate the patient.

Utilizing powerful substances like opium, mercury, arsenic, and strychnine, orthodox therapies earned the name of "heroic" medicine. For most ailments, orthodox physicians practicing during the period from the 1780s to the 1850s advocated bleeding, blistering, purging, and sweating. They often combined extensive bloodletting with the administration of massive doses of dangerous drugs designed to cleanse the system. As disease was defined as loss of equilibrium in the interaction between the individual and the environment, medicine amounted to a set of procedures designed to regulate bodily fluids. Consequently, few disease-specific therapies existed. Medical educators of the early eighteenth century advocated massive bleeding, for example, as a cure for a variety of ailments. The release of several ounces to several pounds of blood was prescribed to reduce inflammation, relieve congestion, alleviate pain, relax muscles, and stop hemorrhage. Physicians also prescribed calomel, the most widely used drug in the first half of the nineteenth century, indiscriminately. When calomel, containing the chloride of mercury, would break down in the intestines into its poisonous components, it served as a violent laxative, producing effects consistent with the system of orthodoxy. While some physicians doubted such harsh therapeutics, the average patient continued to insist upon receiving the treatment that was currently most popular.

Homeopathy entered a largely unregulated medical marketplace created by the political forces of Jacksonian democracy. A popular distrust of the wealthy, elite, and well educated made professional medical societies one of many targets. For the individual physician, membership in orthodox societies represented distinction, prestige, and a license to practice. For the individual seeking alternatives to orthodox treatment, the medical society represented a monopoly. Responding to the equalitarian spirit of the times, state after state repealed laws governing licensure. While this opened the practice of medicine to virtually anyone, including quacks and outright frauds, advocates of deregulation saw diversity in medical practice as a counterpart to religious plurality.

SAMUEL HAHNEMANN AND THE FOUNDATIONS OF HOMEOPATHY

The roots of homeopathy can be traced to German physician and theorist Samuel Hahnemann, a physician who left medical practice due to his disillusionment with heroic therapies. His work as a writer and translator of medical texts, however, ultimately led him back to practice and changed the history of medicine. While translating a treatise on medical treatments by Scottish physician William Cullen, Hahnemann included a footnote disputing Cullen's explanation for the effectiveness of cinchona bark in treating malaria. Cullen maintained that the bitterness and astringent quality of the bark confronted the fever and malaise. Hahnemann suggested another explanation was necessary because other substances decidedly more bitter and astringent were not effective in treating malaria. In an effort to understand the effects of cinchona bark on the body, Hahnemann took repeated doses of the herb until his body responded. He experienced the same fever, chills, headaches, and other symptoms of malaria. Consulting Hippocrates for an answer, Hahnemann concluded that the herb was effective because it caused symptoms similar to those of the disease it was treating. For Hahnemann, this meant the drug that caused illness in a healthy person would cure that same illness in a sick person. This founding principle, which he termed *similia similibus curantur*, or "likes are to be cured by likes," became the cornerstone of homeopathic doctrine.

In direct opposition to the excesses of heroic medicine, homeopathy was organized around a second fundamental principle—that diseases were curable by small doses of particular drugs. Hahnemann's "doctrine of infinitesimals" suggested that the greatest therapeutic benefit came from diluted doses. While regular physicians had no firm theoretical basis for attacking Hahnemann's "like is cured by like" principle, the idea of diluted doses provided an opportunity for orthodox followers to denounce homeopathy as nonsensical and therapeutically ineffective.

For the patient, however, small doses prevented the damaging effects of heroic therapies. Offering an alternative to traditional orthodox practice, homeopathy gained a substantial following among doctors and patients as a safe, effective, and relatively inexpensive form of therapy.

Homeopathy also owed some of its popularity to its philosophical appeal, especially for Transcendentalists and others who had become disillusioned with the rigid materialism of Enlightenment rationality. Hahnemann provided an implicitly spiritual or metaphysical view of healing with references to the "spirit-like" activity of some medicines. He suggested that homeopathic remedies enabled an inner vital spirit to combat illness. This modified form of vitalism required a belief in the interrelationship between the spiritual and material provinces.

In 1810, Hahnemann published these ideas in his most important work, the *Organon of Homeopathic Medicine*. The following year, the first volume of his *Materia Medica Pura* included a guide to the medicines he tested and described based on the symptoms they caused. These "drug provings" provided a system of medical practice based on the law of similars. Hahnemann claimed that orthodox practitioners prescribed drugs not on the basis of *contraria* (drugs opposite in reaction to the symptom), or *similia* (like the symptoms), but *allos*, meaning another basis of prescription. Intended as a derogatory designation, the term *allopath* was soon commonly applied to the regular profession.

THE SECTARIAN CHALLENGE TO ORTHODOXY

Homeopathy was part of a much broader movement that challenged the legitimacy of orthodox practice. The first widespread challenge to regular medicine came from the son of a struggling New Hampshire farmer, Samuel Thomson. Thomson developed his own theory that illness was an imbalance of bodily constituents, normally the result of cold. According to Thomson, curing any disease involved restoring bodily heat by clearing obstructions and providing nourishment from stimulants. Although this was not dramatically different from the orthodox approach to restoring equilibrium, Thomsonians limited therapeutic intervention to herbs and intense steam baths. Thomson quickly enjoyed success as a healer and incurred the jealousy of orthodox practitioners. His motto of making every man his own physician coincided with the prevailing democratizing force of Jack-

HOMEOPATHY AND ITS KINDRED DELUSIONS
OLIVER WENDELL HOLMES

German physician Samuel Hahnemann developed the idea of homeopathy in the late eighteenth century based on the notion of using natural cures for the treatment of physical and mental illness. Homeopathy continues to have millions of resolute adherents who believe the method is more effective than conventional medicine in treating their symptoms. The following document, first presented in lecture form in 1842, is a critique of homeopathy by U.S. Supreme Court justice Oliver Wendell Holmes.

It is necessary, for the sake of those to whom the whole subject may be new, to give in the smallest possible compass the substance of the Homeopathic Doctrine. Samuel Hahnemann, its founder, is a German physician, now living in Paris, at the age of eighty-seven years. In 1796 he published the first paper containing his peculiar notions; in 1805 his first work on the subject; in 1810 his somewhat famous "Organon of the Healing Art"; the next year what he called the "Pure Materia Medica"; and in 1828 his last work, the "Treatise on Chronic Diseases." He has therefore been writing at intervals on his favorite subject for nearly half a century. [Hahnemann died in 1843.] . . .

Does Hahnemann himself represent Homeopathy as it now exists? He certainly ought to be its best representative, after having created it, and devoted his life to it for half a century. He is spoken of as the great physician of the time, in most, if not all Homeopathic works. If he is not authority on the subject of his own doctrines, *who is?* So far as I am aware, not one tangible discovery in the so-called science has ever been ascribed to any other observer, at least, no general principle or law, of consequence enough to claim any prominence in Homeopathic works, has ever been pretended to have originated with any of his illustrious disciples. He is one of the only two Homeopathic writers with whom, as I shall mention, the Paris publisher will have anything to do with upon his own account. The other is Jahr, whose Manual is little more than a catalogue of symptoms and remedies. If any persons choose to reject Hahnemann as not in the main representing Homeopathy, if they strike at his authority, if they wink out of sight his deliberate and formally announced results, it is an act of suicidal rashness; for upon his sagacity and powers of observation, and experience, as embodied in his works, and especially in his Materia, Medica, repose the foundations of Homeopathy as a practical system.

Source: Douglas Stalker and Clark Glymour, eds. *Examining Holistic Medicine* (Buffalo, NY: Prometheus Books, 1985).

sonian America and the belief that the individual could do anything he desired.

Homeopathy presented a much greater professional and economic threat to orthodox practitioners. Whereas Thomsonians operated outside the orthodox medical system, homeopathic practitioners often graduated from orthodox schools and subsequently defected from the ranks of regular physicians. Many homeopaths made a concerted effort to convert established physicians. Strong proselytizing efforts distinguished homeopathy from all other medical sects. Furthermore, although Thomsonianism tended to appeal to rural and poor clients acquainted with traditional herbal remedies, homeopathy flourished among the urban upper class. Homeopaths were generally well educated and carried the reputation of patronage by the aristocracy and social elites of Europe. As a result, homeopaths brought direct economic competition to the regular system.

The most effective denunciation of homeopathy came from the famous physician, poet, and medical educator Oliver Wendell Holmes in 1842. Presented as two lectures for the Boston Society for the Diffusion of Useful Knowledge, the classic assault on "Homeopathy and Its Kindred Delusions" was later published widely. Holmes disavowed the miraculous curing power of homeopathy by placing it in the same category as other medical delusions, including the legendary cure for a form of tuberculosis allegedly provided by the royal touch of the King of England. While Holmes found that the law of similars had some validity, he ridiculed homeopaths for the doctrine of minute doses and Hahnemann's drug provings. Holmes admitted, however, that the real problem with evaluating the merits of homeopathy was that the vast majority of patients recovered under any system. In an admission that seemed equally damning to the regular profession, and a pronounced retreat from heroic medicine, Holmes asserted that 90 percent of the cases commonly seen by a physician would recover if nothing interfered with the power of nature. Regardless, Holmes predicted homeopathy would ultimately fail once its novelty wore off and its failures increased.

Surprisingly, the homeopathic influence in the abandonment of heroic therapies was made especially clear by the 1951 Fiske Award of the Rhode Island Medical Society, given for the best attack on homeopathy. In "Homeopathy, So-called, Its History and Refutation," Worthington Hooker skillfully used mathematics to demonstrate the absurdity of the theory of infinitesimals, while resorting to logic to disprove the claim that the law of similars was the only "law of cure." Yet, Hooker recognized that homeopathy had demonstrated that the healing power of nature could be even stronger than heroic practices. Hooker announced that regular medicine must learn to harness that power. He maintained that it was in this way that the most absurd of all medical delusions might still do service to the cause of science and humanity.

THE AMERICAN MEDICAL ASSOCIATION AND HOMEOPATHY

Despite predictions that homeopathy was doomed, it continued to spread in the 1840s as orthodox practitioners like Hooker became increasingly hostile and defensive. Homeopaths also went on the offensive, claiming their system had a firmer grounding in scientific experimentation than orthodoxy, while criticizing the regular profession for an influx of inferior physicians. The regular profession was in turmoil, and homeopaths more than any other group advertised its shortcomings. The dramatic growth of proprietary medical schools compromised educational standards, faculty disputes ran rampant, doctors were unable to agree on methods of diagnosis and treatment, and citizens were outraged at the attempts of some physicians to regulate medical fees and eliminate competition. Acknowledging these problems, regular doctors sought to regain lost prestige by forming a national professional organization to improve medical education. Physicians saw the improvement of educational standards as an opportunity to promote citizen confidence in orthodoxy, ensure the elimination of inferior physicians and quacks, and inhibit defections to homeopathy.

At the first meeting of the fledgling American Medical Association (AMA) in 1846, no one mentioned homeopathy or other medical sects. The top priority was the improvement of standards and requirements for the medical degree. The following year, however, the formulation of a code of ethics ex-

plicitly asserted that no homeopath could consult with an orthodox physician, even if the patient requested such a meeting. The so-called consultation clause was sometimes carried out to the point of absurdity. It prevented the regular physician from coming to the aid of a patient whose doctor was a homeopath, regardless of how desperate the situation was—this despite the fact that by the early 1850s, the majority of the homeopaths were themselves graduates of orthodox medical schools. Nonetheless, by 1855 the member societies of the AMA had adopted the code of ethics, and the conflict between homeopathy and orthodoxy was officially sanctioned. Intended to separate quackery from orthodoxy, while publicly condemning sectarian practitioners, the code and the growth of the AMA did not bring the end of homeopathy. Enforcement of the code did, however, help to polarize the medical profession for the remainder of the century.

The first major battle between homeopathy and orthodoxy took place in the late 1850s, over the control of wards in newly constructed municipal hospitals. As major cities like Chicago, New York, and Boston made a commitment to provide medical care for the urban masses, homeopathic physicians applied for equal access. While homeopaths campaigned for hospital jobs, orthodox practitioners from 1850 to 1880 nearly unanimously refused to serve alongside homeopaths. With a stranglehold on medical boards, the orthodox community was even able to exclude homeopaths from military service during the Civil War, despite the fact that doctors were almost always in short supply.

ACCOMMODATION AND A NEW CODE OF ETHICS

During the 1860s and 1870s, regular practitioners gradually abandoned the harsh treatment of the age of heroic medicine, and the orthodox and sectarian found common cause to settle some of their disputes. Milder medication replaced heroic remedies, and more physicians relied upon the body's natural healing powers. At the same time, many who considered themselves homeopaths increasingly deviated from the tenets of Hahnemannian medicine, and the homeopathic profession began to fragment. While high-dilution advocates adhered carefully to Hahnemann's doctrines, other more eclectic homeopaths accepted orthodox remedies or dispensed homeopathic drugs in large doses. Some homeopathic graduates of orthodox medical schools experienced the benefits of allopathic treatments and were attracted to an increasingly scientific medicine. The public and sectarians alike responded enthusiastically to exciting advances in surgery, preventative medicine, and pharmacology. Many homeopaths began to blend their teachings with the new orthodoxy, partly in response to patient requests and partly in hopes of achieving greater professional respect.

By the 1880s, the majority of homeopaths were in favor of dispensing both traditional homeopathic treatments and orthodox remedies. The growth of specialization increased the need for interdependence in the profession across sectarian and orthodox lines. Orthodox specialists relied on referrals from homeopaths, just as sectarian general practitioners relied on orthodox hospital administrators for access to facilities. A renewed licensing movement concurrently promoted collaboration between regular physicians and homeopaths to win laws that would protect all of them from competition with poorly trained practitioners, coming primarily from proprietary schools serving as diploma mills.

In an effort to strengthen and unify the profession, discussions of a revised code of ethics officially began at the annual meeting of the Medical Society of the State of New York in 1881. By early 1882, a committee had crafted a new code that abandoned the consultation clause and placed the health of the patient above professional restrictions. Defenders of the new code, usually younger physicians, claimed that the old code was an infringement on the rights of citizens to freely meet with their physician of choice. They argued that since homeopathy had been legalized in every state, it should receive professional recognition.

Despite support for the new code in newspapers and leading magazines, twelve of the fourteen state medical associations that met prior to the 1882 AMA convention passed resolutions condemning their colleagues. At the AMA meeting in Cleveland the following year, every delegate was asked to sign a pledge of allegiance to the old code of ethics. By 1885, the new code became a national issue that threatened to destroy the Ninth International Medical Congress to be held in Washington, D.C. When the AMA decided that only those physicians who accepted the old code of ethics could serve on any committee of the International Congress, prominent new code supporters like Henry Bowditch, who had served as president of the AMA in 1877, were summarily excluded. The new code controversy threatened to destroy what de-

fenders of the old code cherished most—professional respect, integrity, and brotherhood.

While the consultation clause issue divided the orthodox profession into liberal and conservative wings, the homeopathic response was also mixed. Editorials in homeopathic publications warned that the acceptance of orthodox practitioners would threaten the individuality and therapeutic advantages of homeopathy. In 1885, the American Institute of Homeopathy suggested there was reason to be afraid. The AMA's attempts to establish licensing boards, which were dominated by orthodox practitioners, threatened to place the fate of homeopathy in the hands of the enemy.

A resolution to the protracted battle over consultation came at the 1903 AMA meeting in New Orleans. The old code of ethics was replaced with a document that opened up membership to any legally registered and reputable physician who was not supporting an exclusive medical system. This did not explicitly forbid homeopaths from joining the AMA, but it did suggest that they must not practice homeopathy exclusively. The document noted that it was inconsistent with scientific principles for physicians to designate their practice as exclusive or sectarian. The new code, however, avoided any reference to the type of medicine doctors actually practiced, allowing homeopaths to win a share of the scientific and professional benefits of the AMA.

Accommodation by the AMA came at the height of homeopathy's rise. In the two decades following the Civil War, homeopathy had gained the support of local boards of health, the government's medical corps, and the general public. When the regular profession denounced homeopaths, they thrived. By 1900 there were twenty-two homeopathic medical schools, more than 100 homeopathic hospitals, and more than 1,000 homeopathic pharmacies. Advocates of homeopathy included some of the most prominent and respected members of American society, such as William James, Nathaniel Hawthorne, Daniel Webster, William Seward, Harriet Beecher Stowe, Louisa May Alcott, and John D. Rockefeller. At the turn of the century, homeopathic physicians were generally supported in the press; they were famous for their success at treating various infectious epidemic diseases throughout the nineteenth century and prolific in scholarship with more than twenty-nine different homeopathic journals.

Ironically, the more homeopaths gained access to the privileges of the regular profession, the more their numbers declined. By 1910, there were only twelve homeopathic medical schools left, and by 1923 only two remained. Internally, homeopathy suffered from doctrinal disputes and a softening view of orthodox medicine. While earlier advocates of homeopathy could point to a dramatic therapeutic difference with regular practitioners, the alternative to homeopathic practice was no longer so dreadful. Even regular physicians were now using large amounts of homeopathic medicines themselves. Meanwhile, as the orthodox community used scientific knowledge to distinguish between competent practitioner and quack, homeopathic colleges that decided to offer more education in the medical sciences to compete with orthodox schools often compromised training in homeopathic therapies. As a result, graduates from these colleges were less able to practice homeopathy and often prescribed medicines according to the disease categories of orthodoxy. Eventually, many homeopaths gave up homeopathic practice, while homeopathic patients sought other types of care.

Homeopathy was further weakened by socioeconomic factors. First, more money was to be made in specialization than in either homeopathic or orthodox general practice. Specialization was rarely an option for the homeopath because it was incompatible with the spirit of homeopathic doctrine. Second, homeopathy was ill equipped to match the combined resources of the AMA and the rapidly expanding drug industry. By 1910, the AMA had made a deal with patent-drug manufacturers that supplied a constant flow of money in the form of advertising revenue for medical journals. As these same medical journals became mouthpieces for pharmaceutical companies, homeopathy suffered the consequences of bad press. Ultimately, homeopaths found it difficult to compete with the quick fix provided by the proliferation of patent medicines and the acceptance of new drugs into the cabinets of orthodox physicians.

THE FLEXNER REPORT AND REFORM OF MEDICAL EDUCATION

At the turn of the century, a reorganized and strengthened AMA returned to the problem that had originally motivated its formation by making the reform of medical education its top priority. The AMA had two longstanding goals that had not been met effectively since its formation fifty years earlier. First, the AMA hoped to renew licensing laws in order to combat the problem of competition in the medical marketplace. Second, in response to the glut of poorly trained physicians graduating from proprietary

schools, members of the AMA wanted to improve their social, economic, and professional status as a group. In 1904, the AMA established the Council on Medical Education to evaluate the quality of instruction in the nation's 161 medical schools. The initial report, issued in 1907, declared that only 82 schools provided acceptable instruction, while 47 were listed as doubtful and 32 unsatisfactory. Homeopathic schools were largely condemned for their inability to meet requirements of adequate instruction in physics, chemistry, and biology. The first chairman of the council predicted that homeopathy would soon die out for lack of students, once the results were made public.

The report of the council presented one major problem for the AMA. Its own professional ethics code frowned on physicians attacking each other in public. Not only would publication of the council's report create ill will, but it would also be a technical violation of its own code. A new report from the independent and unbiased Carnegie Foundation for the Advancement of Teaching would be necessary to provide the objectivity of a disinterested body. This report could then be published as part of a broader effort to shape public opinion in support of the AMA's objectives.

In 1910, the Carnegie Foundation commissioned Abraham Flexner to conduct an evaluation of sectarian and regular medical schools. The result was his report, "Medical Education in the United States and Canada," colloquially referred to as the Flexner Report on Medical Education. The Flexner Report rated schools according to the same standards. Flexner measured schools by the quality of their laboratories, size of their teaching hospitals, level of endowments, entrance qualifications, and amount of original research produced. Almost all of the homeopathic institutions failed to satisfactorily meet one of these criteria. Flexner criticized homeopathic schools for their failure to undertake progressive scientific work, a lack of resources, and their preference for employing professors who were also in clinical practice. While he was willing to credit homeopathy with playing an important part in discrediting the excesses of orthodox therapies, he argued that the orthodox schools were already doing the work of homeopathy far more effectively. Furthermore, Flexner insisted that adherence to Hahnemannian dogma by homeopaths was incompatible with science. Homeopathy was judged an unfit system for training physicians in scientific medicine.

Although Flexner was equally critical of many regular schools, the Flexner Report was clearly more damaging to homeopathic schools as a whole. He denounced almost all of the existing schools for poor standards and made no allowance for their survival in his plans for reconstructing medical education. Flexner helped seal the fate of many homeopathic schools that were already struggling to meet the financial burdens of operating in a competitive marketplace. Licensing boards and potential students alike subsequently scorned schools with poor ratings.

The impact of the Flexner Report was heightened by internal problems within homeopathy. The report heightened the debate between the pure Hahnemannians committed to the doctrine of infinitesimals and the revisionists who were unwilling or unable to adhere to Hahnemann's rigid formula for therapeutics. Following the publication of the Flexner Report, some homeopaths maintained that homeopathic schools were closing because they did not teach pure homeopathy but instead devoted too much time to medical science. Other purists maintained that the new standards set by Flexner were too high and would require too much money to revamp existing programs.

The Flexner Report created a standard that favored orthodox medical education in an era characterized by a dramatic increase in philanthropic support for schools. In 1920, for example, the struggling Hahnemann Medical College of Philadelphia was unable to obtain funds from the General Education Board of the Rockefeller Foundation, despite the fact that John D. Rockefeller himself continued to consult a homeopath for his personal medical care. The General Education Board appropriated nearly $15 million for medical education by 1920, and by 1929 the total had climbed to $78 million. However, homeopathy colleges were not the recipients of these awards.

DECLINE OF HOMEOPATHY

The 1920s and 1930s brought a reinvigorated attack on all forms of unorthodox medicine. Orthodox practitioners abandoned any reference to their practice as "regular," and those outside the bounds of orthodoxy were no longer designated as "sects" but rather as "cults." The long-time editor of the *Journal of the American Medical Association*, Morris Fishbein, disseminated this representation of unorthodox medicine as cultlike most enthusiastically. In 1925, Fishbein published *The Medical Follies*, a best-selling book attacking the "healing cults." Although Fishbein acknowledged that homeopathy had encouraged positive reforms in

orthodox practice, he concluded that it had ultimately died from internal inconsistencies.

In 1935, the AMA Council on Education outlawed the inclusion of unorthodox systems on the list of approved medical colleges and hospitals. This action eliminated the possibility of homeopathic schools benefiting from the extensive philanthropic support of regular medicine. By this time, the doctrinal split in homeopathy caused sufficient organizational and political weakness to preclude a significant response. In the decades to follow, homeopaths still made efforts to convince the AMA to recognize homeopathy as a specialty in internal medicine, but to no avail. By 1950, all the homeopathic colleges in the United States were either closed or no longer teaching homeopathy exclusively.

Homeopathy encountered a series of forces, peculiar to the American medical scene, that remained insurmountable. Practitioners were weakened from the attack on marginal schools instituted by the Flexner Report, unable to compete with the concentration of resources in fewer institutions, and burdened by a unified condemnation from the AMA and pharmaceutical industry. All the while, the orthodox community never provided scientific evidence that homeopathy failed to generate positive therapeutic results. Meanwhile, in Europe homeopathy maintained a large share of patients and in some countries expanded its base of patients and practitioners.

In the United States, however, homeopathy was on the brink of extinction by the 1960s. Most of its practitioners were over sixty years old. Few physicians were converted to homeopathy partly because it required a high level of therapeutic knowledge and expertise for practice, while demanding greater time and energy from the physician. Some predicted that homeopathy would not survive the twentieth century. With fewer than 200 practicing homeopaths, prospects remained grim.

UNEXPECTED REVIVAL

In the face of internal and external pressures, homeopathy did not die out. In the 1970s, there were only 50 to 100 physicians who specialized in homeopathy, and yet by the mid-1980s approximately 1,000 homeopaths had established practices. Capitalizing on the resurgence of alternative medicine in the 1970s, homeopaths reasserted their position, in opposition to a medical profession increasingly criticized for invasive therapies and limited success in combating major diseases. In the 1990s, studies in major medical journals revealed that patients used alternative medical systems like homeopathy because they found these healthcare alternatives to be more congruent with their own values, beliefs, and philosophical orientations toward health and life. Some see the resurgence of alternative forms of medical care as a testimony to the increased public dissatisfaction with modern medicine and its delivery system. Others suggest that the public evaluation of scientific medicine must be separated from evaluation of physicians.

In addition to the resurgence of homeopathic physicians, since the 1970s dozens of new homeopathic medical schools have been established, sales of homeopathic medicine have increased 2000 percent, and for the first time, some orthodox medical journals have conducted successful clinical trials validating the efficacy of homeopathy. Although homeopathic practitioners continued to be marginalized by the orthodox community, a strong push toward a complementary approach to therapy by organizations like the AMA suggests that homeopathy will continue to thrive in the decades to come.

Eric Boyle

BIBLIOGRAPHY

Coulter, Harris L. *Divided Legacy: The Conflict Between Homoeopathy and the American Medical Association—Science and Ethics in American Medicine 1800–1910.* Berkeley, CA: North Atlantic Books, 1973.

Fuller, Robert C. *Alternative Medicine and American Religious Life.* Oxford: Oxford University Press, 1989.

Kaufman, Martin. *Homeopathy in America: The Rise and Fall of a Medical Heresy.* Baltimore, MD: Johns Hopkins University Press, 1971.

Nicholls, Phillip A. *Homeopathy and the Medical Profession.* London: Croom Helm, 1988.

Starr, Paul. *The Social Transformation of American Medicine.* New York: Basic Books, 1982.

AMERICAN INTENTIONAL COMMUNITIES

Intentional communities—communities devoted with intent, resolve, and commitment to a collective objective—have been a part of the American cultural scene since the early days of European settlement. Some had very idealistic aims and were also called utopian communities. The first British settlers at Jamestown, Virginia, adopted a communal form of organization for a time, as the Pilgrims did later at Plymouth, Massachusetts. Thousands upon thousands of experiments in community have dotted our history ever since.

What is generally regarded as the first true intentional community in America—the first settlement organized from the beginning on explicitly communitarian principles—was Swanendael, or Plockhoy's Commonwealth. In the late 1650s, Peter Cornelius Plockhoy, a Dutch Mennonite, began to publish tracts that envisioned a community in which all residents would be equal, all work would be agreeable, and all points of view would be welcome. In 1663, Plockhoy and a band of some forty followers, with financial backing from the city of Amsterdam, set sail for America and in due course settled near what is now Lewes, Delaware. The fate of the colony is unknown because the Netherlands and Britain soon went to war, and a British detachment razed the colony a year after its founding.

Two other important communes followed Plockhoy's in the seventeenth century: the Labadist Community at Bohemia Manor, Maryland, and one popularly known as the Woman in the Wilderness in what is now Philadelphia. Both survived longer and had more impact on later communities than Plockhoy's did. Both (but especially the Woman in the Wilderness) influenced Johann Conrad Beissel, who in 1732 founded the earliest intentional community of which any built remnant remains, the Ephrata Community, or Cloister, in Lancaster County, Pennsylvania. Celibate renunciates, both men and women, lived lives of austere devotion and hard work, denying themselves worldly pleasures in their spiritual quest, producing marvelous works of choral music, beautifully illuminated manuscripts, and extensive works of prose and poetry published by their own press. Ephrata was not only one of the earliest American communal societies, but also among the longest-lived; it endured communally until 1814, and a few members remained on the premises until the 1890s.

THE SHAKERS

While Ephrata was at its peak, the first members of what was probably the most famous American communal movement of all began their work. The first Shakers (more formally, members of the United Society of Believers in Christ's Second Appearing) arrived from England in 1774 and soon took up the common life near present-day Albany, New York. Their visionary founder, Ann Lee, proclaimed a message of repentance of sin and the abandonment of worldly attachments. Very early, apparently, the movement demanded celibacy of all of its resident members. Although Lee died in 1784, able leaders arose to organize the Shakers into their characteristic village colonies. Eventually, Lee came to be regarded as Christ in the Second Coming (the "Second Appearing" of the group's formal name).

The Shakers grew for several decades, eventually numbering several thousand members in around twenty communal villages, the larger of which had several hundred members each. Following Ann Lee's dictum, they put their "hands to work and hearts to God" and produced some of America's most admired craftworks, including elegantly simple furniture and the exquisite villages themselves, several of which survive as museums. The Shakers did not consider the production of beautiful artifacts, however, to be their chief goal. Instead they, like other monastics, were simply leading dedicated and highly ordered lives in

Shakers dance at a meeting in 1873. The Shakers—so named because they practiced shaking, shouting, dancing, and whirling during their religious services—derived from the radical English sect, the Quakers, and set up communal societies in New England, New York, Kentucky, Ohio, and Indiana. Shakers believe in celibacy, equality, and simplicity, and although their numbers have dwindled, they remain active today. *(Brown Brothers)*

the service of God. The enforcement of celibacy meant that men and women were strictly separated, and a hallmark of Shaker architecture became its system of double doors and stairways—one for each sex. In their early years, the Shakers were well known for their vigorous worship practices, which involved "laboring," or group dancing, which could continue for hours. They also wrote thousands of spiritual songs, including the widely familiar "Simple Gifts."

Despite their disciplined lives set apart from the "world," as the general society was called, Shakers were not antimodern. On matters of gender and racial equity they were more than a century ahead of their time, accepting African-American members on an equal basis with all others and affirming the full equality of men and women. Gender equality was reflected in the Shakers' governance of each village with a ministry team of two brothers and two sisters, and a similar four-member ministry group over the whole movement. The Shakers were also inventive folk,

credited with such creations as the circular saw, the clothespin, and the flat broom. They embraced technology readily, driving cars and trucks, for example, when they became available. Today's Shakers use computers.

The latter half of the nineteenth century was marked by a decline in the number of members, a trend that accelerated during the twentieth century. By mid-century, the end of Shakerdom seemed inevitable, as village after village closed. In 1947, the headquarters village at Mount Lebanon, New York, was shuttered. For several years two villages—Canterbury, New Hampshire, and Sabbathday Lake, Maine—continued to operate with only a few members each. In 1965, the leaders at Canterbury closed the society to new members; Sabbathday Lake continued to welcome newcomers. Sabbathday remains the only surviving Shaker location, with fewer than ten members, although inquirers do visit and occasionally a new

The Rappite House in New Harmony, Indiana. George Rapp, a German linen weaver, established the utopian community of Harmony (also spelled "Harmonie"), first in Pennsylvania and then in southern Indiana in the early 1800s. Rappites renounced marriage and lived in celibacy. In 1825, Rapp sold the entire village to Robert Owen, who used the land, houses, and work buildings to launch his own utopian society. *(Library of Congress)*

member does join. At present the Shaker existence is tenuous.

HARMONISTS AND RAPPITES

Not too many years after the arrival of the first American Shakers came several groups of German immigrants who sought the freedom to live communally and practice their faith in America. One of the earliest and largest groups was the Harmony Society, which arose in the German province of Wuerttemberg in the late eighteenth century. The Harmonists constituted a particularly radical wing of the Pietist movement, which had recently arisen to challenge the formality and cold intellectualism of the established Lutheran church. The Pietists sought a heartfelt religious experience that included personal conversion and a striving for Christian perfection; some wanted to reform Lutheranism, but others sought to sever their ties with an institution they considered incapable of real transformation. Several separate groups ended up leaving Germany in their religious quest.

Into this environment came George Rapp (1757–1847), whose powerful Pietist convictions and leadership prowess won him some thousands of followers by about 1790. For several years tension between the civil authorities and the Rappites was intense, and eventually they decided to emigrate. In 1804, George Rapp and his associates purchased a tract of land north of Pittsburgh, Pennsylvania, on which they founded the communal village of Harmony. For a decade they built up their isolated village, but in 1814 Rapp decided that the group should move west. They purchased a large tract on the Wabash River, just upstream from the Ohio, in southern Indiana, which today remains one of America's most pristine museum villages. They achieved great prosperity in their new home, with extensive farms and industries, and soon they seemed permanently settled there. But in 1824 George Rapp decreed yet another exodus, this time to a place called Economy just a few miles from the original Harmony in Pennsylvania. In that last location the Harmonists achieved even greater prosperity and built the most extensive settlement yet. Eventually, however, the society began to fray. Celibacy, which had been introduced at the original Harmony, meant that the movement quit producing potential new members from within. A charismatic visitor who called himself the Count de Leon led a large group of disgruntled members out of the community in 1832. Rapp's death in 1847 led to notable organizational changes. Community life continued for several decades, but after the deaths of the old-line Rappites one John Duss seized control of the organization in the 1890s and squandered what was by then its vast wealth. In 1905, just a century after its arrival in America, the Harmony Society was dissolved.

INSPIRATIONISTS AND AMANA

Another notable group of communal Pietist immigrants whose story to a degree paralleled that of the Harmonists was the Community of True Inspiration, also a product of the German Pietist unrest of the eighteenth century. Its distinctive contribution to communal Pietism was its embrace of the precept that a few persons, in the pattern of the biblical prophets, could speak with divine inspiration. Several of these inspired "instruments" helped shape the society's history—and none more so than Christian Metz, who, in 1843 and 1844, oversaw a migration from Germany to New York State, where the group founded a community called Ebenezer. As had been the case with the Harmonists, the Inspirationists, soon numbering more than 1,000, came to feel a need to move west, and in 1855 they began to resettle on a large tract of land in eastern Iowa. Calling the new location Amana, they built up seven villages under Metz's able direction. Eventually, however, spiritual restlessness among some members and economic problems exacerbated by the Depression forced an abandonment of the fully communal way of life at Amana. In 1932, the society decommunalized its

economy. Its surviving industries, including the flagship appliance-manufacturing company, became private enterprises. Nevertheless, many Amanans stayed on. The Inspirationist church continues to operate (albeit without an inspired leader for more than a century), the factory turns out refrigerators and microwave ovens, and the Amana Society still has extensive land and business holdings. The colonies, now accessible by interstate highway, have become the leading tourist attraction in Iowa, marketing their own past to millions of visitors.

NOYES AND THE ONEIDANS

Many other immigrant colonies, albeit smaller than those of the Harmonists and Amanans, also flourished in the nineteenth century—the Zoar Society in Ohio (another product of German Pietism), Bishop Hill in Illinois (founded by dissenting Swedish Lutherans), and many more, all with fascinating stories. At the same time, home-grown prophets proved as capable as any of the immigrant leaders of bringing believers into the common life. Among them none was more successful, flamboyant, and famous (notorious, his detractors would say) than John Humphrey Noyes, the founder of the Oneida Community. Noyes was converted in a revival in 1831and began to study for the ministry. In 1834, he concluded that he was freed from sinfulness and was morally "perfect"; his community eventually developed as a place in which he and others who had transcended the human propensity to sin could build what was actually regarded as the beginning of the Kingdom of God on earth. No part of Noyes's unorthodox theology was more controversial than "complex marriage," in which the community of the saved became a family, with all men married to all women, with all of the sexual privileges that relationship implies.

Community life began in the mid-1840s in Putney, Vermont, but complex marriage scandalized that small town and Noyes was soon indicted for adultery. Later, in 1847, Noyes and his closest disciples then headed for upstate New York, where they settled outside the town of Oneida. Although their situation was financially precarious at first, eventually they built up solid industries; animal traps were a major success, followed by the silverware that has made "Oneida" a household word. Through their publications, they were a beacon among the intentional communities and social reformers of the day. Eventually, however, pressures—especially the inevitable external attacks against a community founded on such radical principles—took their toll on the community. In 1879, the community abandoned complex marriage, and in 1881 its successful industry was transformed into a joint-stock corporation. The Mansion House—where hundreds of members lived under one roof—survives and continues to be inhabited in part by descendants of the original Oneidans.

SECULAR INTENTIONAL COMMUNITIES

Religion was not the only basis for organizing intentional communities in the nineteenth century. The first of several secular movements to receive wide notice was the New Harmony of Robert Owen. Owen made a fortune as a mill-owner in Scotland and became renowned as a social theorist and reformer, one who held that workers, having created wealth, had a right to a share of their productivity. New Lanark, his company town, was publicized as a workers' paradise. In his prolific writings, he envisioned cooperative villages in which all would share in production and in the fruits of the community's enterprises under conditions of universal social equality.

Owen had hoped to inaugurate some grand communitarian experiments in Scotland, but land there was prohibitively expensive. When word reached him that George Rapp's Harmony Society was selling its entire town of New Harmony and its 20,000 acres, he seized the opportunity and purchased the property early in 1825. But as a community the experiment was short-lived. Owen flung the doors of his community open to all, attracting deadbeats as well as industrious idealists. It turned out that a diverse lot of people did not necessarily work harmoniously together. By 1827, the communal phase of New Harmony was over. The influence of the experiment, however, was enormous. New Harmony attracted a large contingent of intellectuals and became an important center of scholarship, particularly in geology and natural science. Its progressive schools became models for educational reformers. It was the home of the first American trade school. Its library for workers inspired some 160 other such institutions. Over a dozen other communal experiments based on Owen's ideas were started around the country. Owen himself remains a major figure in the history of socialism and social reform. In short, the influence of Owenite New Harmony extended far beyond its short communal lifespan.

One of the best-known American communities of all was Brook Farm, which was founded by George Ripley and others at West Roxbury, Massachusetts (now a part of the city of Boston), in 1841, as a direct outgrowth of the Transcendentalist ferment then at its peak. The New England Transcendentalists, of whom the leading light was Ralph Waldo Emerson, sought both free mental exploration and direct experience of the material world, and Ripley proposed to bring the diverse values of the movement together in a rural social experiment. Although many of the Transcendentalists declined to join the project, a goodly contingent of free-spirited and intelligent young adults jumped in and created what by all accounts was a fulfilling round of manual labor, intelligent conversation, and lively socializing. Especially prized was the community's school, which attracted students from far and wide.

In 1844, Brook Farm announced its reorganization as the Brook Farm Phalanx. By that time, the social ideas of the Frenchman Charles Fourier had developed an American following, and for a time Brook Farm became the intellectual center of Fourierism, which proposed to organize society in a manner that would be tightly prescribed but wonderfully fulfilling to its members. Under Fourier's system, exactly 1,620 persons would constitute a "phalanx," or community, and live and work in a "phalanstery," a huge structure surrounded by a large tract of open land. Brook Farm had a short-lived career as a phalanx because its grand phalanstery burned to the ground just as it was being completed in 1846, and the community could not survive that crushing blow. However, dozens of other phalanxes were founded from Massachusetts to Texas before the movement ran its course toward the end of the century. Most were short-lived, with only a handful lasting more than three years. Fourier's sweeping ideas, however, have influenced later communitarians and cooperators, especially those who founded cooperative stores and workshops throughout the country.

Another French-inspired secular communitarian movement shared the heyday of Fourierism. In 1839, Etienne Cabet published the utopian novel *Voyage en Icarie* (Journey in Icaria), a massive work along the lines of Thomas More's *Utopia*. Hundreds of readers of the work found it so inspiring that they determined to make it a built reality. Taking personal leadership of the movement he inspired, Cabet, like so many other European utopians, concluded that America was the best site for his project. In 1848, the first Icarians headed for Texas, where Cabet had purchased a million acres in the Red River Valley. For a variety of reasons the site was utterly unworkable, and when Cabet himself arrived in 1849, he and those willing to try again found a more congenial location—Nauvoo, Illinois, the home of the Latter-day Saints who had lately left for Utah. They bought much of the town

Founded by Transcendentalists in West Roxbury, Massachusetts, in 1841, the Brook Farm Institute of Agriculture and Education, as it was formally known, combined manual labor with progressive educational techniques, such as nonpunitive discipline, intellectual discourse, and open-ended study hours. Among Brook Farm's many literary residents was Nathaniel Hawthorne, who immortalized the community in his 1852 novel, *The Blithedale Romance*. *(Brown Brothers)*

from the Mormons and moved in. The lives of the Icarians were strictly regulated, but they developed a society that valued education, cultural pursuits, and gender equality. However, divisions soon erupted, not least because Cabet's authoritarian ways alienated a majority of his followers. In 1856, the anti-Cabet majority evicted the founder and his loyalists. Cabet then founded a new Icaria just outside St. Louis. A financial crisis at Nauvoo forced the remaining communitarians to move to Iowa, where cheap government land was available. In 1881, some members of New Icaria moved to California and founded the last colony, Icaria Speranza, north of Santa Rosa. It was dissolved in 1886, and in 1898 the last Iowa Icarians dissolved their community as well.

Secular communities would continue to be founded ever afterward. In 1885 a group of San Francisco Socialists moved to the Sierra Nevada and, with devoted physical labor, built the Kaweah Cooperative Commonwealth, a dynamic little utopia whose life

was cut short when the federal government preempted the colony's land, without payment, to create Sequoia National Park. A notable cluster of Socialist and Anarchist communities grew up in Washington State; among them were the Puget Sound Cooperative Colony, located at Port Angeles, founded in 1887; Equality, near Bellingham, 1897; Burley, on Puget Sound, 1898; Freeland, on Whidbey Island, 1899; and the most notable of them all, the Home colony, which for more than twenty years after its founding in 1896 was a bastion of American Anarchism. Ruskin Colony, in Tennessee, published the *Coming Nation*, the nation's leading Socialist newspaper, in the 1890s, and the Llano Colony, first near Los Angeles and later in Louisiana, was a key center of American socialism in the 1910s through 1930s. Economic reformers also founded a number of cooperative settlements, including ten or so devoted to embodying the single-tax principles of Henry George. (Fairhope, Alabama, and Arden, Delaware, were prominent examples.)

LATE-NINETEENTH-CENTURY RELIGIOUS COMMUNITIES

The latter part of the nineteenth century was rife with all kinds of religious communities. One of the most extensive networks of communities in American history was (and is) that of the various groups of Latter-day Saints (LDS). The Mormons had experimented with communal forms as early as the 1830s, but under Brigham Young in Utah in the 1870s, the United Order of Enoch, as it was known, was launched in earnest. Well over 100 United Order organizations were formed, some of them thoroughly communal in structure and others only loosely cooperative. Although the main Mormon church eventually gave up on communal living as an ideal, the legacy of the United Order lives on in the church welfare system, cooperative stores, and close-knit relations among believers. Moreover, dozens of Mormon splinter groups, many of them retaining the practice of polygamy that the main church abandoned early in the twentieth century, continue the communal tradition today. The polygamy-practicing splinter LDS settlement at Colorado City, Arizona, is the largest intentional community in the United States today, with over 5,000 resident members.

HUTTERITES

In 1874, just as the United Order was being launched in Utah, what would become the largest communal movement in North American history took root on the American plains. Founded in 1528 as a radical Anabaptist movement, the Hutterites had, after many migrations, settled in the Ukraine in 1770 with the understanding that they could live in their own communities and not be drafted into military service. When the special privileges were lifted in 1871, however, the Hutterites moved yet again. They arrived in South Dakota in 1874, organizing themselves into three separate subgroups (Schmiedeleut, Dariusleut, and Lehrerleut) and living in colonies of around 100 members each.

World War I was a difficult time for these German-speaking pacifists, and amid severe persecution most of them left the United States for the western provinces of Canada. In the 1930s, they began to return to the United States, and today they operate freely in both countries. With a high birth rate and strong retention of their young people, the Hutterites have seen explosive growth, today numbering over 40,000 in over 400 colonies. They embrace modern, large-scale agricultural technology but culturally remain largely isolated from the outside world. Their communitarianism is thorough; private property is limited to a few intimate personal items. By any standard (size, longevity, prosperity), the Hutterites are the leading American communal success story, exceeded in scope only by traditional religious communities of monks and nuns. Another similar movement, the Bruderhof, was founded in Germany in 1920 in explicit imitation of the Hutterites. It came to the United States in 1954 and now has over 2,000 members in several colonies in the United States and abroad.

The Hutterites were not the only refugees from eastern Europe who settled in intentional communities in the United States in their era. Shortly after their arrival came a large wave of Jewish community-building, fueled by the influx after 1880 of large numbers of refugee Jews fleeing persecution. Although most of the colonies, based on agriculture and light industry, were soon dissolved, traces remain, especially in southern New Jersey, where several former colonies (Woodbine, Brotmanville, Norma) continue their existence as small towns.

The turn of the twentieth century saw the rise of a number of communities led by independent religious visionaries. In the 1890s, Cyrus Teed, known as "Koresh," established his Koreshan Unity community at Estero, Florida, which lasted several decades and whose buildings have been preserved as a state park; the movement was best known for Teed's teaching that the earth is hollow and we live on the inside of it. Zion City, founded north of Chicago by the faith-healing evangelist John Alexander Dowie in 1901, may have had more than 5,000 resident members at its peak. The House of David was founded in 1903 at Benton Harbor, Michigan, by Benjamin and Mary Purnell, as one of many groups descended from the work of the English mystic Joanna Southcott. It was best known to the general public for its barnstorming baseball teams whose players never cut their hair or beards. Zion City continues as a noncommunal town, its independent Dowieite church still strong, while the House of David, now divided into two factions, continues to lead a tenuous existence in Benton Harbor.

NEW AGE RELIGIONS

The turn-of-the-century era also saw the beginnings of religious communalism grounded in Asian, esoteric, and New Age religions. Theosophy, a blending of Asian and Western mystical religious traditions, established several communal centers, the largest and best-known of them at Point Loma, California (today part of San Diego), where several impressively exotic buildings were erected and a wide variety of educational and cultural activities were pursued for several decades after 1897 under the leadership of Katherine Tingley. Theosophy also gave rise, indirectly, to the Camphill movement, which later in the twentieth century created a network of communities dedicated to caring for handicapped and retarded persons.

A later manifestation of the spiritual quest, the loosely defined New Age movement also gave rise to several communal centers, such as the far-flung Emissary communities, whose headquarters, Sunrise Ranch in Colorado, has been operating since 1945. The Vedanta Society, one of the early Hindu movements to establish an American foothold, had communal ashrams (Hindu religious retreats) operating in the first decade of the new century, and Buddhist monastic communalism began in the 1930s with the work of Dwight Goddard, a Baptist missionary to China who converted to Zen Buddhism and promoted his new religion upon his return to the United States. After changes in American immigration laws in 1965, many Asian teachers arrived on American shores, and Asian-based religious communities mushroomed. Hundreds of communal centers representing most major branches of Hinduism and Buddhism operate today.

Working artists have long congregated in various attractive locales, and for a few decades at the beginning of the twentieth century some of them went a step further and formed intentional communities. The Roycrofters, under the commercially savvy leadership of Elbert Hubbard, turned out a commercially successful line of books and furniture from their colony at East Aurora, New York. In 1902, Byrdcliffe was founded and funded by a patron, Ralph Radcliffe Whitehead; it made Woodstock, New York, the center of the arts, which it has been ever since. Rose Valley, near Philadelphia, had as many as sixty residents during its brief communal life from 1903 to 1908. Some communal colonies of the arts continue to operate quietly today.

A surge of commune-founding followed the onset of the Depression after 1929. The federal government, as a part of its general poverty-fighting program, sponsored around 100 collective settlements under the Division of Subsistence Homesteads and later the Resettlement Administration. At the same time, independent activists promoted self-sufficient living in small communities. Ralph Borsodi, a zealous advocate of self-sufficiency, formed what he called the School of Living. Arthur Morgan similarly promoted all kinds of small communities as an antidote to the ills

of the day; the intentional communities of mid-century owe much to his leadership. As always, independent visionaries appeared with their own communal solutions to the ills of the day. The most prominent of them in the 1930s was Father Divine, whose followers considered him God in the flesh and who lived by the thousands in Divine's "heavens," as the communities were called.

THE 1960S AND 1970S

The era from the early 1960s through the mid-1970s saw the greatest outpouring of communal living that the country has ever seen. Mostly young persons affected by the cultural and political upheavals of the day banded together in huge numbers and formed thousands of urban and rural communes. Such early examples as Tolstoy Farm, an anarchist enclave in eastern Washington State (founded 1963), and Drop City, an art colony outside Trinidad, Colorado (founded 1965), offered exciting new lifestyle visions and opened their doors to all who would come. In 1966, Lou Gottlieb, a member of the Limeliters folk-music group, opened his 31-acre Morning Star Ranch north of San Francisco to one and all, and there soon ensued a veritable flood of communes on the West Coast. By about 1967, communes were turning up everywhere. They came in many styles and lived by many philosophies. The largest of them all, the Farm, founded in 1971 near Summertown, Tennessee, embodied the spirit of the day in classic form. Led by Stephen Gaskin, an eclectic spiritual teacher whose outlook embraced, among other things, the use of psychedelics, Farm members were strict vegetarians who eschewed modern conveniences and dedicated themselves to building a new society and helping the less fortunate.

Coming as they did at a time of sweeping social change, the 1960s communes saw a good deal of social experimentation. Many of them tolerated, or advocated, the use of drugs, especially marijuana and LSD. Unconventional patterns of sexual conduct were widely embraced, although practice probably was not as flamboyant as theory. Rejection of the values of mainstream society was bedrock.

Amid the countercultural communes that got a great deal of attention in the press were a good many religious communities, some with rigid standards of belief and behavior. The Shiloh movement, the Children of God, and many others took in thousands of earnest young Christian believers—and often were the focus of a good deal of controversy for their alleged tight control of their members' lives and their intense spiritual energy. Other communal groups grounded in Asian religions—the International Society for Krishna Consciousness; the Unification Church—were similarly intense and similarly controversial. But many of them continue to exist today.

By the end of the twentieth century, two new, or at least newly named, types of communities were occupying important niches in the larger fabric of communitarianism. One was cohousing, usually found in urban or suburban locations, in which clustered homes were built in a way that allowed owners as much privacy or community as they chose. They had complete (but small) individual homes as well as shared facilities, which typically included workshops, child-care facilities, tool sheds, guest rooms, and a kitchen and dining room large enough for the whole community to use. The other was the ecovillage movement, whose communities were usually located in rural areas and sought to promote lifestyles that were cooperative, largely self-sufficient, and environmentally as benign as possible. Ecovillages often used alternative building technologies (such as straw-bale construction), engaged in organic farming, and tried to minimize energy consumption.

And so the story continues. Hundreds of intentional communities from the American past are still active. Reba Place (founded in 1957 in Illinois), Twin Oaks (1967, Virginia), Jesus People USA (1974, Illinois), the Celo Community (1937, North Carolina), and a host of others are all quite alive and well. They stand as a testimony to the human imagination and to idealism. Their members put their lives and fortunes on the line to affirm what they saw as the essential humanity of all. Historically, communities have often been short-lived. Still, the tendency for the communities to break apart fairly quickly has not deterred new generations of seekers. As long as optimism remains in the human race, intentional communities will be with us.

Timothy Miller

BIBLIOGRAPHY

Communities Directory: A Guide to Intentional Communities and Cooperative Living. Rutledge, MO: Fellowship for Intentional Community, 2000.

Dare, Philip. *American Communes to 1860: A Bibliography.* New York: Garland, 1990.

Hostetler, John A. *Hutterite Society.* Baltimore, MD: Johns Hopkins University Press, 1997.

LeWarne, Charles Pierce. *Utopias on Puget Sound, 1885–1915.* Seattle: University of Washington Press, 1975.

Miller, Timothy. *American Communes, 1860–1960: A Bibliography.* New York: Garland, 1990.

———. *The Quest for Utopia in Twentieth-Century America.* Vol. 1. Syracuse, NY: Syracuse University Press, 1998.

———. *The 60s Communes: Hippies and Beyond.* Syracuse, NY: Syracuse University Press, 1998.

Pitzer, Donald E., ed. *America's Communal Utopias.* Chapel Hill: University of North Carolina Press, 1997.

Stein, Stephen J. *The Shaker Experience in America.* New Haven, CT: Yale University Press, 1992.

Ethical Culture Movement

Founded by Dr. Felix Adler in 1876, Ethical Culture is a religious, educational, and social movement. The early history of Ethical Culture developed in response to the evils wrought by the industrial revolution. With a twofold commitment to both theory and practice, Ethical Culture has sought to anchor its social activism in moral ideals and a critical understanding of the sources of human oppression.

In accordance with a predominant current of nineteenth-century thought, Adler interpreted religion as an evolving phenomenon. He aimed to bring religion into modern times by creating a movement exclusively committed to ethical ideals, while eliminating supernatural belief and unscientific practices. Human dignity and interdependence lay at the heart of Adler's ethics. The mission of Ethical Culture then and now is to expand and deepen reverence for the worth of others as a vehicle to underscore one's own. It works to make primary the ethical factor in all relationships of life, ranging from the family to society, and ultimately the international arena.

Ethical Culture Philosophy

On its philosophical side, Ethical Culture was born in what the historian of religion Sidney Ahlstrom has called "the Golden Age of Liberal Theology." It was a period in which religious thinkers were compelled to respond to Darwinism and its implication that man evolved by natural processes, and so lacked a special status conferred by divine creation. Science had great prestige in the nineteenth century, and liberal theologians sought to validate their religious speculations by harmonizing them with the scientific spirit and discoveries of the age. Adler was among these modernizers but remained troubled that science, which adequately described physical processes, could not sanction the absolute worth of the person. With Ethical Culture, Adler sought to create a new religious movement that would be "ultra-scientific without being anti-scientific."

Three major influences informed Adler's philosophy. Adler received his doctorate from the University of Heidelberg in 1873 and was greatly influenced by the moral and idealistic philosophy of Immanuel Kant, whose ethical thought he transformed in a more organic and social direction. Through creatively reworking Kant's concept of the "reality-producing processes of the mind," Adler found the transcendental reality by which to ground the absolute worthiness of the person.

Adler immigrated to the United States in 1857 at the age of six. He became inspired by the American democratic experience for which Ralph Waldo Emerson was a major spokesperson. Emerson had called for the emergence of a "purely ethical religion" in America, and Ethical Culture can be understood as a realization of Emerson's hopes. Adler also drew from Emerson's transcendentalism in his own construction of a spiritual universe, but paralleling his critique of Kant, he found Emerson's ideal of the "over soul" not sufficiently social.

Adler's background in Reform Judaism provided the third major influence on his thought. Adler's father, Rabbi Samuel Adler, who played a major role in liberalizing Judaism in Germany, later served as the second rabbi at the newly established Temple Emmanuel in New York. The Reform Judaism of the late nineteenth century was dedicated to the concept of "ethical monotheism" and was permeated with ideals of progress, rationalism, and universalism drawn from the European Enlightenment. The German Jewish community in America could be characterized by its meteoric economic success, a commitment to building social welfare institutions, and its desire for equality in Protestant-dominated America. Adler and many of his early followers who came from Reform Judaism reflected these cosmopolitan, high-minded sensibilities that were to animate Ethical Culture in its formative period. Ethical Culture attracted families identified with the German-Jewish elite who had

Born in Germany in 1851, Felix Adler established the Society for Ethical Culture in New York City when he was twenty-five years old. The Ethical Culture Movement emphasized the importance of moral values and judgment regardless of a supreme being. *(New York Society for Ethical Culture)*

which many of Adler's well-positioned followers were inspired to improve the conditions of the disadvantaged.

ETHICAL CULTURE AND SOCIAL REFORM

Ethical Culture was among several influential social reform movements that flourished in late nineteenth-century urban America and attracted an extraordinary cluster of talented visionaries and organizers. Among figures who were within the orbit of Ethical Culture in its early phase and worked with it toward common goals were such luminaries as Jacob Riis, Jane Addams, Lillian Wald, Booker T. Washington, W.E.B. Du Bois, Thomas Davidson, William James, and Walt Whitman. Samuel Gompers, the founder of the American Federation of Labor, was an enthusiastic member of the New York Society for Ethical Culture. Adler anticipated the Christian Social Gospel movement through his early emphasis on the moral dimension of Jesus' teaching. Like the Social Gospel movement, Ethical Culture was committed to applying religion to social reform, especially in the cities. Both movements were open to accepting new knowledge gleaned from the social sciences as an adjunct to liberal faith.

The problems of labor and industrial society consumed the passions of Adler and his followers. Endemic poverty, crowded, substandard housing, child labor, and deficient schools were among the problems these social reformers confronted. For some twenty years Adler had named "the social or labor question" as "the chief moral question of the day." According to Horace Friess, Adler's biographer,

> It was the growing edge of a new stage of society that he [Adler] saw in the general state and future prospects of industrial workers. It was a concern for the entire education and development of the workers, for their homes and families, their life structure and it was concern, as well, that they have a voice in the making of economic decisions. These economic, intellectual, and moral dimensions led Adler to view "the liberation of labor" as of crucial ethical moment to all society.

Within its first two years, Ethical Culture undertook several projects in the service of its mission that became characteristic of its approach to social reconstruction. In 1877, Ethical Culture hired several nurses to visit the poor in their homes and dispense their services free of charge. This program of "visiting nurses" later became a component of New York City's

prospered in the professions manufacturing and banking. Among them were Joseph Seligman, Lionel Sutro, Joseph Price, Henry Morgenthau, and Louis Bamberger.

Although Adler preached his own brand of ethical idealism from the Ethical Culture platform, he emphasized that Ethical Culture was founded on total freedom of conscience in matters of ultimate belief. This freedom, and Ethical Culture's dedication to social justice, were often expressed in the slogan "diversity in the creed, unanimity in the deed." For both Adler and his followers, religious devotion needed to be expressed in and through the world of social realities, with a view toward progressively transforming them by the light of the ideal. Adler referred to this work as "social reconstruction," implying that it was neither revolutionary nor simply reformist. In practical terms, much of the early work of Ethical Culture reflected a top-down approach to social change in

health services and was permanently organized through the work of Lillian Wald and the Henry Street Settlement.

Around the same time, Ethical Culture established the first free kindergarten for the working poor on the Lower West Side of Manhattan. The Workingman's School eventually grew into an eight-grade elementary school, and then a high school, which, in contrast to the public and elite private schools, was dedicated to a progressive pedagogy of industrial education in which theory would be combined with practice. This early effort reflected Adler's lifelong commitment to education as a primary vehicle for social reform. The Workingman's School became the Ethical Culture School as members of Ethical Culture enrolled their own children and so diversified its class character. Adler's elaborated vision for the school, his "Fieldston Plan" (named for the area of the Bronx where the school was located), included prevocational training along with a broad liberal arts education. Though never fully realized within the confines of a single school, it did serve as a blueprint for such "magnet schools" as the High School of Music and Art and the Bronx High School of Science, among other outstanding components of New York City's public education system.

In the 1880s, as new waves of European immigration brought destitution to America's cities, Adler became a vocal member of New York State's Tenement House Commission. He advocated for humane, healthful living conditions, and he challenged the subterfuges of exploitative landlords, as he argued that profits on rent above 3 percent should be condemned as usury. His work with this state program inspired him to found the Tenement House Building Company, with E.R.A. Seligman, economist at Columbia College and Ethical Society member, as president. By 1887, the company had built six model tenements, which eventually benefited 3,500 families, on Cherry Street on New York's Lower East Side. These early projects reflected Ethical Culture's mode of activism in which, under Adler's inspiration, with the support of benefactors, the society would establish institutions that evolved to take on lives of their own, as their origins in the Ethical Movement receded to the background.

EXPANSION AND THE SETTLEMENT HOUSE MOVEMENT

In the 1880s, Adler recruited four professional lieutenants who moved Ethical Culture beyond New York City. William Mackintire Salter, S. Burns Weston, Wal-

ter Sheldon, and Stanton Coit came from liberal Protestant backgrounds. After pursuing graduate studies in Germany at Adler's behest, they respectively became the founding lecturers (later called "leaders") of Ethical Societies in Chicago, Philadelphia, St. Louis, and London, England.

In those urban venues, they continued the work Adler had begun in New York City. Weston devoted himself to settlement house work in Philadelphia, while Sheldon, building upon the traditions of freethinking Germans who had settled in the St. Louis area, created the Self-Culture Halls Association that replaced the educational work of the settlement houses without their emphasis on direct social action. In Chicago, Salter, concerned about legal representation for the poor, helped to found the Bureau for Justice, which in time evolved into today's Legal Aid Society.

Although the Settlement House movement is usually associated with Lillian Wald and Jane Addams, the first settlement house in the United States, Neighborhood Guild, today known as the University Settlement, was founded by Coit in New York in 1886. Based on a British model, and together with Madison House and the Hudson Guild, it marked Ethical Culture as a pioneer in this influential effort to teach immigrants American values, train them in needed job skills, and provide venues in which newcomers could learn the habits of democratic self-governance.

Adler's interest in childhood development went beyond the confines of formal education. Inviting new advances in children's psychology, the New York Society initiated the Visiting and Teaching Guild for Crippled Children and the Mothers' Society to Study Child Nature, the latter growing into the Child Study Association. Adler combined his interest in children with his analysis of the labor problem in his long presidency of the National Child Labor Committee, which he helped to found in 1894. Adler railed against the powerful commercial and industrial interests that exploited children in factories while denying them education. With the documentary assistance of the famed photographer Lewis Hine, Adler's committee paved the way for early legislation protecting the rights of the child.

In the last decades of the nineteenth century, there was no religious leader more sympathetic to the cause of labor in New York City than Felix Adler. Though he supported the trade union movement and its demands, his critique went far beyond advocacy of bread-and-butter issues. Adler believed that the labor movement was pivotal to bringing society to a new stage of development. But as an idealist he averred that without the intellectual and moral education of both owners and workers, the movement limited itself to the materialism he saw represented by both capitalism and socialism.

VOCATIONALISM AND WOMEN'S RIGHTS

Never a barricades activist, Adler possessed a temperament that found its expression in theoretical exposition, precise and eloquent oratory, organization, and mediation. In a series of twelve lectures given at the Summer School of Applied Ethics in Plymouth, Massachusetts, in 1894, Adler produced his most elaborate assessment of the labor problem. These lectures, which Adler considered his finest work, brought together scholars, among them Woodrow Wilson, as well as activists to discuss conditions and remedies of the labor problem.

At the center of Adler's commitment to labor was his theory of vocationalism. This meant that the worker needed to be fitted to his specific task to ensure that his or her work would serve as a vehicle for authentic personal growth. Moreover, in a way consistent with the organic character of all of Adler's ethical theorizing, each vocation needed to stand in right and mutually fruitful relations with other callings.

In 1910, the commitments of Ethical Culture were challenged when the garment trades called an industrywide strike involving 75,000 workers. Significantly, Ethical Culture members took leadership roles on both sides of the mediating process. Ethical Culturist Julius Cohen served as lawyer for the manufacturers, while Henry Moskowitz, who joined Adler in professional leadership in 1907 and helped to found Madison House, worked tirelessly with his wife, Belle, to help reach a solution. Moskowitz called upon department store magnate A. Lincoln Filene, whose interests had been adversely affected by the strike. Filene, a fellow Ethical Culturist, in turn prevailed upon a young Boston lawyer, Louis Brandeis, to serve as arbitrator. Brandeis, Adler's brother-in-law, served under Adler's chairmanship of the Council of Conciliation, which grew out of the strike settlement.

Adler, in a way that expressed his Victorian values, did not support women's suffrage, asserting that it would worsen an already faulty electoral system. Although he supported separate social spheres for women and men, he nevertheless advocated for women's education and the need to learn a trade as a hedge against spousal abandonment. Despite his conflicting views, Adler recruited as a colleague the Unitarian Anna Garlin Spencer, in 1894. Spencer was a suffragist, pacifist, and vice president of the Women's International League for Peace and Freedom. Unable to find a satisfying professional place in Ethical leadership, she resigned her position ten years later to become a founder of Columbia University's School of Social Work.

NEW LEADERSHIP

The year 1894 also saw the entry of John Lovejoy Elliott into the ranks of Ethical Culture's leadership. Elliott was chosen to become Adler's successor as the senior leader of the New York Society, upon Adler's death in 1933. Adler and Elliott provided a study in complementary contrasts. Elliott, who hailed from Illinois, came from an abolitionist family with deep Midwestern roots. While Adler was philosophical and aloof in his personal relations, Elliott immersed himself in the grit of human experience. Never a high-minded orator, Elliott's personalism exemplified a new style of Ethical Culture leader as social worker.

Elliott chose to live in the proletarian, rough-and-tumble neighborhood of Chelsea, on New York's Lower West Side among the Irish immigrant poor. Believing in the inherent goodness of the common man, he was committed to helping the powerless learn to help themselves.

Elliott's work centered on building the Hudson Guild Settlement, which brought him into daily contact with the destitute, youth gangs, and criminals. With financial assistance from Ethical Culture's uptown members, Elliott was able to build printing shops and create an employment bureau, a model tenement of its own, and a 500-acre farm in western New Jersey.

Through his prominence and success as a spokesperson for the disadvantaged, Elliott developed notable associations and friendships, which he used to good advantage. Frequently, he would appeal to New York's mayor Fiorello La Guardia or Eleanor Roosevelt to help win bail or a pardon for a prisoner whose case he was championing. Elliott's intercession on behalf of imperiled individuals took him to Berlin in 1938 to help secure the release from the Nazis of Dr. Wilhelm Boerner and Walter Eckstein, leaders of the Vienna Ethical Society. This experience inspired the New York Society to establish programs to help refugees adjust to American society while supplying them with needed food and clothing. Out of this work grew the Good Neighbor Association, a national effort with Elliott as chairman, New York Society member James Hart as executive, and Eleanor Roosevelt as honorary chairman. Though well launched, the association's work was cut short in 1941 by America's entry into World War II.

Through his productive career, Elliott bridged two worlds: He was a beloved figure to members of Ethical Culture and its young people, and a local hero to the poor on whose behalf he so arduously labored.

THE MOVEMENT DECLINES

Elliott's style and commitments came at a time of change in the class character and philosophical underpinnings of Ethical Culture in the decades preceding Adler's demise. Idealism, which had been the regnant philosophy in nineteenth-century Europe, reached a dead end on America's shores, to be replaced by variants of naturalism, instrumentalism, and pragmatism. William James and John Dewey were the major exponents of this distinctly "American" approach in philosophy, inspiring former leader Edward Ericson to observe that Ethical Culture was "the movement that Adler built and Dewey, through his followers, so quickly inherited." With this shift in ground, Ethical Culture began to assume the mantle of a "humanist" organization, a term Adler shunned for its emphasis on human ends devoid of the spiritualizing dynamics inspired by transcendental ideals.

As new immigrants found their way to Ethical Culture, Adler's idealism simultaneously receded. The movement became a broad tent under which liberals, agnostics, atheists, Socialists, and activists could find a welcoming home. Adler's death also spurred a problem of succession and focus for the Ethical Movement, as preoccupation with institutional concerns grew, while the self-confidence characteristic of Ethical Culture in early path-breaking decades began to diminish. The social mission of Ethical Culture continued nevertheless as the defining center of its identity and activity.

ETHICAL CULTURE'S ACHIEVEMENTS

Although its precise origins are somewhat vague, there can be no doubt that Ethical Culture played a pivotal role in the founding of the National Association for the Advancement of Colored People (NAACP) in 1909. Elliott, Spencer, Salter, and Moskowitz were signatories of the NAACP's founding charter and represented Ethical Culture's early interest in race relations. Adler, who was a frequent lecturer at black colleges, organized the world's first international conference on race, held in London in 1911. Adler himself was one of the two American delegates to that conference; WE.B. Du Bois, the great

African-American intellectual and activist, was the other.

Roger Baldwin, who was first introduced to Ethical Culture in St. Louis and later affiliated with the New York Society, founded the American Civil Liberties Union in 1920 as a response to government repression during the Palmer Raids and to render support to conscientious objectors to World War I. Elliott was a key participant in the ACLU's founding group, initiating a long-standing relationship between the two organizations.

Between 1893 and Adler's death in 1933, sixteen new individuals entered leadership, full or part time, to carry forward Ethical Culture's mission. Most of these leaders, such as David Muzzey, a noted historian who taught at Columbia University for many years, and Percival Chubb, who worked in Societies in England, New York, and for decades in St. Louis, distinguished themselves as educators and orators. Another activist to be added to the list that included Elliott, Spencer, and Moskowitz was Henry Neumann. Neumann became a leader of the Brooklyn Society in 1911 and served the Ethical movement professionally as a much-beloved personality until his death in 1966. Neumann, whose pacifism had caused rifts in the Ethical movement during World War I, was not less committed throughout his life to advocating for democratic socialism in the mold of Norman Thomas.

It was the youngest of the new generation of leaders recruited under Adler's tutelage who would go furthest in identifying Ethical Culture with progressive social change in the mid- and late decades of the twentieth century. Algernon D. Black, a son of working-class Russian Jews, was born in 1900. Educated at the Ethical Culture schools and receiving his B.A. in economics from Harvard, Black personified an activism that blended moral idealism with a strong economic analysis of social injustice.

A man of dynamic and charismatic presence and grandiloquent oratory, Black became synonymous with Ethical Culture for uncountable thousands who heard him from the Ethical platform and for decades as a commentator on New York's WQXR radio station. Although his activist commitments ranged broadly, Black became identified primarily with the causes of racial justice, workers' rights, affordable housing, civil liberties, and antifascism, and he was a forceful paragon of the democratic left in America, the Cold War era, and the civil rights movement. Though never a strong institution builder within Ethical Culture, Black taught ethics for four decades at the Fieldston School, and his skills as a storyteller helped to mold the values of generations of children.

In the 1930s, Black spoke out forcefully against fascism in Spain, as he did against the Nazi onslaught in Europe several years later. Often a polarizing force in a movement hesitant about ideological zeal, Black supported a Worker's Fellowship in the New York Society, which many suspected had been infiltrated by the Communist Party in the 1940s.

Typical of Black's activism was the early assistance he gave to striking silk workers who were trying to organize in Paterson and Lodi, New Jersey. In 1941, Black became the founder and chairperson of the Citizens Committee for Harlem, and he was a prime mover in the development of the New York State, and later, the National, Committee Against Discrimination in Housing. Black served for years on the board of the NAACP and became vice president of the organization in 1950.

Both the leadership and laity of Ethical Culture have found the cause of civil liberties close to the center of the movement's commitment to preserving human dignity and freedom. Black, who had worked on behalf of labor with Roger Baldwin, served for years on the board of the American Civil Liberties Union, as John Elliott did before him, and as colleague Sheldon Ackley would later. His dedication to civic activism was duly recognized when Mayor John Lindsay of New York appointed Algernon Black as the chairperson of the controversial and short-lived Civilian Police Review Board.

No project reflected the scope of Black's political vision and the depth of his humanism more than the creation of the Encampment for Citizenship. In the mid-1940s, Black initiated the Work Camps for Democracy, which blossomed into the Encampment for Citizenship soon after World War II. Infused with the energies of suffragist Anita Politzer and the enthusiastic endorsement of Eleanor Roosevelt, the Encampment served as a radical experiment in democratic living and action in the years before the dawn of the modern civil rights movement. The Encampment brought together in a residential setting first college-age and then high school students from different racial, ethnic, and class backgrounds for classes and workshops in progressive community action. Classes and workshops were held in various sites in the United States, and participants were invited to Hyde Park, New York, to meet with Mrs. Roosevelt. For fifty years, the Encampment nurtured distinguished alumni of its own, including the activist congressman Allard Lowenstein; David Rothenberg, guiding light

of the ex-prisoners' support organization the Fortune Society; Simeon Golar; and Eleanor Holmes Norton. Golar and Norton would become commissioners for human rights in New York City, and later Norton served as Washington, D.C.'s, nonvoting representative to Congress.

The role of Ethical Culture in providing a voice against the repression of the McCarthy era cannot be overstated. According to a movement historian, Howard B. Radest, "When McCarthyism was at its height, the New York Platform was one of the few places where public criticism was heard." Black's protest was the most outspoken of all, but he was joined in denouncing the Red Scare by Neumann and his colleague in New York, the liberal Deweyan Jerome Nathanson.

During the 1960s, Ethical Culture plied its work on the progressive landscape, in civil rights, in organizing against the American war in Vietnam, and in safeguarding civil liberties. Primarily through its national organization, the American Ethical Union, Ethical Culture continued to support public education, the separation of church and state, the rights of nontheistic conscientious objectors, and women's rights, and was especially active in securing a woman's right to a safe and legal abortion. Often this work was carried forward in coalition with kindred organizations, such as the Unitarian-Universalist Association and the American Humanist Association.

In the last decades of the twentieth century and into the current one, the cutting edge of Ethical Culture as a social movement has been more difficult to sustain. Unlike its golden period in the nineteenth century, many human services that it had pioneered have been absorbed by government programs, especially since the decades of the New Deal and the Great Society. Moreover, peopled primarily by middle-class professionals today, Ethical Culture lacks the formidable financial resources it once claimed, while volunteer activism has become broadly characteristic of the contemporary American ethos.

Although the history of Ethical Culture is most readily recounted through the initiatives of its illustrious individuals, it has always been a congregational movement, fulfilling the social and religious needs of its members and associates.

Today, Ethical Culture remains a progressive redoubt standing against the irrationalism and intensive subjectivism of the postmodern era. Its thirty societies in the United States serve as vital communities for humanists sensitive to the pressures of excessive consumerism in American life. Through its moral education programs for children, its humanistic ceremonies celebrating the life passages of birth, marriage, and death, and its enduring emphasis on the primacy of ethics and human dignity, Ethical Culture remains a distinctive and significant movement on the American landscape.

As Ethical Culture looks to the future, it rests upon a proud historical legacy. As the only "religion of humanity" founded in the nineteenth century to endure into the twenty-first, Ethical Culture, though never claiming more than 6,000 members, has served as a pioneering "gadfly" movement in American social history. Through its platforms, schools, camps, and numerous social institutions it has founded but which have achieved independent lives of their own,

Ethical Culture has improved the well-being of countless thousands, while inspiring many more to live meaningful lives of deeper moral and social commitment.

Joseph Chuman

BIBLIOGRAPHY

Friess, Horace. *Felix Adler and Ethical Culture*. New York: Columbia University Press, 1981.

Kraut, Benny. *From Reform Judaism to Ethical Culture: The Religious Evolution of Felix Adler*. Cincinnati, OH: Hebrew Union College Press, 1979.

Radest, Howard B. *Toward Common Ground*. New York: Ungar, 1969.

HEALTH FOOD MOVEMENT

CHARACTERISTICS OF THE HEALTH FOOD MOVEMENT

From its origins in the nineteenth century, the American health food movement has been loosely organized and diverse in character. Some scholars argue that the movement is more accurately described as a consumer lifestyle consisting of the similar yet disconnected food choices of millions of individual shoppers. On the contrary, the historical and contemporary significance of the health food movement is much more meaningful than the creation of a mere "market niche." The health tradition, in fact, has a long history of activist leaders and committed followers, cogent belief systems and ideologies, a network of organizations, independent businesses, and corporations that distribute nutritional information and health food products, and increasingly, millions of adherents whose everyday food choices are informed by ethical, environmental, political, and nutritional considerations.

Several important trends have marked the health food movement from its inception. The health food tradition is rooted in three major American reform movements of the nineteenth and twentieth centuries. Its leaders, ideologies, and organizations emerged during the Second Great Awakening, became popularized and institutionalized from the late nineteenth century through the Progressive Era, and matured in the wake of the cultural and political upheavals of the l960s and 1970s. The contemporary cultural climate and political issues of these major reform eras determined the character of health reforms in each period. For instance, Protestant reformers such as William Metcalfe, "moral physiologists" including Sylvester Graham and William A. Alcott, and new religious sects such as the Seventh-day Adventists led by Ellen G. White and James Harvey Kellogg preached a message of health for morality and salvation, giving the movement a distinctly religious and ethical tone dur-

ing the nineteenth century. Public health, sanitation, and disease prevention occupied the attention of health reformers during the Progressive Era. The cultural and political radicalism of American youth, their critique of mass, homogenized food production, and their concern for the environment intertwined to inspire and popularize the natural foods movement of the 1960s and 1970s.

Health reformers in every period have been both reactionary and visionary. Consistently throughout the nineteenth and twentieth centuries, they critiqued America's food production and distribution system, challenged conventional medical doctors, and questioned the authority of scientific experts to decide matters of health, nutrition, and healing. Health reformers have just as often offered idealistic, ethical, and moral visions for individual and societal reform. Arguing that the solution to societal ills lay in cultivating the relationship between physical health, spiritual well-being, and human potential, health reformers in every period have optimistically searched for a holistic way to maximize human performance. Eating certain healthy foods and abstaining from others, they believed, could result in a physically healthy and spiritually enlightened society. By the end of the twentieth century, environmentally minded health food advocates argued that by choosing carefully the foods they consumed, Americans could live their politics "365 days a year, three times a day," contributing to personal vitality while taking social responsibility in an interdependent global community.

THE "CHRISTIAN PHYSIOLOGISTS" AND THE HOLISTIC TRADITION

The nineteenth-century American health food movement emerged from the religious revivalism of the Second Great Awakening. Reformers like the Protestant minister William Metcalfe, temperance and health food advocate Sylvester Graham, and physician William A. Alcott encouraged Americans to follow dietary restrictions and other hygienic reforms (temperance, loose clothing, fresh air, exercise) as part of a plan for improved moral, spiritual, and physical health. Their ideas about health were rooted in the common belief that caring for the body, "the temple of God," was a sacred, religious duty. Historians consider these three "Christian physiologists" to be the founders of the American health food tradition.

Metcalfe, an English immigrant and founder of the Bible Christian Church in Philadelphia (1817), was one of the first reformers to argue for a direct correlation between food choices and spiritual health; in addition, he brought vegetarianism to the United States through his sermons and his book *Abstinence from the Flesh of Animals* (1827). In 1830, Metcalfe hired temperance reformer Sylvester Graham (1794–1851) to lecture at the Bible Christian Church. Combining his teachings on temperance with Metcalfe's proscriptions for health, Graham developed a regimen for healthy living based on strict dietary and hygienic guidelines. He claimed that all "stimulation" was potentially health threatening and warned Americans to avoid "flesh foods," alcohol, tea, coffee, spices, and frequent sex; the proper diet, Graham contended, consisted of wheat bread and grains, fresh fruits, vegetables, and nuts. Graham was especially critical of commercially processed breads, arguing that greedy bakers contaminated bread with "bean flour, peas and potatoes, chalk, pipe clay, and the plaster of Paris." Instead of purchasing bread in the market, Graham advised Americans to bake their own whole-grain "Graham bread." His holistic teachings, more secular than religious in nature, became so popular that contemporaries labeled them "Grahamism."

Although Graham's name became synonymous with the early health food movement, he did not work alone. His contemporary and cohort, Connecticut physician William A. Alcott (1798–1859), played an important role in the movement, warning Americans to stay away from "stimulating" foods, especially meat. Influenced by his cousin Amos Bronson Alcott, who founded the vegetarian commune Fruitlands, William Alcott argued that a "vegetable diet lies at the basis of all reform, whether civil, social, moral, or religion." In approximately 100 publications on diet, health, and ethics, he steadfastly advanced his simple argument: you are what you eat! Alcott warned Americans that "diseased food causes disease in the people who use it."

Graham and Alcott proactively advocated self-responsibility for disease prevention and health, but their philosophies also represented the popular reaction and disgust that Americans held for the painful and ineffective conventional medical treatments of the day, such as blistering, bleeding, and purging. It is likely that the broad appeal of the Christian physiologists relied on their ability to synthesize useful practices from both conventional and alternative medicine and offer the public more choices for health care. For instance, Graham and Alcott combined ideas from Shradrach Ricketson's *Means of Preserving and Preventing Disease* (1806) and botanist Samuel Thomson's *New Guide to Health; or Botanic Family Physician* (1822); they also incorporated homeopathy and hydrotherapy into their teachings.

In 1837, Graham and Alcott took the first steps toward institutionalizing the health food movement. They founded the American Physiology Association to promote holistic health reforms and established a health food store that sold Graham bread, fruits, nuts, and vegetables grown in "virgin, unfertilized soil." They also sponsored "physiological boarding houses," requiring tenants to follow a vegetarian diet, sleep on hard beds, take cold baths, and exercise moderately.

INSTITUTIONALIZING THE HEALTH FOOD MOVEMENT

As Grahamism reached the apex of its popularity at mid-century, American reformers supplemented its holistic philosophy with hydrotherapy (water treatments that included bathing, exercising, massage, and sweating). Joel Shew, a New York physician, opened the first hydropathic establishment in 1844, and by 1870, 200 "water-cure" institutions existed in the United States. The most important of these resorts, Our Home on the Hillside, opened by James Caleb Jackson (1814–1895) in Dansville, New York, offered visitors a combination of Grahamism, hydropathic cures, and social activities such as lectures, concerts, dances, and plays. Our Home also marketed a line of health foods, including a coffee substitute, Graham bread, and Granula—a nonperishable alternative to Graham bread.

One of the most important visitors to Our Home was Ellen G. White, a founder and prophetess of the Seventh-day Adventist Church (SDA). White had begun to incorporate the ideas of the early Christian physiologists into the doctrines of the SDA church by the late 1840s, but after a visit to Our Home followed

REVIEW OF *HYDROPATHY; OR THE WATER CURE*

Hydropathy, or the water cure, became a popular medical treatment in the mid-nineteenth century. Joel Shew began his hydropathic practice in 1844 in New York and a year later expanded his practice to New Lebanon Springs, New York. Shew was a prolific writer and contributor to many publications on hydropathy and water cures.

10. *HYDROPATHY; or the Water Cure: Its principles, processes and modes of treatment.* Compiled in part from the most eminent authors, ancient and modern, on the subject. Together with an account of the latest methods adopted by Priessnitz, & c. By Joel Shew, M.D. Third edition. John Wiley, 161 Broadway.

Hydropathy, as a curative science, has certainly made greater progress in the last few years than has either Allopathy or Homeopathy, and we think for the general preservation of health, as well as a remedy for most disorders of the system, its growing reputation is deserved. That the medical science has been so backward in improvement in an age when all others have made such rapid advances, may be taken as evidence of the existence of some radical error in principles, and want of confidence in its professors—certain it is, that when personally afflicted, none show so great distrust of the efficacy of remedies they daily prescribe others, as physicians themselves. That many acute diseases will temporarily yield to a certain course of treatment, and that experience in relation to the physical condition of the patient as a guide to the application of those remedies seems to be the sum total of medical science as it exists. Beyond that there is no help in medicine. How helpless does the profession appear in the presence of the prevailing epidemic, which now for the third time is devastating the country! That Hydropathy, which eschews all drugs, is the true system, we do not assert; on the other hand, with many constitutions it does not agree at all. In very many, however, it is of great service, and few can read the work of Dr. Shew without being attracted by its merits.

Source: "Hydropathy; or the Water Cure: Its Principles, Processes and Modes of Treatment. By Joel Shew, M.D." *The United States Democratic Review* 25:133 (July 1849).

by several prophetic visions on health, White convinced her parishioners to fund and build the Western Health Reform Institute in 1866 (later renamed the Battle Creek Medical and Surgical Sanitarium). Destined to become the leading scientific institution of the health food and vegetarian movements, the San (commonly used name for this first Seventh-day Adventist health institution in Battle Creek, Michigan) functioned in obscurity until 1876, when Dr. James Harvey Kellogg (1852–1943) assumed leadership, announcing that the institution would become a "university of health" where "people learn to stay well." To fulfill this mission, Kellogg established an experimental kitchen at the San where he churned out the nation's first popular cold breakfast cereals—Granola and Sanitas Corn Flakes, a palatable peanut butter, and high-protein meat substitutes like Battle Creek Steaks and Battle Creek Scallops. Through institutions like the Battle Creek San, which had hosted 300,000 visitors by 1943, including President William Howard Taft, J.C. Penney, and Montgomery Ward, SDAs institutionalized, popularized, and legitimized the health food movement of the nineteenth century, creating an infrastructure of research institutions, hospitals, and health food stores staffed by experts trained in health and nutrition.

Noting the popularity of the health food movement in his book *Eating for Strength* (1888), Dr. M.L. Holbrook wrote: "In no period of the world's history has there ever been so deep an interest in the subject of foods as at the present. . . . It would almost seem as if the time had nearly arrived when mankind would eat to live, would feed themselves so as to nourish their bodies most perfectly and render themselves capable of the most labor, and least liable to diseases." Holbrook's reference to food as the basis of worker efficiency and disease prevention signaled a turning point in the movement as Progressive Era health reformers, armed with scientific expertise and a determination to bring order to America's burgeoning immigrant-industrial cities, turned to public health issues such as sanitation, disease prevention, and regulation of industrial food production. By the 1930s, the holistic health message of Grahamism and the Christian physiologists, though institutionalized by the SDA Church, had faded into obscurity in the mind of the American public behind the harsh realities of world war, a decade of cultural liberalism, and the Great Depression.

JOHN HARVEY KELLOGG (1852–1943)

John Harvey Kellogg, a leading advocate of healthy living and nutrition, was born on February 26, 1852, in Tyrone, Michigan, to John Preston Kellogg and Anne Jeanette Stanley, devout Seventh-day Adventists. In 1866, at the Health Reform Institute, Kellogg was educated in the water cure, known as hydrotherapy, which he later rejected. After receiving medical training at Bellevue Medical College in New York and becoming a medical doctor, Kellogg became editor of the Seventh-day Adventist monthly, *Health Reformer*, renamed *Good Health* in 1879. Dr. Kellogg returned to Michigan and in 1876 became superintendent of the Battle Creek Sanitarium.

Kellogg developed a "biologic living" dietary approach that was based on the notion of "natural living," vegetarianism, asceticism, and abstinence. Later, with his brother Will, Kellogg produced and marketed corn flake and rice flake cereals sold through mail order. The company, initially known as Sanitas Food Company, grew dramatically. Conflicts between the two brothers led to a formal split in 1906. Despite legal challenges, Will gained rights to the renamed W.K. Kellogg Company, which would become a multinational cereal company. John, less successful in his business than Will, established the Battle Creek Food Company, which sold a variety of health foods, including coffee substitutes and soybean-derived milk. By 1907, Kellogg was excommunicated from the Seventh-day Adventist Church because of his independence of thinking and differences over his business ventures. A prolific writer, Kellogg actively participated in the eugenics movement, founding the Race Betterment Foundation. Kellogg died at the age of ninety-one on December 14, 1943. At the time of his death, Kellogg held more than thirty patents for food products and various exercise, diagnostic, and therapeutic machines.

Immanuel Ness

THE "COUNTERCUISINE"

By the mid-twentieth century, the health food movement consisted of a few institutions, such as the SDA church, local vegetarian societies, and determined individuals such as J.I. Rodale and Adelle Davis. Generally referred to as "health nuts" in the popular culture, they kept the movement alive until the late 1960s, when America's youth, swept up in a maelstrom of cultural and political radicalism, recognized

that "the personal is political," consciously reconsidered their food choices, and reinvigorated the health food movement.

The SDAs continued to play an important role in the health food movement throughout the twentieth century by establishing research institutions such as Loma Linda University, health food corporations like Worthington Foods, the vegetarian restaurant chain Country Life, and numerous publications on health and nutrition. Independent health food stores served similar functions in communities across the nation; distributing health food products, including meat substitutes, teaching interested Americans about alternative food choices, and serving as community centers for health food advocates.

Although they were dismissed as "crackpots" and conspiracy theorists by scientists and the medical professionals during the 1950s, pioneering health food reformers such as J.I. Rodale and Adelle Davis continued to criticize America's system of "unnatural" food production and encouraged consumers to search for alternatives. Rodale, founder of the Rodale Press and publisher of *Organic Gardening and Farming* and *Prevention*, lambasted mechanized monoculture agriculture and decried the use of dangerous agrochemicals in food production. Americans, he argued, should turn to "organic farming": a system of sustainable agriculture that acknowledged the ecological interdependence of soil, plants, animals, and people. Davis, also a critic of food production, argued that food corporations were poisoning Americans with dangerous additives like cyclamate.

Most Americans refused to hear the warnings of these "health nuts." Although Rodale preached organic and Davis warned about the dangers of additives, middle-class Americans baked casseroles with canned soups, enjoyed canned vegetables and processed cheeses, and gobbled down convenience foods—a Swanson's TV Dinner of turkey and stuffing could be had for only ninety-eight cents. Most important, Americans "cooked out" and consumed massive amounts of meat: sales of outdoor cooking equipment had topped 30 million dollars a year by the mid-1950s, and meat consumption rose from 121.7 pounds per year in 1930 to 160 pounds per year in 1970.

As historian Warren Belasco has written in *Appetite for Change: How the Counterculture Took on the Food Industry, 1966–1988* (1989), "In the late 1960s, young cultural rebels began to turn against mainstream foodways" to develop a countercuisine. The counterculture's experimentation with health foods began with a rejection of standardized, fabricated, convenience foods like canned vegetables, Tang, Carnation Instant Breakfast, and Pringles, in favor of fresh fruits and vegetables, whole grains, beans, brown rice, and yogurt. Finding grains, rice, and beans in bulk at natural food stores and cooperatives, scooping out what one needed, and labeling the product fit well with the youth culture's search for eccentric, "authentic" experiences. At the same time, the product diversity, absence of brand names, and minimal packaging became a means by which to reject mass food production and homogenized supermarkets like Safeway, Giant, and A&P. Between 5,000 and 10,000 food cooperatives opened between 1969 and 1979, grossing an estimated $500 million per year.

The countercuisine became increasingly politicized after 1970 as activists considered the consequences of diet for American society and the environment; radicals criticized food production, and extremists such as Dick Gregory suggested a connection between poor diet and American intervention in Vietnam. Events at People's Park, an oil spill off the California coast, smog alerts in Los Angeles, news stories on DDT and cyclamates, and Paul Ehrlich's book *The Population Bomb* (1968), which predicted soil erosion, worldwide famine, and nuclear war from "runaway food and population pressures," catapulted environmentalism to the top of the radical agenda. Francis Lappé's *Diet for a Small Planet* (1971), in turn, directly linked food choices to environmentalism by explaining the global ecological consequences of a meat-based diet. Lappé argued that the nation's vegetable protein crops (grains and soy beans) should be consumed directly by humans instead of stock animals. Explaining that "an acre of cereals can produce five times more protein than an acre devoted to meat production; legumes can produce ten times more; leafy vegetables fifteen times more," Lappé claimed that by adopting a more agriculturally efficient vegetarian diet, Americans could alleviate world hunger. Lappé's hope that collective personal choices could make a social impact, her evidence that a vegetarian diet was nutritionally adequate, and her collection of recipes inspired and guided a generation of vegetarians and health food advocates. Dick Gregory, in *Dick Gregory's Natural Diet for Folks Who Eat: Cookin' with Mother Nature* (1973), argued that diet was at the root of America's foreign policy problems: "I think one of the reasons we have so much overweight and overeating in these United States is that America is insecure. In her security, America raids the refrigerators of Southeast Asia, wipes out the pantry of Latin America, munches

and snacks on the freedom of people all over the world."

MAINSTREAMING THE MOVEMENT

By the mid-1970s, the values and consumer preferences of the counterculture had become a powerful political lifestyle, defining health foods as foods with no synthetic ingredients, minimal processing, in as close to a whole and natural state as possible. As a result, the counterculture laid the foundation for the growth of the multibillion-dollar natural foods industry. Mo Siegel, founder of Celestial Seasonings Corporation, was one of the first "hip" capitalists to turn the tastes and philosophies of the countercuisine into big profits. His company had its beginnings in 1969 when Siegel, a nineteen-year-old hippie, and his friends conjured their first blend of teas called "Mo's 36 Herb Tea" in a barn outside of Boulder, Colorado, packaged it in hand-sewn muslin bags, and sold it to the Green Mountain Grainery—one of Boulder's health food stores. The success of hip entrepreneurs like Siegel depended on their ability to appeal to counterculture values by marketing their companies as socially useful and morally legitimate institutions. Siegel, for example, advertised his company's mission statement—"to create and sell healthful, naturally oriented products that nurture people's bodies and uplift their souls, and to make the world a better place by unselfishly serving the public"—and it quickly paid off. In 1970, he earned $2,000; in 1973, the year that Celestial Seasonings incorporated, the company made a profit of $1.3 million; by 1978, the company employed 200 people and earned $9 million per a year.

The success of Celestial Seasonings and other hip health foods corporations represented the mainstreaming of the health food movement and the birth of the "Lifestyles of Health and Sustainability Market" (LOHAS), a $230 billion industry, in 2002. Several factors propelled the health food movement into mainstream American culture after 1980. Many medical doctors, including Andrew Weil, Dean Ornish, and Julian Whitaker, argued for healthy eating as a central component of preventative and alternative medicine, giving the holistic philosophies of health foods reformers the authority of scientific expertise. The American Dietetic Association officially endorsed vegetarianism in the 1990s, and the U.S. government replaced the four food groups guidelines, which had emphasized the importance of meat and dairy products, with the food pyramid, informing the public that a healthy diet consists predominantly of vegetables, legumes, and fruit. Finally, Congress passed the Federal Organic Foods Production Act in 1990, and the United States Department of Agriculture implemented the legislation in 2002. At the core of the LOHAS market are 10 million vegetarians and 8,000 natural foods retailers, including the natural foods giants Wild Oats Corporation and Whole Foods Corporation. One-half of conventional grocers now carry organic foods, and Americans' fast-food choices include wraps, smoothies, and garden burgers. As the health food movement approaches full circle from its religious infancy through its grassroots adolescence to its current status as an important retail market, it faces many complex challenges heading into the twentieth century. As a progressive force in American society, health reformers must deal with new and pressing issues such as the genetic modification of food, the preservation of community-based organic farms and natural foods outlets, and the co-opting of natural foods concepts by multinational corporations.

Amy L. Scott

BIBLIOGRAPHY

Belasco, Warren J. *Appetite for Change: How the Counterculture Took on the Food Industry, 1966–1988.* New York: Pantheon Books, 1989.

Ehrlich, Paul R. *The Population Bomb.* New York: Ballantine Books, 1968.

Engs, Ruth Clifford. *Clean Living Movements: American Cycles of Health Reform.* Westport, CT: Praeger, 2000.

Gregerson, Jon. *Vegetarianism: A History.* Fremont, CA: Jain, 1994.

Gregory, Dick. *Dick Gregory's Natural Diet for Folks Who Eat: Cookin' with Mother Nature.* New York: Harper & Row, 1973.

Holbrook, Martin Luther. *Eating for Strength.* New York: M. L. Holbrook & Co., 1888.

Lappé, Frances Moore. *Diet for a Small Planet.* 10th Anniversary Edition. New York: Ballantine Books, 1982.

Maurer, Donna. *Vegetarianism: Movement or Moment?* Philadelphia: Temple University Press, 2002.

Money, John. *The Destroying Angel: Sex, Fitness & Food in the Legacy of Degeneracy Theory, Graham Crackers, Kellogg's Corn Flakes & American Health History.* Buffalo, NY: Prometheus Books, 1985.

Whorton, James C. *Crusaders for Fitness: The History of American Health Reformers.* Princeton, NJ: Princeton University Press, 1982.

COUNTERCULTURE MOVEMENT
1960s–1970s

Mention of "hippies" or "the counterculture" often conjures an image of long-haired young men wearing tie-dyed tee-shirts and young women dressed in "granny" skirts, smoking marijuana, enamored of rock and roll, and flaunting their sexual freedom to the dismay of their elders. This reduction of the counterculture to the hedonistic pursuit of "sex, drugs, and rock and roll" often obscures the complexity, diversity, and seriousness of the phenomenon. Scholars are only now beginning to examine the counterculture as an important form of social protest during the 1960s and 1970s.

LOCATING THE COUNTERCULTURE

What place should the counterculture occupy in the history of American social movements? Who were the "hippies," and what did they contribute to the panoply of movements for social change that arose in the 1960s? This question has proved difficult to answer because the counterculture was a diffuse phenomenon that defies categorical understanding.

The cultural radicalism of the hippies and the instrumentalist politics of the New Left originated among distinct populations of radical youth in the early and mid-1960s. However, hippies and New Leftists interacted intensely with one another during the mid-1960s, as youth radicalism grew exponentially on college campuses and in urban, bohemian enclaves. However, by the late 1960s, neither formation constituted a discrete population. So many New Leftists incorporated countercultural styles, projects (such as communal living), and analysis into their organizing efforts, and so many hippies likewise found themselves moved to participate in demonstrations and to speak out against the machinations of corporate America that the two formations became integral parts of a larger whole. Therefore, it is most accurate to say that the counterculture and the New Left be-

came *tendencies* within a larger movement of Euro-American youth activists, known at the time simply as "the Movement." What, then, distinguished these two tendencies from one another?

The New Left took a materialist approach to the analysis of the problems of American society, seeing inequality and individual alienation as problems primarily of *structure*, and only secondarily as problems of individual *consciousness*. They adopted Marxism's insistence that individual beliefs and feelings derive from the way in which society organizes power, work, and resources. People who lack the resources to force other powerful people to heed their concerns *feel* powerless and insignificant because elites exclude them from participation in decision making about what should be produced, how it should be produced, and how valuable such work is to society as a whole. These fundamental "relations of production," in turn, structure all other social relationships, even those not directly pertaining to work. Accordingly, New Leftists sought to reverse these feelings of powerlessness by organizing poor people for united action.

Counterculturalists developed an analysis of America's social ills as originating primarily in the repressive organization of individual *consciousness*. In their view, inequalities of social structure figured more as the effect, rather than the cause, of the profound alienation from which all Americans suffered. For most citizens, the material abundance and technological sophistication of the post–World War II period seemed to confirm the power of science to explain the universe in rationalistic terms. Yet, hippies noted profound incongruities between public and private life. They argued that urban life alienated citizens of industrial civilization from the natural world, and thus from their own fundamental

These "hippies" gathering at a site in Sultan, Washington, on September 3, 1968, for the Sky River Rock Festival, find themselves dancing in mud created by heavy rains. *(AP Wide World Photos)*

nature as members of an animal species. Furthermore, they argued, the heavily bureaucratized routines and authoritarian structure of work, and the emotionally empty practice of modern religion, reduced human beings to what they regarded as a state of spiritual passivity.

To compensate for this alienation, advanced industrial society offered Americans the opportunity to participate in a consumerist regime, driven not by genuine demand, but by a propagandistic marketing apparatus. As a result, said the hippies, Americans lived in a conformist society, and one increasingly devoid of genuine beauty and opportunities to develop individual creativity. Furthermore, the deluge of con-

sumer products and marketing messages, combined with the anxieties attendant to career and property ownership, made genuine alternatives to the status quo increasingly difficult to imagine.

The appropriate response, as hippies saw it, was to liberate the instinctual, human animal from the self-imposed repression attendant to "progress." The individual quest to recover their repressed, animal instincts, to experience spiritual ecstasy, and to infuse daily life with artistic beauty, generosity, and genuine fellow feeling, would prepare the individual to initiate new ways of organizing all of the facets of social life. The new, liberated society would rise spontaneously amid the old.

THE COUNTERCULTURE'S DIVERSE FORMS OF OPPOSITION

Hippies agreed widely on the need for the liberation of consciousness. However, they never reached consensus on the best means by which to accomplish that liberation. Two primary schools of thought about countercultural praxis emerged among the most committed cultural radicals.

Beginning in 1966, a group known as the Diggers became the most celebrated advocates of anarchism as the most effective means by which to transform the American consciousness. The Diggers defined freedom as the complete absence of imposed rules. They believed that imposed authority of any kind robbed individuals of the freedom to organize their lives according to the dictates of self-knowledge and experience. Imposed rules also robbed individuals of the *responsibilities* that came with freedom: to deal with others in complete good faith, honesty, and with brotherly generosity; to accept others' difference from oneself; and to accept the consequences that followed from one's choices.

The Diggers charged that Americans suffered from an unhealthy dependence on leaders and institutions to make choices for them. Americans, they said, also behaved hypocritically in their private lives—for example, proclaiming the sanctity of the family while practicing adultery. It would be better, said these hippie anarchists, to abolish *both* institutions and allow free individuals to negotiate relationships on a more authentic basis.

Most of the founding Diggers had been members of the radical San Francisco Mime Troupe. Dissatisfied with the Troupe's structure and practice, several members, including Peter Berg, Emmett Grogan, Judy Goldhaft, and Peter Cohon (later, Coyote), broke away to experiment with the application of theatrical techniques to the process of changing people's consciousness on a massive scale. Instead of presenting plays on a stage, which audiences could regard as fictions separate from the realities of everyday life, the Diggers proclaimed themselves "life-actors."

They practiced a theater of the streets in which there was to be no dividing line between the audience and the actors, and in which participants could experience, at firsthand, a utopian world in which goods changed hands without money and in which life-actors followed their own deepest impulses, and not a script written and directed by others. The Diggers regarded the hippies of the Haight-Ashbury district as a population who lacked only the Diggers'

dynamic example in order to become the crest of a rising wave of liberated individual consciousness, which would gradually engulf all members of "straight" (unliberated, nonhippie) society.

Anarchist hippies, however, were a minority in the counterculture. More numerous were those who attempted to achieve the liberation of human consciousness through the disciplined practice of mysticism: the conviction that religious faith requires not only belief in God, but also the direct experience of complete union with the Godhead, achieved through a process of mental discipline. Mystical hippies sought to reverse what they regarded as the spiritual death encouraged by scientific rationalism. They cultivated a seemingly limitless variety of religious beliefs in their efforts to counteract advanced industrial civilization's loss of faith in the spiritual and the metaphysical.

For some mystical hippies, the search for complete union with the Infinite took the form of a commitment to an established religious tradition or collective, such as Krishna Consciousness, the monastic forms of Buddhism, or the youth-oriented Christianity of the Jesus People. Frequently, however, mystical hippies followed spiritual teachers who advocated a syncretic philosophy, borrowing and combining concepts from diverse religious traditions, old and new. In addition, countercultural mystics sometimes pursued union with the Infinite through use of the powerful mind-altering drugs, especially LSD.

As students of the counterculture, we must not discount (as some authorities did at the time, and as some still do today) the seriousness of purpose with which countercultural youth sometimes approached the use of such drugs. At the same time, we must also realize that the risks inherent in LSD use were not then fully understood. Even those who approached its use with great reverence and respect for its mind-altering power sometimes suffered disabling psychotic reactions, occasionally leading to suicide. Such outcomes were more likely among those who used the drug not for religious purposes but simply for the thrill of the experience.

Through their pursuit of direct connection with the Godhead, mystical hippies sought, as did the anarchist Diggers, to transform the consciousness of all human beings. Widespread spiritual enlightenment would, they believed, lead to the withering away of institutions and practices that promoted human alienation. In their place would arise new forms of community and society promoting the sacredness of human life and the natural environment, and emphasizing the spiritual dimension of life over pursuit of material possessions.

ORIGINS

Although participants in the counterculture often sincerely believed that they had created the forms of countercultural radicalism from whole cloth, historical analysis shows that their originality lay less in their creation of new cultural forms and more in their capacity to combine existing cultural forms in new and imaginative ways. According to historian Laurence Veysey, the division of the counterculture into anarchistic and mystical schools of thought followed a pattern evident, since the nineteenth century, in the American tradition of cultural radicalism. A brief examination of two major influences on the counterculture reveals the debt that its proponents owed to earlier generations.

Historian Timothy Miller has carefully traced some elements of hippie communalism to the Catholic Worker movement and the School for Living, both of which originated during the era of the Great Depression. The Beats, a movement of literary experimentation and social criticism during the 1950s, provided another link between the hippies of the 1960s and older forms of American bohemianism. Few in number compared to the counterculture, the Beats nevertheless bequeathed to hippies their oppositional stance toward mass culture and conventional morality; an admiration of, and identification with, the marginalized people who lived by their wits "on the street"; a rich vocabulary of slang that they had appropriated from African-American jazz musicians; and a fascination with Asian mysticism. From both the Beats and the avant-garde artists of the 1950s working in other media, hippies inherited the belief that inspired art could serve as a vehicle for discovering the repressed elements of the self, revealing heretofore unimagined possibilities for human relationships through the transgression of conventional limits and the questioning of conventional wisdom.

DEVELOPMENT

The first countercultural enclaves took shape in 1965, mostly in urban settings and in college towns. Each enclave developed according to its own timetable and cultivated a distinctive local character. The most renowned of the early enclaves was the Haight-Ashbury district of San Francisco. The Haight was home to many students and faculty members of San Francisco State College; and, after authorities forced the Beats out of the North Beach district in 1962, many

migrated there in search of inexpensive accommodations. New coffeehouses sprang up; soon, new rock and roll bands appeared, such as the Grateful Dead and the Jefferson Airplane, which played the "acid rock" influenced by Ken Kesey's experiments with electronics and light shows as accoutrements enhancing the effects of LSD. "Head shops," offering drug paraphernalia, books on Asian philosophy, and whimsical handicrafts, began to occupy long-vacant storefronts.

By late 1966, a "New Community" had taken shape, with its own psychedelic newspaper, the *San Francisco Oracle*, setting forth a vision of social change through mystical practice, and a rival faction, the Diggers, urging residents of "Psychedelphia" to become "life-actors," and realize *today* their vision of a new society through immediate, concrete activity.

The rapid growth of the enclave caused considerable tension between hippies and long-time residents. Meanwhile, the national media sensationalized developments in the Haight, portraying it, alternately, as a paradise of love and idealism in a heartless, competitive society, or as a sinkhole of moral depravity, addiction, and violence. A tidal wave of youthful seekers descended on the neighborhood during the spring and summer of 1967, far exceeding the number that could have been successfully integrated into the community. Many established hip bohemians, including most of the Diggers, left the neighborhood in search of less crowded environs, to escape the rapid rent increases that followed on the neighborhood's popularity and to escape the escalating violence of the drug trade, which organized crime had rationalized and commercialized.

A belief in a coming apocalypse—that straight society was an environmentally unsustainable way of life and one suffering a crisis of legitimacy in the face of rising popular discontent—pervaded both the counterculture and the New Left by 1968. Some New Leftists responded to this expectation of impending apocalypse by aligning themselves—at least, rhetorically—with Third World, anti-imperialist movements abroad, and militant, antiracist movements at home. Law enforcement agencies responded with increased efforts to infiltrate, destabilize, and destroy movement organizations. Many hippies responded to the expected apocalypse by leaving the cities to establish rural communes, in which they hoped to create new lifeways that would flourish in the free social spaces of postapocalyptic America.

THE RURAL DIASPORA

Counterculturalists founded thousands of communes from 1968 to 1975. Writing separately, Timothy Miller and sociologist Judson Jerome converge on a rough estimate that perhaps as many as 30,000 rural and urban communes existed in the early 1970s, with a population approaching a million persons. By any estimate, the 1960s and 1970s witnessed the greatest surge in communal experimentation in the history of the United States.

These communes varied tremendously in terms of their social organization, longevity, and population size. Although many communal groups of a dozen or so kindred spirits formed, and then vanished, during the course of a summer, leaving no trace of their existence, other communes proved remarkably resilient. Several of the best-known hippie communes overcame the long odds against longevity and still exist today, even if in much-altered form, including Twin Oaks, in Louisa, Virginia; The Farm, in Summertown, Tennessee; and Black Bear Ranch, in Siskyou County, California.

Longevity should not be misinterpreted as a measure of a commune's "success." As historian Donald E. Pitzer has persuasively argued, the communal sharing of resources usually constitutes only one stage of a social movement's life cycle, and if prolonged beyond the point of its usefulness, communalism can become a barrier to a movement's continued development. Longevity *does* indicate, however, hip communards' devotion to their chosen way of life, long after the time when the wave of commune foundings crested in the early 1970s.

Both hippie anarchists and hippie mystics founded communes. What sustained these new communities, and what was everyday life like within them?

THE SOCIAL RELATIONS OF COUNTERCULTURAL COMMUNITIES

Communards traded the security of steady income in the mainstream economy for the expected social warmth of collective life. Since cash was usually scarce, its conservation was essential to the survival of the commune. Furthermore, the countercultural critique of consumerism made a virtue of the simple life. Freed from the time constraints of regular jobs, many hippie communards found both pleasure and profit in the manual labor of raising and preserving food; repairing vehicles, clothing, and shelters; and scavenging building materials, auto parts, used clothing, and sundry household items from the enormous stream of waste created by the consumer economy. Support from federal and local welfare programs also figured into the bottom line of many communes (although some, like The Farm, refused all such aid on principle).

Land ownership frequently proved a vexing question for idealistic commune-dwellers. The anarchist influence on countercultural thinking questioned the ethics of individual land ownership, arguing that land was a resource that belonged to all. At times, this ethic led to the declaration of "open land," upon which anyone might erect a dwelling and claim membership in the community. Lou Gottlieb, the legal owner of one of the earliest open-land communes, Morning Star Ranch, attempted to divest himself of mastery over the land by deeding it to God—local authorities having found his property in violation of numerous zoning regulations. More often, however, communalists accommodated themselves to the realities of land tenure, renting farmsteads or large urban houses, or benefiting from the donation of property to the group by a member or outside benefactor. Just as surely as the gift of land (or successful completion of mortgage payments) could lend long-term stability and a sense of rootedness to a commune, the loss of land could mean the demise of the community when landlords or benefactors experienced a change of heart.

In addition to the economies of scale that communal living provided, and in addition to the savings realized through simple living, some hippie communes, urban and rural, identified niches in the commercial economy that they were uniquely suited to fill. One of the more successful practitioners of this variety of hip capitalism was the Twin Oaks commune, which developed a successful hammock-making business. Other communes proved less fortunate: The Farm, for example, invested heavily in an expansion of its commercial agricultural production in 1978, at precisely the time when commodity prices plummeted. Losses from this reversal, in addition to a host of other pressures, finally forced a reorganization of the commune in 1981.

Anarchist communards, like those who occupied Black Bear Ranch from 1968 to 1974, resisted all efforts to stabilize governance by resort to formal political hierarchy. Nevertheless, some communes developed sophisticated systems of governance and accounting, such as Twin Oaks' work-credits system. The mystically inclined hippies of The Farm developed a complex corporate and political hierarchy as their ranks swelled in the late 1970s. By the end of that decade, it had become the largest of all countercultural communes, with a population of perhaps 1,500 and with members branching out to found satellite communes in dozens of other locations.

Most communes fell in between the extremes of anarchistic decentralization and large-scale bureaucratization. The organizational structure of the Johnson's Pastures commune in Guilford, Vermont, took a variety of forms over time, as a high rate of membership turnover left the property in the hands of successive groups of relative newcomers. Further adding to the commune's difficulties was a struggle for control of the property between the tightly disciplined followers of a charismatic spiritual leader and the freewheeling successors to the original communards.

Day-to-day governance in most hip communities generally proved to be a matter of face-to-face interactions, rather than the sophisticated coalition-building and calculated organization of an institutional power base that characterizes the life of bureaucratic institutions. Among the Diggers, many (but not all) of whom lived in communal houses in San Francisco, the group's direction was left to the initiative of individual members, who derived influence from their perceived "personal heaviness"—that is, their demonstrations of fidelity to the group's anarchistic ideals, ability to conceive of new group projects that were both ideologically and aesthetically compelling (they were, after all, skilled practitioners of the theater arts), and the articulateness with which they justified their actions. Later, many communal groups sought to reach decisions through the development of consensus—sometimes through the application of "encounter-group" techniques and sometimes through interminable meetings, in which a single obstinate member could thwart the process. Perhaps the single most frequent form of communal governance was the exertion of peer pressure, whether manifested in the negative, as the threat of ostracism, or in the positive, as a live-and-let-live attitude that regarded efforts to impose one's own views as contrary to the spirit of the community.

Although most scholars have focused on the governance of individual communes, Barry Laffan argued that the Johnson's Pasture community occupied a specific niche within a larger network of increasingly more specialized movement organizations in southern Vermont and western Massachusetts in the early and mid-1970s. In terms of recruitment, Laffan located Johnson's Pastures within a national circuit of places known, by word of mouth, to be hospitable to itinerant members of the counterculture. Simultaneously, the recruitment of members depended not only on the personal contacts of existing members, but, as the local counterculture grew more specialized and institutionalized in the mid-1970s, on the commune's reputation as a haven for "street hippies," drawing misfits who did not feel at home in other local groups. In short, over time Johnson's Pastures became a low-status commune in an increasingly status-driven regional network.

The entire range of human reactions to life in close quarters, from the most admirable to the most despicable, found its expression in the hippie communes. At their best, the communes fostered a sense of community and intimacy that was rare—and, indeed, continues to prove sorely lacking—in the atomistic modern world.

CLASS, RACE, AND ETHNICITY

As the example of Johnson's Pastures suggests, the counterculture brought together youthful seekers from a range of class backgrounds. Among many residents of the Haight-Ashbury enclave, the Hell's Angels motorcycle gang enjoyed a reputation as outlaws willing to defend their autonomy from the depredations of corrupt "Establishment" authorities, including the police. For a time, several of the Diggers (whose members came from both white-collar and blue-collar families) maintained an alliance with the biker "heavies," and one of their number, Bill Fritsch, actually joined the Angels.

As the mass media of the time frequently remarked, many other members of the counterculture came from middle-class, and even wealthy, backgrounds. If the power of the counterculture resided more in the attractiveness of its ideas than in the strength of its numbers, then one reason was because it drew on the articulateness of both middle-class, university-educated youth and the insights of cultural radicals from decidedly less privileged backgrounds.

Several commentators have noted the prominence of youth of Jewish heritage in the countercultural population, which necessarily paralleled their prominence in the movement as a whole—for example, among white students who "went South" to participate in Freedom Summer in 1964. A significant number of residents at both Black Bear Ranch and The Farm hailed from Jewish families, as did, for example, several of the leading figures on the staff of the Haight-Ashbury's first psychedelic newspaper, the *San Francisco Oracle*.

One factor that brought so many of Jewish heritage into the counterculture was the prominence of many of their parents in the radical politics of the Depression era. In many cases, this created a family tradition of strong commitment to social justice. The counterculture, as one segment of the youth revolt of the 1960s, thus can be understood only partially as a revolt of "youth" against parental authority. Although many youthful radicals, including many hippies, did quarrel with their parents over the appropriateness of their chosen form of rebellion, this did not always lead to total and permanent estrangement. For example, the correspondence that passed between members of the Black Bear Ranch commune and their parents demonstrates that, in many instances, sharp conflicts were but one dimension of a larger and enduring intimacy.

If the counterculture was perhaps more diverse in terms of social class than once was thought, it remains quite evident that hippiedom held significantly less allure for people of color than for white Americans. Many participants at the time, and many scholars since, have attributed this phenomenon to hippies' embrace of voluntary poverty, a stance available only to the economically privileged. Hippies, so this reasoning goes, had renounced the material possessions that impoverished minorities had never been able to enjoy.

Yet, this analysis presumes that the material acquisitiveness of the predominantly white middle class of the time constituted the universal standard of human dignity—a presumption that, once articulated, clearly stands open to debate. This analysis also obscures the existence of distinct forms of cultural radicalism among people of color during the 1960s and 1970s. Although the political nationalism of groups such as the Black Panthers has received more scholarly attention than the contemporary movements of African-American and Latino cultural radicalism, we will better understand the historical context of the counterculture by placing it in the context of the diverse manifestations of cultural radicalism of a multicultural society.

GENDER

The counterculture took shape during the years immediately prior to the advent of the women's liberation and gay liberation movements. Like nearly all people at the time, hippies simply presumed that what we today call gender—masculinity and femininity—derived directly from biological maleness and femaleness, even if society molded those raw characteristics into "sex roles" that reflected its particular values at a given point in history. Although the popular memory is of hippie men as "longhairs" rel-

atively indifferent to the prescribed masculine "sex role" embodied by John Wayne, the counterculture regarded the recovery of "natural" masculinity and femininity as integral to its program of liberation. All hippies agreed that conventional sex roles were repressive, and they believed that the liberation of the consciousness of the individual would facilitate the regeneration of authentic manhood and womanhood.

Counterculturalists disagreed sharply among themselves, however, over the appropriate means and ends toward that goal. Hippies' ideals and practices regarding the recovery of authentic masculinity and femininity depended primarily on their commitments to anarchist or mystical forms of social change. Hip anarchists suspected conventional forms, such as monogamous marriage, the nuclear family, and private property, as the primary means by which modern society robbed individuals of their autonomy. Thus, their gender ideal celebrated the manliness and womanliness of the "outlaw" who disregarded conventional morality. They championed the sexual revolution as not only an end to unwarranted restraint on individual sexual choice, but also as a vehicle for a more general liberation from all forms of unjust authority.

Hippie mystics thought of freedom not so much as the absence of rules, but as the recovery of awareness of the laws of nature from the hubris of an advanced industrial society beguiled by scientific rationality. Through mystical practice, they sought to reconnect men and women to the metaphysical dimensions of self and cosmos, including the transcended forms of masculine and feminine "energy" often conceptualized as yang and yin. Some mystics supported the practices of the "sexual revolution" as a means of ecstatic union with the Infinite. Others, like the followers of Stephen Gaskin at The Farm, saw the sexual revolution as another instance of modern society's lack of appreciation for the power of women's fertility and maternal nurture. Gaskin advocated that men adopt a chivalrous, "knightly" reverence toward "ladies," expressed in a willingness to commit to lifelong monogamous marriage. Other mystics, such as practitioners of Krishna Consciousness, distrusted the body and sensual indulgence as distractions from the discipline necessary to achieve union with the Infinite. They advocated total sexual abstinence as the ideal.

When the women's liberation movement (and, for a time, elements of the gay liberation movement) articulated an analysis of gender as a political and social, rather than reflexively biological, phenomenon, they called into question the dominant countercultural assumption that freewheeling sexual expression would return relations between women and men to their presumptively harmonious, "natural" state. Although some men and women in the counterculture (including, for example, a minority of the residents of Black Bear Ranch) embraced this analysis, and some vehemently rejected it, many more responded more selectively, adopting some insights and practices and discarding others.

At Black Bear, most men moved toward a more equal distribution of household labor after women residents began meeting as a group to discuss the inequities of the commune's sexual division of labor in 1971. It took much longer, however, for some Black Bear women to gain the necessary skills to participate fully in tasks, such as woodcutting, once regarded as men's work. Similarly, the radical-feminist analysis of sexuality as a political process prompted a few of the women residents of Black Bear to create a "women's house" and to experiment, tentatively, with lesbianism as a form of sisterly solidarity. But in the main, most women residents appear not to have found this alternative compelling.

Thus, although the counterculture quite justifiably drew some of radical feminists' and gay liberationists' strongest criticism, and although elements of the counterculture offered resolute resistance to that criticism, preliminary evidence indicates that many more hippies proved at least moderately willing to adapt to that criticism as part of their commitment to social change through the transformation of individual consciousness.

THE FADING OF THE APOCALYPSE

The great wave of commune foundings crested in the early 1970s. At various points in time after 1968, however, members of the movement reassessed the earlier expectation of an imminent, apocalyptic collapse of straight society that would facilitate rapid social change. As sociologists Jack Whalen and Richard Flacks have shown, this reassessment often did not amount to activists' recantation of their radical beliefs. Rather, it entailed a modification of the timetable for social change. Increasingly, New Leftists and hippies now expected change to come slowly, over a period of generations.

In light of this reassessment, it made sense to seek a more stable livelihood, one that would sustain their activism over an entire lifetime. Some left the communes to resume interrupted education toward conventional careers, such as law, that might be utilized as a means of social advocacy. Others sought to establish unconventional careers, such as the practice of "alternative" medicine, that bore the strong imprint of the counterculture's efforts to infuse daily life with religious ecstasy.

Of course, not everyone left the communes that had become so important as an expression of the countercultural quest for liberation. Those who carried on the communal lifeway sought to strengthen the economic foundations and governance mechanisms of their communities so that they might serve as vehicles for the invention and preservation of alternatives that might find a wider acceptance in future generations.

Thus, although the counterculture might not prove as visible today as it was in its heyday, its influence has diffused into the larger society through the large numbers of ex-participants who, in innumerable ways, still seek to spread peace and justice through the transformation of individual consciousness—if sometimes by less flamboyant means than they did in their youth. And though less visible today than in decades past, the many communes and "alternative" practices that still thrive on the margins of American society also bear witness to the power and vitality of the countercultural critique of American society.

Tim Hodgdon

BIBLIOGRAPHY

Blue Mountain Ranch Commune Staff. *January Thaw: People at Blue Mountain Ranch Write about Living Together in the Mountains.* New York: Times Change Press, 1974.

Braunstein, Peter, and Michael William Doyle, eds. *Imagine Nation: The American Counterculture of the 1960s and '70s.* New York: Routledge, 2001.

Cohen, Allen, ed. *The San Francisco Oracle: The Psychedelic Newspaper of the Haight-Ashbury, 1966–1968.* Facsimile edition. Berkeley, CA: Regent, 1991.

Coyote, Peter. *Sleeping Where I Fall: A Chronicle.* Washington, DC: Counterpoint, 1998.

Digger Archives. http://www.diggers.org.

Fike, Rupert, ed. *Voices from The Farm: Adventures in Community Living.* Summertown, TN: Book, 1998.

Hodgdon, Tim. "Manhood and the Age of Aquarius: Masculinity in Two Countercultural Communities, 1965–1983." Ph.D. diss., Arizona State University, Tempe, 2002.

Laffan, Barry. *Communal Organization and Social Transition: A Case Study from the Counterculture of the Sixties and Seventies.* New York: P. Lang, 1997.

Miller, Timothy. *The Hippies and American Values.* Knoxville: University of Tennessee Press, 1991.

———. *The 60s Communes: Hippies and Beyond.* Syracuse, NY: Syracuse University Press, 1999.

Monkerud, Don, Malcolm Terence, and Susan Keese, eds. *Free Land, Free Love: Tales of a Wilderness Commune.* Aptos, CA: Black Bear Mining, 2000.

Ohle, David, Roger Martin, and Susan Brosseau, eds. *Cows Are Freaky When They Look at You: An Oral History of the Kaw Valley Hemp Pickers.* Wichita, KS: Watermark, 1991.

Perry, Charles. *The Haight-Ashbury: A History.* New York: Vintage, 1985.

Pitzer, Donald E. "Developmental Communalism: An Alternative Approach to Communal Studies." In *Utopian Thought and Communal Experience,* ed. Dennis Hardy and Lorna Davidson, pp. 68–76. Enfield, UK: Middlesex Polytechnic, 1989.

Rochford, E. Burke, Jr. *Hare Krishna in America.* New Brunswick, NJ: Rutgers University Press, 1985.

Veysey, Laurence. *The Communal Experience: Anarchist and Mystical Counter-Cultures in America.* New York: Harper & Row, 1973.

Whalen, Jack, and Richard Flacks. *Beyond the Barricades: The Sixties Generation Grows Up.* Philadelphia: Temple University Press, 1989.

Zablocki, Benjamin. *Alienation and Charisma: A Study of Contemporary American Communes.* New York: Free Press, 1980.

AMERICAN BUDDHISM

American Buddhism has undergone four developmental phases, evolving from a topic of intrigue and exoticism in the travel narratives "Oriental Tales" and critical missionary accounts of the early national period, to a religion imported and practiced predominantly by Asian immigrants during the nineteenth century, to a central component of an eclectic and trendy counterculture spirituality, and, finally, to a revered spiritual discipline for both Asian immigrants and American-born converts during the last four decades of the twentieth century. Including practitioners of the three major forms of Buddhism—Theravada (predominant in Southeast Asia), Mahayana (predominant in China, Korea, and Japan), and Vajrayana (predominant in Tibet and Mongolia)—American Buddhism is the result of a social movement forged by Asian immigrants and teachers, American converts, and sympathizers who found wisdom in the Dharma (the teachings of Buddhism's founder, Siddhartha Gautama, 563–483 B.C.E.). The history of Buddhism in America is as complex as the immigrant cultures and teachers who transplanted it and as diverse as the individuals who practice it. Yet four categories of analysis—orientation, encounters, exclusion, and passages—laid out by Thomas A. Tweed and Stephen Prothero in *Asian Religions in America: A Documentary History* (1999) provide the most compelling framework for understanding the forging of a uniquely American Buddhism.

ORIENTATION 1784–1840

Americans, whose attention initially turned eastward with the intention of capturing lucrative Asian markets, have long been fascinated by the contrasts in worldviews and religious beliefs between the peoples of the East and the West. Americans, however, drew their first impressions of Asian cultures and religions from reading the culturally biased travel narratives of traders, encountering artifacts brought back from China, and perusing reports by missionaries who labeled Buddhists as spiritual degenerates and atheistic heathens. In addition, the popular, fictional work "Oriental Tales" of this period whose authors sought to portray the exoticism of Asian cultures, such as Benjamin Franklin's "A Letter from China," further informed Americans' opinions about Buddhism. As a result, Americans lacked a learned understanding of Buddhist traditions and beliefs. Hannah Adams's *A Dictionary of Asian Religions* (1817) constituted the most sophisticated treatment of Buddhism by an American writer of the period. Adams, in an effort to understand Asian religions without comparing them to Christianity, argued that Buddhism was a venerable spiritual discipline practiced by one-third of the world's population.

ENCOUNTERS 1840–1924

Americans gained direct access to Buddhist teachings after 1840 when publications such as *The Dial*, the voice of Transcendentalists and advocates of religious liberalism, published translations of Buddhist texts, including portions of the *Lotus Sutra*. Influenced by *The Dial*'s translations of "Ethnical Scriptures," popular American writers such as Ralph Waldo Emerson, Henry David Thoreau, and Walt Whitman included references to Buddhist traditions in their writings.

Anglo converts to Buddhism, however, were rare. By far the most important transmitters of Buddhist tradition to America during this time period were the Asian immigrants who transplanted their ethnic religions in the West Coast's booming cities. Between 1850 and 1924, 368,000 Chinese immigrants and 270,000 Japanese immigrants entered the United States. Chinese merchant societies set aside space for worship on the upper floors of their properties, and immigrants established makeshift "joss houses" (God houses) in which they practiced Chinese folk religions that blended elements of Confucianism, Taoism, and Buddhism. San Francisco's Chinatown had at least eight temples by 1875, and historian Ferenc Szasz estimates that Chinese immigrants had established 400 temples on the West Coast by 1900. Japanese Buddhists, led by Dr. Shuye Sonoda and Reverend Kakuryo Nishijima, teachers of the True Pure Land Buddhism, established the Buddhist Mission to North America (BMNA) in 1898. In an effort to demonstrate their Americanism during World War II, a time of persecution and hardship for Japanese Americans interned in prison camps, the leaders of the BMNA renamed their institution the Buddhist Churches of America.

Zen, the most influential form of Japanese Buddhism in America, was introduced at the 1893 World's Parliament of Religions: a seventeen-day conference of 200 international delegates, organized by American religious liberals, and held in Chicago in conjunction with the Columbian Exposition. Historians define the Parliament of Religions as a decisive event in the history of American religious pluralism. Indeed, the meeting marked the beginning of a Buddhism that reached beyond Asian immigrant communities and sparked a dialogue between Buddhist teachers and potential American converts. Contacts crucial to the growth of Buddhist institutions in America were forged at the meeting. Paul Carus, for instance, the most important Buddhist sympathizer of the Gilded Age and the director of Open Court Publishing Company, met Japanese Zen master Soyen Shaku and Anagarika Dharmapala, the Theravada Buddhist delegate from Ceylon.

The ties forged at the conference marked a turning point in American Buddhism. Shaku's student D.T. Suzuki moved to the United States, where he worked with Carus for ten years, translating the Buddhist texts published by Open Court. Dharmapala traveled across America lecturing at events set up by Carus, and Carus himself wrote more than sixty books following the conference. Carus, intending to popularize Buddhism in America, borrowed from the philosophies of Dharmapala and Suzuki to create a marketable American Buddhism. Dharmapala, in a speech titled "The World's Debt to Buddha," had already explained to an American audience the pragmatism of Buddhist thought and practice: "In the religion of Buddha are found a comprehensive system of ethics and a transcendental metaphysic embracing a sublime psychology. To the simpleminded it offers a code of morality, to the earnest student a system of pure thought. But the basic doctrine is the self-purification of man." Carus repeatedly employed Dharmapala's logic to argue that Buddhist doctrines fit well in a modern America characterized by progress, reason, and scientific expertise.

EXCLUSION 1924–1965

Although the 1893 World's Parliament of Religions pointed to a future of religious pluralism and transnational spiritual dialogue, it took place amidst a general atmosphere of intolerance toward Asian immigrants. Workers in the West who feared competition from Chinese laborers in mining, agriculture, transportation, construction, and small business, and middle-class reformers who believed there were ineradicable racial and cultural differences between Asians and whites had convinced Congress to pass the Chinese Exclusion Act in 1882, effectively stemming Chinese immigration and excluding Chinese from U.S. citizenship. American policymakers targeted Japanese immigration with the 1907 Gentleman's Agreement. Discriminatory immigration restriction based on national origins culminated in the First and Second Quota Acts of 1921 and 1924, respectively, which established quotas of fewer than 100 for both China and Japan.

As a result of federal legislation, the Asian immigrant populations in America stagnated, as did ethnic Buddhist organizations. By 1906, the Census Bureau counted only 62 Chinese temples and 141 shrines in twelve states. Yet Asian-born leaders, such as D.T. Suzuki, expanded the reach of American Buddhism by converting Anglo Americans. Asian leaders opened Zen centers in Los Angeles, San Francisco, Chicago, and New York, published books, and delivered lectures on the East and West coasts. D.T. Suzuki, the most well known and influential Buddhist teacher of this period, contributed to the fashionable "Zen boom" among American elites during the 1950s. He taught at Claremont Graduate School and Columbia University, helped establish the Cambridge Buddhist Association in Massachusetts, appeared on television, and was the subject of at least nine articles in the popular press. Suzuki's lectures and books appealed to a diverse group of American writers and thinkers, including Alan Watts, J.D. Salinger, Jack Kerouac, Allen Ginsberg, Gary Snyder, Trappist contemplative writer Thomas Merton, neo-Freudian psychologists Erich Fromm and Karen Horney, and the humanist psychologist Abraham Maslow.

PASSAGES 1965–Present

Intellectuals Frederick Spiegelberg and Alan Watts, American converts such as Gary Snyder, Beat writers Jack Kerouac and Allen Ginsberg, and Asian teachers Shunryu Suzuki and Chogyam Trungpa did much to popularize Buddhism as a viable spiritual alternative in postwar American society. In fact, this diverse group ensured Buddhism's inclusion in the spiritual experimentation of the 1960s counterculture and the holistic approach of the human potential movement during the 1970s. In 1951, Frederick Spiegelberg, a Stanford professor of comparative religions, became the director of the American Academy of Asian Studies in San Francisco and invited the former Episcopalian priest and popularizer of Zen Buddhism Alan Watts to join the faculty. Under Spiegelberg's and Watts's leadership, the academy formed the center of the San Francisco Renaissance in the 1950s and 1960s, providing a welcoming intellectual and cultural space where the adventurous soul could explore his or her consciousness through such diverse vehicles as Asian religion, humanist psychology, experimental poetics, and popular drugs.

Jack Kerouac, the most famous of the Beat writers, attended lectures at the academy. In *The Dharma Bums* (1958), he captured the spontaneous experimentation that characterized the San Francisco scene in the 1950s and expressed the hope that Zen Buddhist practice might form the basis of a new spirituality in America society. Japhy Ryder, the central character whom Kerouac based on Zen practitioner Gary Snyder, exclaims:

> I see a vision of a great rucksack revolution thousands or even millions of young Americans wandering around with rucksacks, going up to mountains to pray . . . all of 'em Zen Lunatics who go about writing poems that happen to appear in their heads for no reason. . . . What we need is a floating zendo. . . . Yessir, that's what, a series of monasteries for fellows to go and monastate and meditate in, we can have groups of shacks up in the Sierras or the High Cascades or even Ray says down in Mexico and have big wild gangs of pure holy men getting together to drink and talk and pray.

The teachings of Watts and Spiegelberg at the American Academy of Asian Studies and the popularization of Zen by Beat authors created a demand among Anglo Americans for instruction in Zen practice, prompting Shunryu Suzuki (1905–1971) to found the San Francisco Zen Center in 1962. With the founding of the San Francisco Zen Center, Tassajara Zen Mountain Center, and Green Gulch Farm in Marin County, California, American Buddhism became an institutional reality, offering American converts an unprecedented opportunity for advanced Zen training and a monastic regimen in the United States.

The institutionalization and popularization of American Buddhism escalated after 1965, when Congress passed the Hart-Cellar Act, abolishing the restrictive national origins quota system. Asian teachers, including Tibetan meditation master Chogyam Trungpa, immigrated to the United States. From his base of operations in the hip city of Boulder, Colorado, Trungpa did more than anyone else to shape the nature of Tibetan Buddhism in the United States, propelling the least known form of Buddhism before 1970 to one of the most popular in recent years. Aided by Beat poet Allen Ginsberg, Trungpa masterminded the establishment of the Buddhist-Poetics-Humanist Psychology community in Boulder, institutionalizing this hybrid counterculture spirituality into an experimental educational enterprise: the Jack Kerouac School of Disembodied Poetics (1974) and the Naropa Institute (1976), now Naropa University.

Trungpa had fled Tibet in 1959 after the Chinese government launched a campaign of ruthless oppression that eventually killed or drove into exile a third of the entire Tibetan population. After studying religion and mastering English at Oxford University, Trungpa established a meditation community in the Scottish Highlands. He felt at home in the mountains, but upon determining that "the Scots were slightly missing the point," Trungpa accepted an invitation to teach a religious studies course at the University of Colorado, moving his operation to Boulder in 1970.

Initially, Trungpa attracted students largely from the communes that surrounded Boulder. The new practitioners congregated at the Kharma Dzong meditation center, dropped acid, listened to Trungpa's lengthy lectures, and attempted to meditate on images from the *Tibetan Book of the Dead*. Trungpa and his student poet Allen Ginsberg concluded that, by combining the philosophy and practices of Tibetan Buddhism, the teachings of Humanistic Psychology, and the spontaneous poetic style of the Beats, they could fundamentally change the way students perceived the world.

Trungpa and Ginsberg became visible members of Boulder's growing counterculture community when they launched the Jack Kerouac School of Disembodied Poetics. Its first summer session offered courses and workshops in Eastern and Western disciplines of meditation, philosophy, psychology, poetry, creative writing, theater, dance, music, and visual arts. Prominent poets, artists, and scholars volunteered to teach that summer, including Allen Ginsberg, William S. Burroughs, Ann Waldman, Harvey Cox, Ram Dass, and Gary Snyder. Organizers of the school's first sum-

At St. Charles Borromeo Church in Bloomington, Indiana, a Buddhist monk greets the Dalai Lama on August 23, 1999. The Dalai Lama is the spiritual leader of Tibetan Buddhists, a branch of Buddhism that has attracted a large number of followers in the United States. *(AP Wide World Photos)*

mer session expected a maximum of 200 locals to participate in the workshop, but the prospect of enlightenment offered by Beat poets, hallucinogenic drugs, and Eastern religious gurus drew 2,000 people from across the nation.

Realizing the marketability of their alternative educational and spiritual experiment, Trungpa and Ginsberg founded Naropa Institute, a contemplative college that offered degrees in buddhist studies, Western psychology, and secular meditation. Instead of directing students toward a career path and a life of acquisitive materialism, Naropa would offer them a life of contemplation and service to the community. Required courses in Naropa's degree programs included spontaneous prose writing, history of the Beat

poets, sensory awareness, body movement, transpersonal psychology, organic gardening, and insight meditation. In addition, Naropa's summer writing program continued to draw America's most famous radical poets and authors to Boulder. Beyond establishing Naropa Institute, Trungpa adapted traditional Tibetan teachings to American culture to meet the needs of his American students. In 1977, for instance, he developed Shambhala training, a secularized path to spiritual awakening based on meditation practice, and he established an international network of Shambhala Meditation Centers that together constitute the largest Tibetan organization in the Western Hemisphere.

The accretion of temples, universities, meditation

centers and retreats, publishing houses, and periodicals founded by Buddhist teachers and practitioners provided an institutional base for Buddhist Sanghas (communities) within America's diverse religious landscape, simultaneously popularizing aspects of Buddhist philosophy and spiritual practices to American consumers. In addition, American Buddhism continues to evolve as a social movement as "Engaged Buddhist" activists, inspired by world-renowned leaders like the Fourteenth Dalai Lama, Tibetan Tenzin Gyatso, and Vietnamese Zen Buddhist Thich Nhat Hanh, agitate for a politics that privileges environmentalism, social justice, world peace, and international human rights.

Amy L. Scott

BIBLIOGRAPHY

Coleman, James William. *The New Buddhism: The Western Transformation of an Ancient Tradition*. New York: Oxford University Press, 2001.

Cox, Harvey. *Turning East: Why Americans Look to the Orient for Spirituality—And What That Search Can Mean to the West*. New York: Simon and Schuster, 1977.

Kerouac, Jack. *The Dharma Bums*. New York: Viking Press, 1958.

Melton, J. Gordon. *American Religions: An Illustrated History*. Denver, CO: ABC-CLIO, 2000.

Prebish, Charles S., and Kenneth K. Tanaka. *The Faces of Buddhism in America*. Berkeley: University of California Press, 1998.

Queen, Christopher S., ed. *Engaged Buddhism in the West*. Somerville, MA: Wisdom, 2000.

Schumacher, Michael. *Dharma Lion: A Critical Biography of Allen Ginsberg*. New York: St. Martin's, 1992.

Seager, Richard Hughes. *Buddhism in America*. New York: Columbia University Press, 1999.

Szasz, Ferenc Morton. *Religion in the Modern American West*. Tucson: University of Arizona Press, 2000.

Taylor, Eugene. *Shadow Culture: Psychology and Spirituality in America*. Washington, DC: Counterpoint, 1999.

Tweed, Thomas A., and Stephen Prothero, eds. *Asian Religions in America: A Documentary History*. New York: Oxford University Press, 1999.

Ueda, Reed. *Postwar Immigrant America: A Social History*. New York: Bedford Books of St. Martin's, 1994.

Waldman, Anne, and Marilyn Webb, eds. *Talking Poetics from Naropa Institute: Annals of the Jack Kerouac School of Disembodied Poetics*. Boulder, CO: Shambhala, 1978.

Williams, Peter W. *America's Religions: From Their Origins to the Twenty-First Century*. 3d ed. Chicago: University of Illinois Press, 2002.

9

ANTIWAR/PROTEST
MOVEMENTS

INTRODUCTION

When most people think of the American antiwar movement, the images that come to mind usually include the Vietnam War, student radicals, mass marches in Washington and New York, and the burning of draft cards. But antimilitarism in the United States has a long history that transcends the events of the 1960s. With roots in Christian pacifism and secular movements of political opposition that date back to the earliest years of American history, antiwar movements have grown and evolved to include a diverse constituency with a variety of political and religious beliefs and a wide range of strategies and approaches. The contemporary American antiwar movement represents the result of centuries of development and struggle.

Before there was a "movement," there were simply antiwar sentiments—brought over to the American colonies by members of the historic peace churches (the Quakers, the Mennonites, and the Brethren) and fostered by a growing colonial aversion to the carnage of the European imperial wars. Through the first half of the nineteenth century, pacifism largely remained the domain of personal religious witness. Antiwar protests, on the other hand, against wars like the War of 1812 and the 1846 Mexican-American War, grew out of the secular political divisions of their times. Although the influence of these two strains of American antimilitarism, political and religious, has varied since then, this distinction between principled pacifism and pragmatic antimilitarism continue as a defining feature of American antiwar struggles.

So, too, did the link between peace and social justice. Early-nineteenth-century pacifist leaders made the initial connection between these two concerns by building strong alliances with other antebellum evangelical movements for social and political change. The most visible merging of these efforts can be seen in the "nonresistance" policies advocated by members of the radical abolitionist movement led by William Lloyd Garrison. After the Civil War, women's rights activists took on the antiwar cause as part of their broad "maternalist" political agenda that defined women's Progressive Era reform. Bohemians, Socialists, and other radicals linked antimilitarism to the struggle for working-class solidarity before and during World War I, and responded to the political repression during those wartime years by fighting to defend basic civil liberties and constitutional rights. The antiwar movement of the 1920s and 1930s similarly linked its goals to those of the surging labor movement, while pacifists from the 1940s through the 1960s made concrete connections between their nonviolent protests against war and the developing black freedom struggle. Struggles for peace and fights for social justice have often gone hand in hand.

In spite of these strong threads of continuity, the history of the American antiwar movement is just as strongly marked by change. Before 1915, there were antiwar efforts, pacifist groupings, and antiwar organizations, but no organized protest movement had arisen in a form that people would recognize today. Most pacifists of the pre–World War I era focused on pursuing a style of individual "nonresistance" through personal acts of religious witness and fidelity. Secular antimilitarists, on the other hand, generally saw themselves as constructive political actors, but not as leaders of social movements. In fact, many of these antiwar advocates saw their work as supporting the status quo of American politics rather than opposing it. Indeed, during the late nineteenth and early twentieth centuries, the most prominent American antiwar efforts were led not by pacifists or by dissidents, but by members of America's professional and business elite, who focused their attention on building institutional structures to mediate international conflict and promote global trade.

World War I changed everything. In response to

the carnage that defined the European conflict, a national, organized antiwar movement emerged in the United States for the very first time. This movement drew upon the initiative of Progressive reformers, women's suffragists, Socialists, pacifists, and radical activists and intellectuals. Its opposition to U.S. involvement in the war was both principled and pragmatic. But most significantly, the leaders of the World War I–era peace movement used the political skills and experiences they had gained in other struggles to create national political organizations capable of mobilizing vast numbers of people. In the years before the United States' 1917 entry into the war, they organized mass demonstrations for peace never before seen in this nation's history. Afterward, in the face of state repression and a national Red Scare, the number of antiwar advocates shrank but their efforts continued. In the process, activists created the framework for modern American antimilitarism: a mass-based movement standing in opposition to U.S. overseas policies and linked to progressive and radical struggles for social and political change.

The antiwar movement continued to evolve over the course of the twentieth century. Certainly, strategies changed. In the 1930s, for example, inspired by Mohandas Gandhi's organized resistance campaigns against British colonial rule in India, American activists began to incorporate the tactics of nonviolent direct action into their work for peace. Pacifist practice moved beyond the traditional doctrine of passive nonresistance—of simply refusing to fight—to include the more active Gandhian tactics of nonviolent resistance to war.

The political focus of antiwar efforts changed as well. The end of World War II forced pacifist and nonpacifist activists to turn their attention toward the threat of nuclear arms. Such efforts culminated in the massive "ban-the-bomb" movement of the late 1950s and early 1960s, which were then overshadowed by the increasingly militant and widespread opposition to the Vietnam War—the movement that most people think of when then they think of "the American peace movement." Although the mass base of the Vietnam War–era antiwar movement was unprecedented, it was built on the leadership and example of those activists who had come before to wage a far-reaching and persistent fight against U.S. Cold War policies. Activists in the decades since have used the experiences and lessons of the 1960s to continue the struggle against nuclear weapons, the American culture of violence, and U.S. military intervention overseas. The recent mass protests throughout the nation against the United States' unilateral war on Iraq represents simply the latest evolution of the movement's broad antiwar agenda.

As the essays in this section show, perhaps the most striking characteristic of the American antiwar movement is its longstanding diversity: in goals, in membership, and choice of political tactics. Over the course of its history, American antiwar efforts have embraced people from a variety of political and philosophical backgrounds—from absolute pacifists opposed to violence and war of any kind to individuals politically opposed to specific wars, to social and political reformers intent on finding constructive ways to promote peace. Members of these movements have spanned the political spectrum from right to left and have often linked the antiwar struggle to other campaigns for social change, including abolitionism, antipoverty crusades, and struggles for women's rights. This diversity of purpose has been a source of weakness and strength. At times, as during the 1930s and 1960s, this range and variety helped create a vital and broad-based movement with significant political impact. At other historical moments, these differences created deep divisions that undermined efforts to build and sustain political influence and support. At almost all times, antiwar efforts have been minority campaigns of dissent that operated from the margins of national politics and culture. Nevertheless, the antiwar movement has played an integral role in America's protest tradition, reflecting the nation's values and perspectives even as it has worked to challenge and reform the meanings of patriotism and loyalty in American life.

Marian B. Mollin

ANTIWAR MOVEMENT: OVERVIEW

Antiwar movements in the United States have historically embraced people from a variety of political and philosophical backgrounds—from absolute pacifists opposed to violence and war of any kind to individuals politically opposed to specific wars, to social and political reformers intent on finding constructive ways to promote peace. Members of these movements have spanned the political spectrum from right to left and have often been linked to other struggles for social change, including abolitionism, antipoverty crusades, and both early and contemporary struggles for women's rights. This diversity of purpose has been a source of both strength and weakness. At times, as during the 1930s and 1960s, this range and variety has helped to create a vital and broad-based movement with significant political impact. At other historical moments, these differences have created deep divisions that undermined efforts to build and sustain political influence and support. At almost all times, antiwar efforts have been minority campaigns of dissent that operated from margins of national politics and culture. Nevertheless, the antiwar movement has played an integral role in America's protest tradition, reflecting the nation's values and perspectives even as it worked to reshape and reform some of the most basic assumptions of American life.

PACIFISM AND ANTIMILITARISM IN EARLY AMERICA

Although the antiwar movement as we know it today did not emerge until the cataclysmic years of World War I, pacifism and antimilitarism have a long heritage in the history of American political dissent. Pacifism came to colonial America through the historic peace churches, the Religious Society of Friends (Quakers) and Anabaptist sects like the Mennonites and the Brethren, and until the twentieth century pacifism was primarily religious in orientation. Building on the Christian principles of loving one's enemy and turning the other cheek, religious pacifists adopted a stance of "nonresistance" by resolutely upholding the biblical injunction against killing. This position most obviously required refusing to bear arms or join the military. Nevertheless, it did not automatically imply engaging in active resistance to war. Instead, the traditional nonresistant pacifist was expected to submit to violence even as he or she refused to participate in it.

It is important to differentiate between principled pacifism and the more pragmatic political efforts individuals and groups have made to influence U.S. foreign policy and international affairs. In fact, when looking at the early history of American antimilitarism, one is struck by how little pacifism influenced antiwar efforts at all. According to historian Charles DeBenedetti, the Revolutionary struggle for independence, for example, arose in part as a response to a growing cultural revulsion to militarism. Antiwar sentiments grew out of the evangelical religious revivalism of the First Great Awakening and the intellectual currents of Enlightenment thought, and by the mid-1700s had begun to shape Americans' ideas about their involvement with the larger world. Colonists spoke out about wanting to break from the seemingly endless cycle of European wars and to protect themselves from the threat of tyranny posed by British soldiers on colonial soil. Even though Revolutionary War leaders embraced the need for armed resistance to British imperial power, many still described their ultimate goal, in the words of Thomas Paine, as "peace for ever." Those who opposed the Revolutionary struggle, on the other hand, largely opposed it for political, not antimilitarist, reasons. Loyalists supported the British Crown and believed that resistance to colonial rule would endanger the health of American society overall. But, like their patriot counterparts, they were more than willing to take up arms. Antimilitarist and antirevolutionary beliefs did not preclude waging war in battles for independence.

RELIGION AND PACIFISM

There was a Revolutionary War–era pacifist movement, but its emphasis was on religious constancy, not political protest. This was a difficult stance to uphold, even for members of the historic peace churches. Many did not necessarily oppose the war per se, but they overwhelmingly refused to fight, often at great risk to their personal well-being. A number lost property or faced physical persecution for their stance. Most simply tried to live their lives as best as they could according to their faith. For many, this meant turning inward into their religious communities and isolating themselves from the larger outside world. Others, like the Friends, chose to take on a more activist role by providing aid to noncombatants caught in the wake of war, and thus began a long tradition of Quaker social reform.

The distinctly nonpacifist nature of early American antiwar protest similarly characterized opposition to the War of 1812. Relations with England, never particularly good after the Revolutionary War, turned overtly hostile in the early 1800s as the repercussions of the Napoleonic War began to be felt on North American soil. But the decision to declare war on Britain reflected not only frustration with British policies, but also the increasingly partisan divisions that had come to characterize American political life. Thomas Jefferson's political heirs, the Democratic-Republicans, were among the most vocal war hawks of the time. They fondly recalled France's support of their own revolutionary movement a generation before, and they considered themselves ideological brothers to Napoleon's own revolutionary crusade. To declare war on France's enemy thus seemed logical and just. But to the Federalist opposition, mostly New England merchants who depended upon the trans-Atlantic trade and who had strong cultural and economic ties to England, the war was a tragic mistake. They feared that it would bring American commerce to a halt and create an irreparable schism between the United States and what Caleb Strong, governor of Massachusetts, emotionally referred to as "the nation from which we are descended." When President James Madison brought the declaration of war to Congress, not one New Englander voted in support.

Federalist opposition did not stop there. Antiwar sentiment was widespread, especially in the Federalist stronghold of New England, where it reached its peak in 1814. Resistance to the war took many forms, from the public speeches of prominent leaders who decried Anglo-American hostilities to the refusal of New En-gland financiers to purchase war bonds, to public demonstrations among common people reminiscent of the Revolutionary War–era street actions that had undermined British colonial rule. The revolt of the Federalists and their sympathizers culminated in the Hartford Convention of 1814–1815, when Federalists gathered to complain of the federal government's disregard of New England's interests, discussed the possibility of seceding from the Union, and then crafted a public statement that elaborated their grievances about the war.

These acts of protest did little to impede the actual conduct of the war but led almost directly to the downfall of the Federalist Party. A victim of bad timing, the Hartford Convention's statement of dissent came out just as the war came to an end, with Andrew Jackson's symbolic but triumphant victory over the British at the Battle of New Orleans. Although the results of the war were ambivalent at best, nationalists couched the conflict as a second War of Independence and denounced the antiwar Federalists as traitors. With that, the Federalists' political fate was sealed. Their antiwar stance had cost them political influence and power. As a political party, they ceased to exist.

THE NINETEENTH-CENTURY PEACE REFORM

Antiwar sentiments, on the other hand, persisted and spread over the course of the nineteenth century. War continued to be a touchstone for domestic political divisions, most notably in the case of the Mexican-American War. But the nature of peace advocacy also changed as the evangelically based antebellum reform movements gave birth to a nonsectarian strain of pacifism, distinct from that of the historic peace churches but similarly rooted in a principled opposition to violence of all kinds. By the late 1800s, the peace reform had evolved to yet another stage. Peace advocates, influenced by both Gilded Age and Progressive tendencies, embraced the goals of rationality, practicality, and an activist state over spiritual and moral reform. Their focus shifted as they worked to create institutions to prevent and mediate international conflict. Growing efforts to link the emerging struggle for women's rights to the antiwar cause augmented the movement's focus. Together, these ingredients laid the groundwork for the birth of a recognizably modern American peace movement.

The most dominant form of antebellum antimilitarism grew directly out of the religious revivalism of the early 1800s known as the Second Great Awakening. Newly inspired converts quickly translated their religious zeal into action as they organized Bible tract societies, temperance campaigns, antiprostitution crusades, and antislavery associations, seeking to address the social ills of nineteenth-century American life. This movement similarly inspired the men who founded the nation's first two peace organizations in 1815: the New York Peace Society and the Boston-based Massachusetts Peace Society. As David Low Dodge, founder of the fledgling New York society typically proclaimed, "All who love our Lord Jesus Christ in sincerity cannot but ardently desire that wars may cease." The pursuit of peace, he believed, not only would save Americans from the scourge of war, but would turn them away from the temptations of vice, bringing them ever closer to the kingdom of God. Mirroring the strategies of other evangelical reformers, antebellum peace advocates emphasized persuasion and conversion, and recruited volunteers to distribute literature and organize public lectures. Though small in number, they abided in the belief that they could convert society to their aims.

In the years leading up to the Civil War, peace reformers forged strong alliances with other movements for social and political change. By 1838, for example, with the founding of the New England Non-Resistance Society, it became almost impossible to separate advocates of Christian nonresistance from the radical wing of the antislavery movement led by the well-known abolitionist William Lloyd Garrison. In Garrison's eyes, slavery was a form of violent coercion as heinous as war that required personal purity, a commitment to nonviolence, and unceasing agitation to overcome. The Garrisonians' embrace of a more active form of pacifism distinguished them from others who sought to abolish slavery through either force or legislation, and helped link ideas about peace to the abolitionist cause. At the same time, this most "ultra" group of evangelical reformers also began to relate nonviolence and nonresistance to the organized pursuit of women's rights. The leaders of this movement, including early feminists like Elizabeth Cady Stanton, Lucretia Mott, and Sarah Grimké, saw nonresistance as a critical tool in overcoming the oppression faced by women as well as slaves.

Peace reformer Elihu Burritt provided antebellum Americans with another example of how nonviolence could be linked to larger struggles for justice and social change. Like Garrison, Burritt based his nonresistance on an understanding of Christian perfectionism that viewed war as what he called the "sin-breeding sin of sins" and that sanctified the notion of a broth-

erhood of man. This belief in brotherhood, and his background as a blacksmith, led Burritt to embrace a far more inclusive vision of peacemaking—one that inspired him to turn peace advocacy into a trans-Atlantic cause that could be embraced by the working as well as middle classes. In 1846, he traveled to England, where he promoted the idea of an international peace pledge and helped found the League of Universal Brotherhood, which quickly counted over 30,000 members in Britain and 25,000 in the United States. To attract working-class recruits, Burritt argued for peace on economic as well as moral grounds and publicly cast his lot with laboring men. In his eyes, the pursuit of nonviolence needed to be more than just a vocation for the elite: only an organized international working-class brotherhood could help pave the way for universal peace.

The outspoken nature of these antebellum peace leaders, however, belied the general apathy that most Americans felt toward the antiwar cause. Nevertheless, when war with Mexico broke out in 1846, opposition raged, especially in New England and the Old Northwest. For the most part, these clusters of antiwar sentiment stemmed not as much from a principled opposition to war as from pragmatic political concerns regarding the growing power of Southern slaveholding interests in national politics. Northerners overwhelmingly viewed the U.S. incursions into Mexico as part of a larger Southern plot for territorial expansion and believed that acquiring new territories would exacerbate the already tense divisions between the North and the South. Abraham Lincoln, then a young congressman from Illinois, publicly criticized President James Polk for instigating the conflict and lying to Congress. Newspaper editors denounced the conduct of the war. And writer Henry David Thoreau publicized the voice of moral protest and individual conscience when he refused to pay taxes to support what he believed to be an immoral war and then marched off to jail. His essay "On Civil Disobedience" became a powerful statement on the virtue of individual resistance to governmental wrongdoing. Yet, in the tradition of earlier antiwar advocates, Thoreau and others did not justify their position with pacifist ideals. In the 1840s, Christian nonresistance and antiwar agitation were not one and the same.

PACIFISM AND THE CIVIL WAR

The increasing intensity of the national struggle over slavery in the 1850s further undermined the power of the peace reform movement. As the nation headed toward war, pacifist reformers stood on the edge of po-

Many of the participants in the New York City draft riots of 1863 lived in the Five Points area, a poor, largely Irish-American neighborhood in Manhattan. During four days of violence, mobs beat and lynched blacks, resulting in more than 100 deaths. *(Collection of the New-York Historical Society)*

litical irrelevancy. Committed to the emancipation of slaves above all else, even the most devout advocates of nonresistance found ways to tolerate the violence that threatened to divide the nation. Radical abolitionist and feminist Angelina Grimké wrote in 1854 that there was no choice but "to choose between two evils, and all that we can do is take the *least*, and baptize liberty in blood, if it must be so." Even the pacifist William Lloyd Garrison offered his qualified support to John Brown's violent raid on the Harpers Ferry armory. And when the Civil War broke out in 1861, most peace advocates lent their support to it on pro-Union and antislavery grounds. Indeed, the most visible signs of antiwar discontent came not from the efforts of the nation's tiny and largely middle-class

peace community, but from a crowd of nonpeaceable working-class whites who led the New York City draft riots of 1863. This three-day rampage highlighted racial and class resentments among poor white men who could not buy their way out of conscription but had little sympathy for black freedom's cause. Nonresistance as a mobilizing force, however, fell by the wayside as the "war to save the Union" became a war to end slavery.

PRE–WORLD WAR I PACIFISM

Instead, in the aftermath of the Civil War, at the dawn of the Industrial Age, the quest to promote practical alternatives to war rose to replace the pacifist ideal as the guiding force of American peace reform. It was a

CHARGE OF THE POLICE ON THE RIOTERS AT THE "TRIBUNE" OFFICE.

The New York City draft riots of July 1863 were the largest civil disturbance of the nineteenth century. Most rioters opposed both conscription and the Civil War. When police proved unable to quell the violence, President Abraham Lincoln ordered Union soldiers—victorious in the recent Battle of Gettysburg—to New York to patrol the streets. *(Brown Brothers)*

reform shaped by the hallmark values of the Gilded Age—rationality, optimism, and an unabashed celebration of American advancement and power—that stood in striking contrast to the efforts of the prewar reformers. Antebellum peace dissidents had struggled from the political margins as they worked to shape society in God's image and lead the nation away from the sin of war. The Gilded Age reformers, however, drew upon their expertise and connections as members of the educated elite to create a powerful coalition of business leaders, government officials, legal experts, and social reformers. Like other Progressive reformers, peace advocates promoted practical solutions to the "social problems" of their day—in this case the threat of war—by finding "rational" ways to mediate conflict and shape foreign policy. Their emphasis on preventing violence through the arbitration of international conflict dominated peace efforts for almost fifty years, until the outbreak of world war in 1914.

Reaching its peak between the 1880s and the early 1910s, the Gilded Age peace reform firmly linked antiwar efforts to professional internationalism rather than the pacifist idealism of earlier decades. Motivated by the globalization of capital and the search for commercial markets, reformers argued that preventing war was the only way to ensure global trade. Such efforts attracted the support of prominent Americans, like the steel magnate Andrew Carnegie, and cooperation from leading government officials. Even peace-minded clergy couched their quest for peace as a business rather than a moral proposition. As the influential Protestant cleric Josiah Strong characteristically noted in 1898, "We are entered upon the final stage of industrial development, which is the organization of a world-industry. This world-tendency involves also the complete development of a world-life, a world-conscience. And all these involve ultimate international arbitration." The work of Russian czar Nicholas II, who called the First Hague Peace Conference in 1899, seemed to suggest that such mechanisms were possible. The conference's creation of a Permanent Court of Arbitration and its prohibition of the use of certain weaponry as a means to "civilize" and "rationalize" war pointed the way toward a new standard in international affairs.

Nevertheless, a moral pacifist impulse remained as an important undercurrent of antiwar reform. Quakers continued to promote nonresistance as an integral part of their witness for peace, most notably through the work of Alfred H. Love and the Universal Peace Union. Feminists like Elizabeth Cady Stanton and Julia Ward Howe similarly persevered in their belief that women's rights and the pursuit of peace were inseparable goals. Echoing the arguments of other female reformers, feminist peace advocates insisted that women could draw upon maternal concern and, in Howe's words, women's "superior moral force" as powerful weapons against war. By the 1890s, they were joined by the Woman's Christian Temperance Union's Department of Peace and Arbitration, which, as part of the largest grassroots political organization of its time, mobilized its members to work against military conscription, war toys, and schooltime military drills. Finally, there was the influence of Leo Tolstoy, whose writings highlighted a belief in Christian anarchism that upheld the dignity of human life above all else and that denounced violence and force of all kinds. Settlement House leader Jane Addams, one of the most famous social reformers of the Gilded Age, was profoundly influenced by Tolstoy's work. So were a number of other turn-of-the-century reformers, idealists whose desire for peace stemmed from humanitarian concerns.

WORLD WAR I AND THE BIRTH OF THE MODERN AMERICAN PEACE MOVEMENT

World War I came as a shock to those who believed that the Progressive principles of order and law would make war between nations obsolete. Instead they faced the horrifying specter of barbarism rising from the heart of the "civilized world" and the growing realization that their efforts to resolve international conflicts with scientific studies and judicial codes would do little to stop the slaughter then making its way through Europe. A movement that relied on reasonable discussion and governmental cooperation had little relevancy in a world where neither of those forces existed. The genteel respectability of the prewar American peace movement had painted itself into a corner from which there was no apparent escape. Its members could only watch the affairs in Europe with dread and dismay.

Out of this crucible of hopelessness, a new American peace movement was born. It began, first, with the women. On August 29, 1914, less than a month after the war in Europe began, approximately 1,500 women silently marched down New York's Fifth Avenue in a parade of mourning and concern. The Parade Committee hoped to stimulate public opposition to U.S. involvement in the European war. Led by prominent women's rights activists, including Fanny Garrison Villard (daughter of abolitionist William Lloyd Garrison), Harriot Stanton Blatch (daughter of the pioneering feminist Elizabeth Cady Stanton), and Carrie Chapman Catt (leader of the National American Woman Suffrage Association), the parade highlighted the special role feminists believed that women should play in the struggle for peace. As mothers, they saw themselves as uniquely devoted to the preservation of human life. As women, they acutely felt the dangers that war posed to their advancement and safety. As suffragists, they argued that only the enfranchisement of women would inject female morality into the political sphere and lead the world to peace.

The organization they ultimately formed, the Woman's Peace Party (WPP), reflected this feminist perspective as well as a determination born of experience in the growing mass movement to win women the right to vote. The New York branch of the Woman's Peace Party, for example, mirrored the militancy of suffrage protests by staging street demonstrations, leafleting at preparedness parades, and booing and hissing pro-war speakers. Other WPP members, though less confrontational, were equally daring in their deeds—particularly the almost fifty women who traveled to Europe as a female peace-making delegation in the spring of 1915. Internationalism, in fact, became a defining feature of this antiwar effort. So did their public protests, which stood in stark contrast to the staid and respectable demeanor of prewar peace endeavors.

Principled antimilitarism gave birth not only to the WPP, but to numerous other antiwar groups that attracted tens of thousands of men and women to their cause. There was the American Union Against Militarism (AUAM), whose mass meetings and Washington office provided an outlet for those who wanted to act decisively against the growing tide of military preparedness. Chicago activists, including the venerable Jane Addams, by this point one of the most famous women in the nation and a leading member of the WPP, convened the Emergency Peace Federation to defend the Progressive reform agenda from the ravages of war. Christian pacifists, heirs to the nonresistance tradition of the nineteenth century, gathered together in the nondenominational Fellowship of Reconciliation. Smaller local groups similarly tapped into widespread public antiwar desires. For the first time in U.S. history, a truly national movement existed with peace at its center.

The World War I–era antimilitarists were broad thinking and politically savvy. Veterans of successful social reform campaigns and experienced in the workings of political life, this new generation of antiwar activists took themselves seriously as organizers and agents of change. The leaders of the AUAM, for example, could pride themselves on building an organization that had over 15,000 members, distributed literature in the hundreds of thousands, maintained a sizable national mailing list, lobbied in Congress, and published articles in the leading reform-minded journals of the time. Like their antebellum predecessors, these activists saw their antiwar efforts as part of a much larger struggle for social and political change. They believed, on the most fundamental level, that militarism threatened the democratic institutions that they held dear. Only by achieving social justice, they argued, could a lasting peace be forged. The struggles of the suffrage and labor movements, of antipoverty campaigns, and for women's rights—struggles in which they had all taken part—became part and parcel of their antiwar reform.

Up until the moment that the United States entered the war, the Progressive peace movement maintained its fervor, intensity, and public support. In the early months of 1917, as tensions between the United States and Germany reached the breaking point, a sense of urgency took over the anti-intervention campaigns. Mass rallies, lobbying efforts, and full-page newspaper ads alerted the nation to the growing danger and signified the persistence of a public antiwar impulse. But as the inevitability of war grew, the movement experienced critical signs of attrition. Local groups folded. Key members of the WPP and the AUAM resigned. Nevertheless, even on the eve of war, antimilitarist forces were able to hold a rally in New York's Madison Square Garden whose crowd overflowed into the street.

All of this changed when Congress declared war on Germany in April 1917. Public support for the antiwar cause evaporated overnight, its decline aided in part by passage of the Selective Service Act that May and the Espionage Act in June. Conscription brought the heavy hand of the state down upon those men who hoped to avoid participating in the war. But it was the Espionage Act, which empowered the federal government to censor newspapers, ban the mailing of publications, and imprison anyone who "interfered" with the draft or voluntary enlistment, that sent a palpable chill through antimilitarist circles. Not surpris-

ingly, the threatened penalty of twenty years in prison and a $10,000 fine dramatically narrowed the range of acceptable public debate. Activities that had once been legal, though controversial, were now prohibited by law. As Jane Addams recalled after the war, pacifists and antimilitarists essentially became "outlaws." Only the most stalwart dissenters remained within the peace movement's fold. Most other Progressives left, having decided that it was futile to oppose government policy; instead, they worked to influence the conditions of the postwar peace.

Thus, the declaration of war profoundly changed the basic parameters of antiwar activism in the United States. Activists regrouped, first in the new People's Council of America for Peace and Democracy, whose platform called for an early peace, the repeal of conscription, safeguarding the rights of labor, and protecting civil liberties and basic democratic rights. Its leftist orientation attracted members of the Socialist Party and the Anarchist labor movement—radicals who feared that what they considered a capitalist and nationalist war would only undermine their efforts on behalf of the working class. The Espionage Act, however, put these groups on a collision course with the wartime assault on radical dissent. Federal authorities arrested and imprisoned numerous leaders of the Socialist Party and the Industrial Workers of the World (IWW) for sedition. Even those who weren't arrested found it almost impossible to organize and meet. The postmaster general barred antiwar and Socialist publications from the mail, making communication difficult at best. And when the People's Council tried to convene a constituent assembly during the summer of 1917, mobs and local police closed down the meeting halls and drove its leaders out of town. Activists across the country were shocked by the intensity of government repression and by how quickly it had pushed them to the political margins.

Religious pacifists and conscientious objectors to military service (COs), though small in number, found the times trying as well. Federal legislation granted members of the historic peace churches exemption from military combat, for the first time providing a legitimate avenue of nonresistance to pacifist adherents. But the government forced those it granted official CO status to work in the military in noncombatant roles, thus turning them into soldiers who simply did not carry guns. In addition, the federal CO provisions explicitly excluded pacifists not specifically affiliated with the historic peace churches, thus closing off all options except outright resistance. As a result, over 1,400 men, one-third of all those who claimed CO status, spent the war imprisoned in military confinement and subject to physical and psychological abuse.

Given the difficult nature of their wartime task, a number of antiwar advocates turned their attention to the defense of civil liberties and constitutional rights. Two feminist pacifists, Tracy Mygatt and Frances Witherspoon, founded the Bureau of Legal Advice, which furnished organized help for conscientious objectors and free speech victims. The AUAM followed suit with a Civil Liberties Bureau that lay the groundwork for the founding of the American Civil Liberties Union (ACLU). Over the next several years, these two groups provided legal advice and prepared affidavits for thousands of antiwar protesters and COs.

By the time the war ended with the armistice of November 1918, the American antiwar movement had been radically transformed. No longer the domain of eminent men who hoped to use arbitration and the rule of law to make the world safe for global commerce, the movement had become a haven for reformers and radicals, women and men, seeking to create social change by fostering peace. In its recognizably modern form, the peace movement became an organized voice of collective protest that linked social justice to the pursuit of a nonviolent world.

THE ANTIWAR ZENITH OF THE INTERWAR YEARS

The end of World War I, however, did not necessarily mean peace for those involved in the antiwar movement. Building on the political repression of the wartime years, the United States experienced a postwar wave of anti-Communist hysteria—a Red Scare—that effectively stifled whatever political dissent had not already been stamped out. What began in 1919 as a government crackdown on domestic radicalism and the mass deportation of "enemy aliens" (mostly IWW members and Anarchists) continued through the 1920s when the nation entered an era as famous for its political conservatism as it was for its cultural experimentation. Peace advocates, now tied in the public's mind to radical causes, became easy targets. Even the venerable Jane Addams, once one of the most highly esteemed women in the nation, was not immune from attack as "subversive" and "unAmerican." Nevertheless, the antiwar movement, backed by a committed core of experienced leaders, continued to work toward its new postwar goals of disarmament, the abolition of war, and the pursuit of social justice on a national and international scale.

Even within this harsh climate, the antiwar movement tapped a raw nerve in the public psyche. The atrocities of World War I had led to a widespread social and cultural revulsion to war, a sense of disillusionment that, despite the Red Scare, made sizable sectors of the American public open to the message and goals of peace advocates. War stories by Ernest Hemingway, John Dos Passos, and, most famously, Erich Maria Remarque in his best-selling novel, *All Quiet on the Western Front* (1929), spread images of senseless horror that countered the wartime discourse of honor, civilization, and patriotic duty. Scholars published research arguing that collusion and manipulation on the part of the Allies, and especially leading industrialists and munitions manufacturers, had caused a war that was, at its root, about earning profits, not saving democracy. By the early 1930s, even the terms of the postwar peace had come up for public critique. The rise of fascism in Germany and Italy suggested the limits of a war ostensibly fought to make the world "safe for democracy." To many Americans, the solution was clear: make sure that such a war never happened again.

THE WOMEN'S PEACE MOVEMENT

Stripped of their prewar optimism but not of their sense of political influence and power, female activists—leaders and members of the Woman's Peace Party—began a multifaceted campaign for disarmament and the outlawing of war. Feminists had achieved a major victory with passage of the women's suffrage amendment in 1920. Now, convinced that women could act as a united and potent political force, they turned their attention to the problem of war. As in earlier efforts, many of these female leaders argued that women had a unique role to play in the work for peace, not just as mothers but as worldly and experienced political reformers. They saw their work as an extension of "municipal housekeeping"— their earlier (and successful) efforts to reform the state—which they now hoped to take to the international stage.

Through organizations such as the Women's International League for Peace and Freedom (WILPF), the Women's Peace Society, the Women's Peace Union, and the National Committee on the Cause and Cure of War (NCCCW), former suffragists became the backbone of the interwar peace movement. Determined to work on the inside of a political system they had just gained official access to, these women mobilized their vast constituencies, elected political allies, and lobbied Congress in pursuit of their goals. WILPF, the reconstituted successor to the Woman's Peace Party, pursued a primarily legislative strategy. Led by the indomitable Dorothy Detzer, WILPF played a dominant role in the Washington "peace lobby" of the 1920s and 1930s—working tirelessly for universal disarmament under the auspices of the League of Nations and fighting to secure U.S. participation in a world court of justice. WILPF's pursuit of legal alternatives to war was augmented by the efforts of the Women's Peace Union, which sought, unsuccessfully, to introduce a constitutional amendment prohibiting war, and the NCCCW, which, under the directorship of former suffrage leader Carrie Chapman Catt, organized a vast membership of over 5 million women in outreach and educational campaigns.

Paralleling the development of these sizable women's peace efforts was the rise of the nation's first mass student movement. Organized in response to the social conditions of the Great Depression, a diverse coalition of college radicals came together in late 1931 to seek action-oriented solutions to the problems of poverty, joblessness, and economic collapse. By 1933, the movement had pushed the issue of world peace to the center of its political agenda, a decision that facilitated the movement's spread from its center in New York City to campuses across the country. Not surprisingly, college students were among those most disillusioned by the "lessons" of World War I. As youthful idealists, they looked back in horror at the domestic repression that went hand in hand with militarization in the United States. On a more personal level, they feared becoming the next generation of casualties in the next "Great War." Students converted to pacifism and antimilitarism in unprecedented numbers. Beginning in the spring of 1933, tens of thousands took the Oxford Pledge, by which they renounced personal participation in any war. A national student poll that same semester documented the widespread nature of these antimilitarist beliefs: 39 percent of those polled supported the Oxford Pledge, while another 33 percent stated that they would fight only if the United States itself was attacked. Student demonstrations between 1934 and 1936 pushed the campus peace campaigns to a militant edge that reached its peak in April 1935, when 60,000 students boycotted classes as part of a national student strike against war.

Much of the push for this student peace movement came from the ranks of the radical left, Communists and Socialists who saw the antiwar cause as intimately linked to a much wider struggle for social justice and social change. In their opinion, wars were

the work of "vested interests," the businessmen and industrialists who had been implicated in the Nye Committee's 1933 congressional investigation of war profiteering and the munitions industry during World War I. From the perspective of student radicals, undermining the power of ruthless capitalists thus removed a major obstacle to world peace. They threw themselves into the labor movement, providing support and publicity to working-class struggles during a crucial moment in U.S. labor history. This largely white group of student activists also took up the banner of interracial justice by organizing campus campaigns to abolish Jim Crow. As with their antiwar forebears of World War I and the pacifists of the nineteenth century, student radicals saw the struggles for peace and justice as part and parcel of the very same cause.

These connections gained credence in the early 1930s as news of Mohandas Gandhi's nonviolent struggle against British colonial rule in India reached the United States. Pacifist clergy in particular—the third major branch of the interwar peace movement—embraced Gandhi's example with zeal. The Fellowship of Reconciliation (FOR), which had become the leading venue of radical Protestantism in the years since World War I, had been striving for years to apply the precepts of the Social Gospel—the idea that American Christians had the responsibility to use their power and privilege to create a better world—to its work for peace. What Gandhi provided was proof that nonviolence could work as an effective, and "Christian," alternative to war. Quaker lawyer Richard Gregg publicized Gandhi's experimental techniques in his widely read 1934 book, *The Power of Non-violence*, which FOR members studied as they theorized about how to apply these tactics to their work, and thus transformed the meaning of Christian pacifism in the United States. The traditional doctrine of passive nonresistance had long stood at the center of pacifist theology. But many believed it was no longer enough to simply refuse to fight. With Gandhian nonviolence, it was now possible to resist.

Together, Christian pacifists, student radicals, and feminist internationalists built a powerful and far-reaching antiwar movement. By the mid-1930s, they had developed a solid constituency, political allies, and a developing theory of nonviolence that would have surprised the beleaguered pacifists of 1919. The challenges of the late 1930s, however, would put this coalition to the test.

PACIFISM AND NEUTRALITY MEET WORLD WAR II

The antiwar movement of the 1930s, for all of its popular support, faced an insurmountable obstacle to its quest for world peace: the rise of fascism and militarism in Europe and Asia. The threat first appeared in 1931, when Japanese troops invaded Chinese Manchuria. By the mid-1930s, the threat had reached Europe with the Nazis' rise to power in Germany, Mussolini's invasion of Ethiopia, and the carnage of the Spanish Civil War. The world now teetered on the edge of another total war, and peace advocates needed to formulate a response. The bulk of the peace movement initially gathered under the banner of "neutrality." Like their antimilitarist counterparts of World War I, they sought to prevent U.S. involvement in the conflict overseas. But as international tensions deepened, the movement disintegrated, leaving only the most absolute pacifists behind and tainting the movement with a stain of treason that would follow it for years.

At first, however, it seemed that neutrality, specifically *strict* neutrality, would provide a workable solution to the problem of U.S. involvement in the spreading global conflict. Strict neutrality differed from prior practices in that it prohibited *all* trade with belligerent nations. Critics had blamed "neutral" commerce for having aggravated international tensions in the 1910s and pulling the United States into World War I. Now activists worked to implement a stricter definition. In 1935, pacifists from the FOR, WILPF, and the American Friends Service Committee (AFSC) joined with liberal internationalists to form the Emergency Peace Campaign (EPC). Although strict neutrality played a key role in the EPC's program, its ultimate goal was not to isolate the United States from international affairs. On the contrary, EPC leaders believed that strict neutrality had to go hand in hand with an internationalist program that stressed transnational cooperation and political democracy around the globe. In the mid-1930s, activists still believed that such a program held significant promise.

The EPC opened with high hopes. Leaders launched the campaign in April 1936, during the third year of nationwide student strikes for peace and amid continued support for the Oxford Pledge. By the spring of 1937, the campaign had grown enough to launch an ambitious and broad-based "No-Foreign-War Crusade." This "crusade," like other EPC efforts, reflected the coalition's internationalist interpretation of neutrality. Organizers distributed literature, held public meetings, and conducted workshops to educate the public about developments in Europe and Asia. Speakers traveled across the country, and staff members and campaign leaders met directly with senators and congressmen to gain sponsorship and support for neutrality legislation. Although political victories proved elusive, organizers were pleased with the publicity and enthusiasm their efforts gained. There still seemed to be popular support for a movement against war.

But tensions in Europe proved stronger than peace advocates expected, and by 1940 the interwar movement had fallen apart. The Communists left first, convinced by the events of the Spanish Civil War that direct action was necessary to overcome Fascist aggression. By the spring of 1938, nonpacifist internationalists had also abandoned the neutrality effort to advocate on behalf of U.S. intervention in the anti-Nazi struggle. Liberal pacifists joined with Socialists in the short-lived Keep America Out of War Coalition, but they themselves left in 1940 when the coalition allied with the right-wing and isolationist America First Committee. From there, the pacifists and the peace movement were on their own.

This remaining remnant quickly found itself isolated and derided. The Japanese attack on Pearl Harbor in December 1941 only accelerated a trend that had started several years before. As historian Lawrence S. Wittner notes, "Americans now renounced pacifism with the same fervor with which they had previously renounced war." The public viewed antiwar advocates as delusional cowards and blamed them for the appeasement policies that had given Adolf Hitler a foothold in Europe. At a time when supporting the war effort defined the meaning of patriotic service, even principled pacifism was viewed as "un-American." Ostracized from the mainstream of American political life, and even from the radical left, pacifists turned inward—gathering in religiously oriented organizations like the FOR and the AFSC, and the more secular War Resisters League (WRL) and WILPF, for mutual support.

CONSCIENTIOUS OBJECTORS

The status of COs quickly moved to the top of the peace movement's agenda. Prodded by leaders of the historic peace churches, the federal government included provisions in the 1940 Selective Service Act that not only secured exemption from military service for religiously based pacifists, but established Civilian Public Service (CPS) camps where COs would live and engage in work "of national importance." Most

DAVID DELLINGER (1915–)

Born in Wakefield, Massachusetts, on August 22, 1915, David Dellinger is a descendant of old New England families and the son of a well-to-do Boston family. He graduated from Yale University in 1936 and studied at Oxford University, Yale Divinity School, and Union Theological Seminary (1939–1940). Dellinger's dedication to antiwar causes began early in life and would lead him to the forefront of militant, nonviolent activism.

After graduating from Yale, Dellinger went to England in 1937 to study at Oxford. While on vacation, he traveled around England and read and learned about St. Francis of Assisi, an experience that deeply influenced his future. He returned to America and entered the Union Theological Seminary. Dellinger, with other members of the seminary, started the Newark Commune. The commune, located in the ghetto of Newark, functioned as a cultural center for the black and white children of the neighborhood. The commune also served as a buying program that purchased a farm in Chester, New Jersey, and turned it into a communal farm. When World War II broke out, Dellinger refused to register for the draft despite his eligibility for a deferment as a seminary student and, as a result, was sentenced to three years in prison. He held hunger strikes in prison to protest how prisoners were treated. The protests eventually led to more humane treatment and also the desegregation of the federal prison system.

Upon his release in 1945, Dellinger formed the Libertarian Press, a printing cooperative. During the 1940s

and 1950s, he took part in many demonstrations and nonviolent protests. In April 1950, he participated in a two-week fast in Washington to protest the making of the hydrogen bomb. He also participated in sit-ins at the Atomic Energy Commission in Maryland and New York City.

Later, Dellinger actively opposed both the Korean War and the Bay of Pigs Invasion. In 1956, he became editor and publisher of *Liberation*, a major voice of radical pacifism. The magazine focused on the causes of civil rights, anarchism, decentralism, nonviolent direct action, and others.

As an opponent to American involvement in Vietnam, Dellinger was a major link to the North Vietnamese government and facilitated the release of American prisoners of war. He was arrested as a leader of the antiwar demonstration that erupted in riot at the Democratic National Convention in Chicago in 1968 and was charged as part of the "Chicago Seven"—the popular name of the seven radicals accused of inciting the Chicago riots, and was sentenced to five years. The conviction was later overturned.

Emphasizing the need for radical change as well as nonviolence, Dellinger became editor of *Seven Days* magazine (1975–1980). In the 1980s, he moved to Vermont to teach and write. He has continued his activism, speaking at the "Stop the Drug War" rally in Chicago near the 1996 Democratic Convention. He also regularly fasts in an effort to change the name of Columbus Day to "Native American Day."

James G. Lewis

of this work involved menial tasks like digging ditches and building roads, but the almost 12,000 pacifists who entered these camps, largely run under the direction of the peace churches themselves, lived in conditions far superior to those of their World War I forebears. Although not a perfect system, most pacifist leaders viewed CPS as a giant step forward in the government accommodation of COs.

The men who served in the camps, however, were not always so sure. Since COs were drafted just like ordinary Americans, their presence in the camps was anything but voluntary. Unlike soldiers, however, CPS men were not paid for their service. Instead, the peace churches had to raise funds for the camps' operating expenses while the men had to find ways to support themselves and their families. Work assignments proved problematic as well. As a rule, most COs were

happy to donate their skills and energy to important works of service. But as highly educated men with idealistic goals, the work to which they were assigned, generally unskilled physical labor, only added insult to injury. "How can we be content day after day to manicure mountains," one CO complained, "when the world has such crying need for practical real help and help that we want to give." As the war, and their grievances, progressed, growing numbers of COs came to view CPS more as a form of state-sponsored punishment than as an experiment in alternative national service.

Many began to rebel. Inspired by the radical labor movement of the 1930s, men in the CPS camps initiated work stoppages and slowdowns. The more frustrated camp members simply walked out. Leaving the camps did not mean freedom, but rather the opposite, since such noncooperation violated federal law. The COs who walked out simply exchanged one prison for another: CPS for the federal penitentiary. There they joined men who had refused to cooperate—for reasons of conscience, religion, and politics—with the draft in any way or form. Over the course of the war, approximately 6,000 hard-line resisters, uncompromising pacifists, and deserting CPS men—one-sixth of the total federal penal population—served federal prison terms, where they continued their protests, albeit in a different form.

Their biggest challenge was to justify their pacifism in the face of Nazi atrocities and overwhelming popular support for the war. For those who took the biblical commandment not to kill at its word, however, there was little choice. This had always been the position of the historic peace churches. A.J. Muste, the nationally renowned leader of the FOR, named by *Time* magazine as "The Number One U.S. Pacifist" in 1939, echoed these sentiments when he publicly insisted that since "all men were brothers" it was immoral to kill. But he also blamed the rise of fascism on economic domination, global imperialism, and the flawed peace of World War I. Still others pointed to Gandhi, who propagated the view among many throughout the world that war was immoral.

The Color Bar

For the imprisoned COs, Gandhian nonviolence also became a practical tool of transformation and radicalization. Working from an incipient understanding of nonviolent direct action techniques, a group of draft resisters began to demonstrate against racial segregation inside the federal prison system. The color bar was everywhere, even in the Northern institutions. To resisters like the black pacifist Bayard Rustin and the white militant James Peck, segregated dining tables and dormitories were a grievous affront that required an immediate response. By mid-1943, their protests, which included a combination of prolonged work and hunger strikes, had spread through the federal penitentiaries that housed militant COs. Authorities responded by separating the protesters and putting them in solitary confinement, but the resisters sent word of their actions to the outside world, successfully publicizing their efforts to a larger community of support.

The nonviolent prison protests against Jim Crow mirrored similar campaigns being waged in the streets. Pacifists had latched on to the wartime surge in civil rights protests, inspired in part by black labor leader A. Philip Randolph, who led the 1941 March on Washington Movement that forced President Franklin D. Roosevelt's administration to act against racial discrimination in the war industries. The FOR developed close ties to Randolph and, encouraged by Randolph's assertion that the "evil of racism" could be overcome by "nonviolent, good-will direct action," adopted the civil rights issue as one of its own. FOR members helped found the Congress of Racial Equality (CORE) in 1942, which provided pacifists with a venue for constructive wartime work and an outlet for their experiments with Gandhian techniques. CORE's local chapters used pickets and sit-ins to combat segregation at lunch counters, restaurants, movie theaters, and amusement parks, and helped keep pacifism relevant during a difficult time.

The Waning of the Peace Movement

By the end of the war, the American peace movement had dwindled to a small but hardened core of dedicated pacifists. Organizations like WILPF, which had worked to attract nonpacifists to the antiwar cause, emerged battered yet still intact. Purely pacifist organizations, like the AFSC, FOR, and the WRL, actually saw their memberships rise during the wartime years even as their broad bases of support shrank. Isolated pacifists sought each other out for much-needed fellowship. Solidarity helped to strengthen their resolve, while experiments in nonviolent action paved the way toward a new direction in antiwar protest.

The Struggle Against McCarthyism and the Bomb

Ultimately, it was how World War II came to an end that most profoundly shaped the antiwar movement of the postwar years. With the dropping of atomic bombs on the Japanese cities of Hiroshima and Nagasaki in August 1945, the United States simultaneously ushered in the nuclear age and paved the way for the Cold War. The nuclear threat made the struggle against war all the more urgent, as did the growing tensions between the United States and the Soviet Union. Meanwhile, growing fears about Soviet expansionism set off another Red Scare on American soil. At a time when the stakes seemed higher than they ever had been before, the opportunities and tolerance for political debate shrank. Those who challenged U.S. foreign and military policy were deemed subversive and dangerous enemies of the state. Antiwar advocates faced new challenges and unfamiliar threats.

Atomic scientists were among the first to organize

in opposition to the bomb. As the people most directly responsible for its development and most knowledgeable about the consequences of its use, they felt a special responsibility to bring the burgeoning arms race under control. Under the banner of "One World or None," prominent scientists like Albert Einstein, Linus Pauling, and Leo Szilard joined together as the Emergency Committee of Atomic Scientists. From the committee's perspective, atomic weapons made wars dangerously obsolete. "Time is short," they argued, "and survival is at stake." The only solution, they believed, was to prevent international conflict through powerful institutions of world government. The scientists' stature brought them instant acclaim, although their message lost its appeal once the Cold War set in. By the summer of 1946, Americans had replaced their fear of nuclear weapons with an even greater fear of the Soviet threat. The atomic scientists' movement continued but without its necessary support.

THE SOVIET THREAT

More traditional peace constituencies faced even greater obstacles to success as anti-Communism came to dominate American politics, culture, and life. The wartime alliance between the United States and the Soviet Union began to break down in 1945. By 1946, U.S. government officials were characterizing the Soviets as a threat to democracy across the globe. Fears of Communist infiltration quickly consumed the minds of American politicians and the public at large. In 1947, President Harry Truman pushed through a program of loyalty oaths that trickled down to state and local levels. By 1950, the effort to root out Communist subversion, now labeled "McCarthyism" after Senator Joseph McCarthy's anti-Communist crusades, had become a national obsession. The House Un-American Activities Committee (HUAC) held virtual nonstop meetings that interrogated Americans from all walks of life. Congress passed the McCarran Act, requiring Americans who belonged to government-identified Communist or Communist-front organizations to register with federal authorities. Government surveillance and harassment of dissidents increased and spread into the popular culture. Although the United States had a long history of antiradical crusades, McCarthyism brought such efforts to an all-time high.

The Cold War and the Red Scare redefined patriotism and loyalty in ways that undermined almost every organized antiwar endeavor. Public pronouncements equated "peace" with containing Communism

through military strength and deemed any other definition as "unpatriotic." The government did everything it could to neutralize the peace movement itself, using overt political harassment to complement the growing cultural antipathy for dissent.

Communist-led peace campaigns, which criticized U.S. foreign policy without questioning the military buildup of the Soviet Union, only helped to brand non-Communist antiwar efforts, still reeling from their marginalization during World War II, with the indelible mark of subversion. As experiences within the movement suggest, peace activists themselves could do their share to undermine the work and unity of organizations struggling to stay alive.

WILPF, for example, at first appeared to be on sound footing. Although its membership had dropped dramatically over the course of the war, it had managed to survive with the help of strong leaders. In 1946, as a testament to WILPF's vision of feminist internationalism, the Nobel Peace Prize committee granted its prestigious award to one of WILPF's founding members, Emily Greene Balch. WILPF had also begun to reorganize its work—putting a new emphasis on the dangers of the nuclear age—and to renew its membership base. With the advent of McCarthyism, the organization took up the causes of free speech and civil liberties even as its leaders insisted that WILPF's democratic vision was incompatible with Communist doctrine. WILPF publicly prided itself on welcoming all who subscribed to its antimilitarist program.

Despite WILPF's "anti-anti-Communist" stance, conflicts flared in a number of local chapters—Denver, Chicago, and metropolitan New York—as members argued about how to protect themselves from the dual threats of internal Communist subversion and external charges of Communist infiltration. Suspicion ruled as branch leaders investigated new members, pried into the histories of its most active local leaders, and persecuted those whom they believed had Communist ties. The results were disastrous. WILPF lost some of its most able and dedicated organizers. Equally damaging, the atmosphere of paranoia divided and crippled the work of its local chapters and diverted energy away from the organization's national campaigns.

McCarthyism helped turn the late 1940s and early 1950s into the nadir of twentieth-century peace advocacy, not just in WILPF, but in the movement overall. It was not that antiwar activism did not continue. Numerous activists and organizations persisted in their efforts to respond to the arms race, conscription, the Korean War, and the continuing struggle for racial justice. But their numbers were small and their influence too weak to make a dent in public policy or opinion. The combination of paranoia from within and hostility from without took a toll on a movement already struggling in the aftermath of its World War II decline.

THE CIVIL RIGHTS MOVEMENT

Unexpectedly, in the mid-1950s, the situation suddenly changed. Rising concern about the dangers of atomic testing reached a crescendo as the general public gained knowledge about the health hazards of radioactive fallout. Then, in 1955, a bus boycott in Montgomery, Alabama, led by the young Reverend Martin Luther King Jr., ignited the civil rights movement and helped break down the Cold War's barriers to protest. For peace activists who had cut their teeth on the jailhouse demonstrations and interracial struggles of World War II, the Montgomery boycott was a monumental event. As the editors of the radical journal *Liberation* wrote in 1957, "Not since the death of Gandhi [in 1948] has there been so much discussion of nonviolence as there is today." Many pacifists believed that the time was now right to start a nonviolent movement of their own.

These stirrings of discontent brought almost immediate results. In 1955, the first protests appeared in New York City during the municipally mandated civil defense drills. Then, in 1957, a broad coalition of antiwar activists came together to organize the Committee to Stop H-Bomb Tests. Within months, this committee had devolved into two parallel disarmament organizations: the Committee for a Sane Nuclear Policy (SANE) and the Non-Violent Action to Abolish Nuclear Weapons (NVA). SANE harnessed liberal opposition to nuclear weapons testing, and its program of newspaper advertisements, petitions, and literature distribution attracted tens of thousands of members. NVA, on the other hand, with its calls for unilateral disarmament and direct action against the bomb, acted as the new home for a smaller but dedicated group of radical pacifists. Together, these two groups mobilized public sentiment and brought the campaign against nuclear weapons to the front pages of the nation's news. By 1960, the peace movement had been reborn.

The distinct orientations of SANE and NVA (later reorganized as the Committee for Nonviolent Action [CNVA]) highlight the diverse nature of this reconstituted movement. SANE had one basic goal: a comprehensive ban on nuclear testing. Leaders viewed this objective as the first step toward nuclear disarmament and the easing of Cold War tensions but insisted on maintaining their singular focus. This decision was a tactical success. SANE reached out to a large and only moderately politicized community, gathered signatures for its acclaimed newspaper advertisements, and organized enormous marches and rallies—all designed to pressure Congress to pass a nuclear test ban.

CNVA, on the other hand, placed the ban on nuclear testing within a much broader political agenda that challenged the very foundations of the Cold War. Taking Gandhian nonviolence to the next level of protest, CNVA members staged a series of dramatic civil disobedience campaigns: they trespassed on the Nevada nuclear test site, sailed into the Pacific nuclear test zone, blockaded trucks heading into nuclear facilities, and climbed aboard nuclear submarines. These radical pacifists cast themselves as the revolutionary vanguard of the antiwar struggle, not as the leaders of the moderate mainstream. Like the Garrisonian abolitionists of a century before, they saw themselves as the necessary and uncompromising voice of moral protest whose work would broaden the boundaries of political debate.

The combined efforts of SANE and CNVA mobilized a groundswell of opposition to nuclear testing and nuclear arms. SANE was an almost immediate success. By 1958, it counted almost 25,000 members in 130 local chapters. News reports in 1959, which revealed that radioactive fallout, particularly Strontium 90, had been absorbed into the nation's food and milk supply and now appeared in the bones and teeth of children far away from the actual tests, only increased public support for the antinuclear movement. In 1959, SANE and the AFSC co-sponsored an annual series of Easter marches for peace that by April 1961 attracted over 20,000 people. Even CNVA's militant actions garnered sizable support. And although SANE lost its lead in the test ban struggle in the spring of 1960, after anti-Communist purges left the organization bitterly divided, the movement continued to grow. The emergence of Women Strike for Peace (WSP)—which brought over 50,000 concerned housewives and mothers into the streets in defense of their children's futures, and which successfully stood up to the intimidating tactics of HUAC—and the Student Peace Union—which attracted growing numbers of students to the antiwar cause—indicated how antinuclear protests, even in the midst of the Cold War, could move from the political margins into the mainstream of American liberal dissent.

DECLINE OF THE MOVEMENT

These forces won a victory of sorts with passage of the Partial Test Ban treaty in 1963. No one doubted that this was a diplomatic breakthrough. But, as SANE had recognized from the start, the treaty was only a first step that had serious limitations. It did not end nuclear testing; it only moved it underground. Nor did it halt the continued escalation of the arms race or the development of new and more deadly nuclear weapons systems. It did, however, pull the rug out from under the peace movement's efforts. With passage of the treaty, many recruits to the antinuclear cause believed that they had accomplished their primary aim. The impetus for widespread activism disappeared while the organizations, which still believed that much needed to be done, scrambled to maintain some degree of momentum and visibility.

In the wake of their greatest success, the peace movement hit hard times. Groups like SANE and WSP stagnated. Radical pacifists in CNVA bemoaned the test-ban agreement and the movement's subsequent decline. What they failed to recognize, however, were the movement's more subtle successes. SANE and WSP had helped bring the antiwar movement back into the political mainstream—no small feat in the conformist climate of the Cold War. CNVA, with its dramatic acts of civil disobedience, similarly helped to popularize nonviolent direct action techniques beyond those employed in the emerging civil rights struggle. Finally, as historian Charles Chatfield notes, the combined efforts of the movement helped antiwar activists gain political influence as they "forced the government" to admit its mistakes and "acknowledge dangers it had masked." Although activists could not know it at the time, these developments, and the changes they had fostered in the national political culture, would soon help their movement confront a new crisis and build widespread opposition to an unpopular war.

THE PEACE MOVEMENT, THE ANTIWAR MOVEMENT, AND THE VIETNAM WAR

The signs appeared almost immediately. In the fall of 1963 and the spring of 1964, new chants began to punctuate liberal and radical peace gatherings and demonstrations: "End the War in Vietnam, Now!" Since the mid-1950s, the U.S. government had grown increasingly involved in sustaining the anti-Communist state of South Vietnam, the southern half of the former French colony that, in its fight for independence, had unwittingly become a pawn in the Cold War. U.S. military intervention started out slowly, but by 1963 the nation had wholeheartedly committed itself to supporting the brutally corrupt, but ardently anti-Communist, South Vietnamese regime. To a small but growing number of activists, these developments suggested that U.S. foreign policy had taken another dangerous turn. Groups like WILPF, WSP, SANE, the FOR, the WRL, and CNVA turned their attention toward Vietnam, adding it to their long agendas of political concern. Little did they know how quickly the Southeast Asian conflict would overshadow their internationalist and disarmament efforts, consuming the movement and transforming the antiwar struggle.

Pacifists led the way in the years leading up to 1965, although, as in the 1950s, their demands and strategies varied. Radical pacifists favored direct action protests, including burning draft cards and sitting in at military installations, as their tactic of choice. For them, there were no halfway measures. Just as they had espoused "unilateral disarmament" during the ban-the-bomb struggle, they now called for "immediate withdrawal." So, too, did they emphasize acts of personal witness—civil disobedience protests that carried the risk of arrest and jail—which demonstrated commitment through sacrifice and which highlighted the need for individuals to take a moral and uncompromising stance against violence and war. Liberal pacifists, on the other hand, focused their energy on education, lobbying, and outreach. Rather than rejecting the roots of American foreign policy, they simply sought to reform it. They believed that their moderate tactics and call for a "negotiated settlement" to the war would inspire large numbers of Americans to speak out in protest.

But it was the war itself, rather than pacifist leadership, that mobilized people to gather in opposition. In winter 1965, President Lyndon Johnson inaugurated Operation Rolling Thunder, launching massive bombing raids and substantially increasing the number of U.S. troops stationed in Vietnam. Johnson's policies sparked an almost immediate response on the nation's college campuses. Faculty and students at the University of Michigan spontaneously initiated a new form of protest, the teach-in, which spread to over 100 campuses before the semester's end. The teach-ins captured public attention and gave tens of thousands of young people the information they needed to challenge Johnson's foreign policy decisions. An April march and rally, sponsored by the radical Students for a Democratic Society (SDS), similarly gave notice that a new force in antiwar politics had arrived. Much to

SDS's surprise, its march against the war brought 20,000 supporters into the streets of Washington, D.C., making it the largest peace demonstration in the capital city until that time, and the first major demonstration against the war.

Students quickly became the most visible group in this new and evolving movement. In part this was because of the draft, which brought the war home to male students in a very personal way and which became the focus of widespread resistance actions. The existence of organizations like SDS helped as well. Established in the early 1960s to seek broad social change through campus reform and inner-city organizing campaigns, SDS quickly became a vital conduit that linked masses of students in its local chapters to the national antiwar struggle. Then there was the rise of the counterculture, which helped bring youthful rebellion to the forefront of national consciousness. Best known for their promotion of "sex, drugs, and rock and roll," dungaree-clad hippies also embraced the values of "authenticity," "community," and "liberation." Many saw the antiwar movement as yet another venue to express political dissatisfaction and visionary idealism. Although their presence often alienated mainstream America, their gentle nature softened the hard-line politics of student leftists and committed pacifists, and helped attract a wide range of young people to rallies and demonstrations. Before long, hippies and protesters, the student movement, and the antiwar movement came to be seen as one and the same.

The movement against the Vietnam War, however, was about more than just youthful rebellion. In early 1966, religious leaders came together in Clergy and Laity Concerned About Vietnam (CALCAV) to spearhead a faith-based constituency of Americans organized to end the war, and scored a major coup when civil rights leader Martin Luther King Jr. joined their ranks later that year. Mainstream Democrats, prodded by liberal peace groups like SANE, WILPF, and WSP, also began to speak out openly against the war. Their efforts to elect peace candidates in the November 1966 elections brought them into the movement and created valuable local networks of opposition to Johnson's policies abroad. Vestiges of the old labor-oriented left, like the Socialist Workers Party, joined the struggle. So did militant black activists, particularly associates of the Student Nonviolent Coordinating Committee (SNCC), who saw little justice in going to fight against dark-skinned people overseas when they, as black people, had so few rights at home. By the summer of 1966, they, like their white student

counterparts, had endorsed draft resistance as a key strategy in the struggle to end the war. In this movement of movements, all avenues could lead to some form of opposition. The campaign against the war in Vietnam had room for Americans from all walks of life.

Building such a broad-based coalition allowed leaders to mobilize unprecedented numbers of people in protest. The spring 1966 International Days of Protest, for example, drew 200,000 people into the streets in demonstrations across the nation. One year later, over 300,000 rallied in New York and San Francisco to pressure Johnson to end the war. When 100,000 people gathered in Washington, D.C., in an October 1967 March on the Pentagon, nobody blinked—except for the government, who called out federal troops to protect the capital city from protesting citizens. As the numbers suggest, opposition to the war was widespread and growing.

Sustaining a united front, however, was not as easy as the massive numbers of protesters suggest. By late 1967, the antiwar movement was more like a many-headed hydra than a unified and coordinated campaign. Rising frustration over Johnson's continued escalation of the war led to serious tension within the movement. So did the irony that, no matter how many demonstrations people organized, and no matter how large the crowds, how varied their membership, or how militant their actions, the war continued unabated. Divided by constituency, locality, and ideology, activists increasingly found little they could agree on except for their common desire to end the war in Vietnam. Liberal peace advocates, who believed that the only way to end the war was to work through existing political channels, had little to say to radicals who shunned the Democratic Party and called instead for revolution and confrontation. Local activists often found themselves at odds with organizers in the national offices. And pacifists, who had hoped to lead a Gandhian-styled antiwar campaign, instead had to struggle to keep nonviolence in the forefront of the movement's tactics. It proved difficult, at best, to build solid alliances between those who believed that the war was just an aberration, a mistake in an otherwise acceptable political system, and those who believed that the war grew out of the unjust distribution of power that defined American politics and life.

JOHNSON'S ELECTORAL CHALLENGE

The tensions became particularly clear in late 1967 and 1968. That fall, Minnesota senator Eugene Mc-

Carthy rose to challenge President Johnson for the Democratic Party's presidential nomination. The liberal contingent of antiwar protesters rushed to his support. Idealistic young college students shed the "hippie" image, cut their hair, and operated phone lines, ran off press releases, and canvassed door-to-door as part of the "Clean for Gene" brigade. This grassroots effort at democracy-in-action celebrated in March 1968, when McCarthy won over 40 percent of the vote in the New Hampshire primary in a surprising show of popular support. McCarthy's victory paved the way for Senator Robert Kennedy's entry into the presidential contest—now bringing two critics of Johnson's war to the center of Democratic Party politics. Johnson, aware that popular sentiment was running strongly against him, decided not to run again. His surprise announcement on March 31st seemed proof that liberal reform efforts could affect the outcome of the war.

This apparent liberal success, however, came in the wake of a rising tide of violence that brought the radical vision of social change to the forefront of the antiwar struggle. The January 1968 Tet Offensive, when North and South Vietnamese rebel forces attacked American military strongholds in South Vietnam, shocked an American public that had been told by government officials that the end of the war was near. Then the bloodshed and fire came home. On April 4, Martin Luther King Jr. was assassinated in Memphis, Tennessee, setting off a wave of urban riots that left major cities, including Washington, D.C., in flames and convincing many that the age of nonviolent protest had come to an end. That May, a small group of Catholic laity and clergy, known as the Catonsville Nine, raided a Maryland draft board and incinerated the records with a homemade recipe for napalm, the jellied gasoline mixture that U.S. forces were dropping on civilians in Vietnam. Although many antiwar advocates shunned this public destruction of government property, the poet and priest Daniel Berrigan, one of the Nine, insisted that it was better to burn paper than children. Given the intransigence of federal government policies, he and his supporters believed that there were few choices left besides the most militant of actions.

The visibility of such radicalism only increased as the viability of liberal dissent seemed to shrink. Demonstrations, some turning violent, rocked college campuses that spring of 1968. Then, in June, Robert Kennedy was assassinated in front of a crowd of supporters. Along with King, Kennedy had marked the last of the great liberal hopes. Now all such hope

seemed dead. The rioting and police assault on demonstrators outside that August's Chicago Democratic National Convention, and the selection of Johnson's designate, Hubert Humphrey, as the party's presidential nominee, highlighted the obstacles that antiwar forces faced as they tried to make themselves heard. But it was the Chicago street actions, not Democratic Party machinations, that captured the public's attention. Rather than garnering sympathy and support for the movement, television images of militant protesters battling police raised the ire of the general public, who increasingly saw these demonstrations as a dangerous and disruptive force. Although growing numbers of Americans opposed the conduct of the war, in the battle for public opinion, the antiwar movement found itself on the losing end. As the movement became more and more associated with its radical wing, Americans came to hate antiwar protesters as much as they hated the war.

Wracked by internal dissension and external opposition, about all that kept the antiwar forces of the late 1960s together and moving was Washington's continued prosecution of the war. The imperative for action was constant. Republican Richard Nixon came to the presidency on a platform of "Peace with Honor." But when he unveiled his peace plans in May 1969, activists recognized that his peace required continued military support for South Vietnam and quickly mobilized in protest. That fall, the movement staged two of its largest and most impressive demonstrations. The first, the Moratorium, drew from the grassroots organizing experience of antiwar liberals and Democrats involved in the 1968 presidential campaign. On October 15, over a quarter of a million Americans—students, workers, housewives, and politicians—removed themselves from their day-to-day responsibilities and gathered in their cities and hometowns to express their desire to end the war. A month later, a coalition on the left organized the fall Mobilization, attracting more than 800,000 people in two large protests in San Francisco and Washington, D.C. The Mobilization's high point came during the thirty-eight-hour "March Against Death," where a seemingly endless line of participants, each carrying a placard with the name of an American killed in Vietnam, marched from Arlington Cemetery to the White House and placed the placards, one by one, into a series of wooden coffins. The success of these protests belied the disarray that was ravaging the movement. Nevertheless, when Nixon announced the U.S. invasion of Cambodia in late April 1970, the movement rallied in a spontaneous wave of protest.

These demonstrations were, more than anything, displays of reaction rather than proactive programs of organized political dissent, but there was no doubt that they were spreading. The May protests, for example, arose specifically in response to the Cambodia invasion. When they ended in tragedy on May 4 at Kent State University and two days later at Jackson State, after the National Guard and local police shot into crowds of unarmed students, college campuses rose up in revolt. Spontaneous student strikes shut down almost 500 colleges and universities. Veterans similarly began to organize, coming together as Vietnam Veterans Against the War in public demonstrations that stunned the nation and infuriated the president. With each escalation of the war, the protest movement escalated as well. But it was a movement held together by little more than a shared disgust with the war.

McGovern's Campaign to End the War

Protests persisted through the early 1970s, and although militant demonstrations still stood at the center of media coverage of the movement, liberals had actually started to make significant gains. Efforts at education, lobbying, and outreach had begun to influence the contours of congressional political debate. In 1972, Democratic presidential candidate George McGovern openly stated his plans to withdraw U.S. forces from Vietnam. By the time an agreement was reached on the Paris Peace Accords in January 1973, organizers representing the liberal wing of the movement had forged the strongest antiwar coalition ever, gaining support from McGovern's campaign, the labor movement, and traditional pacifist stalwarts like SANE, WILPF, and the AFSC.

It was this last core of pacifists who once again led the struggle in the years between the signing of the peace agreement and the actual end of fighting in Vietnam in 1975. Historians Charles DeBenedetti and Charles Chatfield describe the movement as, over the course of a long decade, having come full circle. What was a peace movement in 1963 was subsumed by 1965 into a larger, but more narrowly defined, antiwar struggle. A decade later, nonpacifist leftists, liberals, and civil rights advocates—the bulk of the movement's constituency—had fallen away, returning to the demands of their daily lives or to other struggles for social and political change. As a result, the antiwar movement reverted to its pacifist roots. But this was not the same pacifist movement that had inaugurated early protests against the Vietnam War. Antiwar coalitions had brought pacifists in touch with activists working on a variety of other concerns and had helped forge vital links between the peace movement and the broader struggles for social change. Pacifist leadership had also been transformed. A younger, experienced, and more radicalized generation now stood at the helm. Skeptical of liberal politics and governmental affairs, they displayed attitudes that reflected the growing cynicism of post-Watergate American life. Nevertheless, the peace activists of the mid-1970s remained a highly empowered group, committed to nonviolence and convinced that citizens had the power to promote change and resist war.

The Antiwar Movement: From Vietnam to the New World Order

In the decades since the end of the Vietnam War, the antiwar movement has had to adjust to dramatic changes in political climate, the global balance of power, and its place in domestic debates over violence and war. Although the movement shrank significantly after 1973, it rallied with an impressive show of strength in the early 1980s. Since then it has struggled to retain influence and support while advancing a nonviolent vision of social and political change.

One theme that continued unchanged from the Vietnam War years was opposition to U.S. military intervention overseas. Activists got an early taste of things to come in 1973, when a U.S.-sponsored military coup toppled the popularly elected Socialist government of Chile. By the late 1970s, the United States was actively working to undermine revolutionary movements in Guatemala, El Salvador, and Nicaragua. Peace advocates sided with the popular insurgent movements, arguing that they comprised the strongest voices for democracy and reform, and that the American government was supporting repressive military regimes under the guise of Cold War conflicts. Acting in solidarity with the people of Central America, peace activists staged vocal demonstrations, waged outreach and educational campaigns, lobbied Congress to cut off funding for military aid, and enlisted help from a wide range of liberal, radical, and religious groups. In all of these efforts, antiwar "veterans" of the Vietnam era shared their experience and knowledge with a new generation of activist volunteers as they struggled to maintain the movement's vital edge.

OPPOSITION TO NUCLEAR WEAPONS

The peace movement's other main focus in the 1970s and 1980s was the revived struggle against nuclear weapons. Even in the midst of the Vietnam War, SANE had not entirely abandoned its goal of ending the nuclear arms race. In 1969, it spearheaded an effective coalition effort to halt the development of antiballistic missiles (ABM), and in 1972 it played a key role, along with the AFSC and CALC, in the successful campaign against the B-1 bomber. These efforts were augmented by the contributions made by radical direct actionists to the antinuclear power crusades that swept the nation with mass demonstrations, and thousands of civil disobedience arrests, in the middle and late 1970s.

This combination of radical and liberal activism laid the foundation for the mass movement against nuclear weapons that emerged in 1979. The Nuclear Freeze campaign built on the mainstream political efforts of SANE and the AFSC. Its goal was limited and, activists believed, achievable: a bilateral and comprehensive freeze on the development and deployment of nuclear weapons. As with the test-ban advocates of the late 1950s, Freeze organizers saw their campaign as the first step toward a nuclear-free future. Designed as a grassroots effort that placed Nuclear Freeze referendums on state and local ballots and that put political pressure on elected officials, the campaign attracted widespread support and mobilized hundreds of thousands of citizens on its behalf. The radical wing of the peace movement, however, like its counterpart from the ban-the-bomb days, called for unilateral disarmament and shunned electoral campaigns. In cities from Minneapolis to Las Vegas to New York, radical grassroots organizers mobilized thousands of citizens to sit in at local munitions makers and military sites. Expanding the boundaries of protest even further, the priest brothers Daniel and Philip Berrigan catalyzed Catholic resistance to the bomb by hammering on nuclear warheads, sparking a series of direct disarmament actions known as the Plowshares movement. The women's movement also joined forces with the antinuclear crusade when, in solidarity with feminist antinuclear efforts in England, it organized a peace camp at the Seneca Army Depot in upstate New York.

Encompassing both the center and left wings of American politics, the antinuclear weapons movement grew at a dramatic pace that ultimately proved difficult to sustain. In June 1982, only three years after the founding of the Freeze, a New York City rally held in conjunction with the United Nations' Second Special Session on Disarmament attracted nearly one million people, making it the largest protest demonstration in American history. Two days later, in a coordinated gesture, over 1,600 protesters risked arrest by committing civil disobedience at the consulates of the world's nuclear powers. This dramatic showing, however, marked the movement's peak. By the mid-1980s, with few legislative victories and no treaties to show for its efforts, the movement to stop the arms race had shrunk down to a declining core of dedicated activists. Activism continued, albeit in a muted, diminished, and increasingly marginalized form.

THE PERSIAN GULF WAR

The antiwar movement persisted in its reduced state through the late 1980s and into the 1990s, when world events rearranged the global dynamics of power and forced peace advocates to adjust their priorities and goals. The first indication that things had changed came in 1991 with the Persian Gulf War. The United States' military conflict with Iraq was qualitatively different from its military engagements of the Cold War years. Protests broke out against what activists described as the unilateral use of U.S. power in the world, with demonstrations that attracted tens of thousands of supporters in the days before the January 1991 declaration of war. It seemed, for a moment, as if the peace movement had been reborn. But once the war began, the tide of public opinion turned. In the new age of conservatism, the tolerance for dissent had dramatically diminished. Pundits described the Gulf War as the nation's remedy for its humiliation in Vietnam and as a preview of the United States' role in what President George H. W. Bush called "the new world order." The media, which no longer considered peace activism a newsworthy item, kept the voices of protest out of the news and isolated from one another. Only the most dedicated activists maintained their involvement through small local vigils, newsletters, and occasional civil disobedience protests. The movement now focused on constraining the U.S. military as much as possible. But with limited public support, such efforts became symbolic at best.

Stymied by the overt celebration of militarism that arose in the wake of the Persian Gulf War, antiwar advocates also had to confront the new world order that arose in late 1991 with the collapse of the Soviet Union and the subsequent end of the Cold War. Although some peace leaders talked of the possibility of a "peace dividend" that would be redistributed out of money saved from reduced military expenditures, no such bonanza appeared. Nor did the nuclear arms race come to an end, despite a number of highly publicized arms limitations treaties. Instead, the United States was left as the sole global superpower, with no clear sense of its new role in the world, but intent on preserving its dominant global position. Peace activists grew increasingly concerned about the unilateral use of U.S. military power and the continued threat of nuclear proliferation but remained unsure about how to organize and around what issues to take a stand.

In the decade that followed the first Gulf War, the American peace movement focused on advancing a multifaceted vision of a world without violence and war. Groups like the War Resisters League and WILPF joined the anti-globalization protests of the early twenty-first century, lending their expertise as organizers and publicists, as well as working to keep the tradition of nonviolent activism alive. Numerous activists similarly continued their work for social justice, tackling issues as diverse as the death penalty, homelessness, inner-city poverty, racism, and environmental abuse, alongside their work for peace.

The terrorist attacks of September 11, 2001, which killed thousands of Americans in New York City, the Pentagon, and on United Airlines Flight 93, which crashed in Pennsylvania, brought a new sense of urgency to these efforts. Fearing that the War on Terror would lead to civil liberties abuses at home, racial discrimination against Arab immigrants, and military actions abroad, antiwar groups mobilized to prevent new national and international crises. Their voices of dissent received little public or media attention in the year that followed the tragedy of 9/11. But by the winter of 2003, in the face of an impending U.S. war against Iraq, it became impossible to ignore their presence on the political stage. Organized under the auspices of established pacifist groups, as well as new broad-based coalitions like United for Peace, which brought together a wide array of labor, racial justice, anti-globalization, feminist, and faith-based activists, the antiwar movement staged a resurgence in numbers not seen since the days of the Vietnam War. Their efforts culminated in a dramatic weekend of protests in February 2003, when a coordinated series of marches and demonstrations brought more than 10 million people out onto the streets in over 600 cities across the globe. From New York to London to Rome, Istanbul, Australia, and Brazil, citizens of the world said "No" to war. Despite this unprecedented display of opposition to war, the national and international antiwar movement failed to prevent the U.S.-led attack and occupation of Iraq that began in March 2003. Nevertheless, the movement had shown its ability to mobilize a vast and diverse constituency of protest.

In the wake of U.S. military operations in Iraq, and the United States' shift to what many observers describe as a "permanent war mode," peace and antiwar activists are now struggling to marshal the energy of the winter's mobilizations and turn it into a sustained and organized movement against violence, injustice, and war. This will not be an easy task. Despite their recent organizing successes, the activists of 2003, pacifist and non-pacifist alike, have few illusions about their political strength. They recognize that their most pressing challenges are to persist, to make their voices heard, and to broaden and deepen their bases of support as they continue their critique of U.S. military policies and the impact of these policies on people's lives at home and abroad.

Marian B. Mollin

BIBLIOGRAPHY

Alonso, Harriet. *Peace as a Women's Issue: A History of the U.S. Movement for World Peace and Women's Rights.* Syracuse, NY: Syracuse University Press, 1993.

Chatfield, Charles. *The American Peace Movement: Ideals and Activism.* New York: Twayne, 1992.

———. *For Peace and Justice: Pacifism in America, 1914–1941.* Knoxville: University of Tennessee Press, 1971.

Cohen, Robert. *When the Old Left Was Young: Student Radicals and America's First Mass Student Movement, 1929–1941.* New York: Oxford University Press, 1993.

DeBenedetti, Charles, with Charles Chatfield. *An American Ordeal: The Antiwar Movement of the Vietnam Era.* Syracuse, NY: Syracuse University Press, 1990.

Early, Frances. *A World Without War: How U.S. Feminists and Pacifists Resisted World War I.* Syracuse, NY: Syracuse University Press, 1997.

Gara, Larry, and Lenna Mae Gara, eds. *A Few Small Candles: War Resisters of World War II Tell Their Stories.* Kent, OH: Kent State University Press, 1999.

Gregg, Richard. *Power of Non-Violence.* Philadelphia: J. B. Lippincott Company, 1935.

Katz, Milton. *Ban the Bomb: A History of SANE, 1957–1985.* Westport, CT: Greenwood Press, 1986.

Lieberman, Robbie. *The Strangest Dream: Communism, Anticommunism, and the U.S. Peace Movement, 1945–1963.* Syracuse, NY: Syracuse University Press, 2000.

Patterson, David S. *Toward a Warless World: The Travail of the American Peace Movement, 1887–1914.* Bloomington: Indiana University Press, 1976.

Robinson, Jo Ann Ooiman. *Abraham Went Out: A Biography of A. J. Muste*. Philadelphia: Temple University Press, 1981.

Steinson, Barbara. *American Women's Activism in World War I*. New York: Garland, 1982.

Swerdlow, Amy. *Women Strike for Peace: Traditional Motherhood and Radical Politics in the 1960s*. Chicago: University of Chicago Press, 1993.

Tracy, James. *Direct Action: Radical Pacifism from the Union Eight to the Chicago Seven*. Chicago: University of Chicago Press, 1996.

Wittner, Lawrence S. *Rebels Against War: The American Peace Movement, 1933–1983*. Philadelphia: Temple University Press, 1984.

———. *The Struggle Against the Bomb*. 2 vols. Stanford, CA: Stanford University Press, 1993–1997.

ANTI-PREPAREDNESS MOVEMENT

Anti-preparedness can be defined simply as the movement against U.S. military preparation before its official entry into World War I. Its roots lay in two closely related national debates about the role and nature of the United States. As the crisis in Cuba during the 1890s grew more serious and voices were raised in the United States for action against Spain, the power governing Cuba, a lively public argument broke out for and against war. Anti-imperialists insisted that the democratic tradition of the United States demanded no foreign wars for the creation of an American Empire. They argued that an empire would necessarily destroy democracy. On the other side, Imperialists like Admiral Alfred T. Mahan and Assistant Secretary of the Navy Theodore Roosevelt (later governor of New York and president of the United States) argued that the United States had earned the right to be a world-class power. The currency of power was a strong military and imperial acquisitions. No clear-cut victory was had by either group, despite the United States' acquisition of the Philippines and Puerto Rico, and the financial guardianship exercised over Cuba as a result of the Platt Amendment.

A second debate was literally fought out inside the United States over the nature of the country. Large corporations came to dominate the American economy in the 1890s and beyond, while citizens, notably workers faced with enormous corporate power, fought to uphold what they considered their individual democratic rights as laid out in the Declaration of Independence and the Bill of Rights in the face of corporate power. Neither of these public debates was resolved when war was declared in Europe in August 1914. Indeed, strife had reached such a level between workers and bosses that it truly became "class warfare" across the nation. So serious was it that a presidential committee, the U.S. Commission on Industrial Relations, conducted hearings from 1913 through 1914 to investigate causes and remedies.

From mid-1914, businessmen such as J.P. Morgan and others who had lost monies since the beginning of hostilities in Europe joined forces with politicians like ex-President Theodore Roosevelt in an attempt to protect their interests. Although Roosevelt and Senator Henry Cabot Lodge (R-MA) championed the idea of protecting America's vital interests rather than business profitability, they eagerly accepted business support. The preparedness faction believed that President Woodrow Wilson had a moral obligation to increase military preparedness. Oddly enough, the first anti-preparedness advocate was President Wilson. In speeches during 1914, a midterm election year, he consistently advocated that the cost of building the military which his opponents wanted would draw America into the European conflict that had nothing to do with the United States, and so the nation would be forced to choose sides. If the United States became involved, according to Wilson, it would lose the status of friendship with some European nations and it would no longer be a disinterested party in their conflict.

In reality, Wilson believed that the war would change global structures both politically and economically, but his reasons for remaining on the sidelines in 1914 were based on domestic American politics. The United States in 1914 was in many aspects a nation of immigrants. In most major cities, anywhere between 60 percent and 85 percent of inhabitants were either foreign-born themselves or had at least one parent born abroad. The majority of first-generation immigrants in that year were from central, southern, and eastern European countries where the war had broken out and raged. President Wilson had little desire to confront the issues surrounding immigrant loyalty to America at that juncture. He recognized that it would be a long process to create the atmosphere necessary to have the loyalty of these new immigrants tested on a battlefield in a country in which they still had relatives. He also knew that the majority of Americans were not in favor of creating a large military for two reasons. First were the budget constraints that military preparedness would place on domestic programs, along with a tax increase to fund military spending. The second was that most Americans associated a large military with European despotism and a threat to democratic principles. Beyond the domestic reasons, Wilson used the political reality of 1914 to back his anti-preparedness stance. Democrats in Congress would never vote for military programs over domestic spending, and most conservative Republicans and Progressives agreed. Along with most of the world, Congress believed that this was going to be a short war and it need not impinge on America. In 1914, using the principles that most Americans held, Wilson easily quieted the preparedness voices in America.

A dramatic change in attitude took place within the administration the following year, though it was not expressed publicly. Germany's use of submarines and attacks on American vessels raised some eyebrows and brought questioning from the press, but the majority of Americans still perceived the threat of war to be a European problem. The sinking of the ocean liner *Lusitania* in May, with the loss, among many others, of 128 American citizens, created public outrage that the war was no longer confined to the Europeans. Still, the American public was unwilling to go to war. By late 1915, the British and French governments were out of money. J.P. Morgan, as their representative in the United States, had trouble floating loans to continue their war effort. Aware that the war was inevitable given the situation in Europe with both sides deadlocked, Wilson began the process of preparing the nation to fight. When the politicians ignored Wilson's preparedness program presented to Congress in 1915, the president had to take action himself. He made a series of speeches during the second half of the year emphasizing that there were many Americans who held "alien sympathies"—a direct attack on immigrants with radical political beliefs. He also made references to labor unions which he believed were centers for immigrant radicals who advocated undermining the government. The most radical union of the day was the Industrial Workers of the World (IWW). Wilson believed and advocated that these organizations of workers were an actual threat to the nation.

In 1916, Wilson ran for reelection. He used the rhetoric of "Americanism" and patriotism during the campaign in the face of criticism by Roosevelt, Lodge, and others who advocated that the time had come to support the Allies in Europe. Behind the scenes, Wilson worked with the Democrats in Congress to change the long-held antiwar stance of the party. During the Democratic Party Convention and on the campaign trail, he talked of "negotiated peace" in Europe and observed that the United States recognized the rights to self-determination and freedom from aggression for all nations. Wilson also spoke out against the anti-preparedness forces in America, stating that they did not have loyalty to the country. He used the term *disloyalty* to characterize any individual or group that expressed a negative opinion of his leadership. Wilson employed ethnicity as a device to demonstrate the differences between loyal Americans and the disloyal. This type of rhetoric served to increase the anger of unions such as the IWW which believed that American entrance into the war would be an excuse to smash labor unions and give industry a free hand against labor. When the election took place in November, Wilson won by a very narrow margin due to his antiwar stance. The Socialist Party, which had great success in the 1912 election, did not have a large following during the 1916 election because Eugene Debs, the living embodiment of the Socialist Party, refused to run because of ill health. Socialists, radical labor, and political groups largely voted for Wilson because he promised to keep them out of the war.

During the campaign, Wilson had claimed that war was the opposite of peace, while gently nudging the nation toward a more warlike stance through events such as preparedness parades in major cities around the country.

The city of San Francisco was the site of a huge Preparedness Day parade on July 22, 1916. Its purpose was to demonstrate support for the Allies and promote patriotism. More accurately, what actually happened in San Francisco reflected a conflict between conservatives and radicals. The Preparedness Day parade became a focus of the ongoing struggle in the city between workers and management, a microcosm of the national situation. The San Francisco Central Labor Council and the Building Trades Council actively opposed worker participation in this demonstration of patriotism, while city employers demanded that their employees take part or be replaced. The radicals set up an anti-preparedness demonstration at Dreamland Rink, a city park, for the evening of the same day.

For workers and radicals, opposition to the preparedness parades was relatively straightforward. They believed preparedness to be a cynical maneuver by big business to hijack patriotism and the nation for their own selfish ends, to crush unionism and worker rights, and to profit from death and injury in war. In San Francisco, such an attitude appeared amply proven by the fact that the Preparedness Day parade was organized by the Chamber of Commerce, an organization dominated by large businesses like Pacific Gas & Electric and United Railways. These businesses had raised $1 million earlier in the year and had revived the city's vigilante heritage with the formation of its Law and Order Committee, the specified goal of both being to rid the city of labor unions. Although the bulk of the energy behind the anti-preparedness movement came from radicals and militant labor, it was also supported by many immigrant and ethnic Americans, especially those who were first-generation Americans, and by veterans of the anti-imperialist and clean government movements of recent history. In San Francisco, these latter people were represented at the Dreamland meeting in speeches by Rudolf Spreckels, a banker, and Fremont Older, publisher of the *San Francisco Bulletin*. Anti-preparedness was a powerful expression of what was believed at root to be a contest between workers and management thinly disguised in Americanism.

The Preparedness Day parade itself went ahead, with thousands of marchers participating more to protect their jobs than through enthusiasm for the cause and thousands also who truly believed in its worth. Rapidly, however, it turned to tragedy. A bomb exploded, killing ten and wounding scores of others. Immediately, five militant city labor unionists were arrested. They included two men later famous as the centerpiece of international campaigns for their release, Warren Billings and Tom Mooney. Radicalism in America was blamed, and the San Francisco Preparedness Day bombing fed into a growing move to tar all dissent in the nation as unpatriotic and anarchistic. Anti-preparedness as a movement was transformed into a series of defense campaigns against government suppression of free speech.

In other cities where preparedness parades were held in 1916, as in Chicago, anti-preparedness dem-onstrations were held. The following year, as the United States moved ever closer to war, significant labor groups like the Chicago Central Labor Council and the United Hebrew Trades, developed their anti-preparedness and labor defense campaigns, giving large rallies and money to denounce the government and employers' drive to war.

During the first months of 1917, it became apparent from the division within the country over the issue of preparedness and the increasing strength of radical labor and political movements that Wilson had not managed to bring the country to a consensus over the war. The anti-preparedness campaign continued with publication of articles in Socialist, radical, and labor journals, such as the IWW's *Solidarity*, the Socialist New York *Call*, and the Anarchist *Mother Earth*. Rallies were held, keeping the momentum of the movement high. Congress passed a series of laws early in the year dealing with patriotism issues.

First, it passed a law restricting incoming immigrants to those who were literate and to deport those who held political beliefs contrary to the majority in the nation. During the following month, it passed legislation outlawing any bodily threats to the president. Congress outlawed the publication of information that could undermine the success of the U.S. military during war. Although the United States did not declare war on Germany until April 6, 1917, the pieces of legislation passed during this winter session were all aimed at the radicals and labor affiliates.

In March, when the state of Idaho passed a law that banned the IWW from any action in labor negotiations that could be determined as unlawful, the anti-preparedness movement gained strength. The fear was that the Idaho legislation would be the beginning of a national ban on labor negotiations, with claims that the unions were using unlawful means to obtain a contract to the workers' advantage. The federal Justice Department started compiling lists of radicals and union members whom they believed to be alien and disloyal to American interests. Nonetheless, the anti-preparedness forces continued to publish articles and speak out against the government, recognizing that arrest and deportation could be imminent.

The declaration of America's entry into World War I in April 1917 signaled the end of the anti-preparedness campaign. It was replaced by anticonscription campaigns. The laws enacted to stop dissent during the preparedness phase of America's involvement with the war were now turned against those who continued to advocate against involvement. For the radicals and labor leaders there was a new fear. They believed that the government was willing to suspend civil liberties and the right to free speech during war. Time would prove their fears justified.

Linnea Goodwin Burwood

BIBLIOGRAPHY

Berkman, Alexander. "The San Francisco Conspiracy." *The Blast* 1: 18 (September 1, 1916): 3–4.

Cooper, John Milton. *Pivotal Decades: The United States, 1900–1920.* New York: W.W. Norton, 1990.

Gentry, Curt. *Frame-up: The Incredible Case of Tom Mooney and Warren Billings.* New York: W.W. Norton, 1967.

Goldstein, Robert Justin. *Political Repression in Modern America from 1870 to 1976.* Urbana and Chicago: University of Illinois Press, 1978.

ANTIWAR MOVEMENT: WORLD WAR I

American opposition to World War I came primarily from two wings of the peace movement—internationalists and liberal reformers—and developed in two distinct phases—before and after the United States entered the war in April 1917. Internationalist peace organizations worked within the framework of established global political power structures to develop international organizations, arbitration, and laws for securing and maintaining peace without trying to produce fundamental social and economic change. Liberal reformers were composed of a coalition of feminists, social workers, labor lawyers, publicists, journalists, clergy members, and others who formulated their own peace organizations or integrated antiwar efforts within their other progressive causes. Unlike the internationalists, they closely connected the achievement and maintenance of peace with substantial political, social, and economic reform. Before the United States entered the war, the peace movement captured a degree of sympathy from the general public, for many Americans initially wanted their country to stay out of what they saw as a strictly European conflict. The opposition movement against the war collapsed when the United States declared war on Germany on April 6, 1917, as it quickly became unacceptable to publicly voice opposition to the country's war effort. Most peace organizations disbanded, became defunct, or shifted their stance to support the war effort, focusing instead on gaining a quick and equitable peace.

INTERNATIONALISTS

Most internationalist peace organizations started in the first decade and a half of the twentieth century. Increased involvement in the foreign arena tangibly launched the United States as an emerging imperial power. U.S. participation in international affairs—notably the Spanish-American War and the costly Russo-Japanese War—spurred pacifist interest in constructing systems to maintain peace between nations that possessed increasingly powerful armed forces. These circumstances helped peace societies to dramatically increase their membership and influence. No doubt, however, the pacifist movements were slow to develop. The American Peace Society, for example—the largest American peace organization in 1900—grew from a small local society in Boston. The nascent expansion of the United States as an international power led to the rapid growth of the organization. By 1907, the American Peace Society expanded to nine chapters, and by 1914, the organization grew in stature to become a bona fide national organization with thirty-one chapters across the country.

During these prewar years, a range of peace advocates emerged to cut across the political spectrum, ranging from internationalists like the American Society of International Law to feminist Jane Addams to Socialists. However, the internationalists certainly had the most influence, power, and momentum of all peace activists. From 1901 to 1914, Americans formed forty-five new peace organizations. Among the most influential of these were the American Society of International Law, the American Peace Society, and the World Peace Foundation. These groups drew the support and participation of elite men like Andrew Carnegie and Elihu Root. In fact, Carnegie established the Carnegie Endowment for International Peace in 1911, which subsidized many of the pacifist organizations and provided the opportunity to engage directly with diplomats and state leaders, often at international conferences and closed meetings. Pacifists typically did not work in public forums or try to gain popular support through rallies and other events, practices pursued by liberal reformers.

In the years before World War I, internationalists tried to maintain peace by setting up a network of global organizations, laws, courts, and conferences providing nations with a framework through which

On August 29, 1914—twenty-six days after the onset of World War I—some 1,500 women conducted a silent peace march down Fifth Avenue in New York City. They favored keeping the United States out of the war. *(Brown Brothers)*

they could peacefully resolve conflicts through negotiation, arbitration, and legal hearings. This approach to promoting peace conflicted with the European system of maintaining a careful balance of power among nations and also required that Americans abandon their hope that isolationism would protect the United States from armed conflict. Two significant examples of peace activist work include participation in the First and Second Hague Peace Conferences in 1899 and 1907. The 1899 conference developed some rules of war and established the permanent Court of Arbitration. The second conference expanded on the war conventions, particularly on rules of neutrality. The work of many internationalist peace advocates before and during World War I laid the conceptual ground-

work for the League of Nations and ultimately the United Nations. The League to Enforce Peace, for example, was founded during the war for the primary goal of promoting a postwar international organization.

Differences within the ranks of the internationalist peace movement focused on the degree to which nations should surrender their sovereignty to an international system of institutions and laws. On the conservative end, some felt that a body of laws and rules of arbitration that nations agreed to would be sufficient to maintain peace without substantially impinging on a nation's sovereignty. On the liberal end of the scale, others felt the Western world required nations to give up part of their sovereignty—partic-

As World War I ravaged Europe, women played a major role in trying to end the hostilities. Pictured here is a delegation of the Women's International Committee for Permanent Peace. Jane Addams stands in the front row, second from the left, above the first "E" in "PEACE." *(© National Archives)*

ularly their ability to unilaterally engage another nation with force—in exchange for a collective security system to prevent armed conflict. Despite these differences, all internationalists worked with the assumption that structured international cooperation was needed at some level.

Internationalists maintained a noticeably conservative approach to advocating peace through working closely within the political establishment. They did not connect peace to social causes or class relations, and they did not look to address issues of inequality. The internationalists did not make their calls for peace on moral grounds but rather on practical arguments that modern armed forces made war economically and politically unfeasible. As America industrialized and expanded its global trade, they argued, interna-

tional peace and stability became increasingly critical to the nation's economy.

The start of World War I in August 1914 seemed to leave many internationalist peace advocates in shock. In the war's first two years, most internationalists abandoned their antiwar stance and supported the Allied cause. The Carnegie Endowment for International Peace played a critical role in this shift as it used its financial power to convince a number of peace organizations to back the Allies. Internationalists justified this switch by arguing that Germany had to be defeated before any meaningful long-term peace could be established. In short, they took up a strategy of peace through victory.

The internationalists therefore turned their attention to securing a stable peace after the war. Their most significant work toward this goal took place when members of the New York Peace Society and other conservative peace activists established the League to Enforce Peace in 1915. Their proposed league was a federation of nations that agreed to use force against any state that refused to submit to international law and arbitration. Under the leadership of former president William Howard Taft, the League to Enforce Peace gained an audience with President Woodrow Wilson in 1916. At that meeting Wilson did not directly endorse the group's proposals, but he did become the first head of state to publicly support a league or association of nations after the war. This marked one of the internationalists' biggest achievements during the war and indicated their focus was not on opposing the war but on developing a postwar peacekeeping infrastructure.

LIBERAL REFORMERS

A range of liberal activists from feminists to social workers to reform-minded clergymen along with many peace activists saw the reaction of the established peace societies as weak, timid, and ineffectual. Frustrated by what they saw as the peace societies' refusal to advocate for an immediate end to the war, many liberal reformers—including peace activists frustrated by their leaders—formed several new peace societies after the start of the war. These new organizations differed from the internationalists in that they were generally much more adamant in their demands that the war end immediately and that the United States stay out of the conflict. They also connected the war to many of the social ills affecting America and the world. Their calls for peace became part of their larger moral crusade for social justice and equity, while the internationalists made their calls for peace on the grounds that it was the key to political and economic stability. By 1916, the liberal reform wing of the peace movement had overshadowed the internationalist wing.

Feminist leaders were among the first to organize protests in the United States against the war and connect it to social and political inequalities. Less than a month after fighting started in Europe, leaders of various women's organizations and suffrage movements and independent feminists, such as Fanny Garrison Villard, organized a 1,500-person march in New York City protesting the war. Many of these leaders built on the success of that march to officially formulate in January 1915 the Woman's Peace Party a meeting in Washington, D.C., attended by 3,000 people. The party appointed Jane Addams—founder of Hull-

House, social worker, and among the nation's leading feminists—as its chair. It became the premiere women's war opposition group in America, claiming 40,000 members in 1917 before the United States entered the war.

Like other reformers, women's groups tied their opposition to the war to their own causes, women's rights and, specifically, suffrage. Some felt that the war, which the general public associated with male bravery, strength, and courage, would emphasize the differences between the sexes at a time when feminists were trying to demonstrate and achieve their equality. Therefore, protesting the war was a necessary part of their feminist and suffrage work. Addams argued that their protest against the war was a natural extension of the work they had engaged in before 1914. Not only was their opposition to the war a politically necessary move, but it fit within their feminist philosophy and feminine role as well. Although fighting for gender equality, many women's rights activists still subscribed to the prevailing theory that women were more nurturing and sensitive than men and therefore better qualified and more naturally inclined to support peace. This view of women also made it socially acceptable for them to engage in peace activities, which in turn helped them become prominent players in the antiwar movement.

This view of women also gave the feminist peace activists the intellectual backing to argue that the male-dominated internationalist peace organizations were an integral part of the state system that caused the war in the first place. They felt that these groups had aimed too narrowly to only restrict war and not trying to achieve fundamental reform that would bring the world a lasting peace. The Woman's Peace Party and other women's organizations claimed that they were in a better position to gain this lasting peace because of their ability and feminine sensibilities. This position clearly put them at odds intellectually with the internationalists and firmly in the liberal reform wing of the peace movement.

During the first year and a half of the war, women's groups and other liberal peace organizations shared the internationalists' approach of using mediation between nations to achieve peace. Although the older, conservative peace societies looked to use mediation as part of an international structure to maintain peace after the Allies defeated the Central Powers, the newer, reform-minded peace organizations wanted to use mediation to end the war immediately. The International Congress of Women at The Hague and the Neutral Conference for Continuous

Mediation were prominent examples of efforts to mediate a quick end to the war. The International Congress of Women convened in April 1915. Presided over by Jane Addams and attended by American and European delegates, the congress called for an ongoing conference of neutral nations that would lead the negotiation of a peace settlement. The Conference for Continuous Mediation also met at The Hague later the same year. Beset with internal problems, the Conference managed to produce a peace proposal in 1916 that featured mediation. No state leader endorsed either proposal.

In 1916, peace activists began to shift their focus from international mediation to anti-preparedness in the United States. Before America entered the war, a public debate raged over how dramatically, if at all, the United States should increase its armed forces, particularly the Army. During the early years of the war, most Americans wanted to stay out of the conflict. In fact, in 1916 the nation reelected President Woodrow Wilson, who made his pledge to keep the nation out of the war a central tenet of his campaign. Even many preparedness supporters—those who argued that the United States should increase its armaments—wanted the country to stay off the battlefield. They felt that a strong military would prevent America from getting dragged into the war. Many peace activists believed, however, that strengthening the armed forces would do just the opposite. Opposing preparedness became one of the main goals of the liberal peace movement in late 1915 and throughout 1916.

A number of prominent liberal peace activists founded the American Union Against Militarism (AUAM) in November 1915. It quickly became the leading anti-preparedness organization in the country as it fought calls for a draft and increased military spending and became one of the most significant peace organizations of the war. The origins of the AUAM came from the Anti-Preparedness Committee, which was founded by reformers in New York. Within a year, it grew from fifteen to 15,000 members and transformed itself into the AUAM. The organization focused on lobbying and publicly arguing against other organizations that supported preparedness. In particular, the AUAM fought against conscription, dramatic military spending increases, and the Plattsburg movement that encouraged reserve officer training for civilians.

In 1916, the AUAM had striking success in preventing a major armed conflict between the United States and Mexico. While in pursuit of Francisco

"Pancho" Villa and his irregular troops, who had killed several Americans in 1916, U.S. and regular Mexican army soldiers exchanged gunfire on June 21, 1916, which cost nine U.S. lives. Much of the press blamed the Mexicans for starting the incident and clamored for full-scale war. President Wilson came close to launching an invasion of the country. The AUAM immediately launched a publicity campaign to prove that the American troops were at least as much at fault as the Mexicans for the incident. The peace organization managed to turn the tide of public opinion, which quickly pressured Wilson to negotiate a settlement with Mexico. The AUAM helped facilitate those negotiations, and the two nations avoided war—although they remained wary of each other. It was a resounding success for the anti-preparedness organization and appeared to provide a model for keeping the United States out of the world war and resolving the horrific conflict. However, it proved infinitely more difficult to negotiate a resolution of the European conflict than the U.S.-Mexico dispute.

THE UNITED STATES ENTERS THE WAR

Just as the start of the war in 1914 had stunned the older, established peace organizations, America's declaration of war on April 6, 1917, shocked the newer, progressive peace societies and threw them in disarray. Within a few months, most of the progressive peace organizations abandoned their antiwar stance and supported the American war effort. Coherent, organized opposition to the war began to fall apart at the beginning of 1917 with Germany declaring unrestricted U-boat warfare on January 31 and the United States breaking diplomatic relations on February 3. By the fall of that year, it became nearly impossible to make antiwar or anti-U.S. involvement statements without facing the active suppression and occasionally violent wrath of private citizens and public officials. President Wilson, who was sympathetic to the peace activists' cause and who received the support of most activists in the 1916 election, called antiwar efforts treasonous in June 1917. The government formed the Committee on Public Information that publicly hounded those who opposed the war. It also passed the Espionage Act in 1917 and the Sedition Act in 1918, which allowed the government to investigate, harass, and arrest individuals making any remotely antiwar statements.

In this difficult political climate which accepted little political dissension, most liberal peace activists gave their support to the nation's war effort. Only a small number of peace organizations and individual

"I DIDN'T RAISE MY BOY TO BE A SOLDIER"

In the early twentieth century, the United States was emerging as an imperial power, to the great dismay of many Americans who wanted the country to stay out of European wars. Much of the opposition to preparation for World War I was to emerge from pacifists, isolationists, Socialists, and Christian denominations. In 1915, "I Didn't Raise My Boy to Be a Soldier" became a popular antiwar song.

Ten million soldiers to the war have gone,
Who may never return again.
Ten million mothers' hearts must break,
For the ones who died in vain.
Head bowed down in sorrow in her lonely years,
I heard a mother murmur thro' her tears:

Chorus:
I didn't raise my boy to be a soldier,
I brought him up to be my pride and joy,
Who dares to put a musket on his shoulder,
To shoot some other mother's darling boy?
Let nations arbitrate their future troubles,
It's time to lay the sword and gun away,
There'd be no war today,
If mothers all would say,
I didn't raise my boy to be a soldier.

(Chorus)
What victory can cheer a mother's heart,
When she looks at her blighted home?
What victory can bring her back,
All she cared to call her own?
Let each mother answer in the year to be,
Remember that my boy belongs to me!

(Chorus)

Source: Al Pianadosi and Alfred Bryan, "I Didn't Raise My Boy to Be a Soldier," Edison Collection, Library of Congress, recording.

activists remained openly opposed to the war, and most Americans viewed these remaining groups as radicals. They only shared their antiwar stance with individual conscientious objectors who refused to join the war effort because of their religious, philosophical, or political beliefs. Antiwar organizations either ceased operations, existed in name only, or shifted politically to the left as Socialists, radicals, far-left reformers, and members of the cultural avant-garde—

among the few people to still oppose the war—filled the ranks of the depleted peace societies.

Peace activists who ultimately dropped their direct opposition to America's participation in the conflict exhibited varying degrees of support for the nation's war effort. At one end of the spectrum was Jane Addams who did not agree with America's involvement in the war but did support charities that tended to soldiers' needs. Nor did she directly try to obstruct the country's cause. At the other end of the spectrum was the Carnegie Endowment for International Peace, which offered its offices to the government's Committee on Public Information. Peace activists who actively supported the war effort saw the conflict as an opportunity to further their reform aims. Some felt that the war might weaken or even destroy some of the social, economic, and political structures that prevented reform. Others calculated that supporting the war would pay political dividends later. For example, the National American Woman Suffrage Association supported the war effort, and in 1918 President Wilson fully endorsed suffrage, claiming it was essential for the war effort.

The peace activists who became war supporters tried to direct the nation to pursue the war in a just manner and for a fair peace. Many formerly antiwar leaders continued with the work of the prewar internationalists to formulate an international structure to ensure a permanent peace. They also demanded that peace come quickly and that it be based on liberal principles and be fair and reasonable for all sides. In addition, they supported relief efforts for victims of the war in Europe. Peace activists—particularly from the liberal reform wing of the movement—focused on preserving freedoms and equality on the homefront. They argued that the nation's political process must be more representative to allow for a broader spectrum of people to be heard. They also demanded an equitable distribution of war costs in the light of widespread rumors of profiteering by industrialists.

In particular, these activists focused on defending individual liberties, especially the rights of dissenters and conscientious objectors. The National Civil Liberties Bureau—which later became the American Civil Liberties Union (ACLU)—of the AUAM led this defense of civil liberties. AUAM members founded the Bureau as part of the original organization after the United States entered the war. By October 1917, the Bureau became an independent entity and was boldly defending the rights of those who objected to the war.

The formation of the National Civil Liberties Bureau signaled the demise of the AUAM and symbol-

At a demonstration in New York City, antiwar activists protest military drills and conscription as a prelude to American involvement in World War I.
(Brown Brothers)

ized the internal division that struck many peace organizations in 1917 and 1918. Moderate members left the organization—including one of the founders, Paul Kellogg—when the majority of the AUAM decided to start the Civil Liberties Bureau. Kellogg and others felt that its work to defend conscientious objectors and war dissenters radicalized the AUAM. The remaining members merged with antiwar Socialists and the Emergency Peace Federation to form the People's Council of America for Peace and Democracy, which campaigned for a quick peace settlement, a repeal of conscription, and civil liberties. It steadfastly opposed the war and urged workers in America not to support the war effort. Not surprisingly, a number

of federal and local authorities hounded the People's Council throughout the war.

What happened to the AUAM illustrated a pattern throughout the peace movement of moderate activists becoming, at least passive, supporters of America's military campaign. They often left their antiwar organizations or transformed them into war-supporting entities. Meanwhile, those that remained steadfast against the war either took over the peace organizations or started new ones. The composition of the remaining antiwar movement slid to the left as Socialists, members of the Industrial Workers of the World, and radicals replaced liberal reformers who generally worked within the nation's capitalist framework.

The liberal reformers who backed the war had hoped that they would be able to influence how the nation pursued its war aims—defending civil liberties at the home front and ensuring a fair and lasting peace abroad. Their vision of how the United States should conduct the war never materialized. The world war turned out to be one of the worst periods for civil liberties in American history, and the punitive terms of the Treaty of Versailles were obviously disappointing to them. On the other hand, stalwart antiwar activists and political radicals accused these liberal reformers of having no principles because they bowed to societal pressure to support the war. The bitterest criticism of the liberal reformers came from Randolph Bourne, a young intellectual. Bourne claimed that these new war-supporters had sold out their principles for mere expediency. He also rhetorically asked, if the peace activists could not prevent the war, how could they manage it in a way that would produce the reforms they wanted?

The number of conscientious objectors was very small, but they were among the most steadfast opponents to the war. They were not an organized group but rather individual men who refused to fight in the war. The Selective Service Act allowed people from generally recognized religious sects whose religious beliefs prevented them from fighting to claim an exemption from combat duty. This narrow standard excluded people who did not belong to a well-known sect or who objected to fighting on political or philosophical grounds. Local draft boards were primarily responsible for deciding who was eligible for an exemption, and the criteria for making these decisions varied widely from board to board. The claims of an untold number of men for conscientious objector status were turned down.

By the end of the war, the army had officially drafted just under 4,000 conscientious objectors. Approximately 2,600 of them had been assigned to either noncombatant roles in the army or had been furloughed out of the army with assignments for industrial, agricultural, or reconstruction work. At war's end, the army had just over 200 conscientious objectors whom it had not assigned to alternative service. The army court-martialed and imprisoned 450 objectors on whom it did not bestow official conscientious status. Another fifty men were also court-martialed but quickly released. Just over 700 absolutist objectors were in military camps but refused to engage in noncombatant duty because they believed that even this service would help conduct a war they fervently opposed. In comparison, local draft boards had given

almost 21,000 men noncombatant status for a variety of other reasons, and an estimated 171,000 people simply evaded the draft.

Most people were conscientious objectors—or at least tried to claim this status—because of either political or philosophical principles, their literal belief in scripture, or a combination of religious, philosophical, and humanitarian beliefs. Of the officially recognized—hence, religious conscientious objectors—half were Mennonites and one-quarter belonged to pacifist sects. Nearly all of the religious objectors had a literal understanding of the Bible.

Several religious denominations, especially the Quakers, Mennonites, and Brethren, organized efforts to try to ensure the civil rights of conscientious objectors, prevent their mistreatment in army camps, and provide any financial assistance they might have needed. Most pacifist churches, such as the Mennonites and the Quakers, held fast to their antiwar beliefs after the United States entered the war. Although these churches were opposed to the war, many felt a moral obligation to provide assistance to those left destitute by the conflict. Members of the Mennonites and Brethren, for example, worked through public charity organizations or founded their own groups, such as the Friends Service Committee. These churches made their sense of obligation to help those hurt by the war an integral part of their antiwar beliefs.

CONCLUSION

The start of World War I facilitated the emergence of a new generation of peace activists who opposed U.S. involvement while advocating a swift and just peace. Most new peace advocates were liberal reformers. Among other groups, leading figures included labor leaders, social workers, feminists, journalists and writers, and Social Gospel clergy who associated their opposition to the war to their ongoing reform work. As the war continued, liberal reformers became more influential than internationalist peace advocates who, since the end of the nineteenth century, had worked to develop an international system of courts, laws, and arbitration to prevent armed conflict between nations. America's entry into the European conflict in 1917 created disarray in the antiwar movement as many peace activists supported the nation's war effort and a fair and equitable peace while also trying to protect the rights and civil liberties of Americans who still opposed the war. Only a small number of peace organizations maintained a principled antiwar stance, moving to the political left—since only radicals, Socialists, and those with an unwavering commitment to opposition to the war or the government's policies remained to fill the breach. These enduring antiwar organizations only shared this stance with individual conscientious objectors and pacifist religious sects.

Eliot Wilczek

BIBLIOGRAPHY

Abrahamson, James L. *The American Home Front: Revolutionary War, Civil War, World War I, World War II.* Fort Lesley J. McNair, Washington, DC: National Defense University Press, 1983.

Chambers II, John Whiteclay, ed. *The Eagle and the Dove: The American Peace Movement and United States Foreign Policy, 1900–1922.* 2d ed. Syracuse, NY: Syracuse University Press, 1991.

Chatfield, Charles. *For Peace and Justice: Pacifism in America, 1914–1941.* Boston: Beacon, 1971.

Chatfield, Charles, and Robert Kleidman. *The American Peace Movement: Ideals and Activism.* New York: Twayne, 1992.

Early, Frances H. *A World Without War: How U.S. Feminists and Pacifists Resisted World War I.* Syracuse, NY: Syracuse University Press, 1997.

Howlett, Charles F., and Glen Zeitzer. *The American Peace Movement: History and Historiography.* 261 AHA Pamphlets, Washington, DC: American Historical Association, 1985.

Kennedy, David M. *Over Here: The First World War and American Society.* New York: Oxford University Press, 1980.

Kuhlman, Erika A. *Petticoats and White Feathers: Gender Conformity, Race, Conformity, the Progressive Peace Movement, and the Debate over War, 1895–1919.* Westport, CT: Greenwood Press, 1997.

Marchand, C. Roland. *The American Peace Movement and Social Reform, 1898–1918.* Princeton, NJ: Princeton University Press, 1972.

Patterson, David S. *Toward a Warless World: The Travail of the American Peace Movement, 1887–1914.* Bloomington: Indiana University Press, 1976.

Zieger, Robert H. *America's Great War: World War I and the American Experience.* Lanham, MD: Rowman & Littlefield, 2000.

WORLD WAR I AND CIVIL LIBERTIES

The definition of civil liberties in America has changed over time. Civil liberties consist of the first ten amendments of the Constitution, known as the Bill of Rights, and natural rights that have been deemed as individual rights after a prolonged period of usage. Civil liberties occur only in democracies; the Founding Fathers believed that inclusion of the Bill of Rights in the Constitution would protect the individual from encroachments by the state. Changes that occurred during the Progressive Era and World War I significantly altered the way in which the Bill of Rights was interpreted. During this time frame, civil liberties were no longer an abstract question with little case law to make them a reality. In the early years of the twentieth century, the rights of the individual came face to face with the needs of the state as expressed through the leaders of the nation.

America's entrance into World War I on April 6, 1917, was preceded by months in which the legislative branch of government had passed a series of laws that diminished the rights of the individual. Many of the laws passed between mid-1915 and American entrance into the war dealt with the need of the state to prepare for war and to isolate those who voiced dissent against war preparations. Because of the ethnic composition of the immigrants who arrived on American shores during the late nineteenth and early twentieth centuries and the fact that their homelands were now at war, Woodrow Wilson's administration worried over the issue of immigrant loyalty to the United States. The president wanted the support of the whole nation if and when the country declared war against Germany. The other group that presented the Wilson administration with problems over the issue of war was the radicals. Many of the radical labor and political movements of this time were composed of first- and second-generation immigrants. Wilson's administration believed that dissent from the radicals would lead to a groundswell of antigovernment feelings within the nation. During the early months of

1917, the legislators prepared the groundwork for the curtailing of civil rights through legislation pertaining to the immigration of radicals and protection of the president from words or actions that could be interpreted as hostile.

RESTRICTIVE CIVIL LIBERTIES

After war was declared, the issue of restricting civil liberties increased. During the years prior to the war, there were countless struggles with municipalities, states, and federal authorities over civil rights, most especially the Free Speech fights waged by the Industrial Workers of the World (IWW). Historians explain the suspension of civil liberties during the war as a necessity inasmuch as the issue of national security became a fundamental concern for the Wilson administration. America's entry into the war changed the discourse of civil liberties from one of conservative interests into a national issue. Shortly after the declaration of war, the congressional conservatives attacked Wilson for his lack of repressive measures when dealing with dissidents, whether it was the leader of the Socialist Party of America (SPA), Eugene Debs, or the social reformer, antiwar voice, Jane Addams. Wilson's response to the congressional criticisms was a proclamation that gave federal agents the right to arrest enemy-aliens, those who wrote or spoke against government policies. The antiwar voices were predominant in both the midwestern and northwestern states. Wilson and his administration wanted to destroy the mechanisms of dissent in the country.

Wilson quickly set up the Committee on Public Information (CPI) with the purpose of creating a national unity of public cooperation against the enemies of the state. One of its main purposes was to maintain multicultural solidarity for the war effort. The CPI quickly assumed a propaganda role, with a simple message that the enemy was everywhere and the good citizen should report any type of un-American behavior to the proper authorities. The CPI's message was patriotism, and its role was to create consensus thinking about the war and American involvement in it, while asking all loyal Americans to act as a policing mechanism against those who dissented. The CPI was only the first agency created to suppress civil liberties during the war.

Directly after the declaration of war, Wilson created the Civil Service Commission (CSC) to investigate the loyalty of government employees. The CSC was given wide latitude to decide where there was a reasonable doubt of loyalty attached to any person then working for the government and those who applied for positions. This committee lasted until 1921, and many people were fired from federal agencies with no cause shown for the CSC actions.

During the following two years, the legislative branch passed a series of laws that would curtail civil liberties further. Wilson sent Congress the Espionage Act in May of 1917, which dealt with the issues of sabotage and spying for foreign powers, but it extended the powers of the federal government over the rights of free speech and a free press also. The Espionage Act broadened the use of the term *treason*, and it allowed the postmaster general to confiscate all materials that could be interpreted as treasonous under the loosely worded law. The law referred to simply treasonous language; however, with the new version of the Espionage Act it became open to interpretation by the postmaster general. Any newspapers, periodicals, or journals that were sent through the mails became scrutinized for language and content. This was especially applied to German-language and radical publications. The Anarchist Emma Goldman's *Mother Earth* and the Socialists' *The Masses* were two of the journals considered treasonous by the federal government, and their mailing privileges were rescinded. The editors of any publication that fit under this new law were liable to fines and federal imprisonment.

On the heels of the Espionage Act there followed another executive order from the president that directly affected the German population living in America. All German aliens over the age of fourteen had to be registered with the federal government and were barred from living or working in areas of the country that had any military importance. This selected group had to get federal permission to move within the country and were also required to report any change in their employment or living circumstances. These new restrictions affected nearly 600,000 Germans living in the country. Over 2,000 of them were considered national security risks and were accordingly interned.

The second piece of national security legislation passed in 1917 was the Trading with the Enemy Act. Although superficially it dealt with trade to either Germany or Austro-Hungary, it contained a domestic clause that allowed the postmaster general to suspend the mailing privileges of all publications that in his estimation were not in the best interests of the nation. This struck at the heart of the radical and labor movements.

In 1918, two acts were passed that gave the government more power over the individual. The first was the Alien Act, which granted the commissioner of immigration the right to deport any nonnaturalized American suspected of actions or beliefs that were not in agreement with the government. The Alien Act also allowed the government to remove from American shores anyone who spoke openly against the government. For the radical and labor movements whose memberships had a large number of first-generation, nonnaturalized citizens on their roles, this act would destroy their movement's base of support. The last act passed during the war period that curtailed civil liberties was the Sedition Act of 1918. This act placed a sweeping ban on any printed or published language that was disloyal to the government or the military. The penalty was federal prison and a hefty fine.

The laws, viewed benignly, could be interpreted as an attempt to unify the nation in a time of war, but the Wilson administration enforced these laws with a great deal of vigor. Albert S. Burleson, the postmaster general, took to heart the Trading with the Enemy Act and began suppressing mailings of journals in which radical and even those who were native-born Americans criticized the war or the administration. He hated the radical and labor movements, and so their journals and newspapers were suppressed without delay. Former congressman Victor Berger, the editor of *Milwaukee Leader*, a Socialist publication, had his newspaper repressed, but he was also convicted of violation of the 1917 Espionage Act and was not allowed to take his seat after being reelected to Congress in 1918.

The Justice Department vigilantly hunted people who were deemed enemies of the state under these new laws. It prosecuted over 2,000 people under the Espionage Act and nearly 1,000 under the Sedition Act between 1917 and 1919. The most famous case prosecuted under the Espionage Act was that of the Socialist and labor leader Eugene Debs for statements he made at an antiwar rally in Ohio. Debs refused to disavow his statements and took the opportunity in court to avow his Socialist beliefs. He was sentenced to ten years in a federal prison. The most famous case prosecuted under the Sedition Act was that of the Anarchists Emma Goldman and Alexander Berkman. The Sedition Act was a more explicit version of the Espionage Act. Goldman and Berkman, neither a naturalized American citizen, had journals that condemned preparedness prior to the war and worked to stop conscription and condemn the government after America entered the war. They were Russian by birth, and after the Bolsheviks overthrew the government of Russia in 1917 and with anti-Russian feelings running high in the government, it was almost inevitable that the two would be tried and convicted for their inflammatory publications. They were the first tried and deported using the Sedition Act.

What occurred during World War I was simply governmental institutions being used to regulate free speech. The entire nation did not agree with the repressive measures being used to counter antigovernment rhetoric; concerned citizens and those who dissented formed organizations to defend the nation from encroachments of and intrusions on civil liberties. A young social worker who refused to register for the draft, Roger Baldwin, formed the National Civil Liberties Bureau in 1917. It was later renamed the American Civil Liberties Union (ACLU). Its purpose was to defend the right to free speech and free opinions against both governmental and private attempts to rescind those rights.

THE COURTS AND CIVIL LIBERTIES

During the war years, the U.S. Supreme Court was very reluctant to take on the issue of civil liberties. With the war raging in Europe and following American involvement, the Court moved very slowly to take on appeals such as the convictions of Victor Berger and Eugene Debs. They did reverse Berger's conviction on court procedural grounds, but Berger was still not allowed to take his seat in Congress. As for Eugene Debs, the Court found in 1919 that his conviction should be upheld on the grounds that the speeches he made against the war and draft registration were impediments to the government carrying out its laws. Later that same session, Justice Oliver Wendell Holmes would use *Schenck v. United States* (1919), another case of a radical convicted under the Sedition Act which restricted free speech when there were circumstances when the right to free speech presented a "clear and present danger" such as during war. Thus, the Supreme Court sided with the Wilson administration that the war activities were of greater importance than the individual's right to free speech,

and therefore the rights articulated in the Constitution could be suspended during certain circumstances. Holmes was criticized for the "clear and present danger" decision by constitutional proponents such as Harvard Law professor Zechariah Chafee and Judge Learned Hand. By mid-1919, during the height of the Red Scare that followed the war, Holmes would become one of the leading Supreme Court voices championing the right to free speech even during times of war.

During these years, when there were complaints that the Justice Department or postmaster general had gone too far in their restriction of civil liberties, the administration did nothing to change the way in which the government was operating. This attitude trickled down to local levels where German Americans were discriminated against. Some states and municipalities outlawed the teaching of German language or German-language books in libraries. German-language books were burned in some places, and other localities forbade the populace to speak German. State and local governments took this opportunity to impose laws similar to the Sedition Act, restricting the rights of radical political groups, especially the Socialists and the Anarchists. They also challenged the right of existence for radical labor movements such as the IWW. The IWW never spoke out against the war because they believed that there was a more urgent war than the one in Europe and that was the war with capitalists. Many states refused to seat Socialists or other political radicals in their state or local legislatures. These different actions were infringements of civil liberties and political repression.

After the Armistice was signed in 1919, there was no immediate change in the government's attitudes toward radical groups within the country. The government continued to use the wartime legislation during the demobilization effort as it feared that there would be social unrest. Although Socialist parties in many states in the South and the Midwest had broken apart, there remained great support in the North and midwestern states. The government did not want a political challenge, and with the creation of the American Communist Party the laws that had been in place during the war were not rescinded. The year 1920 was a terrible year for civil liberties; with the war over, many Americans wanted a return to "normalcy" (a term popularized by Republican presidential candidate Warren G. Harding) as quickly as possible. The country was plagued by labor strikes as the workers who had had not been allowed to negotiate labor contracts during the war believed that the moment had come to allow the workers to share in the profits that were made by big business during the war. The race riots that occurred in over twenty-five cities that year showed the government that the transition from war to peace was not going to be easy.

THE RED SCARE

Federal officials believed that the problems that plagued the nation emanated from some outside force labeled bolshevism. The United States had troops involved with the civil war that was taking place inside the old Russian Empire, and there was a great deal of concern that the revolution taking place in Russia could be transported abroad. It appeared that many of the nations in Western Europe were infected by revolution in the same way that Russia had been in 1917. The American government did not want revolution in this country, so the continued repression of civil liberties was seen as a necessity. In June a series of mail bombs were sent to government officials and business moguls. The new attorney general, A. Mitchell Palmer, was the recipient of such a bomb. The Justice Department's response was to utilize the same legal means that had been used during the war to suppress civil liberties. These were now turned in earnest against the population. This eighteen-month period, 1919 to mid-1920, is called the "Red Scare." It was a short, difficult time in America as the repression and patriotism that had clashed before and during the war acted the final scene of this era where civil liberties were abrogated. The "Palmer Raids," named after Attorney General A. Mitchell Palmer, who authorized them, were carried out against political and labor radicals. Their headquarters were raided, literature was confiscated, printing presses were smashed, and members were arrested under the same acts that had been used against aliens during the war. The atmosphere was filled with propaganda, patriotism, and Americanism during this period. The laws utilized to protect American interests during the war were now used in the courts against Americans. Palmer wanted to eliminate radical labor and political movements through use of the wartime legislation. Labor and political activists were arrested and tried on espionage or sedition charges, and the Justice Department used the Immigration Act of 1917 to set aside those individuals who were not naturalized Americans for deportation. The attorney general claimed that many of these people were Communist agents and that their sole purpose in agitation was to bring the American government down. The American people continued to support the government and the programs of repression until early 1920, after the first boatload of detainees was deported. Several factors led to lessening support for this war against Communism; the press and government officials opposed continuation of the civil rights violations; Palmer had overplayed the role of dissidents in America; the fear of Communist revolutions in Western Europe did not materialize; and by early 1920 most radical political and labor movements in America had been destroyed or severely debilitated. By mid-1920, there were many powerful and respected voices who called for investigation into Palmer and the methods he had used. There were also calls for the negation of the wartime legislation and a resumption of civil liberties. This period of repression ended without any fanfare, but it was only the first in a twentieth century filled with civil liberties abuses.

Linnea Goodwin Burwood

BIBLIOGRAPHY

Cooper, John Milton. *Pivotal Decades: The United States, 1900–1920.* New York: W.W. Norton, 1990.

Cotterell, Robert C. *Roger Nash Baldwin and the American Civil Liberties Union.* New York: Columbia University Press, 2000.

Goldstein, Robert. *Political Repression in Modern America From 1870 to 1976.* Chicago: University of Illinois Press, 2001.

"Why American Civil Liberties Does What It Does." *U.S. News and World Report* 96:1 (March 26, 1984): 76.

ANTIWAR MOVEMENT: WORLD WAR II

Although the American peace movement virtually collapsed following the Japanese attack on Pearl Harbor in December 1941, it had been strong and vibrant in the period between the two world wars. It was aided by the great disillusionment following World War I, especially after writers focused their literary efforts on exposing the dark side of total warfare. Some of these writings included Henri Barbusses's *Under Fire* (1916), Siegfried Sassoon's *Counter-Attack* (1918), Ernest Hemingway's *A Farewell to Arms* (1929), Laurence Stallings's *What Price Glory?* (1924), and Erich Maria Remarque's *All Quiet on the Western Front* (1929). In addition, the poetry of Wilfred Owen (e.g., "Arms and the Boy") and T.S. Eliot (e.g., "The Waste Land") contributed to the antiwar sentiments.

But after Pearl Harbor, there was a rallying around the flag in which nationalism triumphed over any impulse for peace. Anyone who criticized the war was considered un-American. U.S. Senator Burton K. Wheeler, a staunch isolationist, characterized the national mood when he said, "The only thing now to do is lick hell out of them." Of the radical journals, only the *Call* and the *Progressive* called for nonintervention. The *Christian Century*, on the other hand, declared U.S. participation in the war a "guilty necessity."

Jeannette Rankin, the first woman elected to the U.S. House of Representatives, is remembered for being the only member of Congress to vote against the American declaration of war in both World War I and World War II. Although fifty members of Congress had voted against America's entry into World War I, in 1941 she was the sole dissenting voice. "This time I stood alone," Rankin later recalled. "It was a good deal more difficult than it had been the time before." Actively involved in the Women's International League for Peace and Freedom, the Women's Peace Union, and the National Council for the Prevention

of War, Rankin spent the 1930s lobbying against a $616-million naval building bill. If her election to Congress in 1941 represented a second wind for her political career, voting against the war signaled the beginning of the end to her office-holding days.

Between 1919 and 1925, the peace movement was characterized by three main groupings: internationalists, pacifists, and liberal reformers. The movement was comprised of feminists, educators, political reformers, liberal Protestants, and progressive activists. By and large, women were the backbone of the peace groups. Internationalists were associated with the League of Free Nations Association (founded in 1918) and the League of Nations Non-Partisan Association (founded in 1923), the latter of which in 1929 became the League of Nations Association and still later, following World War II, the United Nations Association of the United States of America. Pacifists were represented by the Women's International League for Peace and Freedom (founded in 1919) and the War Resisters League (founded in 1923). Liberal reformers rallied around the National Council for Prevention of War (founded in 1921) and the National Conference on the Cause and Cure of War (founded in 1924).

Peace advocates found credence in the Kellogg-Briand Pact, which was initially signed by the world's major powers on August 27, 1928. Formally known as the Pact of Paris, Kellogg-Briand went beyond the naval disarmament agreements by outlawing war as an instrument of foreign policy. Named after Frank Kellogg, the U.S. secretary of state under President Calvin Coolidge, and Aristide Briand, the French foreign minister, the treaty was supported by those Americans who desired isolationism. Although forty-seven countries, including the United States, were signatories to Kellogg-Briand, the pact lacked bona fide enforcement mechanisms. Nonetheless, peace supporters would cite Kellogg-Briand for political justification long after the treaty was null and void.

The high-water mark of the American peace

On February 25, 1941, members of the Massachusetts Woman's Political Club protested at the White House against the Lend-Lease Act, which provided military support to Great Britain in the early years of World War II. Antiwar sentiment drew wide support in the 1920s and 1930s but collapsed virtually overnight following the Japanese attack on Pearl Harbor on December 7, 1941. *(Brown Brothers)*

movement for the first half of the twentieth century was 1921 with the establishment of the National Council for Prevention of War (NCPW). Founded in Washington, D.C., by representatives of seventeen national peace organizations, the NCPW was active in every state. Its executive secretary, Frederick J. Libby, decided to devote his life to the cause of peace after touring Europe in the aftermath of World War I. The NCPW supported international agreements for the reduction of armaments, advocated a progressive world organization, and worked toward a global system of education for peace. Its *News Bulletin* (1921–1934) and *Peace Action* (1934–1968) kept readers informed about peace issues. In 1936, when the NCPW was at or near its peak, the *Peace Action* had a circulation of 25,000.

As World War II neared, the NCPW lobbied for neutrality legislation and the requirement for a war referendum.

The American League Against War and Fascism, formed in New York City in the autumn of 1933, had as its primary mission the protection of the Soviet Union. According to its manifesto, "Serious struggle against war involves rallying all forces around this peace policy, and opposing all attempts to weaken or destroy the Soviet Union." Although it was a Communist-front organization, it attracted many people who were not Communists, including Norman Thomas of the Socialist Party, Roger Baldwin of the American Civil Liberties Union, A.J. Muste of the Conference for Progressive Labor Action, and the theologian Reinhold Niebuhr. In November 1937, the organization changed its name to the American League for Peace and Democracy.

In February 1938, Norman Thomas opened his "Keep America Out of War" campaign, offering the Left a non-Communist antiwar front. Three months later, he helped establish the Keep America Out of War Congress, which received support from the National Council for Prevention of War. Thomas's slogan was, "The maximum American cooperation for peace; the maximum isolation from war." After Pearl Harbor, the group officially disbanded but was reincarnated as the Provisional Committee Toward a Democratic Peace, taking on a role similar to the People's Council for Peace and Democracy of World War I. The Provisional Committee championed civil rights at home and advocated a more equitable distribution of the war costs. It also stressed the need for a just and lasting peace after World War II.

The America First Committee was formed in 1940 with the purpose of preventing the United States from repeating the mistakes that led to World War I. Charles Lindbergh, Chester Bowles, and Stuart Chase were some of the well-known figures of this organization. Lindbergh, who accepted a medal from Adolf Hitler in 1938, was forced to resign his commission in the U.S. Air Corps Reserve because of what was seen as his pro-German stance. After America's entry into the war, however, Lindbergh served as a consultant for the aircraft industry and even went on missions in the Pacific on behalf of the U.S. Air Force.

Beginning in June 1943, the peace movement had a moderate resurgence. Dave Dellinger, a Socialist, founded the People's Now Committee with the objective of the immediate end of the war. In July of that year, George W. Hartmann of the War Resisters League and Quaker Dorothy Hutchinson organized the Peace Now Movement (PNM) as a conservative counterpart to Dellinger's group. Hartmann and Hutchinson attempted to tap into the America First constituency, but consequently existing peace groups shunned their efforts. In its statement of purpose, the PNM called on the United States to formulate "fair and reasonable" peace terms. The Friends Committee on National Legislation was founded in November to lobby Washington for war relief, civil liberties, and racial justice. Similarly, pacifists such as A.J. Muste and Evan Thomas focused their energies on organizing relief services for war refugees and the families of imprisoned conscientious objectors, while at the same time denouncing the internment of Japanese Americans and the saturation bombing of civilian populations.

Although the peace movement floundered after Pearl Harbor and lost even more momentum after the Holocaust came to public light, pacifists were emboldened. The Fellowship of Reconciliation and the War Resisters League (WRL) actually thrived. Between 1939 and 1945, the WRL, for example, grew from 900 to 2,300 active members, with an income that increased from $5,000 to $20,000. Of the 10 million males ordered to report for military induction, 42,973 were classified as conscientious objectors. A total of 6,086 were imprisoned during the war.

A number of prominent Protestant clergymen maintained their pacifist stance, including Harry Emerson Fosdick, Methodist Bishop Paul B. Kern, and Episcopal Bishops Walter Mitchell and W. Appleton Lawrence. Three out of four Quakers and three out five Mennonites chose conscientious objector status. Jehovah's Witnesses constituted the largest dissent group during World War II, refusing military induction as well as participation in the Civilian Public Service. Consequently, many were imprisoned. As a political force, they were not very strong because they remained aloof from other objectors and pacifists. Jehovah's Witnesses were less against war than they were against being controlled by the government. Although there was the Association of Catholic Conscientious Objectors (founded in 1940) and a chapter of the Women's International League for Peace and Freedom in Rockaway, New York—that was comprised mainly of Jewish members—very few pacifists were representative of the Catholic and Jewish faiths.

Roger Chapman

BIBLIOGRAPHY

Browder, Earl. *The Second Imperialist War.* New York: International, 1940.

Conlin, Joseph R. *American Anti-War Movements.* Beverly Hills, CA: Glencoe, 1968.

DeBenedetti, Charles. *The Peace Reform in American History.* Bloomington: Indiana University Press, 1980.

Fried, Albert. *Communism in America: A History in Documents.* New York: Columbia University Press, 1997.

Giles, Kevin S. *Flight of the Dove: The Story of Jeanette Rankin.* Beaverton, OR: Touchstone, 1980.

Wittner, Lawrence S. *Rebels Against War: The American Peace Movement, 1941–1960.* New York: Columbia University Press, 1969.

Antiwar Movement: Vietnam War

The Vietnam War—America's longest war—left much of Southeast Asia in ruins and divided Americans more than any other event in the nation's history since the Civil War. As the war unfolded on the other side of the globe—with horrific results—at home it gave rise to one of the most resilient, widespread, and diverse social protest movements. The antiwar movement began as a small series of protests, organized mostly by seasoned Old Left activists. Early antiwar actions were often discouraging affairs for planners and participants alike. They received scant media attention and were often overshadowed by even larger pro-war demonstrations.

But years of persistent organizing transformed various scattered actions into a cohesive, mass, nationwide movement, with respectable adherents and a solid base of popular support. By the late 1960s and early 1970s, an increasing number of antiwar actions became more localized, grassroots efforts, as national antiwar coalitions fragmented, then regrouped into new entities, only to split again. Still, the movement would remain a potent force well into the 1970s. Within its ranks were senators and representatives, homemakers, college and high school students, civil rights activists, Maoists, countercultural youths, poets, Vietnam veterans, clergy, business executives, blue-collar workers, scientists, professors, African Americans, Latinos, soldiers and veterans, pacifists, draft resisters, and others.

The movement drew support from hundreds of organizations, but no single group dominated it. Thus, it was far from monolithic. Within its ranks, liberal Democrats vied with Trotskyists. Student militants sometimes split with their seasoned elders. Leaders debated tactics, while ordinary participants created protest signs and banners that reflected their own personal concerns about the war. Countercultural youths who felt a natural rapport with the goals and aims of the movement drifted in and out of marches, while clean-cut supporters of Senator Eugene McCar-thy (D-MN) turned their attention from Democratic Party campaigning to organizing the 1969 Moratorium protests. The killing of four students at Kent State University in Ohio and two students at Jackson State in Mississippi days later in May 1970 further intensified the divisions in American society and left the movement reeling but continuing. Vietnam veterans reenergized the movement when they marched on Washington in April 1971, briefly lobbied members of Congress, and then threw away their medals, ribbons, citations, and other military items on the steps of the nation's Capitol.

Amid all of the national convulsions of the late 1960s and early 1970s, the antiwar movement ground on, ebbing in the early 1970s but never disappearing until the Vietnam War itself ended with the defeat of South Vietnam and the United States at the end of April 1975. But the antiwar movement was not—as some scholars and authors have insisted—simply the result of a generational split between baby boomers and their parents. It was deeper, more complex, and more widespread than that. It cut across virtually all lines, including class, race, gender, and age. Although students played a vital role in the movement, particularly early on, they never dominated it the way that the movement's detractors have suggested. In 1973, a political scientist who studied the era concluded, "No case can be made for the popular proposition that 'youth' was in revolt over the war. . . . The poll data argue that although some young people may have been deeply opposed to the war, 'youth' as a whole was generally more supportive of the war than older people." The antiwar movement was, observed historians Charles DeBenedetti and Charles Chatfield, "a typically American reform effort—a voluntary crusade attracting adherents and impelling them to act out of a felt personal responsibility for social wrongs."

Events in Vietnam

During the 1950s and early 1960s, U.S. involvement in Vietnam deepened at an incremental, yet steady, pace. It began with the Truman and Eisenhower administrations supporting the French war effort, eventually financing 80 percent of it by the early 1950s. With the end of the French war in the spring of 1954, U.S. officials reevaluated and revised America's Indochina policy. After 1954, U.S. officials supported and financed the newly created South Vietnamese government under the leadership of the autocratic president, Ngo Dinh Diem. In 1961, under the newly elected Kennedy administration, the number of U.S. military personnel and advisers in Vietnam escalated sharply, surpassing 16,000 by the end of 1963. Kennedy hoped this increase, coupled with his favored policy of training South Vietnamese soldiers and indigenous ethnic people in rural areas in low-intensity counterinsurgency warfare, would bolster the vulnerable South Vietnamese government. But years of nepotism and repressive policies left the Diem regime even more vulnerable in 1963 than it had been at the time of its inception in 1954. Exacerbating matters for Diem was a press corps of highly talented young journalists, including David Halberstam, Peter Arnett, and Neil Sheehan, whose dispatches often illuminated the rampant corruption in the Saigon regime. With the tacit approval of the Kennedy administration and America's ambassador to Vietnam, Henry Cabot Lodge, Diem's generals staged a coup on November 2, 1963, ousting the unpopular leader. The generals assassinated Diem and his brother, Ngo Dinh Nhu, head of the security forces in South Vietnam. Three weeks later, Kennedy himself would be shot and killed in a motorcade in Dallas, Texas.

President Lyndon Johnson continued following a trajectory set by Dwight Eisenhower and John F. Kennedy, steadily increasing the number of advisers and personnel in Vietnam. Reacting to the potent legacy of McCarthyism, Johnson feared his reputation would not withstand the disaster of "losing" South Vietnam to the Communists. Republican accusations that President Harry Truman had "lost" China to the Communists were still fresh in his mind. Johnson also feared that failing to act in Vietnam would undermine his "Great Society," the most ambitious federal aid programs since the New Deal. In early August 1964, Johnson went on national television, claiming that two U.S. naval destroyers—the USS *Maddox* and USS *C. Turner Joy*—had been attacked by North Vietnamese PT boats. Johnson claimed that two separate attacks had occurred (most historians dispute the second one) but neglected to tell the American public that the two destroyers were involved in a larger U.S.-

backed covert effort to destabilize Communist North Vietnam. Johnson, claiming the attack was an act of Vietnamese Communist belligerence, went before Congress asking for far-reaching powers to take whatever steps necessary—even military force—to repel attacks against U.S. forces and to protect Southeast Asia from Communist aggression. His so-called Tonkin Gulf resolution passed the Senate with only two dissenting votes (Senators Ernest Gruening [D-AK] and Wayne Morse [D-OR], who would go on to achieve heroic status in the antiwar movement) and moved unanimously through the House of Representatives. In February 1965, following a Viet Cong attack on Pleiku that killed nine and wounded more than 100 Americans, Johnson authorized massive air strikes over Vietnam, dubbed "Operation Rolling Thunder." By the end of 1965, nearly 200,000 marines and army troops would arrive in Vietnam.

THE BIRTH OF A MOVEMENT

Antiwar organizers wasted no time in responding to Johnson's resolution. Even before the Tonkin Gulf resolution, an incipient antiwar movement struggled for support. When South Vietnamese president Ngo Dinh Diem cracked down on Buddhist opposition in the spring and summer of 1963, small antiwar protests occurred in New York and other major cities, demanding an end to U.S. aid to the Diem regime. On December 19, 1964, more than 1,500 people braved the frigid winds of New York to hear antiwar speeches delivered by A.J. Muste, A. Philip Randolph, and Norman Thomas. Smaller demonstrations took place in San Francisco, Minneapolis, Miami, Austin, Philadelphia, Chicago, Washington, D.C., Boston, and Cleveland. These early protests were sponsored and organized by the Fellowship of Reconciliation (FOR) and the War Resisters League (WRL), two pacifist groups with long histories. The American chapter of FOR, a religious interfaith pacifist organization headquartered in New York, was founded in 1915. FOR had resisted U.S. military participation in both world wars and called for nuclear disarmament during the Cold War. In 1963, FOR had been at the forefront of monitoring the repression of Buddhists by the Saigon regime, and the organization sponsored antiwar protests immediately after the Tonkin Gulf resolution. The WRL, a more radical and confrontational group than FOR, was founded in 1923. During World War II, it supported conscientious objectors and war tax resisters, and in the Cold War, it sponsored civil disobedience against civil defense drills and nonpayment of taxes used for weapons spending. In a bold move

Flashing the two-finger peace sign, antiwar protesters gather in Berkeley, California, in 1969. Following the emergence of the Free Speech Movement at the college campus in 1964, Berkeley remained one of the centers of the student protest movement. (© Underwood Photo Archives, Inc.)

against escalation in Vietnam, the WRL sponsored a demonstration in New York City on May 16, 1964, at which twelve men burned their draft cards. Other pacifists played a crucial role in the early period, including a group of influential nonviolent radicals—among them, Dave Dellinger, A.J. Muste, and Staughton Lynd—all activists, as well as editors at the radical monthly *Liberation* magazine. Eventually, other Old Left radicals—Trotskyists in the Socialist Workers Party, Communist Party members, and a variety of independent progressives—would also contribute significantly to the antiwar coalition of the 1960s and early 1970s.

The early antiwar movement owed much to these

pacifists and old left enclaves. But other important influences shaped the movement as well. Even before the first antiwar protests, the civil rights movement had already prompted President Lyndon Johnson to begin dismantling repressive Jim Crow institutions in the South. The nonviolent Southern freedom struggle helped define the tactics and agenda of the antiwar movement and furnished it with a steady stream of seasoned organizers. Similarly, the Berkeley Free Speech Movement (FSM) in the fall of 1964 also inspired antiwar activists. The FSM culminated in a semester-long confrontation that pitted a coalition of students, their faculty supporters, and various Bay Area activists against University of California administrators who had banned student political tables near the UC Berkeley campus.

Finally, the burgeoning New Left also influenced the antiwar movement. The New Left, emerging during an era when liberalism flourished across America, appealed to primarily young activists. These radicals were, in the words of sociologist and New Left adherent Richard Flacks, "disaffected from all 'established radicalisms,'" and "self-consciously sought to provide political direction, theoretical coherence and organization continuity to the student movement." The main New Left group of the 1960s, Students for a Democratic Society (SDS), had grown out of the Old Left League for Industrial Democracy in 1960. By June 1962, a group of sixty SDSers gathered at an American Federation of Labor-Congress of Industrial Organizations (AFL-CIO) camp in the woods at Port Huron, on the southern shore of Lake Huron and drafted a sweeping manifesto, the Port Huron Statement. The statement condemned militarism, fanatical anti-Communism, the arms race, racism, excessive corporate power, and public apathy. It called for a politics of "authenticity," which involved more personal empowerment, a deeper interconnectedness, and greater grassroots control of political institutions, dubbed "participatory democracy."

SDS organized the first major antiwar action, a march of 25,000 people in Washington, D.C., on April 15, 1965. On that beautiful spring day, with cherry blossoms in full bloom, the huge crowd gathered at Washington Monument and listened to speeches by the venerable radical journalist I.F. Stone, civil rights activist Bob Moses, Alaska senator Ernest Gruening, and SDS president Paul Potter. Joan Baez, Phil Ochs, and Judy Collins provided the music. Then the huge crowd marched to the nation's Capitol to deliver an antiwar petition. It was, at that time, the largest antiwar demonstration in American history. The march generated headlines across the country and seemed to herald the birth of a new movement. It greatly enhanced the prestige of SDS, which, despite its huge influence on the early antiwar movement, would shortly thereafter abdicate its role as a "single-issue" antiwar organization at its June convention in Kewadin, Michigan. It was an unfortunate move, one that many SDSers would later regret. The decision briefly created a vacuum that other antiwar groups wasted no time in filling.

From its outset, the antiwar movement was strikingly diverse. Just as Walt Whitman said that America was not one nation, but a "teeming nation of nations," so the antiwar movement consisted of many different struggles, each with different aims and tactics that unfolded in communities across the country. Numerous organizations emerged, some lasting only briefly, others enduring through the war's duration. Tactics and strategies varied widely, depending on the participants. Despite a shared conviction within the movement that the Vietnam War was immoral and unjust, and a shared urgency that it had to be ended as soon as possible, it was often difficult to find the cement to coalesce the disparate antiwar forces.

1965: The Year of Vietnam

The array of protests throughout the very busy year 1965 reflected the breadth and diversity of the movement. Prior to SDS's highly successful April 15 march, the radical pacifist Committee for Nonviolent Action (CNVA)—a small group of antinuclear activists around since the 1950s—declared 1965 "the Year of Vietnam." CNVA organized pickets and civil disobedience in various locales on February 7. Meantime, students and faculty at the University of Michigan busily organized the first teach-in on the Vietnam War, held in March 1965. The Michigan teach-in, which offered the war's critics in academe an opportunity to speak out against it, attracted an audience of thousands and inspired countless other teach-ins on campuses across the nation. Other protesters resorted to more desperate acts. On March 16, eighty-two-year-old Alice Herz, a widow who had fled Nazism in Germany, set herself afire in the streets of Detroit. "I choose the illuminating death of a Buddhist to protest against a great country trying to wipe out a small country for no reason," she wrote, referring to Buddhist protesters who immolated themselves in protest against the Saigon regime. Later, she would be joined by Baltimore Quaker Norman Morrison, who set himself on fire in November near the Pentagon, and Catholic activist Roger LaPorte, who immolated himself near the United Nations building.

Most antiwar protesters chose more conventional ways of expressing opposition to the war, listening to speakers at rallies and participating in marches. For the first few years of the antiwar movement, large pro-war demonstrations often overshadowed antiwar gatherings. In many cases, the pro-war counter-demonstrators carried signs denouncing Communism and "peaceniks," and they often spent more time in the media spotlight than the war's foes. "Love it or leave it" and "Go back to Hanoi" were familiar refrains. But the pro-war rallies rarely deterred determined antiwar activists. Following SDS's April 15 event, waves of protests—many spontaneous, local, and grassroots in nature—continued across the country. The year's activities culminated with an equally successful Thanksgiving antiwar march sponsored by the National Committee for a Sane Nuclear Policy (SANE). Throughout the year, new antiwar groups emerged in cities and towns across the country, some headquartered in elaborate offices with telephones and filing cabinets, others based in people's homes and apartments and linked to the outside world by P.O. box. By the end of 1965, there were over thirty different antiwar organizations, each sponsoring events and planning various activities. The following year, 1966, has been characterized by contemporary observers at the time, and historians in more recent years, as a period of slackening and slowdown within the antiwar movement. Fewer demonstrations generated headlines, and the movement seemed to lose its momentum. But a great deal of significant, behind-the-scenes coalition building occurred that year.

Building a National Coalition: The Spring Mobilization

The first national coalition of significance was the Spring Mobilization Committee to End the War in Vietnam. The "Spring MOBE," as it was called, grew out of a two-day meeting in Cleveland, Ohio, in September 1966, organized by the Inter-University Committee for Debate on Foreign Policy, the intercollegiate faculty group that had organized the first campus teach-ins. Originally called the November 8 Mobilization Committee, the group later renamed itself the Spring Mobilization Committee and functioned as an ad hoc national group whose purposes were to forge a coalition of existing peace groups and begin planning national demonstrations for April 15, 1967, in New York and San Francisco. A.J. Muste, a lifelong pacifist and radical activist, became the group's chairman. By this time, Muste, a revered elder father figure of the movement, was in his early eighties and a familiar sight at many early demonstrations, with his lanky frame, trademark hat, narrow tie, and overcoat. Born in the Netherlands in 1885, Muste came to America at age six and had a long history of involvement in a wide variety of progressive causes. In the Great Depression, he briefly embraced Trotskyism but returned to radical Christian pacifism. He remained a devoted antiwar and antinuclear activist during World War II and the Cold War, and maintained ties with the civil rights movement.

Widely regarded as the "founding father" of the antiwar movement and admired by even his harshest critics, Muste was an effective coalition builder whose warm personality lured the finest activists of the era into the fold. He envisioned a unifying, umbrella organization that could bring together the diverse elements of the peace movement. But the aging Muste never lived to see the event he worked so hard to plan. He died of a stroke in February 1967, at age eighty-two. Organizers mourned his loss and soon discovered that keeping the Spring Mobilization together without him would be a difficult task. Liberals affiliated with SANE demanded a purge of Communists and Trotskyists from the coalition. Radical pacifists, such as Dave Dellinger, advocated widespread civil disobedience to protest the war. Activists associated with the Trotskyist Socialist Workers Party (SWP), under the guidance of veteran SWPer Fred Halstead, showed grim determination in exerting their influence in the movement, demonstrating an uncanny stamina at meetings.

But the end result of their hard work, the April 15, 1967, Spring Mobilization to End the War in Vietnam, was a triumph. Over a quarter of a million people assembled at Sheep Meadow in New York City's Central Park, and the gigantic throng marched to the United Nations Building, carrying antiwar signs and banners. The event's success owed much to a rousing antiwar speech delivered by Reverend Dr. Martin Luther King Jr. at the United Nations Building.

DR. MARTIN LUTHER KING JR. AND THE ANTIWAR MOVEMENT

Since 1965, King had had serious misgivings about the war, but in public he remained silent about the matter, fearing he would alienate liberal supporters in high places. Moreover, King felt uneasy about the presence of Communists and other radicals in the leadership of the antiwar movement. Moderate civil rights leaders, such as Roy Wilkins and Bayard Rustin, counseled him against condemning the war publicly. However, younger and more militant African Americans, many of them gravitating toward "black power," were losing faith in King as a result of his silence regarding the war. King's own close associate, Reverend James Bevel, repeatedly advised King to speak out against the war or risk losing his prestige. By 1967, with 380,000 soldiers in Vietnam and no end to the war in sight, King's opposition to the war eclipsed his concerns about the antiwar movement. On April 4, 1967, he delivered an impassioned condemnation of the war at Riverside Church in New York City. In the speech, he concluded, "I would never again raise my voice against the violence of the oppressed in the ghettos without having first spoken clearly to the greatest purveyor of violence in the world today—my own government."

King's speech two weeks later at the massive April 15 Spring Mobilization march elevated the prestige of the antiwar movement to new heights. By 1967, the antiwar movement had evolved from a series of peripheral and scattered actions to a mass protest movement. After April 15, the media and policymakers began taking the movement seriously. New antiwar groups appeared, greater varieties of dissent flowered, and in Washington, D.C., congressional doves took bolder stands against the escalating war in Southeast Asia. Six months later, organizers of the Spring Mobilization planned an equally successful event, the October 21 March on the Pentagon. One hundred thousand peaceful protesters, including GI's and veterans, clergy, minorities, and countercultural peaceniks, listened to speakers at the Lincoln Memorial. Then 35,000 marched to the Pentagon, where spirited youths placed flowers in the rifle barrels of military police.

The antiwar movement entered its renaissance, but it would remain a diverse "movement of movements," more difficult than ever to coalesce. Women, GI's and veterans, draft resisters, students, and minorities all formed key segments in the movement.

WOMEN AND THE MOVEMENT

From the outset, women played an instrumental role in the antiwar movement. Women from all walks of life became active participants. One of the first petition drives against the war was launched by the Women's International League for Peace and Freedom (WILPF). The WILPF, one of the oldest peace groups in America, grew out of the Woman's Peace Party, founded in 1915 by several Progressive women, including social reformer Jane Addams. It remained a formidable antiwar network during the 1960s, planning several events and maintaining chapters across the United States. A much newer organization, Women's Strike for Peace (WSP), held its founding convention in Ann Arbor, Michigan, in 1962, with a far-reaching agenda to end the nuclear arms race. When the Vietnam War began, WSP leaders switched the group's focus to antiwar organizing. Across America, WSP members went door-to-door collecting signatures for petitions, mailed protest letters to policymakers, staged public rallies at city halls, and encouraged neighbors to resist the war. The group's

March on the Pentagon in February 1967 generated much media attention.

Other women's groups had a strong impact. In March 1967, a gathering of fifteen women from Beverly Hills, California, launched Another Mother for Peace (AMP), which began in March 1967 by selling 200,000 antiwar Mother's Day cards to citizens to send to their member of Congress. The group grew rapidly, thanks to celebrity endorsements from liberal celebrities such as Paul Newman and Debbie Reynolds, and eventually it emerged as a powerful antiwar lobbying group. AMP provided support to Daniel Ellsberg and Anthony Russo when they released the Pentagon Papers to the *New York Times* and other media outlets.

Women role models were numerous in the antiwar movement. Perhaps the most effective and highly visible organizer was Norma Becker, a New York public school teacher, single mother of two, and veteran of various civil rights struggles. Becker was a cofounder and coordinator of the Fifth Avenue Peace Parade Committee, a coalition of several New York antiwar groups that organized the Fifth Avenue Peace Parade held on March 26, 1966. The parade drew 50,000 participants and was one of the success stories of the early antiwar movement. Becker would remain a key leader in the movement until the end of the war, assuming important high-level positions in the National Mobilization Committee to End the War in Vietnam (also known as "the MOBE," the successor to the Spring Mobilization) and various draft resistance programs. Becker and other women would always be instrumental in the flourishing struggle against the war, and the rise of feminism in the late 1960s and early 1970s strengthened their position as leaders and contributors to the movement.

THE RELIGIOUS COMMUNITY

Religious opposition remained strong throughout the entire war. The interfaith Fellowship of Reconciliation organized the earliest antiwar actions, immediately following the Tonkin Gulf incidents and resolution. FOR sent fact-finding teams to South Vietnam to probe human rights abuses and eventually revealed the Saigon regime's torture of prisoners in cramped "tiger cages." FOR's executive secretary, Alfred Hassler, actively promoted an interfaith dialogue between Americans and Vietnamese, bringing the renowned Vietnamese Buddhist monk, poet, and activist Thich Nhat Hanh to the United States to speak in 1966 as part of a FOR-sponsored tour.

FOR inspired other religious figures to speak and

act against the war. William Sloane Coffin, chaplain of Yale University, emerged as one of the most eloquent antiwar spokespersons of the era and participated actively in demonstrations and civil disobedience. Along with Dr. John Bennett, president of Union Theological Seminary, and Rabbi Abraham Heschel of the Jewish Theological Seminary, Coffin cofounded Clergy and Laymen Concerned About Vietnam (CALCAV), an interfaith antiwar organization. Under the astute leadership of Richard Fernandez, CALCAV grew rapidly in the late 1960s and early 1970s, attracting thousands of religious dissenters from across the country. The most famous religious resisters were Catholic radicals Daniel and Philip Berrigan. The Berrigan brothers and seven other Catholic activists made headlines on May 17, 1968, when they broke into a draft board office in Catonsville, Maryland, stole 300 draft files, and set them on fire in the parking lot with homemade napalm.

STUDENTS AND THE MOVEMENT

In 1959, a few years before SDS's rise to prominence, the Student Peace Union (SPU) formed at the University of Chicago, founded by pacifists, liberals, and ban-the-bomb activists. By the next year, it had twelve chapters in the Midwest, and in the summer of 1962 the SPU could boast 2,000 members. At the beginning of the war, the SPU, along with FOR and WRL, shifted its attention to antiwar organizing. The SPU tapped into a rich source of activism—the student body of America's higher education system—which would eventually furnish a steady stream of recruits to the antiwar movement. The growth of higher education, which was owing largely to huge government expenditures, meant an unprecedented number of Americans attended universities in the 1960s. The number of students enrolled in colleges and universities climbed from 3.2 million in 1960 to 7.5 million in 1970. Few American students embraced radicalism in the mid-1960s. A *Newsweek* poll of 800 university students conducted in the spring of 1965 found that 90 percent expressed confidence in higher education, corporations, and the federal government, while 80 percent were pleased with college life and expressed confidence in organized religion and the military. Despite widespread conformity on campuses, students formed an important cornerstone of the antiwar movement. They organized the waves of teach-ins in 1965 and 1966. They committed civil disobedience against napalm manufacturer Dow Chemical at the University of Wisconsin-Madison in 1967. And in May 1970, many Americans were shocked and dismayed

by the news of the war coming home when the Ohio National Guard opened fire on students, killing four at the Kent State University campus.

Most accounts of the era downplay the importance of the Student Mobilization Committee to End the War in Vietnam (SMC), likely because of the influence that the Trotskyist SWP exerted over the organization. But it was the SMC—not SDS—which drew significant numbers of students into the antiwar movement on college campuses across the nation. The SMC originated at a national student antiwar conference held in Chicago, December 28–30, 1966. The SMC operated all over the country and remained active through much of the antiwar movement, organizing several successful protests involving university and high school students and GI's.

Meanwhile, liberal college students campaigned for dovish political candidates, especially Minnesota senator Eugene McCarthy when he ran as an antiwar presidential candidate in 1968. Calling themselves "clean for Gene" (to disassociate themselves from countercultural hippies), students flooded into New Hampshire for the primaries and worked many long hours for the campaign. Even though McCarthy lost to Johnson in the primaries, the race was so close that President Johnson announced in March 1968 that he would not seek office again. Many of these young, idealistic liberal students would go on to organize the Moratoriums, a series of protests—candlelight vigils, church services, marches, and other events—held across America beginning in the fall of 1969.

Later in the antiwar movement, President Richard Nixon would single out antiwar students for attack. Nixon repeatedly claimed that the movement was dominated by students, "spoiled bums blowing up campuses," he called them. A highly publicized clash between "hard hat" construction workers and peaceful student demonstrators in lower Manhattan on May 8, 1970, proved a coup for the Nixon administration. A crowd of 200 angry workers descended on the students and began pummeling them with fists, crowbars, and wrenches, leaving seventy youths bloodied and dazed. Nixon used the event as an opportunity to reemphasize that the so-called silent majority was fed up with protesters and countercultural youths.

THE COUNTERCULTURE

The misconception that America's "war at home" was simply a youth protest movement grew out of the highly visible presence of young, countercultural men and women at events. The colorful, psychedelic youth

BOB DYLAN (1941–)

Bob Dylan was born in Duluth, Minnesota, as Robert Zimmerman on May 24, 1941, but grew up in the small town of Hibbing, Minnesota. Dylan learned guitar at the age of ten and the autoharp and harmonica at fifteen. While attending the University of Minnesota, he began performing under the name Bob Dylan and soon dropped out of school. He moved to New York City by early 1961, determined to meet his musical hero, Woody Guthrie, who was bedridden with Huntington's chorea, and to join the burgeoning folk music scene there.

In New York, Dylan became part of the Greenwich Village folk music scene, playing coffeehouses and spending time with musicians like Joan Baez, Phil Ochs, and Tom Paxton. Influenced by Huddie Ledbetter, Bo Diddley, Hank Williams, and Woody Guthrie, Dylan had a profound effect on folk and rock music. Though his earliest circulating recordings date from 1958, his first commercial release was in 1962 and instantly changed popular music. As a lyricist, he captured the cynicism, anger, and alienation of American youth, which reverberated in his harsh vocal delivery and insistent guitar-harmonica accompaniment. Among his many songs of social protest are "Blowin' in the Wind" and "The Times They Are A-Changin'." Dylan's style has evolved from folk ("Don't Think Twice"), to folk-rock ("Highway 61 Revisited"), to country blues ("Country Pie"). His decision to perform with an electric rock-and-roll band in 1965 at the Newport Folk Festival outraged his fans but further influenced popular music. Enigmatic and reclusive, he published an autobiography, *Bob Dylan, Self-Portrait* (1970), and a novel, *Tarantula* (1971).

Dylan is unquestionably one of the towering figures of late-twentieth-century popular music, mixing folk, country, blues, and rock on over forty albums. Although Dylan was an influential pop figure during the youth movement of the 1960s, his first number one hit, "Knocking on Heaven's Door," didn't come until 1973. During the 1980s, he toured extensively and recorded with other artists on several albums. In the 1990s, his songs found a new audience and more acclaim from the music industry: in 1991, he was given a Lifetime Achievement Grammy Award; his 1997 album, *Time Out of Mind*, won three Grammys; and in 2001 Dylan won the Academy Award for Best Song for his "Things Have Changed," from the movie *Wonder Boys* (2000).

James G. Lewis

culture of the 1960s frequently overlapped with the antiwar movement. The "hippies"—as the *San Francisco Chronicle* dubbed them in 1965—rarely proved to be committed activists. Young people with long hair and psychedelic clothing followed drug guru Timothy Leary's advice and began dropping out, living communally among enclaves of kindred spirits in the Haight-Ashbury District of San Francisco, the East Village of New York, and other communities. Their rejection of the dominant culture and all things associated with it, including the Vietnam War, resulted in a natural affinity with the antiwar movement. Some 1960s bohemians were far more political than others. Early in the movement, antiwar folk singers such as Bob Dylan, Joan Baez, Phil Ochs, and Judy Collins appealed to youthful protesters, inspiring many to become involved. In the mid-1960s, the New York Workshop in Nonviolence founded the enduring antiwar periodical *WIN* magazine, a favorite periodical of countercultural antiwar activists.

The earliest heavily publicized wedding of the movement and the new youth culture occurred at the January 14, 1967, "Human Be-In" at Golden Gate Park in San Francisco, a four-hour "Pow Wow" of rock music, Allen Ginsberg chants, and an antiwar speech by activist Jerry Rubin. Janis Joplin performed, as did Jefferson Airplane and the Grateful Dead. Twenty thousand attended. Later that year, "Human Be-In" speaker Jerry Rubin teamed up with SNCC activist Abbie Hoffman, *Realist* publisher and editor Paul Krassner, and other youths to form the madcap, irreverent anarchical Youth International Party, or the Yippies. Not so much a formal organization as a concept, the Yippies attempted to bridge the antiwar movement and the counterculture, with mixed, though often amusing, results. Whether tossing one-dollar bills from the balcony of the New York Stock Exchange and watching traders scramble for them, or attempting to levitate the Pentagon at the October 21, 1967, demonstration, the Yippies always added much-needed humor to the proceedings. Thanks to the Yippies and other vibrant countercultural groups, such as the Diggers, a radical, theatrical collective, the rebellious youth styles of the era heavily colored the antiwar movement by the late 1960s and early 1970s.

AFRICAN AMERICANS AND CHICANOS

Despite pervasive antiwar sentiment in the black community, the antiwar movement attracted few committed antiwar organizers. Even before the war, the militant Muslim Malcolm X linked the U.S. government policies in Indochina with the repression of African Americans at home. A few years later, in January 1967, Reverend James Bevel of the Southern Christian Leadership Conference—Dr. King's group—became national chairman of the Spring Mobilization. Another close associate of King's, Reverend Ralph Abernathy, remained closely aligned to the antiwar movement throughout the 1960s. The Student Nonviolent Coordinating Committee (SNCC), whose sit-ins, civil disobedience, and voter registration had been highly successful in the South, was the first civil rights movement to condemn U.S. policy in Vietnam when it issued an antiwar statement in January 1966. When heavyweight champion Muhammad Ali refused induction, he was stripped of his crown and sentenced to a maximum penalty of five years in jail and $10,000 in fines. Ali's decision energized African Americans, particularly youths, who applauded his antiwar statement: "No Viet Cong ever called me a nigger." Various "black power" luminaries—including Stokely Carmichael and SNCC chairman H. Rap Brown—spoke at antiwar rallies. A 1970 study by journalist Wallace Terry found that widespread antiwar and black power sentiment existed among black GI's in Vietnam. But many black power militants felt estranged from the predominantly white antiwar leaders, who seemed to be ignoring problems in the black community. "We're not inside the peace movement," wrote SNCC leader Ivanhoe Donaldson, echoing the sentiment of other militants. "It's basically all-white. There's no way to relate to that."

Like African Americans, Chicanos (Americans of Mexican descent) often participated in antiwar activities but did not necessarily feel at home in the movement. Many Chicano activists worked in Chicano rights groups, such as La Raza Unida and the Brown Berets. But Chicanos also organized some highly publicized antiwar events. Denver activists founded the Chicano Moratorium Committee, which conducted its first demonstration on February 28, 1970, in East Los Angeles. Five thousand attended, despite heavy rain. Other Chicano Moratorium protests occurred across California, as well Texas, New Mexico, and Colorado. On August 29, 1970, the Chicano Moratorium held its biggest demonstration in Los Angeles. Twenty thousand people showed up. Clashes occurred between police and Chicano protesters. In a shootout at a local tavern, Los Angeles police shot and killed Ruben Salazar, popular columnist for the *Los Angeles Times*. By 1971, Chicano protest shifted away from the war and more toward issues having to do with community organizing and "brown pride." Although few Chicanos rose to positions of prominence and authority in the

antiwar movement, their presence left an indelible mark.

ANTIWAR POLICYMAKERS

"I like to believe that the people in the long run are going to do more to promote peace than our governments," said President Dwight Eisenhower in 1959. "I think the people want peace so much that one of these days government had better get out of their way and let them have it." In the 1960s and 1970s, dovish politicians not only followed Eisenhower's advice, but they took the next step and actively supported the antiwar movement. U.S. undersecretary of state George Ball had opposed U.S. involvement in Vietnam from the time he joined the Kennedy administration in 1961. But his was a lone voice, and few in official Washington shared his concerns. Senator J. William Fulbright (D-AR), chairman of the Senate Foreign Relations Committee, emboldened many political doves when he conducted a series of televised Senate hearings critical of the war in January and February 1966. Fulbright had supported the Tonkin Gulf Resolution but gradually turned against the war the following year. His hearings enabled the war's moderate opponents, such as George Kennan, architect of the containment policy, and Lieutenant General James Gavin, to criticize the war from a respectable platform.

The Vietnam War caused deep divisions within the Democratic Party, often splitting the party in half. Senators Eugene McCarthy and Robert Kennedy (D-NY) ran for the presidency in 1968 on antiwar platforms. Kennedy's campaign was cut short by the assassin's bullet on June 5, 1968, and McCarthy's campaign floundered after Vice President Hubert Humphrey entered the race. But antiwar protesters targeted Humphrey during the 1968 Chicago Democratic National Convention for his pro-war position. During the convention, an antiwar platform drafted by Democratic doves was narrowly defeated. Four years later, George McGovern, the Democratic Party's 1972 presidential candidate, ran as an outspoken peace candidate. By this time, the Democratic Party opposed the war, and many politicians spoke at antiwar events. In addition, a growing number of Republicans, including Senator Mark Hatfield (R-OR), Representative Paul McCloskey (R-CA), and Senator George Aiken (R-VT), strenuously opposed the war in and out of the halls of Congress.

THE DRAFT

In 1966, General Lewis B. Hershey, director of the Selective Service, stepped up the draft call from less than 10,000 to more than 30,000 per month, to meet the growing demand for troops in Vietnam. Hershey also supported draft deferments for university students, whom he regarded as "socially useful" members of society. The draft was widely unpopular among the nation's youth, and it became a lightning rod for antiwar protests. An antidraft movement was already under way before Hershey's decision. In May 1964, twelve men had burned their draft cards in an anticonscription protest. During the October 1965 Days of International Protest in New York City, pacifists organized a gathering at the Whitehall Street Induction Center, where one of the speakers, David Miller, a Catholic Worker activist, decided to burn his draft card instead of speak. The crowd of 500 applauded him. Miller was the first person to publicly burn a draft card since Congress had passed a law the previous summer making the act a felony. Miller's act touched off other draft card burnings. Of all the tactics employed by antiwar activists, draft card burning was one of the most controversial. Beginning with David Miller's defiant draft card burning in 1965, the media frequently spotlighted the draft card burners, and conservatives called for strict punishments against them. When Bruce Dancis and other activists at Cornell University burned draft cards in the spring of 1966, their actions generated a great deal of publicity and sparked similar protests elsewhere. Draft card burning divided the antiwar movement. Many liberal doves, as well as members of the Socialist Workers' Party, whose organization opposed civil disobedience, condemned draft card burning. Radical pacifists such as Dave Dellinger and Brad Lyttle supported and actively encouraged draft card burning as an important, symbolic form of resistance. Draft card burning hit a peak in 1967 and began to decline in the years that followed, as anti-draft organizers began to advocate the less dramatic approach of draft card "turn-ins," where young men simply returned their draft cards to authorities.

The first sizable antidraft demonstration occurred at the Spring Mobilization protest on April 15, 1967. Before the march, 175 men gathered in Sheep Meadow in Central Park and burned their draft cards in an action organized by antidraft organizer Bruce Dancis and a handful of Cornell students. Demonstrators held their flaming cards high as crowds of onlookers clapped.

On March 8, 1967, antiwar activist David Harris and a group of his friends met in Palo Alto, California, and founded a group they called "The Resistance." They planned a series of demonstrations where young men could proclaim their independence and return their draft cards to the U.S. government. Across the country, activists opened local offices of the resistance and participated in the planning by recruiting draft resisters in their area. On October 3, 1967, more than 1,500 men returned their draft cards in the first "turn-in" demonstration planned by the Resistance. Two weeks later—October 17, 1967—3,000 protesters confronted a phalanx of club-wielding police in an antidraft protest at the Oakland induction center. The event, sponsored by several Bay Area antiwar organizations, quickly deteriorated into a violent melee, despite the efforts of Harris and other pacifists to keep it peaceful. Still, most antidraft protests remained nonviolent. Building on the success of its first "turn-in," the Resistance organized others, including one on December 4, where 475 participated, and April 3, 1968, which drew 630 draft resisters. David Harris ultimately went to prison for organizing the Resistance. Author Tom Wells noted that "the Resistance contributed to a grass-roots movement of more than half a million young men who violated Selective Service laws."

Thousands of draft resisters left the United States, settling in Sweden, Great Britain, Mexico, Canada, and elsewhere. The largest recipient of these young expatriates was Canada because culturally, it had much in common with the United States, and yet it provided a safe haven for young men fleeing the draft. During the Vietnam War, approximately 50,000 Americans—many young men and women opposed to the war—moved to Canada. In 1968, American draft resisters in Canada founded numerous antiwar organizations, the most influential being Amex, an antidraft organization. Amex published a newspaper of the same name, which went out to draft resisters across the country. The expanding Canadian anti–Vietnam War movement attracted numerous American expatriates, who brought a sense of urgency to planning protest activities. On college campuses from British Columbia to the maritime provinces, the new immigrants marched, spoke out, and organized.

Back in the United States, Dr. Curtis Tarr replaced General Hershey as head of Selective Service in 1969, and he looked for ways to quell the mass antidraft movement, as well as widespread allegations that the government was singling out the poor for the draft. He introduced a random lottery and scaled back deferments, which Nixon ultimately revoked in 1971. By that time, however, the draft had slowed substantially, thus removing much of the wind from the sails of the antidraft movement.

GI'S AND VETERANS

Reflecting the wider sentiments of the American public in 1965, most soldiers and veterans supported America's Vietnam policies. But a few bold ones turned against the war. In November 1966, Lieutenant Henry Howe was arrested and later court-martialed for attending an antiwar protest at Texas Western College. The following year, Captain Howard Levy, a U.S. Army physician, refused to train Special Forces medics bound for Vietnam. He was court-martialed and convicted, and served twenty-seven months in prison. In Fort Hood, Texas, three privates—Dennis Mora, James Johnson, and David Samas—refused orders to go to Vietnam in June 1966. "We want no part of the extermination," the so-called Fort Hood Three declared. Several antiwar activists came to the defense of Levy and the Fort Hood Three, planning demonstrations and generating much media attention. Like Captain Levy, the Fort Hood Three would each spend two years in prison. But their resistance emboldened the antiwar leaders, who were encouraged that dissent was finally making its way into the military.

Near military bases, activists opened up coffeehouses for antiwar GI's. In 1967, Fred Gardner, a reservist and former *Harvard Crimson* editor, opened the doors of the first GI coffeehouse, the UFO, in Columbia, South Carolina. He then traveled to Texas to open the Oleo Strut, a GI coffeehouse a few miles from Fort Hood. Despite harassment and persecution from military authorities and local police, nineteen coffeehouses were operating by 1970. Along with coffeehouses, GI underground newspapers helped spread antiwar sentiments through the military. GI activist David Cortright described the underground GI papers as "often short-lived and appearing in the form of barely readable mimeographed sheets." Two early GI underground papers were *FTA* at Fort Knox, Kentucky, and *Fatigue Press* at Fort Hood, Texas. Eventually, papers with such titles as *Open Sights, The Ally,* and *Left Face* could be found on military bases all over the United States and Vietnam.

Veterans also became involved in greater numbers as the war dragged on in Vietnam. In September 1965, U.S. Army Special Forces Sgt. Donald Duncan, who had trained soldiers in Vietnam, refused a promotion and resigned from the army to become involved with the antiwar movement. Duncan used his unique status as an ex–Green Beret to legitimize his resistance against the war. He became an editor at the radical periodical *Ramparts* and remained constantly in demand as a speaker at antiwar protests throughout the 1960s and 1970s.

In June 1967, six veterans who marched at the Spring Mobilization in New York founded Vietnam Veterans Against the War (VVAW). By the early 1970s, VVAW boasted 30,000 members, with chapters in every state of the union and Vietnam. The organization's first national demonstration, Operation RAW (Rapid American Withdrawal) in September 1970, was a highly publicized march of more than 150 Vietnam veterans from Morristown, New Jersey, to Valley Forge, Pennsylvania. VVAW conducted the Winter Soldier war crimes hearings in January and February 1971, attracting little media attention. But the organization next staged perhaps the most profoundly moving protest of the entire antiwar movement, Operation Dewey Canyon III (the title spoofed Operation Dewey Canyon II, code name for the U.S. military's "limited incursion" into Laos in February 1971). Well over a thousand veterans came to Washington, D.C., in April 1971 for a week of lobbying, guerrilla street theater, and marches. The week climaxed on Thursday with a powerful televised speech by VVAWer (and future U.S. senator) John Kerry, denouncing the war before the Senate Foreign Relations Committee. Then, the following day, Friday, April 23, 1971, perhaps as many as 1,500 veterans lined up on the steps of the nation's Capitol (surrounded by a makeshift wood and barbed-wire wall in preparation for the tumultuous upcoming May Day demonstrations). One by one, the veterans threw their medals, citations, ribbons, and other symbols of war, many of them making short and memorable statements, while network news cameras whirred and newspaper still cameras clicked. Images of the demonstration were played and replayed on television and in newspapers, searing it into the collective psyche of the American public.

The GI and veterans movement would flourish in the early 1970s, becoming arguably the most vibrant and active segment of the later antiwar movement. In June 1971, an alarmed Marine Corps Colonel Robert D. Heinl Jr. acknowledged in the respected *Armed Forces Journal* that the numerous GI and veterans protest movements had resulted in a crisis of morale in the U.S. military.

Members of the Vietnam Veterans Against the War march in Washington, D.C. *(© Underwood Photo Archives, Inc.)*

THE PEAK OF THE ANTIWAR MOVEMENT

The antiwar movement reached its zenith between 1968 and 1971. In these years, the movement had matured and had become increasingly decentralized. If the early years were characterized by national protests, planned by unified coalitions, in heavily populated cities such as New York, Washington, D.C., and San Francisco, the later years witnessed a more localized flowering of the movement, in communities across the country. This trend was accelerated by the fall 1969 Moratorium, a series of nationwide protests, some occurring in small towns in places like Kansas and Georgia, which had never had protests before.

1968

A year of trauma and upheaval, 1968 began with the Communist Tet Offensive in Vietnam at the end of January, and the intensity never subsided. The Tet Offensive was huge, as desperate North Vietnamese Army and Viet Cong soldiers battered virtually every major city and district capital in South Vietnam, surprising American commanders and their South Vietnamese allies. Like a sleeping giant suddenly awakened, U.S. forces struck back with unprecedented ferocity, pummeling rural and urban areas from the air and battling Communist forces on the ground. Scenes from the bloody battles—including unforgettable footage of South Vietnamese police chief

Nguyen Loc Loan assassinating a bound and un-armed Viet Cong prisoner—were played and re-played on American television sets. Most Americans had believed President Johnson's promises in late 1967 that the war was going in America's favor and would soon end. Although Tet ended in disaster for the Communists, it rattled the confidence of the American public and greatly enhanced the prestige of the antiwar movement.

But the assassinations of Reverend Dr. Martin Luther King Jr. in April and Senator Robert Kennedy in June (while campaigning for president on an antiwar platform) left the movement reeling and many activists dispirited. In April, radical students seized control of Columbia University in New York, which intensified the highly charged atmosphere. Many of the students were SDSers and outspoken antiwar militants. The tense takeover ended in late April when police forcefully evicted protesters from campus buildings, beating students and innocent bystanders in front of television cameras. As the mood of the country grew more polemical, a tiny but vocal minority of activists embraced violence and political extremism. These radicals had grown impatient with traditional methods of protest, which failed to reverse—much less end—the Vietnam War, and they vowed to "bring the war home." Beginning in 1968, militant revolutionary sects began attracting handfuls of antiwar activists. Between January 1969 and April 1970, 40,000 bombing incidents or bomb threats occurred, damaging $21 million in property and killing forty-three people. Police and federal agents never learned the identity of most of the perpetrators.

Demonstrations occurred frequently in 1968, but most of them remained peaceful. The antiwar movement reached a feverish climax in August in Chicago, during the Democratic National Convention. After the April 15, 1967, marches, the Spring Mobilization had again changed its name—this time to the National Mobilization Committee to End the War in Vietnam, or MOBE for short. The MOBE and several other organizations spent months planning protests for the Democratic National Convention, scheduled for August 21–26, 1968. Chicago's crusty mayor and political boss, Richard Daley, learned of the protests and responded by filling Chicago's streets with 12,000 uniformed and heavily armed police officers, and kept 6,000 Illinois National Guardsmen stationed nearby on standby. MOBE organizers Dave Dellinger, Tom Hayden, and Rennie Davis hoped the coalition would inspire antiwar Democrats to revolt against the pro-war faction of the party, ideally in the streets. The

Yippies planned a "Festival of Life," which they envisioned would include rock music, drugs, skinny dipping, and their own presidential candidate, a pig called "Pigasus."

Chicago 1968 assumed a historical significance beyond the actual events that occurred during the convention, due largely to the heavily televised drama coming out of the city each day. Delegates clashed with each other on the convention floor. At night, phalanxes of police, with clubs swinging, charged into crowds of taunting protesters. The streets were filled with smoke and blood. The Yippies' "Festival of Life" was poorly attended but heavily covered by the media. The MOBE's huge rally in Grant Park and many marches deteriorated into pandemonium. Young activists climbed atop statues and waved the National Liberation Front flag, provoking more police charges. True to their word, activists were bringing the war home, and in the process, the Democratic Party itself unraveled, shaking public confidence in the party's nominee, Hubert Humphrey.

After Richard Nixon's narrow presidential victory over Humphrey in November 1968, eight organizers of the Chicago Democratic National Convention protests were indicted on charges of conspiracy and crossing state lines with intent to commit riot. The trial of the Chicago Eight—later the Chicago Seven (defendant Bobby Seale was removed from the trial when he refused to cooperate, even after being bound and gagged)—proved to be heavily publicized high drama. Beginning in August 1969, the trial quickly deteriorated into a courtroom free-for-all, with the presiding judge, Julius Hoffman, exchanging insults and epithets with the defendants. The trial lasted four months. The seven defendants were found not guilty of conspiracy but were convicted of intent to riot and sentenced to five years in prison. A federal appeals court later overturned the charges against the defendants.

The Moratorium

The events in Chicago, coupled with Richard Nixon's victory in November, left many activists feeling dispirited and weary. Newly elected president Richard Nixon had promised that he had a "secret plan" to end the war in Vietnam, but he waited until July to reveal that he planned a gradual withdrawal of U.S. forces from Southeast Asia. During that time, movement activists regrouped and planned more events. After Chicago, antiwar activists worked tirelessly to mount the largest, most ambitious protest of the antiwar movement, the Moratorium. The head of the

National Guardsmen spray tear gas at antiwar demonstrators at Kent State University in Ohio, on May 4, 1970. The demonstration—sparked by President Richard Nixon's announcement that the Vietnam War would be expanded into Cambodia—led to the deadliest moment of the peace movement when Guardsmen opened fire on students, killing four and injuring nine. *(© Underwood Photo Archives, Inc.)*

Moratorium, Sam Brown, who had organized young volunteers for Senator Eugene McCarthy's 1968 presidential campaign, proposed a day of actions across the nation, where Americans took the day off school or work to protest the war. The Moratorium also drew support from the more radical wing of the peace movement. Co-sponsoring the fall events was the MOBE, by now re-christened "the New MOBE." The SWP-backed Student Mobilization Committee (SMC) also contributed significantly to organizing events around the country.

The October 15, 1969, Moratorium proved enormously successful. An estimated 2 million citizens participated in events across the country. They marched, listened to speeches, distributed pamphlets, read the names of Americans and Vietnamese killed in the war, showed films, attended church services, and conducted candlelight vigils. Church bells pealed for the dead. Millions of middle-class Americans who

had never before protested in their lives wore black armbands to signify their unhappiness with the war. In Boston, more than 100,000 flooded the Common for the largest demonstration in that city's history. A second Moratorium in mid-November drew even more participants. During the groundswell of protest, newspapers across the country began publishing a series of reports, written by journalist Seymour Hersh, about a massacre in the Vietnamese hamlet of My Lai. On March 16, 1968—almost a year and a half before the story broke in America—Army Lt. William Calley Jr. and a number of his men herded 500 Vietnamese civilians together—men, women, and children—and systematically slaughtered them. My Lai fueled antiwar sentiment. So did a photo spread that fall in *Life* magazine, reminiscent of a high school yearbook, showing row after row of American soldiers killed in one week in Vietnam.

CAMBODIA AND THE WAR AT HOME

President Nixon was disturbed by the numerous media revelations about the conduct of the war throughout 1969. Particularly troubling to him was a story that first appeared in the *New York Times* in June reporting that the U.S. government was conducting a secret bombing campaign of Cambodia. Nixon had broadened the scope of the bombing to wipe out enemy sanctuaries in Cambodia and to destabilize the Communist Khmer Rouge guerrillas within its borders. At the end of April 1970, President Nixon made a televised speech announcing that he was sending American troops into Cambodia to destroy Vietnamese Communist positions in the country. The announcement immediately touched off a wave of protests at colleges and universities across the nation. Antiwar actions spread to 350 campuses, and some of them would remain closed for the rest of the year. On Monday, May 4, 1970—following a weekend of protest at Kent State University in Ohio, where an ROTC building was burned to the ground—Ohio National Guardsmen opened fire on a crowd of more than 1,000 students, killing four and injuring nine. Nine days later—on the evening of May 13—police opened fire on protesters at Jackson State in Mississippi, killing two students in the dorms. Both incidents, especially the more highly publicized Kent State, sent shock waves through the antiwar movement and undermined the momentum of the spring student strike movement. By the fall, most campuses would return to business as usual, but the traumatized nation would never be the same.

THE LAST HURRAH

The movement enjoyed a spectacular revival in the spring of 1971. A flurry of highly publicized protests occurred, starting in April, indicating the continued power of the antiwar movement. VVAW's "Operation Dewey Canyon III," a week of protest activity in Washington, D.C., April 19–23, 1971, involving more than a thousand Vietnam veterans, represented a huge coup for the movement. The medal-throwing ceremony on Friday, April 23, made countless headlines and dominated the network nightly news. The next day, April 24, between a half million and three quarters of a million people attended the largest demonstration in the history of the antiwar movement. A week later, thousands of protesters swept into the nation's capital for the May Day protests. During the numerous scattered actions, a record number of activists were arrested for civil disobedience. Crowds

Locking arms in solidarity, veterans of the Vietnam War demonstrate on the steps of the Supreme Court Building in Washington, D.C., on April 22, 1971. The next day many publicly tossed away their war medals, a powerful symbolic action that galvanized the peace movement. *(© Underwood Photo Archives, Inc.)*

swept through the city, disrupting traffic, trashing neighborhoods, interrupting government offices, and generally wreaking havoc. Numerous scuffles broke out between police and demonstrators. On May 3 alone, Washington police arrested 7,000 people. Numerous other actions followed throughout 1971, with military and veteran dissent now dominating the antiwar agenda.

A powerful boost to the movement came in June 1971, when Defense Department "whiz kid" Daniel Ellsberg, onetime National Security Council operative, senior liaison officer to the U.S. Embassy in Vietnam, ex-Marine, and former Cold Warrior, leaked the Pentagon Papers to the *New York Times*. The Pentagon Papers, a forty-seven-volume, 7,000-page study of the Vietnam War (from 1945 to 1968) was commissioned by Secretary of Defense Robert McNamara. Compiling the study involved the combined efforts of thirty-six Defense Department analysts, including Ellsberg and Harvard professor and Defense Department official Leslie Gelb. In addition to the *New York Times*, portions of the study appeared in the *Washington Post* and the *Boston Globe*. News of the released documents provoked a furor among conservatives who wanted to see Ellsberg convicted of treason, while antiwar activists felt vindicated by the findings of the massive study. The Pentagon Papers revealed a lengthy and systematic pattern of lies and deceit extending to the highest levels of government. The Justice Department tried to halt publication of the Pentagon Papers, and the leak upset President Nixon, who believed it would undermine his policymaking abilities in Vietnam. The leak prompted a secret organization called "the Plumbers"—a shady group of Nixon administration supporters sometimes called the Committee to Reelect the President (CREEP)—to break into the offices of Ellsberg's psychiatrist, Dr. Lewis Fielding, and steal Ellsberg's files. Nixon's obsession with leaks eventually led to the burglary at the Watergate office complex on June 17, 1972. Nixon's "plumbers" broke into the Democratic Party headquarters looking for files linking Democratic presidential candidate George McGovern with antiwar organizations and leaders. The burglars were caught, and slowly the extent of Nixon's involvement in the various break-ins, wiretaps, and other dirty tricks became known. The Impeach Nixon campaign of 1973 and 1974 grew largely out of the efforts of antiwar organizers.

DECLINE OF THE ANTIWAR MOVEMENT

When used to refer to the tumultuous protest movements of the period, the term "the 1960s" is a misnomer. Most of the protest movements of the era spilled into the 1970s, and the antiwar movement was no exception. It flourished until the early 1970s. Even throughout 1972, organizers could still mobilize significant demonstrations. At the Republican National Convention, thousands of protesters flooded into Miami to, as the posters for the event declared, "confront Nixon at Miami Beach." Various groups were busily planning a Counter-Inaugural demonstration, which occurred in Washington, D.C., on January 20, 1973, and attracted an impressive 100,000 participants. But the mass movement phase of the antiwar movement was effectively over after the 1973 Counter-Inaugural demonstration.

Decline did not come suddenly, and it occurred for many reasons. President Nixon's policy of "Vietnamization"—that is, replacing American combat forces with South Vietnamese soldiers—undermined the momentum of the movement. Gradually, Nixon withdrew U.S. forces while stepping up the air war.

In June 1969, Nixon told Americans that he was withdrawing 25,000 of the 543,000 soldiers from Vietnam. The policy continued over the next few years, with painful slowness, but steadiness. Troop levels plummeted to 340,000 by the end of 1970 and then dropped to 156,000 at the beginning of 1972. By this time, most of the U.S. troops were used for support purposes, to bolster the vulnerable Army of the Republic of Vietnam (ARVN). Nixon continued the air war, pushing it to its most intense and concentrated extremes in 1972 and 1973, and pledged his support to the Thieu regime in South Vietnam. The Saigon government continued to enjoy billions of dollars in aid in 1973 and 1974, but because the flow of American body bags coming home from Vietnam had now slowed to almost a halt, antiwar sentiment ebbed substantially.

The gradual withdrawal of troops from Vietnam increased public confidence in Nixon so that the president enjoyed a hugely lopsided victory over his opponent, antiwar South Dakota Democrat George McGovern, in the 1972 presidential elections. In the fall, Nixon launched Operation Linebacker, an intense bombing campaign over North Vietnam designed to pressure the North Vietnamese to sign the Peace Accords in Paris. The bombing stirred antiwar sentiment around the world, including in the United States. The recently formed Indochina Peace Campaign (IPC), founded by Jane Fonda and Tom Hayden, lobbied and organized some effective antiwar campaigns. But when Vietnamese and American leaders put pen to paper at the Paris Agreements in January 1973, formally ending the war in Vietnam, they effectively eliminated the raison d'être of the antiwar movement. Many antiwar organizations folded immediately; a few held out until 1975. In sporadic, local actions, people gathered to protest U.S. aid to the Thieu regime in South Vietnam and to halt the bombing of Cambodia.

But the movement suffered even before the Paris Peace Accords. During the late 1960s and early 1970s, Nixon's paranoia, coupled with the repressive surveillance and harassment campaigns against the movement carried out by the Federal Bureau of Investigation (FBI) and other federal and local law agencies, had a chilling effect on dissent. The Internal Revenue Service audited prominent antiwar activists, the FBI sent undercover agents provocateurs into the movement to encourage violence, and federal agents tapped telephones, photographed participants, and hounded their families and places of employment. "The surveillance was far more extensive than generally known," noted historian Terry Anderson.

Sectarian infighting within the movement also contributed to its demise. In some cases, liberals and radicals could not work together. Other times, internecine battles erupted over such insignificant matters as appropriate slogans for marches, or the order of speakers at a rally. In the early 1970s, the national coalition split in two, at a time when unity was needed the most. The two organizations—the SWP-dominated National Peace Action Coalition (NPAC) and the radical pacifist People's Coalition for Peace and Justice (PCPJ)—were simply fragments of the once mighty MOBE. Extremist revolutionary sects—always infinitesimal in number—also damaged the movement's credibility. Marchers who insisted on carrying Viet Cong flags and chanting "Ho-Ho-Ho Chi Minh" hindered the movement's ability to reach out to a large segment of the American public.

Ultimately, however, the antiwar movement left a profoundly indelible impact on America. It changed Vietnam policy, limiting America's options and military involvement in Southeast Asia, as movement chroniclers Tom Wells, Melvin Small, Thomas Powers, and others have demonstrated. It introduced new forms of dissent into the arena of America democracy. An alliance of many different groups emerged and challenged the U.S. war effort in Vietnam, with a scope and tenacity unprecedented in the history of American social protest movements. It ushered in an epic struggle over what sort of nation the United States ought to be, and it inspired other protest efforts in the process. In the end, the efforts of countless antiwar activists—in thousands of different communities across the United States—diminished American militarism, while at the same time greatly enhanced the nation's democratic traditions.

Andrew Hunt

BIBLIOGRAPHY

Anderson, Terry. *The Movement and the Sixties: Protest in America from Greensboro to Wounded Knee.* New York: Oxford University Press, 1994.

DeBenedetti, Charles, with Charles Chatfield. *An American Ordeal: The Antiwar Movement of the Vietnam Era.* Syracuse, NY: Syracuse University Press, 1990.

Dellinger, Dave. *More Power Than We Know: The People's Movement Toward Democracy.* Garden City, NY: Anchor/Doubleday, 1975.

Flacks, Richard, and Jack Whalen. *Beyond the Barricades: The Sixties Generation Grows Up.* Philadelphia: Temple University Press, 1989.

Foley, Michael S. *Confronting the War Machine: Draft Resistance During the Vietnam War.* Chapel Hill, NC: University of North Carolina Press, 2003.

Hall, Mitchell K. *Because of Their Faith: CALCAV and Religious Opposition to the Vietnam War.* New York: Columbia University Press, 1990.

Halstead, Fred. *Out Now! A Participant's Account of the American Movement Against the Vietnam War.* New York: Monad, 1978.

Hunt, Andrew. *The Turning: A History of Vietnam Veterans Against the War.* New York: New York University Press, 1999.

Powers, Thomas. *Vietnam: The War at Home.* New York: Grossman, 1973.

Robinson, Jo Ann. *Abraham Went Out: A Biography of A.J. Muste.* Philadelphia: Temple University Press, 1981.

Small, Melvin. *Johnson, Nixon and the Doves.* New Brunswick, NJ: Rutgers University Press, 1988.

Small, Melvin, and William D. Hoover, eds. *Give Peace a Chance: Exploring the Vietnam Antiwar Movement.* Syracuse, NY: Syracuse University Press, 1992.

Swerdlow, Amy, and Catharine R. Stimpson, *Women Strike for Peace: Traditional Motherhood and Radical Politics of the 1960s.* Chicago: University of Chicago Press, 1993.

Tracy, James. *Direct Action: Radical Pacifism from the Union Eight to the Chicago Seven.* Chicago: University of Chicago Press, 1996.

Wells, Tom. *The War Within: America's Battle over Vietnam.* Berkeley: University of California Press, 1994.

Wittner, Lawrence S. *Rebels Against War: The American Peace Movement, 1933–1983.* Philadelphia: Temple University Press, 1984.

Zaroulis, Nancy, and Gerald Sullivan. *Who Spoke Up? American Protest Against the War in Vietnam, 1963–1975.* Garden City, NY: Doubleday, 1985.

DRAFT RESISTERS IN CANADA DURING THE VIETNAM WAR

One of the specters of the war in Vietnam and the attendant "War at Home" in the United States was the image of the young draft resister migrating to Canada to avoid military service. Throughout the late 1960s and early 1970s, the popular press was filled with stories about "draft dodgers" who had abandoned family, friends, and country for exile in the United States' northern neighbor. These press articles told a common tale of intergenerational rupture, separation, and estrangement generated by America's military involvement in Southeast Asia. Yet decades after the fall of Saigon, and President Jimmy Carter's 1977 blanket amnesty, the migration of thousands of young men, women, and families to Canada has become only a footnote in the history of the Vietnam era.

It is estimated that between 30,000 and 100,000 Americans went to Canada between 1965 and 1975. Sociologist Renee Kasinsky puts the figure at 40,000 based on her estimates of the number of draft-aged American males who entered Canada as landed immigrants between 1965 and 1975. This number, however, tells only part of the story. Along with the draft-aged men went thousands of women who made the journey into exile as girl friends, wives, and as expatriates in their own right, with their own political reasons for migrating. Determining how many Americans stayed in Canada after the granting of amnesty in 1977 is even more difficult than calculating how many made the initial move across the border.

Going to Canada did not endear draft resisters to the organized movement against the draft in the United States. The leadership of the so-called Resistance articulated a strategy of noncompliance and noncooperation with the Selective Service and local draft boards. In their view, massive civil disobedience would force the government to take an even harder line against draft resisters, in effect criminalizing an entire generation of young American men. This in turn would create a moral and political crisis, which would make the continuance of the draft impossible. Noncooperation was a strategy that demanded all draft-aged men risk criminal prosecution and imprisonment. Making the journey across the border was a rejection of this strategy. The young men who came to Canada did so for many different reasons; some went as a political act, some because they did not want to go to jail, others because it just seemed like the easiest way to avoid military service. Although the reasons for coming to Canada were subjective, many resisters felt that crossing the border was a way of rejecting the United States, American imperialism, and the corrosive political and cultural climate of the late 1960s.

For the Canadian government, the migration of thousands of young, middle-class, and educated draft resisters was a windfall. Draft resisters, after all, were the very type of immigrant that the Canadian government deemed ideal for its increasingly communications- and technology-oriented society. In addition, the government reaped an important symbolic benefit in allowing draft resisters entry in that it demonstrated Canadian independence from the United States, and by default, opposition to the war in Vietnam. This independence had its limits, however, as the Royal Canadian Mounted Police monitored and shared intelligence on draft resisters with the Federal Bureau of Investigation in the United States. Nor were all young Americans resisting U.S. militarism afforded easy entry into Canada. U.S. deserters, many who were working-class, African American, or who had little or no postsecondary education did not experience a warm welcome. In many cases, their status was in doubt, and on numerous occasions border officials actively sought to deny deserters entry.

The antidraft movement in Canada emerged out of the nascent student movement and as such was part of the Canadian New Left. The Student Union for Peace Action (SUPA), a broadly based student group in the tradition of the Students for a Democratic Society (SDS), was among the first Canadian groups to offer aid and assistance to the growing numbers of young Americans who were drifting across the border to avoid the Selective Service draft. In 1966, SUPA produced the first pamphlet, *Escape to Freedom*, written by draft-resister Richard Paterak, that gave advice to Americans interested in coming to Canada. In addition to publishing the pamphlet and distributing it in the United States through SDS chapters, SUPA made room in their offices to counsel and support the growing numbers of young Americans arriving in Toronto. Another draft resister, Mark Satin, was hired to coordinate SUPA's antidraft program and to develop more comprehensive information on the practical and legal aspects of migration to Canada. Along with other SUPA staff in 1967, Satin compiled *The Manual for Draft-Age Immigration into Canada*, a book that would become the bible for thousands of Americans who made the move north.

SUPA's initial antidraft efforts would also grow and expand, becoming a separate organization, the Toronto Anti-Draft Programme (TADP), in late 1966. TADP would be the largest and longest lasting of the antidraft organizations in Canada. Over the years, it would offer draft resisters and deserters from the U.S. military assistance in finding housing, employment, and help in adjusting to life in a foreign, if relatively familiar, country. In addition to the TADP, many other groups aided draft resisters and military deserters. These included among others, the Union of American Exiles, the American Deserters Committee, the Montreal Council to Aid War Resisters, and Red, White and Black, to name only a few. Most major Canadian cities had at least one organization that provided assistance, support, and draft counseling to the steady flow of young Americans. In addition to the student movement, Canadian church groups were a major source of funding and volunteers for antidraft organizations. The Canadian Friends Committee (the Quakers), the United Church, Mennonite Central Committee, Canadian Council of Churches, and other religious groups were deeply involved in aiding resisters and working and supporting the peace movement in Canada.

Out of one of these resister organizations emerged *AMEX*, a newspaper dedicated to the political and social concerns of American expatriates in Canada. As a newspaper, *AMEX* followed in the tradition of the alternative and underground press of the late 1960s that provided a forum for debate, connections, and expressions of dissent rather than a pseudoprofes-

sional journalism. In its early years of publication, *AMEX* argued that draft resisters should assimilate into Canadian society, that they should learn about Canadian history, read Canadian literature, and reject the American past. In tone and spirit, the contributors to *AMEX* were advocates of English Canadian Nationalism, a movement that sought to limit and reduce American political power and influence in Canada. For some draft resisters, Canadian Nationalism was an important vehicle to express opposition to U.S. imperialism and to make a political commitment to their homeland. Yet as the 1970s progressed, *AMEX* shifted its focus away from advocating assimilation into Canada to the campaign for amnesty in the United States. Long-time *AMEX* editor and pro-amnesty advocate Jack Colhoun, noted that the ascendancy of the pro-amnesty group within the newspaper was due in large part to the fact that the Canadian nationalist elements had drifted away from involvement in resistance politics to involvement in a range of other political activities.

As a group, the young Americans who came to Canada were participants in the larger youth and countercultures that blossomed in Canadian cities during the late 1960s and early 1970s. In Vancouver, draft resisters were a significant part of the hippie scene in the city's west end and artsy Kitsilano neighborhood. In Toronto, draft resisters were a significant presence at the Rochdale College, Toronto's experiment in alternative higher education, as well as in the bohemian neighborhood along Baldwin Street. As Americans settled in the social spaces of Canada's largest cities, they also became involved in a wide variety of political and cultural movements. American expatriates would play key roles in a wide variety of movements such as the Canadian labor movement, the women's movement, the urban reform movement, the lesbian and gay movement, and the alternative school movement. In some cases, these Americans brought with them activist politics honed on U.S. college campuses and through involvement in the civil rights movement and in antiwar activities during the 1960s. For others, however, coming to Canada was part of a process of politicalization that saw them become more active in causes and social movements as a result of leaving the United States.

The status of draft resister was resolved in 1977 when then-President Jimmy Carter provided a blanket amnesty, thus allowing American resisters to repatriate themselves. Though many resisters returned, thousands stayed behind, becoming a significant part of Canadian civil society over the last decades of the twentieth and the first years of the twenty-first century.

David S. Churchill

BIBLIOGRAPHY

Baskir, Lawrence M., and William A. Strauss. *Chance and Circumstance: The Draft, the War and the Vietnam Generation.* New York: Alfred A. Knopf, 1978.

Colhoun, Jack " 'The Exiles' Role in War Resistance." *Monthly Review* (March 1979).

Hagan, Jon. *Northern Passage: American Vietnam War Resisters.* Cambridge, MA: Harvard University Press, 2001.

Haig-Brown, Robert. *Hell No We Won't Go!* Vancouver: Raincoast Books, 1996.

Kasinsky, Renee G. *Refugee from Militarism: Draft-Age Americans in Canada.* New Brunswick, NJ: Transaction Books, 1976.

Surrey, David. *Choice of Conscience.* New York: Praeger, 1982.

Antiwar Movement
Twenty-First Century

In the aftermath of the terrorist attacks on the World Trade Center and the Pentagon on September 11, 2001, a new and vibrant antiwar movement took shape in the United States, protesting U.S. military intervention first in Afghanistan and then in Iraq. Unlike the movement against the Vietnam War in the 1960s and 1970s, the new antiwar movement was very diverse, bringing together people of all ages and a range of political viewpoints and affiliations. As renowned progressive analyst Noam Chomsky stated, "Antiwar opposition here has been completely without precedent in scale and commitment."

Compared with the antiwar movements of earlier decades, the movement of the early 2000s consolidated rapidly. Although the September 11 attacks and the resulting increase in nationalism and conservative sentiment temporarily sidetracked the global justice movement, the infrastructure developed by the movement laid the groundwork for much early antiwar organizing. Whereas the initial protests against the Vietnam War in the early 1960s drew at most hundreds of demonstrators and numbers did not reach the hundreds of thousands until the war was well under way, early twenty-first-century demonstrations drew hundreds of thousands in the United States and millions worldwide before the Iraq War of 2003 had begun. The protest movement against the Vietnam War developed over a period of more than a decade, while the Iraq antiwar movement emerged almost instantly. And it was not only activists who were moving at a more rapid pace. The active phase of the United States' military engagement lasted less than two months, given the government's understanding that the American people would no longer tolerate a long war involving multiple U.S. casualties.

DIVERSE ISSUES, DIVERSE PARTICIPATION

As previously noted, the contemporary antiwar movement has brought together a wide range of participants, ranging from left organizations to global and social justice activists to moderates and even some conservatives. This classification is for discussion purposes only. Many individuals and groups belong to more than one coalition, and the major coalitions frequently endorse each other's actions and jointly sponsor demonstrations.

Cadre-Initiated Coalitions

As happened during the Vietnam War, some of the earliest opposition to the wars in Afghanistan and Iraq came from the far left and from those already heavily involved in activism. Left cadre organizations quickly drew upon their ability to rapidly mobilize members and widely publicize events. International Act Now to Stop War and End Racism (ANSWER) formed on September 14, just days after the terrorist attacks in New York City and Washington, D.C. While ANSWER is officially a coalition, including groups such as the Free Palestine Alliance, the Muslim Student Association of the U.S. and Canada, and the Kensington Welfare Rights Union, it is closely affiliated with the International Action Center (IAC) and the Workers World Party (WWP).

Not in Our Name (NION), a large coalition endorsed by many individuals and groups, is associated with Refuse and Resist, which in turn is affiliated with the Revolutionary Communist Party (RCP). Formed in March 2002, NION played a key role in antiwar organizing, especially on the East Coast, including a major demonstration on October 6 of that year. NION also initiated an antiwar statement signed by more than 100 celebrities, including Jane Fonda, Martin Luther King III, Tony Kushner, Gloria Steinem, and Alice Walker (published as an ad in the *New York Times,* the *Los Angeles Times,* and dozens of other papers), as well as a Pledge of Resistance reading in part: "Not in our name will you wage endless war; there can be no

Antiwar demonstrators near the United Nations in New York City were among the hundreds of thousands who gathered worldwide on February 15, 2003, to protest the threatened U.S. invasion of Iraq. *(AP Wide World Photos)*

more deaths, no more transfusions of blood for oil. . . . We pledge to make common cause with the people of the world to bring about justice, freedom and peace. Another world is possible and we pledge to make it real."

The International Socialist Organization (ISO) was heavily involved in mobilizing against U.S. intervention in Afghanistan in the wake of September 11 and—though not as visible as ANSWER or NION—continued to organize against the war in Iraq.

Global and Social Justice Activists

Although their decentralized, consensus-based process did not allow them to mobilize as quickly as ANSWER, local peace groups and global justice activists also began networking and organizing immediately after September 11. In New York City in particular, veteran activists and ordinary citizens (including family and friends of people killed in the World Trade Center attacks) came together to proclaim, "Our grief

is not a cry for war." Utilizing electronic mailing lists, websites, independent media centers, and other infrastructure developed in the course of organizing against the World Trade Organization, the International Monetary Fund (IMF), and the World Bank, global justice activists mobilized large numbers of protesters in the United States and worldwide, forming antiwar groups in cities and towns across the country.

Although the large coalitions focused on mass rallies, many global and social justice activists favored direct action. Among the most active groups in this tradition were Direct Action to Stop the War (DASW) in the San Francisco Bay Area and the M27 Coalition in New York City. Many—but not all—direct action proponents identified politically as Anarchists or anti-authoritarians, and most mass protests included features familiar from global justice actions. These groups were organized on a consensus model, with no paid staff or formal fund-raising.

Peace and social justice organizers formed United for Peace and Justice (UPJ) in October 2002. According to the coalition's unity statement, UPJ opposes the Bush administration's "drive to expand U.S. control over other nations and strip us of our rights at home" and "its use of war and racism to concentrate power in the hands of the few, at home and abroad." The coalition includes activists working on human rights, feminist, antiracist, civil rights, environmental, and antipoverty issues. Although initially it was particularly strong in New York City, UPJ came to include more than 600 participating groups from around the country, including Black Voices for Peace, Global Exchange, and the Institute for Policy Studies. UPJ is more participatory and directly democratic than the cadre groups, and embraces multiple tactics. The coalition came to effectively occupy a "middle ground" between the cadre organizations and direct action proponents, and the more mainstream antiwar activists.

In addition, many preexisting organizations such as the War Resisters League, the American Friends Service Committee, and Veterans for Peace were active in organizing against the wars in Afghanistan and Iraq, often joining new coalitions such as UPJ. The National Network to End the War Against Iraq, a broad yet less widely known coalition comprised of some 150 peace and justice, student, and faith-based organizations throughout the country, was formed in 1999 to end "the illegal, unjust, and inhumane war being waged against the people of Iraq." Unlike the more moderate coalitions discussed below, the network opposed sanctions as well as military action, and multilateral as well as unilateral intervention. Similarly, Voices in the Wilderness, formed in 1996, also opposed sanctions against Iraq and in September 2002 organized an Iraq Peace Team to "witness, understand, and expose the situation of the civilian population of Iraq."

The Mainstream

As war with Iraq loomed closer, several progressive organizations and national advocacy groups came together in the fall of 2002 to form Keep America Safe: Win Without War (WWW), a coalition that explicitly spoke to the mainstream. Its members supported the U.S. government's goal of removing Saddam Hussein from power but favored sanctions, weapons inspections, and multinational efforts under the auspices of the United Nations rather than unilateral U.S. military intervention. "We are patriotic Americans who share

the belief that Saddam Hussein cannot be allowed to possess weapons of mass destruction," read a WWW statement. "But we believe that a pre-emptive military invasion of Iraq will harm American national interests." Member groups ranged from progressive to conservative, but tended to be moderate liberals. Among these were the National Association for the Advancement of Colored People (NAACP), the National Council of Churches, the National Gay and Lesbian Task Force (NGLTF), the National Organization for Women (NOW), Physicians for Social Responsibility, the Sierra Club, and Working Assets. Among the more conservative was Business Leaders for Sensible Priorities, a group of Republican business executives who published an open letter to President Bush in the *Wall Street Journal* in January 2003 reading in part, "You are waltzing blindfolded into what may well be a catastrophe. . . . War is the most extreme action a society can take. It can only be unleashed after exploring every other road. You have not explored all the roads."

Religious activists of all denominations were well represented within the antiwar movement, many motivated by faith-based principles of nonviolence. Along with a range of traditionally liberal Christian groups, pagan activists (prominently represented in the global justice movement) were active participants. Muslim and Arab individuals and organizations joined antiwar coalitions in unprecedented numbers, responding to scapegoating and attacks on their civil liberties in the wake of September 11. Jewish activists—a traditionally progressive constituency—also opposed the war in Iraq but decried the anti-Semitism that developed among some factions of the antiwar movement as the issue of U.S. military intervention in the Middle East became linked with the Israel/Palestine conflict. While extremists on one side voiced frank hatred of Israel and the Jewish people, those on the other branded any criticism of the actions or policies of the Israel state as expressions of anti-Semitism.

Although activists have utilized computer networking for the past decade, the contemporary antiwar movement has witnessed the explosion of a new type of Internet-based organizing. The most prominent online organization is MoveOn.org, which was formed in September 1998 by Joan Blades and Wes Boyd, two Silicon Valley entrepreneurs seeking to oppose the impeachment of former president Bill Clinton. Relying on a network of some 2 million online activists worldwide, MoveOn seeks to "bring ordinary people back into politics," circumventing the in-

Carrying a poster mocking President George W. Bush, Gary Wallinga (right) and Judy Dorn protest the possible war against Iraq, in St. Cloud, Minnesota, on February 15, 2003. *(AP Wide World Photos)*

fluence of big money and big media. The group broadened its scope to include issues such as campaign finance reform, sensible energy policy, and judicial nominations. The MoveOn Peace campaign began as 911Peace.org, an online petition started by Eli Pariser calling for a peaceful response to the September 11 terrorist attacks. After the two efforts merged, MoveOn rapidly raised hundreds of thousands of dollars in small increments for antiwar television, radio, and billboard ads, coordinated some 6,000 candlelight vigils worldwide, and raised money for humanitarian relief in Iraq.

Labor

In contrast to its position during the Vietnam War, sections of the organized labor movement came out against unilateral U.S. military action in Iraq, forming U.S. Labor Against the War (USLAW). In part, this shift can be traced to organized labor's decreased faith in the federal government's willingness or ability to support a decent standard of living for working people. Following the lead of several local labor councils, in February 2003 the largest U.S.-organized labor federation, the American Federation of Labor-Congress of Industrial Organizations (AFL-CIO), passed a statement opposing war in Iraq, claiming that President Bush had not made a compelling case for unilateral action against Saddam Hussein without the broad support of international allies. Various local unions were active participants in antiwar demonstrations, with teachers and healthcare workers, for example, protesting the vast amounts of money being spent on war rather than social services. Said USLAW's Bob Muehlenkamp, "Unions can no longer afford to talk about jobs and benefits without addressing issues of war and peace."

Students and Youth

Unlike the Vietnam War movement, which began (and is still often regarded) as largely a student and youth phenomenon, the contemporary antiwar movement is much more multigenerational. Yet university, community college, and high school students, as well as nonstudent youth activists, remained prominent participants. The National Student and Youth Peace Coalition organized a large antiwar rally in Washington, D.C., in April 2002. The Campus Antiwar Network was founded at two conferences in Washington, D.C., and San Francisco in January 2003 and soon counted members at more than 100 schools. Student global justice groups such as United Students Against Sweatshops (USAS) and Students Transforming and Resisting Corporations (STARC), emerging out of the resurgent student activism of the 1990s, saw resisting U.S. militarism as part of their global activist agenda. Campaigns to remove ROTC/JROTC and military recruiters from campuses—popular in the 1980s before the federal government passed legislation denying funding to schools that did not welcome the military—experienced a new revival.

Perhaps because of the lack of a draft and the greater economic challenges facing today's students, antiwar sentiment was not as widespread as it was during the Vietnam era. On some campuses there was a sort of role reversal, with professors—many of whom had been students themselves during the Vietnam War days—taking the lead in protesting the wars in Afghanistan and Iraq. The new movement included people of all ages, and media coverage of the mass protests in early 2003 often noted the participation of families with children, as well as older peace and social justice activists. Once the war in Iraq began in March 2003, the most prominent disruptions took place on the streets rather than on the campuses.

People of Color and Women

Although polls consistently showed that African Americans and Latinos were more likely to oppose war compared with whites, people of color have not been well represented at mass antiwar protests. Chicana activist Elizabeth (Betita) Martinez noted that people of color face more challenges to make ends meet and have more to lose when they protest government policies (especially if they are immigrants). Many activists of color felt that white activists failed to recognize and respond to the continuing war at home against communities of color, and some also criticized white antiwar activists for failing to take leadership from people of color. In addition, blacks make up a disproportionate share of people in the military, and some African Americans hesitated to appear as if they did not support U.S. troops. Even so, many people of color found ample reason to oppose war. In the words of former member of Congress Walter E. Fauntroy (D-DC), an African American, "We know that every bomb that explodes is robbing our children and their families of five things: income, education, health care, housing, and justice." In cities such as Washington, D.C., African-American groups, including Black Voices for Peace, played a prominent role in antiwar organizing. In Oakland, New York City, and elsewhere, youth of color were active in efforts to tie war abroad with social and economic justice struggles at home.

The contemporary antiwar movement is perhaps more demographically diverse than any other in our history, having benefited from identity-based organizing in the 1970s through the 1990s.

The current movement includes a roughly equal representation of women and men, and many even believe women make up a majority of its leadership. Nationwide polls taken during the run-up to the war in Iraq consistently showed that women were less likely than men to support military intervention. During the war in Afghanistan, some women were conflicted as the oppression of women under the Taliban

Dressed in skeleton masks and star-spangled top hats, members of the group Americans Against War march in Paris, France, on March 15, 2003. France was one of the leading nations opposed to the U.S.-Iraq War. *(AP Wide World Photos)*

regime garnered widespread media attention. But by the time of the Iraq War, many women had taken the position that unilateral U.S. military action would not improve the lives of women and children in Iraq. Women have been active participants in all facets of the movement, and in addition some have formed women-focused groups such as CODEPINK: Women for Peace, a grassroots peace and social justice group seeking social change through creative protest and nonviolent direct action. Another woman-led effort, the Lysistrata Project, organized more than 700 readings in March 2003 of the Greek play by Aristophanes in which the women of Athens and Sparta withhold sex from their men until they make peace.

Cultural Voices

The Vietnam War protests initially were closely associated with the youth counterculture, but the contemporary antiwar movement is not linked to a specific cultural style. On the grassroots level, groups such as Art and Revolution and Reclaim the Streets—best known for their prominent role in the global justice movement—added music, art, and puppets to mass antiwar demonstrations. On the popular culture front, many musicians spoke out against the war in Iraq. Thurston Moore of the alternative rock group Sonic Youth developed an Internet website called Protest -records.com offering free downloads of antiwar songs. Musicians protesting the war encompassed all ages and many musical styles: Harry Belafonte, the Beastie Boys, Chumbawamba, Mos Def, Zack de la Rocha of Rage Against the Machine, Michael Franti and Spearhead, Lenny Kravitz, Cat Power, Boots Riley of the Coup, Pete Seeger, Russell Simmons, Bruce Springsteen, and Eddie Vedder of Pearl Jam. Perhaps most famously, Natalie Maines of the country rock band the Dixie Chicks ignited a storm of controversy when she told London concert-goers that she was embarrassed that President Bush hailed from her home state of Texas.

Actors Janeane Garofalo, Danny Glover, Dustin Hoffman, Edward Norton, Sean Penn, Tim Robbins, Susan Sarandon, and Martin Sheen spoke out against the war, in some cases risking their careers. The Baseball Hall of Fame canceled a ceremony celebrating the anniversary of Robbins's baseball movie, *Bull Durham,* while a United Way chapter in Tampa, Florida, scrapped a charity event featuring Sarandon after receiving complaints about her antiwar stance. Behind the cameras, directors Spike Lee and Martin Scorsese voiced their opposition to war, while iconoclast Michael Moore made antiwar comments during the Academy Awards ceremony. More than 100 musicians, actors, writers, and others joined Artists United to Win Without War (affiliated with WWW), which aims to encourage public debate and activate citizens through use of the media.

A BRIEF CHRONOLOGY

In the days immediately following September 11, 2001, activists began to organize against anticipated U.S. retaliation against the Taliban, known sponsors of the Al-Qaeda terrorist network. ANSWER formed mere days after the terrorist attacks, as did local groups in several cities. Activists decried the U.S. rush to war as well as the crackdown on civil liberties at home (including the hastily passed USA PATRIOT Act, which, among other things, removes restrictions on wiretapping and online surveillance without probable cause), stepped up registration and detention of immigrants, and attacks against Arabs and Muslims. The first large antiwar protests took place in late September and October of that year. A march called by ANSWER on September 29 brought out an estimated 20,000 people in Washington, D.C., and 10,000 in San Francisco. Some 10,000 attended a protest organized by the New York Peace and Justice Coalition on October 7.

In April 2002, the National Student and Youth Peace Coalition and ANSWER both held rallies in Washington, D.C., coinciding with antiglobalization protests against the IMF and World Bank. The National Coalition for Peace and Justice and the Emergency National Network first came together for the D.C. demonstrations. ANSWER publicized its rally as a pro-Palestinian demonstration (following a recent Israeli incursion into the Jenin refugee camp and several West Bank towns), a focus the other groups declined to adopt.

As antiwar sentiment grew, more than 150 cities and towns passed antiwar resolutions. Although the movement experienced a lull in the summer of 2002, it quickly revived as the Bush administration threatened military intervention in Iraq. By the fall of 2002 and the winter of 2003, activists in the United States and around the world had mobilized antiwar demonstrations larger than any seen since the Vietnam era. On October 6, NION organized a massive rally in New York City, and protests occurred the same day in San Francisco, Seattle, Chicago, and dozens of other cities and towns.

ANSWER called another large demonstration in Washington, D.C., for October 26. Organizers estimated that 100,000 marched around the White House, while 50,000 demonstrated in San Francisco; protests also took place in Berlin, Rotterdam, Barcelona, and several cities in Italy. During the weekend of October 26 representatives from some 50 groups met and formed United for Peace and Justice. A subset of these organizers also started Win Without War.

In the early weeks of 2003, President Bush set firmer deadlines for Saddam Hussein to surrender weapons of mass destruction, and antiwar activists stepped up their organizing. Although the largest mass demonstrations took place in New York City, San Francisco, Washington, D.C., Boston, and Los Angeles, *War Times* newspaper reported antiwar activities in some 2,400 cities and towns across the country. On January 18 ANSWER sponsored a large rally in Washington, D.C., which brought out an estimated 125,000 protesters. A like number marched in San Francisco, and demonstrations also took place in numerous countries around the world, including Argentina, Canada, Egypt, Germany, Italy, Japan, Mexico, the Philippines, Russia, and the United Kingdom.

The most extensive international days of protest took place during February 14–16. In New York City police denied UPJ organizers a permit to march in Manhattan—a denial supported by the federal Department of Justice, citing security concerns. Nevertheless, on February 15 dozens of unpermitted "feeder" marches (among them students, people of color, LGBT people, performing artists, healthcare workers, and educators) departed from various points around the city to converge outside the United Nations for a rally estimated at up to half a million people; tens of thousands attempting to get to the rally site were corralled into pens of police barricades. Marches and rallies took place across the United States, including a rally of some 100,000 in Los Angeles. The following day, ANSWER, NION, UPJ, and Bay Area United Against War jointly sponsored a march and rally in San Francisco (pushed back a day so as not to conflict with the traditional Chinese New Year's parade), which brought out as many as 250,000 people.

Internationally, 750,000 people rallied in London in what police said was the largest demonstration in British history. In Rome, 1 million demonstrators heard a communiqué from Mexico's Zapatistas read by the mother of Carlo Giuliani, a global justice activist killed by police during protests in Genoa in July 2001. "The attack on Iraq is just one page in the script of terror which the power of money has prepared for the entire planet," proclaimed the statement by Subcomandante Insurgente Marcos. "It is not justice, nor democracy, nor liberty which drives this terror. It is fear. Fear that the entire world will refuse to accept a policeman which tells it what it should do, how it should do it, and when it should do it. . . . Fear that the world will refuse to be treated like plunder. Fear of that human essence which is called rebellion. Fear that the millions of human beings who are mobilizing today throughout the world will be victorious in raising the cause of peace."

Elsewhere 500,000 demonstrated at the Brandenburg Gate in Berlin; 200,000 protested in Sydney; 70,000 turned out in Amsterdam; and 35,000 gathered in Stockholm. In Israel, 2,000 Israelis and Palestinians marched together in Tel Aviv, while 5,000 Turks in Istanbul demanded that their leaders not support the U.S. war, and protesters clashed with police in Athens. In all, an estimated 10 million to 30 million people demonstrated during the weekend in some 900 cities. Long-time antiwar protester David McReynolds said the demonstrations "exceeded anything I can recall in my 73 years," while the *New York Times* acknowledged that there were now two world superpowers: the United States and global public opinion.

Despite the outpouring of antiwar sentiment, President Bush declared that weapons inspections were not sufficient and that Saddam Hussein must abdicate power and leave Iraq. He made it clear that the United States was preparing to act with or without the support of the United Nations. In the run-up to war, activists in the United States and around the world increasingly turned to direct action. A notable example was the group of Westerners who traveled to Iraq to act as "human shields" in an attempt to stave off U.S. bombing.

A national antiwar student strike took place on March 5, with thousands of high school and college students from some 400 schools around the country walking out of class. On March 8 (International Women's Day), thousands of CODEPINK women protested in Washington, D.C., and twenty-five were arrested in front of the White House, ending a months-long peace vigil. In the days leading up to the war, eight antiwar protesters in Seattle were arrested for blocking a highway and disrupting the morning commute, while seven were arrested in Portland, Oregon, for blockading the city's federal building. In Chicago, eleven antiwar activists locked themselves together at the headquarters of Boeing to protest the corporation's production of equipment used by the military. Beginning in mid-March, San Francisco antiwar activists organized by Direct Action to Stop the War (DASW) blocked buildings and intersections in the city's financial district on several occasions, leading to dozens of arrests.

Antiwar protesters also took direct action in other countries. Two activists in Sydney, Australia, scaled the city's famous Opera House to paint "No War" on the building's white sails. Irish protesters painted peace signs on a U.S. navy plane at Shannon International Airport, while British activists repeatedly breached fences and damaged runways at air force bases. In Italy and Turkey antiwar activists blocked trains and trucks carrying U.S. military equipment. In Brazil, dock workers refused to load or unload U.S. and British ships for a day, and the Greenpeace ship *Rainbow Warrior* blockaded a section of a naval base in Spain to prevent a U.S. warship from leaving for the Persian Gulf.

Activists vowed to interrupt "business as usual" if war started, and when President Bush declared on March 19 that the "decapitation" bombing campaign had begun in Iraq, they made good on their pledge. On March 20, antiwar activists sprang into action, implementing the civil disobedience plans they had been formulating over the preceding months. Tens of thousands of protesters, largely mobilized by DASW, "called in sick" and shut down dozens of intersections and corporate, government, and media sites in downtown San Francisco, often locking themselves together to make it more difficult for police to remove them. "They succeeded this morning—they shut the city down," said one harried police chief. "They are moving faster than us. They're highly organized, but they are totally spontaneous." The decentralized, leaderless actions carried out by autonomous affinity groups resulted in more than 2,000 arrests by the end of the week (although most of the charges were later dropped). In New York City, protesters laid down in Times Square. In Washington, D.C., protesters forced the closure of Potomac River crossings during the morning commute, while in Chicago they shut down Lake Shore Drive during the evening rush hour (resulting in some 500 arrests). Similar disruptions also took place in other cities, including Atlanta, Boston, and Philadelphia, in addition to numerous planned and spontaneous protest rallies from Bangor, Maine, to Fairbanks, Alaska.

Actions continued over the following days and weeks, along with more marches and rallies in numerous cities, including demonstrations by 20,000 in Los Angeles and a quarter million in New York City on March 22. On March 27, New York protesters mobilized by the M27 coalition (made up of members from some thirty-five progressive groups including UPJ) held a "die-in" on Fifth Avenue in front of Rockefeller Center in downtown Manhattan, resulting in some 200 arrests. Other decentralized affinity group actions took place that day throughout the city, including a "die-in" staged by CODEPINK in front of Tiffany's jewelry store and an occupation of the New York University student center.

By the end of March, activists had shifted their strategy away from disruption of traffic, instead focusing on corporations that stood to profit from the war (such as Bechtel, the Carlyle Group, Chevron-Texaco, and Halliburton), media outlets that uncritically supported President Bush's actions (including Fox News and Clear Channel Communications), and military facilities (such as Vandenberg Air Force Base and the Concord Naval Weapons Station, both in northern California).

On April 7, activists from DASW, in conjunction with members of the International Longshore and Warehouse Union, picketed at the Port of Oakland outside the terminals of American Presidential Lines and Stevedoring Services of America, which had received contracts to ship military supplies and run a port in Iraq. Police opened fire on protesters and longshoremen with rubber and wooden bullets and concussion grenades, injuring many and prompting lawsuits and calls for investigation of police misconduct (including one from Amnesty International). It proved to be, according to the *New York Times*, "the most violent [clash] between protesters and authorities anywhere in the country since the start of the war in Iraq."

Surrounded by body bags symbolizing the deaths of soldiers in the U.S.-Iraq War, Zoe Roller and Lola Basque lie down in a "die-in" in San Francisco on April 2, 2003. *(AP Wide World Photos)*

Antiwar protests continued throughout the spring and into the summer, although they grew smaller as the first phase of the war drew to a close. Rallies called by ANSWER in Washington, D.C., San Francisco, Seattle, and other cities on April 12, for example, drew a fraction of the crowds that came out in January and February. Once the war started, President Bush enjoyed an increase in support as the country experienced the common "rally 'round the flag" effect. Even many who opposed the war were concerned about appearing not to support U.S. troops, were pleased that the United States and Britain minimized civilian casualties, and wished for a quick end to the war. After Hussein's regime was toppled, President Bush declared victory on May 1, but U.S. troops continued to play a police role in the country as Iraqi resistance continued, leading some to label the situation a quagmire in the making. With no weapons of mass destruction found, troop morale declining, and a few more U.S. soldiers being killed each week by Iraqi fighters, President Bush's approval rating slipped as the summer wore on, and there was increasing pressure to bring the troops home.

CAUSES AND CONFLICTS

With the number of diverse participants comprising the contemporary antiwar movement, various conflicts have come to the fore. The chief causes of contention can be divided into two broad areas: disagreements over strategies and tactics, and debates about the scope of issues that should be part of the movement's agenda.

Organization and Tactics

The debate over tactics among antiwar activists echoed a common theme within the global justice movement, whereby moderate organizers expressed concerns that illegal direct actions (especially those that included property destruction) would discourage the involvement of mainstream participants, including organized labor and religious groups. The cadre groups, as well as moderate antiwar organizations like Win Without War and U.S. Labor Against War, favored large antiwar marches. Indeed, these mass protests were the most visible expressions of antiwar sentiment and provided an opportunity for participation by thousands of people who did not consider themselves "activists." But as President Bush pressed on with his plans for war in Iraq despite a huge international outpouring of dissent, many activists felt that marches and rallies were not enough. They began organizing direct actions aimed at stopping "business as usual," including traffic blockades and attempts to shut down military, corporate, and media targets. Moderate activists argued that this type of direct action alienated the mainstream, while the militants countered that it was necessary to "raise the stakes" and impose real costs on institutions that supported or stood to profit from war. After a round of disruptive direct actions in the days immediately preceding and following the start of the war in Iraq, however, even many radicals came to agree that traffic blockades were angering and alienating citizens (many of whom already opposed the war), and shifted toward more specific targets.

Another debate concerned the level of direct democracy in organizing and decision making. Grassroots activists (many coming out of the global justice

movement) favored a more participatory, consensus-based organizing style. On the other side, cadre groups (in particular ANSWER but NION as well) were criticized for their centralized, top-down organizing methods and their lack of transparency. ANSWER was accused of attempting to impose other agendas on the antiwar movement, opportunistically using antiwar organizing to promote party-building, and taking credit for the efforts of other activists. In November 2001, the ISO was accused of attempting to "hijack" student antiwar organizing conferences in Berkeley, Boston, and Chicago. At the same time, large moderate coalitions such as WWW were criticized for relying on traditional top-down organizing, employing professional staff, and focusing on fund-raising, as well as relying too heavily on electoral politics.

The Antiwar Agenda

The diverse constituencies opposed to U.S. wars in Central Asia and the Middle East were motivated by myriad different causes, and many sought to include other issues in their antiwar organizing. Principled pacifists (including religious activists) opposed military intervention and its attendant carnage across the board, while many first-time protesters were motivated solely by opposition to the current war in Iraq. But more seasoned activists coming from other movements typically felt that U.S. militarism was intrinsically connected to other causes they cared about.

In the months after September 11, 2001, the burgeoning antiwar movement broadly agreed on three major issues: stopping the outbreak of war, ending racial scapegoating of Arabs and Muslims, and opposing the crackdown on civil liberties in the United States. Many also added opposition to any U.S. intervention in the Middle East and support for Palestinian liberation, although these issues proved to be more contentious.

The cadre-initiated coalitions, ANSWER and NION, were subject to criticism for promoting an anti-imperialist line (along with less apparently relevant issues such as support for Mumia Abu-Jamal, a former Black Panther who was accused of killing a police officer and for appearing to be anti-American). Whereas Socialist and Communist cadre groups had played a major role in Vietnam-era organizing, many veteran activists recalled how interorganizational conflict over party lines had contributed to the demise of that movement. During the 1991 Persian Gulf War, too, the movement split over support for Hussein, promoted by the International Action Center (ANSWER's parent group). By the late 1990s, cadre-style organizations had fallen out of favor among grass-roots activists, and they were not key players in the global justice movement.

ANSWER had an excellent capacity for mass organizing and was able to activate many volunteers and mobilize huge numbers of people for major marches and rallies in Washington, D.C., New York City, and San Francisco. Many (perhaps most) who participated in antiwar demonstrations were not experienced activists and often knew little of the initiating organizations' background or affiliations—much less agreed with their party lines. Although some refused to participate in protests organized by ANSWER or NION, others felt it was important to support all antiwar protests, regardless of who initiated them. Many agreed with Bob Borosage, co-director of the Campaign for America's Future: "[H]istory shows that protests are organized first by militant, radical fringe parties and then get taken over by more centrist voices as the movement grows. They provide a vessel for people who want to protest."

In the fall of 2002, several critical articles appeared in the press, featuring both "red-baiting" from the right and accusations of authoritarianism from the left. Some argued that the movement would never grow and attract new participants as long as it was associated with extreme positions such as the IAC's support for Slobodan Milosevic and other dictators. (It should be noted, however, that even among the radical fringe there was minimal overt support for the Taliban or Saddam Hussein, comparable to the earlier antiwar movement's support for the Vietnamese National Liberation Front). Todd Gitlin, a former president of Students for a Democratic Society, called ANSWER's prominent role "a gigantic ruination for the antiwar movement," while LA Weekly editor Marc Cooper called on "more mature segments of the left" to "step into the forefront of the peace movement and displace those who can only see evil in America."

The cadre groups were not the only ones calling for broad opposition to U.S. imperialism and capitalism. In fact, Anarchists demanded "No war between nations, No peace between classes." The revolutionary wing of the antiwar movement argued that war in Iraq was a first step in the consolidation of the U.S. role as the world's sole superpower, exemplified by the new National Security strategy's "preemptive" strike policy announced by President Bush in September 2002. Such concerns were strengthened by mounting U.S. threats against Syria, Iran, and North Korea.

For global justice activists, opposition to U.S. militarism dovetailed with their anticorporate and environmental agenda, especially the belief that war in the Middle East was spurred on largely by the desire for access to oil and lucrative rebuilding contracts for well-connected corporations.

Fearing that such a radical agenda would discourage labor, religious, and minority participation, moderate activists countered with attempts to promote the idea that "peace is patriotic." They emphasized that the majority of people who opposed the war were not anticapitalist, were concerned about terrorism, believed Hussein should be condemned and removed from power (albeit by means other than war), and did not see the United States as a bastion of evil.

While the ANSWER coalition remained small, United for Peace and Justice managed to bring together national organizations and local groups as divergent as Greenpeace and the National Council of Churches. "If we're going to be a force that needs to be listened to by our elected officials, by the media, by power, our movement needs to reflect the population," said UPJ organizer Leslie Cagan. "It needs to be large, it needs to include the people who could be described as mainstream—but that doesn't exclude the people who are sometimes thought of as the fringes."

Some feared that taking on other issues would alienate potential participants, whereas others found that just such a strategy was needed to mobilize underrepresented constituencies such as working people and people of color. Organizers condemned the scapegoating and racial profiling that took place in the wake of September 11, 2001, winning support from Arabs and Muslims. Some felt that President Bush was using fear of terrorism to consolidate power by cracking down on domestic dissent. Antiwar activists and others made connections between the exorbitant cost of war and the lack of financial support for social programs at home. Some went so far as to assert that President Bush was using the war to divert attention from shrinking civil liberties and a failing domestic economy. On tax day, April 15, rather than calling for yet another mass rally, UPJ called for a weekend of local actions, including teach-ins and nonviolent civil disobedience. "We think it's an appropriate time for the peace movement to start focusing on the social justice part of this war," said UPJ's Leslie Cagan. "Where is the money coming from?"

THE FUTURE

By the summer of 2003, the antiwar movement increasingly began to look inward and plan for its long-term future. Although activists were disappointed that the movement did not succeed in stopping the war in Iraq, they were encouraged that protests appeared to delay it and heartened by the resurgence of political activism. As military engagement dragged on, many believed that opposition would strengthen, and also emphasized the need to be prepared to counter further U.S. military interventions.

Although many single-issue antiwar protesters pulled back as the war wound down, long-term activists argued for broadening the movement's focus. DASW in San Francisco, comprised largely of global justice activists, expanded its goals to encompass uprooting the system behind the war in Iraq and "the war at home" (including racism, poverty, and corporate globalization), and creating socially just, directly democratic, ecological, peaceful alternatives. UPJ has also broadened its agenda to include global justice issues. However, it remains to be seen to what extent newly mobilized antiwar activists will move on to other issues once the war is over.

ANSWER held an antiwar meeting in May 2003 that drew 800 participants, while UPJ hosted its own organizing conference in June 2003, bringing together more than 500 attendees representing over 300 organizations. The UPJ conference adopted a new structure and put in place a steering committee made up of representatives from national and local antiwar groups (mandated to include a broad spectrum of social groups). Although friction between the major antiwar coalitions remains, activists will continue to come together to express opposition to the continued American military presence in Iraq and future U.S. wars, uniting behind the demand to "Bring the Troops Home Now." Indeed, coalition members and non-aligned activists frustrated with intramovement divisions and conflicting events have called on the large coalitions (in particular UPJ, ANSWER, NION, and USLAW) to find ways to work together.

Meanwhile, Win Without War and MoveOn largely turned their attention to the presidential and local legislative races. Electoral politics proved to be a point of contention among activists, with the more radical element arguing that politicians—Democrats included—cannot be relied upon to oppose war and crackdowns on civil liberties in the name of national security. In fact, only one member of the House of Representatives—Barbara Lee (D-CA), representing Berkeley and Oakland—voted against President Bush's resolution to use the military to pursue the War on Terrorism in the wake of September 11. As the 2004 presidential campaign heated up, several Democratic candidates including Carol Moseley Braun, Howard Dean, Dennis Kucinich, and Al Sharpton came out strongly against the war in Iraq, while the Green Party maintained its clear antiwar stance.

The ultimate duration and outcome of U.S. military intervention in Iraq remains uncertain. Yet it is clear that the contemporary antiwar movement remains active in its opposition to U.S. policy in the Middle East.

Liz Highleyman

BIBLIOGRAPHY

Bloom, Steve, et al. "An Open Letter to Activists Concerning Racism in the Anti-War Movement," February 13, 2003. *Znet.* http://www.zmag.org.

Cockburn, Alexander. "No to War! Is Anyone Listening?" *Working for Change*, January 9, 2003.

Cooper, Marc. "A Smart Peace Movement Is MIA." *Los Angeles Times*, September 29, 2002.

Corn, David. "Behind the Placards: The Odd and Troubling Origins of Today's Anti-War Movement." *LA Weekly*, November 1, 2002.

Ferguson, Euan. "One Million. And Still They Came." *London Observer*, February 16, 2003.

Ferguson, Sarah. "NYC Peace Activists Vow to Face Down Bush's War." *Village Voice*, February 12, 2003.

Gitlin, Todd. "Who Will Lead?" *Mother Jones*, October 14, 2002.

Goldberg, Michelle. "Peace Kooks." *Salon.com*, October 16, 2002.

———. "The Antiwar Movement Goes Mainstream." *Salon.com*, December 12, 2002.

———. "Rage or Reason." *Salon.com*, March 27, 2003.

Greenwood, David Valdes. "The Protest Movement Grows Up." *Boston Phoenix*, April 3, 2003.

Hutchinson, Earl Ofari. "Why Aren't More Blacks Protesting the War?" *Baltimore Sun*, April 8, 2003.

Klein, Naomi. "Privatization in Disguise." *The Nation*, April 15, 2003.

Mendoza, Martha. "Police Open Fire at Anti-War Protest, Longshoremen Injured." *San Jose Mercury News*, April 8, 2003.

Moberg, David. "Unions Against the War." *In These Times*, December 16, 2002.

Parrish, Geov. "Anti-War Movement Draws New Blood." *In These Times*, October 15, 2002.

———. "The Six Day War." *Working for Change*, March 31, 2003.

Vitale, Louis, and Bernie Galvin. "Why We Are Taking to the Streets." *AlterNet*, March 20, 2003.

Waskow, Arthur. "Pro-Israel, Pro-Peace, Anti-Occupation: Is There Anti-Semitism in the Anti-War Movement?" *Sojourners Magazine*, May-June 2003.

Zernike, Kate, and Dean Murphy. "Protesters Across the Nation Try to 'Stop Business as Usual.'" *New York Times*, March 20, 2003.

———. "Antiwar Movement Tries to Find a Meaningful Message." *New York Times*, April 20, 2003.

10

RADICAL AND POOR PEOPLE'S MOVEMENTS

INTRODUCTION

Poverty has been a feature of American life from colonial times to the present. So have the collective struggles of poor people to end their penury. From spontaneous and inchoate riots for bread in early colonial towns to well-organized and disciplined Unemployed Councils in the 1930s, poor people's efforts have taken many forms. Poor people have marched on City Hall and Washington, organized unions, rioted in the streets, sat in at lunch counters and government offices, created settlement houses, taken freedom rides, constructed activist organizations, and formed political parties. Sometimes, poor people's efforts have achieved groundbreaking reforms, such as the labor and antipoverty legislation of the New Deal and Great Society. At other times, poor people's activity has victimized racial and ethnic minorities, as in the riots against Catholics during the economic depression of 1857 or the Civil War draft riots that targeted African Americans. Whatever their form and content, the movements of poor people have demonstrated repeatedly that millions of Americans have been and remain excluded from their United States' unparalleled economic abundance, yet they refuse to accept their fate quietly.

The ebb and flow of poverty in the United States has followed both cyclical and secular trends. Panics, depressions, and recessions have increased the number of the poor, while booms and times of economic stability have pulled numerous people out of penury. In the longer run, industrialization and the penetration of the market economy into more and more aspects of life expanded inequalities of wealth and enlarged the pool of poor people during the nineteenth century. At the same time, industrialization and commercialization created the conditions for poverty's elimination, and the second half of the twentieth century saw an uneven decline in the number of poor people and proportion of this economic demographic in relation to the rich, in no small part due to the movements of poor people.

Movements against poverty have reflected the form they took. In the eighteenth and nineteenth centuries, poor people struggled against the impact of expanding markets. Poor farmers protested against high commodity prices, low crop prices, currency devaluations, railroad monopolies, land speculation, monopolistic grain elevators, usurious banks, debtors' prison, trusts, inattentive political parties, government inaction, and wealth inequality. Urban poor people protested against high prices, debtors' prison, trusts, inattentive political parties, government inaction, and wealth inequality; they also fought against high rents, low wages, long hours, dangerous working conditions, unemployment, and graft. Both urban and rural poor people fought for public education. Their movements included public protests of various kinds, marches, meetings, riots, initiative and referendum campaigns, and political parties. The outlook of most poor people's organizations in the eighteenth and nineteenth centuries was backward looking, focused on land redistribution as the key to poverty elimination, even among city dwellers. By the end of the nineteenth century, industrialization, urbanization, the commercialization of agriculture, and ubiquitous market relations had made land redistribution irrelevant for most poor people, even farmers. Instead, poor people focused their demands on various forms of government aid; the idea of the welfare state—a government that takes responsibility for the well-being of its citizens—was born. Poor people's movements from the late nineteenth century demanded that the government provide relief aid, tenement elimination and affordable housing, clean water, an end to child labor, unemployment insurance and workmen's compensation, public works to provide employment and services, a minimum wage, and work-hour limits. Later, child care, job training, public transportation, public investment, and universal healthcare were added to the list of demands. Many of these demands were met, as well as an expansion of political and social rights, such as greater access to political participation and the end of racial, ethnic, and gender exclusion.

In addition to fighting poverty and its associated problems, poor Americans have had to struggle against a pernicious ideology that locates the cause of poverty in individual incapacities. Rather than understanding poverty as the result of social, political, and economic circumstances as well as individual effort, many Americans blame the victims. The poor, they say, are poor because they lack the moral and intellectual capacities to lift themselves out of poverty. In a society that glorifies wealth, poor people are stigmatized as unfit to enjoy the full benefits of citizenship. With few resources to court politicians, finding allies to build the political and cultural clout necessary to tilt public policy in their favor is extremely difficult. In addition, many poor people have accepted the dominant characterization that equates poverty with indolence, stupidity, and amorality. This ideological burden has constituted one of the greatest barriers to the mobilization of poor people. Overcoming it has required that poor people find a way to universalize their plight and put forth an argument based on identifiable rights—the right to a minimum wage or unemployment relief—to justify their demands and win sympathy from nonpoor Americans.

Poverty has been an equal opportunity scourge in America. Certain ethnic and racial groups, and women, have suffered disproportionately, but no group has completely escaped the ills of economic destitution. Despite the common notion that poor people are predominantly nonwhite, the bulk of the poverty-stricken has been and is, in fact, white. The movements of poor people have reflected the country's racial and ethnic diversity. Rarely, however, have racial and ethnic groups fought their poverty side by side. More often, movements against poverty have foundered on the shoals of racism and sexism. For a time, Southern black and white farmers fought together in the Populist Party, but the party eventually collapsed in a wave of racist reaction that perpetuated Jim Crow throughout the South. Communists were more successful in uniting black and white unemployed people in the 1930s, but black people were excluded from many of the New Deal programs aimed at eliminating poverty. Thus, for the most part, poor people's movements have been racially and ethnically exclusive.

Where they have not included people of color or ethnic minorities, white poor people's movements have at best ignored and at worst targeted them. For example, the Equal Rights Party in New York in the 1830s largely ignored African-American citizens in its antimonopoly campaigns against high prices, but later bread, meat, rent, and fuel rioters often attacked Catholics and African Americans who supposedly stole from white poor people. Never have the all-too-often spasms of violence against nonwhite people done anything to eliminate white people's poverty. The movements of poor people of color, on the other hand, have done much to improve the conditions of all Americans. These movements have usually been part of larger movements against exclusion from political, economic, and social participation. Puerto Ricans in the Young Lords in the 1960s fought police brutality, racist hiring practices, and poverty. The political mobilization of freed slaves after the Civil War led to the passage of the Fourteenth Amendment, expanding the rights of all Americans. The War on Poverty grew out of the civil rights movement of African Americans, but the massive elimination of poverty achieved by the program aided the poor of all races and ethnicities.

The achievements of poor people's movements are many, but so, too, are the failures. Despite the efforts of so many dedicated people for so long, poverty remains a serious problem in the United States. At the turn of the twenty-first century, it is a growing problem, made worse by the glorification of business and the increasing hostility to the welfare state. The poor of today do not suffer the same afflictions as the poor of a century ago. Still, the poor suffer not only deprivation and humiliation, but also disease, mental illness, and shorter life expectancy. If the past is any guide, the contradiction between America's abundance and the persistence of its poverty will revive poor people's movements. For while the past has proven that economic growth can reduce poverty, it has also demonstrated that only an organized political movement can eliminate it.

Aaron Brenner

POOR PEOPLE'S MOVEMENTS

Perhaps the greatest truism in American history is that the United States from colonial times has been a very rich and abundant country with large numbers of poor people. During the 1700s and 1800s, the existence of an impoverished class was largely covered up in a popular ideology that glorified the prosperous, self-reliant "yeoman farmers" and enterprising mechanics, the democratic producing masses, and the independent, sober, and thrifty common man. Poor people's movements in the antebellum period both developed in response to the increase in economic insecurity and poverty that accompanied early industrialization and sought through land reform, free public education, and other reforms to make real the vision of a society where no one had to be poor.

PRE–CIVIL WAR ERA

The antebellum history of indentured servitude and slavery went against the popular ideology of a middle class, as did the ravages of industrialization through the nineteenth century. Wealth in natural resources meant little for those without the tools or capital to make use of those resources. Antebellum movements of workers against imprisonment for debt, in support of "hard currency," and for free land often drew their support from those who found themselves paid in valueless currency, made to pay exorbitant rents in expanding urban areas, and beset by periodic economic crises, called depressions and recessions in the twentieth century, which sometimes drove them into destitution.

Cities like New York, whose population rose from 130,000 in 1820 to 1 million in 1860 and 4 million in 1900, became centers of the visible poor, living in slum neighborhoods that were repositories of periodic epidemics and rioting. With the disappearance of property qualifications for white male suffrage after the 1820s, political radicals sought to lead movements of the poor. One such movement was the Equal Rights Party, popularly called Locofocos, in New York, which campaigned on a program of antimonopoly price reductions of "bread, meat, rent and fuel" in the depression of 1837. Riots such as the Locofoco flour riot against high prices were common, although riots of the poor in the mid-nineteenth century often took the form of "native" Protestants attacking "immigrant" Catholics seen as taking jobs. Such riots fueled the anti-immigrant and anti-Catholic Know-Nothing movement of the 1850s, whose xenophobic anti-Catholic message became an important force in national politics by pitting nativist Protestant whites against new Catholic immigrants. The Know-Nothings briefly competed with the new antislavery reform-oriented Republican Party to challenge the Democrats before the Civil War.

The depression of 1857, which gave impetus to the Republicans, led to major slum riots in New York, a mass demonstration of the unemployed in front of the Wall Street Stock Exchange, attacks on police stations, and the use of U.S. Marines to oust rioters who had briefly occupied City Hall, demanding work and food.

The Civil War, which brought price inflation and conscription, also heightened strikes and riots among the poor, in both the Union and the Confederacy. In 1863, bread riots among the poor took place in the Confederate capital, Richmond, Virginia, and in Mobile, Alabama, along with antidraft riots in a number of Southern cities. Confederate law gave draft exemptions to large slaveholders.

In the more widely industrialized North, strikes of workers were common, and army troops were often used to suppress these strikes, particularly when they were against munitions or transportation facilities. Although these strikes cannot be seen as poor people's protests, they were responses to the forging of an industrial working class under wartime conditions and a harbinger of postwar labor struggles.

CIVIL WAR DRAFT RIOT

Perhaps the most important riot of the poor in the nineteenth century, which highlighted the social and ethnic divisions of the American poor, was the New York City draft riot of 1863. Just as big slaveholders were exempt from the Confederate draft if they chose to be, wealthy men in the Republic could purchase an exemption for $300. In July 1863, shortly after the great Union victory at Gettysburg, a mob of predominantly Irish immigrant labors attacked the new army recruiting station in New York and went on to loot homes of the wealthy, and hunt and kill all free blacks they could find, sometimes hanging or burning the victims, sometimes drowning them in the Hudson and East rivers, until Union troops returning from Gettysburg suppressed the riot.

Smaller "draft" riots with a similar social composition took place in Boston, Newark, New Jersey, and other cities. Although the riots were spontaneous rather than inspired by Confederate agents, as many abolitionists and supporters of the Republic contended, they were essentially a "war of the poor against the poor." The spirit of these riots would reappear in the postbellum period in various ways, primarily in "race riots" of poor whites against blacks. In addition, the mobilization of poor white communities in Boston, Philadelphia, and other cities against school integration in the second half of the twentieth century reflected the hostility of the white working class toward desegregation in urban areas, while middle-class suburbanites retained racially segregated schools.

INDUSTRIALIZATION AND WORKING-CLASS PROTEST

The pattern of spontaneous strikes by workers and rioting among the poor continued in the postwar period, as rapid industrialization and mass immigration produced larger cities, slums, and depressions. In the long depression of the 1870s, the unemployed held demonstrations demanding relief in Chicago, New York, and other cities, and often joined solidarity demonstrations for strikes, most importantly in the Great Railroad Strike of 1877, the first nationwide industrial strike. During the depression, the press used the term *tramp* to demonize the wandering unemployed, and some handguns were advertised as "tramp specials." Widespread looting by the poor and armed clashes by workers with police and state militias followed until President Rutherford B. Hayes

used federal troops, which had recently been withdrawn from the South, to suppress the strike.

Symbolically, Hayes's actions represented the abandonment of nearly 4 million impoverished former slaves in the South and the concentration of federal military force against workers and the poor in the North and marginalized native peoples in the West, who were soon to be in the "reservation stage" of Indian removal.

Many members of the working poor, especially women and immigrants, flocked to the Knights of Labor, which accepted unskilled workers, women, and minorities, in the postwar period. On May 1, 1886, a new labor organization, the American Federation of Labor (AFL), whose leaders were influenced by the growing European Socialist movement, called for strikes throughout the country in support of the eight-hour day, which the Knights also took up.

In solidarity with one of the strikes at the Mc-Cormick Harvester Company in Chicago, a large crowd of workers and the poor gathered on May 4, 1886, in Haymarket Square. When police marched against the demonstration, a bomb was hurled at them, and a bloody riot ensued. Eight organizers of the demonstration, who had no proven connection with the bomb thrower (who was never found), were tried for murder. Despite international protests that included English writers William Morris and George Bernard Shaw, four were executed. When the Illinois Supreme Court refused to hear the appeal of the eight Haymarket defendants, Shaw wrote with characteristic sarcasm, "If the world must lose eight of its people, it can better afford to lose eight members of the Illinois Supreme Court."

POVERTY REDUCTION AS A SOCIAL CAUSE

In 1886, Henry George, the author of *Progress and Poverty* (1879) (an enormously popular work that asked why there was so much more visible poverty in a period of unprecedented economic growth and technological advance), ran a strong race for mayor of New York, finishing second, ahead of Republican Theodore Roosevelt, as the candidate of New York's labor unions. In *Progress and Poverty* and in his subsequent career as a reformer, George saw mass poverty as the result of the huge increase in land values that accompanied an industrialization that compelled both workers and small businessmen to pay usurious rents to a class of landlords who produced nothing and invested in nothing productive. George's solution to poverty and inequality was a "single tax"—essentially a progressive tax on land—that would take away the "unearned increment" that the marketplace had given landlords. With the proceeds from the single tax, George proposed to fund public works that would provide jobs for the unemployed and other social improvements.

RURAL POVERTY AND THE POPULIST MOVEMENT

The existence of mass urban poverty spawned a powerful literature in the 1880s and 1890s, both realist and utopian, including such works as William Dean Howells's *A Hazard of New Fortunes* (1890), Stephen Crane's *Maggie: A Girl of the Streets* (1893), Edward Bellamy's Socialist utopia, *Looking Backward* (1888), and Ignatius Donnelly's capitalist dystopia, *Caesar's Column* (1891). However, the most important political movement that arose in the period, Populism, addressed the rural social dislocation and poverty created by the new boom-bust national economy, which saw agricultural production expand enormously in response to greatly increased urban markets, the "transportation revolution" represented by the railroads, and great advances in agricultural technologies. However, farmers saw the prices of their crops drop while the costs of farm implements, transportation, and grain storage increased sharply, reducing large numbers to tenants and, in the South particularly, sharecroppers and farm laborers.

To fight against this downturn, western and southern farmers in the 1880s formed farmers' alliances, which attempted to form farm distribution cooperatives and crop insurance plans, and made various legislative proposals, including public ownership of railroads and grain storage facilities and currency expansion ("free silver") to assist debtors. The alliances sent thousands of circuit-riding lecturers through the countryside to mobilize farmers and were a movement much more of small indebted farmers fighting against a commercializing agriculture that drove them into debt than of those already poor. Nonetheless, the movement became the center for campaigns against monopoly, the trusts, and the banks.

The alliance campaigns were an important part of the background to passage of the Sherman Anti-Trust Act in 1890; however, the failure of the alliances to influence the Democratic and Republican parties through pressure-group politics led to the creation of the People's (Populist) Party at Omaha in 1892. The preamble to the party's platform, written by Ignatius Donnelly, summed up the rage of the new poor of industrial America: "We meet in the midst of a nation brought to the verge of moral, political, and material ruin . . . the newspapers are subsidized or muzzled; public opinion silenced; business prostrate, our homes covered with mortgages, labor impoverished, and the land concentrated in the hands of capitalists . . . the fruits of the toil of millions are boldly stolen to build up colossal fortunes. . . . From the same prolific womb of governmental injustice we breed two classes—paupers and millionaires."

Although the Populists' message appeared apocalyptic, the onset of major industrial depression in 1893 gave it great force. Unable to make much headway in the rapidly industrializing core regions of the country, the Northeast and the Mississippi Valley Middle West, the Populist Party gained power briefly in the 1890s in plains states like Kansas and mountain states like Colorado. In the South, where white farmers belonged to a Southern Alliance and blacks to a Colored Farmers' Alliance, Populists fought fierce battles against the post-Reconstruction Democratic Party, which represented the interests of landlord planters and merchants and cotton factors who held the notes of the tenants and croppers. In the South, the struggle between Populists and those they called Bourbon Democrats—the white upper class—assumed the character of an open class struggle, as the conservative Democrats used heightened racist appeals, mass disenfranchisement of blacks and, to a much lesser extent, poor whites, and outright terrorist violence to suppress the Populist movement. For the Populists, the plantation owners and farmer slaveholders controlling the Democratic Party were equivalent to the Bourbon kings and aristocrats ruling France before the French Revolution.

The Populists had few practical programs for northern labor and the urban poor beyond antimonopoly rhetoric and a call for greater democracy, thus limiting the possibility that they would become a mass Farmer-Labor party replacing one of the two major parties. The decision of party leaders to form a coalition with the Democrats in 1896, supporting the candidacy of William Jennings Bryan, who mixed Populist and evangelical rhetoric with a narrow focus on the Populist program of currency expansion, doomed the party in two ways. Bryan led the Populists down to defeat with him and coopted an important part of their style and in a watered-down form some of their issues. Repressed in the South, many Populists joined the Democrats, acquiescing in white supremacy and seeking to represent poor white interests in what was now a one-party region. In the West, some Populists became active in the new Socialist

LOOKING BACKWARD
EDWARD BELLAMY (1888)

Edward Bellamy, a nineteenth-century utopian Socialist, originally published Looking Backward, 2000–1887 *in 1888, from which the following passage is excerpted. The work predicts that in the future all of the world's social ills will be abolished, including war, class divisions, crime, and mental illness.*

As to the final outcome of the labor troubles, which was the phrase by which the movement I have described was most commonly referred to, the opinions of the people of my class differed according to individual temperament. The sanguine argued very forcibly that it was in the very nature of things impossible that the new hopes of the workingmen could be satisfied, simply because the world had not the wherewithal to satisfy them. It was only because the masses worked very hard and lived on short commons that the race did not starve outright, and no considerable improvement in their condition was possible while the world, as a whole, remained so poor. It was not the capitalists whom the laboring men were contending with, these maintained, but the iron-bound environment of humanity, and it was merely a question of the thickness of their skulls when they would discover the fact and make up their minds to endure what they could not cure.

The less sanguine admitted all this. Of course the workingmen's aspirations were impossible of fulfillment for natural reasons, but there were grounds to fear that they would not discover this fact until they had made a sad mess of society.

They had the votes and the power to do so if they pleased, and their leaders meant they should. Some of these desponding observers went so far as to predict an impending social cataclysm. Humanity, they argued, having climbed to the top round of the ladder of civilization, was about to take a header into chaos, after which it would doubtless pick itself up, turn round, and begin to climb again. Repeated experiences of this sort in historic and prehistoric times possibly accounted for the puzzling bumps on the human cranium. Human history, like all great movements, was cyclical, and returned to the point of beginning. The idea of indefinite progress in a right line was no chimera of the imagination, with no analogue in nature. The parabola of a comet was perhaps a yet better illustration of the career of humanity. Tending upward and sunward from the aphelion of barbarism, the race attained the perihelion of civilization only to plunge downward once more to its nether goal in the regions of chaos.

This, of course, was an extreme opinion, but I remember serious men among my acquaintances who, in discussing the signs of the times, adopted a very similar tone. It was no doubt the common opinion of thoughtful men that society was approaching a critical period which might result in great changes. The labor troubles, their causes, course, and cure, took lead of all other topics in the public prints, and in serious conversation.

The nervous tension of the public mind could not have been more strikingly illustrated than it was by the alarm resulting from the talk of a small band of men who called themselves anarchists, and proposed to terrify the American people into adopting their ideas by threats of violence, as if a mighty nation which had but just put down a rebellion of half its own numbers, in order to maintain its political system, were likely to adopt a new social system out of fear.

As one of the wealthy, with a large stake in the existing order of things, I naturally shared the apprehensions of my class. The particular grievance I had against the working classes at the time of which I write, on account of the effect of their strikes in postponing my wedded bliss, no doubt lent a special animosity to my feeling toward them.

Source: Edward Bellamy. *Looking Backward, 2000–1887* (Boston and New York: Houghton Mifflin, 1926).

---

movement, particularly after the formation of the Socialist Party of America (SPA) in 1901.

MOVEMENTS OF THE UNEMPLOYED

As the depression of the 1890s deepened in 1894, Jacob Coxey, a radical greenbacker and champion of public works for the unemployed, caught press attention by leading an "industrial army," a march of the unemployed from Ohio to Washington. Other "industrial armies" (the concept was derived from Bellamy's *Looking Backward*) also marched on Washington, including an army of Polish immigrants from Chicago. Often the armies were greeted enthusiastically by unionized workers, as was Coxey's at Homestead, Pennsylvania, scene of the great steel strike against Andrew Carnegie and his lieutenant Henry Clay Frick two years before. But the marches also produced many clashes with local police, especially in the West, and often dissipated because of a combination of police harassment and lack of food and other provisions. Coxey, riding a white horse, made it to Washington and led his army of 500 strong to the capital steps, only to see the police break up his demonstration and arrest him for trespassing. Other industrial armies from around the country suffered similar fates when they reached Washington. In August 1894, police authorities destroyed Coxey's campsite, which served as the center for all the protests, driving away more than 1,200 demonstrators.

Although Coxey was vilified in the press and largely forgotten, his march would live on in the much larger Bonus March of World War I veterans in 1932, to which the Hoover administration would respond much as Grover Cleveland had in 1894. In addition, Coxey would outlive those who mocked him, passing away in 1951 at the age of 97 and contending with a great deal of justification that New Deal jobs programs like the Works Progress Administration (WPA), the Civilian Conservation Corps (CCC), and the National Youth Organization (NYO) had vindicated him.

SETTLEMENT HOUSE MOVEMENT

As the twentieth century dawned, both Socialists and non-Socialist reformers addressed the question of poverty. Although it could more accurately be seen as a movement for rather than of poor people, settlement houses in urban slum areas, of which Chicago's Hull House, founded by Jane Addams in 1889, became the best known, provided a variety of social and educational services for the immigrant poor while publicizing the misery of life in the sweatshops and tenements.

Jacob Riis's *How the Other Half Lives* (1890), which used the relatively new medium of photography to chronicle conditions among Lower East Side Jewish immigrants in the 1880s, helped to create a genre that would become a part of early twentieth-century exposé journalism. Popularly called muckraking, these photographic and journalistic profiles focused primarily on political and business corruption. Distinguished photographers Alfred Stieglitz and Lewis Hine would make urban poverty a major theme in their work. Hine particularly was involved in the National Child Labor Committee, which grew as the number of children engaged in work grew. In 1900, the U.S. Census showed that 1.7 million children worked in mills and other manufacturing installa-

tions. This was a conservative figure, for parents routinely lied about the ages of the children as reformers began to have some success in northern industrial states in enacting minimum age requirements for workers.

WORLD WAR I AND THE RISE OF RACISM AND ETHNOCENTRISM

The pre–World War I era might best be called an era of the discovery of poverty. New "progressive" magazines with predominantly middle-class subscribers regularly gave their readers accounts of urban poverty that was often just one neighborhood and one economic crisis away. Traditionalists continued to blame poverty on the poor, claiming that it was the fault not of society or the nation's economic system but of poor people themselves that they were poor.

First, racism served as both an explanation of poverty and an ideology to oppress the poor. Mounting violence in the South against poor blacks both helped to consolidate the system of segregation and disenfranchisement in the wake of the defeat of populism and served as a foundation for racist ideology and practice throughout the nation. A new generation of southern politicians, simply called demagogues in the northern press, appealed to poor whites with a theatrical politics that mocked the wealthy and incited hatred and violence against blacks.

Politicians like Senator James Vardaman (D-MS), and later Senator Theodore Bilbo (D-MS) and Representative John Rankin (D-MS), Senator Ben "Pitchfork Ben" Tillman (D-SC), and later Senator Ellison DuRant Smith (D-SC) and Senator James Strom Thurmond (R-SC), Senator Hoke Smith (D-GA), former Populist leader Senator Tom Watson (D-GA), and later Georgia governors Eugene Tallmadge and Lester Maddox, preached a politics of inciting the "war of the poor against the poor" in which a huge increase in lynching and the nationally publicized Atlanta race riot of 1906 were the best-known early examples. The spread of lynch law to the North in 1909 led a group of white and black progressives and Socialists to found the National Association for the Advancement of Colored People (NAACP). Although the NAACP could not be considered a poor people's movement, it nevertheless sought to regain civil rights lost since the end of Reconstruction and to prevent further erosion of the rights of an impoverished people.

In the North, portrayals of the immigrant poor as violent criminals, Anarchists, and Communists served as the backlash against social reformers' attempt to awaken a social conscience against poverty. The American Protective League lobbied for immigration restriction and encouraged the work of "scientific racists" who portrayed Italian, Greek, Slavic, and Jewish immigrants from Eastern and Southern Europe as genetically inferior to Northern Europeans and a menace to the nation's "racial stock" and future. President Woodrow Wilson, whose Democratic Party particularly depended on the votes of new immigrants, spoke disparagingly of "hyphenated Americans" (those who called themselves Irish-Americans, Italian-Americans, etc.), sought to extend segregation to federal offices following his election to the presidency, and praised the racist film *Birth of a Nation*, which glorified the Ku Klux Klan (KKK) of the Reconstruction period, when it was released in 1915.

World War I intensified these trends as conservatives called for 100 percent Americanism and expanded political attacks on progressives, Socialists, and the Industrial Workers of the World (IWW). Known as the Wobblies, the IWW was a revolutionary workers organization that organized lumberjacks, miners, garment workers, dockworkers, and other impoverished workers who were seeking to improve wages and working conditions. The KKK also revived and spread rapidly, in both the North and the South, after the war, feeding on the postwar red scare against Socialists, Anarchists, and members of the new Communist Party, as well as the wave of race riots against blacks, particularly returning servicemen, in what was called the red summer of 1919.

POVERTY AND INEQUALITY IN THE POST–WORLD WAR I ERA

World War I stimulated a huge expansion of U.S. industry through the implementation of mass production technologies and electrification. The increase in wealth brought the growth of inequality, as the labor movement was thrown back from its wartime highs. For example, the Keating-Owen Child Labor Bill of 1916, outlawing child labor, was declared unconstitutional by the U.S. Supreme Court (*Hammer v. Dagenhart*, 1918), and the political climate glorified both business and pro-business governments, denounced Communists, and mocked prewar progressives as "tired radicals" whose criticisms of business had been proven wrong by history.

What followed heightened inequality and increased conflicts between whites and blacks, among Protestants, Catholics, and Jews, and between urban and rural populations, along with exacerbating the al-

ready deep divisions over social issues such as Prohibition, religion, and personal morality. With the American public deeply divided over social issues and participation in electoral politics declining, conservative Republican administrations were free to pursue policies summed up by President Calvin Coolidge's famous phrase, "the business of America is business. He, who builds a factory, builds a temple. He, who works there, worships there."

This rather religious vision of American public life that linked prosperity to capitalism remained axiomatic in American national politics. In his 1929 inaugural address, President Herbert Hoover issued a statement that his generation of Americans was closer to the eradication of poverty than any generation in history—a contention that would prove wildly erroneous just seven months later, when the stock market crash rapidly accelerated the decline of what was already a stagnating economy. The Hoover administration's commitment to business-as-usual politics intensified what was to become the worst industrial depression of modern history. In the process, the poor became more visible than at any time in U.S. history, constituting at best a large minority and at worst a substantial majority of the population.

DEPRESSION AND THE NEW DEAL

The Great Depression saw a rediscovery of poverty and the creation for the first time in U.S. history of poor people's movements seeking to transform society. At the center of the movements was the Communist Party USA (CPUSA), which in the aftermath of the Russian Revolution represented a new leftist force in the United States, the Socialist Party of America, which under its new leader Norman Thomas remained a significant force, and various radical movements in rural areas drawing upon the experience of populism. Together, these movements influenced the government of Franklin D. Roosevelt, which, in 1932, proclaimed a "New Deal" for the "man at the bottom of the economic heap, to enact major social welfare legislation to provide protections for workers, the unemployed, and the poor generally." In short, the New Deal was a series of government-led economic and social programs created to jump-start the economy.

By the winter of 1930, demonstrations of the unemployed, sometimes spontaneous, often led by Communists and other radicals under such slogans as "Work or Wages" and "Fight—Don't Starve," broke out in front of city halls in Philadelphia, Cleveland, Los Angeles, and other cities. The Communist movement globally declared March 6, 1930, International Unemployment Day, and tens of thousands participated in demonstrations in the United States. In New York, Boston, Milwaukee, and other cities, the demonstrations led to major clashes with the police. In the wake of the demonstrations, the press, which had been downplaying the economic crisis (the term *depression* was at first a euphemism for what had previously been called panics and crises), began to acknowledge the severity of the situation.

THE COMMUNIST PARTY AND THE POOR

Following up on the success of the demonstrations, CPUSA activists organized unemployed councils throughout the country and established a loose national organization, Unemployed Councils USA. The councils organized local campaigns for increased relief and demonstrations against evictions, which often led to violent clashes with police, particularly when council members sought to block the evictions of African Americans in Chicago and other major cities. Nationally, the councils focused on petition drives for a practical reform, unemployment insurance, so much so that American Federation of Labor conservatives, in opposing old age pensions and unemployment insurance at the AFL's 1932 convention, mocked them as "Communist programs."

In response to the press's contention that "nobody was starving," the councils organized "hunger marches," the most famous of which led to a bloody clash with police at the Ford Motor Company at Dearborn, Michigan, in 1931. The following year, Angelo Herndon, a young African-American Communist, was arrested and charged with "attempting to incite insurrection" for leading a multiracial hunger march in Atlanta, Georgia, in 1932. Sentenced in 1933 to twenty years on a Georgia chain gang, Herndon became the focus for civil liberties agitation throughout the country. The result was a 5–4 decision by the U.S. Supreme Court in 1937, which was then retreating from its all-out opposition to New Deal labor and social legislation, which declared the Georgia anti-insurrection law unconstitutional.

Communist organizing among the poor and unemployed stirred others on the left. The Socialist Party, through the Socialist-led mass organization, the League for Industrial Democracy (LID), organized unemployed groups in Chicago, Baltimore, and other cities, often pursuing similar goals—that is, negotiating improved welfare conditions and an end to evictions—as the Communists did, but with less militant tactics. In 1935, Socialists under the leadership of David Las-

ser established a national organization of the unemployed, the Workers Alliance of America, which was to include many Communists in grassroots campaigns. In spite of the bitter rivalry between the Communist and Socialist parties, the Workers Alliance was to become a sort of informal union representing workers in the New Deal's WPA and a lobby for federal relief and other social programs for the poor.

Communists also sought to mobilize sharecroppers in the Deep South, establishing a Share Croppers Union in 1931, which built a base of strength among impoverished black sharecroppers in Alabama. Socialists organized a Southern Tenant Farmers Union (STFL) under the leadership of H.L. Mitchell, which mobilized predominantly white tenant farmers and fought to reform New Deal agricultural policies, which, given the influence of Southern Democrats, practically favored large landlords and commercial agriculture.

In 1935, left-leaning members of the Agricultural Adjustment Administration's (AAA) legal staff attempted to override the southern plantation owners' policy of replacing black sharecroppers with whites by issuing a ruling from Washington headquarters that the same people had to be kept on the land. In response to landlord policies of removing tenants and croppers along with the acreage reduction for which they received benefit payments, the AAA had issued an order (often violated) that, in order for benefit payments to be received, the same number of people had to be kept on the land. In order to remain in compliance, southern landlords then began to replace blacks with whites, sometimes at a smaller share than blacks had received.

Afraid to alienate powerful conservative forces, including the Southern Democrats and the Cotton Council of the South, AAA administrators fired rebellious legal staffers. Lee Pressman, one of these staffers, went on to become general counsel of the CIO and was regularly attacked by anti–New Deal and antilabor media as a Communist agent seeking to foment industrial strikes to advance Communist political agendas.

Communists also pioneered in campaigns to organize predominantly migrant workers in the Central Valley of California in the middle 1930s. One of these became the center of John Steinbeck's famous early novel, *In Dubious Battle* (1936), which was critical of the growers, the Communist organizers, and the political power structure. Subsequently, many of these Mexican-American migrant workers were replaced by poor white tenant farmers from Oklahoma and Arkansas fleeing the dustbowl in the late 1930s. Their plight drew national attention in James Agee's nonfiction *Now Let Us Praise Famous Men* (1941), John Steinbeck's novel *The Grapes of Wrath* (1939), and the work of WPA photographers and became a symbol of poor people victimized by society.

Campaigning to organize tenants, sharecroppers, and migrant laborers, Communists faced violent repression and were on the whole unsuccessful. Yet, the party influenced subsequent New Deal legislation and provided an important precedent for the later United Farm Workers' union-organizing drives led by Cesar Chavez, which gained widespread public support and won some important victories in the 1960s and 1970s.

LABOR MILITANCY

For a brief period, the struggles of the agricultural workers and the rural poor seemed to be advancing significantly when they were taken up by the left-leaning Food, Tobacco, and Agricultural Workers Union/CIO in the late 1930s. Although the union pursued far more moderate policies than the various sharecroppers' unions and farm labor organizers, it held out the possibility of bringing the substantial resources of the CIO to the task of organizing the rural poor. However, the postwar Taft-Hartley law encouraged national CIO leaders to abandon their southern organizing drive, purge their unions of Communists and other radicals, and expel unions whose members refused to go along with the purges.

Under such slogans as "organize the unorganized" and "black and white, unite and fight," Communist, Socialist, and other unemployed groups supported the strike wave that began in the summer of 1934 and served as a counterweight to employers who sought to use the unemployed as strikebreakers. The demonstrations of Communist-led unemployed councils and the mounting strikes led the National Council of Mayors in the fall of 1934 to call upon the Roosevelt administration to enact national welfare legislation.

Although the legislation would fall far short of what Communists, Socialists, and other militants had been calling for, it represented the most important and far-reaching social legislation in U.S. history. First, the WPA funded a wide variety of public works projects, providing millions of jobs to the unemployed. Conservatives in Congress triumphed by insisting that the WPA pay its workers low "security wages" rather than the prevailing wage in industry. Conservatives also restricted appropriations for the WPA and other New Deal agencies providing jobs (the Public Works

Administration and the NYA, which provided both jobs and work study grants for youth), so that, at their peak, some New Deal jobs programs could not reach more than a third of the unemployed. Still, the programs both saved millions of people and enriched the country by building public hospitals, roads, and recreational facilities; establishing federal theater, arts, and music projects; and engaging in other activities for low-income people that private enterprise, even in prosperous times, had considered unprofitable.

The New Deal government saw these jobs programs as temporary. As a long-term solution to poverty, the administration enacted old age pension and unemployment insurance legislation, the latter particularly associated with the campaigns of the Communist-led unemployed councils in 1935. Defined as an attempt to expand the power of labor to confront powerful businesses and corporations and increase workers' purchasing power, the National Labor Relations Act of 1935, in large measure a response to the growing strike wave and the fears that Communist-influenced strikers might create a revolutionary situation if reforms were not enacted, established a National Labor Relations Board to supervise union elections and outlaw unfair labor practices. The Rural Electrification Administration (REA) was also established in 1935 to provide electricity for rural areas too poor to get power from private companies.

THE CONGRESS OF INDUSTRIAL ORGANIZATIONS AND THE STRUGGLE FOR A WELFARE STATE

In 1935, the formation of the Committee (later Congress) on Industrial Organizations ushered in the organization of large, inclusive industrial unions, including Steel Workers, Auto Workers, and Electrical Workers, who, unlike the AFL, strongly supported social welfare legislation for the working class and poor. President Roosevelt addressed these constituencies when he ran for reelection in 1936, denouncing the "economic royalists" of big business and the "nine old men" of the U.S. Supreme Court, and contrasting what his administration had done for the industrial workers and the poor with the Hoover administration's actions in 1932 and promising to do more.

Roosevelt's great victory further stimulated union-organizing drives, leading to the victory of the United Auto Workers (UAW) in the General Motors Sit-Down Strike in the winter of 1937 and the victory of the Steel Workers in gaining recognition from U.S.

Steel. Subsequent New Deal legislation helped to break down distinctions between urban and rural labor, employed and unemployed, and to establish in a rudimentary way what would later be called a welfare state. Legislation included the Bankhead-Jones Farm Tenant Act of 1937, which created the Farm Security Administration, providing loans for family farmers and establishing "sanitary camps" to protect migrant agricultural laborers from exploitation, as well as the Fair Labor Standards Act of 1938, which established minimum wages, established the forty-hour week, and outlawed child labor.

The administration's commitment in 1935 to provide federal aid for families with dependent children (the Depression had produced widespread desertion by male heads of households in a society that still placed large obstacles, in the best of times, to full-time women workers) and later to subsidize the poor with food vouchers redeemable at stores (the Food Stamp Plan, enacted in 1939) represented the triumph of both the labor and unemployed movements. Although the Depression was not over and unemployment never dropped below 10 percent until the United States approached entry into World War II, American financier Jay Gould's arrogant boast of the 1880s, "I can hire one half of the working class to kill the other half," had finally been shattered by a remarkable coalition of liberals and radicals, labor, and unemployed organizers.

After sixty years of defeats in major strikes, beginning with the railroad strike of 1877, industrial workers had won great victories in the late 1930s. After facing for that same period a Supreme Court and a federal judiciary that routinely declared unconstitutional minimum-wage laws, protective legislation for women, anti–child labor laws, and legislation regulating business on the principle of "freedom of contract," workers and the poor now began to see a judiciary willing to accept government legislation on their behalf.

OPPOSITION TO WELFARE STATE PROGRAMS

A great backlash from business and conservative forces opposed efforts to build strong welfare state programs. The WPA was vilified as a center of waste and inefficiency, and the industrial unions were condemned as seedbeds of Communist revolution. An informal coalition of Republicans and Southern and other conservative Democrats came into existence by 1938 to oppose New Deal policies, and the recession of 1937–1938 increased their numbers in Congress.

Faced with a congressional committee system that gave great power to anti–New Deal Southern Democrats with seniority garnered from the fact that they did not have to run in competitive elections, Roosevelt made a limited and unsuccessful attempt to oppose anti–New Deal Democrats in the Democratic primaries of 1938. The press, which was overwhelmingly anti–New Deal, called Roosevelt's actions a "purge," comparing them with the great political purges sweeping the Soviet Union. Meanwhile, a member of the conservative coalition, Representative Martin Dies (D-TX), became the leader in 1938 of the new House Un-American Activities Committee, whose stock in trade from its inception was to strike at unions, New Deal agencies, and various advocacy groups as the "Trojan horse," to use Dies's phrase, of Soviet-directed Communist revolutionaries. Another prominent conservative, Senator Harry Byrd (D-VA), led a committee on government appropriations, popularly known as the "economy committee," which sought to expose waste and cut New Deal budgets. Conservative newspapers spread the story that high New Deal official and WPA administrator Harry Hopkins had said, "we will tax and tax, spend and spend, elect and elect," which Hopkins denied, but which became a mantra for conservatives who saw the New Deal as a machine taxing business and the productive middle and upper classes to support radical unions and bribe the undeserving poor to keep them in power.

Even before the U.S. rearmament program began, the conservative coalition scored its first important victory when it eliminated the WPA's federal theater project, which was accused of radical influences and mismanagement in 1939. Once the United States entered the war and Roosevelt, in a highly publicized speech, announced that "Dr. New Deal," necessary to fight the Depression, was now to be replaced by "Dr. Win the War," a politically strengthened congressional conservative coalition eliminated the WPA entirely, struck down the Farm Security Administration, and abolished the Food Stamp Plan (which would be resurrected in the 1960s) on the grounds that they were no longer needed. When the National Resources Planning Board, a major New Deal planning agency, came forward for proposals to establish a comprehensive postwar welfare state, focusing on publicly supported housing, education, transportation, and healthcare, the conservative coalition eliminated the appropriation for the board.

Roosevelt used a number of the board's recommendations to develop his goal for a "second bill of rights," stressing economic and social security, which he ran on in 1944 and which the press dubbed the "Economic Bill of Rights." However, the increased strength of the conservative coalition, the effect of the war in stimulating a vast expansion of American big business, and the political unreliability of the Democratic Party to advance New Deal goals—represented by the influence of powerful Southern Democrats and urban machines much more interested in local patronage than in social policy—made the realization of these goals very unlikely. Roosevelt's acceptance of Harry Truman, a centrist machine Democrat from Missouri, as a replacement for Vice President Henry A. Wallace on the ticket in 1944 and Truman's accession to the presidency on Roosevelt's death as the war ended inaugurated a new postwar period of conservative politics in which organized labor was contained and the poor became largely invisible once more.

CIVIL RIGHTS MOVEMENT AND THE WAR AGAINST POVERTY

The civil rights movement was to become the most important force in U.S. society opposing postwar developments. The civil rights movement was often led by middle-class-based groups, black southern ministers, the NAACP, and even more radical groups like the northern-based Congress of Racial Equality (CORE) and the Student Non-Violent Coordinating Committee (SNCC), whose leadership cadre came largely from college students, intellectuals, and professionals. In addition, the movement depended on hundreds of thousands of mostly poor African Americans in the South and many in the North for its achievements. Poor blacks, in the tradition of Mississippi sharecropper Fannie Lou Hamer, who was nearly murdered when she tried to register to vote in the early 1960s, became heroes and heroines of the struggle.

Initially, the developing Cold War political climate set back the struggle for civil rights, as political purges in the unions, arts, sciences, and professions, were spurred on by the Truman administration's establishment of an "Attorney General's list" of subversive organizations in 1947. The Taft-Hartley Act, passed in 1947, made all union officials sign an annual oath that they were not members of the Communist Party, spread through the country, leading to the expulsion of many of the most qualified union organizers. These policies generated a political climate that made advocacy of the rights of workers, the poor, and minorities open to charges of subversion and treason and

eliminated many of those who had led the successful struggles for the poor in the 1930s from public life.

Henry Wallace's public career was destroyed by his Progressive Party presidential candidacy in 1948; moreover, his running mate, Senator Glen Taylor (D-ID), was hounded out of the Democratic Party and the Senate in the aftermath of the campaign. The Wallace campaign sought to revive New Deal policies and connect them with civil rights and anti–Cold War positions. Governor Strom Thurmond of South Carolina, candidate of the segregationist National States Rights Party, who ran for president in opposition to the Truman administration's attempt to appeal to African-American and New Deal voters by offering to advance civil rights, was welcomed back into the Democratic fold and became a major leader of southern segregationists in the U.S. Senate within a decade.

This move away from pro–civil rights positions continued in the Democratic Party during the Korean War as the Democrats watered down their party's civil rights plank in 1952 and presidential candidate Adlai Stevenson chose Senator John Sparkman (D-AL), a centrist on most domestic issues and a supporter of segregation, as his running mate

Although the Supreme Court's historic *Brown v. Board of Education* (1954) decision overturned the juridical basis of southern segregation and made the federal judiciary the principal governmental ally of the civil rights movement in subsequent struggles, it did not bring about school integration until a mass social movement developed. At Montgomery, Alabama, such a movement launched a boycott against the city's bus system, which lasted over a year, produced as its spokesman the Reverend Martin Luther King Jr., and resulted in a victory both in the courts and in the solidarity shown by the African-American population. At the time, the average annual income of black workers in Montgomery was less than $1,000, which made the great majority of those who participated in the bus boycott, laborers, domestics, and the children of laborers and domestics, very poor by U.S. government statistical definitions of poverty.

Indeed, local segregationist elites throughout the South formed White Citizens Councils, which sought to coerce blacks from supporting the civil rights movement by threatening them with loss of jobs and evictions. Ironically, the mechanization of southern agriculture was forcing more and more blacks out of the rural South and, given deeper discriminatory policies against them in southern industry, to the North, so that many poor rural southern blacks had very little to lose, save their lives, which a revival and expansion of KKK activity put at risk.

On February 1, 1960, four black college students organized a sit-in at a Woolworth's lunch counter in Greensboro, North Carolina, which sparked a wave of sit-ins that spread to southern stores, movie theaters, churches, and public swimming pools, led to mass arrests by segregationist police, and ultimately involved more than 50,000 people. Although the leaders of the protests were clearly young middle-class activists, the majority of participants were drawn from the segregated black poor. From the sit-ins came a heightened emphasis on direct action and a new slogan, "freedom, now," which rejected the gradualism that both the Eisenhower administration and its Democratic opposition preached and the NAACP and the Urban League, the leading establishment civil rights organizations largely indifferent to the plight of the black poor, had accepted.

The sit-ins saw the creation of the SNCC, made up of militant black and white college students who would interact with hundreds of thousands of poor southern blacks in anti-segregation and community organizing drives and voter registration campaigns in the early 1960s. Initially founded as a support group for civil rights activity with connections to the old Socialist LID and the political action apparatus of the United Automobile Workers Union, the predominantly white and middle-class Students for a Democratic Society (SDS) worked with SNCC, had many members who held joint membership in both organizations, and took the experiences it garnered from the southern-based civil rights movement to create an Economic Research and Action Project (ERAP), which launched community-organizing projects among the urban poor in northern cities in 1964, developing concepts and tactics that would reappear in the Johnson administration's War on Poverty.

The southern civil rights movement, under the leadership of Dr. Martin Luther King Jr. and the Southern Christian Leadership Conference (SCLC), was attempting to mobilize poor people to fight a nonviolent war against a violent enemy. The campaign sought to turn national and international public opinion toward compelling the federal government to end a system of segregation that had, in principle, been illegal since the *Brown* decision. The civil rights movement launched a full-fledged boycott against discrimination in public accommodations and employment in a major southern city, the steel city of Birmingham, Alabama. In May 1963, thousands of blacks, mostly young and poor, demonstrated against police dogs, fire hoses, and police beatings, filling the jails and gaining national and global attention. The fact that there were many cities like Birmingham in both the North and the South, where minority workers were essential to the service and industrial economy, convinced northern business leaders to support legislation to end southern segregation.

GOVERNMENT RESPONSES TO THE CIVIL RIGHTS MOVEMENT

In the early 1960s, the Kennedy administration announced support of legislation to end segregation and sought to channel the energies of young civil rights activists into voter registration drives in the South. The Democratic Party expected this direction would work to its advantage, since segregationist Southern Democrats were now deserting the party in droves. With this in mind, it supported voter registration drives such as Mississippi Freedom Summer, which took place in 1964, after the assassination of President John F. Kennedy and after his successor, Lyndon Johnson, had enacted a comprehensive civil rights bill banning discrimination against minorities and women in public accommodations and employment.

Events in the Mississippi Freedom Summer, the brutal murder of three civil rights activists, two white and one black, further undermined the de facto system of disenfranchisement that had been in existence in much of the Deep South since the end of the nineteenth century. These events, along with the SCLC campaign in 1965 at Selma, Alabama, provided public support for passage of Lyndon Johnson's Voting Rights Act, which became the basis for the restoration to southern blacks of voting rights lost after Reconstruction.

THE GREAT SOCIETY

The events of Mississippi Freedom Summer, the close cooperation among middle-class civil rights activists and the African-American poor, along with the realization that the Kennedy and Johnson administrations were using the activists as unsupported cannon fodder while they continued to negotiate with and reward southern segregationists, bred a deep anger and alienation. These feelings exploded when the National Democratic Party, at its Atlantic City Convention in August 1964, refused to seat a delegation from the integrated Mississippi Freedom Democratic Party, which the civil rights movement had created, over the segregationist regular Democratic Party.

As he prepared to run for the presidency in his own right, Lyndon Johnson had called for the creation in the United States of a "Great Society," a term he used in a speech at the University of Michigan commencement in the spring of 1964, which became a catchphrase for his administration. As an important part of the Great Society, Johnson called for "an unconditional War on Poverty." With establishment liberals like Johnson's running mate, Hubert Humphrey, beginning to use such terms as a "Marshall Plan" for the cities, Johnson in his inaugural address in January 1965 made the war on poverty a high priority, something that no one in American history had ever done, short of Franklin D. Roosevelt's call for a New Deal and his commitment in his second inaugural to policies to elevate the suffering of "one third of the national, ill-housed, ill-clothed, and ill-fed." Never before in U.S. history had the question of poverty and the poor been broached in this way.

In 1964, Johnson had established an Office of Economic Opportunity (OEO) under the leadership of Sargent Shriver, brother-in-law of the late John F. Kennedy, to direct an antipoverty campaign. Kennedy had raised the issues of poverty and hunger in the 1960 campaign, focusing his attention on the white rural poor of Appalachia. Although conservative Senator Barry Goldwater (R-AZ) joked that most of the millions whom Kennedy claimed were going hungry were on diets, Kennedy did try to extend benefits under the existing, federally supported Aid to Families with Dependent Children (AFDC) welfare system, whose numbers began to grow sharply as the urban poor suffered from suburbanization, "urban renewal," declining public transportation and education systems, and the export of jobs to Taft-Hartley "right to work" states and suburban areas.

In addition, the civil rights movement, which focused on employment issues, in both the North and the South, had connected the campaign against segregation with the struggle against poverty, a point made clear by the 1963 March on Washington, whose official slogan was "Jobs and Freedom."

Building on modest Kennedy administration policies like the Manpower Development and Training Act (1962) and the Community Mental Health Centers Act (1963), which in a limited way established job training and expanded social work services for the poor, the Johnson administration in 1965 in effect created a series of new programs whose purpose was to provide education, healthcare, housing subsidies, job training, everything, as critics on the left noted, but the jobs themselves, to the poor.

The New Deal's food stamp plan was revived and in its early years expanded very liberally to a large number of low-income people, including college students. Although comprehensive national health insurance, which had come out of the New Deal's wartime program and Truman's 1948 presidential campaign, was not realized, the Johnson administration established Medicare, a Social Security–style healthcare for retirees (whose out-of-pocket healthcare expenses had driven many below the poverty line), and a federal-state "Medicaid" program of public healthcare for the poor who passed a means test. The administration also established the Head Start program, providing educational and recreational programs for poor preschoolers, federally supported legal services to the poor, a "model cities" program for rehabilitation of slum areas, a Jobs Corps, along with a number of other job training programs, and a great increase in federal aid to education, some of it targeted to the poor, under the Elementary and Secondary Education Act of 1965 and the Higher Education Act of 1965.

The OEO sought to coordinate a number of these activities at the community level, seeking to ensure that the programs were both democratic and reflected the specific needs of communities through a policy of "maximum feasible participation," that is, the involvement of community activists and organizations in the development of antipoverty programs. As a result, community-based antipoverty organizations sprang up in urban areas throughout the country and became a battleground for a variety of radical activists and patronage-hungry politicians, many of whom were members of African-American and Latino minorities closed out by the existing political machines.

The escalation of the Vietnam War, however, would ultimately undermine the War on Poverty. Johnson, in spite of the enormous victory the liberal Democrats had won in the elections of 1964, which temporarily broke the veto power that the conservative coalition had over progressive initiatives since World War II, now found himself negotiating with his political opponents to limit funding for antipoverty and other Great Society programs in order to maintain congressional support for rapidly rising military expenditures.

The Johnson administration found that this strategy was untenable. The strongest supporters of its antipoverty program, both in mainstream politics and in the activist groups and community-based organizations, were also the strongest opponents of the Vietnam War, which increasingly became the great cause for a new center-left coalition of liberals and radicals.

The bitterest enemies of Johnson's antipoverty program and his administration generally were the most loyal supporters of the Vietnam War escalation, Cold War politics generally, and a social conservatism that demonized welfare and saw the social protest movements of the period as both subversive and perverse.

Unlike Roosevelt, who was able to disappoint radical activists on many issues and still maintain their loyalty and love, Johnson found himself by 1967 hated by the activists whose grassroots support was necessary to both mobilize the poor and educate workers and sections of the middle classes of the need to support a program as ambitious as the Great Society.

As a result, the urban poor experienced what might be seen as a revolution in rising expectations, as the antipoverty program, to take a phrase from one of its early Johnson administration critics, Daniel Patrick Moynihan, was both "oversold and underfunded." What the urban poor did learn by 1965 was that to put down Viet Cong insurgencies against the South Vietnamese and American troops and fight a containment war, the administration was ready to spend very big money. Beginning with the Los Angeles Watts riot of 1965 and continuing in major urban ghetto riots in Detroit and Newark, New Jersey, in 1967, slum dwellers launched their own insurgencies against slumlords, tenements, unsanitary conditions, price-gouging storekeepers selling inferior products, and the long hot summer of life in the ghetto. In the short run, money did pour in to keep the peace, providing jobs particularly for unemployed youth, but the medium-term effects were to escalate white fears of northern urban black violence and to undermine the great success of the civil rights movement five years earlier in turning the violence of the segregationist white power structure against itself.

That these riots, suppressed by police and National Guard units, were not "race riots" in the American sense but, like nineteenth-century uprisings of the white poor, riots of the poor against poverty, meant little to many whites who associated poverty with blacks and were willing to listen to conservative politicians like Richard Nixon. Nixon began to revive his political career with calls for law and order in the streets, self-reliance and accountability among the poor, and the creation of an undefined program of "black capitalism" to replace Great Society programs that were fostering both dependency and unrealistic expectations that led to violence.

Actually, Great Society programs, when compared to New Deal programs, were fostering capitalism, though not necessarily minority capitalism. Storekeepers redeemed food stamps, housing developers were paid "market value" rent subsidies to build housing for the poor, universities and employers received generous government grants for their involvement in administration-supported education and job programs, and the officials of the local antipoverty agencies reaped the greatest benefits from the programs. The Johnson administration's siding with Democratic political machines against community activists helped to turn many community antipoverty agencies into corrupt political machines led by men whom the poor came derisively to call "poverty pimps." Most of all, the establishment of major social programs like Medicaid and section 8 housing benefits to the poor when they were not available to moderate- and low-income people above the poverty line bred resentment and divided lower-income groups.

Yet, by any statistical standard, the Great Society programs, given their limitations and the fact that an administration hostile to them took power in 1969, were remarkably successful in lowering the formal rates of poverty and providing through Affirmative Action–based education and employment programs a large expansion of African American and other minority middle classes.

As the Johnson administration retreated on the war on poverty in order to escalate the war in Vietnam, Martin Luther King Jr. became both an eloquent critic of the Vietnam War and a champion of a real War on Poverty. In 1966, King had led an unsuccessful campaign against de facto segregation and discrimination in Chicago, the leading industrial city of the North.

Here he had challenged the powerful political machine of Johnson's close ally, Mayor Richard J. Daley of Chicago, who used black ward healers in what was a much more sophisticated power structure. As his alienation from the administration and his fear of where the advocates of black power and violent confrontation were leading the country grew, King devoted his energies to building a poor people's movement, a broad coalition of poor whites, blacks, Latinos, Native Americans, Asian Americans, and others, and planned a great encampment of the poor, a nonviolent super version of Coxey's 1893 march and the 1932 Bonus March to revive the War on Poverty and in effect save the Great Society from itself in 1968.

It was in solidarity with this campaign that King went to Memphis to support a strike of black sanitation workers in April 1968. Following King's assassination in Memphis, riots of the black poor swept urban areas throughout the country and gave impetus to Nixon's emerging "law and order" presidential campaign. The assassination of Robert F. Kennedy in Los Angeles in June 1968, following his victory in the Democratic presidential primary, removed the only candidate with a program of uniting labor with white and minority low-income groups and youth, thus saving what he saw as his brother's domestic legacy from Lyndon Johnson, who had become his bitterest political enemy.

Kennedy had surprised many who had known him in Washington by his focus on the Bedford-Stuyvesant slum district of New York, his meetings with militant community activists, and his strong identification and support for Cesar Chavez and the United Farm Workers (UFW). As a senator from New York, Kennedy had also sought to expose the abuses against Native Americans, statistically the poorest group in the nation. At the time of his assassination, he had built a bond with poor blacks, Latinos, Native Americans, and others greater than his brother or any contemporary American politician.

CONSERVATIVE BACKLASH

At the Republican National Convention in 1968, Nixon revealed his position on the ghetto riots by choosing Spiro T. Agnew, the governor of Maryland, as his running mate. Agnew was well known for ordering state police to shoot to kill when riots followed the King assassination and berating local civil rights leaders for failing to keep their people "in line." Just as Democrat Adlai Stevenson had called Nixon in 1952 a "white-collar McCarthy," to appeal to the anti-Communist hysteria during the Eisenhower administration, so Agnew was used by Nixon to appeal to those frightened by the ghetto riots and antiwar protests.

Whereas Franklin Roosevelt had appealed to the "forgotten man at the bottom of the economic heap" in 1932, Nixon appealed to a "silent majority" of law-abiding nonprotesters who had been abandoned by "limousine liberals" appealing to lawless elements. Songs like Merle Haggard's "Welfare Cadillac" captured the mood of what analysts called the "white backlash"; that is, the poor, meaning the nonwhite poor, were getting something for nothing at the expense of the hard-working middle classes. The demonstrations at the Democratic Convention in Chicago in August 1968, together with the ensuing massive police repression against the demonstrators, seemed to ensure the end of the Great Society and the defeat

of Lyndon Johnson's hand-picked successor, Hubert Humphrey.

Nixon, however, would face great opposition from a wide variety of his opponents—civil rights activists, Great Society liberals, antiwar activists, feminists, environmentalists, and a growing welfare rights movement—leading to the initiation of conservative reform and unprecedented repression to defeat his real and perceived enemies and maintain his power.

GOVERNMENT REPRESSION

The failed promises of the Great Society could be seen most forcefully in the activities of a group that the Nixon administration, through the Federal Bureau of Investigation (FBI) and its relationship with state and local police authorities, would search and destroy, the Black Panther Party. Founded in Oakland, California, in 1966 as a revolutionary black power organization, the Panthers, who denounced police brutality, bore arms, and called for the right of armed self-defense and self-determination for black ghettoes, functioned as the far left of the black power and community control movements of the late 1960s. Although they became the most important symbol of "black violence" for the mass media in the period, their political strength was based on practical social welfare programs that they organized for the poor in urban slum areas. These included free clinics, free breakfast programs for hungry children, alternative schools, voluntary sanitation projects, and militant protests against slum landlords and local storekeepers. The Black Panthers also became the model for a variety of other activists among the minority poor, particularly Mexican-American activists in the Southwest who formed the "Brown Berets" (the Panthers' informal uniform was a black beret and a black leather jacket) and the Young Lords Party, a Puerto Rican group.

Founded as a street gang in Chicago in the 1950s, the Young Lords transformed themselves into a militant group working among the Puerto Rican poor through contacts with Black Panther leaders in the mid-1960s. In New York City in particular, the Young Lords emerged as a significant force in protests against police brutality and in the creation of voluntarist social services for the poor. Less confrontational in their style than the Black Panthers, the Lords developed relationships with progressive Catholic clergy (as did the Panthers with some urban African-American ministers) and a number of individuals associated with the Lords, including Pablo Guzman, a young attorney for the New York chapter, Geraldo Rivera, and Juan Gonzalez, went on to long-term careers in New York and national media.

The fate of the Black Panthers was to be quite different. In 1969, Chicago police raided Panther headquarters and killed Panther leaders Fred Hampton and Mark Clark on information provided by an FBI infiltrator, who had served as head of security for the Chicago Panthers. In Los Angeles, the FBI provoked an armed conflict between Black Panthers and members of a rival organization, the cultural nationalist organization US, led by Ron Karenga. Black Panther leader Bobby Seale was one of the leaders of the Chicago Democratic Convention demonstrations arrested by the Nixon administration and tried in federal court. Because of his protests, Seale was separated from the seven other defendants and bound and gagged. The national leadership of the Black Panther Party was regularly arrested, re-arrested when charges had to be dropped, and either given long prison sentences or forced to flee the country.

Many local leaders were also arrested, tried, and convicted on dubious charges. Others were killed in shootouts with the police, usually under very questionable conditions. By the early 1970s, the group had for all practical purposes been destroyed, although individuals in various parts of the country sought to keep its social welfare activities alive. Today Amnesty International and other international human rights organizations regard those Black Panther leaders who remain in U.S. jails as political prisoners.

ORGANIZING LOW-WAGE WORKERS

A significantly more moderate movement of the working poor that enjoyed broad support among liberals and the general labor movement, the UFW under the leadership of Cesar Chavez sought to organize migrant farm workers, mostly Mexican Americans, who were at the very bottom of the economy in terms of incomes and benefits, in California and other parts of the country. The farm workers' grape strikes in California against Gallo Wine and lettuce strikes against Central Valley growers won the support of Senator Robert Kennedy, who brought his great celebrity and influence with liberals to the UFW. Eventually, large numbers were drawn to consumer boycotts and pickets against supermarkets and liquor stores that sold the products harvested by nonunion migrant labor.

After winning important victories in the late 1960s, the farm workers suffered significant defeats in the early 1970s when Teamster leader Frank Fitzsimmons, a Republican and strong supporter of the national Nixon administration and the local Reagan administration in California, joined with growers to launch raids against the UFW, sending goon squads into California to break UFW strikes. Local police and California State police, with the enthusiastic support of Governor Ronald Reagan, arrested many strikers. The election of liberal Democrat Edmond G. (Jerry) Brown as governor of California in 1974 led to significant reforms that partially revived the UFW, although the organization never regained what it had lost, nor did it recover its momentum from the late 1960s. Farm workers today remain generally nonunion and among the most exploited of America's working poor.

WELFARE RIGHTS MOVEMENT

Through the 1960s, Great Society programs and increased militancy among the poor led to a liberalization of the AFDC federal system, as the federal government encouraged states to provide access to benefits to larger numbers of people. Stirred also by Legal Services attorneys petitioning for such benefits and sociological studies that showed that large numbers of low-income people had been routinely denied benefits to which they were entitled, through a failure to inform them of such benefits, various bureaucratic subterfuges, or simply the social stigma of applying for "welfare," state and local authorities accepted higher numbers of applicants. Whereas only 55 percent of those who applied for welfare received benefits in 1960, the percentage had risen to 70 percent in 1968. Also, the number of applicants grew spectacularly. In 1960, 745,000 families had received benefits. By 1972, the number had risen to 3 million and federal payments for the program had grown from 1 billion in 1970 to 6 billion in 1972.

While this amounted to less than three months of Vietnam War spending, the numbers provided ammunition for conservative politicians, who blamed rising taxes on a corrupt welfare system.

The agitation of the late 1960s led to the formation of a National Welfare Rights Organization (NWRO), led by activists and academics who advocated a radical transformation of U.S. public policy for the poor. In early 1966, scholar activists Richard Cloward and Frances Fox Piven joined with George Wiley, a leader of CORE, and other antipoverty activists to found the NWRO, which they envisioned as a national organization that would provide leadership, strategies, and coordination for the struggles of the urban poor.

Led by civil rights veterans skilled in the tactics of nonviolent civil disobedience and dismayed by the nationalist and separatist currents developing in

Renowned scholar Frances Fox Piven was one of the founders of the National Welfare Rights Organization. She has written some of the most influential sociological works on poverty, the unemployed, and poor people's movements. *(Frances Fox Piven and Richard Cloward Archives)*

CORE, SNCC, and other civil rights groups, the NWRO developed a guerrilla war strategy of mass mobilization to disrupt public institutions (similar to the unemployed councils disruptions of city halls and welfare bureaus in the 1930s) to maximize political pressures through confrontations. Winning over and recruiting activists in existing antipoverty agencies, especially Volunteers in Service to America (VISTA), which was seen as a domestic Peace Corps, NWRO groups grew rapidly in the late 1960s and led welfare recipients in sit-ins and other protests against welfare offices, but dissipated quickly.

With an anti-organizational outlook similar to groups historically connected to Anarchist movements and an emphasis on relentless pressure-group politics to achieve reforms, the NWRO groups won many short-range victories in terms of expanding benefits for the poor but had no way to consolidate these victories. Campaigning successfully to educate the poor about "special grants" for supplementary benefits that often existed in the local welfare laws, the

NWRO, after gaining many of these increased benefits for welfare recipients, saw welfare departments across the country eliminate them and replace them with flat grants.

Internal leadership conflicts between George Wiley and others over questions of strategy and organization further undermined the NWRO, as did its failure to develop effectively its coalition with the Southern Christian Leadership Conference's Poor People's Campaign, which continued with limited effect under Ralph Abernathy's leadership following the assassination of Martin Luther King Jr. The NWRO and welfare rights activists generally were also harmed by the anti-welfare rhetoric and policies of the Nixon administration, which expanded benefits for many Great Society programs benefiting middle-class groups while it sought to stigmatize the poor and abolish the OEO.

Under Nixon, the Department of Health, Education and Welfare (HEW) began to restrict or reverse rights that AFDC families had gained in regard to access to benefits and privacy protections. Conservative politicians, most notably Governor Reagan of California, whose state, together with New York, contained half of the nation's AFDC recipients, launched campaigns to purge the welfare rolls of "cheaters," introduced more stringent eligibility requirements, and reduced appropriations. In 1969, the Nixon administration itself proposed a far-reaching "welfare reform," to replace the AFDC system with a Family Assistance Plan (FAP), which would provide a minimum federal guaranteed income of $1,600 for a family of four (less than a third of what welfare rights activists regarded as a fair minimum income in most of the country).

Daniel Patrick Moynihan, a former Great Society official whose controversial 1965 report attributing poverty largely to the now discredited "social pathologies" of black families, departed the Johnson administration due to this and other criticisms of the Johnson antipoverty program. He later served as an adviser to the Nixon administration, which believed that increased welfare benefits produced greater numbers of dysfunctional families and would only increase expense and dependency rather than permit the poor to "reform" themselves.

Thus, the argument over "welfare reform" said that the existing system was "destroying" the poor by creating a "permanent underclass." The FAP received a wide variety of opposition from southern conservatives, who found the $1,600 standard too high and a potential threat to the southern low-wage structure.

On May 18, 1970, members of the National Welfare Rights Organization stormed the office of the U.S. Department of Health, Education and Welfare, which Secretary Robert Finch had abandoned. Such direct action aimed to raise welfare benefits and mobilize the poor. *(AP Wide World Photos)*

The program's defeat took place in an atmosphere of mounting political backlash against the "undeserving poor," who were increasingly seen as "welfare queens"—minority women bearing children for the sole purpose of gaining welfare benefits and living dissolute lives subsidized by the taxpayers. When George McGovern ran for president in 1972 with a commitment to provide a guaranteed annual income in the form of a "negative income tax" (cash payments of $1,000 per person to low-income people below a certain level, which would have eliminated the welfare bureaucracy and provided a higher level of support for the poor), the Nixon campaign accused him of threatening to place half the nation "on welfare."

As the Nixon administration found itself em-broiled in the Watergate crisis after 1972, and the "stagflation" economy combined recession and infla-tion, the NWRO collapsed of its own internal and philosophical divisions, and movements of the poor, like all other social movements of the 1960s, save per-haps the environmental movement, found themselves in retreat. The huge inflationary wave of 1974 that followed the so-called energy crisis in the aftermath of the Arab-Israeli War of 1973 and the formation of the Organization of the Petroleum Exporting Coun-tries (OPEC) led debt-ridden cities to launch draco-nian cutbacks of social services. The best example was the New York City fiscal crisis of 1975, which led to the creation of a dictatorial New York State Emer-gency Financial Control Board. The board fired thousands of city employees and raised the cost of public transportation and access to various city facilities. Not only were the reforms advocated by welfare rights activists not instituted, but the value of public assistance payments to AFDC families in real dollars began to decline steeply from the early 1970s to the program's final elimination in 1996.

The 1950s and 1960s had been good times in terms of the national economy. The 1970s and 1980s were not. In spite of attempts to purge welfare rolls and restrict benefits, the "entitlements" under AFDC had seen the number of families rise from 3 million in 1973 to 11 million in 1980, of which 8 million were children.

Low-income women with dependent children found themselves the primary victims of the retreat from the Great Society and were now also blamed for the "welfare mess" as they sought to support children on reduced public assistance grants. Increasingly, two-income families struggled to keep their heads above water on the installment plan as inflation increased interest rates, while female pink-collar workers were in growing numbers compelled to live on public assistance.

THE NEW RIGHT AND THE ATTACK ON THE POOR

By the 1980s, liberal sociologists and some politicians began to write of the "hyper-segregation" of millions of marginalized minority poor living on public assistance in drug- and crime-infested slums without expectation or hope of ever working in the above-ground economy. Although these contentions were exaggerated in that the majority of the poor remained working poor and the majority of those on public assistance went in and out of employment with the vagaries of the economy and the limits of their skills, the crusade against welfare begun by conservative politicians in the 1970s and made into national policy by the Reagan administration greatly increased the hardships of low-income people. It did this primarily by freezing minimum wages, undermining unions, and eliminating housing subsidies, which created a mass homelessness problem for the first time since the Great Depression and generally made life for the bottom 20 percent of income earners far worse then it had been at any time in the post–World War II era.

In the Reagan years, the "new poor," were largely outside of the political process. The great majority were children, who, unlike the majority of low-income adults who do not vote, were not legally entitled to vote. Indeed, even such moderate political scientists

as Walter Dean Burnham noted by the late 1970s that "the massive class skew in electoral participation which is America's chief peculiarity" was growing sharply. By contrast, in Italy, for example, a country with a very strong labor movement and a large working class, 75 percent of people with less than five years of formal education voted.

In the United States, the number was 8 percent. In West European countries, voter participation averaged in excess of 75 percent. In the United States except for presidential elections, the numbers were routinely well below 50 percent, with the nonvoting majority drawn overwhelmingly from low-income people. In the 1980s and 1990s, these trends would continue, producing presidential elections where around 50 percent of the eligible voters voted and off-year congressional elections where the numbers dropped below 40 percent. In state and local elections, the turnouts were even lower, creating elections where the top 20 percent of income earners often constituted a majority.

The top 20 percent of income earners, augmented by members of the religious and socially conservative New Right, constituted the core constituencies of the Reagan administration. The administration in its first term sharply reduced AFDC spending, at a time when the sharpest postwar recession created the highest unemployment since the Great Depression, threw more than 1 million people off AFDC rolls, and reduced benefits for many others. The Comprehensive Employment and Training Act (CETA) jobs program, which the Carter administration enacted in December 1973 to deal with mounting unemployment, was eliminated, removing public jobs for 300,000 people.

Huge tax cuts that benefited corporations, upper-income people, and, to a much lesser extent, moderate-income people, combined with a spectacular rise in military spending to produce runaway deficits, which made the United States, which had been the leading creditor nation of the world from 1919 to the 1980s, the leading debtor nation by 1985. In 1986, for example, the deficit was $283 billion, more than the total deficit had been at the end of World War II. Although unemployment subsided after 1982, and inflation by late 1970s standards was relatively low, nearly half the new jobs created paid wages that were below the poverty line for a family of four. Meanwhile, despite declining wages and the growth of poverty, the administration actively opposed public birth control policies and promoted the much bally-hooed revival of the male-headed nuclear family.

In this atmosphere, new advocacy groups for the

poor, especially the homeless, emerged, but no poor people's movement could or did exist where homelessness joined unemployment as a real menace for the working poor. An author rewriting Edward Bellamy's *Looking Backward*, a treatise on poverty in late-nineteenth-century America, at the end of the 1980s might come to the conclusion that the world of 1988 was actively trying to become the world of 1888. Homeless people were once more on the streets in significant numbers, and religious and secular groups were encouraged to develop food banks, shelters, and other voluntary programs to help them get on their feet. In New York City subways, some of the homeless even hawked a newspaper, *Homeless News*, filled with Horatio Alger and Social Darwinist solutions to their plight and chronicles of their success.

Scandals plagued a new generation of robber barons since they made their money largely through mergers and acquisitions, not through creating industrial corporations that produced goods. As forced urban gentrification drove large numbers of low-income people from rental apartments, the Reagan administration sold off or, in some highly publicized cases, leveled federally supported public housing complexes that it claimed were centers of drug addiction and crime. Urban development programs were reserved largely for the middle class, with federal and local government assistance. Meanwhile, local governments promoted expensive housing for affluent people and supported gentrification and commercial development projects in order to increase their tax base in response to federal government cutbacks.

Just as in the Progressive Era, the plight of children, who now constituted more than two-thirds of those officially poor, rather than child laborers as they had a century before, became a major cause for advocates of the poor. Marian Wright Edelman, leader of the Children's Defense Fund, sought to expose the size and effects of child poverty in the mass media and fight against Reagan and Bush administration policies in Congress and the courts.

Advocates for the homeless engaged in demonstrations, acts of guerrilla theater, and lobbying campaigns to increase welfare benefits for the homeless, improve and expand the capacity of public shelters, and, in cities like New York, restore the system of "welfare hotels," the elimination of which had thrown thousands of their inhabitants into the streets. Unlike the Communist movement–influenced unemployed councils of the 1930s or the civil rights movement–influenced welfare rights campaigns of the 1960s and 1970s, there were no movements involving masses of poor people, as conservative political forces sought to roll back the New Deal and what was left of the Great Society in the last two decades of the twentieth century.

CONTINUED ATTACK AGAINST THE POOR: ROUTINIZATION OF POVERTY AND INEQUALITY

As was true at the end of the nineteenth century, forces seeking to awaken a social conscience and institute reforms concerning poverty competed with anti-immigrant, openly racist groups who blamed economic inequality and stagnation on millions of new non-European immigrants, both documented and undocumented. Of the 20 million new immigrants entering the United States legally since the Hart-Celler Act of 1965 ended the quota system favoring Northern Europeans and largely excluding non-Europeans, about half migrated from Latin America and the Caribbean and a quarter from Africa, Asia, and the Near East.

In states like California, immigrants, both documented and undocumented, became scapegoats for conservative politicians who mounted "English-only" campaigns, opposed bilingual education, campaigned to remove all welfare benefits from undocumented immigrants, and campaigned to sharply restrict benefits for legal immigrants. Patrick Buchanan, a right-wing speech writer in the Nixon and Reagan administrations, made Latino immigrants a central feature in his declaration of a "culture war" against "multiculturalists," minority interest groups, and all others who were undermining the United States as a "European nation" and the principal guardian of Western civilization. In his speeches Buchanan singled out Latinos, saying that in California and the Southwest illegal immigrants named "José" (which he used as a generic epitaph) were taking jobs from American citizens. Buchanan also called for greatly increased border patrols and even suggested the possibility of building an electronic fence across the U.S.-Mexican border to thwart immigrants.

In 1994, anti-immigrant forces successfully passed in a state referendum Proposition 187 in California, which denied illegal immigrants and their children access to public assistance, public education, and healthcare. Calling itself Save Our State (SOS), the petition group, with the support of Governor Pete Wilson and much of the state's conservative Republican establishment, made racist appeals, accusing those who defended the rights of undocumented workers as aiding and abetting an "illegal alien invasion" that threatened to turn California into a "Third World country."

Although the proposition was challenged in the courts and declared unconstitutional by the California State Supreme Court, the sweeping Republican victory in the 1994 congressional elections led to federal enactment of some of its major provisions. Passed by the Republican-dominated Congress, whose most important leader was the skilled conservative House Speaker Newt Gingrich, and signed into law by President Bill Clinton, the Illegal Immigration Reform and Immigrant Responsibility Act (1996) increased the border patrol, expanded Immigration and Naturalization Service (INS) powers to deport immigrants, and sharply increased penalties for illegal immigration.

The legislation upheld that the government would do everything in its power to keep undocumented immigrants out and restrict legal immigrants, but employers were minimally penalized. In fact, employers could report undocumented workers to the INS when they sought improved wages and working conditions.

Millions of low-income, minority, union, and liberal voters (the core groups of the Democratic Party since the 1930s) hoped that they had put an end to the Reagan-Bush era and its war against labor, civil rights, and the poor when they elected Bill Clinton to the presidency in 1992. Within two years, the Clinton administration sharply alienated these groups and opened the door to the restoration of long-term Republican control of Congress for the first time since the 1920s.

First, Clinton's much-trumpeted call for a national health system was defeated by Republicans in Congress with the support of the insurance companies that controlled the private managed care insurance system. Clinton's attempt to enact an economic stimulus package that would have aided labor and the poor was also defeated. As the administration went from one defeat to another, it was obvious that the president was not able to enact key legislation.

DISMANTLING THE WELFARE STATE

Clinton's failure to promote a progressive social agenda and his support of the North American Free Trade Agreement (NAFTA) created disillusionment and malaise both within the labor movement and among liberal Democrats. In a campaign filled with attacks on his administration, including references to White House corruption and sex scandals, the Republicans, issuing a conservative manifesto they called a "Contract with America," in 1994 regained control of both houses of Congress for the first time since 1954 in an election where 38 percent of the eligible voters went to the polls.

In his 1992 election campaign, Clinton had made the vague promise to "end welfare as we have known it." While many of those who voted for him assumed he meant a return to Great Society job training and education programs, along with a more tolerant approach to welfare recipients, none of this materialized in the first two years of his administration. When the Republican majority came forward with legislation to eliminate AFDC and put into law the view that welfare was itself a major social problem, not a solution to poverty, Clinton divided his own party and supported them. That the president was running for reelection in August of 1996, when the legislation was signed, may have explained his behavior.

Assaults on the welfare state had permeated the mass media since the Nixon administration, became national policy in the Reagan administration, and after a quarter of a century, served as conventional wisdom in U.S. politics. The poor were still the largest group of nonvoters, and children ineligible to vote were the majority of those receiving AFDC benefits. Also, Clinton knew that those most hostile to welfare reform would not vote against him and bring conservative Republican Bob Dole into the White House.

The term *welfare reform,* used by both the Republican majority and the Clinton administration, covered up what was essentially the first full-fledged removal of a major social guarantee of the New Deal era.

Minimum wages had been frozen in the Reagan-Bush era, but not abolished, as some conservatives had wished. Social Security and unemployment benefits had also been restricted but not eliminated. Unions were weakened tremendously, but the NLRB system remained in place against any attempt to revert to the antilabor abuses that were routine in the pre–New Deal era. Called the Personal Responsibility and Work Opportunity Reconciliation Act (PRWORA), the legislation eliminated the AFDC, with its "safety net" concept, and replaced it with a Temporary Assistance to Needy Families (TANF) program, which would provide block grants to states, with a five-year limitation on benefit payments to individuals.

Block grants were used widely in the Reagan administration to undermine federal social programs by both reducing their funding and turning over, in the

On March 23, 1995, police arrest antipoverty leaders—including National Organization for Women president Patricia Ireland (far right)—for protesting welfare reform proposals under consideration by Congress. The proposals were enacted into law in 1996. *(AP Wide World Photos)*

form of the grants, decisions as to the distribution of funds to state authorities. The PRWORA abandoned entirely in theory and practice the AFDC principle that public assistance was part of a "safety net" below which people would not be allowed to fall. The legislation made putting recipients to work as quickly as possible its highest principle, without regard to the value of the work or its effects on workers. Along with the five-year limitation on benefits, recipients were required to find some work within the first two years or lose support. Those who could not find work in the private sector were compelled to work in "workfare" programs for their benefits (without minimum wage protections) in public sector jobs, or be removed from the rolls. Previous rules, which allowed women receiving AFDC benefits to attend college, were removed and replaced with narrow vocational education.

While welfare rolls were reduced sharply to the delight of conservatives and the Clinton administration, researchers by the end of the twentieth century were citing the grim human costs of "welfare reform" for those willing to listen. First, the General Accounting Office of Congress reported that the wages earned by those who had left the welfare system for jobs were on average below the poverty level and, for many, well below that level. Reports also showed that more than 25 percent of those who got jobs soon lost them. Like the old system, but without its security, large numbers of people went on and off TANF hoping that their five years of eligibility would not run out. Many also found their health benefits far more haphazard than under AFDC Medicaid. One news story at the end of the Clinton years highlighted the case of a Brooklyn, New York, woman working at a job in order to keep her health benefits for herself and her family. Fearing the loss of those benefits if she lost her job, she delayed seeking medical attention and died of a condition that may have been treatable had she sought medical assistance earlier.

"Welfare reform" did spark a revival of organizing among the poor at the end of the twentieth century. While the PRWORA cut off welfare benefits to legal immigrants, the American Federation of Labor-Congress of Industrial Organizations (AFL-CIO), under the leadership of the reform-oriented John Sweeney, revived with limited success organizing drives among low-income workers. It also reversed labor's historic opposition to immigration by seeking to organize undocumented workers and actively defending both their rights and the rights of legal immigrants.

Labor also vigorously protested the attempt by many city administrations to replace municipal workers with "workfare" clients. New York, the nation's largest city, was the worst offender in this regard. After the passage of PRWORA, Mayor Rudolph Giuliani removed through attrition and other means 22,000 municipal workers and replaced those in unskilled positions in sanitation, city parks, hospitals, and welfare offices with workfare clients. At the same time, since PRWORA barred benefits for higher education, more than 20,000 recipients formerly under the AFDC system dropped out of the City University of New York. Critics noted that New York paid less than 15 percent of the wage of a full-time unionized municipal employee to workfare workers and no benefits.

Community-based welfare rights groups sprung up throughout the country to resist welfare reform, reviving many of the tactics of the Welfare Rights Organization of the 1960s. Perhaps the most significant was the Philadelphia-based Kensington Welfare Rights Union (KWRU), founded a few years before "welfare reform" by Cheri Honkala, a former "welfare mother" committed to building an alliance between welfare recipients and the labor movement. Using civil rights nonviolent civil disobedience tactics and the disruptions of NWRO groups, KWRU launched a Poor People's Economic Human Rights Campaign, affiliated itself with the American Federation of State, County, and Municipal Employees (AFSCME), which has a large female membership, and used sit-ins, tent cities of the poor, and other time-honored tactics and peaceful picketing of welfare offices to publicize their view that public assistance was a human rights issue.

Honkala became a national leader of the Labor Party, a new party founded by progressive trade unionists, which has made a constitutional amendment to establish the right to a job as a major issue. Honkala led a Freedom Bus across the country in 1998 to show increased urban and rural poverty. At the end of the national fact-finding tour, Honkala and KWRU leaders brought the findings, including the accounts of the poor themselves, to the United Nations (UN) to argue that U.S. policy toward the poor constituted a violation of the United Nations' 1948 Charter on Human Rights.

The election of 2000 produced little discussion of poverty or the rights of poor, except in Ralph Nader's Green Party campaign for president, which called for repeal of the Taft-Hartley law and highlighted the disastrous effects of public policy on the nation since the election of Ronald Reagan in 1980. Certainly, the low turnout and the active campaign to keep poor and minority people away from the polls by the Republicans in Florida contributed to George W. Bush's victory in the electoral college, even though he received more than 500,000 fewer votes than Democratic presidential contender Al Gore.

Although millions of potential Nader voters returned to the Democratic fold by election's end, Ralph Nader's nearly 3 million votes represented the most important challenge to establishment politics, raising questions of the rights of labor, minorities, and the environment since Henry Wallace's 1948 campaign. The combined Nader-Gore vote represented a solid victory over the combined Bush-Buchanan vote, however irrelevant that might be in the electoral college.

The crushing defeat of the 2000 Republican ticket in California, a state that pioneered in anti-welfare, anti-immigrant politics for much of the last four decades of the twentieth century, was seen by some as a harbinger of future politics. Latino voters in larger numbers than ever before voted against politicians whose stock in trade had been to scapegoat them as illegal immigrants and the undeserving poor. (In the state's ever-changing political climate, however, Republican Arnold Schwarzenegger was elected governor in the October 2003 recall vote without the majority support of Latinos.)

Although the turnout remained abysmally low, the decisive defeat of the Republican ticket in states like Illinois, Michigan, and New Jersey, and a much greater than usual defeat in New York, suggested that those states that, together, house a majority of those on public assistance, and a disproportionate number of low-income "working poor," had turned sharply away from the anti–social welfare anti-taxation philosophy that Ronald Reagan made the center of U.S. domestic policy, George Bush faithfully continued, Bill Clinton softened, and George W. Bush has attempted to harden.

Both presidential and congressional majorities for conservative and Republican politics now depend on a new Solid South, along with agricultural, mountain, and Southwestern Taft-Hartley "right to work" states. A labor–poor people's political coalition could perhaps once more make social welfare, social justice, and social equality, into principles and policies at the center of American politics.

The damaging effects of September 11 on the ability to organize and mobilize against poverty are unquantifiable. Large increases in military spending will not likely trickle down to the poor. Moreover, efforts to increase the rights of immigrant workers through organizing low-wage workers from Latin America, China, and South Asia could be halted by the ongoing efforts to significantly expand internal security agencies and reduce the formal rights of noncitizens and those citizens who associate with them. Although the future of the poor people's movement remains uncertain, the poor continue to mobilize to improve their conditions on an everyday basis, which inevitably will lead to a new surge of organizing and militancy in the future.

Norman Markowitz

BIBLIOGRAPHY

Barbuta, Domenico. *American Settlement Houses and Progressive Social Reform: An Encyclopedia of the American Settlement House Movement.* Phoenix: Oryx, 1999.

Bartlett, Donald, and James Steele. *What Went Wrong?* New York: Simon and Schuster, 1992.

———. *America: Who Really Pays the Taxes?* New York: Simon and Schuster, 1994.

Bernstein, Irving. *The Lean Years: A History of the American Worker, 1920–1933.* Boston: Houghton Mifflin, 1960.

Brown, Elaine. *A Taste of Power: A Black Woman's Story.* New York: Anchor Books, 1994.

Burnham, Walter Dean. *Critical Elections and the Mainsprings of American Politics.* New York: Norton, 1970.

Carter, Dan. *From George Wallace to Newt Gingrich: Race and the Conservative Counter-revolution.* New Orleans: LSU Press, 1999.

Churchill, Ward. *Agents of Repression: The FBI's Secret Wars Against the Black Panther Party and the American Indian Movement.* Boston: South End, 1988.

Cleaver, Eldridge. *Soul on Ice.* New York: McGraw-Hill, 1967.

Cleaver, Kathleen, and George Katsiaficas, eds. *Liberation, Imagination, and the Black Panther Party: A New Look at the Panthers and Their Legacy.* London: Routledge, 2001.

Davis, Mike. *City of Quartz.* New York: Vintage Books, 1992.

Doherty, John L., comp. *Lewis Wickes Hine's Interpretive Photography.* Chicago: University of Chicago Press, 1978.

Feldstein, Stanley, and Lawrence Costello, eds. *The Ordeal of Assimilation: A Documentary History of the White Working Class.* Garden City, NY: Anchor, 1974.

Ferriss, Susan, and Ricardo Sandoval. *Fight in the Fields: Cesar Chavez and the Farmworkers Movement.* New York: Harcourt Brace, 1997.

Foner, Philip. *History of the Labor Movement of the United States.* Vol. 1. New York: International, 1947.

———. *The Panthers Speak.* New York: International, 1995.

Georgakas, Dan Detroit. *I Do Mind Dying: A Study in Urban Revolution.* Cambridge, MA: South End, 1998.

Goodwyn, Lawrence. *Democratic Promise: The Populist Movement in America.* New York: Oxford University Press, 1976.

Jones, Charles, ed. *The Black Panther Party Reconsidered.* Baltimore, MD: Black Classic, 1998.

Katz, Michael. *In the Shadow of the Poor House: A Social History of Welfare in America.* New York: Basic Books, 1996.

Kelley, Robin D.G. *Yo Mama Is Dysfunctional.* Boston: Beacon, 1997.

———. *Hammer and Hoe: Alabama Communists during the Great Depression.* Chapel Hill: University of North Carolina Press, 1990.

Lee, Chana Kai. *For Freedom's Sake: The Life of Fannie Lou Hamer.* Urbana: University of Illinois Press, 1999.

Moynihan, Patrick. *Maximum Feasible Misunderstanding.* New York: Free Press, 1969.

Murray, Charles. *Losing Ground.* New York: Basic Books, 1984.

Patterson, James. *America's Struggle Against Poverty, 1900–1980.* Cambridge, MA: Harvard University Press, 1983.

Naison, Mark. *Communists in Harlem During the Depression.* New York: Grove, 1983.

Phillips, Kevin. *Arrogant Capital: Washington, Wall Street, and the Frustration of American Politics.* Boston: Little, Brown, 1994.

———. *Wealth and Democracy, a Political History of the American Rich.* New York: Broadway Books, 2002.

Piven, Frances Fox, and Richard A. Cloward. *Poor People's Movements: Why They Succeed, How They Fail.* New York: Pantheon Books, 1977.

———. *Why Americans Don't Vote.* New York: Pantheon Books, 1988.

Roberts, Dorothy. *Killing the Black Body.* New York: Pantheon Books, 1997.

Rosales, F. Arturo. *Chicano: The History of the Mexican American Civil Rights Movement.* Houston, TX: Arte Publico, 1997.

Savage, David. *Turning Right: The Making of the Rehnquist Supreme Court.* New York: John Wiley, 1992.

Schwantes, Carlos. *Coxey's Army: An American Odyssey.* Lincoln: University of Nebraska Press, 1985.

Terkel, Studs. *Hard Times.* New York: Pantheon Books, 1970.

Theoharis, Jeanne, and Athan Theoharis. *These Yet to Be United States: Civil Rights and Civil Liberties in America since 1945.* Belmont, CA: Wadsworth/Thompson Learning, 2003.

Torres, Andres, and Jose Velasquez, eds. *The Puerto Rican Movement.* Philadelphia: Temple University Press, 1998.

Zinn, Howard. *A People's History of the United States.* New York: HarperCollins: 1996.

Zuchino, David. *The Myth of the Welfare Queen.* New York: Scribner, 1997.

SETTLEMENT HOUSE MOVEMENT

An offshoot of Christian Socialist theory and experiments in communitarian approaches to meeting the needs of the urban poor already in operation in Britain, the settlement house movement in the United States was a response to rapid urbanization and industrialization and the changing face of labor at the end of the nineteenth century. The movement thrived from the 1890s through the end of World War I. It provided a foundation for a spectrum of Progressive social reform causes and campaigns primarily designed to better the lives of immigrants, tenement dwellers, and sweatshop and factory workers who increasingly populated American cities.

THEORY AND ORIGINS

With many exceptions, settlement house movement activists were primarily college-educated reformers of Anglo-American descent; among them were religious men and many able women. In tackling problems like dilapidated and crowded housing, exploitative work conditions, lack of sanitation, and inferior education, they sought to implement improvements through political means and the application of social-scientific methods. Many gained inspiration from the example of Samuel Barnett's Toynbee Hall (which had opened in 1884 in the East End of London) and approached their work with a secularized sense of missionary calling.

In theory, the leaders of the movement embraced the idea of the mutual good and enlivened democracy that could come from native-born middle-class reformers living and interacting among the ethnic immigrant poor. They were keenly interested in replacing older models of charity and philanthropy with models of direct interaction across cultures and classes—an arrangement thought to fulfill the potential of the privileged as much as benefit those they came to serve.

Among the first settlements founded in the United States (in 1889) were Jane Addams's Hull-House in Chicago and the New York College Settlement on the Lower East Side of Manhattan. The New York College Settlement was begun as the first experiment of the College Settlement Association, which had been organized by Vida Scudder and a small group of Smith College alumni and soon involved other graduates of eastern women's schools. By 1893, Lillian Wald's Henry Street Settlement was founded in New York, with a particular emphasis on public health and nursing.

In the next two decades, hundreds of settlement houses and neighborhood agencies were created across the country, but the movement was centered primarily in the cities of the Midwest and Northeast. The National Federation of Settlements (founded in 1911) helped coordinate the movement's direction and concerns.

SETTLEMENT INNOVATIONS AND SERVICES

Influenced by the teaching of John Ruskin, William Morris, and others, several settlements placed an emphasis on the uplifting power of aesthetics and opportunities for self-expression as well as practical matters of achieving greater social equity. The residents of Hull-House, in particular, established a wide range of cultural as well as social programs to help elevate the lives of the primarily Irish, Italian, Greek, Russian, Polish, and eastern European immigrants whom they served. They sponsored ethnic festivals, encouraged appreciation of traditional crafts such as embroidery and weaving, taught pottery making and book arts, and offered studio space to artisans trapped in the daily drudgery of factory production. Musical evenings were offered as neighborhood entertainment, and community theater productions were mounted. Meanwhile, settlement supporters worked for the incorporation of music and the arts into public school curricula.

JANE ADDAMS (1860–1935)

Jane Addams was a leader of the settlement house movement in the United States and a key public proponent of Progressive Era reform. As an intellectual and activist, she helped formulate the Progressive response to urbanization and industrial capitalism. Through her many writings and her work as a negotiator and as a founder and leader of organizations, she influenced public consciousness and created a groundswell of popular support for a multifaceted reform agenda. In the World War I era she became a leading organizer of the international peace movement.

Addams founded Hull-House in Chicago with Ellen Gates Starr in 1889 and directed the settlement until the end of her life. In addition to her local work in education, sanitation, and civic reform, she was a national leader within the suffrage and women's rights movements and an advocate for the labor movement and social justice causes. Among the hundreds of organizations in which she was an officer or had a founding role were the National Women's Trade Union League, the National Federation of Settlements, the National American Woman Suffrage Association, and the National Association for the Advancement of Colored People. She was a stalwart, along with her friends Florence Kelley, Julia Lathrop, and other allies, in lobbying campaigns for protective labor legislation, factory and consumer regulation, the living wage and the eight-hour day, children's rights, and juvenile justice.

Many of the programs Addams originally advanced as an activist were codified in the 1920s and 1930s through the professionalization of social work, the passage of state and federal reform legislation, increased gains for unionization and collective bargaining, and the creation of New Deal agencies. They were revisited in the antipoverty programs of the 1960s.

As a champion of cultural pluralism, nonpartisan mediation, and a maternalist brand of feminism, Addams was alternately criticized for being too moderate and too radical. She devoted the last portion of her life to the peace movement, arguing the connection between militarism, poverty, and political repression. Her opposition to intervention by violent means alienated her from many of her former activist colleagues who supported entry by the United States into World War I. Building on her ties in the American Union Against Militarism (later the American Civil Liberties Union) and international networks of suffrage supporters and women reformers, she helped convene and chaired the International Congress of Women at The Hague, which gathered together over 1,500 women from a dozen European countries and the United States in April 1915 in opposition to the war. She subsequently led the delegation from the congress to meet with the heads of warring nations to urge nonviolent resolution. Through this activism was born the International Committee of Women for Permanent Peace, which became the Women's International League for Peace and Freedom (WILPF) in 1919. Addams served as its president until her death in 1935. During the 1920s, WILPF strongly supported the principles of international alliance and economic aid manifested in the League of Nations. In explicit recognition of her role in creating an international women's peace movement, Addams was awarded the Nobel Prize for Peace in 1931.

Addams was much buoyed in her public career by her decades-long relationship with Hull-House patron and volunteer Mary Rozet Smith. She died of cancer in Chicago in 1935 in the midst of the Depression and was buried in her hometown of Cedarville, Illinois.

Addams's writings include *Democracy and Social Ethics* (1902); *Newer Ideals of Peace* (1907), *Twenty Years at Hull-House* (1910); *Women at the Hague* and *The Overthrow of the War System* (both with others, 1915); *Peace and Bread in Time of War* (1922); and *Why Wars Must Cease* (with others, 1935). Swarthmore College and the University of Illinois, Chicago, hold major collections of her papers, including settlement house and peace movement records. The *Jane Addams Papers* microfilm edition includes those materials as well as others from hundreds of repositories.

Barbara Bair

Encouraging literacy, debate, and literary appreciation were other aspects of settlement life. Settlement volunteers organized lending libraries, book clubs, and lecture series. They offered newly arrived immigrants and striking workers literacy courses and English-language training, and they helped facilitate lifelong learning and stimulate political discussion by sponsoring working people's debating societies.

Child welfare, early child development, and education were a special focus of the settlement house movement from its inception. Settlement teachers offered innovative approaches to kindergartens and day care. They opened gymnasiums, led physical education classes, and urged cities to establish playgrounds, parks, and open spaces. They sponsored boys and girls clubs, offered field trips to rural settings and museums, and ran afternoon and summer arts and recreation programs for children. Parenting skills and family health care were a closely related concern. Settlement workers organized mothers' clubs and taught cooking, sex education, and nutrition classes. Some settlements operated dispensaries (free or low-cost medical clinics) and pharmacies, or helped provide home health and midwifery services, as well as access to job training or work referral services.

Although a majority of settlement services were directed at immigrant neighborhoods, some settlements operated separate branches for black residents. In African-American neighborhoods, community-based social services were implemented through mutual aid societies and neighborhood associations and, later, through such organizations as the National Urban League (founded in New York in 1911), which provided services to migrating workers. The Phyllis Wheatley Settlement in Minneapolis and the White Rose Mission and Industrial Association (founded in New York in 1897 by Victoria Earle Matthews) were created to provide residences for young African-American women entering the city to work. The White Rose Home offered a distinguished lecture series, a kindergarten, and training classes in skills that would gain women jobs in domestic service, which then was the leading job sector for African-American working women. In Atlanta, Lugenia Burns Hope, the founder of the Atlanta Neighborhood Union, was one of the prominent activists in the settlement and municipal reform movements.

MUNICIPAL REFORM AND LABOR ACTIVISM

Beyond the boundaries of their wards, settlement activists were instrumental in instigating civic reform as well as in supporting organized labor. They helped expose corruption in city politics, develop community gardens, provide sanitation to tenement alleys, improve public health, and monitor safety and work conditions in factories and sweatshops. Settlement houses were used as meeting places for arbitration and union meetings and as clearinghouses for information during strikes, most importantly during general strikes in the needle trades in New York and Chicago in 1909–1911. In coalition with the National Women's Trade Union League (WTUL), the International Ladies' Garment Workers' Union, and other labor organizations, settlement activists and their wealthy patrons (many of whom were also supporters of the suffrage movement) helped provide legal aid

and food relief as well as a middle-class presence on the picket lines, in the jails, and in the courtrooms. Leading women labor organizers like Mary Elisabeth Dreier, Margaret Dreier Robins, Leonora O'Reilly, and Mary Kenney O'Sullivan all had close ties to the settlement movement, and many were also advocates of feminist causes.

BROADER REFORM

Settlement movement members were deeply involved outside their own cities as leaders in the wider social justice movements of their day. Beyond the labor and public health movements, they helped foster the suffrage and temperance movements, consumers' rights, and, increasingly in the World War I era, the international peace movement. Founding and working within reform organizations like the National Consumers League, the National Child Labor Committee, the Immigrants Protective League, the Juvenile Protective Association, and the WTUL, they helped mount anti-vice and anti-prostitution campaigns, supported protective labor legislation (including restrictions on work hours and child labor), and were primary advocates for juvenile justice, penal reform, and pure food and drug laws, as well as vocal critics of civic corruption—all functions that earned them the title of "civic housekeepers." Others, especially those who worked closely with the labor movement or who had emerged primarily out of the Anarchist and Socialist movements, were dedicated to a more militant and radicalized brand of social change.

TRANSITIONS, LIMITATIONS, AND DECLINE

Although many settlements still exist in modern form as neighborhood centers and community-based anti-poverty agencies, the settlement movement as a whole began to decline markedly in the 1920s.

In many ways, the movement was phased out by its own success. Many of the kinds of social services and educational, investigatory, and regulatory functions first provided by settlement workers—or created through their political lobbying and support—were superseded by the routinizing of city services and the burgeoning of a social welfare state. Reforms once pioneered through the settlements were absorbed into the formal operations of governmental agencies (such as the U.S. Children's Bureau, created in 1912), incorporated into public school systems, or legalized through federal and state legislation (such as the Sheppard-Towner Act, passed in 1921). During Franklin D. Roosevelt's administration, many settlement innovations were bureaucratized in the programs of the New Deal.

The social conservatism of many of the old-elite leadership of the settlement movement and an essential blindness to the negative economic consequences of many of their programs—from protective legislation to housing codes—sometimes proved a barrier between activists and the working poor they sought to benefit. Top-down policies that movement leaders advocated also sometimes crossed the line between social reform and social control. Established leaders failed to adequately delegate or yield internal positions of power to immigrant women within the hierarchies of settlement leadership, and their settlement microcosms did not reflect the very kind of ethnic diversity at top levels that they theoretically championed in society at large. The settlement movement failed to meet the needs of a changing city population; namely, to adequately extend its vision of democracy from ethnicity and cultural pluralism to race. Despite the presence of some settlements in African-American neighborhoods, and the overlap between the movement and such organizations as the National Association for the Advancement of Colored People, the national movement was effectively segregated, to the virtual exclusion of African-American concerns, and local agencies were often so poorly funded that they were short-lived.

Just as frustration with the prescribed roles and relations of women helped foster the power of the settlement movement, so did wider opportunities for middle-class and working women help signal its decline. The advent of coeducation, the ratification of the Nineteenth Amendment granting women the vote, the rise of social work as salaried labor, the opportunity for some positions of responsibility in city and federal bureaucracies and within union leadership, and a renewed social emphasis on marriage attracted potential residents to other options and made low-paid or volunteer work and collective living appear less desirable. As Judith Ann Trolander has pointed out, as social work was professionalized, settlement work also changed in nature, becoming increasingly clinical and masculinized. The original emphasis on children was lost, as was the milieu of communalism and alternative lifestyle. Neighbors instead became clients. Immigration restriction, racial violence and polarization, and the social consequences of World War I with its antipacifism and the breakdown of alliances between liberals and the American Left also took its toll. Private systems of funding broke down. And generations changed. The proper Victorian behavior and elitist ideas of aesthetic uplift manifested among many of the old-school settlement house leaders distanced them from young working girls for whom dance halls, theaters, and other sources of mass entertainment were among the joys of life. Working people and the poor began increasingly to speak for themselves. The movement's original leaders grew elderly, and the focus of advocacy changed for many of them from local and national to international concerns.

Barbara Bair

BIBLIOGRAPHY

Addams, Jane. *Twenty Years at Hull-House.* New York: Macmillan, 1910.

Barbuto, Domenica M. *American Settlement Houses and Progressive Social Reform: An Encyclopedia of the American Settlement Movement.* Phoenix, AZ: Oryx, 1999.

Carson, Mina. *Settlement Folk: Social Thought and the American Settlement Movement, 1885–1930.* Chicago: University of Chicago Press, 1990.

Davis, Allen F. *Spearheads for Reform: The Social Settlements and the Progressive Movement, 1890–1914.* New York: Oxford University Press, 1967.

Muncy, Robyn. *Creating a Female Dominion in American Reform, 1890–1935.* New York: Oxford University Press, 1991.

Philpott, Thomas Lee. *The Slum and the Ghetto: Immigrants, Blacks, and Reformers in Chicago, 1880–1930.* Belmont, CA: Wadsworth, 1991.

Trolander, Judith Ann. *Professionalism and Social Change: From the Settlement House Movement to Neighborhood Centers, 1886 to Present.* New York: Columbia University Press, 1987.

Wald, Lillian. *Windows on Henry Street.* Boston: Little, Brown, 1934.

THE UNEMPLOYED ORGANIZE

When the U.S. stock market crashed on "Black Thursday," October 29, 1929, few people would have predicted that the economy would remain stagnant for another twelve years or that a second world war would be responsible for reinvigorating U.S. industry and the economy. The years between Black Thursday and the Japanese attack on Pearl Harbor on December 7, 1941, marked the beginning and end of the period referred to as the Great Depression. Some of the most significant economic policies, including Social Security and unemployment insurance, were implemented during this decade under President Franklin D. Roosevelt's (1933–1945) New Deal initiatives. By the time the United States declared war on Japan and officially entered World War II, the government had assumed the role of caretaker of its citizenry to a degree unthinkable prior to the stock market crash. After having weathered the 1930s, the majority of U.S. citizens believed that the government should provide a safety net for its citizens so that great numbers of them would never again suffer long-term unemployment, homelessness, and starvation.

Sheer desperation forced most people to change their minds about governmental intervention. It took many years of debate, discussion, and protest, however, for the people to agree that Franklin Roosevelt's New Deal policies were necessary. Prior to the onset of the Depression, Presidents Calvin Coolidge (1923–1929) and Herbert Hoover (1929–1933) and the majority of the presidents before them subscribed to the theory of laissez-faire economics, albeit in different ways and to different degrees. Supply, they thought, would adjust to demand, and vice versa; the federal government should not directly intervene in the economy even in times of crisis. Even two years into the Depression, President Hoover advised people to do their best to weather the current period of instability. Eventually, the market would balance itself. In a statement representative of Hoover and his advisers'

thinking, historian Franklin Folsom in *Impatient Armies of the Poor: The Story of Collective Action of the Unemployed, 1808–1942* (1991) writes that Charles W. Schwab, chairman of the board of Bethlehem Steel, advised people in 1931 to "Just grin, keep on working, stop worrying about the future and go ahead as best you can. We always have a way of living through hard times."

PRIVATE CHARITY AND GOVERNMENT RELIEF

Government relief was, for Hoover, simply out of the question. Private charities, which had for generations provided food, shelter, and clothing for the needy in times of distress, should continue to carry the burden of providing relief. Even though private agencies were quickly overwhelmed, Hoover refused to commit federal resources to provide relief to the poor. He believed that doing so, even temporarily, would set a dangerous precedent. Citizens would quickly become dependent on the government dole and lose not only their motivation to work but also their competitive spirit. Competition and innovation were, for Hoover, the hallmarks of American industry. He refused to authorize government relief payments because he believed dependence on the dole would dampen that spirit and create a lethargic and hopeless citizenry. Eventually, even Hoover conceded that some amount of governmental intervention was unavoidable. He did not, however, authorize Congress to devote monies to feeding, clothing, or providing shelter for the growing numbers of homeless in the United States. Instead, and in line with his philosophy, Hoover created the Reconstruction Finance Corporation to prevent further bank closures. Voters thought he offered too little too late. Roosevelt won the election of 1932 by promising Americans a "New Deal" and by offering people hope that the government would indeed

On March 8, 1933, the Emergency Unemployed Relief Fund distributed $27,000 to 1,300 desperate men in New York. *(Brown Brothers)*

intervene and that their dire situations would improve as a result.

By the time Roosevelt took office in 1933, the United States had suffered through three years of economic depression. Although Roosevelt disliked the idea of increased government intervention, unlike Hoover, he believed desperate circumstances required desperate measures and he took action. As governor of New York, he had committed state funds to help relieve suffering, and he intended to continue to do so with federal funds as president. The U.S. government, according to Roosevelt, had an obligation to intervene. Furthermore, developments worldwide suggested to him and his advisers that government intervention might prevent radical political movements from gaining a foothold among the more desperate of the population. Extremists on the left and the right had supplanted ruling bodies in Russia, Germany, and Italy during the 1910s and 1920s. If the U.S. government wanted to prevent revolutionary movements or Fascist dictatorships from gaining a foothold, it needed to provide some reason for its people to remain loyal. Roosevelt's fears were not unfounded. In the months after the stock market crashed, Communists, Socialists, and other radical groups gained popularity, especially among the desperate unemployed whose numbers grew at an alarming rate between 1929 and 1933.

The economic collapse of the 1930s witnessed the largest percentage of unemployed, and the largest corresponding movement of the unemployed, in U.S. history. During 1933, the worst year of the Depression, the first year of Roosevelt's presidency, the unemployment rate reached just over 25 percent. Even those lucky enough to find a job often worked less than full time. Widespread unemployment and underemployment created what historian Irving Bernstein calls a society "adrift." People who grew up during the Depression remembered moving "all of the sudden" to follow leads on jobs, because they were evicted from their apartments, or because they lost their homes. Men left their wives and children for months at a time to find work. Many men and women traveled by freight train creating the popular image of the wandering "hobo." Eviction and foreclosure caused people to take any available shelter. One woman recalled that she and her family lived in a garage for seven years. Others were not as lucky. A number of squatter settlements derisively labeled "Hoovervilles" in honor of then president Herbert Hoover emerged as increasing numbers of people lost their jobs and were evicted. One survivor of the Depression described a Hooverville in Oklahoma City that measured ten miles square. People, she recalled, lived in rusted-out car bodies, made shacks out of orange crates, and lived in holes in the ground. Others remembered constant hunger and the threat of starvation; hospitals routinely treated people who fainted from hunger. In order to escape the bitter cold of the winter months, still others migrated to southern states to avoid the freezing temperatures.

UNEMPLOYED ACTIVISM

People coped with the Depression in a number of ways. While many moved around in search of employment, others became apathetic. Most relied on family members, neighborhood associations, and churches to help make ends meet and turned to private charities only after they had exhausted all of their resources. People were ashamed to ask charities for money or food. Only the "pariahs" of society, namely, paupers, beggars, drunkards, and prostitutes, depended on relief. Turning to the almshouse or workhouse, the most common public relief agencies in existence in the early years of the Depression, was viewed as a last resort, and yet, as the Depression worsened, even these institutions-of-last-resort were overwhelmed with requests. As people realized that the economic slump was not short-term or temporary, as President Hoover predicted, feelings of desperation and hopelessness took over. Irving Bernstein includes in *A Caring Society: The New Deal, the Worker, and the*

Great Depression: A History of the American Worker, 1933–1941 (1985) the observations of two people who witnessed that hopelessness take over in New York and Chicago. Herman Shumlin, a Broadway producer, described the despair engraved on the faces of the men he saw waiting in breadlines: "I'd see that flat, opaque, expressionless look that spelled . . . human disaster." Similarly, Lewis Andreas, a medical doctor, described a march of the unemployed down Chicago's Michigan Avenue:

> A very scraggly march of the unemployed. Just a mass of people flowing down that street. In their minds, I think, a point was reached: We're not gonna take it anymore. I remember it particularly because of the silence. No waving of banners, no enthusiasm. An undercurrent of desperation.

Organizing and participating in a parade, march, or other demonstration designed to draw attention to your own condition of destitution was not easy. Yet desperation drove people to take action. Sociologists Frances Fox Piven and Richard Cloward find that some of the earliest expressions of discontent among the unemployed consisted of mob looting. People began to simply demand food. For example, 300 people in Henryetta, Oklahoma, demanded that a local storekeeper give them food and insisted that they were not begging. In New York City, 1,100 men broke out of the bread line they waited in to mob delivery trucks scheduled to deliver baked goods to a hotel nearby. According to Piven and Cloward, the organized looting of food became a nationwide phenomenon.

In addition to mob looting, people began in the early months of 1930 to demand that local governmental offices provide relief. In the years following the stock market crash of 1929, a number of groups emerged to organize protests against rising unemployment, to demand that the government respond more aggressively to the Depression, and to simply find ways to help the poor survive. Historian Roy Rosenzweig estimates that over 2 million people engaged in some form of protest in the 1930s. Radical political organizations were at the forefront of the early unemployment movements in the United States. Communists, Socialists, and the lesser-known Musteites—followers of labor leader Abraham J. Muste—for example, organized demonstrations and parades and formed unemployment councils and workers' committees to combat unemployment. They also helped people obtain relief, avoid eviction, and find work, without the stigma more often associated with asking charitable associations for assistance. Communists, Socialists, and other radical groups were so popular during the early years of the Depression that Rosenzweig argues in a 1975 article, "Radicals and the Jobless," that, in 1933, "radical revolution seemed as likely as liberal reform."

Although only about 5 percent of the unemployed participated in organized movements, those who did challenged both the societal assumptions regarding the causes of joblessness and poverty and the capitalist system itself. Given the assumptions that had to be overcome, it is perhaps not surprising that the first organized efforts to challenge the condition of unemployment were waged by the Communist Party. The Communists organized the unemployed in the United States and other countries throughout the 1920s, focusing on the jobless in what historian Daniel Leab, in a 1967 article, "United We Eat," calls "chronically depressed" areas. In the months after the stock market crash, the Party gained popularity and expanded its efforts. Using the slogan "Fight Don't Starve," Communists began to organize unemployment councils in industrial centers throughout the United States. Communist Party organizers found recruits for the unemployment councils on bread lines, outside factory gates, in "flophouses," and outside relief offices. Housewives participated in Communist-inspired demonstrations in which they carried empty pots and pans.

One of the Communist Party's more successful organizing efforts of the early 1930s was the International Unemployment Day it held on March 6, 1930. Earlier that year, people had staged successful demonstrations in Chicago, Philadelphia, and Cleveland. The Communist Party decided to organize a demonstration to protest growing unemployment worldwide. Piven and Cloward report in *Poor People's Movements: Why They Succeed, How They Fail* (1977) that rallies and marches were held more or less simultaneously in most major cities in the United States. One of the larger and more volatile demonstrations of the day occurred in New York City, where over 35,000 people gathered in Union Square to protest widespread unemployment. Organizers had promised the police that the demonstrators would remain in Union Square. When thousands of people began to march toward City Hall, New York City, police rushed into the crowd with clubs. People described the ensuing confrontation as a "scene of battle." Despite or perhaps because of the violence, Mayor Jimmy Walker formed a committee soon thereafter to collect and distribute funds to the unemployed.

The New York City demonstration exhibited another characteristic unique to Communist organizing efforts of this period. Not only were Communists among the first groups to make demands on behalf of the unemployed, but they also paid particular attention to the unique circumstances African Americans found themselves in during the Depression. Few organizations in the United States in this period acknowledged the fact that, as bad as the Depression was for the men who had been accustomed to a steady income, it was much worse for African-American men and women who suffered from high levels of unemployment and underemployment during times of prosperity. In preparation for International Unemployment Day, Communists organized the Upper Harlem Council of the Unemployed and purposefully recruited African-American unemployed workers to participate in the protest. Historian Mark Naison, in *Communists in Harlem during the Depression* (1983), finds that Communists, by using slogans like "Negro-White Unity," made "blacks feel welcome in New York's first protest against Depression conditions."

GROWING POVERTY AND RISING RESISTANCE

The period 1931–1932 witnessed several similar marches in different locations throughout the United States as people began to demand that the government do something about the widespread distress caused by growing unemployment. Some of the marches were spontaneous, others locally organized, and still others a result of the efforts of the Communist Party. In March of 1932, Communists spearheaded a march of unemployed auto workers in Detroit known as the Ford Hunger March. The auto industry suffered enormously after the stock market crashed. Prior to the crash, auto factories produced over 5 million cars. By 1932, they were producing only 1.5 million. As a result, people in Detroit experienced the devastating effects of widespread unemployment earlier than people in most other cities. They had exhausted all of their resources and faced mass evictions and foreclosures on their homes by 1931. In November 1931, unemployed auto workers staged a hunger march on the Briggs plant in Detroit. The Communist-sponsored Unemployment Council in Detroit proposed that a similar and larger march take place at Ford. Unemployed workers numbering 3,000 gathered a short distance from the Ford employment office, located in nearby Dearborn, on March 7, 1932. As they marched toward the office, they carried signs that read "Give Us Work" and "Tax the Rich and Feed the Poor." Dearborn police arrived on the scene, along with some guards from Ford's private security force, to disperse the crowd. They fired tear gas into the crowd and threatened to shoot. The unemployed responded by throwing stones at the police. More police were called in, and eventually shooting broke out. Five people died and several were wounded before the hostilities ended. The ensuing funerals gained national press coverage. The *New York Times* reported that more than 30,000 people attended the funerals.

Just months later, some of the Ford marchers joined veterans of World War I in perhaps one of the most well known unemployment demonstrations of the early 1930s. Again organized largely by Communists, "Bonus Marchers" marched at the Capitol building from as far away as Portland, Oregon, to demand that the government pay them their war bonuses early. Thousands of unemployed, mostly men, some with their wives and children, made their way to Washington on foot, by train, or by any means possible. Most, one observer recalled, were middle-aged and middle-class men, all now unemployed. They wore overalls or their old military uniforms. Franklin Folsom, in *Impatient Armies of the Poor*, describes a contingent traveling by freight car from Minnesota. The contingent posted a sign outside the car that read, "Pennsylvania Railroad #36865—Destination Washington, contents livestock, 55 veterans."

Once they arrived in Washington, it was clear that many of the veterans intended to stay. Even though some accepted President Hoover's offer to pay their way home, most of the veterans chose to stay in Washington. Some lived in abandoned buildings throughout the city, but most gathered in an area southeast of the Capitol called Anacostia Flats and set up a "Hooverville" within view of the Capitol building. Estimates of how many people lived in Anacostia Flats varied widely from as low as 11,000 to upward of 22,000. Nevertheless, it is clear that thousands of people gathered at the Capitol on June 17, the day before Congress was to adjourn, to demand their bonuses. President Hoover not only refused to meet the veterans' demands, but he sent the U.S. Army to disperse them from the Capitol and to level the settlements at Anacostia Flats. General Douglas MacArthur commanded the troops who threw tear gas into the crowd and set fire to their belongings. The public was outraged. Some blamed the Communists for inciting a riot. Others blamed Hoover for not responding to the needs of the unemployed. According to Piven and

Cloward, a reporter for the *Washington News* voiced his disgust over the situation, writing "What a pitiable spectacle is that of the great American Government, mightiest of the world, chasing men, women, and children with Army tanks. . . . If the army must be called out to make war on unarmed citizens, this is no longer America."

Communists also began in 1930 to organize resistance to evictions. Small bands of people would use strong-arm tactics to prevent city officials from putting people's furniture out on the street. The Communists' Unemployed Councils were particularly active in combating evictions in Chicago where members would meet each morning and wait to hear who in the neighborhood had been evicted. Once they got word, they would go, as a group, to the evicted person's apartment and simply carry furniture back into the residence. City officials, marshals, and police found it difficult to counter the actions of the Unemployed Councils because, at least at that moment, the person who had removed the furniture was outnumbered. Members of the Chicago Unemployed Councils were often arrested and occasionally beaten for their actions. Eventually, however, the mayor of Chicago ordered a moratorium on evictions, and some of the unemployed eventually found work on the city's relief rolls.

In effect, the Communists launched a multipronged attack against unemployment. In addition to demonstrations and anti-eviction action, they also turned people's utilities back on and helped them apply for the limited relief that was available. The Unemployed Council's "gas squads" and "electric squads" went to people's houses after their utilities were turned off because of nonpayment and simply turned them back on. The "electric squads" simply rerouted wires around electric meters to reestablish the connection. Communists also helped people apply for relief. A woman in New York City recalled standing in line for three days "in the rain" outside the Home Relief Bureau with no success. After the Unemployed Council intervened on her behalf, she received a rent check one week later. Communists were particularly successful in obtaining relief payments for people because relief workers were not accustomed to dealing with aggressive, organized tactics. Most of the people who applied for relief were ashamed, meek, and generally not very demanding because of the stigma associated with being "on the dole."

Other politically motivated groups organized demonstrations and helped the unemployed make ends meet. The Socialist Party, for example, organized

Unemployed Leagues and Workers Committees. Unlike the Communists' Unemployed Councils, the Socialists' Leagues and Workers Committees drew upon the already existing network of settlement houses, ethnic neighborhood associations, and churches to organize their efforts. Socialists were particularly successful in Chicago, where, by 1931, they operated eight locals on Chicago's northwest side alone. By 1932, there were sixty Workers Committees operating in the city representing over 35,000 members. Like the Communist groups, the Socialist-sponsored groups helped people obtain relief and also attended to other immediate needs. They helped families in Chicago obtain coal for their furnaces and gain admittance to local hospitals when they needed medical attention. Also in 1932, the Socialists organized 35,000 people to protest a pending decision by Chicago authorities to cut the amount of relief the city distributed. Not only did Socialists help people successfully navigate the local relief system, but the Chicago Board of Public Relief agreed to have its local supervisors meet with members from the Socialist Workers Committees to discuss the needs of the unemployed in their respective areas.

Unlike Communist organizations, which lost some momentum by 1934, Socialists gained momentum throughout the early 1930s. Historian Roy Rosenzweig argues in a 1979 article, "Socialism in Our Time," that, by 1935, Socialists had organized "a locally based unemployment movement of significant dimensions" in New York, Pennsylvania, Indiana, New Jersey, Maryland, and Oregon. Rosenzweig finds that at that point Socialists claimed as many as 450,000 "adherents." In addition to continuing to obtain immediate relief for the unemployed, Rosenzweig argues that the Socialist Party's efforts "raised the political and social consciousness of its members by altering their views about public relief, by introducing them to principles of trade union organizing, by fostering interracial cooperation, and by reinforcing weakened bonds of community solidarity."

Finally, another movement-oriented group that deserves mention is the "Musteites." The Musteites, like the Communists and the Socialists, were a left-oriented group that followed the philosophy of Abraham J. Muste, a prominent labor leader. In the early 1930s, Musteites worked more closely with Socialists and trade unionists than with Communists. In fact, in some locations, the Musteites organized unemployment leagues in direct opposition to the Communist-sponsored Unemployed Councils. One of the more significant of the Musteites' contributions to the fight to combat widespread unemployment came in 1929 when they organized the Conference for Progressive Labor Action (CPLA). The CPLA launched a successful educational campaign the next year to promote unemployment insurance. It also joined with the Unemployed Citizens' League in Seattle, a movement of several thousand jobless, both to protest growing levels of unemployment and, like the Communists and the Socialists, to obtain food and supplies and help people apply for relief. In 1932, the CPLA and the Seattle-based Unemployed Citizens' League obtained 120,000 pounds of fish, 10,000 cords of firewood, and eight carloads of potatoes, pears, and apples from local merchants. Merchants either donated the food or had the unemployed work for them in exchange.

The Musteites, like the Socialists, organized unemployment leagues in various locations. Despite early success in Seattle, they sustained the most support in Ohio and Pennsylvania. In August of 1933, the Musteite-sponsored unemployed leagues in Ohio marched on the state capitol building in Columbus to demand more state aid. Musteites reached the height of their success in the spring of 1933, just as President Roosevelt took office. At that point, in Ohio alone, the Musteites had organized 187 unemployed leagues with over 100,000 members. In Pennsylvania, they had organized over 40,000 members into unemployed leagues. The Musteites, even more than the Socialists and Communists, found it difficult to gain a national following. They attempted to hold a national convention in Ohio in 1933, but fights broke out when the Musteites refused to recite the Pledge of Allegiance. A group took the podium in response and called the Musteites "reds." The group advised the attendees to come back the next day and pledge their support to both America and to "a militant fight for the jobless." One Musteite organizer recalled that even people who did not mind being called "reds" were reluctant to join the organization because being labeled a "red" or a "radical" made it even more difficult for them to find jobs. By 1934, the Musteites had lost a great deal of support. They had trouble raising enough money to buy gas for their cars and the postage necessary to distribute information about unemployment, much less to sustain a movement.

CONCLUSION

As Roosevelt's New Deal initiatives took hold during his first term in office, the Socialists gradually began to operate as a "national lobby for higher relief appropriations." Ironically, the Socialists' and Communists' success in influencing Roosevelt and his New

Deal policies proved responsible for both organizations' diminished popularity as the 1930s wore on. Many people began to look not to these radical political organizations but to Roosevelt and to the U.S. government to solve their problems. To Hoover's horror, Roosevelt delivered. Within two months of taking office, the new president set up the Federal Emergency Relief Administration (FERA) to dispense relief directly. He also put people to work by creating the Civilian Conservation Corps and the Works Progress Administration. Unlike Hoover, Roosevelt did not shy away from government intervention. His New Deal programs combined direct relief payments with government-sponsored employment and were intended to feed people, put them to work, and get the economy moving.

Although New Deal initiatives did alleviate some suffering and put many people to work, they failed in significant ways. Those people who suffered the worst from the Depression, namely, sharecroppers and tenant farmers in the South, were excluded from New Deal initiatives. Furthermore, New Deal policies failed to fully reinvigorate the economy, and the unemployment rate remained high throughout the 1930s. Nevertheless, once Roosevelt began to thoroughly commit the government to providing relief for its citizens, there was less need for Socialist- and Communist-inspired lobbying efforts, protests, electric squads, eviction parties, and others of their more successful programs. People began to believe in their government again. Roy Rosenzweig, in "Socialism in Our Time," describes the loyalty exhibited by jobless miners who "displayed the Blue Eagle, symbol of FDR's recovery program, on the entrance to the abandoned coke ovens they used as homes." Despite a loss in popularity and despite the fact that their efforts did not, as the Communists hoped, spur a worldwide revolution against capitalism, Socialists, Communists, and Musteites were very influential in publicizing the plight of the unemployed and in demanding that the U.S. government take action on their behalf. Coming together under the umbrella of the Socialist-organized Workers Alliance of America, the three groups became, according to Roy Rosenzweig, "FDR's left force." They maintained an agreement with Harry Hopkins, who administered the FERA, "to always ask for more" than they knew Roosevelt would give.

Whether Communist, Socialist, or Musteite, their efforts were both needed and appreciated. Each of these groups gained members simply by providing the help other agencies, whether private, local, charity, or religious, did not provide or were too overwhelmed to provide. Historians and contemporaries alike argue that the greatest contribution of these radical movements of the early 1930s was that they were the only organizations to step to the forefront to help alleviate the suffering of the poor. Rosenszweig relates Albert J. Muste's assessment of the situation at the time: "When you looked out on the scene of misery and desperation during the depression, you saw it was the radicals, the left-wingers . . . who were DOING SOMETHING about the situation, who were banding together for action, who were putting up a fight." Once Roosevelt took office and initiated New Deal programs that were designed with similar intentions, the Communists, Socialists, and Musteites lost a great deal of support. In the end, people preferred a reformed capitalist system to the revolution that radicals advocated.

Lisa Phillips

BIBLIOGRAPHY

Bernstein, Irving. *A Caring Society: The New Deal, the Worker, and the Great Depression: A History of the American Worker, 1933–1941.* Boston: Houghton Mifflin, 1985.

Folsom, Franklin. *Impatient Armies of the Poor: The Story of Collective Action of the Unemployed 1808–1942.* Boulder: University Press of Colorado, 1991.

Leab, Daniel J. " 'United We Eat:' The Creation and Organization of the Unemployed Councils in 1930." *Labor History* 8 (1967): 300–315.

Naison, Mark. *Communists in Harlem during the Depression.* Urbana: University of Illinois Press, 1983.

Piven, Frances Fox, and Richard Cloward. *Poor People's Movements: Why They Succeed, How They Fail.* New York: Pantheon, 1977.

Rosenzweig, Roy. "Radicals and the Jobless: The Musteites and the Unemployed Leagues, 1932–36." *Labor History* 16 (1975): 52–77.

———. " 'Socialism in Our Time:' The Socialist Party and the Unemployed, 1929–36." *Labor History* 20 (1979): 485–509.

TENT CITY MOVEMENTS

At the turn of the millennium, the phrase "tent city movements" has increasingly come to denote intentional communities organized by the homeless. These communities serve both as an alternative to sleeping on the streets or in regimented shelters, and as a form of political protest against the material conditions and social policies that create and perpetuate homelessness.

HISTORICAL BACKGROUND

The numbers of homeless or precariously housed Americans grew in the nineteenth and twentieth centuries along with industrial capitalism, urbanization, fluctuating labor markets, and an inadequate housing supply. Workers moved to areas that promised jobs, where the tight housing supply was marginally supplemented by working-class families taking in boarders and slumlords expanding spaces within already densely packed tenements. Skid rows became centers for the urban indigent, featuring cheap hotels and restaurants, single room occupancies (SROs), missions, and hiring halls. Men, women, and children without shelter huddled near heated grates on city streets, depended on passing boxcars for transportation and bedding, or joined fellow homeless in ramshackle shantytowns erected near cities' edges. Local governments alternated between tolerating transients during periods of labor demand and enforcing vagrancy and other laws to rid their communities of the homeless.

In the early decades of the twentieth century, transient male laborers often erected "jungles" or tent camps near dumps, railroad crossings, and rivers, far from officials' eyes. These encampments ultimately became important venues for the organizing efforts of the era's most legendary labor union, the Industrial Workers of the World (IWW), who with Western harvest and timber workers shared leads on work and agitated for workplace justice and the end to the domination of capital.

Workers evicted from company or landowner housing for strike and organizing activity often created tent cities for emergency shelter and to maintain community solidarity in their collective protests. Evicted from their homes during the 1913–1914 strike against Colorado Fuel and Iron, owned by Rockefeller's Standard Oil Corporation, coal miners and their families created the Ludlow tent colony to protest labor conditions. On April 20, 1914, National Guard troops fired into tents and burned the colony to the ground, killing two women and eleven children. The incident, known as the Ludlow Massacre, prompted demonstrations across the country against Standard Oil.

During the Depression, the numbers of homeless, hoboes, and encampments ballooned. While the self-governing "Hoovervilles" of the 1930s were rarely the site of radical organizing on behalf of the poor, their name and visibility came to signify the president's indifference and the federal government's failure to address the problems of joblessness and poverty.

The "Bonus Army" of 1932 created the most famous tent city of the period, erected for explicitly political goals, as 25,000 unemployed men camped at the edge of the nation's capital, demanding early payment of their military service bonus. The Hoover administration sent the army to disband and destroy the protest. Troops burned the Bonus Army homes and the transients' hopes that the federal government would assist them.

Other protests emerged out of the ranks of the unemployed in the 1930s, resisting evictions and refuting the notion that the jobless were responsible for their condition. Demands for federal assistance led the New Deal to aid homeless and unemployed workers through the Federal Transient Bureau and the Farm Security Administration, which created rural work camps. Still, most cities in the 1930s tried to send transients on their way and toughened vagrancy laws.

In the 1930s, when Southern sharecroppers and tenant farmers, like supporters of the Southern Tenant Farmers Union, were thrown off the land for organizing, they sought solidarity in makeshift tent camps. Even as late as 1960 in Fayette County, Tennessee, white property owners evicted more than 400 African-American tenant families for participating in the Fayette County Civic and Welfare League, which had initiated a voter-registration drive. With support of an African-American property owner, the families formed a community known as "Tent City." A smaller tent city arose in nearby Haywood County, where dozens of families had also been evicted for their political work. The Justice Department filed suit against landowners and merchants in Fayette County who had violated the civil rights of the tenants, and in July 1962 they were enjoined from interfering with the rights of citizens to vote.

MODERN TENT CITY MOVEMENTS

Post–World War II efforts to renew downtown areas, in decline because of suburbanization, often targeted skid row areas, traditional haunts of low-income people and transients. "Planning" and "renewal"—or gentrification—of urban cores translated into intensified struggles for poor people in need of housing. The demolition or conversion of SROs, which accelerated in the 1970s and 1980s, deindustrialization, deinstitutionalization, and defederalism combined to swell the ranks of the homeless, which included unprecedented numbers of women, children, and families. At the same time, officials, often pressured by merchants and new upper-income city residents, increasingly cracked down on the presence of the homeless and supported anti-homeless legislation.

This struggle over urban spaces catalyzed new forms of activism to challenge existing inequities and champion new housing policies. In the immediate aftermath of the assassination of Martin Luther King Jr. in April of 1968, the Southern Christian Leadership Conference spearheaded the "Poor People's Campaign" that culminated in the creation of an encampment on the Washington Mall. The central goal of "Resurrection City," which housed approximately 2,500 protesters, was to pressure the Johnson administration to fulfill the promises of the much vaunted War on Poverty. On June 24, police and National Guardsmen forcibly disbanded the protesters' community, arresting hundreds.

The 1970s marked the emergence of several important groups that built on the momentum of the Poor People's Campaign. Unions for the homeless

sprung up in Philadelphia, Chicago, Baltimore, Boston, and Los Angeles, demanding living wages and affordable housing. Activist Mitch Snyder and Washington, D.C.'s Community for Creative Non-Violence, brought national attention to the struggles of the homeless, leading pray-ins, eat-ins, and the occupation of buildings. Similar groups such as Seattle's Operation Homestead, formed in many cities; while for the most part focusing on local issues and strategies, activist groups occasionally joined forces to influence national policy. The National Coalition for the Homeless, founded in 1984, organized 250,000 to appear in Washington, D.C., in October 1989 with its Housing Now! March. These actions combined with litigation by advocates pressured Congress to hold hearings and support a patchwork of new programs in the 1980s, but the government provided little funding for new housing.

Building on historical efforts by the homeless to assert autonomy through independent communities, the modern tent city movement has taken a stand to highlight the lack of affordable housing and to reclaim public spaces that have increasingly excluded the poor. Since the 1980s, tent cities have materialized in cities as diverse as Las Vegas, San Diego, San Jose, and Corpus Christi. Tent city activists have built on elements of the civil rights, women's, gay liberation, environmental, and poor people's movements to draw attention to their marginalization and inability to obtain minimal shelter, and to create solidarity in a self-governing community. Some tent cities were designed as short-term political protests. Homeless activists, for example, erected tent cities in front of the Illinois, California, and Washington state capitols to lobby for funding. Others have sought to create more permanent communities to provide an alternative model of shelter that fosters self-governance, empowerment, and autonomy.

The pioneers of the contemporary tent city movements are vocal critics of the shelter system, and more broadly of charity-based approaches to poverty; furthermore, they frequently examine the systemic roots of homelessness, critiquing capitalism and the high unemployment rates that sustain it. Residents of tent cities argue that their itinerant housing provides a preferable alternative to overcrowded and unsanitary shelters and more effective security for their few remaining material possessions. Tents and lean-tos, however ramshackle, tend to provide greater privacy than is afforded in most shelters. Tent communities, moreover, embrace both gay and straight couples, and in some cases, children, while shelters almost universally enforce gender segregation while excluding same-sex couples. In addition, while nationally only a handful of shelters allow pets, they are a visible feature of tent city landscapes. While the majority of shelters are open to residents only at night, tent cities accommodate the variable hours of the working poor.

At the same time, residents emphasize that the collective nature of tent city living protects them from assault. They note that, while crimes perpetrated by "transients" receive amplified media attention, crimes against the homeless go largely unreported in local and national media and are frequently acknowledged only in the pages of the country's approximately thirty newspapers published by and for the homeless. Notably, within days of the forced closure of the Las Vegas tent city in July 2001, a former resident of the encampment was severely beaten and robbed by three assailants, and another homeless man was beaten to death.

Homeless activists erected tent cities with pointed political goals to move individuals out of the relative isolation of urban doorways to become a more visible presence to city officials and residents. Many of these efforts have negotiated small victories, including city promises to expand shelter beds and housing units. In 1993, the city of Eugene sanctioned a three-year experiment to allow the homeless to camp on a parking lot near the University of Oregon's Autzen Stadium. When funding ran out, the Centennial Car Camp closed, but the city was forced to continue to allow some scattered legal camping on unused public parking lots. Squatters who created Camp Paradise in Santa Cruz refused to budge for a year until in early December 2001 a rainstorm flooded away the tent city. Although police had ticketed the campers, the city did not aggressively pressure the camp to disband and after the flood provided motel vouchers until the campers could find a new site. The camp's success in garnering much local support inspired city council members to reform Santa Cruz's homeless services, including allowing a homeless campground.

More often, the tent city movement has met resistance from neighbors, police, and elected officials. In 1991, officials disassembled a Santa Ana, California, camp after allowing it to exist for a year, and in 1992, Marin County, California, officials shut down a camp that sprang up after the city closed a National Guard Armory shelter. As the homeless have been driven out of some spaces and ingeniously occupy other public sites, city officials enact new rules or conduct sweeps. When over a hundred people living in Tompkins Square Park on Manhattan's Lower East Side pro-

Squatters—people who take over abandoned land or property—seized this building in New York City before being evicted by police in 1995. *(AP Wide World Photos)*

tested the city's efforts to remove them, the city closed and fenced off the park for "renovations." The police in Washington, D.C., tore down temporary shacks erected each day in Lafayette Park. San Francisco, which by the early twenty-first century had gained the reputation as the most hostile city in America toward the homeless, alternated its methods of removing the homeless just as quickly as the homeless found new places to camp. In December 2001 officials fenced off the area that had housed a tent city under Highway 101.

It is not simply the transitory nature of the accommodations that garners resistance from local communities and authorities. In fact, officially sanctioned tent cities have long been embraced as an answer to housing and prison shortages, to attract low-wage laborers, and to house state troops called to quell civil dissent. In Alaskan fishing towns like St. Petersburg, city-sanctioned tent cities have long served to accommodate seasonal workers. In California, in the absence of both affordable conventional housing and sustainable wages, 1,100 state-sanctioned and licensed tent cities serve a fraction of the state's estimated 700,000 migrant farm workers on a seasonal basis. In the late 1990s, as an answer to overcrowded jails, Phoenix, Arizona, launched a pilot tent city jail, housing as many as 1,580 inmates. What distinguishes the embattled tent cities of otherwise homeless individuals from these provisional accommodations is the extent to which they visibly signify their collective rejection of officially sanctioned strategies for managing the poor and as a critique of the social and economic conditions that create and perpetuate homelessness.

WEST COAST EFFORTS

Although cities grew determined to eliminate encampments of more than a few people, a number of coalitions persisted on the West Coast to sustain the new tent city movement. Three tent cities have been the most visible and have served as models for other embryonic efforts.

In January 1985, activist Ted Hayes and seventy-three homeless men, women, and children established a shantytown in Central City East, or Skid Row, in Los Angeles. From its inception, "Justiceville" had strained relations with city authorities and social service providers alike. Despite efforts by advocates and a thirty-five-day fast by Hayes, the city closed Justiceville/Homeless, USA, on May 10. For the next eight years LA's homeless, including former members of Justiceville, lobbied government and businesses and engaged in civil disobedience to demand attention to the plight of the homeless. In November 1993 the Dome Village, originally known as Genesis One, opened as an innovative effort to provide a structural alternative for those unable or unwilling to live in traditional shelters. The twenty Omni-Sphere domes softened the harsh downtown skyscraper landscape and provided community and living spaces for many shunned by traditional service providers. The self-governing project sought to empower and engage residents in productive activities to help transition them out of homelessness. The village spawned a number of micro-enterprises, created a CyberDome computer learning center, and cultivated an organic garden.

During the Goodwill Games held in Seattle in the summer of 1990, a group of homeless men and women decided to camp out on the waterfront in clear view of tourists and the city's major daily newspaper. To underscore the need for affordable housing, on Thanksgiving activists created a tent city beside the Kingdome, which prompted city officials to provide more indoor shelter space. Campers organized as the

Seattle Housing and Resource Effort (SHARE) and formed alliances with churches and other community groups, including the homeless group Operation Homestead, to address the need for low-income housing. SHARE organized shelters, laundry and storage facilities, and new housing units. In 1993, a group of women within SHARE formed Women's Housing Equality and Enhancement League (WHEEL) to advocate for homeless women's concerns.

As in other cities, Seattle's homeless made some headway while seeing other gains erode. Activists periodically camped out in front of municipal buildings to demand lodging lost by redevelopment efforts in the 1990s. As a new mayor in 1998 held a housing summit to address the needs of the homeless, his police force began its regular bulldozing of campsites above I-5. In response, SHARE/WHEEL reconstituted Tent City on Beacon Hill in June. Even as police closed the site, Mayor Paul Schell promised new funds to eliminate homelessness. SHARE set up two more tent communities in 1999 to provide shelter during the WTO protests; this time activists, banding together with advocates from local faith communities, strategically located their encampment on church properties to strategically resist the city government's attempts to raze the settlement.

When winter response shelters closed in March 2000, the group again raised a tent city, which persisted through thirteen forced moves by the city on threats of zoning violations against private landowner hosts. In August, El Centro de la Raza invited the tent city and its 100 residents to locate at its center for the next six months. Because the city rejected El Centro's application for a tent-city permit, residents moved to a church and battled the city in court. In September 2001, a King County superior court judge ruled that because the military, Scouts, and disaster-relief groups had histories of establishing safe encampments, the city could not discriminate against the homeless group's permit efforts. A new federal law that appeared to allow churches to ignore land-use codes while engaged in religious practices also strengthened Tent City's cause. In March 2002, Seattle and Tent City representatives signed an agreement that allows the community to remain in one commercial or residential spot for up to three months.

Influenced by the Los Angeles and Seattle movements, Portland's latest tent city movement was initially catalyzed by a Multnomah County circuit court decision in September 2000. Striking down the city's ban on outdoor camping, which dated back to 1981, Judge Stephen L. Gallagher ruled that the ordinance

Staking tents beneath an overpass, homeless people built the community of Dignity Village in Portland, Oregon, in 2001. *(Photo by Bryan Pollard)*

constituted "cruel and unusual punishment," and effectively punished "the status of being homeless" and impeded homeless people's right to travel. With the city intent on appealing the decision, on December 16, 2000, with support from *street roots*, a nonprofit newspaper largely staffed and distributed by homeless people and covering issues of concern to the homeless, a core group of eight homeless individuals pitched their tents on public land under the Morrison Bridge in downtown Portland. Despite Gallagher's decision, the threat of arrest impelled five early moves even as the "camp's" population steadily grew, until a formal agreement was struck with the city authorizing the camp's temporary location under a freeway.

The relative stability of new, albeit temporary, legitimacy enabled the birth of Dignity Village, as residents created community coalitions and partnerships, held press conferences, teach-ins, and public meetings, and developed a website to foster more effective

outreach to the immediate community, as well as to other national and international tent cities. Villagers worked in concert with University of Oregon architectural students and with the City Repair Project to develop architectural plans for a permanent settlement at a fraction of the cost of conventional low-income housing. The plans included communal gardens, a "piazza" for gatherings, wind power generators, composting toilets, and a gray water irrigation system as an expression of the village's ecological consciousness and commitment to sustainability.

Forced in September 2001 to relocate to a fenced enclosure abutting the city's leaf composting yard outside the city center, with the help of City Repair, Portland's Rebuilding Center, Americorp volunteers, and other supporters in the community, the village erected a communal hall and domed conference room out of salvaged materials. In the spring, villagers banded together with Portland's Environmental Middle School, greenscaping the blacktop with communal vegetable beds and container gardens scattered throughout.

The village has variously participated in arts and theater projects, has entertained a barrage of local and international reporters interested in its experiment in community, has fashioned a partnership with a Japanese tent city, and is the site of a literacy project in partnership with Washington State University Vancouver. In February 2004, Portland city officials granted the village campground status, making it legal for the sixty residents to remain in their self-regulated tent community.

Homeless advocates debate whether tent cities can ultimately affect larger social change needed to address the lack of affordable housing in the United States. Others worry that the attention and resources devoted to the camps will detract from other efforts to develop adequate and humane emergency and long-term low-income housing. The latter argument, which tends to focus almost exclusively on the quality of housing, generally fails to adequately acknowledge the challenge that tent cities, with their emphasis on self-determination, pose to the country's core political assumptions. It must be noted, however, that many homeless themselves prefer shelter beds or more independent living on the streets to tent city accommodations. But tent city activists believe that they are creating community and "homes," while engaged in a political project to draw attention to homelessness.

Desiree Hellegers and Laurie Mercier

BIBLIOGRAPHY

Barak, Gregg. *Gimme Shelter: A Social History of Homelessness in Contemporary America.* New York: Praeger, 1991.

Blau, Joel. *The Visible Poor: Homelessness in the United States.* New York: Oxford University Press, 1992.

Casey, Juliet V. "Three Attack, Beat Homeless Man." *Las Vegas Review-Journal,* July 3, 2001.

Crouse, Joan M. *The Homeless Transient in the Great Depression: New York State, 1929–1941.* Albany: State University of New York Press, 1986.

Dignity Village (Portland, OR). http://www.outofthedoorways.org/index/html.

Dome Village/Justiceville (Los Angeles, CA). http://www.domevillage.org/dm/new/index/htm.

Gaura, Maria Alicia. "Paradise Lost: Santa Cruz's Shantytown Flooded Out." *San Francisco Chronicle,* December 9, 2001.

Kaiman, Beth. "Roving Tent City Can Build on Its Legal Foundation." *Seattle Times,* March 28, 2002.

Lelchuk, Ilene. "City Closes Homeless Tent Town." *San Francisco Chronicle,* December 5, 2001.

Olsen, Lise. "Incentives Help Workers' Camps but Shantytowns Remain a Fixture." *Seattle Post-Intelligencer,* July 23, 1998.

Riddle, Amanda. "Arpaio Opens Tent City for Juveniles." *The Associated Press State & Local Wire,* November 9, 1998.

SHARE/WHEEL Tent City (Seattle, WA). http://www.insideshare.org/tentcity.

Weinman, Richie. "The Village Grows, the Dignity Dwindles." [Portland] *Oregonian,* November 25, 2001.

General Index

Epstein, Abraham, **4:**1240
Equal Employment Opportunity
    Commission (EEOC), **1:**161; **2:**400
    Clinton's appointments to, **1:**246–247
Equal Pay Act (1963), **2:**369
Equal Rights Amendment (ERA),
    2:364–365, 373–376, 402
Equal Rights (journal), **2:**364
Equal Rights Party, **3:**1117
Equality Begins at Home, **4:**1371
Equality (journal), **3:**957
Equality League of Self-Supporting
    Women, **1:**301
ERA. *See* Equal Rights Amendment
Era Club, **1:**314
Erdman Act (1898), **2:**537
Erdrich, Louise, **2:**754–755
ESL. *See* English as a Second Language
Espionage Act (1917), **3:**1045, 1068,
    1074
Ethical Culture
    decline of, **3:**1011
    founder, **3:**1007
    and labor movement, **3:**1009–1010
    leaders, **3:**1009
    legacy, **3:**1011–1012
    new leadership, **3:**1010–1011
    philosophy, **3:**1007
    Settlement Houses, **3:**1009–1010
    and social reform, **3:**1008–1009
Ethnic Studies, **4:**1209
Ethnocentrism, **3:**1121–1122
Ethology, **4:**1313
Ettor, Joseph, **2:**529, 530
EU. *See* European Union
Eugene (Oregon), homeless camp, **3:**1154
Eugenics movement
    American Eugenics Society, **3:**901
    historical roots, **3:**899–900
    ideology, **3:**900–901
    Margaret Sanger and, **2:**356–358;
        3:901
    opposition to, **3:**902–903
    reform, **3:**903
    revival of, **3:**903–904
    target populations, **3:**901–902;
        4:1246–1247
European Union (EU), **4:**1459, 1467
Evan, Thomas, **3:**1079
Evangelicalism
    abolition movement and, **1:**19–20,
        31–32, 49–50, 52
    labor movement and, **2:**466
    politics and, **4:**1402
    women and, **3:**948–949
    See also Christianity

Evangelism
    Oxford Group Movement and,
        3:908–909
    televised, **3:**951
Evans, George Henry, **2:**469, 470
Evans, Hiram, **4:**1437
Evans, Romer v. (1996), **3:**854; **4:**1325,
    1352, 1366
Everett Massacre, **2:**531
Everglades, **2:**746
Evers, Medgar, **1:**184, 185
Evictions of planters, **3:**814–816
Evolution
    Darwinism, **3:**934
    teacher arrested for teaching, **3:**950
    theories of, **3:**899–900
Ex-Gay Movement, **4:**1371
Exodusters Movement, **1:**114; **3:**773–776
Exotic Dancer's Union, **3:**861
Experimental Negotiating Agreement,
    2:546

F

"The Factory Bell" (poem), **2:**470
"Factory Girl's Reverie" (fiction),
    2:689–690
Factory inspections, **1:**319
Factory work, **1:**315–317, 324–325
    Lowell System rules, **2:**465
    women in, **2:**505
Fair Employment Practices Committee,
    1:152, 161, 168, 202; **2:**541
Fair Labor Standards Act (1938), **2:**369,
    374–375, 522
Fair Trade Coffee campaign
    coffee crisis, **4:**1497–1499
    competition and sustainability,
        4:1501–1502
    ethical consumption and fair trade,
        4:1499–1500
    making a fair trade market,
        4:1500–1501
    overview, **4:**1497
Fairfax, Francis, **4:**1380
Fall, Albert, **2:**703
Faludi, Susan, **2:**433
Falwell, Jerry, **3:**855, 856; **4:**1400, 1402
Familistere, **1:**287
Family and Medical Leave Act (1993),
    2:655
Family Assistance Plan, **3:**1132–1133
Family planning. *See* Birth control
    movement
Family Research Council, **4:**1404
Family roles, 1830–1840, **1:**19

Family values
    post–World War II, **2:**370
    Religious Right and, **3:**852
Fantasia Fair, **4:**1381
Farah Manufacturing Company, **2:**685
Fard, Wallace D., **1:**145, 229; **3:**935–936
The Farm, **3:**1005, 1024–1025
    See also Gaskin, Stephen
Farm Animal Reform Movement,
    4:1316
Farm ownership, **3:**822–823
Farm Sanctuary, **4:**1316
Farm Security Administration, **1:**166;
    3:1125
Farm worker boycotts, **2:**683–685
Farm Workers Labor Movement,
    3:822–834
Farmer-Labor Party, **1:**350; **3:**818–821
Farmers' Alliance Movement, **3:**783–786
Farmers' Protective League, **3:**826
Farming, organic, **3:**1017
Farrakhan, Louis, **1:**230, 241, 242–243;
    4:1210
FAS. *See* Federation of American
    Scientists
Fashion industry
    sweatshop labor and, **2:**554
    See also Women's clothing
Father Divine, **3:**953–954, 1005
Faubus, Orval, **1:**180
Fauntroy, Walter E., **3:**1104
Fauset, Crystal Bird, **2:**367
FBI. *See* Federal Bureau of Investigation
FCC v. Pacifica Foundation (1978), **3:**850
Federal Administration on Aging,
    4:1242
Federal Bureau of Investigation (FBI)
    and American Indian Movement,
        2:711, 712, 714, 715–723
    and Black Panthers, **1:**200, 203,
        213–214, 233; **2:**715; **3:**1130
    COINTELPRO. *See* COINTELPRO
    and Industrial Workers of the World,
        2:531
    investigation of Martin Luther King
        Jr., **1:**188
    during McCarthy era, **1:**169, 171
    and militia groups, **4:**1441
    RESMURS investigation, **2:**719–721
    surveillance of Vietnam War
        activists, **3:**1095; **4:**1187–1188
    and Wounded Knee siege (1973),
        2:712, 714
Federal Bureau of Narcotics, **3:**873
Federal Coal Mine Health and Safety
    Act (1969), **2:**646, 649

Milk, Harvey, **4**:1356
Millennialism, **3**:943, 969–970
Miller, David, **3**:1089
Miller, Elizabeth Smith, **1**:269
Miller, Herman, **3**:904
Miller, William, **3**:931
Miller v. California (1973), **3**:848
Miller v. Johnson (1995), **1**:248
Millet, Kate, **2**:407
Million Man March, **1**:242–243; **2**:396
Mills, Samuel, **1**:13
Milwaukee Leader (newspaper), **3**:1074
Mime Troupe, San Francisco, **3**:1022
Mine Owners' Protective Association,
   2:494
Miners, free *vs.* convict, **1**:124
Miners for Democracy, **2**:634
Miners' League, **2**:492
Miners' Union of the Coeur d'Alenes,
   2:494–495
Mineta, Norman, **1**:247
Minimum Drinking Age Law (1984),
   3:870
Mining
   black lung movement, 646–649
   child labor, **2**:516
   claim-patent system, **2**:490, 491
   Comstock unions, **2**:491–493
   dangers of, **2**:494
   Idaho, **2**:493–496
   laws, **2**:489, 490–491
   miner strikes, **2**:494
   miner wage reduction, **2**:491–492,
      493
   "people's" mines, **2**:489–490
   privatization, **2**:489, 491–492, 494
   union camps, **2**:492
   wildcat strikes, **2**:648–649, 676–677
   women in, **2**:490
Mining Law (1872), **2**:490
Minneapolis Teamster's strike, **2**:564,
   593–595
Minnesota
   opposition to the Nonpartisan
      League, **3**:804–805
   White Earth reservation, **2**:700–701
Minnesota Farmer-Labor Party. *See*
   Farmer-Labor Party
Minor, Virginia, **1**:297
Minor v. Happersett (1874), **1**:274
Minutemen, **4**:1440–1441
Miscegenation, fear of, **1**:8, 50, 101
Miss America Pageant, **2**:401, 425
Missionaries
   colonial America, **2**:697, 698, 750;
      3:926, 961

Missionaries *(continued)*
   decline of Protestant American, **3**:965
   evaluating western, **3**:964–965
   gender and, **3**:962–963
   globalization and, **3**:961–962
   overseas, **3**:963, 964
   youth and, **3**:963–964
Missionary Review of the Word (journal),
   3:963
Mississippi
   African-American migration from,
      3:775–776
   civil rights at University, **1**:184–185
   Freedom Riders imprisoned,
      1:183–184
   Freedom Summer, **1**:190–193;
      3:1127–1128
   racist violence, **1**:191–192, 209
   voting rights, **1**:191
Mississippi Freedom Democratic Party,
   1:181, 191, 192–193
Missouri, Gaines v. (1938), **1**:162
Missouri Compromise (1850), **1**:58, 94
Mitchell, George, **2**:707
Mitchell, H.L., **3**:1123
Mitchell, John, **3**:874
Mitchell, O. M., **1**:43
Mitchell, Wisconsin v. (1993), **1**:248
Mitchell v. MNR (2001) (Canada), **2**:736
Miyamoto, Nobuko Joanne, **4**:1220
MNR, Mitchell v. (2001) (Canada), **2**:736
Mobilization Committee to End the War
   in Vietnam, **3**:1092
Model Christian Neighborhood
   (Stowes), **1**:287–288
Mohawk (Richard Billings), **2**:715
Mojave Desert, **4**:1296
Molly Clubs, **4**:1379–1380
Mondragón, Celedonio, **4**:1227
The Monkey Wrench Gang (Abbey, 1975),
   4:1280
Monroe, Sarah, **2**:469
Montezuma, Carlos, **2**:701
Montgomery (Alabama), attack on
   Freedom Riders, **1**:183, 205, 209
Montgomery Bus Boycott, **1**:152, 172,
   177–178, 204, 209
Montgomery Improvement Association,
   1:178
Montgomery Race Conference of 1900,
   1:129
Moody, Dwight L., **3**:966
Mooney, Tom, **2**:676
Moore, Ely, **2**:469
Moore, Fred H., **2**:580, 581
Moore, Richard B., **2**:570

Moore v. Dempsey, **1**:138
Moor's Charity School, **2**:697
Moraga, Cherrie, **2**:411
Moral Majority, **4**:1402
Moral panics, **3**:844
Moral reform movement
   and child welfare, **3**:864
   due to cultural anxieties, **3**:863–864
   overview, **3**:843–844
   women and, **1**:264–265, 343; **3**:949
   See also Anti-abortion movement;
      Anti-drug movement; Obscen-
      ity and pornography; Prostitu-
      tion reform; Religious Right;
      Temperance movement
Moral suasion, **1**:4, 20, 35, 63, 67, 97
   failure of, **1**:103–104
Moral uplift, **1**:67–68
Moreno, Luisa, **2**:621, 622
Morgan, Arthur, **3**:1005
Morgan, Robin, **2**:400, 407, 440
Morgan v. Virginia, **1**:203, 208
Morlan, Robert, **3**:802–803
Mormons
   communal living, **3**:1004
   and dress reform, **1**:269
   founder, **3**:931
   lynching of, **3**:931
   and utopianism, **1**:262; **3**:923
Morning Star Ranch, **3**:1005, 1024
Morris, Glen, **2**:722
Morrison, Toni, **1**:247
Morrison, United States v. (2002), **2**:450
Moscow Treaty (2002), **4**:1296
Moses, Robert, **1**:191, 192
Moskowitz, Henry, **3**:1010
Moss, Thomas, **1**:331–332
Most, Johann, **2**:499
Mother Earth (magazine), **2**:501; **3**:1074
Mother Jones. *See* Jones, Mary Harris
   (Mother Jones)
Mothers Against Drunk Driving
   (MADD), **3**:870
Mother's Milk Project, **2**:745
Mother's pension, **1**:338
Mother's Society to Study Child
   Nature, **3**:1009
Motion Picture Association of America,
   3:850
Mott, James, **1**:56
Mott, John R., **3**:962, 966
Mott, Lucretia Coffin, **1**:55, 56, 92, 263,
   266
   and abolition movement, **1**:290
   and woman suffrage, **1**:290, 319
Moultrie, Mary, **2**:641

Biographical Index